D0138490

ENCYCLOPEDIA OF
AMERICAN BUSINESS HISTORY

VOLUME II

CHARLES R. GEISST

An imprint of Infobase Publishing

Encyclopedia of American Business History

Copyright © 2006 by Charles R. Geisst

Facts On File, Inc.
An imprint of Infobase Publishing
132 West 31st Street
New York, NY 10001

Library of Congress Cataloging-in-Publication Data

Geisst, Charles R.
Encyclopedia of American business history / Charles R. Geisst.
p. cm.
Includes bibliographical references and index.
ISBN 0-8160-4350-7 (hardcover : alk. paper) 1. United States—Commerce—History—Encyclopedias. 2. Business enterprises—United States—History—Encyclopedias. 3. Industries—United States—History—Encyclopedias. I. Title.

HF3021.G44 2005
338.0973'03—dc22   2005003309

Text design by Cathy Rincon

Cover design by Cathy Rincon

Illustrations by Sholto Ainslie

Printed in the United States of America

VB Hermitage 10 9 8 7 6 5 4 3 2 1

This book is printed on acid-free paper.

CONTENTS

VOLUME I

CONTRIBUTORS   iv

LIST OF ENTRIES   vi

INTRODUCTION   ix

ENTRIES A–M   1

VOLUME II

ENTRIES N–Z   293

CHRONOLOGY   491

SELECTED PRIMARY DOCUMENTS   495

GENERAL BIBLIOGRAPHY   565

INDEX   569

N

Nader, Ralph (1934–) *consumer advocate and political candidate* Ralph Nader was born in Winsted, Connecticut, on February 27, 1934, a son of Lebanese immigrants. An exceptional student, he graduated from Princeton University with honors in 1955 and acquired his law degree from Harvard Law School three years later. Nader then commenced a successful practice in Hartford, specializing in automobile accidents, and also taught at the University of Hartford. In the course of litigation, Nader became convinced that traffic accidents were due more to faulty engineering than human error. He carefully collected statistics and published his findings in numerous magazine articles. By 1964, this activity brought him to the attention of the U.S. Department of Labor, which appointed him to a landmark study of auto safety in America. The following year he published his famous tome, *Unsafe at Any Speed,* which excoriated the automobile industry for shoddy safety concerns. In retaliation, Nader's personal life fell under scrutiny by private detectives hired by General Motors president James M. Roche. When the truth emerged, Roche publicly recanted, and Nader became an instant consumer celebrity. He subsequently expanded his inquiries to mines, oil and gas pipelines, and environmental practices, with a view toward tarring corporate America as indifferent to public safety. No mere radical, Nader was thorough and precise in collecting data, and exacting in his presentations. In 1967, his revealing investigation of the MEAT PACKING INDUSTRY resulted in the new Wholesome Meat Act of that year.

The thrust of Nader's evolving political thesis was that American business was too obsessed with profit to give consumer safety more than lip service. In time he extended similar accusations against the government as a silent and willing partner in these transgressions. His message resonated strongly with the public, and legislators were pressured to invoke new and stricter health and safety laws. Throughout the decade of the 1970s, Nader expanded his litany of complaints and his host of public supporters to investigate pesticides, food additives, color televisions, and X-ray machines. With few exceptions his endeavors resulted in a bevy of new laws to protect the average citizen. In time he acquired considerable renown and controversy as the nation's most outspoken consumer advocate and a relentless proponent of corporate accountability. He also surrounded himself with a new generation of consumer activists, Nader's Raiders, to keep the pressure upon elected officials. But having failed to stop the North American Free Trade Agreement of 1993, which he felt imperiled both American jobs and consumer safety, Nader decided to take his crusade to the next level by entering politics.

While closely allied to progressive causes, Nader was no friend to the Democratic Party, and he accused it of having sold out to corporate interests, like the Republicans. To that end he received the Green Party's nomination for the presidency in 1996; he won considerable public

Ralph Nader (Getty Images)

sympathy but only 700,000 votes. In fact, neither major party ever took him as a serious contender. However, circumstances subsequently forced Nader into the headlines during the 2000 presidential election between Democratic vice president Al Gore and Republican challenger George W. Bush. When polls predicted an extremely close race, Democrats pleaded with Nader to withdraw his candidacy in competitive states lest he siphon off badly needed votes from Gore. Nader defiantly and unapologetically refused, declaring that the two parties were so close philosophically it did not matter which side won—consumers were sure to lose. In November 2000, the Green Party amassed 2.6 percent of votes cast. However, this included a tally of more than 90,000 votes at Gore's expense in Florida, enough to tip the balance to the Republicans and assure Bush's victory. Nader, formerly the darling of left-wing causes, was now publically lambasted as a spoiler. But the former consumer crusader shrugged off such complaints and continued railing against the government's alleged capitulation to corporate America. His legacy as an advocate is secure, but his future with the Green Party—still roiled over its indirect role in Bush's election—remains less certain. "You have to keep up the pressure, even if you lose," Nader declared. "The essence of the citizen's movement is persistence."

Further reading

Graham, Kevin. *Ralph Nader: Battling for Democracy.* Denver, Colo.: Windom Pub., 2000.

Martin, Justin. *Nader: Crusader, Spoiler, Icon.* Cambridge, Mass.: Perseus Pub., 2002.

Nader, Ralph. *Crashing the Party: Taking on the Corporate Government in an Age of Surrender.* New York: Thomas Dunne Books/St. Martin's Press, 2002.

John C. Fredriksen

National Association of Securities Dealers (NASD) A professional trade group of securities dealers, originally organized during the New Deal. It is a self-regulating body that oversees the activities of the over-the-counter bond markets and also conducts the NASDAQ stock market, short for National Association of Securities Dealers Automated Quotations system.

The predecessor of the NASD originally was formed in 1933 as a response to the New Deal's call for professional associations to be formed in order to fight the Depression. The securities industry responded quickly to the idea that trade groups could help pull their economic muscle together and fight the economic slowdown, an idea originally charged to the NATIONAL RECOVERY ADMINISTRATION, an agency created by the National Industrial Recovery Act. Even after the NIRA was declared unconstitutional by the Supreme Court in 1935, the investment banking industry favored the idea of a national trade group that would oversee what at the time was known as the over-the-counter, or unlisted, securities market—the place where stocks not listed on one of the exchanges traded. Since the National Industrial Recovery Act encouraged trade group associations, the Investment Bankers' Conference organized itself as a competitor of the older Investment Bankers' Association.

Congress obliged by passing the Maloney Act in 1937, which created the NASD. Introduced by Senator Francis T. Maloney, a Democrat from Connecticut, the act was an amendment to the Securities Act of 1934, allowing securities dealers to form national groups to better regulate themselves and arrange codes of conduct and trading. The Maloney Act provided for organization and basic trading rules to apply to the vast membership of what became the NASD. More than 6,000 brokers and securities houses joined, and the organization was originally responsible for overseeing trading in more than 3,000 securities. The group remained self-regulating but was still only a trade group as opposed to the Securities and Exchange Commission, which had the power of law behind it.

The NASD expanded its authority and reputation considerably by organizing the over-the-counter market into the NASDAQ in 1972. The market was computerized, with dealers linked through a central computer over which they could enter quotations and trade securities among themselves and with the public. Once operating well, the new market drew many new listings to the NASDAQ marketplace since more efficient trading of stocks could be ensured.

In 1998, the NASDAQ announced a merger with the AMERICAN STOCK EXCHANGE in order to compete for business with the NEW YORK STOCK EXCHANGE. NASDAQ's trading system of using market makers linked by computer is in direct competition with that of the NYSE, which still employs the specialist system for selling securities on the exchange floor.

The market suffered when 30 member firms were fined more than $1 billion in 1997 for manipulating prices and maintaining spreads between bid and offer prices favorable to market makers, not customers. As a result, the market announced that it was shifting to quoting prices in decimals rather than fractions in an attempt to provide cleaner prices for the public. The market shared in the success of the market rise in the later 1990s. It rose dramatically during the 1990s, and its major index rose to over 5,000 before falling 80 percent when the overall market bubble burst in 2000–01.

See also STOCK MARKETS.

Further reading

Geisst, Charles R. *Wall Street: A History.* New York: Oxford University Press, 1997.
Ingebretsen, Mark. *NASDAQ: A History of the Market That Changed the World.* New York: Forum, 2002.

National Bank Act (1864)   Legislation passed during the Civil War designed to provide some structure to U.S. banking and currency. The law created a national currency for the country, making it more difficult for state banks to issue their own money, as had been the case in the 19th century. National banks were created that became note issuers, replacing the state banks. The law was, in fact, a currency act, although it did create a new class of bank.

The act also created the office of comptroller of the currency, which became responsible for overseeing banks that registered with it, allowing them to use the name *national bank*. The banks had capital requirements and other regulations that they had to observe in order to meet the new designation. The new national banks took over the function of issuing currency under the auspices of the comptroller. They were also required to hold one-third of their assets in TREASURY BONDS, which had to be deposited with the comptroller, who in turn issued national banknotes, using the bonds as collateral.

The act helped the United States consolidate a sloppy currency situation and helped reduce fraud in the old payments system. In the past, when the state banks issued money, a great deal of fraud occurred, and many merchant banks made a specialty of helping customers detect counterfeit notes. Detecting bogus BANKNOTES was an art prior to the Civil War. After 1864, the situation improved dramatically since the note issuance process now was more uniform and had a central regulator for the first time.

But the act fell far short of developing a central bank for the United States because there was still no lender of last resort in the country. The actual supply of money could become less than what was needed, especially if the economy required a dose of extra money and credit. This would be referred to as inelasticity in the money supply, and it became a political issue before World War I.

Between 1865 and 1913, the major New York banks usually decided among themselves the proper course of remedial action to be taken when the stock market collapsed or a large bank failed. But for all the shortcomings, the comptroller of the currency remained the only regulator of banking until the FEDERAL RESERVE was created in 1913.

See also GREENBACKS; MCFADDEN ACT.

Further reading

Friedman, Milton, and Anna Schwartz. *A Monetary History of the United States*. Princeton, N.J.: Princeton University Press, 1963.
Myers, Margaret. *A Financial History of the United States*. New York: Columbia University Press, 1970.

National Labor Relations Act (NLRA)   A major, revolutionary labor act passed during the NEW DEAL and signed into law by President Roosevelt in 1935. The NLRA's major sponsor was Senator Robert F. Wagner of New York. The law, also known as the Wagner Act, was predicated on the principle that in an industrial democracy workers must be allowed to organize and bargain collectively with management through their own representatives. In the year following its passage, the act became known as the Magna Carta of organized labor.

The major difference between the atmosphere the act created and that which preceded it was significant. Labor and management were now to bargain with each other in an atmosphere in which the fundamental rights of labor were recognized. Although organized labor already was well developed in the United States, employers often disciplined and blacklisted union members, causing a great deal of industrial strife in the early 1930s. In order to offset these problems and discourage even more problems in the future, the act was passed during the New Deal.

The NLRA guaranteed workers the right to join unions without fear of reprisal or dismissal. The National Labor Relations Board (NLRB) was created to ensure that the provisions of the act were carried out. It has three members who are charged with interpreting the act. The NLRB is an independent judicial administrative agency that has the power to enforce its own rulings. After the TAFT-HARTLEY ACT was passed in 1947, the NLRB was overshadowed to an extent, limiting its ability to interpret the Wagner Act.

The law nevertheless gave employees the right to organize, to engage in strikes when necessary, and to bargain collectively. Employees were also given the right to participate in the negotiation of their wages, working conditions, and number of hours worked per week. After the act was passed, many of the large industries became unionized and recognized the collective needs and demands of their workforces. Successful campaigns were launched in the automobile, steel, electrical, manufacturing, and rubber industries to sign workers up in unions. As a result, by 1945 union membership reached 35 percent of the workforce.

The Wagner Act was similar in tone to the National Industrial Recovery Act of 1933, which later was declared unconstitutional. However, the constitutionality of the Wagner Act was upheld in 1937, and it has become the cornerstone of labor relations in the United States along with the Taft-Hartley Act.

See also Lewis, John L.; Meany, George; National Recovery Administration.

Further reading

Derber, Milton. *The American Ideal of Industrial Democracy, 1865–1965* Urbana: University of Illinois Press, 1970.

Gross, James A. *The Making of the National Labor Relations Board: A Study in Economics, Politics and the Law.* Albany: State University of New York Press, 1974.

National Negro Business League (NNBL)

A professional and political organization that was first convened in 1900 at the Tuskegee Institute by Booker T. Washington (1856–1915). Next to Washington's educational endeavors and role as an African-American political boss, the NNBL was arguably the most important contribution the Tuskegee principal made toward institutional and organizational self-help activities in the black community.

From the NNBL's inaugural meeting of more than 300 aspiring and established African-American business men and women, the organization, during Washington's lifetime, held annual gatherings in northern and southern American cities to allow black entrepreneurs to network and share success stories. About 3,000 like-minded black capitalists attended the 1915 anniversary Boston gathering, representing 600 chapters from 36 American states and West Africa. On this occasion, the NNBL claimed major success in stimulating black capitalism in America as it cited the growth in African-American businesses from 1900 to 1915: banks from two to 51; drugstores, 250 to 697; mortuaries, 450 to 1,000; wholesale companies, 149 to 240; and retail outlets, 10,000 to 25,000. The NNBL, moreover, spawned many other significant business entities and commercial associations such as the National Bankers Association, the National Association of Negro Insurance Companies, the National Association of Funeral Directors, and the National Association of Real Estate Dealers, all of which met in tandem with annual NNBL meetings.

Booker T. Washington and his followers continued to sustain the organization, despite using it for political purposes and relying on both Andrew Carnegie and Julius Rosenwald for support in order to keep the NNBL afloat. With Washington's death, the next 85 years were difficult ones for the NNBL as internecine leadership struggles for control of the organization extended into the 1920s; hard times came during the Great Depression; and the NNBL never quite consummated the revivalism begun in the 1950s under the leadership of Ohio businessman Horace Sudduth, Tennessee physician Dr. James E. Walker, and North Carolina insurance magnate C. C. Spaulding. A brief moment of optimism came in the 1960s as the organization changed its name to the National Business League and, from its headquarters in Washington, D.C., under the leadership of businessman Berkeley Graham Burrell, developed a "Project Outreach" to provide management and technical assistance to African Americans and other minority business firms and companies. Burrell received support from the Nixon administration, the Department of Commerce's Office of Minority Business Enterprise, and the Office of Economic Opportunity.

The NNBL was unable to hold its centennial anniversary at the turn of the 21st century. One member explained the developmental problem as one of having "politicians trying to run a business organization." The remnants of this once important African-American business organization are evident today in many southern cities, and the NNBL is now quartered in New Orleans, Louisiana.

Further reading

Kijakazi, Kilolo. *African-American Economic Development and Small Business Ownership.* New York: Garland Publishing, 1997.

Walker, Juliet E. K. *The History of Black Business in America: Capitalism, Race, Entrepreneurship.* New York: Macmillan, 1998.

Washington, Booker T. *The Negro in Business.* Boston: Hertel Jenkins, 1907.

Maceo C. Dailey

National Recovery Administration (NRA)

A federal agency created by the National Industrial Recovery Act of 1933 (NIRA). The agency was designed to combat the intense and destructive competition between American businesses and replace it with a consensual self-government of business and industry. The agency was modeled on the War Industries Board (WIB), an agency operating during World War I that had a similar mission.

The NRA was headed by General Hugh JOHNSON, formerly a member of the War Industries Board. The NRA had as its symbol a blue eagle, and that became the nickname for the agency. The eagle decal was displayed on many business windows and became an unofficial symbol of the country's efforts to emerge from the Great Depression. Detractors referred to it as the "Roosevelt buzzard."

As part of the NRA program, the Roosevelt administration suspended the antitrust laws for two years and authorized industry to form government-recognized trade organizations that would reduce internecine competition, devise codes of competition, and dictate fair labor practices. More than 500 codes were drawn up, although many were not adhered to. One positive by-product of the codes was the elimination of child labor.

Another organization, created by the securities industry under the guidelines, was known originally as the Investment Bankers Conference and today survives as the NATIONAL ASSOCIATION OF SECURITIES DEALERS after being formally established by the Maloney Act in 1937. The basic assumption made by the NRA was that competition between companies was actually hindering economic recovery during the Depression rather than helping, and antitrust laws were put in a state of suspension so that the new, larger trade organizations were not accused of breaking the laws. The suspension of the antitrust laws suggested to some that the NEW DEAL was attacking the basic structure of American business.

In May 1935, the NIRA was declared unconstitutional by the Supreme Court and with it the NRA as well. In the case of *Schecter Poultry Corporation v. United States,* the Supreme Court ruled that congressional authority had been usurped to the executive branch and that the law was unconstitutional as a result. Even severe economic conditions did not warrant the transfer of power to the presidency. The NRA was not reorganized and passed out of existence the same year. Although generally considered a failure, the NRA experience provided a foundation for other reforms and better-designed regulatory agencies during the years that followed.

Further reading

Bellush, Bernard. *The Failure of the NRA.* New York: W. W. Norton, 1976.

Brand, Donald R. *Corporatism and the Rule of Law: A Study of the National Recovery Administration.* Ithaca, N.Y.: Cornell University Press, 1988.

Johnson, Hugh S. *The Blue Eagle from Egg to Birth.* Garden City, N.Y.: Doubleday, Doran, 1935.

New Deal   The name given to the first administration of Franklin D. Roosevelt, covering the period 1933–37. The term was used to suggest that legislation and social programs would be enacted to address the needs of working and middle-class citizens, not just those in upper-income brackets. It was first used in Roosevelt's nomination acceptance speech before the Democratic National Convention in 1932. Social and economic legislation was passed, especially before 1936, encompassing a wide spectrum of programs ranging from securities legislation to social security programs.

During the first 100 days of Roosevelt's administration, the White House proposed and Congress passed sweeping legislation concerning the financial markets and banks. The objective was to pass legislation that would end the Depression and help stimulate the economy while proscribing practices, especially in the securities business, that many believed were responsible for the economic slowdown. Among this legislation were the SECURITIES ACT OF 1933, the BANKING ACT OF 1933, the Agricultural Adjustment Act, and the National Industrial Recovery Act, all passed by June of 1933. The SECURITIES EXCHANGE ACT was passed in 1934, regulating stock exchanges for the first time. After the first round of legislation was complete, the second 100 days began, and Congress passed the National Labor Relations Act and the Social Security Act and created the WORKS PROGRESS ADMINISTRATION. All were designed to either regulate sectors of the economy or create jobs for the unemployed.

The legislation also created a myriad of new government agencies, all known by their initials. They ranged from the AAA (Agricultural Adjustment Agency) to the WPA (Works Progress Administration). They become known as the "alphabet agencies," and some eventually were dismantled. Others, like the Social Security Administration, became permanent. Others would follow, such as the FEDERAL NATIONAL MORTGAGE ASSOCIATION in 1938, during Roosevelt's second administration.

A serious blow was dealt to the New Deal when the National Industrial Recovery Act, passed in June 1933, was declared unconstitutional by the Supreme Court in 1935. The agency it created, the NATIONAL RECOVERY ADMINISTRATION (NRA), had been instituted to develop a code of fair practice for various businesses, which were voluntarily participating in the program. The companies participating in the process were writing codes of conduct for their respective businesses, including specific standards of quality, working hours, minimum wages, and price floors for goods they produced. When it was declared unconstitutional it was generally assumed that the NRA was benefiting business and that many businesses were in favor of it.

The AAA was declared unconstitutional in 1936, joining the NRA. After the Supreme Court packing controversy in 1937, only a few significant pieces of legislation were passed, including the Housing Act of 1937 and the Fair Labor Standards Act in 1938. Reform slowed when it became apparent that the Depression was continuing, especially when a severe RECESSION occurred in 1937.

While not successful in ending the Depression, the New Deal nevertheless provided a great deal of social legislation that became part of the bedrock of society, especially Social Security. Much of this legislation, when combined, is referred to as the "safety net" erected to prevent economic institutions and society in general from crashing again. It also helped establish a firmer hand of government in public affairs than had been the case previously, leading to more REGULATION in general. Much of the apparatus established by the New Deal became useful as World War II approached, and many government agencies began to direct their attention toward the war effort, especially the Reconstruction

Finance Corporation, actually founded in 1932, that helped many companies finance and build facilities to aid the war effort.

Further reading

Leuchtenburg, Willam E. *Franklin D. Roosevelt and the New Deal, 1932–1940*. New York: Harper & Row, 1963.

Loucheim, Katie, ed. *The Making of the New Deal: The Insiders Speak*. Cambridge, Mass.: Harvard University Press, 1983.

Rosenof, Theodore. *Economics in the Long Run: New Deal Theorists and Their Legacies, 1933–1993*. Chapel Hill: University of North Carolina Press, 1997.

Schlesinger, Arthur M. *The Coming of the New Deal: The Age of Roosevelt*. Boston: Houghton Mifflin, 1959.

newspaper industry   Over the course of three centuries, the newspaper industry has served two disparate—and sometimes conflicting—roles: It has been a bulwark of American democracy and grown into the $55 billion industry that it is today. The tension between these two roles has given rise to a key question that has dominated newspaper publishing since the colonial era: How can the industry balance its civic responsibilities as a quasi-public institution in a democracy with the profit-making motives of a business enterprise?

Since the days of the Massachusetts Bay colony, the nascent newspaper business was at the center of the struggle over the political and religious character of the colonies. Benjamin Harris, who had established a bookstore and coffeehouse in Boston, printed the first colonial newspaper, *Publick Occurrences both Forreign and Domestick,* in 1690. The paper, which was not licensed by the colonial authorities, was shut down after just one issue. Two items in particular had annoyed the authorities: one of them a reference to a sexual scandal in the French royal family, the other involving mistreatment of prisoners by Indian allies.

Like *Publick Occurrences,* many of the earliest "newspapers" were little more than newsletters published by proprietors of coffeehouses and pubs, which became centers of political debate—and eventually dissent—in colonial America.

The second colonial newspaper was published by John Campbell, the postmaster of Boston. Campbell, who launched *Boston News-Letter* in 1704, began a colonial tradition whereby the postmaster also served as publisher. The colonial post office was a center of news, with first access to European newspapers—much as it would be in small-town America for years to come. The postmaster enjoyed "francking privileges" and could send his newsletters throughout the colonies free of charge. He was also "a safe" choice as a publisher, since he owed his job to the colonial authorities. Moreover, the colonial government often awarded printing jobs to newspapers. Thus, Campbell submitted his paper, which was available only through subscription sales, for "precensorship" to the authorities.

By the 1720s, there were three competing newspapers in Boston. The best of these papers, *The New England Courant,* was published by James Franklin, whose brother Benjamin Franklin was an apprentice printer and the author of satirical essays under the pseudonym "Silence Dogood." The *Courant* was launched during a period of growing dissent—focused on religious, rather than political, freedom. James was jailed in 1722 for publishing a series of attacks on the government, which was led by Increase Mather and his son Cotton, leaving the publication of the paper to his teenage brother Benjamin. Silence Dogood wrote "an eloquent plea for freedom of the press."

The Franklins successfully resisted repeated efforts by the Mathers, themselves religious publishers, to censor their paper, thus effectively ending censorship in Massachusetts. Benjamin Franklin later bought the *Pennsylvania Gazette.*

By the 1720s, newspapers were being published in several major colonial cities, including

Philadelphia and New York. It was in New York City that another major battle in the war for a free press was fought. In 1733, opponents of Governor William Cosby, one of the most corrupt administrators in the colonies, launched the *New York Weekly Journal.* When the paper attacked the local authorities and demanded a more representative government in New York, Cosby asked a grand jury to indict the *Journal's* editor, John Peter Zenger. Though the grand jury refused, Cosby had Zenger arrested and jailed. When Zenger came to trial in 1735, he was defended by Andrew Hamilton, a famous Philadelphia lawyer, who admitted that Zenger had published articles critical of the government—a crime under colonial law. But Hamilton argued that to be found guilty "the words themselves must be libelous—that is, false, scandalous, and seditious—or else we are not guilty." In an eloquent speech, Hamilton asserted the right for "the liberty—both of exposing and opposing arbitrary power . . . by speaking and writing truth."

The jury, which was composed of ordinary citizens, returned a verdict of not guilty. Although truth was not accepted as a defense in seditious libel cases until after the passage of the Sedition Act of 1798, Zenger's vindication demonstrated that the "average colonialist" was opposed to authoritarian government.

Eventually, the British authorities gave up trying to license newspapers, and by 1750, there were 14 weeklies in the six most populous colonies. Colonial papers, weeklies generally, were accepting advertising and had grown sufficiently in circulation to enrich a few publishers.

Colonial newspapers were radicalized by the Stamp Act of 1765, which imposed a tax on paper, a burden that fell particularly hard on newspaper publishers. While such taxes had long been levied on English papers, in the colonies the tax sparked calls of "taxation without representation." Although the Stamp Act was repealed a year later, by then most newspapers were committed to revolution.

Newspapers were highly partisan during the prerevolutionary and postrevolutionary period and were generally more interested in commentary than in news. Isaiah Thomas, who became one of postrevolutionary America's greatest publishers, founded the *Massachusetts Spy* in an attempt to create one of the few moderate, nonpartisan publications. Eventually, even the *Spy* went underground and became anti-British.

In the years after the Revolution, newspapers remained an important forum of debate, with most papers representing either a Federalist or a Republican point of view. The *Federalist Papers,* for example, were first published in newspapers. Another major debate between the Republicans and the Federalists centered on guarantees of individual rights, including freedom of the press, which the Republicans supported and the Federalists found "impracticable." Out of this struggle grew the Bill of Rights and the First Amendment, which states: "Congress shall make no law. . . . abridging the freedom of speech or of the press."

Freedom of the press—and its precise definition—has been debated since the passage of the Bill of Rights. On a number of different occasions, especially the passage of the Sedition Act in 1798 during the administration of Theodore Roosevelt, the government has sought to rein in the freedom of the press. The press also, especially in wartime, often has exercised self-censorship. Significantly, the concept of press freedom predated by decades the notions of "fairness" and "responsibility" that became canons of journalistic ethics only in the 20th century.

Until the late 18th century, most newspapers were read primarily by the educated elite; these early papers sold for as much as eight cents or for an annual subscription fee that was out of the reach of many ordinary Americans. The partisan press reached its peak during the presidency of Andrew Jackson, who was known for actively manipulating the press and rewarding sympathetic journalists and editors by giving them political appointments.

Ironically, by the early 19th century, the newspaper industry began to serve as a force of democratization. Though the industry was centered in Philadelphia and New York, by 1820 there were more than 500 newspapers in the United States; of these 24 were dailies. And the 1830s also saw the rise of the penny press and a more independent cadre of newspaper publishers. In 1833, Benjamin Day began publishing the *New York Sun,* the first daily paper that was designed to appeal to the urban working class. The *Sun* was sustained more by circulation and advertising than by political patronage. It also emphasized human interest stories, rather than the political and economic stories that had been the mainstay of earlier papers. Day introduced formatting changes such as large type and wider column widths to make the paper more legible. Most importantly, from a marketing perspective, Day sold his paper for just a penny.

Other papers, especially in New York City, followed the *Sun's* example. James Gordon Bennett's *New York Herald* was another journalistic path breaker. For one thing, the *Herald* combined the sensationalism of the *Sun* with the political and commercial coverage of more traditional papers. Bennett also became the first publisher to announce his paper's independence from political affiliations and his determination to "record facts, on every public and proper subject, stripped of verbiage and coloring . . ." After the development of the TELEGRAPH in 1844, the *Herald* became the first newspaper to use that technology to gather reports from other cities. By 1860, the *Herald* was selling 60,000 papers daily.

Bennett's *Herald,* as well as two other New York papers, Horace Greeley's *New York Tribune* and Henry J. Raymond's *New York Times,* were all institutions run by strong-willed and eccentric men who established the American newspaper as a capitalist, moneymaking business. Greeley's *Tribune* employed a large editorial staff with correspondents in six American cities, as well as Europe and Latin America. Greeley's paper mounted a slew of editorial campaigns, including

a fight against SLAVERY. The *New York Times* was considered one of the new breed of higher quality newspapers from its founding in 1851, though it did not become the "paper of record" until the 20th century. While the penny press did not always live up to its promise of dispassionate coverage, it established a new culture of aggressive, deadline-driven reporting.

In 1848, six New York papers banded together to form the Associated Press of New York, the nation's first wire service. Because the AP was funded by several papers of different political bents, the AP itself sought to present "objective" reports to which its client papers could add their own slant. Partly to defray their rising editorial costs, by the mid-19th century the mass market papers cost two pennies instead of just one.

While the newspapers of the mid-1800s eschewed political affiliations, they espoused the views of their owners. Perhaps the starkest ideological fault line in the newspaper industry in the years before the Civil War involved editorial policies on slavery. Many papers took sides for or against slavery. The abolitionist movement also spawned a number of journals, including a few black-owned newspapers. The most well known of these was the *North Star,* which was published by Frederick Douglass.

The Civil War sparked a number of important changes in the newspaper industry. Washington, D.C., became the center of political coverage. Feature syndication started during this period. The Civil War was the first war to be covered by photographers. However, it was not until the development of screen printing in the 1890s that photographic images could be reproduced in newspapers and magazines. Toward the end of the Civil War new printing innovations did enable newspapers and magazines to duplicate illustrations economically for the first time. (During the Gold Rush of 1899, *the Seattle Times* printed extensives graphic guides and maps on the gold fields. And in 1901, the *Chicago Daily News* pioneered the use of color.)

Because battlefield reporters were worried that the new telegraphic technology used to transmit dispatches might fail, they began packing the important news into the top of their stories, leaving the details for last. Thus, the old chronological news reporting style was replaced by what we now think of as the "inverted pyramid."

Following the Civil War, the growth of the RAILROADS opened the West to settlement, and the spread of heavy industry fostered a boom in both immigration and urbanization, which fueled ever greater demand for mass-market newspapers, while industrialization and the beginnings of a consumer culture (in particular the advent of the department store) fostered the growth of advertising.

The industry and the news gathering process also benefited from a number of technological advances that not only speeded printing but also made it possible to file stories from remote locations. Until the beginning of the 19th century, printing and the production of paper were handicraft businesses. Paper was produced literally from rags, not wood, and type was set by hand. The years after the Civil War saw a revolution in technology, including the invention of paper made from wood pulp in a paper-making machine. Other innovations included the linotype machine, which tripled the speed of typesetting, halftone photoengraving, which made it possible to print photographs for the first time, and the telephone and the telegraph.

A new generation of newspaper tycoons sought to appeal to the growing cadre of working-class readers with a renewed focus on sensational, crusading news stories. Publishers such as Joseph Pulitzer and William Randolph Hearst would become leading pioneers of what became known as yellow journalism.

Pulitzer, a Hungarian immigrant who got his start in the newspaper business by founding the *St. Louis Post-Dispatch*, bought the *New York World* in 1883. Pulitzer's mission, he said at the time, was a paper that would "expose all fraud and sham, fight all public evils and abuses." The

World embraced diverse crusades ranging from the Standard Oil monopoly to the conditions of tenement housing in New York City. Pulitzer commissioned R. F. Outcault to draw the first cartoon comic, and he devised and published the first opinion poll. He is credited with adding sports news and so-called women's news. Pulitzer, who would found both the eponymous journalism prizes and the Columbia University School of Journalism, also exhorted his editors to "always tell the truth, always take the humane and moral side . . ." William Randolph Hearst, whose family owned the *San Francisco Examiner,* bought the *New York Morning Journal* in 1895 to compete against Pulitzer's *World*. Mounting a vigorous campaign to steal both readers and advertisers from the *World,* Hearst spent lavishly to attract star talent, many from the *World,* and undercut the *World*'s advertising rates. By the turn of the century, both papers were publishing morning, evening, and Sunday editions.

In their frenzied competition, the *World* and the *Morning Journal* pushed the boundaries of sensationalism and journalistic ethics, giving rise to the term *yellow journalism*. As tensions between Cuba and its colonial ruler escalated, Hearst and Pulitzer exploited—some say they even fueled—the impending crisis to boost circulation. Hearst dispatched writer Richard Harding Davis and artist Frederic Remington to Cuba. When they arrived to find things quiet and asked to be sent home, Hearst is said to have replied: "Please remain. You furnish the pictures and I'll furnish the war." When the battleship *Maine* exploded mysteriously in Havana harbor, sparking the Spanish-American War, both papers pinned the blame on the Spanish and splashed the story across their front pages. Within days, Hearst launched a subscription campaign to raise money for a memorial, which was eventually built at Columbus Circle. Not to be outdone, Pulitzer built a statue to Pomona at the east end of 59th Street and Fifth Avenue. A similar subscription campaign by the Hearst newspapers helped fund Mount Rushmore. To whip up support for both the war and the memorial, Hearst's papers also published distorted accounts of Spanish atrocities. Hearst's tactics prompted former president Grover Cleveland, who had resisted intervening in Cuba during his presidency, to charge Hearst with exploiting the deaths of the men who had died on the *Maine* as an "advertising scheme for the *New York Journal.*" Indeed, within days of the explosion, circulation of both papers exceeded 1 million readers.

In 1900, advertising as a percentage of revenues jumped to 55 percent, up from 29 percent in the 1830s (today, ads account for 70 to 80 percent of newspaper revenues). The development of newspaper chains was another major trend in the early 20th century, led by Edward Wyllis

William Randolph Hearst (LIBRARY OF CONGRESS)

Scripps. Scripps launched the *Cleveland Press,* the first paper in what was to become a cross-country chain of newspapers that numbered 23 by the start of World War I. The Scripps chain pioneered a number of innovations: Editors were often offered stock. Scripps wrote the editorials for his papers himself. He also launched a wire service, United Press Association. Like Pulitzer, Scripps saw himself as something of a crusader for the working class. He even experimented with ad-free newspapers as a way to resist the pressure of advertisers.

The years between World War I and the end of the Great Depression marked a period of massive consolidation in the newspaper industry. For example, inspired by Scripps's success, Hearst, too, began to buy newspapers—more than two dozen by 1934. Hearst also launched a news service, International News Service. The merger of the Hearst news service and the Scripps news service in 1958, resulted in United Press International, which was the major competitor to the Associated Press.

Three other newspaper chains were launched in the early 20th century: the Newhouse Newspapers, founded by S. I. Newhouse; Gannett Newspapers, founded by Frank Gannett; and the Knight-Ridder chain, which got its start when John Knight rescued his father's *Akron Beacon Journal* from near-bankruptcy during the Depression and began buying a slew of midwestern papers.

The turn of the century also saw the rise of the *Wall Street Journal,* which would become the first national newspaper. The business press—in the form of so-called price currents, which were little more than pamphlets that reported on commodity prices, the movement of ships, and exchange rate fluctuations—dated back to the founding of the colonies. General interest newspapers, which had catered to the colonial elite, had recognized the importance of business subscribers and issued supplements, often for free, that listed information on commodity prices, insurance premiums, and shipping news. The most successful and influential of the shipping papers, the *General Shipping and Commercial List* (which eventually became the *New York Shipping and Commercial List*) was launched in 1815 and was published until the early 20th century, when it was merged with the *Journal of Commerce*.

On Wall Street, the first financial newsletters began soon after traders began selling stocks and bonds under a sycamore tree at the corner of Wall and Broad Streets in 1789. By the late 19th century, a number of hand-written financial bulletins were hand-delivered to subscribers every day. The *Wall Street Journal*, which quickly became the premier business journal, was founded on a technological innovation intended to improve the production of these bulletins. In 1882, Charles Bergstresser convinced Charles Dow and Edward Jones, two of his colleagues at the Kiernan News Agency, a leading financial publisher of the day, to defect and form their own company. He did so after Kiernan had refused to give Bergstresser an equity interest in one of his inventions, a stylus that could record the news onto 35 bulletins simultaneously. Dow Jones & Co. soon bought the first financial printing press on Wall Street. The company was also first to use the telegraph to transmit financial news from London and Boston to New York. In 1889, Dow Jones introduced the *Wall Street Journal*, Wall Street's first afternoon newspaper. (A paper by the same name had ceased publication a decade earlier.) The same year, the company introduced the original Dow Jones Industrial Average; of the first 12 companies on the list, only General Electric survives. By that time the company was already producing both bulletins and a financial ticker that transmitted the latest stock prices.

Success also fostered a battle between the business side and the editorial side of the paper. As the *Wall Street Journal* became more and more successful, Edward Jones, who was in charge of advertising, filled the front page with ads. Dow, who was in charge of editorial content, objected. In 1899, Jones sold his interest in the company to Dow, beginning a tradition whereby the editorial department would function independently of the financial side of the paper.

By the start of the 20th century, the newspaper industry had become big business. At the same time, journalists and newspaper publishers thought of themselves as a profession with responsibilities to the reading public. When Adolph S. Ochs bought the near-bankrupt *New York Times* in 1896, he stressed accuracy, objectivity, and depth. This new "objectivity" was also synchronous with the spirit of progressivism, rationalism, and professionalism that gripped the rapidly industrializing nation of the early 20th century. In 1922, the major dailies organized the American Society of Newspaper Editors, which adopted a professional code of ethics known as the "Canons of Journalism." Similar codes had been adopted by regional publications beginning in 1910. Though the canons were voluntary, they stressed fairness, impartiality, independence, and "fidelity to the public interest." Newspapers did, indeed, sometimes have a substantial impact, as, for example, when coverage of the Triangle Shirtwaist factory fire helped to highlight unsafe working conditions and inspired changes in municipal laws.

But sensationalism was not dead. During the roaring 20s, cities saw the rise of a new breed of newspaper, the tabloids, which countered the sobriety of mainstream papers such as the *New York Times* and the *Wall Street Journal* with a new era of sensationalism. The tabloids were smaller in size than conventional papers, so they could easily be read on bus and subway, and used large headlines and photography. The archetype of the new tabloid was the *New York Daily News*, which was founded by Joseph Patterson in 1919.

The 1920s also saw the rise of broadcast media. Radio began to threaten the department store advertising base of the newspapers. Competition and financial pressure led to a further consolidation of the newspaper industry that continues to this day.

Interpretive journalism emerged, in part, as the print media's response to the spot-news

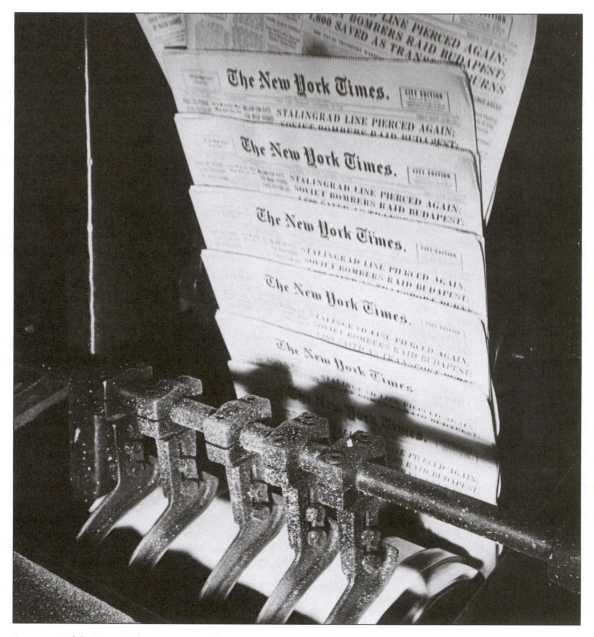

Pressroom of the New York Times, *1942* (LIBRARY OF CONGRESS)

advantage enjoyed by broadcasters. Interpretive journalism also was an answer to the Achilles heel of objective reportage. A nothing-but-the-facts approach to journalism failed to lend meaning to complex news events; it also left journalists open to manipulation by public officials who could garner headlines merely by holding a press conference. Columnists pioneered interpretive journalism in the 1910s and 1920s. The seriousness of the Depression also bolstered interpretive journalism; President Roosevelt, for example, made his economic advisers available to journalists to help explain new economic policies. Senator Joseph McCarthy's success in manipulating the postwar press further discredited "objectivity." (Indeed, it was interpretive reporting by Edward R. Murrow on his *Hear It Now* broadcast that was credited with helping to bring down McCarthy.)

By the second half of the 20th century, competition from new forms of broadcasting and new technology combined to undermine regional, independently held newspapers. Computer and satellite technology fostered a boom in regional printing and the first national newspapers. The *Wall Street Journal* began printing regional editions in the mid-1970s, and Gannett launched *USA Today* in 1982.

The growth of the national papers, chains, and eventually publicly held companies signaled the decline of independent regional newspapers. Just after World War II, Walter Lippmann traveled to Iowa on the occasion of the 100th anniversary of the *Des Moines Register and Tribune*. In his remarks to an audience of Iowa publishers and editors, he said: "There is I believe, a fundamental reason why the American press is strong enough to remain free. That reason is that the American newspapers, large and small and without exception, belong to a town, a city, at the most to a region."

At the time of Lippmann's address, three-fourths of all American dailies were independently owned. But by the turn of the 21st century, a handful of media corporations had come to dominate the news media, and all but a few daily papers had gone public. By selling shares to the public, newspaper companies were able to raise much-needed capital. However, the strategy also gave newspaper editors (and managers) a new focus: shareholders and profit margins, rather than readers.

To resist being swallowed up by chains, a number of newspapers formed joint operating agreements, and in the 1950s, one-newspaper towns began to flourish. The Newspaper Preservation Act of 1970 provided some protection against antitrust prosecutions and was intended to protect weak newspapers by allowing two publications to share advertising, management, and printing resources, while maintaining separate editorial staffs. Some newspapers also bought local television stations. However, in 1975 the FEDERAL COMMUNICATIONS COMMISSION banned future purchases by media companies that would result in a company owning both a newspaper and a television station in the same market; the rule has come under fire in recent years as media conglomerates have sought to weaken FCC rules governing ownership.

By the late 20th century, the most successful newspapers were highly profitable businesses, garnering net profits of 15 to 25 percent, substantially more than many U.S. businesses, which rarely see double-digit margins. A handful of prominent family-controlled newspapers, including the *Washington Post* and the *New York Times*, also went public, but used large blocks of shares to retain family control and to blunt the pressures of the stock market.

The pressures of public ownership sharpened the debate about the watchdog function of newspapers. "News has become secondary, even incidental, to markets and revenues and margins and advertisers and consumer preferences," note the authors of *Taking Stock: Journalism and the Publicly Traded Newspaper Company*. Significantly, the biggest—and riskiest—stories of the late 20th century, Watergate and the Pentagon Papers, were broken by the *Washington Post* and the *New York Times*, which are still controlled by family members.

See also ADVERTISING INDUSTRY; BARRON, CLARENCE W.; MUCKRAKERS.

Further reading

Auletta, Ken. *Backstory: Inside the Business of News.* New York: Penguin, 2005.
Bezanson, Randall P., Gibert Cranberg, and John Soloski. *Taking Stock: Journalism and the Publicly*

Traded Newspaper Company. Ames: Iowa State University Press, 2001.

Meyer, Philip. *The Vanishing Newspaper: Saving Journalism in the Information Age.* Columbia: University of Missouri Press, 2004.

Andrea Gabor

New York Stock Exchange In the 18th century, stock traders conducted an outdoor market on Wall Street in lower Manhattan to trade stocks and commodities. The market was very limited both by location and by weather, and when it became impossible to trade outside, the traders often moved indoors to coffeehouses, also located on Wall Street. This general locale became the site of stock trading in New York City.

In 1791, the early stock market suffered a serious setback because of speculation by William DUER, a former finance official during the Continental Congress. Duer speculated heavily in land and became overextended in his dealings, causing the market to collapse. As a result, the traders realized that they needed to form an organization to control their own membership and organize the market. A meeting was held under a buttonwood tree and was known as the Buttonwood Agreement. It became the foundation for the New York Stock & Exchange Board in 1817 and its successor, the New York Stock Exchange.

The post-Buttonwood brokers would meet daily to transact business in the securities of the day—mostly government bonds. From those humble beginnings emerged one of the world's largest marketplaces, home to more than 3,000 listed securities and a daily volume in excess of a billion shares. With 1,366 seat-holders (memberships), the New York Stock Exchange (NYSE) has attracted most of the world's largest corporations to its listings and counts among its members firms representing most of the financial capital in the securities industry. The NYSE's marketplace is built upon a specialist system of executions. Each security listed is assigned to a specialist unit that is charged by the exchange to maintain a "fair and orderly market." Over the years this has come to mean that the specialist must buy securities from sellers when there are no public bids and sell to buyers when there are no public offerings in a method that maintains the continuity of the marketplace. In fact, the specialist is involved in less than 20 percent of all transactions, with the balance involving customer meeting customer at the prevailing market price. As the industry has grown, these specialist units formerly numbering more than 100 have merged to about two dozen in recent years as the supply of capital for these functions are available only to the largest entities in the industry.

The NYSE has grown exponentially since its founding. Stock tickers were first used in 1867, and the exchange experienced its first million-share day in 1886. Although it experienced many panics in the 19th century, the 1929 crash was the worst day in its recorded history. After World War II, individual investors began returning to stock investments, and volume and activity began to increase. In 1972 the first salaried full-time chairman, James Needham, took office, and in 1975 the first consolidated TICKER TAPE was introduced along with negotiated commissions.

Technology has greatly changed the structure of the floor and the method of order entry. Whereas once all orders were delivered by hand to the trading posts and either executed or left on the specialist book for later execution (for which the specialist received a small fee), today most orders arrive electronically. The NYSE has developed a Dot System for automatic delivery of all small lot orders directly to the specialist post and a Super Dot for large-size orders to follow the same route. As a result of these changes, the role of the retail floor broker, that individual who walks around the floor executing orders, has been vastly diminished. The role of the broker who has the ability to handle or execute professional large-size institutional orders continues to be an important part of the daily volume on the floor of the NYSE.

In recent years, with the growth of electronic entities that look like stock exchanges but have none of the mandated regulatory functions of an exchange, the New York Stock Exchange has been the target of more and more competition. In fact, many of these electronic networks (ETNs) have applied to the Securities and Exchange Commission for status as exchanges. Expanded trading facilities have also led to increased volume. By the late 1990s, volume was well over a

Trading floor of the New York Stock Exchange, 1955 (LIBRARY OF CONGRESS)

billion shares per day, greatly fueled by the increased number of MUTUAL FUNDS doing business and the increased volume generated by hedge funds.

The New York Stock Exchange has also indicated a desire to demutualize (go public) to put itself in a better position to compete in the quickly changing financial services industry. Under the current structure, the NYSE is run by the votes of 1,366 members, and all decisions go through an arduous path of committees, boards, and staff. As a public corporation, decisions would be made and implemented quickly, a very necessary requirement in today's changing world. The question of going public does not resolve the question of the role of the NYSE as a regulator of the firms in its membership and as the organization charged with overseeing the business principles of its members. Many feel that a publicly owned NYSE cannot be both a competitor and a regulator in the securities industry at the same time.

See also AMERICAN STOCK EXCHANGE; NATIONAL ASSOCIATION OF SECURITIES DEALERS; STOCK MARKETS.

Further reading

Clews, Henry. *Fifty Years in Wall Street*. New York: Irving Publishing, 1908.

Eames, Francis. *The New York Stock Exchange*. New York: Thomas G. Hall, 1894.

Geisst, Charles R. *Wall Street: A History*. New York: Oxford University Press, 1997.

Sobel, Robert. *The Big Board: A History of the New York Stock Exchange*. New York: Weybright & Talley, 1975.

Lee Korins

Norris, George W. (1861–1944) *politician*

Norris was born on a farm in Sandusky County, Ohio, and attended local public schools. He graduated from Baldwin University in Ohio and Valparaiso University's law school in 1883. He taught school for two years before moving to Nebraska, where he began practicing law. He then became a county attorney and a district judge before being elected to Congress as a Republican in 1903. He served in the House of Representatives until 1913, when he successfully ran for the Senate, beginning a 30-year career in the upper house.

Norris became best known as a liberal Republican while serving in the Senate, carrying the torch as one of that body's last Progressives. He became known during and after World War I as an ardent opponent of big business on many occasions, criticizing bankers for the profits made during World War I. He also became an opponent of many of the large UTILITIES combines assembled during the 1920s, especially those of J. P. Morgan Jr. He opposed selling the Muscle Shoals power production plant on the Tennessee River to Henry FORD in 1921, maintaining that the project should remain in the public sector.

His greatest contribution to the NEW DEAL, with which he was ideologically aligned, came when he led the movement, at the behest of Franklin Roosevelt, to create the TENNESSEE VALLEY AUTHORITY (TVA) in order to keep Muscle Shoals permanently in the public realm. Norris had been opposed to private ownership of utilities, especially in rural areas, since many of them had higher operating costs than publicly owned utilities. As a result of his sponsorship, the first of the TVA's dams built was named the Norris Dam.

During his terms in the Senate, Norris held many important committee assignments and chairmanships. Among them were chairman, Committee on the Five Civilized Tribes of Indians, Committee on Patents, Committee on Agriculture and Forestry, and Committee on the Judiciary.

As he drifted further from the Republican Party, Norris won a seat in the Senate as an Independent in 1936. He served until 1943, when a reelection bid failed. Known as the "Father of the TVA," Norris died in McCook, Nebraska, in 1944.

See also MORGAN, JOHN PIERPONT, JR.

Further reading

Lowitt, Richard. *George W. Norris: Persistence of a Progressive, 1913–1933.* Urbana: University of Illinois Press, 1971.

Norris, George W. *Fighting Liberal: The Autobiography of George W. Norris.* New York: Macmillan, 1946.

North American Free Trade Agreement

(NAFTA) A comprehensive trade agreement that will eliminate TARIFFS and remove many nontariff barriers in trade among Mexico, Canada, and the United States. By 2004, most tariffs were phased out. By 2009, tariffs on the previously exempted products, mostly agricultural, will be eliminated. Most trade between the United States and Canada has been tariff-free since 1998 due to the Canada-U.S. Free Trade Agreement (CUFTA). Negotiations began in 1991, and NAFTA was passed by Congress in November 1993. The agreement went into effect on January 1, 1994. The three countries have a combined GDP of $9.5 trillion and a population of 396 million, creating a trade block that rivals the population and economy of the European Union.

Early economic analysis predicted gains for all three countries. However, since the United States and Canada already had a free trade agreement prior to NAFTA, most of the spectacular gains have been made in the trade with Mexico. According to the Dallas Federal Reserve Bank, exports to Canada increased 56 percent, exports to Mexico were up 89 percent, and U.S imports from Mexico and Canada increased 137 percent and 56 percent, respectively, by 1998. Total U.S.-Mexico trade increased 141 percent from 1993 to 1999. Without the agreement, U.S. exports to Mexico would have declined, and U.S. imports would have barely grown. Foreign direct investment, especially from the United States, in Mexico has increased as a result of this agreement. Approximately 80 percent of U.S.-Mexican trade is intraindustry. For example, the United States imports Volkswagens from the plant in Puebla, Mexico, and exports Cadillacs to Mexico. In addition, the trade agreement has facilitated production sharing, as in the maquiladora industry at the border. Certain industrial sectors experienced the most change. For example, the U.S. computer and tractor industries benefited greatly, and the Mexican textile industry boomed.

In current U.S. trade policy making, the president is required to obtain permission to negotiate from Congress, and the agreement must be approved by Congress. Historically, permission to negotiate was readily obtained. However, NAFTA created concern among many groups, especially unions and environmental groups. To receive permission, President George H. W. Bush promised to address some of the environmental and labor concerns. In 1993, a moderate Democrat, President Bill Clinton, created a pro-NAFTA coalition and moved away from the labor wing of the Democratic Party to gain congressional approval of the agreement with the following additions and side agreements. To address environmental concerns, the Border Environment Cooperation Commission was formed to encourage a clean-up of the border. The North American Development Bank was created to provide assistance for communities adjusting to the effects of NAFTA. The North American Agreement on Environmental Cooperation was designed to strengthen environmental cooperation and enforcement of domestic laws. These commissions are designed to promote a development that is sustainable, robust, and competitive.

In addition, the North American Agreement on Labor Cooperation was signed to improve the working conditions and living standards in the three countries, to ensure the enforcement of the respective labor laws, and to provide a venue for problem solving and dispute settlement. In the NAFTA text, under chapter eight of the agreement, parties can impose trade restrictions if increased imports harm a domestic industry. To implement this possibility, they created the Understanding on Emergency Action. Representatives from each country compose the Working Group on Emergency Action. This working group reports to the Free Trade Commission. The NAFTA secretariat provides technical support.

See also FOREIGN INVESTMENT; MULTINATIONAL CORPORATION.

Further reading

Mayer, Frederick W. *Interpreting NAFTA: The Science and Art of Political Analysis.* New York: Columbia University Press, 1998.

Orme, William A. *Understanding NAFTA: Mexico, Free Trade and the New North America.* Austin: University of Texas Press, 1996.

Jennifer Holmes

O

office machines   The office as we know it—rooms filled with people, in buildings designed just to house business facilities—came into existence only in the second half of the 19th century. One of the reasons companies and governments could bring large numbers of office workers together was the emergence of new classes of tools that made it possible for workers to be more productive or to do new things. These tools included adding machines, calculators, telephones, and punch-card tabulating equipment in the 19th century; in the 20th century, computers, photocopiers, PCs, fax machines, and, toward the end of the century, cell phones, laptops, and the INTERNET. Each of the new machines altered the "look-and-feel" of offices and what was done in them. The process of new machines and offices coming into American life began in earnest after the Civil War, although some office buildings had existed before, such as the old War Department building next to the White House, which housed most of the U.S. government during that conflict.

Offices in the 1600s and 1700s were typically the "studies" ministers had in their homes or churches, or a few small rooms in government buildings that housed a secretary or clerk who copied documents. The wealthy would often also have either a study or a library in which they worked, such as the famous library Thomas Jefferson had off his bedroom at Monticello. During the 18th and early 19th centuries, offices often were sparse rooms shared by a number of employees, housing a few books and several desks. Abraham Lincoln, while practicing law in the 1840s and 1850s, shared such an office with a colleague on the second floor of the courthouse in Springfield, Illinois. There were no such things as office buildings filled with hundreds of offices.

In the 1860s, a "typical" American office normally had two types of people: a person who in time would be called a manager, supervising the work of a few people, and others who were either clerks or accountants. High technology consisted of quill pens, paper, and a few reference books. There were no file cabinets, three-ring binders, TYPEWRITERS, or telephones. All of those things would begin arriving in the second half of the 1870s and by 1900 be widely deployed. Between 1875 and the end of the century, large organizations came into being, what we would eventually call corporations, with hundreds, even thousands of employees, multiple layers of management, and the need to coordinate activities across many states, even the entire United States. To a large extent that became possible because of a new collection of information technologies that came into use. The TELEGRAPH, invented before the Civil War, became a popular tool of big business, driving down operating costs for firms and technology. The telephone did the same, beginning at the end of the 1880s.

While the typewriter made it possible to rapidly create large amounts of new text, the telephone had an even more profound effect on how people did their work. Prior to the arrival of the telephone, if an individual wanted to have a quick conversation with someone in another location, one either had to write a note to be mailed or delivered by hand or personally travel to the other building or town to have the discussion. So the amount of this kind of activity that could be done was quite limited. But once many businesses used telephones, it became much easier to dial someone up, resulting in more conversations per day than before, all of which became possible in a practical manner by the early 1920s. By World War II, one could not imagine an office without a telephone.

Before discussing some of the new technologies we should understand what the business requirements were that led to their adoption. As organizations became larger, they needed new ways to record information in a cost-effective way. The typewriter addressed that need very nicely. Time clocks that employees would use to punch in and out collected additional information needed to pay those who were compensated by the hour. Businesses also needed to store and retrieve information as the volume of data required to operate an enterprise increased. During the 1880s and 1890s, a variety of new ways to do so reached the market. The most important innovation was the shift to cards for storing information as opposed to large ledger books. That allowed clerks to sort, merge, and organize data differently, first with hand-written cards

(e.g., 3 x 5 cards) and later with punched cards (what people would eventually call computer cards). These had holes representing different pieces of information (usually numbers) that could be read and sorted by tabulators and other specialized equipment. It was in this period that file cabinets and three-ring binders were invented. Analysis of numeric data was a third activity that managers also wanted to automate in order to understand efficiency and control processes. In support of this activity, adding and calculating machinery proved useful. The first widely available devices began appearing in the 1880s, followed by more specialized equipment that did specific tasks. These devices included billing and bookkeeping "appliances" and tabulating machinery to sort and tabulate results from punch-cards. These various devices had keyboards much like a typewriter by which clerks entered data upon which the machine would perform calculations, total results, and publish answers.

During the period from the 1870s to the end of World War I, continuous improvements in such equipment added functions, lowered their purchase price, and led to their wider use. The other reason for their rapid spread came from management; as they were able to obtain information more rapidly and easier than before, they wanted more of it. This in turn led to more data collection, which inspired manufacturers of such equipment to advance their technologies with newer models richer in function, capacity, and speed.

Large firms emerged in this period that became major information processing manufacturers of office equipment. Burroughs Corporation became the largest provider of adding and calculating machinery in the nation by the early years of the 20th century and years later (1950s) became an early supplier of computers. National Cash Register (NCR) began life in the 1880s as a manufacturer of a mechanical cash register; in the 1960s it also was a major supplier of computers and by the end of the 1970s, of point-of-sale (POS) systems for retail stores. In the late 1880s and early 1890s, Herman Hollerith (an ex-government census taker) introduced to the market punch-card equipment and tabulators, mainly used by large government agencies for tabulating results of population census data, and insurance and railroad companies to tabulate mountains of information. Hollerith's firm became the core piece of what eventually became INTERNATIONAL BUSINESS MACHINES (IBM). His punched cards were used as input and output for early mainframe computers and remained in use until the end of the 1980s.

In the period from 1885 to the start of the Great Depression at the beginning of the 1930s, literally thousands of types, brands, and models of office equipment came onto the market and became widely deployed in most offices of midsize to large government agencies and corporations. An office supply catalog of 1928 listing a variety of machines included adding and calculating machines, billing machines, bookkeeping machines (for accounting), accounting and tabulating machinery, check protectors and writers, coin-changing devices, cash registers, dictating machines, typewriters, duplicating machines, addressing machines, scales, time recording devices, and intercommunications equipment, to mention a few.

During the 1930s and 1940s, advances in the use of technologies available to office managers

Typewriting department at National Cash Register, Dayton, Ohio (LIBRARY OF CONGRESS)

slowed, first because demand went down during the Great Depression and then because supplies of equipment were limited during World War II. But by the 1930s, it would have been difficult to walk through an office without seeing some "hardware," at a minimum a telephone and a typewriter or adding machine. Between the 1880s and World War II, this technology created whole new classes of employees; the most important were secretaries, filing and other office clerks, and accountants. Hundreds of thousands of new jobs were created that were clearly of the type that were later referred to as information-age positions. The creation of the role of secretary in its modern form took place in this period and became the near-total monopoly of young women, often well educated, who learned to type, make telephone calls, and collect, store, and retrieve information and reports. They came to dominate the office as a hub, as as source of information, and as facilitators of various work activities largely based on a knowledge of organizational operations and people. Men continued to manage offices with minor exceptions, and men made up the overwhelming majority of the new class of accountants. Accounting, which pushed the demand for new technologies in the years before World War II, also became more sophisticated as new equipment made it possible to collect additional data and to analyze it quickly. Cost accounting procedures, for example, which document the cost of manufacture, delivery, and sale of products, came into their own in this period, along with inventory control.

After the end of World War II, a new era began in the development of office equipment and of changes in the role of offices. While improvements in adding and calculating equipment and punch-card machinery continued in the late 1940s and all through the 1950s, the central event was the development of commercial computers that came on the market in the early 1950s. The key systems of the day came from Univac, with its famous UNIVAC machines, and a series of computers from IBM in the 1950s. Other firms that were providers of "office appliances" in the prewar period entered the market, such as Burroughs and NCR, but also vendors of electronic appliances, such as GE and RCA. By the middle of the 1960s, the old office appliance firms dominated the new computer market, and from then on the story of computers involved either these old office appliance vendors or new firms born in the 1960s.

While computers are discussed elsewhere, it is important to understand four technological trends that affected the office during the second half of the 20th century. First, mainframes gradually became less expensive, grew easier to use, gained a larger capacity, and were more reliable—all of which encouraged large organizations to use them. Second, beginning in the late 1960s, software tools made it easier to write programs to do specific tasks, such as accounting activities, and commercially available products came to market. These were accompanied by the ability to interact with computers online by using terminals. Third, equipment, software, and telecommunications became more modular, beginning in the 1960s with the arrival of minicomputers and in the 1970s with personal computers. All of these developments meant that ever smaller organizations could afford to use computers and that this technology could be deployed across the economy in all kinds of organizations. Even the humble hand calculator, also equipped with computer chips, moved from being a $700 device from H-P in the early 1970s to being nearly a throwaway product that cost $5 in the early 1990s and was the size of a credit card. Fourth, as computer chips became increasingly inexpensive and available, beginning in the 1960s, computing began to appear inside many devices and equipment used in all functions of organizations, from computer-driven robotic painting machines in automotive factories to the humble digital watch that became so fashionable to wear in the 1970s. Typewriters acquired memory in the 1980s, while a decade earlier, the first word processors had arrived on the market, the most popular of which were from Wang. Telephones in the 1980s acquired a variety of functions made possible by the computer chip: call forwarding, answering machine functions, combined fax and phone operations, recording, and so forth.

Another variation of the office became possible due to all these technologies. Clustering employees together in large rooms to do similar work had been an early form of the modern office, with "typing pools" of dozens of typists already appearing by the early 1880s and continuing right into the 1980s in word processing departments. Insurance claims clerks, who processed data on clients' claims using adding and other calculating equipment, were also clustered in large rooms. Census takers for the U.S. government, using tabulating and other equipment, filled cavernous rooms beginning in the 1880s. Telephone companies created "call centers," also in the 1880s, that continue to be used in many industries today; a number of employees sit in a room in front of a bank of telephone switches (1880s–1970s) or of terminals attached to mainframe computers (1960s–present) doing similar work, whether troubleshooting a problem, taking an order, or responding to a customer's question or complaint. It did not matter if they were in one's state or halfway around the world; fiber-optic cables and computers made telephone calls clear and cost effective. What all these "bull pens" and other centers had in common was a high reliance on a common set of office equipment and a similar suite of functions that people performed. All of the jobs created in the process were a direct result of the existence of the various technologies needed to perform the work at hand.

By the end of the 1980s, a walk through an office in the United States would probably show a telephone, perhaps a typewriter but more likely a personal computer, and possibly in the corner either a fax machine or a photocopier, both of which now had computer chips that governed the variety of activities that they performed. In the half century between the end of World War II and the end of the millennium, the role of offices and people in them fundamentally transformed in large part because of the combined and increased use of telecommunications and computer-based office equipment. In 1950, the work of a business office felt very much like it had in the 1920s and 1930s. Secretaries typed reports and letters and answered the phone. Managers reviewed letters, read reports, and became extensive users of the telephone. Clerks still filed reports and documents in what now were large banks of file cabinets, while the "IBM Room" produced pay checks and monthly accounting reports. A quarter of a century later, some things had changed. The most important changes involved use of online systems in which filing clerks sat down at terminals and used their computers to retrieve increasing amounts of information stored in databases. Office managers still used the telephone but were also increasingly reliant on large boxy fax machines.

In the next 15 years, a massive change occurred that was facilitated by the arrival of new office equipment. Machines that could do word processing—what today is done on laptops using word software—increased the shift of clerks to data collection roles in which they entered data and retrieved it using computers. Secretaries also did this, often becoming the most technically competent people in the office. Organizations and individual managers and employees deployed PCs first to create and use spreadsheets (mainly for accounting), then word processing, and finally to look up information, thanks to the arrival of useful database management software in the 1970s and 1980s. These various applications led everyone in the office to increasingly have direct access to computers to enter information and to retrieve it. In turn, that led to a sharp decline in the number of office clerks and secretaries, a trend that has continued to the present as office automation makes it possible to do more with fewer people. Employees in business increasingly became more reliant on data (information) with which to do their work and to make decisions. The process management movement of the 1980s and 1990s would not have been possible without massive amounts of specific information about how tasks were being done, and the results of that work delivered in a timely fashion to workers and managers alike.

A third development in this short period of time was the increased convergence of telecommunications with computing. Online systems were one part of that process; another involved the ability of PCs to hook up to commercial and private databases by way of a telephone dial-up to access new sources of information with which to work, or to transmit data within an enterprise. E-mail began in this period, leading to a continuing shift away from letters and other paper documents moving about an enterprise. PCs acquired telecommunication capabilities, while the costs of long distance telephone calls began dropping, another trend that has continued unabated to the present. A long distance phone call in 1975 might have cost nearly 40 cents a minute; in 1990, it had dropped to under 30 cents and in 2004 to between 5 and 7 cents. Meanwhile, computing equipment increasingly acquired the ability to mix and match document text with graphics, to present material in color, and to attach still and moving pictures and sound. PCs by the millions flooded the market from such vendors as IBM, Compaq, and Apple. By 1990, more than half the American workforce either had access to a PC or used one on a regular basis; nearly half also had one at home. The democratization of computing was well on its way. It seemed that everyone had access to a computer.

In the early 1990s, telephones became more portable, along with computers. First came telephones that could be used in automobiles (originally called radio phones) that allowed salesmen and service personnel to communicate with their offices. Then came the less expensive, smaller cell phones, which were first adopted by middle and upper management, then by sales and consulting personnel, and by the early 2000s, by more than a third of the American public. At the same time, PCs became smaller and lighter. IBM

introduced what came to be known as the laptop, and soon all vendors had their versions. Laptops, equipped with modems that allowed people to access company files and their firm's e-mail system, in combination with cell phones, made working in a physical office less necessary. People could do a great deal regardless of location. The technology also caused many people to work longer hours because they could and did check their business e-mail at home after dinner, or could call a colleague on a weekend when a brainstorm occurred. Increasingly in the 1990s, more employees began working out of their home offices. While reliable statistics on how many did so are difficult to come by, at least 10 percent began working this way. The group cohesion that working in an office created in prior years was put at risk, but companies saved billions of dollars by downsizing the number of offices they owned and maintained.

From the early 1970s forward another evolution in office functions took place involving a variety of telecommunications. As offices acquired terminals attached to mainframes, these were linked together either through telephone dial-up or by way of dedicated phone lines. Large enterprises also created their own internal telephone networks, which allowed employees to start communicating with each other by using what eventually would be called e-mail. E-mail instantly became the choice over these dial-up and private lines in the 1970s and expanded in the 1980s and 1990s to the point that it is now ubiquitous. At the same time, the U.S. Department of Defense built a highly robust, secure network in the early 1970s that scientists, military personnel, and defense contractors could use. That network was opened to academics by the late 1970s and to others who knew how to access the network. By the mid-1990s, this network was called the Internet. The development of software tools (called browsers) in the mid-1990s made it easier to access and use the Internet. Use of the Internet expanded rapidly to the point that by the early years of the new century, more than two-thirds of office workers used it primarily for e-mail and looking up information. By the early 2000s, having an enterprise home page was considered business as usual, with information about one's company or agency, its services and products, and contact data. In the 1970s private networks sold information over telephone lines (such as financial data), and these services also migrated to the Internet.

Deployment of the Internet is not yet as extensive as the use of terminals and telephones. An office worker in the early 2000s had sufficient technology to be essentially free of having to work in an office. Cell phones and laptops, PDAs to hold information, and the Internet for e-mail and information-gathering all made the use of mobile workers in the 1990s essential for the modern office.

See also GATES, BILL; JOBS, STEVE.

Further reading
Chandler, Alfred D., Jr., and James W. Cortada, eds. *A Nation Transformed by Information: How Information Has Shaped the United States from Colonial Times to the Present.* New York: Oxford University Press, 2000.
Cortada, James W. *Before the Computer: IBM, NCR, Burroughs, & Remington Rand & The Industry They Created, 1865–1956.* Princeton, N.J.: Princeton University Press, 1993.
———. *The Digital Hand.* 2 vols. New York: Oxford University Press, 2004–2006.
Yates, JoAnne. *Control through Communications: The Rise of System in American Management.* Baltimore: Johns Hopkins University Press, 1989.

James W. Cortada

options markets Organized markets for put and call options, originally on common stocks, which developed alongside the securities markets in the 1970s. Along with futures and swaps, options markets are part of the derivatives markets that have developed mostly in Chicago and New York to help investors hedge risk on commodities, securities, and other underlying instruments.

Puts and calls (options to sell and buy) were traded informally on an over-the-counter basis since before the Civil War. Originally, a broker would arrange for an investor to buy or sell a put (option to sell) or call (option to buy). The investors on both sides of the deal would then wait to see if the buyer would exercise the right to the stock at the predetermined price. But options quickly became vehicles for manipulation and fraud. Stock market operators used them in stock watering schemes and as ways in which to manipulate the price of a stock.

In the FUTURES MARKETS, options on futures contracts were banned on the major markets, including the CHICAGO BOARD OF TRADE, in the 19th century. As stock trading grew more popular over the years, trading became more uniform as options were traded on an over-the-counter basis, but the market was often illiquid and lacked REGULATION.

In the late 1960s, volatile STOCK MARKETS created the need for more uniform options on a broader array of widely held common stocks that investors could use for hedging purposes. Organized option exchanges were developed in Chicago at the Chicago Board Options Exchange in 1973 and then at the AMERICAN STOCK EXCHANGE in 1974. The BLACK-SCHOLES options model helped investors and traders value options more precisely and led to their faster development. Each exchange listed options on the stocks it wanted to trade. Despite the fact that the markets are derivatives markets, the Securities and Exchange Commission is the regulator of equity options because they represent common stocks. After 1975, options on futures contracts again were permitted when the COMMODITY FUTURES TRADING COMMISSION was established by Congress.

Options also were developed for other financial instruments, including bonds, stock indexes, and precious metals. The markets continued to expand rapidly although not all stocks have options listed. In order to qualify for an options listing, a stock must fulfill a requirement laid down by the respective exchanges, not unlike those that the stock exchanges demand of a company before its stock can be listed. Currently, most options contracts use a variation of the Black-Scholes model for valuation.

Further reading

Geisst, Charles R. *Wheels of Fortune: The History of Speculation from Scandal to Respectability.* New York: John Wiley & Sons, 2002.

Owens, Michael J. (1859–1923) *inventor and businessman* Michael Joseph Owens was born in Mason County, (West) Virginia, on January 1, 1859, a son of Irish immigrants. After obtaining a rudimentary education, he left school at 10 to secure an apprenticeship at J. H. Hobbs, Brockunier, and Company, a leading glass manufacturer. Owens displayed an amazing aptitude for glasswork, and by 15 he was an acknowledged master of the art of glassblowing. Over the years he also assumed a prominent role in the American Flint Glass Workers Union, and helped bring about the closure of Edward Drummond Libbey's New England Glass Company in 1888. When that firm reopened in Toledo, Ohio, as the Libbey Glass Company, Owens was allowed to join as a blower of lamp shades. Within a few years he advanced to the important post of blowing room foreman and plant supervisor in recognition of his considerable talents. Owens and Libbey eventually reconciled their differences and struck up a cordial working relationship, with Owens providing technical and engineering inspiration and Libbey lending his financial and marketing expertise. By 1896, Owens had perfected his first mechanical innovation, a device to facilitate rapid tumbler and lamp-chimney production. The entire process was semiautomatic at best and required skilled handling, but it greatly enhanced factory output. Owens's success induced Libbey to underwrite the founding of Owens's new Toledo Glass Company, which placed a continu-

ing strong emphasis on research and development in glass manufacture. Moreover, it provided Owens with both the revenue and resources necessary to pursue his technical innovations.

Owens's success as an inventor further facilitated his growing business relationship with Libbey, who continued financing his inventions and sharing the profits from licensing. His greatest technical achievement occurred in 1899, when he finally perfected an automatic device for the MASS PRODUCTION of bottles. This entailed an intricate multiplicity of tasks such as gathering the molten glass, transferring it to a mold, puffing hot air to form the bottle, and severing it on a conveyor belt to the cooling oven. Such a machine quickly dispensed with several highly skilled technicians and thereby increased factory output while dramatically reducing labor costs. Given the relatively crude state of mechanization of the day, it was a true triumph of engineering. Consequently, the Owens Bottle Machine Company was founded in 1903, which significantly impacted the ability of consumers to enjoy a wide range of liquid products at their pleasure. When Owens subsequently licensed his technology to other firms, both he and Libbey profited handsomely from the revenues.

Owens continued manufacturing glass with great success, and in 1912 he became apprised of Irving W. Coburn's attempts to perfect the cutting of sheet-drawn windowpanes. He prevailed upon Libbey to purchase Colburn's patents, even threatening to leave the company if Libbey failed to do so, and spent the next four years perfecting his own sheet-drawing process. His efforts proved successful, and in 1916, the partners formed a new organization, the Libbey-Owens Sheet Glass Company. Again, this new technology greatly increased the output of high-quality windowpanes for consumers while greatly lowering costs. Owens continued producing glass and tinkering with his devices until his death in Toledo on December 27, 1923. In his long career he wielded a tremendous influence upon glassware production in the United States and around the world, singlehandedly transforming it from a highly skilled art into a modern manufacturing process. He owed much of his success to financial and legal backing from Libbey, but the inspiration for change and innovation was purely his own.

Further reading

Floyd, Barbara, Richard Oram, and Nola Skouson. "The City Built of Glass." *Labor's Heritage* 2, no. 4 (1990): 66–75.

Lamoreaux, Noami R., and Kenneth L. Sokoloff. *Location and Technological Change in the American Glass Industry during the Late Nineteenth and Early Twentieth Centuries.* Cambridge, Mass.: National Bureau of Economic Research, 1997.

Walbridge, William S. *American Bottles Old and New: A Story of the Industry in the U.S.* Toledo: Owens Bottle Company, 1920.

John C. Fredriksen

P

Panama Canal Water passage connecting the Atlantic and Pacific Oceans through the Isthmus of Panama. Originally envisaged by the Spanish in the 16th century, American interest in a canal officially did not begin until after the Civil War. Various attempts were made at crossing Central America through Nicaragua before the war, including one by Cornelius VANDERBILT, but always proved unsuccessful. The Americans and British both desired to build a canal in the 1840s and almost went to war over disputed claims in Nicaragua. But it was not until 1914 that the 51-mile canal was actually opened for ship travel.

The need for a canal became more urgent when gold was discovered in California at Sutter's Mill in 1848. A group of New York businessmen built a railroad across the isthmus in 1855 with permission of the Colombian government, which ruled Panama at the time. Then in 1878 a French company directed by Ferdinand de Lesseps began digging a canal for the first time. De Lesseps had directed construction of the Suez Canal, but after numerous setbacks, the French company went bankrupt in 1889. A second French company continued the effort in 1894 but was technically incapable of making much

progress. Five years earlier, in 1889, an American company began work on a canal across Nicaragua but also ran out of money. Only after the Spanish-American War did the United States government become interested in a Panama canal project. In 1902, President Theodore Roosevelt accepted a French offer to complete the project, and the following year the United States signed a canal treaty with Colombia.

The United States sent troops to Panama to protect the isthmus from Colombia and in 1903 officially recognized the Republic of Panama as an independent country. The chief engineer overseeing the construction was General George W. Goethals, a West Point graduate. More than 40,000 people worked on the canal at its most intense period, and it was finally completed in 1914. The approximate cost to the United States was about $380 million, and the canal saved more than 8,000 miles on the ship route between the East and West Coasts of the United States. In 1971 the United States and Panama began negotiations for a new treaty to replace the one signed in 1903. The original treaty was replaced with two, one allowing Panama to take control of the Canal Zone and the other to take official control of the

The Panama Canal under construction (LIBRARY OF CONGRESS)

canal at the end of the 20th century. The United States retained the right to defend the neutrality of the zone. The treaties were approved in Panama in 1977 and by the U.S. Senate in 1978, and both took effect in 1979. On December 31, 1999, full control of the canal was handed over to Panama.

Further reading

Haskin, Frederic J. *The Panama Canal*. New York: Doubleday, Page, 1913.

McCullough, David. *Path between the Seas: The Creation of the Panama Canal, 1870–1914*. New York: Simon & Schuster, 1999.

Pan American Airways An American airline founded by Juan Trippe in 1927. Originally, the airline was a one-route mail carrier flying from Miami to Havana, Cuba. Its premiere flight was on a chartered Fairchild airplane. In 1929, Pan Am began flying the mail route from the United States to Mexico City. The company then won other contracts to fly to the Caribbean and South America and, in 1931, from Boston to Maine. Within a short time of being founded, the company began using seaplanes, which were ideally suited for some of its more difficult routes.

After buying planes from the BOEING CO., Pan Am began offering a cross-Pacific service on its Pacific Clipper. When a flight was interrupted by war in the Pacific, the plane had to return to New York by circling the globe, becoming the first commercial flight to do so. During the war, the airline did long-distance contract flying for the government, reinforcing its credentials as the most experienced long-haul airline in the country. After the war, when jet engines became easier to produce, Trippe was the first customer for them, anticipating the commercial possibilities of flying customers to distant locations as quickly as possible. In 1958, Pan Am's clipper *America* inaugurated jet service to Paris from New York using a Boeing 707 and became the first commercial jet service.

Pan Am's jet services, plus its use of the Boeing 747, the original jumbo jet, opened the market for relatively inexpensive jet service to all and gave Pan Am the unofficial designation as America's flagship air carrier. The company's success could be clearly seen in Manhattan, where the Pan Am Building towered above Grand Central Station in midtown, with a heliport on its roof. The airline also used Boeing 727s to help evacuate American personnel from Vietnam at the fall of Saigon.

The plane blown up by a terrorist bomb over Lockerbie, Scotland, in 1988 was Pan Am Flight 103, and the company was severely affected by the incident. It continued to fly but only with increasing financial difficulties. The company remained the country's best-known international airline until 1991, when those financial problems forced it to shut down operations.

See also AIRLINE INDUSTRY; AIRPLANE INDUSTRY; EASTERN AIRLINES.

Further reading

Daley, Robert. *An American Saga: Juan Trippe and His Pan Am Empire.* New York: Random House, 1980.

Robinson, Jack E. *American Icarus: The Majestic Rise and Fall of Pan Am.* New York: Noble House, 1994.

patents and trademarks The Patent and Trademark Office (PTO) is an agency of the U.S. Department of Commerce that examines and issues/registers patents and trademarks. The Patent Office was created in 1790 and, for more than 200 years, has represented federal support for the progress of science and the useful arts. In 1870, the Patent Office also took charge of issuing trademarks, creating the modern-day PTO.

Patents give inventors a legal monopoly if an invention or device is novel, useful, and nonobvious. A patent is the governmental grant of an exclusive right to make, use, or sell an invention for a specified period, usually 17 years. In contrast, a trademark is a word, phrase, logo, or other graphic symbol that distinguishes one manufacturer's product from another. The main purpose of a trademark is to aid consumers in identifying brands and products in the marketplace and is akin to a guarantee of a product's authenticity. A trademark's duration is indefinite, as long as it continues to represent goods in commerce.

The Constitutional Convention of 1789 created a federal patent system rooted in the Constitution itself. Article I, Section 8, authorizes Congress to award exclusive rights for a limited time to inventors. Thomas Jefferson was a significant contributor to the early federal establishment of the patent system. However, the patent system fully realized its potential in 1836 with the establishment of a formal system of patent examination, complete with professional examiners. Patents on critical inventions in American history, such as the light bulb and the telephone system, came to symbolize the technological development of the 19th century.

In the 20th century, the patent system underwent significant changes. In the 1920s and 1930s, the public viewed large companies as having too much power via patents that dominated their respective industries. Courts became less willing to enforce patent rights until the 1940s, as the nation became involved in the war effort. The military called on inventors to quickly create a large number of new technologies. By the time the war had concluded, Congress favored a stronger patent system, which resulted in the 1952 Patent Act, the first major revision in the patent code since the 19th century. The result of the Patent Act of 1952 was a period of strong protection in which the patent office issued patents freely in comparison to its earlier, more rigorous examinations.

Although patents were being issued more freely to inventors, the federal court system was reluctant to uphold patent rights. In addition to being reluctant to uphold these rights, circuit courts also differed as to the doctrine and attitudes toward patents. Again, Congress responded to these developments by passing the Federal Courts Improvements Act, creating the Court of Appeals for the Federal Circuit (CAFC) in 1982. One of the original, primary functions of the CAFC has been to hear all appeals involving patents. As a result, patents are more likely to be upheld, and injunctions against patent infringers are more easily realized than earlier in the century.

Trademarks differ from patents in that they do not seek to protect something new. In fact, a trademark does not require any degree of inventiveness, only that a distinctive mark is used in commerce. Trademarks were protected in the United States through common law until 1870, when Congress enacted the first federal trademark statute. That statute was later struck down by the Supreme Court, and in its place Congress enacted the Act of 1881, which based protection for trademarks in the COMMERCE CLAUSE of the U.S. Constitution. The trademark statute was modified in 1905 and again in 1920 until, in 1946, Congress enacted the Lanham Act (15 U.S.C. §1051 et seq.), which continues to govern the protection of trademarks today.

In addition to administering the laws related to patents and trademarks, the PTO advises the secretary of commerce, the president of the United States, and the administration on patent, trademark, and copyright protection as well as all trade-related aspects of intellectual property.

Further reading

McManis, Charles R. *Unfair Trade Practices in a Nutshell.* St. Paul, Minn.: West Publishing, 2000.

Merges, Robert, et al. *Intellectual Property in the New Technological Age, 2nd ed.* New York: Aspen, 2000.

Margaret A. Geisst

Penney & Co., J. C.   A department store chain founded by James Cash Penney (1875–1971) in 1902. Born in Missouri, he worked for eight years in a Missouri dry goods store before moving west. His original store was called the Golden Rule Store and was opened in Kemmerer, Wyoming. The name was derived from his fundamental belief that customers should be given a good deal. By 1913, he had 36 stores, and the company was incorporated as J. C. Penney. During World War I and the early 1920s, the chain began to expand rapidly as store managers were allowed to open new stores, keeping one-quarter of the profits, as soon as they were successful. The simple concept led the store to its massive expansion, making it the second-largest retailer in the country by 1970.

The stores proliferated during the general chain store expansion of the 1920s. Penney opened its 500th store in 1924, but the stores were still selling mostly clothing and shoes. Store executives were active in fighting the anti–chain store movement during that decade. By 1930, the company had expanded to 1,250 stores, located mostly in towns and cities serving a wide clientele. After World War II, it moved into the suburbs that were expanding rapidly at the time and added more merchandise to its offerings. The expansion was successful, and by 1980 the company had more than 3,100 stores and employed more than 365,000 people, recording sales over $9 billion. It also expanded into mail-order sales, competing with Montgomery Ward and SEARS, ROEBUCK & CO. International expansion also took place, with smaller chains acquired in Belgium and Italy. Penney also diversified by purchasing a drug store chain and an insurance company. By the mid-1970s, Penney was a staple of retailing and considered an anchor store in most malls throughout the country.

Penney was replaced by K-MART in the late 1970s as the second-largest retailing chain to Sears, Roebuck. After slipping in the ranks of retail CHAIN STORES, the company began a comeback in the 1990s. By the end of the decade, stores totaled 1,075 and were located in all 50 states and Mexico. The company also owned a smaller retail chain in Brazil. Its drugstore expansion also continued to be positive when it acquired the Eckerd Drugstores group, which operates 2,650 stores throughout the United States.

Further reading

Beasley, Norman. *Main Street Merchant: The Story of the J. C. Penney Company.* New York: Whittlesey House, 1948.

Hendrickson, Robert. *The Grand Emporiums: The Illustrated History of America's Great Department Stores.* New York: Stein & Day, 1980.

Penney, J. C. *Fifty Years with the Golden Rule.* New York: Harper & Brothers, 1950.

pension funds   Funds set aside by employers and/or employees to provide benefits for employees upon retirement. Pension funds in one form or other have existed since ancient times, although the current funds in the United States evolved from the 19th century. Originally, pension funds were provided by government employers for those who served in the armed forces. Disabled veterans have received a pension since the Revolutionary War and retired military personnel since the early 19th century. Today there are several categories of pension—public, private, and personal.

In 1875, the first private pension plan in the United States was begun by American Express Co., then a transport company. In 1880, the RAILROADS became the first industry to offer a pension to their workers, and they were followed by other industries. Private plans grew during the first three decades of the 20th century until the Great Depression. Many private plans failed due to weaknesses in the market, and Congress was

forced to react. It passed the Old Age, Survivors, Disability and Hospital Insurance Program in 1935, better known as Social Security. Becoming operational two years later, Social Security was, and is, known as a nonfunded pension plan. Contributors' funds are used to pay recipients; the contributions are not invested. Social Security was meant to augment private plans, not to serve as an individual's sole source of retirement funds.

Most private plans are funded, in contrast to Social Security. This means that the contributions made on behalf of the employee are invested in the market until retirement. Private plans may be of two general types—defined benefit or defined contribution. Under a defined benefit plan, the retiree is guaranteed a specific income during retirement. Under a defined contribution plan, the employee is required to make specific payments, while the amount of payout at the end is not guaranteed. In a contributory plan, the employee and the employer make contributions to the fund, while in a noncontributory plan, only the employer does so. Private defined contribution plans are covered by insurance provided by the Pension Benefits Guaranty Board, or Penny Benny, created in 1974.

Penny Benny, a federally created agency, was created by the Employee Retirement Income Security Act (ERISA) in 1974. Private plans purchase insurance from the agency, and if they cannot provide benefits at a future date, the insurance is used to do so. The act also helped establish employee stock ownership plans (ESOPS), which allowed employees to purchase shares in the companies they worked for through a trust established by the company itself, enabling employees to become shareholders in the company that they work for. The ESOP invests in the stock of the employer, which sponsors the plan. Over the last 30 years, ESOPS have become increasingly popular as a means of compensating employees and allowing them greater participation and interest in corporate affairs.

ESOPs were developed by an attorney, Louis Kelso, in the early 1950s, and the first one was introduced in 1956. In the 1970s, the idea was given considerable impetus when Congress passed the Employee Retirement Income Security Act, or ERISA. The act governed employee benefit plans and established guidelines by which ESOPs could be established. Among their benefits, the plans are able to borrow money in order to purchase stock, effectively becoming leveraged ESOPs. In this respect, their use becomes similar to other sorts of leveraged buy-outs of company stock, such as a leveraged buy-out or a management buyout, except that in this case the buyers are the employees. During the 1980s, when buyouts became popular on Wall Street in general, ESOPS were used by employees and companies to protect their interests against hostile takeovers by unwanted suitors who often threatened company pension plans as a result of their successful takeovers.

Technically, an ESOP is established when a company creates a trust and makes annual contributions to it. The contributions are then allocated to employees, depending upon certain conditions such as length of service. Employees receive the bulk of their share of the plans at termination of duty, retirement, or death. By 1999, almost 12,000 companies had established these plans, covering almost 9 million employees.

ERISA also allowed personal pension plans, which can be created by individuals independent of an employer. Individual retirement accounts (IRAs), Keogh plans for the self-employed, and 401k plans are examples. Individuals can put aside a specific dollar amount or percent of their income, and the plans are directed by the individual herself rather than by an investment manager. Some of these plans are also portable and may be carried from employer to employer rather than terminated when an employee leaves for another position. The personal plans were created in part to augment Social Security, which was under financial pressure in the early 1970s.

Beginning in the 1980s, Congress allowed pension plans to become portable, meaning that they could be funded by employees, regardless of employer. These plans, known universally as 401k plans, became extremely popular since employees could control the investments. However, with the decline of the stock market that began in 2000, many of these plans were seriously eroded since many of them were heavily invested in equity investments rather than being balanced with other investments.

Further reading

Blackburn, Robin. *Banking on Death or Investing in Life: The History and Future of Pensions.* New York: Verso, 2002.

Brown, Jeffrey R. *The Role of Annuity Markets in Financing Retirement.* Cambridge, Mass.: MIT Press, 2001.

Clark, Robert Louis, Lee A. Craig, and Jack Wilson. *A History of Public Sector Pensions in the United States.* Philadelphia: University of Pennsylvania Press, 2003.

Kelso, Louis O., and Patricia H. Kelso. *Democracy and Economic Power: Extending the ESOP Revolution.* New York: Ballinger, 1986.

petroleum industry   The petroleum industry in the United States was created to exploit what would become a recurrent theme in its history, diminishing supplies of consumer products that were increasingly in demand, accompanied by rising prices. At the mid-point of the 19th century, petroleum products were illuminants, principally derived from animal tallow and spermaceti whales, and were long the most widely used source in candle making. The amount of light produced and the limited lifetime of candles made them less desirable than oil lamps, which had been in use for millennia but were improved through enhanced lamp design and the use of fuels that produced more light and burned longer, product characteristics in special demand in factories and urban homes. The most desirable fuel, whale oil, was in diminishing supply, as over-hunting thinned herds, decreased yields, and led to mounting prices. Substitutes, including camphene, distilled from turpentine, were developed during the 1830s, but extreme volatility limited their use until lamp improvements during the following decade lessened the risk of explosion.

Anticipating opportunity in this situation, inventors and entrepreneurs in Europe and America experimented with the refining of oils extracted from coal and shale, developing refining processes that yielded commercially useful oil, though its flash point was commonly so low that consumers generally viewed the product as hazardous. Coal oil proved to be popular, prompting the construction of about 400 plants in urban centers of the United States by 1860.

In the United States, several groups of scientists and entrepreneurs sought improved lamp design and a raw material more accessible and cheaper to process than coal and shale. One group, including members in New York City and at Yale University, was especially venturesome, particularly after Professor Benjamin Silliman Jr.'s laboratory experiments demonstrated that refining could extract at least half of the light fractions of crude oil, often found in surface seepages, notably in northeastern Pennsylvania. In 1857, the Pennsylvania Rock Oil Company hired Edwin L. Drake, a one-time railroad conductor, to drill on leases it had acquired in the vicinity of Titusville, in northwestern Pennsylvania. After a transfer of the properties to the Seneca Oil Company, Drake commenced operations, proceeding slowly and with frequent delays until August 28, 1859, when the crew brought oil to the surface. Drake's well, modest by comparison to later discoveries in Pennsylvania and elsewhere, demonstrated that it was possible to discover and produce crude oil in commercial qualities by drilling. An industry was born.

Its early years were no less turbulent than the decades that followed. As oil men drilled along Oil Creek and in other creeks and valleys in the region, they brought in wells that ranged from token producers to what were at the time described as elephant wells. The well brought in by New York oilman Orange Noble in 1863, flowed 3,000 barrels per day for a few months, then tapered off to 300 barrels less than two years later. In the meantime, it and several other wells flooded the market for crude oil, driving prices downward throughout what became known as the Oil Producing Region of Pennsylvania. Prices, between $18.50 and $20 per barrel early in 1860, dropped to $4 by mid-year. By the end of the following year, prices stabilized briefly at $2.00. Thereafter, price volatility continued to define the economics of oil as exploration and production spread to other parts of Pennsylvania and New York, and then to West Virginia, Ohio, Indiana, California, Kansas, Oklahoma, Texas, Arkansas, Louisiana, and other states.

During the first decade of activity, refiners typically clustered in cities that were accessible by water and rail as well as in the producing regions. Many of the plants were small, and little more complicated than moonshiners' stills. For the most part, all of the processors aimed at yields of kerosene, which enjoyed a cost advantage over competing illuminants. By the 1870s, however, several notable changes, among them the construction of more efficient 500- and 600-barrel capacity operations, gave the larger refiners who could raise $100,000 or more for such plants significant cost and price advantages over smaller operators. From that time, refiners such as Charles Pratt & Co. of New York City and Standard Oil of Cleveland improved market position and emerged as leading purchasers of crude oil. During the late 1870s and early 1880s, Standard, led by John D. ROCKEFELLER and his associates, built a vast refinery capacity at multiple sites and bought out or merged with leading competitors, to the point that the company controlled about 90 percent of American refinery capacity by the mid-1880s.

The emergence of Standard as the dominant American refiner prompted widespread objection and criticism, notably by smaller competitors and wholesalers; the latter lost valuable commissions when Rockefeller's company expanded into wholesale operations in both the United States and abroad. With allies of their own in the press and in politics, Standard's critics unleashed a barrage of litigation and legislative attacks, keeping the company and Rockefeller in the headlines for more than four decades. Controversy over the company and its competitive methods increased when it expanded its operations into pipelines and oil production during the 1880s and 1890s, taking it into court in most producing states and deepening its political problems.

Finally, during the first decade of the 20th century, the vast company was sued under the SHERMAN ACT in a federal court in Missouri. When the case reached the U.S. Supreme Court in 1911, the Court broke up Standard Oil into 33 components. As the new companies, including

An Oklahoma well strikes oil (LIBRARY OF CONGRESS)

Standard of New Jersey, Indiana, California, and Ohio, defined their marketing areas, they emerged as competitors in contiguous territories. They joined a number of new companies that formed after the discovery of massive quantities of oil in the Southwest, most notably at Spindletop, near Beaumont, Texas, in 1901 and in other sections of Texas, Oklahoma, Arkansas, New Mexico, and Louisiana. Gulf Oil and Refining, the Texas Company, Shell, Sun, and other new companies proved to be aggressive competitors, fighting for both regional American and foreign markets, further paring the dominance of the Standard group.

With the shift of production and processing westward, oil operations were increasingly managed from new oil centers, including Houston and Tulsa. The political climates of Texas and Oklahoma could not have been more supportive of the new industry. In Texas, the Railroad Commission first assumed regulatory responsibility for pipelines, then became the enforcer of early environmental regulations such as the limitation of run-off oil into rivers and streams. The commission also attempted, with less success, to limit drilling on small tracts and to slow the pace of field development to lessen waste and social disruption that often stemmed from the boom-type development of petroleum resources.

During the second and third decades of the 20th century, additional improvements in refining and processing increased the efficiency of plants, as continuous process production appeared after its development by the Nobel brothers in pre-revolutionary Russia. Further advances processed crude oil at higher temperatures and pressures, removing a greater proportion of the light fractions that yielded gasoline, in soaring demand because trucks and automobiles were rolling off assembly lines in growing numbers. By 1920, more than 9 million vehicles were registered in the United States and were served by more than 140,000 gas stations by the end of that decade.

Growing demand for petroleum products was more than matched by new discoveries of oil reservoirs. Areas of northern and central Texas, Oklahoma, Louisiana, the Texas Panhandle, and the Permian Basin of Texas and New Mexico came into production to supplement new discoveries in California and in the Texas Gulf Coast area. In California, Shell's discovery at Signal Hill in 1921 launched a new chapter in California oil, while the opening of the Greater Seminole Field in Oklahoma during 1926 sustained that state's strong flow of crude oil. Most notably, the Permian Basin region opened during the mid-1920s, with a long series of commercially significant discoveries stretching into the 1950s, when it became—as it remains—the principal oil-producing region in the lower 48 states. By the late 1920s, the new discoveries had long since replaced long-standing reserves and often flooded markets at least briefly with enough new crude oil to lower prices significantly. Typically, the effects were short-lived as producers negotiated voluntary limitations on production.

Voluntary measures were impossible to negotiate after the giant East Texas Field began producing on October 3, 1930. Running through five counties, the vast reservoir was cheap to penetrate, while a large proportion of the leases were in the hands of hundreds of independent producers who drilled quickly, on as little land as possible, and sought a quick return of capital from the high-gravity, low-sulphur crude. The impact of the discovery was fast and widespread, driving the price of oil as low as a dime a barrel, destabilizing markets, and lowering the asset values of large companies that held substantial reserves elsewhere, kept in storage. Many operators and companies were pushed to the edge of financial failure.

Some large leaseholders, including Humble Oil and Refining (an SONJ subsidiary) and H. L. Hunt, the largest independent in the field, supported production restrictions in the interest of long-term gain. Other large companies, including Gulf and Texaco, like many of the independents, needed crude oil and the income it generated in the short term and opposed intervention by the Texas Railroad Commission, originally created in 1891 to set shipping rates on intrastate railroad lines. The divisions among oil and gas producers prompted litigation at every step. When the commission issued orders limiting production, the matter ended up in both state and federal courts, losing in both jurisdictions in 1931. In August, local officials requested a martial law decree, which Governor Ross Sterling, once head of Humble, issued. By October, Texas National Guard troopers were in the field, attempting to enforce commission restrictions. Several months later, a federal judge declared that action illegal. And so it went from field to court and back.

The passage of the National Industrial Recovery Act in 1933 provided federal support for restrictions by making illegal the interstate shipment of oil produced in excess of a state regulatory body's limits. In 1934, federal courts accepted the commission's authority and that of comparable bodies in Oklahoma and other states to restrict production to prevent economic waste. After the U.S. Supreme Court struck down the NIRA, the Connolly Hot Oil Act of February 1935 reestablished federal enforcement of state regulatory limitations. In the same year, creation of the Interstate Oil Compact facilitated cooperation among state regulatory agencies. By then, the East Texas Field was declining to some extent, but the bill was of continued importance because other significant discoveries in Texas and elsewhere would have swamped oil markets had regulators been unable to control production.

The device used would prove to be historically important: Refiners provided estimates of their demand for feedstock, and the Texas Railroad Commission set state production to match a portion of it. Regulators in other states—excepting California and Illinois, which lacked agencies—adjusted their figures accordingly. The Texas body was fixed with responsibility for sustaining prices and allotting production. Its system was long observed by oilmen and politicians around the world, leading foreign producers to create a comparable international body when they created the Oil Producing and Exporting Countries organization after World War II. In the meantime, volume and hence price were determined by a previously obscure group of three elected officials in Austin, Texas.

Exploration continued at a diminished pace during the first half of that decade, though notable additions to crude oil reserves were made in Texas and Louisiana, along with additional discoveries of natural gas. Long-distance pipelines were constructed to connect gas fields with urban centers in those states and in the middle west. Of longer-term consequence, the increasingly abundant gas would supply essential feedstock for the nascent petrochemical industry, which appeared during the late 1930s when Shell and Esso began to produce 100 octane aviation fuel to feed synthetic rubber and other processing companies.

World War II demand for gasoline forced state regulators to open up the valves, with the East Texas Field producing at maximum capacity because of its proximity to refinery and pipeline systems. To facilitate shipments to East Coast refineries, the federal government paid for the construction of the Big Inch and Little Big Inch pipelines, which linked Gulf Coast fields with middle-western pipelines, connecting to lines that carried crude oil to refineries along the East Coast. Gasoline was rationed during the conflict, in some measure to conserve short supplies of rubber required to produce tires.

Gasoline rationing was ended officially the day after Japan surrendered in 1945. Response to pent-up demand put a record number of vehicles on American highways—26 million in 1945 and 40 million by 1950. With the beginning of the interstate highway system in 1956, nearly 43,000 miles of super-highway would be created to carry the swelling number of cars and trucks. Conversion of coal-users to natural gas and fuel oil swelled the markets for both commodities, with the former increasing nearly threefold in interstate shipment between 1946 and 1950. Fuel oil

was increasingly competitive, until 1958 it was cheaper than coal per unit of heat generated. During succeeding decades, demand for crude oil continued to soar, from 5.8 million barrels per day in 1948 to 16.4 million barrels per day in 1972.

Though new oilfields were discovered in Alaska, Louisiana, Texas, and other states after World War II, supply did not keep up with demand. U.S. production peaked at 11.3 million barrels per day in 1970, leaving a balance of more than a million barrels per day to be secured from foreign fields, principally in Mexico, South America, and the Middle East. Imports grew from 3.2 million barrels per day in 1970 to 4.5 million two years later and 6.2 million in 1973. Increasingly, American refiners looked to foreign sources for feedstocks.

American companies, with the general support of the government, had been involved in the creation of concessions and spheres of interest in Venezuela, Colombia, Mexico, and the Middle East. With the famous "Red Line Agreement" of 1928, U.S. companies acquired the right to purchase nearly one-quarter of the crude produced in the Middle East, excluding Kuwait and Persia. During the 1930s, Texaco, Esso, Mobil, and Chevron signed concession agreements with Saudi Arabia; Gulf Oil participated in a concession in Kuwait; and Esso and Mobil were included in an Iranian concession. As these concessions were developed during the postwar period, they produced increasing volumes of low-cost crude oil, with Middle Eastern production soaring 15-fold between 1948 and 1972.

The vast amounts of foreign crude kept refineries supplied, but they also depressed domestic prices, even after voluntary limitations on imports began during the second Eisenhower administration. Domestic drilling slowed, both in response to imported crude and because domestic exploration yielded few large new discoveries—with two notable exceptions. The Prudhoe Bay Field of Alaska, on pipeline in 1977, 10 years after its discovery, proved to be almost as vast as the East Texas Field. The second major play began in the waters of the Gulf of Mexico in 1947, with Kerr-McGee's discovery in Block 32, nearly 11 miles off the shore of Louisiana. Thereafter, offshore exploration, including expensive and time-consuming projects by Shell and other companies, continued to be a major source of domestic crude oil.

However, oil-finders abroad continued to locate even larger fields, including discoveries in Algeria in 1956 and Libya in 1959, and along the west coast of Africa and in the North Sea. Mounting consumption in Europe and Asia absorbed much of the new production, to the point that spare crude oil production capacity was nominal by 1972. In response, producing countries drove harder bargains with buyers, acquiring a larger ownership in firms that still held concessions and nationalizing the companies during the first half of the 1970s. Libya, Saudi Arabia, Kuwait, and other producing countries also worked through the Oil Producing and Exporting Countries organization. The Arab members of this group cooperated in a boycott of shipments to the United States and the Netherlands after both nations supported Israel during the 1973 Yom Kippur War, and they coordinated production for most of the rest of the decade to increase their profit.

Results of tighter supply and higher prices appeared at gas pumps in the United States and other countries. During late 1973, for example, retail gasoline prices rose by nearly 40 percent in the United States. Occasional shortages and price boosts occurred thereafter, notably after Iraq attacked Iran in 1980 and after the Iraqi invasion of Kuwait in 1990. Price fluctuations were more common when oil was traded on a short-term basis, becoming notably volatile after the New York Mercantile Exchange began to sell crude oil futures in 1983. Prices on NYMEX moved rapidly in both directions, reaching $31.75 in November of 1985 before falling to $11 several months later.

Extreme price volatility prompted major companies to retrench, cutting labor forces and

Texaco gasoline station, 1936 (New York Public Library)

launching large-scale merger and acquisition programs to realize economies of scale. Exxon, one of the biggest, cut its labor force by 40 percent during the 1980s. Others were caught up in the widespread restructuring of the American industry. Mobil acquired Superior Oil, a large independent producer, before it merged with Exxon. Texaco bought Getty before it was purchased by Chevron, which also acquired ARCO. Phillips got General American, a large crude oil producer, then merged with Conoco.

From the 1970s onward, major changes occurred in the downstream sector of the industry as petrochemical complexes, especially those along the coastline of the Gulf of Mexico, continued to expand. In the face of increasingly strong foreign competition, the American installations pursued economies of scale and diversification of product strategies. Refineries also changed, most often to meet environmental standards and to produce locally mandated fuel blends. Overall, American refining capacity declined by about one-quarter after 1970 as the cost of meeting these requirements made some installations unprofitable and others lost indirect subsidies such as foreign-import entitlements as federal policies changed.

With every merger, the overall industry workforce contracted, a trend that also reflected the decline of onshore exploration beginning in 1983. By the mid-1990s, the total industry workforce in the United States was about half of what it had been 20 years earlier. In the end, many of the sizable independents had disappeared, and the Seven Sisters, the largest multinational oil companies, were only four in number. They—Exxon/Mobil, British Petroleum, Shell, Chevron—were looking far afield, in newly independent states that were once part of the Soviet Union and in most other parts of the world, for crude oil. Their searches and those of French, Chinese, Norwegian, and other national companies were often successful, but the continued increase in worldwide demand left little cushion against short-term disruptions of supply, such as that which began with the war between the United States and Iraq in 2003. Supplies—and fears of shortages—were endemic, with an accompanying price volatility that was almost as sharp as that of the early days of Pennsylvania oil.

See also AUTOMOTIVE INDUSTRY; CHEMICAL INDUSTRY.

Further reading

Giddens, Paul H. *The Birth of the Oil Industry*. New York: Macmillan, 1938.

Olien, Roger M., and Diana Davids Olien. *Oil and Ideology: The Cultural Creation of the American Petroleum Industry*. Chapel Hill: University of North Carolina Press, 2000.

Williamson, Harold F., and Arnold R. Daum. *The American Petroleum Industry: The Age of Illumination, 1859–1899*. Evanston, Ill.: Northwestern University Press, 1959.

Williamson, Harold F., Arnold R. Daum, Ralph L. Andreano, Gilbert C. Klose, and Paul A. Weinstein. *The American Petroleum Industry: The Age of Energy, 1899–1959*. Evanston, Ill.: Northwestern University Press, 1963.

Yergin, Daniel. *The Prize: The Epic Quest for Oil, Money, and Power*. New York: Free Press, 1991.

Roger Olien

pharmaceutical industry When Europeans first settled North America, there were few apothecaries, and medicines were usually prepared at home. Apothecaries would prepare each medicine for an individual patient or customer. There was no manufacturing industry in the sense of preparing large amounts of materials for many patients. Medicines were prepared using botanical and chemical ingredients, frequently imported from Europe and sold to anyone who asked for them. Early manufacturing began on a local scale; the population was too scattered, transportation limited, and knowledge unstandardized to support large-scale manufacturing.

The first move to a manufacturing industry in America was a direct result of the Revolutionary War. As the Revolution began, individual apothecary shops were unable to meet the demands of large armies. Andrew Craigie was appointed the first apothecary general of the Colonial army, with one of his first tasks being the establishment of a laboratory and storehouse in Carlisle, Pennsylvania, to prepare medicines and medical supplies for the military.

Philadelphia was the birthplace of American pharmacy and pharmaceutical manufacturing. By 1786, Christopher Marshall Jr. and Charles Marshall were manufacturing muriate of ammonia and Glauber's salt, a cathartic. By 1818, a precursor firm to Powers & Weightman began manufacturing quinine. Other manufacturing pharmacies in New York, Baltimore, and Boston were small concerns serving only regional markets.

Three conditions were necessary for the growth of an American pharmaceutical manufacturing industry: a sizable population, an ability to transport raw materials and finished goods, and the need for standardized products. By 1830, immigrants arriving in New York City from Europe were flooding the interior of the country. By 1860, the population of the 33 states in the Union was more than 31 million. RAILROADS were being built, and by 1860, there were more than 30,000 miles of track; in 1869, the East and West Coasts were linked by the first intercontinental railroad. The increasing population provided a market of considerable size, and the transportation system could quickly move products almost anywhere in the growing country. In 1848, the United States passed the first law restricting importation of substandard medicinal products. There was a growing awareness of the need to standardize such products so that quality and consistency could be assured. The time was right for the transition of pharmaceuticals from the status of a cottage industry to that of large-scale pharmaceutical manufacturing.

Although an unfortunate misnomer, the American patent medicine industry was an important part of the manufacturing industry in the 1800s. Patent medicines had secret formulas and extravagant claims but were not really patented since a patent requires public disclosure of ingredients. The popularity of these products was largely a consequence of the distrust or unavailability of physicians. The accepted therapies of the period were supposed to restore the body's balance, typically by bleeding, blistering, purging, or vomiting. There were few physicians except in the cities, and in many cases their high fees were prohibitive except in the most dire of situations. Patent medicines were easy to obtain since almost every type of mercantile establishment sold them; in the rural areas, traveling shows would bring medicine and entertainment at the same time. Many patent medicines were little more than alcohol or colored water, and others contained what would later be identified as dangerous ingredients, including morphine, opium, and cocaine.

Advertising greatly aided the growth of patent medicines. In addition to the traveling show, manufacturers advertised heavily in local newspapers. Some manufacturers developed other ways to advertise their wares. For example, the Lydia Pinkham Company solicited letters about health care issues from women, assuring the writers that only women would read the letters and provide a personal response. The passage of the Pure Food and Drug Act in 1906 ended many of the worst abuses of the patent medicine industry.

The Civil War marked the emergence of a cohesive manufacturing industry that was separate from the pharmacy. Once again, the military's need for medicines constituted a critical mass of potential customers. Several companies, such as Frederick Stearns & Company, founded in 1855, and E. R. Squibb, founded in 1858, were

Typical 19th-century advertisements for medicines promising relief (LIBRARY OF CONGRESS)

major suppliers to the Union army. Military veterans, such as Eli Lilly of Indianapolis and A. H. Robins of Richmond, began their companies after returning from the war.

Most companies of this period bore the name of the founder, and companies were typically called a "house," such as the House of Squibb, noting the personal nature of the enterprise. John Wyeth, William Warner, Louis Dohme, Silas Burroughs, and Henry Wellcome were pharmacists, while Walter Abbott and W. E. Upjohn were physicians. A few, such as E. Mead Johnson and Hervey Parke of Parke Davis, were businessmen. The eponymous nature of the industry was important in the days prior to REGULATION of products, since it was the name and reputation of the individual that guaranteed the standards of the product. Many companies produced the same standard items, with the only differentiation in the marketplace being the name of the manufacturer.

During the post–Civil War period innovation usually focused on new and improved dose forms rather than on entirely new medicines. For example, Upjohn manufactured and marketed a friable pill that was developed to dissolve in the stomach rather than pass unchanged through the body. William Warner's company developed a process to make sugar-coated pills, and Walter Abbott developed dosimetric granules. John Uri Lloyd took a different approach and manufactured botanical "specifics" for the eclectic physicians of the period. Throughout the 19th century and the beginning of the 20th century, there were few national manufacturing companies such as Squibb and Lilly; most remained specialty or regional manufacturers, and few were engaged in research.

The American pharmaceutical industry of the early 20th century was predominantly a manufacturing industry. Individual companies started by serving a geographical region with an assorted line of standard products or by championing a specific dose form or manufacturing process. The catalogs of the larger manufacturers ran to several hundred pages; many pharmacies would

identify themselves as a supplier of Squibb products or those of Lilly, Wyeth or Parke Davis. When one company brought a new product to market, it could be quickly copied and supplied by a number of other companies.

Some manufacturers marketed their products only to physicians and pharmacists and identified themselves as "ethical" to distinguish themselves from producers of patent medicines and other products sold directly to the consumer. In 1939, no single ethical drug manufacturer had a sales volume as great as the large department stores in New York and Detroit, and the total sales volume for all 1,100 pharmaceutical companies was $150 million at the manufacturing level.

Scientists, such as Pasteur and Koch, had discovered the causes of some diseases by the end of the 19th and beginning of the 20th centuries. These discoveries led to the development of serums and vaccines, or biologics, to treat diseases such as rabies and diphtheria. Diphtheria was one of the most common childhood diseases of the period, and a specific serum to treat it was a major breakthrough. The H. K. Mulford Company was the first to produce reliable serum in the United States, and by 1895 health departments in major cities, such as Cincinnati, Boston, and St. Louis, were also producing serum. Tragedy struck in 1901 when serum produced by the St. Louis Health Department was contaminated and a number of children died. Similar tragedies with the use of other biologics were reported in the United States and in Europe; the response was the passage of the first U.S. law to regulate the safety of biological medicines in 1902. Parke Davis & Company, H. K. Mulford, and Lederle Antitoxin Laboratories were among the forerunners in producing a broad array of serums, antitoxins, toxoids, and vaccines.

The Food and Drug Law of 1906 was passed primarily to address unsanitary conditions exposed by Sinclair Lewis's *The Jungle*. Although the law initially focused on the abuses in the food industry, it was broadened to include the problems of the patent medicine industry. The

Department of Agriculture's Bureau of Chemistry, headed by Harvey W. Wiley, was assigned to enforce the law. The law, however, covered only adulterated or misbranded products in interstate commerce. The 1912 Shirley Amendment broadened the law so that medicines could not be labeled with any false statement, a hallmark of the patent medicines of the period. Reputable manufacturers were in favor of the regulations, since they had analytic laboratories and could already meet the requirements of the law.

The first association of pharmaceutical manufacturers, the American Association of Pharmaceutical Chemists, was formed by family-owned small businesses in 1910, largely as a result of the new regulations. A second association was formed by larger companies in 1912. The agenda of the two associations was similar: to share information on common problems such as taxes and regulation, and to develop high manufacturing standards. In the 1950s, the two groups merged and in 1994 became the current Pharmaceutical Research and Manufacturers of America (PhRMA).

The Department of Agriculture's Bureau of Chemistry became the Food and Drug Administration in 1931, when new regulatory power was sought to strengthen the 1906 act. In 1937 Massengill, a respected family firm in Tennessee, marketed a new liquid form of sulfanilamide using diethylene glycol as the solvent—but without testing the product for toxicity. The combination was deadly, and more than 100 people, mostly children, died as a consequence. In response, the Food Drug and Cosmetic Act of 1938 was quickly passed, requiring manufacturers to prove that a new medicine was safe before interstate marketing could begin. The law also required labeling that led to the distinction between products that could be sold only on prescription and those that could be sold over the counter (OTC) for self-treatment.

At the beginning of World War I, America was dependent on other countries for many of its medicines. Important botanicals, such as morphine and belladonna, were primarily grown elsewhere. Germany was the leader in developing new medicines using synthetic chemistry and protecting its markets through patents in countries with major markets. With the outbreak of hostilities, American scientists were able to determine how to produce important medicines such as the first chemotherapeutic agent, Salvarsan, used to treat syphilis; procaine, the first injectable local anesthetic; and barbital, a barbiturate used as a sedative. After the war the patents were seized as alien property and auctioned. Sterling bought the trademark for Bayer aspirin through this process.

A number of the ethical manufacturers either started or expanded their research programs after the war. Some companies forged alliances with academic institutions to carry on basic research, while others, notably Lilly, Squibb, and Merck, established corporate institutes for basic research, in addition to the analytical services undertaken by others. In spite of the growing interest, most new developments continued to come from European companies, and at the beginning of World War II the United States was once again dependent on imports for medicines.

During World War II, the focus of pharmaceutical research was determined by the government and was characterized by teams from the pharmaceutical industry, academia, and the government working together. The debilitating disease of malaria was common in most of the combat areas during World War II in the Pacific theater. The world supply of medicinal-grade quinine had come from the East Indies (now Indonesia), which had been conquered by the Japanese military. The only alternative was Atabrine, a complex synthetic chemical patented by Germany's I. G. Farben. In less than a year, the process was duplicated by Winthrop scientists. Winthrop and other companies provided millions of tablets for Allied forces during the war.

The basic work on blood transfusions done by clinicians and academics was applied to the need to produce and ship millions of units of blood products. The pharmaceutical industry developed techniques and production facilities devoted to processing the fragile material into dried plasma and albumin. The American Red Cross collected more than 13 million pints of blood that was processed by 11 companies, including Abbott, Hyland, Lederle, Lilly, Parke-Davis, Squibb, and Wyeth.

Another example of teamwork was the development of penicillin. The early research was coordinated by a group of three East Coast companies (Merck, Pfizer, and Squibb), but the team quickly expanded to add a Midwest group (Abbott, Lilly, Parke Davis, and Upjohn) plus three companies unaffiliated with either group (Lederle, Reichel Laboratories, and Heyden Chemical). In 1943, the total production was limited to the military. In 1944, six additional companies (Ben Venue, Cheplin, Commercial Solvents, Cutter, Sterling, and Wyeth) were added to build production capabilities, enabling the War Production Board to authorize civilian distribution.

After the war, the industry was still relatively small, and many companies still had founding family connections. Some companies, such as G. D. Searle, focused their efforts by region or specialty, while others, such as Eli Lilly, Parke Davis, and E. R. Squibb, marketed a broad line of products. A number of companies entered the industry for the first time. Bristol Laboratories, a manufacturer of toiletries including the laxative Sal-Hepatica and Ipana toothpaste, acquired Cheplin Laboratories, a wartime producer of penicillin. Pfizer, a chemical company, used its involvement in the penicillin effort to launch its pharmaceuticals business.

Many companies, adopting research as the engine of growth, invested heavily to take advantage of new scientific and technological discoveries. Growth was spurred by the discovery of new products, many providing effective treatments for the first time. A vigorous search for new antibiotics soon produced streptomycin (Merck, 1945), chlortetracycline (Lederle, 1948), and chloramphenicol (Parke Davis, 1949). This was the period of miracle drugs.

In addition to antibiotics, the immediate postwar period was marked by major advances in a number of therapeutic areas, including vitamins, antihistamines, and hormones. With the exception of antibiotics, most of the attention was on treating symptoms. By the 1960s, research was increasingly focused on addressing problems associated with heredity, diet, and environment. Major discoveries included the first oral contraceptives, nonsteroidal anti-inflammatories, and the anxiolytics beginning with Librium.

Until the emergence of the postwar research industry, most medicines were available from a number of different companies. Manufacturers typically made products that were listed in the *United States Pharmacopoeia* or the *National Formulary* under their own brand names. Pharmacists had the option of deciding which manufacturer's line of standard products to use in filling prescriptions. However, in an attempt to control a growing counterfeit problem in the early 1950s, states passed laws to restrict the choice of products to the prescribing physician. If a physician wrote a prescription using the generic name, then any manufacturer's product could be used; otherwise, only the specified brand name could be used. Repeal of the antisubstitution laws in the 1970s was fueled by the desire to contain costs and the reduced risk of counterfeiting. However, substitution was not popular with patients, physicians, or pharmacists.

In the 1980s, the cost of medicines once again became a legislative force, culminating in passage of the Drug Price Competition and Patent Term Restoration Act, also known as the Waxman-Hatch Act. The law provided for an extension of patent life for time lost due to regulatory delays while streamlining the approval of generic products. The law modified and simplified the Abbreviated New Drug Application process, which resulted in an easier entry to the market for generic manufacturers.

In 1952, the Humphrey-Durham Amendment to the Food, Drug and Cosmetic Act (FDCA) established the criteria for distinguishing between the two categories of medicines in the United States—prescription and nonprescription. The criterion was that products that needed to have professional oversight were to be available only by prescription, while products that could be labeled for safe use by the public could be available without a prescription.

In 1962, tragedy again struck. Senator Kefauver's congressional hearings on marketing practices and pricing in the pharmaceutical industry were transformed by the publication of the story of birth defects due to the use of a sedative, thalidomide. The 1962 FDCA amendments added the requirement that any new product had to be tested for efficacy and approved by the Food and Drug Administration prior to marketing. While these requirements would not have changed the outcome of the thalidomide tragedy, since the product was an effective sedative and was never marketed in the United States, they did change the industry by significantly lengthening the time that it took a new medicine to reach the market.

The American biotechnology industry was largely formed by academics working in molecular biology rather than as a part of the established pharmaceutical industry. Genentech, established in 1976, was the first biotech firm that specialized in the pharmaceutical field. Genentech focused its research on insulin and growth hormones, licensing Lilly to market its first product and the first human biotech medicine, Humulin (human insulin), in 1982. Genentech soon built an organization that included research, development, and marketing. A number of other companies, Biogen in 1978, Amgen in 1980, and Immunex in 1981, were established to discover new medicines. Other companies' strategy was to do the research and then license potential medicines to the pharmaceutical industry to develop and market. Today the lines between the biotech industry and the pharmaceutical industry have blurred or disappeared through internal growth, MERGERS, and acquisitions.

Like most other industries, the pharmaceutical industry has gone through cycles of merger and acquisition. Such unions have been formed to allow companies to gain new skills, technologies, and products that translate to economic growth and success. Merck, for example, gained skills in vaccines with the acquisition of H. K. Mulford and continued its transition to a company specializing in pharmaceutical chemicals with the acquisition first of Powers-Weightman-Rosengarten in 1927 and of Sharpe & Dohme in 1953. Others companies increased their size by licensing products from European discoverers. Many of the early tranquilizers were discovered by the French firm Rhone Poulenc; Smith Kline & French licensed rights to Compazine, while American Home licensed Pherergan. As the decision making shifted from physicians to health maintenance organizations and insurance companies in the 1990s, several pharmaceutical companies diversified by acquiring prescription plan companies, as in Merck's acquisition of Medco.

The American pharmaceutical industry of the 21st century bears little resemblance to its roots. Perhaps this is most evident by the names of the companies. Few companies bear the name of their founder or place of founding. Instead, new names are constructed, such as Aventis and Novartis, or glided past the point of easy historical recognition, such as GlaxoSmithKline and AstraZeneca.

Further reading

Higby, G. J., and E. C. Stroud, eds. *The Inside Story of Medicines.* Madison, Wisc.: American Institute of the History of Pharmacy, 1997.

Mahoney, T. *The Merchants of Life.* New York: Harper & Bros., 1959.

Sneader, W. *Drug Discovery: The Evolution of Modern Medicines.* New York: John Wiley & Sons, 1985.

Dennis B. Worthen

Phillips curve An economic model showing a trade-off between inflation and unemployment. In 1958, economist A. W. Phillips (1914–75) gave the formulation of the Phillips curve, relating the rate of wage inflation to the excess demand for labor. In its short-run form, a trade-off exists between wage inflation and unemployment. As the unemployment rate decreases and the excess demand for labor increases, an upward pressure on wages exists.

While the Phillips curve concept has evolved since 1958, originally it was widely interpreted to posit a stable wage inflation-unemployment trade-off. But monetary policy makers specify inflation targets in terms of output prices. As a result, it was necessary to transform the wage change-unemployment relationship to a price change-unemployment relationship. Accordingly, the expectations-augmented form of the Phillips curve (a non-market-clearing view) asserts a trade-off between unemployment and unexpected price inflation. This transformation assumes that prices are set with a mark-up over unit labor costs so that they move in step with wages.

With this view, the power of policy to alter economic activity depends on how price expectations are formed. Specifically, the inflation-unemployment trade-off vanishes when expectations are realized. At this point, the unemployment rate returns to its natural rate. This version predicts that the potential success of monetary policy depends on the speed of adjustment of price expectations. In addition, policy makers may determine the level of unemployment associated with a target rate of inflation. Alternatively, the Phillips curve was interpreted as offering a number of inflation-unemployment combinations from which policy makers could choose. Given economic circumstances, they could choose a particular mix of inflation and unemployment that would minimize social cost.

Policy makers could also use the framework to estimate the effects of policies that were intended to produce a more favorable Phillips curve, such as a policy that would lower the amount of unemployment associated with a certain level of excess demand. An alternative, market-clearing version of the Phillips curve assumes a labor market in equilibrium. Deviations of unemployment from the natural rate

result from misperceptions about inflation. The unemployment rate returns to its natural rate when misperceptions end. Empirical evidence in the 1960s and 1970s seemed to validate Phillips's empirical estimation. But in the 1990s, as the U.S. economy combined low and stable rates of wage and price inflation with a decline in the unemployment rate, professional and public confidence in the Phillips curve waned.

Today, many economists view the Phillips curve as offering no trade-off at all. The problem with the Phillips curve, according to some economists, is that it focuses on empirical estimates of price-based specifications. For instance, with the unemployment rate decreasing in the 1990s, nominal wages increased around 4 percent annually during the last half of the decade, but the annual rate of price inflation fell. During the last half of the 1990s, the Phillips curve framework did not explain the unemployment–price inflation tradeoff.

Further reading

Humphrey, Thomas M. *From Trade-offs to Policy Ineffectiveness: A History of the Phillips Curve.* Richmond, Va.: Federal Reserve Bank of Richmond, 1986.
Matthews, Peter H., and Ivan T. Kandilov. "The Cost of Job Loss and the 'New' Phillips Curve." *Eastern Economic Journal* 28, no. 2 (spring 2002): 186–202.

Thomas R. Sadler

Ponzi, Charles (1882–1949) *swindler* Ponzi loaned his name to a classic fraudulent scheme in which new investors' money is used to pay off older investors who may demand that their investment be cashed out. He acquired a fortune of $9.5 million in 1920, before his enterprise fell apart in the summer of that year. The notoriety of his actions caused his name to be linked with a common speculative scheme called "a Ponzi scheme."

The ingredients specific to his enterprise were the sale of promissory notes paying a 50 percent return in 45 days, and the payment of the returns on his notes for a time, while relying on new investors to purchase more notes. However, the general scheme—whereby the initial entrants do well and the latter ones take losses—had been common to other speculative episodes. For example, John Law's early-17th-century venture involving the Bank of Paris and his land speculation company, "the Mississippi Company," used the same general method to create a fortune before it collapsed.

Ponzi's activities centered about Boston, at a time when New England was fertile ground because of the large number of immigrants living in the area. Land speculation in Florida was taking on visibly dramatic proportions in the national media, while the U.S. economy was experiencing the 1918–19 and 1920–21 recessions. To facilitate the growth of his operation Ponzi purchased 38 percent of Hanover Trust Company stock, before the Massachusetts commissioner of banks got involved. The bank collapsed after Ponzi's first overdraft to pay the returns on his promissory notes. Another swindle involved selling postal reply coupons to immigrants, claiming that they could resell them for a fortune. That scheme was exposed after the *New York Times* ran an exposé. He was arrested on August 12, 1920. His Lexington mansion and other assets were seized.

Ponzi had sufficient background and education to swindle the unsuspecting. Born in Italy to a well-to-do family, he envisioned his goal as one of getting rich. Seeking to avoid the stigma of having to work, his varying schemes were uniformly illegal. After serving out a prison term in Massachusetts, Ponzi died in a Rio de Janeiro hospital, "leaving an estate of $75 to cover funeral expenses." Because of his various schemes, his name has become forever linked to frauds that pay old investors with new investors' money.

Further reading

Dunn, Donald. *Ponzi: The Boston Swindler.* New York: McGraw-Hill, 1975.

Frazer, William, with John Guthrie. *The Florida Land Boom: Speculation, Money, and the Banks.* Westport, Conn.: Quorom Books, 1995.

William Frazer

predatory pricing   As treated under the federal ANTITRUST laws, predatory pricing is the offense of setting below-cost prices temporarily in order to drive competitors out of business or extort them into raising their own prices. Progressive and New Deal lawyers as well as small-business persons believed that predatory pricing historically was relatively easy for large firms with deep pockets, such as Standard Oil.

The SHERMAN ACT prohibition on predatory pricing was strengthened in 1914 by passage of the CLAYTON ACT, which expressly addressed the offense of charging low prices in a targeted market in order to destroy a rival, while raising one's prices elsewhere in order to finance the predation campaign. This statute repeatedly was used to condemn aggressive price cutting. Beginning in the 1960s, however, many economists began to argue that predatory pricing is expensive, extremely risky, and unlikely to succeed except in a narrow range of circumstances—namely, for a clearly dominant firm in a market in which new entry is very difficult or impossible. Indeed, many economists have come to believe that "classical" predatory pricing, or creating a monopoly by temporarily charging prices below cost, does not exist.

In 1975, Harvard professors Phillip Areeda and Donald Turner responded to these concerns with a very strict test for predatory pricing, requiring proof of prices below cost, and also that the predator could reasonably predict monopoly returns that would exceed the costs of the predation. The federal courts have largely adopted this test, with the result that there have been almost no successful predatory pricing lawsuits since the mid-1970s.

Further reading

Areeda, Phillip E., and Donald F. Turner. "Predatory Pricing and Related Practices Under Section 2 of the Sherman Act." *Harvard Law Review* 88, no. 697 (1975).

McGee, John S. "Predatory Price Cutting: The Standard Oil (N.J.) Case." *Journal of Law & Economics* 1, no. 137 (1958).

Herbert Hovenkamp

Public Utility Holding Company Act (1935)

Symbolic of Franklin D. Roosevelt's Second New Deal, which focused on long-term social welfare, the Public Utility Holding Company Act (PUHCA) was designed to eliminate unfair business practices and abuses by electrical and natural gas holding companies. Written by the president's close associates Benjamin Cohen and Thomas Corcoran, the bill also represented Roosevelt's continuing reform of Wall Street.

The background to PUHCA was in the technology of the utility industry, which facilitated the use of corporate holding companies. When combined with economies of scale, the utility industry moved toward consolidation in the 1920s. By 1932, only three holding companies controlled nearly 50 percent of all American electrical output. Given the states' ineffectiveness in regulating utility companies, more and more critics charged the utility companies with high rates, unreliable service, and excessive profits. With the onset of the Great Depression and utility companies going into receivership, the federal government opted to regulate them.

Although opposition was strong and effective in watering down the original bill, Roosevelt had Congress pass the Federal Power Act (establishing a federal utility regulatory structure) and the Public Utility Act of 1935. Title I of the latter law is known as the Public Utilities Holding Company Act. PUHCA required federal control and REGULATION of interstate public utility holding companies. Utility companies were given an "exclusive service territory" in return for their commitment to providing reliable service at a regulated rate. A "death sentence" provision provided that all holding companies that were more than twice removed from their operating subsidiaries could be abolished by the Securities and Exchange Commission (SEC). This meant that out-of-state ownership of utility companies would be difficult, if not impossible. The SEC was given authority, moreover, to regulate most financial transactions of UTILITIES. From its passage until the 1970s, PUHCA worked very well.

In 1978 and 1992, the Public Utilities Regulatory Policies Act and the Energy Policy Act increased competition in the utility industry to the point that further reform is being called for today, which in effect would replace the SEC with a new federal regulatory agency.

See also DEREGULATION; INSULL, SAMUEL; MORGAN, JOHN PIERPONT; SECURITIES EXCHANGE ACT OF 1934.

Further reading

Abel, Amy. "RS 20015: Electricity Restructuring Background: Public Utility Holding Company Act of 1935," Committee for the National Institute for the Environment, 1999.

Funigiello, Philip J. *Toward a National Power Policy: The New Deal and the Electric Utility Industry, 1933–1941*. Pittsburgh: University of Pittsburgh Press, 1973.

Michael V. Namorato

Public Works Administration (PWA)

The PWA was set up under Title II of the National Industrial Recovery Act (June 1933) of Franklin D. Roosevelt's First NEW DEAL. Designed to provide jobs for the unemployed as well as to help in stimulating economic recovery from the Great Depression, PWA was based on a matching principle whereby the federal government put up 30 percent and the local/state governments 70 percent in secured loans. PWA reflected the personality of its director, Harold Ickes, secretary of the interior throughout the Roosevelt presidency.

Committed to setting up a stable federal agency that would build public works projects of permanence and bring a fair return on the federal government's investment, Ickes methodically decentralized PWA into state and local committees, meticulously reviewed construction plans, and insisted that every dollar expended be accounted for. Although "Honest Harold's" PWA was cumbersome in organization and in spite of PWA and Ickes's rivalry with Harry Hopkins and other New Deal relief agencies such as the WORKS PROGRESS ADMINISTRATION (WPA), PWA still accomplished much. On average, PWA employed approximately 144,000 workers per year, helped in creating 600,000 related jobs, and pioneered in establishing precedents for federal aid to municipalities. PWA, also reflective of Ickes, sought to help black people with its emphasis on no discrimination in jobs or salaries.

Almost from the beginning, PWA had difficulties. Given its organization and director, it moved too slowly for Franklin D. Roosevelt, with the result that PWA funds were taken to set up the Civil Works Administration under Harry Hopkins in 1933. As the WPA developed, it secured more funding, until in 1939 PWA became a victim of the Reorganization Act of 1939, whereby it was turned over to the Federal Works Agency. Nevertheless, its work was impressive, and it spent nearly $6 billion for roads, tunnels, bridges, hospitals, and other major public works. Among its most notable accomplishments were the Hudson River's Lincoln Tunnel, the New York Triborough Bridge, the George Washington Bridge, and Chicago's State Street subway.

Further reading

Ickes, Harold. *Back to Work: The Story of PWA*. New York: Macmillan, 1935.
Watkins, T. H. *Righteous Pilgrim: The Life and Times of Harold Ickes*. New York: Henry Holt, 1990.
White, Graham, and John Maze. *Harold Ickes of the New Deal*. Cambridge, Mass.: Harvard University Press, 1985.

Michael V. Namorato

Pullman, George M. (1831–1897) *inventor and businessman*   Born in Brockton, New York, Pullman went to work at 14 when his father died. He became a cabinetmaker and later a construction worker. After moving to Chicago in 1855, he saw an opportunity to improve the sleeping cars currently in use by the RAILROADS. Three years later he designed two coaches for the Chicago and Alton Railroad. A larger car, the Pioneer, followed in 1865. It was used in Abraham Lincoln's funeral, on the train that carried his body from Washington to Springfield, Illinois. As a result of the trip, the Pullman sleeping car became extremely popular, and orders increased substantially from the railroads.

Later in the 1860s, he also introduced dining cars and then added parlor cars in 1875. In 1867, he organized the Pullman Palace Car Company, which later became simply the Pullman Co. Often leasing the cars to railroads, Pullman observed that service for them could be provided by former slaves, and he began hiring them to serve as porters and waiters. These men became known as "Pullman porters." The company became the biggest employer of blacks in the country at the time and a magnet for black immigration to Chicago, where the company had its operations at the time.

His business ventures in railroad cars continued to succeed. By 1890, Pullman supplied most of the sleeping cars in the United States from his headquarters in Pullman, Illinois—a planned town that he built for his company and workers. He created it to be free of civil unrest and violence, but the undertaking eventually failed. Labor unrest plagued the venture, and in 1894 it underwent what became known as the "Pullman strike," which was broken by federal troops with machine guns. Pullman's relations with his labor force were poor. When sales declined in 1894, he slashed wages by 25 percent. His workers protested unsuccessfully, and Pullman fired several of their spokesmen. They then went on strike and were aided substantially by the American Railway Union, led by Eugene DEBS. Railroad workers refused to work on any train with Pullman cars attached; as a result, President Grover Cleveland sent troops to break the strike. Violence stemming from the strike was estimated to have cost more than $80 million. Debs was subsequently jailed, and troops were sent to Illinois to protect the mails and the company's headquarters.

Pullman's company continued to be highly successful despite the labor problems. In addition to his company, he also owned the Eagleton Iron

Works and was president of the Metropolitan Elevated Railroad, both in New York City.

See also WESTINGHOUSE, GEORGE, JR.

Further reading

Buder, Stanley. *Pullman: An Experiment in Industrial Order and Community Planning, 1880–1930* New York: Oxford University Press, 1967.

Leyendecker, Liston. *Palace Car Prince: A Biography of George Mortimer Pullman.* Boulder: University Press of Colorado, 1992.

Papke, David Ray. *The Pullman Case: The Clash of Labor and Capital in Industrial America.* Lawrence: University Press of Kansas, 1999.

R

Racketeer Influenced and Corrupt Organizations Act (RICO) The Racketeer Influenced and Corrupt Organizations Act (18 U.S.C. § 1961 et seq.), commonly known as the RICO act, was passed by the U.S. Congress in 1970. RICO was intended to provide a more effective means to prosecute members of organized crime. In particular, the RICO act enables the prosecution of those persons who do not personally commit any crimes but who control a criminal enterprise that engages in a pattern of racketeering activity.

RICO also provides the government with broad power to cause the forfeiture of property belonging to any person convicted under the act. In addition, RICO allows the victims of proscribed criminal activities to bring a civil suit against the wrongdoer. Under the act, victims can recover three times their actual damages plus costs and attorneys' fees.

Between 1970 and the mid-1980s, RICO was used almost exclusively by U.S. prosecutors against the leaders of organized crime families throughout the United States. Defendants prosecuted under the act protested that it violated their due process rights, arguing that convictions could be based upon mere conversations with known members of organized crime and that the act allowed for the forfeiture of all their assets, even if the government had no proof that all of the defendant's assets were the proceeds of organized crime. The objections to the act's broad application, however, largely fell on deaf ears because the objections were a natural and necessary result of the act's intended scope, that is, a broad legislative enactment that would effectively eliminate the economic base of organized crime.

In the mid-1980s, civil litigators began to extend the act to areas that were previously thought beyond the reach of RICO. Instead of alleging that a "Godfather" figure was controlling a Mafia family for purposes of engaging in a pattern of extortion, murder, and arson, plaintiffs in civil class actions alleged that a chief executive officer was controlling a Fortune 500 company for purposes of engaging in a pattern of mail and wire fraud. Usually, these latter claims were based upon allegedly false advertisements that were circulated through the U.S. mails or wires. With the advent of this type of creative pleading, suddenly every business or consumer fraud claim had the potential to be a RICO claim.

Although the use of RICO in the business and consumer fraud context complied with the express wording of the statute, many members of the judiciary believed that Congress never intended to "federalize" common law fraud when RICO was originally passed.

During the late 1980s and early 1990s, a plethora of ad hoc rules and theories designed to limit RICO's civil applications were adopted by the various U.S. district courts across the country. Many of these rules and theories conflicted from district court to district court. As a result, application of the civil RICO Act during this period was complicated, burdensome, and inconsistent. It was used to prosecute violators of securities laws in some instances, notably when Michael Milken of DREXEL BURNHAM LAMBERT was charged with infractions of the law during the insider trading scandal of the late 1980s.

Many of the inconsistencies in civil RICO applications have since been resolved by the U.S. circuit courts of appeal and the U.S. Supreme Court. Even without the inconsistencies, however, the complicated and burdensome rules applicable to pleading and proving a RICO claim remain. RICO can have extensive power when employed either civilly or criminally, and it can reach almost any factual situation involving long-term criminal activity. The courts have not, however, made it easy to take advantage of RICO's power and breadth. The exceptional results that can be achieved under the act require exceptional effort.

Further reading

Welling, Sarah N. *Federal Criminal Law and Related Actions*. St. Paul, Minn.: West Group, 1998.

Jeffrey Grell

Radio Corporation of America

From 1919 to 1985, the Radio Corporation of America (RCA) was one of the primary American consumer electronics and telecommunications research and manufacturing firms, playing important roles in consumer, military, and government work and in computer and related fields. Long dominated by David SARNOFF, it was spawned by—and decades later taken over by—GENERAL ELECTRIC.

RCA was formed out of a post–World War I shared business and government desire to build an important American company in the developing wireless business. General Electric established RCA as a subsidiary on October 17, 1919, transferring to it important wireless patents, including those for the Alexanderson Alternator long-distance transmitter. RCA then took over the transmitters of the American Marconi company and other firms. In a series of complex arrangements, RCA was organized as a patent holding company, with patents cross-licensed among GE (30 percent), Westinghouse (20 percent), AT&T (10 percent), UNITED FRUIT (4 percent), and others. GE and Westinghouse took substantial ownership shares in RCA.

Based on this patent pool, RCA marketed consumer radio receivers manufactured by GE and Westinghouse beginning in 1922 and operated long-distance (maritime and international) wireless telegraphy and telephony stations. In 1926, RCA formed the National Broadcasting Company as a wholly-owned subsidiary, initiating regular national radio network service through a handful of its own stations and many other affiliates. While Owen D. YOUNG and Edward Nally of GE were primary early leaders, day-to-day operational control soon fell to David Sarnoff, who became president in 1930.

While no engineer, Sarnoff recognized the importance of staying on the cutting edge of fast-changing technology and strongly supported research in sound motion pictures, recording methods, facsimile radio, and all types of electronic vacuum tubes. His RCA became a wholly separate firm when GE and Westinghouse were forced in a 1932 antitrust consent decree to spin off their stock holdings.

The most public research effort was the innovation of television, which had moved from semimechanical to all-electronic methods by about 1930. Over the next decade, the company spent nearly $50 million, a huge sum at the time, to research and perfect black-and-white television, initiating experimental broadcasts in New York City in 1935 and presenting television as a finished product at the 1939 New York World's Fair. RCA pushed heavily for the Federal Communications Commission's (FCC) final approval of commercial television operations beginning July 1, 1941.

The Japanese attack five months later froze television expansion for the duration of the war. As with most other American industry, RCA converted almost wholly to military equipment manufacturing during World War II. Radios, fuses for bombs, radar, and both underwater and airborne electronics systems dominated company activity while broadening its expertise. Annual sales rose from $110 million in 1939 to $237 million in 1946. Postwar international tensions underlay growing military contracts that built on the company's wartime experience. RCA entered the computer field in the 1940s and expanded operations in the 1950s and 1960s. Research and manufacturing costs were high, however, and profits scarce amid strong competition.

The postwar decade was dominated by television's growth, with RCA and its NBC subsidiary playing central roles. At the same time RCA pioneered development of color television, which was approved for operation by the FCC in December 1953. Due to the high cost of receivers, color developed only slowly, and RCA did not achieve profits in the field (which it dominated) until the early 1960s. A venture into 45 rpm records was less successful, and attempts at manufacture of a broader line of consumer products were soon spun off as well.

With the retirement of David Sarnoff in 1969, RCA appeared to lose its direction and certainly its competitive edge. His son Robert took the helm and soon wound down the company's struggling computer venture after a loss exceeding $500 million (some reports suggested $2 billion). In turn, he pursued acquisitions that blurred the company's technology focus and was forced out

in 1975, to be followed by two further CEOs, each of whom pursued a different strategy while being unable to staunch the growing flow of red ink. Subsidiaries were bought and sold, often at a loss. Divisions of the firm (most particularly the Princeton, New Jersey-based research center) pulled in different directions or overlapped in their efforts. An attempt to revive the company's great consumer electronics successes—with a video disc recording system—failed as the technology was already dated. After two short-lived predecessors, board member (since 1972) Thornton Bradshaw took over the reins of RCA in mid-1981. RCA's NBC network was struggling, profit margins had declined in color television, and many nonelectronic acquisitions were put on the block, some after only a handful of years. Under Bradshaw, RCA refocused on its technology core.

By this time RCA had become a potential takeover target, thanks in part to more than $2 billion in cash from the sale of subsidiaries. Break-up value of the company was several times its share price. In December GE made a friendly takeover deal to RCA, which both company boards quickly approved, as did shareholders, despite controversy about the price ($6 billion) paid. Thus, within 15 years of David Sarnoff's death, RCA disappeared into the GE conglomerate, its name preserved merely as a marketing vehicle for the French Thomson consumer electronics combine.

See also RADIO INDUSTRY; TELECOMMUNICATIONS INDUSTRY; TELEVISION INDUSTRY.

Further reading

Archer, Gleason L. *History of Radio to 1926.* 1938. Reprint, New York: Arno Press, 1971.

Barnum, Frederick O. *"His Master's Voice," in America: Ninety Years of Communications Pioneering and Progress: Victor Talking Machine Company, Radio Corporation of America, General Electric.* Camden, N.J.: General Electric, 1991.

Bilby, Kenneth. *The General: David Sarnoff and the Rise of the Communications Industry.* New York: Harper & Row, 1986.

Sobel, Robert. *RCA.* New York: Stein & Day, 1986.

Christopher H. Sterling

radio industry Radio is a lifestyle medium. Today the business of radio is that of a mass media industry targeting audiences with similar characteristics and interests. Radio programming goes where you go and fits into your schedule and whatever you are doing. There are more than five radio sets per household and more than 12,000 stations, and revenues total more than $18 billion per year.

The foundation of this industry was a revolutionary technology. The earliest historical period of significance to the foundations of radio broadcasting ranges from the mid-1800s to the turn of the century. This pre-broadcast period was a fascinating time in U.S. history. It followed the Civil War. It was a time of massive population growth and urbanization. For the first time in the history of this nation, its manufactured goods were worth more than its agricultural products. This era of U.S. history is known as the Industrial Age. It had such an effect on society that many of the names that dominated the age are still familiar today: Andrew CARNEGIE, Russell Herman Conwell, Andrew Mellon, J. P. Morgan, John D. Rockefeller, William Randolph Hearst, and Joseph Pulitzer. Adding the names of the electric and electronic media pioneers of the same era—James Clerk Maxwell, Heinrich Hertz, Guglielmo Marconi, Reginald A. Fessenden, and Lee De Forest—communicates some idea of the environment in which radio began. These radio pioneers, whose names are obviously not well known, worked in the shadow of the industrial giants. Radio was almost entirely new compared with other evolving industries (such as manufactured goods), but it began within the ideology of the same Industrial Age.

The TELEGRAPH was the most important development of the electronic media in the Industrial Age. During the mid-1800s, telegraphy—the transmission of coded signals—provided the world's first instantaneous information service. The telegraph was the first practical medium that kept the agrarian and the growing urban communities throughout the nation in touch with the rest of the world. The telegraph enhanced the currency of the frontier press by overcoming the obstacles of time and distance. The audience's interest in rapidly delivered information inspired the growth of commercial enterprises.

Samuel F. B. MORSE is credited with the development of the telegraph system, which he patented in 1840. The frontier success of the telegraph naturally led the way for voice communication telephony. Alexander Graham BELL is credited with developing the analog transmission of the human voice over wire. Bell's early experiments led to several important contributions: the carbon microphone, the magnetic receiver (the basis for loudspeakers), and the electronic tube amplifier. Bell announced his successful voice transmission experiments in 1874 and patented his work shortly thereafter. Bell not only produced important technological developments for the electric media, but also founded the AMERICAN TELEPHONE AND TELEGRAPH CO. (AT&T), which would later make significant contributions to the foundations of electronic communication.

Early telecommunication experimentation was not limited to telegraph land lines. The telegraph grew to include transmission of the human voice—telephony and wireless telegraphy evolved into radio telegraphy. There were several inventors whose individual contributions would be combined to produce an over-the-air radio signal. James Clerk Maxwell, a Scottish physicist, was first to publish a theory of radiant energy, which remains the basis of the modern concept of electronic media. Maxwell's ideas attracted the attention of German physicist Heinrich Hertz, who first demonstrated Maxwell's theories by projecting a signal into the air—paving the way for radio. Hertz's achievement is recognized by the use of his name as the unit of measurement for radio frequency. Guglielmo Marconi was the most prominent and well-known experimenter in the industrial history of radio. Marconi, however, was more than an inventor, he was also an entrepreneur. He established the British Marconi Corporation, the Canadian Marconi Corporation, and the

American Marconi Corporation. In 1901, in his most famous experiment, he succeeded in sending a signal through the windy skies from Cornwall, England, to Newfoundland, Canada. Marconi was the first person to use radio as a device to both send and receive information.

Reginald A. Fessenden, a Canadian, took his work to the United States. He was, like most of the earlier radio pioneers who preceded him, primarily an inventor. While Marconi was sending wireless Morse code signals, Fessenden was the first to be successful at voice and music transmission. His first broadcast was from Brant Rock, Massachusetts, on December 24, 1906.

Lee De Forest, who also worked with voice transmission, is often referred to as the "father of radio"—a title he gave himself. He developed the Audion tube, a three-electrode vacuum tube that facilitated voice transmission. In his most famous experiments, he projected speech via radio. He conducted a number of tests in New York and in Europe—his most famous from the Eiffel Tower. This transmission, produced in 1908, was reported to have been received as far as 500 miles away. De Forest, like many of his forerunners, was an inventor and not a business person.

At the turn of the 20th century, several major corporate players were beginning to emerge, including the GENERAL ELECTRIC CO., whose engineer, Charles Steinmetz, developed the alternator to assist Fessenden in his first voice experiments; American Telephone and Telegraph, which eventually acquired the Audion tube from De Forest; and the Marconi companies. These corporations were primarily interested in the commercial value of the patent portfolio. They had the financial resources to see the patents developed into systems—a goal beyond the reach of most of the individual experimenters, who had the vision but lacked adequate financial backing. The prehistory of broadcasting was a complex period of lawsuits, counter-suits, litigation, financial development, competition, and experimentation. Everyone, inventors and corporate interests alike, seemed to hold patents to one or another important element of radio technology, and few were willing to share. Radio at this stage was still a laboratory experiment, but its importance as a means of point-to-point information communication—particularly in marine and ship-to-shore communication—was becoming increasingly apparent.

The first dramatic illustration of wireless radio as a maritime technology was produced by the sinking of R.M.S. *Titanic* on April 15, 1912. There was a ship near the *Titanic,* but its radio operator was not on duty when the *Titanic* struck an iceberg. By the time contact was established, the airwaves were jammed with irrelevant signals. This disaster riveted the nation's attention on the new technology, which was thus catapulted into prominence. The Radio Act of 1912, which governed radio for the next 15 years, was a direct result of the *Titanic* disaster.

As World War I approached, the applications for radio technology shifted. Business and industry were nationalized and focused on war production. On April 6, 1917, when the United States entered World War I, all wireless stations were closed. On April 7, they were reopened under the control of the U.S. Navy. Spurred by its military importance and with rivalries set aside, the technology advanced rapidly.

Following the war radio came into a new era—the Roaring Twenties. The pooling of patents to facilitate the war effort brought together previously competitive ideas and set the stage for commercial development. The move transformed the nature of radio from maritime and defense communication into commercial broadcasting in the 1920s. The radio industry grew rapidly during this decade, producing increased chaos on the air. Rival stations interfered with one another's signals by alternating wavelengths, increasing power, and changing hours of operation at will. The result was the passage of the 1927 Radio Act and the Communications Act of 1934, which regulated radio for the next 62 years.

The 1920s increased the influence of corporate radio. In an effort to protect the United States against a growing British monopoly in radio, which was controlled by Marconi, after World War I the American government pushed for the sale of Marconi's American interests to General Electric. With that sale GE, on October 17, 1919, organized the RADIO CORPORATION OF AMERICA (RCA) to manage what had been Marconi investments. In other words, a British monopoly was exchanged, with government approval, for a U.S. monopoly. Shortly thereafter, RCA formed alliances with Western Electric and its parent corporation, AT&T. Corporations were now a part of the radio landscape, and each operated a pioneering station. Most prominent among the stations were KDKA and WJZ, owned by Westinghouse; WEAF, owned by AT&T; and WJZ, WJY, and WDY, owned by RCA. There were other stations, but those owned and operated by corporations played key roles in the development of network broadcasting.

KDKA Pittsburgh earned a place in the history of radio with its broadcast of the November 2, 1920, election returns. KDKA claimed this broadcast was "the world's first scheduled broadcast," but other stations were experimenting at the same time. Charles D. Herrold pioneered sta-

Father and daughter listening to the radio, ca. 1930 (LIBRARY OF CONGRESS)

tion KQW in San Jose, California, with intermittent broadcasts beginning as early as July 1909. Professor E. M. Terry of the University of Wisconsin set up station WHA (with call letters 9XM, which designated experimental status) to broadcast weather and market reports. Station WWJ, owned by the *Detroit News,* went on the air August 22, 1920, with voice and music. CFCF in Montreal, Canada, and PCGG in the Netherlands both began broadcasting in November 1919. Historian Asa Briggs noted that during 1920, "regular concerts began to be broadcast in Europe from the Hague." Although the focus is generally on KDKA, other stations were claiming "firsts." Wireless experimentation was evolving throughout the world.

WEAF, the AT&T flagship station, led advances in technology and operational patterns. Its technical operations contributed to the development of an important tool that today we take for granted: the control board, which routes, balances, mixes, and controls the audio. The New York station made more significant advances that would have a national impact: It started to sell advertising, and it was the first station to conduct network broadcasting. WEAF was licensed to operate a toll station (to sell commercial time) on June 1, 1922. On August 28, 1922, WEAF conducted the first commercial program. It was a 10-minute speech for real estate company the Queensboro Corporation. The broadcast was so controversial that the trade magazine *Radio Broadcast* editorialized against it. Despite the debate, little seemed to stem the tide. No station during the 1920s was well financed by advertising revenue, but WEAF's toll broadcast set an important precedent and gave the fledgling broadcast industry an impetus—a financial reason to improve. By the end of the decade, an important precedent had been established and continues today: advertising support for commercial media development.

Besides inaugurating the toll broadcast, WEAF was first to provide network broadcasting. AT&T already had telephone lines spreading all over the country. Linking chains of stations together for purposes of programming seemed only logical. Thus the first network was born. AT&T's first experiment was to link two stations—WEAF New York and WNAC Boston—together on January 4, 1923. Other network experiments followed, but the one that focused public attention was a 22-station national hookup that linked stations coast-to-coast. The broadcast occurred in October 1924 and featured a speech by President Calvin Coolidge. By the end of 1925, AT&T had 26 stations linked into the network.

At the same time AT&T was making its debut into network broadcasting, RCA, under the leadership of David SARNOFF, was starting its system. The first RCA network broadcast was in December 1923, between stations WJZ, the RCA-owned New York City station, and WGY of Schenectady, New York, owned by General Electric. In September 1926, RCA formed a separate unit to conduct its broadcast and network operations: the National Broadcasting Company (NBC). Shortly thereafter (1926), AT&T sold its broadcast interests to RCA in an attempt to improve relations with RCA, Westinghouse, and General Electric. The sale immediately placed RCA in the dominant position. With the combination of its own operation based on its station WJZ and the newly acquired and financially successful WEAF, NBC now had two major network chains. The newly purchased WEAF-based AT&T network became known as the NBC Red network, and the older WJZ-based RCA network became known as the NBC Blue. Although the two networks would become similar in size during the mid-1930s, the Red network held the dominant position.

The creation of NBC's chief rival of the time, the COLUMBIA BROADCASTING SYSTEM (CBS), began with George A. Coates. Coates was a promoter who had taken up radio's cause and became involved in the anti-ASCAP (American Society of Composers, Authors and Publishers) controversy. Coates, along with the newly formed National Association of Broadcasters (NAB), was seeking to free the struggling broadcasters from the financial demands placed upon them by ASCAP for music rights on material performed on the radio. He teamed with Arthur Judson, the business manager of the Philadelphia Orchestra, who had been turned down when he tried to sell programming to RCA. The two of them formed a network, the United Independent Broadcasters, Inc. UIB debuted September 18, 1927, but its financing was weak, so it was soon looking for additional backing. The joining of UIB and Columbia Phonograph Corporation was motivated by Columbia's desire to sell records. Columbia was afraid that RCA would merge with the Victor Talking Machine Company and then dominate the record industry (RCA did merge with Victor in 1929). So, UIB and Columbia merged on April 5, 1927, creating a 16-station lineup. The agreement gave UIB a temporary financial boost and a name change—to the Columbia Phonograph Broadcasting System (CPBS-UIB).

The Congress Cigar Company of Philadelphia was one of the successful advertisers at CPBS. The vice president of that company was William S. Paley. Paley and his family purchased the network in September 1928, and by 1929, thanks to some creative financing, the company was showing a profit. The name Columbia was retained. It purchased its first key station, WABC New York, in 1928; a decade later the Columbia Broadcasting System (CBS) purchased the stock of the American Record Corporation, and several other record labels.

The programming schedule offered by NBC, CBS, other smaller networks, and individual independent stations was irregular at first, but it grew with the stations and the audience during the 1920s and 1930s. Historically, programming included sporting events, political speeches, and the personalities of radio programming. But early programming was primarily live music. Performers were willing to appear in hopes that the publicity would increase their own popularity. The networks even had their own live orchestras in the studio. The programs were designed for stu-

dio performance. Large studios were draped with curtains; although the performers would not be seen, they dressed in formal attire for the program events. Programming schedules occupied primarily the evening hours and expanded with the increased audience and the capability of the technical operation.

Radio had a significant effect on those living during the Great Depression and into World War II. Broadcast historians most often call this period radio's "golden age." The comedy and drama programs, such as *Suspense, Amos 'n' Andy, The Shadow, Little Orphan Annie, One Man's Family,* the *March of Time,* the *Lone Ranger,* and a host of others propelled the popularity of radio. During the 1930s and into the early 1940s, radio was beginning to attract more and more advertisers, while other industries continued to struggle. In the politically charged climate of the Depression and war, radio was a popular source of respite and entertainment and the major platform for the discussion of issues. It was a window on the world, a break from a provincial existence and the difficult challenges of the day. President Roosevelt used radio and his Fireside Chats to inspire an audience during troubled times. The episode of Orson Welles's *Mercury Theater of the Air* broadcast on October 30, 1938—an adaptation of H. G. Wells's *War of the Worlds*—was a dramatic example of the power of entertainment and news-styled programming.

During the 1930s, the NEWSPAPER INDUSTRY began to worry about radio detracting from its readership. Some historians have referred to this competition as the "press radio war." It was really a state of intense business rivalry. In 1933, newspapers began to put pressure on the radio industry to eliminate and/or limit news programming. The consensus reached was called the Biltmore Agreement, and while it curtailed news, both NBC and CBS continued with their commentary programs. By December 1938, the Biltmore Agreement fell apart, and the commentators and their support staffs were transformed into news organizations that would cover the events of World War II. Commentators became news anchors and reporters, providing eyewitness accounts and observations about the war.

Radio news was the major program innovation of World War II. Radio newspeople filled the airwaves with reports from the front. Edward R. Murrow, later known as the "dean of broadcast news," took the sounds of the war into every American home. Elmer Davis, H. V. Kaltenborn, Robert Trout, Douglas Edwards, William L. Shirer, Chet Huntley, and other commentators turned to reporting the events of the war. They portrayed the war as they saw it. It was the nation's first eyewitness radio news. As the war expanded, so did the news organizations at NBC and CBS. They established news bureaus throughout the globe, their staffs expanded, and the number of program hours dedicated to news grew dramatically. By the end of the war, CBS radio alone had grown from a mere handful of commentators to almost 170 reporters and stringers, who filed almost 30,000 broadcast reports. World War II marked the beginning of a new era for radio journalism and information gathering. Today radio and television networks program and use the organizational principles they developed.

During the war the radio industry grew slowly. FM technology was still in its pioneering stages, and both FM and television growth were frozen by the FEDERAL COMMUNICATIONS COMMISSION. Edwin Howard Armstrong is considered the father of FM (frequency modulation) broadcasting. He was born December 18, 1890. Early in his career, Armstrong and a rival were working on similar circuitry and wound up in a bitter patent conflict. However, Armstrong's primary concern, and his contribution to the science of radio, was his effort to eliminate the static that interfered with the transmission of AM (amplitude modulation) radio.

Armstrong worked on FM throughout the 1920s and applied for patents on FM in 1930. The patents were granted in December 1933. His FM radio demonstrations were impressive. There

was no static in his signal. Armstrong was dedicated to his system and promoted it as a replacement for AM radio. The impact of FM radio was not immediately confrontational; some scientists saw it as an improvement of the existing signals but gave little thought of it replacing AM. Sarnoff opposed FM. RCA already had two AM radio station networks, but RCA did couple FM with television audio. However, as Armstrong pushed his position, those who had a financial investment in AM radio began to fight back. The conflicts prompted legal delays in the allocation of spectrum space, and as corporate engineers began developing other systems, more conflict resulted. Armstrong spent most of his fortune defending his FM system as a revolutionary technology that would make AM obsolete. FM's development was so slow that Armstrong became despondent, and in 1954 he took his own life. FM would be delayed several decades before it would achieve Armstrong's vision and replace AM.

Today's FM radio audience share is about 75 percent. When the programs of radio's golden age converted to television, radio switched to music. New music styles and formats created programming suitable to every lifestyle. The AM radio audience is primarily limited to news and talk radio. Contemporary radio is characterized by intense competition, with each station competing for a smaller share of the general audience market but a more sizable share of a specific target audience. For example, the audience who supports country-western music. The radio networks of historical significance are gone. They provided only news programming through the last half of the century. Today's radio networks, such as Westwood One, and group owners, such as Infinity Broadcasting, provide satellite-linked music and talk programming to stations across the nation on a contract basis. Perhaps the most prominent trend in the current radio industry is group ownership. The passage of the Telecommunications Act of 1996 removed the old FCC restrictions on ownership. This new REGULATION promoted an immense exchange of radio station properties. Owners who were previously limited to a handful of stations now own hundreds of them.

The technology of radio continues to grow as does its popularity. Satellite radio offers 24-hour service. Digital radio offers CD-quality sound to the car, home, and office. Radio goes where audiences go and has its strengths in localism and an ability to fit into a personal way of life.

Further reading

Barnouw, E. *A Tower in Babel: A History of Broadcasting in the United States*. New York: Oxford University Press, 1966.

Godfrey, D. G., and F. A. Leigh. *Historical Dictionary of American Radio*. Westport, Conn.: Greenwood Press, 1998.

Marconi, D. *My Father Marconi*. New York: McGraw-Hill, 1962.

Sterling, C. H., and J. M. Kittross. *Stay Tuned: A History of American Broadcasting*. 3rd ed. Mahwah, N.J.: Lawrence Erlbaum Associates, 2002.

Donald G. Godfrey

railroads   As a form of transportation, railroads had been experimented with since the late 18th century. They became practical only with the development of the steam engine. Originally, railroads were powered by horses or, in some cases, sails, but only when steam engines were introduced did rail lines begin to be constructed. At first, railroads competed with canals and TURNPIKES for freight and passengers, but by 1828, when the first American passenger railroad, the Baltimore & Ohio, opened, railroads slowly began to overtake the canals and develop into the predominant form of transportation.

The railroads built in the 1840s overtook canals in mileage, although the steam engines were imported from Britain. Wood, rather than iron, was used extensively in construction of the roads themselves. By 1850, an estimated $300 million was invested in railroads, making them the most capital-intensive industry in the country. New England accounted for the most miles completed in the 1850s, when the railroads began to expand from the Northeast into the Midwest. By 1860, more than 30,000 miles had been completed and capital investment tripled. Building was very slow during the Civil War but intensified once the conflict was over. Transcontinental links were of paramount importance during the late 1860s, and the first coast-to-coast link was completed at Promontory, Utah Territory, in 1869, when the Central Pacific and the Union Pacific lines were joined. The rapid building helped link the country's distant markets and also helped develop several midwestern cities as major centers of commerce, notably Chicago.

Rapid expansion also gave rise to scandal and controversy. The management of the ERIE RAILROAD by Jay GOULD and Jim FISK in New York and the famous "Erie wars" gave the railroads a bad reputation. They distributed more than $1 million to members of the New York legislature to gain passage of laws favorable to them. Also, the Crédit Mobilier scandal, beginning in 1872 during the Grant administration, was a major blemish upon congressional funding of a transcontinental rail link. The scandals gave the impression that the only investors who profited from the railroads were senior management, who were often accused of looting them, while ordinary investors earned only a normal return. The capital intensiveness of the railroads finally led many of them to enter pooling arrangements after the Civil War, whereby price rigging of freight rates became common. As the railroads expanded westward, the controversy grew.

After the Civil War, the Pennsylvania Railroad grew to be the largest in the country. It grew mainly by consolidating with other lines. Serving all markets was not practical for the railroads as their routes became longer, extending through many states. Farmers began to organize to fight what they considered to be unfair treatment by the railroads, since the rate schedules were often illogical and cost small farmers more money than larger customers who received more favorable rates. The Grange movement opposed the railroads and precipitated several lawsuits against them, charging monopolist behavior in setting rates. The Supreme Court ruled favorably for the Grangers in *Munn v. Illinois* in 1877 but later reversed itself in *Wabash Railway Co. v. Illinois* in 1886. In 1877, a national railroad strike occurred when the Pennsylvania Railroad and several others cut wages of their workers by 10 percent. The stoppage became the first in the country that could be classified as a general strike; it lasted about a month.

Railroads made significant strides toward uniformity of equipment and safety in the 1880s, anticipating federal regulation of some sort. Despite the court cases favorable to the farmers, REGULATION was in the hands of the states in the absence of federal antimonopoly laws and railroad regulation. The growing power of the railroads finally led Congress to create the INTERSTATE COMMERCE COMMISSION (ICC) in 1887. The body became the first government-created regulatory agency designed to curtail the power of the private sector, if necessary. The immediate impact of the commission was muted by the Panic of 1893, which created a depression forcing many railroads into BANKRUPTCY along with thousands of other businesses. Although the ICC was not a powerful body, it nevertheless marked a significant shift toward the beginnings of regulation in the United States. The continued opposition to big business by farmers and organized labor also

The Potomac railroad yards in Alexandria, Virginia (LIBRARY OF CONGRESS)

gave rise to the Populist movement in the late 19th century.

During the first decade of the 20th century, the railroads suffered several setbacks, including an unfavorable ruling in *U.S. v. Northern Securities* (1904). The ruling dismembered a monopoly that controlled much of the rails in the Pacific Northwest. The Hepburn Act (1906) and the Mann-Elkins Act (1910) gave the ICC increased powers, and the federal government operated the railroads during World War I. After the war, the railroads began to slowly decline as other forms of transportation vied for freight and, later, passengers. The U.S. Post Office granted airlines the right to carry long-distance mail in the 1920s, creating airmail. The passing of the Interstate Highway Act in 1956 also helped diminish railroads' importance as long-distance trucking began to capture a larger and larger share of freight hauling. Congress overhauled the rail system by creating the National Railroad Passenger Corp. in 1971 (Amtrak) and the Consolidated Rail Corporation in 1976 (Conrail). DEREGULATION of the rails was completed in 1980, when the STAGGERS RAIL ACT was passed. Large mergers of several rail systems followed as the railroads fought to consolidate and maintain their portion of freight haulage.

Further changes to the regulatory environment occurred in 1996, when the ICC was abolished and replaced by the Surface Transportation Board (STB). By the end of the 20th century, the railroads were mainly large, consolidated systems formed by merger. Passenger transportation was mainly in the hands of Amtrak and related state-operated systems.

See also HARRIMAN, EDWARD HENRY; HILL, James J.; SCOTT, THOMAS A.

Further reading

Chandler, Alfred D., Jr. *The Railroads: The Nation's First Big Business.* New York: Harcourt Brace, 1965.

Fogel, Robert W. *Railroads and American Economic Growth.* Baltimore: Johns Hopkins University Press, 1964.

Klein, Maury. *Unfinished Business: The Railroad in American Life.* Hanover, N.H.: University Press of New England, 1994.

Kolko, Gabriel. *Railroads and Regulation, 1877–1916.* New York: Greenwood Publishing, 1977.

Saunders, Richard. *Main Lines: Rebirth of the North American Railroads, 1970–2002.* DeKalb: Northern Illinois University Press, 2003.

Raskob, John J. (1879–1950) *businessman*
Born in Lockport, New York, Raskob's father and grandfather were cigar makers. Upon graduating from high school, he attended a business college and studied accounting and stenography, afterward getting a job as a stenographer at a manufacturing company. In 1898, he took a job in Nova Scotia with a steel company before returning to the United States two years later. He was introduced to Pierre DuPont, who at the time worked for the Johnson Company in Ohio. DuPont took a liking to him and hired him as his secretary.

When DuPont became the treasurer of the reorganized DUPONT DE NEMOURS & CO. in 1902, he made Raskob his private secretary. DuPont taught his secretary how to reorganize the firm and also showed him the intricacies of corporate organization. The two created the new DuPont Company's accounting department. In 1914, he became the company's assistant treasurer and then was elected to the company's board and the executive committee. Raskob then invested in GENERAL MOTORS, which was undergoing a change in organization and management. He joined the board of General Motors in 1915 and served as the company's vice president of finance from 1918 to 1928 while still serving as DuPont's chief financial officer. He also became a close colleague of William C. DURANT.

After GM was reorganized again in 1920, Raskob played less of a role in the company but still helped design its dividend policy and some other financial policies as well. He remained with DuPont until he retired in 1946 but resigned from GM in 1928 to pursue other interests. From

1928 to 1932, he served as chairman of the Democratic National Committee. After serious differences of opinion with the administration of Franklin D. Roosevelt, he resigned the position and became a founder of the American Liberty League, a conservative political organization opposed to many New Deal policies. He also was the major force, with Al Smith, behind the construction of the Empire State Building in New York City. The building, the world's tallest upon completion, was built following the construction of the Chrysler Building by Walter CHRYSLER.

Raskob was also associated with the stock market in the 1920s. Raskob was an active investor during the market's historic rise in 1929. An interview, published in the *Ladies' Home Journal* in August 1929 was entitled "Everyone Ought to be Rich," and Raskob gave his reasons why the stock market was a sound place to make one's fortune.

Further reading

Burk, Robert F. *The Corporate State and the Broker State: The DuPonts and American National Politics, 1925–1940.* Cambridge, Mass.: Harvard University Press, 1990.

Colby, Gerard. *DuPont Dynasty.* Secaucus, N.J.: Lyle Stuart, 1984.

recession Slowdown in the rate of economic growth, as reflected in the gross domestic product (GDP), from previous levels. Traditionally, a recession has been defined in the financial markets as two consecutive quarters of negative growth in the leading economic indicators, suggesting that the economy has slowed considerably from previous quarters. As part of the business cycle, it has been assumed that a recession would normally occur about once every seven years as the economy moved through stages of expansion before naturally slowing down.

In the post–World War II era, recessions have occurred in 1945–46, 1949, 1954, 1956, 1960, 1970, 1980–83, 1991–92, and in the year follow-

ing the bursting of the stock market bubble beginning in 2000. Previously, the stock market crash of 1929 had caused the Great Depression, when economic growth remained at low levels for three years before rebounding modestly in the mid-1930s, only to plunge again in the late 1930s. The term *depression* has been applied only to the economic slowdown of the 1930s. Prior economic slowdowns used a different terminology, but no single term was used consistently.

The United States suffered severe economic slowdowns several times before the Civil War. During the 19th and early 20th centuries these events were known as "panics." Slowdowns, or panics, occurred in 1807, 1837, 1857, 1873, 1882, 1893, 1903, 1907, and 1920. Traditionally, these periods were known as panics because they followed significant stock market declines, which at the time were attributed to a loss of investor confidence. Some were clearly more severe than others, with the Panics of 1837, 1857, 1873, and 1893 the most severe and longest. Many of the problems were exacerbated by the lack of a central bank in the United States, which made the supply of money inelastic and unresponsive to economic conditions.

The difference in terminology reflects the state of economic information in the 20th century versus that in the 18th and 19th. The federal government improved its compilation of economic statistics markedly in the 20th century, and the results were a better understanding of those factors capable of causing an economic slowdown. In the 18th and 19th centuries, much of the information surrounding panics was anecdotal or based solely upon banking and stock market performance. As a result, a complete picture never emerged of the root causes of many slowdowns, and many commentators instead relied on anecdotal evidence or attributed panics to the actions of individuals such as the ROBBER BARONS or shrewd stock market operators.

Beginning in the 1920s, Herbert Hoover asked the newly formed National Bureau of Economic Research, a private research group, to begin providing more raw data and analysis of the economy. Other private companies, such as the AMERICAN TELEPHONE & TELEGRAPH CO., also kept their own surveys and analyses of the economy—and the modern period of studying the economy was born. The term *panic* disappeared from serious studies of the economy and instead was used to describe stock market plunges.

Considerable debate has centered on recessions and depressions. Some arguments credit the application of John Maynard Keynes's theories by various administrations, beginning with Franklin D. Roosevelt, as helping to prevent further depressions after the Great Depression of the 1930s. Regardless of the debate, recessions continue to occur, although a depression of the magnitude of the 1930s has not been witnessed again in the United States. But the recession of the late 1970s and early 1980s proved to be one of the most enduring since the 1930s. It also was accompanied by high inflation, a relatively rare occurrence during a recession. For that reason, the term *stagflation* was coined, indicating a recession beset with inflation at the same time.

Further reading

Eckstein, Otto. *The Great Recession: With a Postcript on Stagflation*. Amsterdam: North-Holland, 1978.

Heilbroner, Robert. *Beyond Boom and Crash*. New York: Norton, 1978.

Kindelberger, Charles. *Panics, Manias & Crashes, 4th ed.* New York: John Wiley & Sons, 2000.

Reconstruction Finance Corp. (RFC) Government agency founded in 1932 during Herbert Hoover's administration to help maintain economic stability during the Depression. The original purpose of the RFC was to aid financing in small business, agriculture, and industry. The scope of the agency was expanded during Franklin D. Roosevelt's first administration. Its first loan, to a Chicago bank, was controversial, evoking charges of cronyism and political

favoritism, although the agency would exist for 25 years.

During FDR's first two administrations, the agency became the major lender to many businesses both large and small. Its chairman was Jesse Jones, who presided over the agency for most of the NEW DEAL and until World War II began. It merged with two other agencies to form the Federal Loan Agency, which made billions of dollars in loans to industry and business during World War II. Jones became secretary of commerce in 1940, and Henry Wallace became head of the agency in 1945, when it was returned to the Federal Loan Agency. After the war, a congressional investigation was held after charges of political favoritism were leveled at the agency. As a result, its status as an independent agency was abolished in 1953, and it was transferred to the auspices of the Department of the Treasury. It was out of business a year later and totally abolished in 1957.

Throughout the 1930s and World War II, the RFC was the major lender in the country, dispensing more than $50 billion worth of loans to all types of companies, large and small. It was one of the few agencies able to change its function from peacetime to war and then switch back to peacetime again while keeping within its original mandate. Its activities dominated finance for more than a decade, often supplanting banks and Wall Street as a provider of funds during the later 1930s and 1940s.

Further reading

Jones, Jesse. *Fifty Billion Dollars: My Thirteen Years with the RFC*. New York: Macmillan, 1951.

Olson, James. *Herbert Hoover and the Reconstruction Finance Corp., 1931–1933*. Ames: Iowa State University Press, 1977.

regional stock exchanges Boston, Philadelphia, Chicago, San Francisco, Los Angeles, and Cincinnati are homes to the regional equity exchanges that remain in operation in this country. Most of these exchanges came into existence to trade a specific type of security (for example, those of oil, gold, timber, mining companies) many years ago, and these are the survivors. At one time, exchanges also existed in Hartford, Pittsburgh, Baltimore, Washington, D.C., New Orleans, Denver, Seattle, Portland, Detroit, and a number of other locations that have long since faded from memory.

The remaining regionals are a result of MERG-ERS of two or three exchanges that could not exist on their own. The regional stock exchanges for many years were havens for transactions that a major investor might not want to execute on the New York or American exchanges. It was a way to trade "around the book"; in other words, to avoid the notoriety of a big trade in New York. In 1975, with the advent of the Securities Amend-ments Act, which for the first time eliminated fixed-rate commissions, the regionals came into their own as national exchanges that were part of the National Market System. They listed most of the issues traded on the New York and American exchanges. Through a new communication sys-tem that linked all exchanges, called the Inter-market Trading System, they could guarantee any customer using their floor an execution at or better than the displayed quote on the major exchanges. When they did not wish to trade at or better than the displayed market, they could for-ward the order through the Intermarket Trading System (ITS) to the displaying exchange and fill the order at the best bid or offer.

With this capability in hand, they then turned and offered major broker-dealers the opportunity to become specialists on their respective floors. As many of these firms took advantage of these opportunities and internalized the order flow from their own customers in issues in which they specialized, regional volume expanded, and many new players were attracted to these grow-ing market centers. These developments cost the NEW YORK STOCK EXCHANGE almost 20 percent of its order flow and made the regionals a viable group of markets in the emerging marketplace.

The revenues from this enhanced activity allowed two of them, Philadelphia and the Pacific, to ven-ture into listed options with separate exchanges and enhance their revenue through these ven-tures. Many of the significant changes in the mar-ketplace came from the innovations created by the regional retail executions and continuous net settlements.

The role of the regionals continues to change as technology has created many more competitors than just the New York and American exchanges. The Pacific Exchange has merged its equity busi-ness with a major electronic communications net-work. The Chicago Exchange ventured into the NASDAQ world of over-the-counter dealer issues. The Cincinnati Exchange has become an all-elec-tronic automated marketplace, and Boston and Philadelphia continue to discuss affiliation with other entities in the business.

See also NATIONAL ASSOCIATION OF SECURITIES DEALERS; STOCK MARKETS.

Further reading
Geisst, Charles R. *Wall Street: A History*. New York: Oxford University Press, 1997.

Lee Korins

regulation   The practice of using laws to con-trol the activities of certain industries or sectors of society. Attempts at government regulation began shortly after the Civil War and initially were aimed at the RAILROADS. As the country expanded, certain industries were expanding quickly, posing problems for the states and the federal government. In an attempt to control the private sector, many government units began passing laws designed to control railroads in, or passing through, their jurisdictions.

The first significant government attempt to regulate the railroads came with the establish-ment of the INTERSTATE COMMERCE COMMISSION in 1887. From the last quarter of the 19th century to the beginning of World War I, the idea of regulat-ing industry was fostered by the Progressive movement, and many of its general ideas found their way into federal legislation. As Congress moved to enact labor laws at the behest of the labor movement, pass antitrust laws, and create the FEDERAL RESERVE, the influence of government in the private sector became more extensive. By the 1920s, it was clear that the LAISSEZ-FAIRE attitude of the 19th century was no longer viable as society grew larger and more complex.

In the aftermath of the stock market crash in 1929 and the Great Depression that followed, the administration of Franklin D. Roosevelt began in 1933 to institute more federal regulation over industry than had ever been experienced before. The banking, securities, and UTILITIES industries all had stringent regulations imposed by Congress, while workers in general benefited from Social Security legislation passed during FDR's first administration. At the same time, some states also passed their own laws aimed at regulating certain industries, some of which, such as the INSURANCE INDUSTRY, were regulated primarily at the state rather than the federal level. In many cases, industries were regulated at both the federal and state levels.

During the Depression, it also became obvious that the role of government would have to be stronger in the future to avoid the industry abuses that many believed were the root causes of the economic downturn. The economic theories of John Maynard KEYNES in particular emphasized government spending as a means of stimulating the economy; his ideas became popular for more than a generation since they dovetailed with the general trend toward regulation.

As many industries became larger, they found themselves regulated closely. Airlines and other forms of interstate transportation were closely regulated, as were communications, energy, financial services, and some technologies. Often the regulation extended to imposing curbs on ownership by foreign investors, while at other times regulation was more closely related to the NEW DEAL model of regulation over domestic ownership and control of certain types of activities,

such as the pricing or selling of goods and services. Many government agencies became involved in the regulatory process, including the FEDERAL COMMUNICATIONS COMMISSION, the FEDERAL TRADE COMMISSION, the Securities and Exchange Commission, the Federal Reserve, the Interstate Commerce Commission (later the Surface Transportation Board), the TENNESSEE VALLEY AUTHORITY, and the Office of Thrift Supervision.

Beginning in the 1970s and carrying through to the 1990s, DEREGULATION became popular as Congress sought to allow many industries greater freedom than before. As the population grew and many businesses grew larger as well, theory leaned toward more self-regulation than close government supervision. Often, there were too many businesses in some industries to regulate them effectively, and self-regulation was seen as a practical remedy to government supervision, which often was bureaucratic and time consuming. In some cases, especially that of the securities and banking industries, the original New Deal regulations were thought to be outdated and ineffective. The new deregulatory environment did not wipe out regulations but did allow many companies greater self-regulation and freedom to operate.

Often when regulations were relaxed or rolled back, merger trends appeared, allowing any company to merge with others or the consolidation of entire industries in the name of greater economies of scale and efficiencies, which smaller companies found hard to achieve.

Further reading

McCraw, Thomas K. *Prophets of Regulation.* Cambridge, Mass.: Harvard University Press, 1984.

Schwartz, Bernard, ed. *Economic Regulation of Business and Industry: A Legislative History of U.S. Regulatory Agencies.* New York: Chelsea House, 1973.

Wolfson, Nicholas. *The Modern Corporation: Free Markets Versus Regulation.* New York: Free Press, 1984.

Resolution Trust Corporation (RTC) An agency of the federal government created by the FINANCIAL INSTITUTIONS REFORM, RECOVERY, AND

ENFORCEMENT ACT (FIRREA) on August 9, 1989, and designed to fund the cleanup of the savings and loan crisis. During the 1980s, the savings and loan industry suffered its worst disaster since the Great Depression. By the end of the decade, hundreds of technically failed institutions were still open and awaiting resolution.

The federal deposit insurance fund for savings and loans, the Federal Savings and Loan Insurance Corporation (FSLIC), the thrift institutions' equivalent of the FEDERAL DEPOSIT INSURANCE CORPORATION, had become insolvent and thus unable to complete the failure resolution process. The RTC was assigned this task. Before it ceased operations on December 31, 1995, the RTC closed 747 institutions with $402.6 billion in assets—at a cost of $87.5 billion. Taxpayers provided $81.9 billion to cover this cost, with the remainder provided by private funds.

During its brief existence, the RTC faced enormous challenges and generated considerable controversy. The process of getting failed institutions back into private hands involved managing and selling houses, apartments, office buildings, shopping centers, hotels and motels, raw land, and more. Yet the RTC was required to do this while simultaneously maximizing sale values, minimizing disruptions to local real estate markets, and maximizing preservation of affordable housing. As if this was not difficult enough, the necessary funds had to be authorized by Congress. Initially, only $50 billion was authorized. This quickly proved insufficient. Congress authorized additional funds, but only after needless and costly delays. By the late 1990s, it was estimated that the total cleanup bill exceeded $150 billion.

Early in the resolution process, it became clear that RTC procedures and controls were deficient. This led to a controversy over how best to avoid extra costs from being incurred. Although the RTC did help clean up the savings and loan mess, no public accounting was ever made to enable a determination of how much extra taxpayers paid due to unnecessary funding delays and inappropriate disposition practices.

See also SAVINGS AND LOANS.

Further reading

Barth, James R. *The Great Savings and Loan Debacle.* Washington, D.C.: American Enterprise Institute, 1991.

Ely, Bert. "The RTC in Historical Perspective." *Housing Policy Debate* 1, no. 1 (1990): 53–78.

Federal Deposit Insurance Corporation. *Managing the Crisis: The FDIC and RTC Experience, 1980–1994.* Washington, D.C.: FDIC, August 1998.

James R. Barth

Reuther, Walter P. (1907–1970) *labor leader*

Born in Wheeling, West Virginia, into a German immigrant and trade unionist family, Reuther was originally a die maker by trade. At a young age, he moved to Detroit to finish his education and take a job at a Ford plant. He worked for the FORD MOTOR COMPANY from 1927 to 1932 and then worked abroad for three years, including time in a Soviet factory designed by Henry FORD.

After returning to the United States, he helped organize workers for the UNITED AUTOMOBILE WORKERS (UAW) when the union was founded in 1935. Two years later, he and other UAW organizers were assaulted by Ford security guards outside a Ford plant in a bloody confrontation that made him a national figure. His slogan during the strike, "Unionism, not Fordism," was a direct challenge to industry and sealed his reputation as a champion of workers' rights.

He rose quickly in the UAW hierarchy and became vice president in 1942. Four years later he became president. In 1945, he led a strike against GENERAL MOTORS, demanding a 30 percent pay raise for his workers and also demanding that the company open its books for outside scrutiny, an unheard of demand at the time. Reuther was a long-time advocate of negotiated pension and worker benefits and wages tied to productivity. While president of the union, he held the post of president of the Congress of Industrial Organizations. He also helped orchestrate the merger of the two largest unions. When the CIO merged with the AMERICAN FEDERATION OF LABOR in 1955, he became vice president of the combined organization, a post he held until 1967. The UAW withdrew from the AFL-CIO in 1968 but rejoined in 1981.

Throughout his life, Reuther championed workers' causes and was a member of the noncommunist left. He was one of the first labor leaders to lend his support for putting industry on a wartime footing during World War II. He also supported Lyndon Johnson's Great Society programs and the Civil Rights movement of the 1960s and opposed American involvement in Vietnam. Acting as an emissary for the union movement, he traveled extensively around the world preaching the virtues of trade unionism. He served as an adviser to several Democratic presidents.

Reuther survived several attempts on his life throughout his career. One attack left an arm severely injured. He died in an airplane crash in Michigan in 1970. He is remembered as one of the major figures in American labor.

See also GOMPERS, SAMUEL; LEWIS, JOHN L.; MEANY, GEORGE.

Further reading

Barnard, John. *Walter Reuther and the Rise of the Auto Workers.* Boston: Little, Brown, 1983.

Cormier, Frank, and William Eaton. *Reuther.* Englewood Cliffs, N.J.: Prentice Hall, 1970.

Howe, Irving, and B. J. Widick. *The UAW and Walter Reuther.* New York: Random House, 1949.

Lichtenstein, Nelson. *The Most Dangerous Man in America: Walter Reuther and the Fate of American Labor.* New York: Basic Books, 1995.

Revson, Charles (1906–1975) *cosmetics manufacturer* Charles Haskell Revson was born in Somerville, Massachusetts, on October 11, 1906, the son of Russian immigrants. After passing through public schools in Manchester, New Hampshire, he relocated to New York City to sell dresses for the Pickwick Dress Company. After a brief stint in Chicago as a salesman he returned

to New York to sell nail polish for the firm Elka. In 1932, when the company refused to appoint Revson a national distributor, he left to found his own cosmetics firm in concert with chemist Charles Lachman. At that time, nail polish was restricted to the color red, but Lachman had devised a new formula—creamy, opaque, and nonstreak—that could hold a variety of different colors. Revson immediately perceived a decisive sales advantage, so in 1932 he and Lachman founded the Revlon Company. The firm arrived in the midst of the Great Depression but nonetheless flourished owing to the popularity of the permanent wave hair style. Because this, in turn, led to a dramatic increase in beauty salons, Revson catered solely to that market instead of smaller distributors. He also insisted on charging top dollar for an extremely high-quality product. Revlon sales boomed accordingly, and by 1941, Revson enjoyed a near monopoly of lipstick sales to 100,000 salons. His success skyrocketed again when he introduced different colored lipsticks reflecting the season or mood of the wearer. He then orchestrated a brilliantly conceived advertising campaign entitled "matching lips and fingertips" that promoted color-coordinated lipstick and nail polish for the first time. Women found the combination appealing, and by the end of World War II, Revlon was the number two cosmetics producer in the United States behind Estee Lauder.

The decade of the 1950s witnessed the true marketing genius of Revson come of age. Counter to the staid, prudish mores of the time, he adopted ads and themes that bordered on the sexually explicit. The best example of this was the "Fire and Ice" campaign of 1952, orchestrated to usher in a new line of makeup, which succeeded brilliantly. Revson also recognized the marketing power of the new television milieu, and in 1955, he became sole sponsor of the popular quiz show *The $64,000 Question*. The show closed down five years later amid the general scandal involving prearranged answers, but Revson was never implicated. The impact on makeup sales proved dramatic, however, and the company stock rose by 200 percent by 1956.

Throughout the 1960s Revson again sought to trump the competition by greatly diversifying his product line. Eventually he manufactured and marketed skin-care products, shampoo, hair spray, perfume, lotions, and even a line of men's products. Once Revson became cognizant of the need for cheaper perfumes to cater to younger women, he introduced an inexpensive scent named "Charlie," which became one of the most successful items in cosmetics history. He also displayed considerable business acumen by acquiring the U.S. Vitamin and Pharmaceuticals Company for $67 million and within a few years completely diversified its product line. A decade later, the gamble paid off handsomely, and the new firm accounted for 27 percent of Revlon's annual income.

One secret to Revson's surprising success was his unyielding emphasis on quality. He personally oversaw the manufacture, testing, and marketing of virtually thousands of products—and usually tried most of them on himself. He was also relentlessly demanding upon his staff and workers, and Revlon earned the reputation of a "revolving door company" with a high turnover of workers and staff. Revson himself deliberately cut a larger than life figure with an opulent lifestyle that included expensive yachts, lavish parties, sumptuous residences and—what he relished most—numerous high-profile enemies in the cosmetics industry. By the time Revson died in New York City on August 24, 1975, he had transformed Revlon from an $11,000 company into an international cosmetics giant grossing $606 million annually—one of the 200 most profitable corporations in America.

Further reading

Abrams, George J. *That Man: The Story of Charles Revson*. New York: Manor Books, 1977.

Allen, Margaret. *Selling Dreams: Inside the Beauty Business*. New York: Simon & Schuster, 1981.

Tobias, Andrew E. *Fire and Ice: The Story of Charles Revson, the Man Who Built the Revlon Empire*. New York: Quill, 1983.

Vail, Gilbert. *A History of Cosmetics in America*. New York: The Association, 1947.

John C. Fredriksen

robber barons   Term given to industrialists and bankers of the 19th century. It was originally used by journalist Matthew Josephson in a 1934 book of the same title to describe the careers of Cornelius VANDERBILT, JAY GOULD, J. P. Morgan, and Andrew CARNEGIE, among others.

As portrayed, a robber baron was an extremely wealthy, successful industrialist who created large industries without much consideration for the public welfare. The descriptions are replete with example after example of how the wealthy cajoled and connived their way to power and how they flaunted it once they became established. This was done in the absence of federal laws limiting corrupt behavior, and continued even after many of the laws were passed.

The concept was very similar to the earlier work of journalist Gustavus Myers, whose own book, *The History of the Great American Fortunes*, was one of the first comprehensive muckraking books. The popularity of the easily recognized term can be seen in its continuing general use since the Josephson book was published. More recently, individual works have reexamined the careers of many of the robber barons and concluded that both Myers's and Josephson's critiques were too left of center and often slanted. However, they were an integral part of muckraking literature and strongly reflected both the Populist and Progressive traditions.

Since World War II, the term *muckraking* has faded and has been replaced by investigative journalism. While not as ideological as some muckraking exposes, investigative journalism also attempts to uncover hidden business practices and motives. More recently, the term *robber barons* has been attacked as being ideologically charged against business and deceptive, since many of the so-called barons also were major contributors to industrial growth and were sometimes major philanthropists. The acceptable side of capitalism in these cases has been omitted from the critique in favor of sensationalist headlines and groundless attacks.

See also MUCKRAKERS; NEWSPAPER INDUSTRY.

Further reading
Josephson, Matthew. *The Robber Barons.* 1934. Reprint, 1962.
Myers, Gustavus. *The History of the Great American Fortunes.* Chicago: Charles H. Kerr, 1910.

Robinson-Patman Act An act named after Senator Joseph T. Robinson of Arkansas and Representative Wright Patman of Texas, who proposed legislation directed at large CHAIN STORES, particularly the GREAT ATLANTIC & PACIFIC TEA CO. (A&P). Small grocers and other retailers, who were politically well organized, convinced Congress that these large chains were forcing suppliers to sell to them at a significantly lower price than the smaller dealers could obtain. This injured competition by driving the smaller dealers out of business, leaving the large chains with near monopolies.

The statute, which amended part of the 1914 CLAYTON ACT, actually made it unlawful for a seller to sell the same commodity to two different business buyers at different prices when the two buyers competed with each other. For example, it forbade Farmer Brown from selling milk to A&P for 10 cents per gallon while charging smaller grocers 15 cents per gallon. As the statute was initially proposed, the violator of this "price discrimination" provision was Farmer Brown, even though the farmer was supposedly yielding to the buying power of the large chain store. However, a late amendment to the Robinson-Patman Act made it unlawful for a buyer to induce the unlawful price discrimination.

The act, which became law in 1936, reflected the revolution in product distribution that occurred before and during the New Deal era. Large merchandisers who owned multiple stores were able to purchase goods in quantity at low prices, and thus undersell traditional family owned stores. Further, the Robinson-Patman Act reflected Congress's policy conclusion that injuring small dealers was a bad thing, notwithstanding the general benefit obtained by consumers from lower chain store prices. Thus, the Robinson-Patman Act is considered to be the most "special interest" of all the ANTITRUST statutes and has been severely criticized by both moderate and conservative antitrust scholars. The statute remains on the books, however, and is actively enforced by private plaintiffs.

See also PREDATORY PRICING; SHERMAN ACT.

Further reading
Hovenkamp, Herbert. *Antitrust Law.* Chicago: West Wadsworth, 1999.
Palamountain, Joseph C. *The Politics of Distribution.* Cambridge, Mass.: Harvard University Press, 1955.
Rowe, Fred M. *Price Discrimination Under the Robinson-Patman Act.* Boston: Little, Brown, 1962.

Herbert Hovenkamp

Rockefeller, John D. (1839–1937) *industrialist and philanthropist* Born near Ithaca, New York, Rockefeller was the son of a peddler with a spotty work history. At age 14, his family moved to Cleveland, and two years later, Rockefeller began working for a small produce firm. The city provided him with a new interest since it was the home of the early oil industry. Before entering the oil business, he first formed a partnership in the grain business with a friend, Maurice Clark, selling his interests soon after and using his profit to become an oilman.

Rockefeller and Clark began trading in oil several years after it had been discovered in Titusville, Pennsylvania, in 1859. In 1863, Rockefeller bid $72,000 for a Cleveland refinery and made the transition from commodities to the oil refining business. The oil business brought many railroads to Cleveland, and many of the lines soon began competing for business by offering favorable rate schedules, which Rockefeller and his partners, Henry FLAGLER and Samuel Andrews, used to their full advantage. Flagler in particular negotiated favorable rates, but it was depressed economic conditions in the new industry that helped Rockefeller expand the business.

A recession after 1869 caused economic hardship in the oil business but presented Rockefeller with an opportunity. Borrowing heavily, he began buying many smaller oil companies that faltered during the hard times. In 1870, a new company was formed in Ohio, with the existing partners being the new shareholders. Rockefeller's plan was to offer new shares in the company only when capital for expansion was needed. The Standard Oil Company was born with Rockefeller, Flagler, William Rockefeller, Andrews, and William Harkness as the only shareholders. Its capital was $1 million, and the company controlled 10 percent of the industry's refining capacity.

Standard Oil and some other oil producers joined with several railroads in a venture called the South Improvement Company. Their objective was to set favorable shipping rates for themselves while precluding other competitors. When the arrangement became public knowledge two years later, there was a loud outcry against the companies involved for rigging freight prices. But the clandestine arrangement proved successful for Standard Oil since it allowed Rockefeller to effectively double his company's market share in a short period of time. In 1882, the Standard Oil Trust was established in Ohio. By using the trust form of organization, Standard Oil was able to own the out-of-state companies also owned by Rockefeller. Standard Oil was able to expand even more, and Rockefeller and his partners became extremely wealthy as a result.

In 1889, Standard Oil was sued by the attorney general in Ohio for antitrust violations, and the trust finally was dissolved by Ohio in 1892. The company subsequently shifted its headquarters to New Jersey, where corporate laws were more lenient, allowing the company to own out-of-state companies. A holding company was used to control the vast enterprises. In 1899, Standard Oil of New Jersey was reorganized to become the holding company for the Standard Oil enterprises. The holding company held stock in 37 various companies. It became the largest company in the world and remained so until the establishment of U.S. STEEL in 1901. By the end of the 19th century, it controlled an estimated 90 percent of domestic oil production and distribution.

Rockefeller began to retire from the oil business in the mid-1890s. Like Andrew CARNEGIE, he began philanthropic activities. In 1890, he established the University of Chicago and had donated $35 million to its development by the beginning of World War I. He was drawn back into an active defense of his company when it was sued by the Justice Department for antitrust violations. A campaign had been mounted over the years by politicians and the press, arguing that the company violated ANTITRUST laws and needed to be made accountable. The rates demanded by the company from the RAILROADS over the years and accounts of the company forcing smaller competitors out of business eventually saw the company charged with predatory pricing policies. But it was only with the presidency of Theodore Roosevelt that the company successfully was challenged in court.

In 1906, in the heyday of the trust busting era, the company was charged with violating the SHERMAN ACT. The U.S. Supreme Court ordered the breakup of the company in 1911 in a landmark decision. Standard Oil was ordered to divest itself of 33 of its companies, which were ordered to become independent and with no corporate ties to each other. Standard Oil of New Jersey remained the largest of the new, independent entities. In 1972, the company adopted its current name, the Exxon Corporation. Other notable companies created at the time of the divestiture were the Atlantic Richfield Company,

John D. Rockefeller (NEW YORK PUBLIC LIBRARY)

Chevron, Amoco, and the Mobil Corporation, the latter of which merged again with Exxon in the late 1990s to form Exxon Mobil.

Like many other industrialists of his day, Rockefeller held that competition was ruinous and inefficient. He shared this view with Andrew Carnegie and J. P. Morgan, among others, although his philanthropic activities help temper public opinion of him, especially after he began to withdraw from active management of the company. In addition to the University of Chicago, Rockefeller founded the Rockefeller Foundation in 1913 with a grant of $100 million. The purpose of the foundation was to provide assistance for international humanitarian needs and to promote peace. He also established the Rockefeller Institute for Medical Research in New York City in 1901. It was the first institution in the United States devoted solely to biomedical research. It subsequently was renamed Rockefeller University.

Many members of the Rockefeller family also made a contribution to business and public life, continuing the family dynasty. His only son, John D. Rockefeller Jr., bought the land on which the United Nations stands in New York and also developed another city landmark, Rockefeller Center. Nelson A. Rockefeller, Rockefeller's grandson, served as governor of New York from 1959 to 1973 and as vice president under Gerald Ford. The elder Rockefeller lived a long life and saw many of his children succeed in business on their own. He died in 1937.

See also EATON, CYRUS; MORGAN, JOHN PIERPONT.

Further reading

Chernow, Ron. *Titan: The Life of John D. Rockefeller, Sr.* New York: Random House, 1998.

Hawke, David. *John D.: The Founding Father of the Rockefellers.* New York: Harper, 1980.

Manchester, William. *A Rockefeller Family Portrait: From John D. to Nelson.* Boston: Little, Brown, 1958.

Moscow, Alvin. *The Rockefeller Inheritance.* Garden City, N.Y.: Doubleday, 1977.

Nevins, Allan. *John D. Rockefeller: The Heroic Age of American Enterprise.* New York: Charles Scribner's, 1940.

Rockefeller, John D. *Random Reminiscences of Men and Events.* 1937. Reprint, Tarrytown, N.Y.: Sleepy Hollow Press, 1984.

Tarbell, Ida. *A History of the Standard Oil Company.* New York: McClure Phillips and Co., 1904.

Rothschild, House of   French banking house with branches in Britain and Germany that was a major supplier of investment funds to the United States in the 19th century. Although the family owned and operated bank was primarily a European institution, it nevertheless helped finance much of the early American infrastructure along with BARING BROTHERS, the British merchant bank.

N. M. Rothschild & Sons, the English branch of the European bank, was founded in 1798 by Nathan Rothschild, who had been sent to Britain to deal in cotton for the family interests. It was the English branch that became the conduit for much of the European money that was to find its way to North America. The bank performed what today are called merchant banking operations, and one such operation was to act as agent for many Continental investors who wanted to invest in the United States. After the War of 1812, the bank competed with Baring when investing in the United States, mostly in state and city government bonds, U.S. TREASURY BONDS, and other foreign investments.

Like most foreign banks, the Rothschilds did not establish branches in the United Sates but preferred to appoint a domestic agent who would act on their behalf. Until 1837, Rothschild's main agent in the United States was L., J., & S. Joseph, a New York bank that failed during the Panic of 1837. The business was then assumed by a young employee of the Rothschilds who was in New York waiting to make a connecting voyage to Cuba, August Belmont. Belmont stayed in New York establishing himself as the bank's New York agent through August Belmont & Co. and became a popular figure on Wall Street.

Over the next 50 years, Belmont invested money supplied by the Rothschilds in many infrastructure investments, mainly state and U.S. Treasury bonds as well as in RAILROADS, shipping, and real estate. The bulk of the investment was done before the Civil War, especially in state and local government bonds.

The bank's influence began to wane with the death of Belmont in 1890, although the Belmont bank continued under the guidance of his son, August Belmont II. By World War I, that influence had almost completely disappeared as the United States began exporting capital rather than importing it. The Rothschild bank would remain prominent in European and international, rather than American, financial affairs after that time.

See also BELMONT, AUGUST; BELMONT, AUGUST, II; FOREIGN INVESTMENT.

Further reading

Ferguson, Niall. *The House of Rothschild, Money's Prophets, 1798–1848.* New York: Viking Press, 1998.

Lottman, Herbert R. *The French Rothschilds: The Great Banking Dynasty through Two Turbulent Centuries.* New York: Crown, 1995.

rubber industry   The rubber industry in the United States dates back to the 19th century. In 1839, Charles Goodyear discovered that natural rubber, when mixed with sulfur powder at high temperatures, created an elastic and durable material. The process he named vulcanization made practical the use of rubber for a variety of purposes. Following this discovery, rubber companies began to proliferate in New England. The rubber industry of the 19th century consisted of small companies that focused primarily on the manufacture of rubber footwear and raincoats, but also produced hosing, belts, and insulating material. The rubber industry was dominated by small firms until 1892, when the United States Rubber Company (later Uniroyal) was created through the combination of 11 smaller companies and soon became the largest rubber company in the United States.

Decades after the rubber industry originated in the Northeast, the rubber tire industry emerged in Akron, Ohio. Dr. B. F. GOODRICH established the first rubber company in Akron in 1870, focusing initially on the manufacture of pneumatic bicycle tires. The bicycle craze of the late 19th century created a mass market for rubber tires and encouraged new competitors to enter the field. Akron quickly became the center of the rubber tire industry. By 1909, Akron was home to 14 rubber manufacturing companies. With the spread of automobile ownership, the manufacture of automobile tires became an increasingly important segment of the industry. Concentration of the industry in the Akron area increased through the 1920s such that, by 1930, approximately two-thirds of all tires produced in America came out of Akron.

During the 1930s, the rubber industry suffered from a decline in demand along with most producers of durable goods. The decade also witnessed the first successful attempt to create a union among the workers in the industry. Rubber manufacturers were staunchly antiunion and had successfully fended off earlier attempts to organize their industry. This changed during the 1930s following the passage of the National Industrial Recovery Act of 1933, which granted workers the right to join unions and bargain collectively with management. Soon, rubber workers were flocking to join the newly formed United Rubber Workers (URW). The URW successfully organized the industry, but only after a fierce battle with management that witnessed the first use of the sit-down strike, an aggressive tactic soon adopted by organizing drives in other industries. For the next 50 years, the URW acted as a powerful bargaining organization in the industry.

Since its emergence in the 19th century, the rubber industry had relied on the importation of natural rubber. Both World War I and World War II heightened concern in the United States about dependence upon imports of this crucial raw material, most of which came from Southeast Asia. Limited research on synthetic rubber had been conducted in the 1920s and 1930s. However, on the eve of World War II the American rubber industry still produced 99 percent of its product from crude rubber. When the war in the Pacific cut off supplies from Southeast Asia, the United States had stockpiles of crude rubber to last about a year. The war thus provided the impetus for intensive chemical research to develop an improved synthetic rubber. The federal government launched a synthetic rubber program in which it invested $673 million to fund the construction of plants to produce GR-S (government rubber-styrene); by late 1943, American factories were turning out synthetic rubber. The federal government constructed 44 synthetic rubber factories during the war, which were operated and later purchased by leading rubber manufacturing firms. Synthetic rubber became established as the primary raw material for the industry in the 1950s, as rubber manufacturers invested in laboratories to further research the development of improved synthetic rubber and rubber-based products.

Another major technological advancement in the American rubber tire industry came about in the late 1960s with the conversion to radial tires. American tire manufacturers had traditionally constructed tires on a bias principle, with plies of rubber fabric arranged at an angle of between 25 and 40 degrees. In France, Michelin had built radial tires since the 1940s, but American manufacturers were slow to embrace this method of construction and the capital investment it necessitated. Radial tires, in which plies are arranged at a 90-degree angle and reinforced with a rubber-coated steel belt, had advantages over bias tires. Radial construction reduced friction on the road, thus lessening wear on the tire and improving fuel efficiency, a consideration that was especially important during the 1970s.

For most of the 20th century, the rubber tire industry was one of the most centralized industries in the United States. Decentralization of the industry was a protracted process. The first steps occurred in the 1930s with the expansion of branch factories and establishment of new factories in the South and Midwest. The government-built factories constructed during World War II continued this pattern. Although still the major center of tire manufacturing, Akron's share of rubber tire production declined as newer factories increased total production. This pattern accelerated after the 1960s as firms began to close existing factories in Akron. The new factories constructed for the manufacture of radials in the 1970s and 1980s were concentrated in the South and other parts of the Midwest. The rubber industry gradually abandoned Akron, with its aging and inefficient plants and high-wage unionized labor force. Akron, while retaining the major research facilities and corporate headquarters, produced fewer and fewer tires. By the mid-

1980s, tire manufacturing had become concentrated in the South, and no major tire factories were in operation in Akron.

Further reading

French, Michael J. *The U.S. Tire Industry: A History.* Boston: Twayne, 1991.

Love, Steve, and David Giffels. *Wheels of Fortune: The Story of Rubber in Akron.* Akron: University of Akron Press, 1999.

Susan Allyn Johnson

S

Salomon Brothers Investment banking firm founded by Arthur, Percy, and Herbert Salomon in 1910 in New York City. The original firm began as a money broker between brokerage houses and banks on Wall Street and slowly began trading in bonds during World War I. The firm became a primary dealer in Liberty loans during and after the war, while it continued to expand its operations in the corporate bond market.

The firm became known as Salomon Brothers & Hutzler after taking in Morton Hutzler as a partner in the first year of its operations. He owned a seat on the NYSE and became the firm's link to the wider stock business, although its primary emphasis remained bonds. It arranged for its first corporate bond underwriting during the Depression, but it was not until the late 1950s that its business began to boom. In the 1970s, the firm helped develop the market for mortgage-backed securities for the federally related mortgage assistance agencies and became the leader in that burgeoning field. In 1981, it was acquired by commodities trader Phibro (formerly Philipp Brothers) and became Phibro Salomon. In 1985, Salomon bought out the Phibro stake and again became Salomon Brothers, now a publicly traded company.

In 1991, Salomon ran afoul of the FEDERAL RESERVE and the Treasury because of its behavior at an auction for U.S. Treasury notes when it cornered the market for the issue. The firm received relatively mild sanctions, but its management structure was changed, with Warren Buffett, a major investor, helping to reorganize the firm. Although the firm was rebuked, it did not lose any of its important Fed designations as a primary dealer in Treasury securities, which would have made it difficult to continue in the Treasury bond business.

In 1997, Salomon was acquired by the Traveler's Group, the insurance company run by Sanford WEILL, which also owned broker Smith Barney, and the two firms were combined to form Salomon Smith Barney. When Traveler's merged with CITIBANK to form Citigroup a year later, Salomon became the investment banking subsidiary of the new financial conglomerate, Citigroup. In 2003, the name was finally dropped by Citigroup after Citigroup was included in a $1.4 billion settlement with regulators over irregularities in its business practices during the stock market bubble of the late 1990s. The Smith Barney unit continued under its own name.

See also INVESTMENT BANKING.

Further reading

Geisst, Charles R. *The Last Partnerships: Inside the Great Wall Street Money Dynasties.* New York: McGraw-Hill, 2001.

Mayer, Martin. *Nightmare on Wall Street: Salomon Brothers and the Corruption of the Marketplace.* New York: Simon & Schuster, 1993.

Sarbanes-Oxley Act   Officially known as the Public Company Accounting Reform and Investor Protection Act, this law was passed by Congress in 2002 in response to several accounting and financial scandals at major U.S. corporations, among them ENRON and WORLDCOM. During the late 1990s, it was discovered that these companies and several others had overstated their earnings, using questionable and fraudulent accounting techniques to inflate their earnings during the bull market in stocks. As a result, new legislation was proposed to strengthen the existing securities laws to prevent further problems. The bill was sponsored by Senator Paul Sarbanes, Democrat of Maryland, and Representative Mike Oxley, Republican of Ohio.

The law addressed the problem of accounting by public corporations and the responsibility of auditors to investors. The law created the Public Accounting Oversight Board, which has the broad responsibility of administering the act. The board is required to have five "financially-literate" members, appointed for five-year terms. Two of the members must be or have been certified public accountants, and the remaining members must not be and cannot have been CPAs. The board's members serve on a full-time basis. No member may receive money from an accounting firm while sitting.

The board's main responsibility is to govern public accounting firms that audit public companies and prepare their financial statements. The board, under section 103 of the act, is responsible for registering public accounting firms and establishing, or adopting by rule, "auditing, quality control, ethics, independence, and other standards relating to the preparation of audit reports for issuers." It also is empowered to conduct inspections of accounting firms, conduct investigations and disciplinary proceedings, and impose sanctions if necessary. The chairman of the oversight board is selected by the Securities and Exchange Commission.

In addition to the regulations governing accountants, the law also requires the SEC to establish standards for lawyers practicing before the commission. It also prohibits attorneys, accountants, or anyone involved with financial statements to "impede, obstruct or influence" federal investigation of irregularities. This was inserted into the law because of the problems at the Enron Corporation, especially when employees were discovered to have destroyed financial and other documents prior to the firm's bankruptcy in late 2001.

On the company side of the law, all company audit committees must have at least one financial expert as a member. Accountants serving as auditors cannot provide any other financial service to the companies they serve while completing the audit—an attempt to reduce conflicts of interest, especially when auditors also provided consulting services to companies at the same time they served as auditors.

See also FINANCIAL ACCOUNTING STANDARDS BOARD; GENERALLY ACCEPTED ACCOUNTING PRINCIPLES; SECURITIES ACT OF 1933; STOCK MARKETS.

Further reading

Greene, Edward F., et al. *The Sarbanes-Oxley Act: Analysis and Practice.* New York: Aspen Publishers, 2003.

Lander, Guy P. *What Is Sarbanes-Oxley?* New York: McGraw-Hill, 2004.

Sarnoff, David (1891–1971) *broadcasting executive*   Born in Russia, Sarnoff moved with his family to New York in 1900, where he left school at age 15 to help earn money for their support. Despite his lack of formal education, Sarnoff is considered the father of both radio and television in the United States. He went to work for the Marconi Wireless Telegraph Co. of America as an office boy and soon became a telegraph operator. He was on duty at the company when the *Titanic* sank in 1912 and was the first to receive messages from the S.S. *Olympic,* the rescue ship that was first on the scene. For the next three days, he was the sole source of information about the survivors, as all other telegraph stations were forced off the air by a presidential order.

In 1915, Sarnoff proposed a radio music box that would receive broadcasts over the airwaves. He suggested that it be sold for $75 or less so that all homes could purchase one. It was not until 1919 that his vision began to be taken seriously, when the Marconi Co. became the RADIO CORPORATION OF AMERICA, owned by GENERAL ELECTRIC. In 1921, he was appointed general manager of the company that was first headed by Owen YOUNG of GE. He also created the first sports broadcast when he had the company cover a prizefight between Jack Dempsey and Georges Carpentier in New Jersey. A year later, the National Broadcasting Co. was proposed as the official broadcast arm of RCA, and the company was officially incorporated in 1926. The fight broadcast helped to sell radios, and by the end of the 1920s the company's sales were more than $200 million.

In 1932, an antitrust decree from the Justice Department ordered a separation of RCA from GE, allowing RCA and its broadcasting company to emerge as an independent. Sarnoff became president of RCA in 1930. At the 1939 World's Fair in New York he predicted widespread television broadcasts. Experiments had already proven successful, but a better technology was required to make it universally popular. From 1939, Sarnoff was in direct and often fierce competition with William Paley, the driving force behind the COLUMBIA BROADCASTING SYSTEM, and the competition produced many innovations in television programming.

David Sarnoff (LIBRARY OF CONGRESS)

Sarnoff served with the U.S. Army Signal Corps during World War II and left the service with the rank of brigadier general—after which he was fond of being called "general." After the success of black and white television, color television was introduced in 1954 using the standards RCA had developed rather than those of its major competitors. Sarnoff retired from RCA in 1970 and died in New York in 1971.

See also RADIO INDUSTRY.

Further reading

Bilby, Kenneth. *The General: David Sarnoff and the Rise of the Communications Industry.* New York: Harper & Row, 1986.

Lewis, Tom. *Empire of the Air: The Men Who Made Radio.* New York: Harper Collins, 1991.

Sarnoff, David. *Looking Ahead: The Papers of David Sarnoff.* New York: McGraw-Hill, 1968.

savings and loans Also referred to as thrift institutions, savings and loans traditionally are limited service banks that take customer deposits and make mortgage loans. Because of their limited functions, they have not been considered banks by the FEDERAL RESERVE but have been treated as institutions that provide long-term funds to the mortgage market and not as part of the money creation process, as are commercial banks.

The first savings and loan, or S&L, in the United States was the Oxford Provident Building Association, established in Philadelphia in 1831. Modeled after similar British institutions, the early associations were local or regional in nature and took deposits from members of an association or trade group. Most of the associations were also mutual rather than stock companies, meaning that they were owned by their depositors.

S&Ls were state chartered until 1932, when Congress created the FEDERAL HOME LOAN BANK BOARD. The board itself comprised 12 regional home loan banks around the country, similar in organization to the Federal Reserve. The board, located in Washington, D.C., has regulatory authority over thrifts that choose to join. Federally chartered thrifts, as they are called, may borrow from their regional bank and have their reserve requirements set by it as well. Those that do not join are referred to as state chartered.

The thrifts maintained a close hold on residential mortgage lending, but their numbers declined over the years. More than 7,000 existed in the mid-1930s, but their numbers declined to about 3,500 by the late 1980s. Consolidation of the industry and several crises helped reduce their numbers. Their first serious postwar crisis occurred in the late 1970s as savers began to withdraw their deposits in search of higher interest rates in money market mutual funds. The thrifts could not respond by offering higher rates because the amount of interest they could pay was limited by banking regulations. As a result, many of them became disintermediated, and the entire industry lost money in 1980–81, causing the DEPOSITORY INSTITUTIONS ACT of 1982 to be passed. Although

the legislation liberalized thrift assets and liabilities and allowed them greater flexibility in their activities, poor management, fraud, and imprudent investments led to another crisis in 1988. Losses on commercial real estate lending and JUNK BONDS led to another industry-wide shakeup when the FINANCIAL INSTITUTIONS REFORM, RECOVERY AND ENFORCEMENT ACT (FIRREA) was passed in the summer of 1989.

The FIRREA imposed new, more stringent requirements on the thrifts, and many more went out of business or were acquired by larger financial institutions. As a result, the industry was seriously shaken as many thrifts changed their charters to that of savings banks, allowing them greater flexibility in their borrowing and lending activities, but still not converting to full-fledged commercial bank status. Today, the thrifts still make mortgages and take deposits but also generally make commercial real estate loans, consumer loans, and issue CREDIT CARDS. They now also extend across state lines and are larger than their predecessors on average, having access to a wider customer base and thus to greater funds.

Further reading

Pizzo, Stephen, Mary Fricker, and Paul Muolo. *Inside Job: The Looting of America's Savings and Loans.* New York: McGraw-Hill, 1989.

Seidman, Lewis William. *Full Faith and Credit: The Great S & L Debacle and Other Washington Sagas.* New York: Times Books, 1993.

White, Lawrence J. *The S & L Debacle.* New York: Oxford University Press, 1991.

Schiff, Jacob (1847–1920) *banker* Born into a prominent family in Germany, Schiff began his working career at age 14 as an apprentice in a commercial firm in Frankfurt. He traveled to the United States in 1865 to work in a New York brokerage office and became a citizen in 1870. In 1872, he decided to return to Germany, where he became the manager of a branch bank. In 1875, he married the daughter of Solomon Loeb of the Kuhn Loeb banking house and returned to the United States in that same year as a full partner in KUHN LOEB & CO.

Schiff was raised in a tight-knit Jewish social circle that included the Rothschild and Warburg banking families, and he learned the principles of close-relationship banking from them during his early years. He carried the same principles to New York when he emigrated. He quickly became one of the best-known bankers of his generation and a leader of the American Jewish community.

The period 1890–1920 became known as the "Age of Schiff." He was the most prominent banker of his generation, especially after J. P. Morgan died in 1913. He became the managing partner of Kuhn Loeb and helped the firm establish its reputation, initially in railroad financing. He also helped E. H. HARRIMAN gain control of the UNION PACIFIC RAILROAD and helped arrange financing for the Southern Pacific Railroad, Royal Dutch Petroleum, Shell Transport and Trading, and most notably the Pennsylvania Railroad. He financed more than a billion dollars worth of securities for the railroad, including its tunnel under the Hudson River and its Pennsylvania Station in New York City. He also was an adviser to Theodore Roosevelt, although, like many other German-American bankers, he opposed the establishment of the FEDERAL RESERVE.

Schiff helped the Japanese government raise money during the Russo-Japanese War of 1904–05 and had various interests in life insurance companies in New York that were the subject of the Armstrong investigations in 1905. He was also a strong believer in the GOLD STANDARD. He opposed the massive Anglo-French loan, led by J. P. Morgan & Co. in 1915, on the grounds that the proceeds might fall into the hands of the Russian government, which had a strong record of anti-Semitism before the Russian Revolution of 1917. His opposition earned him and his firm enmity in some quarters, where he was labeled as a German sympathizer. Throughout his tenure at the bank, Kuhn Loeb was known primarily as a bond house and participated in few equity financings.

Schiff was a strong supporter of Jewish causes in both the United States and Europe. Schiff is also remembered for his philanthropy, especially to Harvard University, Tuskegee Institute, the American Red Cross, and to many Jewish causes, including the Hebrew Union College in Cincinnati.

See also INVESTMENT BANKING; LEHMAN BROTHERS.

Further reading

Adler, Cyrus. *Jacob H. Schiff: His Life and Letters.* 2 vols. New York: Doubleday Doran, 1929.

Birmingham, Stephen. *"Our Crowd:" The Great Jewish Families of New York.* New York: Harper & Row, 1967.

Cohen, Naomi W. *Jacob Schiff: A Study in American Jewish Leadership.* Hanover, N.H.: University Press of New England, 1999.

Schwab, Charles M. (1862–1939) *industrialist* Born in Williamsburg, Pennsylvania, Schwab attended St. Francis College in Loretto before taking an unskilled laborer job at the Edgar Thomson Steel Works, a subsidiary of the Carnegie Steel Company. After beginning his career as a stake-driver at $2 per day, he steadily worked his way through the ranks. In 1887, he was made superintendent of the Homestead Works in Pennsylvania and superintendent of the Thompson plant two years later. He was put in charge of repairing relations at Homestead after the bitter riot in 1892. Five years later he was named president of Carnegie Steel Co. and was earning more than $1 million per year.

It was a speech by Schwab in 1900 that prompted J. P. Morgan to make his bid to buy Carnegie Steel, paving the way for the formation of U.S. Steel. After the U.S. STEEL CORP. was formed in 1901, Schwab became its first president; after subsequent disagreement with Elbert GARY, he became disillusioned and resigned in

1903. In 1904, he reemerged in the industry by buying a small steel maker named Bethlehem Steel. He intended to make the small company a major competitor of U.S. Steel.

Bethlehem grew and became very successful after Schwab introduced the open-hearth process of making steel at his plants. His greatest success came during World War I, when he traveled to Britain under an assumed name to sell his products to the British. After consulting with Lord Kitchener, the war secretary, he obtained a large order for steel, and later submarines, to be supplied by Bethlehem. Since American companies were forbidden to sell finished war products to Britain, he sold the parts for the submarines instead.

During the war, Bethlehem Steel took orders exceeding $500 million from the Allies. During the 1920s, he remained salaried at Bethlehem, although he began making other investments as well. He invested in International Nickel and Chicago Pneumatic Tool, among others. But his investments in stocks were uniformly disastrous, and by the early 1930s he had lost almost all of his $200 million fortune. He died in penury in New York City.

Under Schwab's direction, Bethlehem emerged as a major steel producer, although U.S. Steel would remain the largest firm in the industry. The company was finally liquidated in 2003, a victim of imported steel and declining capital investment.

See also CARNEGIE, ANDREW; STEEL INDUSTRY.

Further reading

Berglund, Abraham. *The United States Steel Corporation.* New York: Columbia University Press, 1907.

Grace, Eugene G. *Charles M. Schwab.* New York: privately published, 1947.

Hessen, Robert. *Steel Titan: The Life of Charles M. Schwab.* New York: Oxford University Press, 1975.

Scott, Thomas A. (1823–1881) *railway executive* Born in Fort Loudon, Pennsylvania,

Scott's father was a tavern owner. He left school at age 16 to work as a clerk in a general store until he secured a job working for Major James Patton, his brother-in-law and the collector of tolls in Pennsylvania for public roads and canals. He was chief clerk in the state toll collector's office from 1847 until 1850, when he went to work for the Allegheny Railroad.

In 1860, he was named vice president of the Pennsylvania Railroad. When the Civil War began, he was asked by the secretary of war to transport men and munitions between Baltimore and Harrisburg, Pennsylvania. The railroad connecting the two points, the North Central, was vital to protecting Pennsylvania from attack, and Scott took a telegrapher named Andrew CARNEGIE with him on his journey. In 1861, he was named an assistant secretary of war in charge of RAILROADS and transportation. The next year he was named an assistant quartermaster general for the government. A year later, Scott helped Carnegie found the Keystone Bridge Company.

Under the guidance of J. Edgar Thompson as president and Scott as vice president, the Pennsylvania Railroad grew substantially. Scott personally helped consolidate the railroad, especially in western Pennsylvania and the Midwest, in order to counter Jay Gould's attempts to expand the ERIE RAILROAD. In 1871, the Pennsylvania Railroad expanded into the South by taking over lines extending south of Richmond, Virginia. In the same year, the troubled UNION PACIFIC RAILROAD was also brought into the Pennsylvania's control when Scott assumed the presidency of the line. When Thompson died in 1874, Scott succeeded him as president.

When Scott assumed the presidency, the Pennsylvania was the largest railroad line in the world. Upon assuming the office, he helped the company's finances by paying off and restructuring its debt and reducing its operating costs. But a ruinous battle with John D. Rockefeller damaged his reputation and the railroad's preeminence. In 1877, Rockefeller declared that he would no longer use the railroad for shipping the

Standard Oil Company's products because of a prior dispute. As a result, the Pennsylvania lost almost 70 percent of its oil shipping revenues. Rockefeller gave the business to the New York Central and the Erie.

A serious strike by workers in 1877 also damaged the railroad's reputation. Scott decided to cut workers' wages and increase tonnage on the trains, prompting workers to strike. Militia were called in to aid local police in quelling the disturbance; they fired on strikers, causing many deaths and further strikes. A year after the disturbance, Scott suffered a stroke and died in 1881.

Scott was considered the greatest railroad manager of his day and the organizational force behind the Pennsylvania Railroad. After the Civil War, he also became an astute capitalist, investing in oil producing properties in Pennsylvania and California. One of his investments later became the Union Oil Company of California.

See also GOULD, JAY.

Further reading

Alexander, Edwin P. *On the Main Line: The Pennsylvania Railroad in the Nineteenth Century.* New York: C. N. Potter, 1971.

Bruce, Robert V. *1877: Year of Violence.* Indianapolis: Bobbs-Merrill, 1959.

Wilson, William B. *History of the Pennsylvania Railroad.* Philadelphia: Kensington Press, 1898.

Sears, Roebuck & Co.   Merchandise catalog company and mass retailer founded in Chicago by Richard W. Sears (1863–1914) and Alvah Roebuck in 1886 as the R.W. Sears Watch Co. The company changed its name to Sears, Roebuck & Co. in 1893 and began to expand into the mail order sale of household items and clothing. The initial thrust of the effort was aimed at rural areas where retail stores were in short supply. The company's major competition came from Aaron Montgomery WARD, whose Chicago-based Montgomery Ward practiced the same business strategy. By the mid-1890s, the company was producing large catalogs full of every conceivable consumer good.

Juilius Rosenwald was hired from the clothing business as a vice president to help in expanding the operation, and he and Sears sold stock in the company in 1906. The stock issue was an enormous success, underwritten by Rosenwald's friends at LEHMAN BROTHERS and GOLDMAN SACHS. The 1920s were a pivotal period in the company's history, as rural areas began to decline in population and their inhabitants moved to the cities. The company stock was added to the DOW JONES INDUSTRIAL AVERAGE in 1924. Sears's expansion was led by a vice president, Robert E. Wood. As a result, Sears opened its first retail store in 1925, and within four years, there were more than 300 operating. By 1933, 400 were in operation.

The company maintained the catalog in addition to the stores. Its success led it to expand into other areas. In 1931, it opened the Allstate Insurance Co., which also used a branch system to reach customers. In the 1970s, it added the financial service company and broker Dean Witter and real estate company Coldwell Banker. It also developed a new credit card named Discover, in addition to its already famous Sears credit card, which provided installment credit to shoppers on a revolving basis and was designed to compete with Visa and Mastercard.

After suffering competition from newer, rapidly expanding chains such as Wal-Mart and K-Mart, the company revamped its operations, selling Allstate, Dean Witter, and Coldwell Banker. It also built the Sears Tower in Chicago, at that time the world's tallest building, to serve as its headquarters but later moved its operations out of Chicago. The company began to suffer slower sales in the 1990s, and much of its revenue came from its credit card division rather than from retail sales. It was dropped from the Dow Jones Industrial Average in 1999 and replaced by Home Depot. With Sears still losing ground to the likes of Wal-Mart and Target, the management of K-Mart announced in 2004 that it would merge with Sears to make the third largest retailer in the United States.

See also CHAIN STORES; WALTON, SAM.

Own Your Own Home

Long Life and Happiness

To get the full share of Good Health, Long Life and Happiness for yourself and kiddies, to get the most out of life as our Creator intended it should be, A HOME OF YOUR OWN is an absolute necessity.

It promotes happiness and contentment, for it is the most pleasant and natural way to live. It has the correct environment made up of the natural instead of the artificial.

Green grass, trees, shrubbery, flower and vegetable gardens all your own, provide a pleasant pastime, and an abundance of the things we all crave. It is the real life that leads to happiness, for you, and those you love.

Best of all, a home of your own does not cost you any more than your present mode of living. Instead of paying monthly rental, by our Easy Payment Plan you may have all these luxuries at a lower cost and, in the end, have a beautiful home instead of worthless rent receipts.

Our plan is simple. It has already enabled thousands of people to get out of the renter's class. This plan will put you in your own home and give you your independence.

On the following pages you will find over 100 designs of homes. Some of them will surely meet with your ideas of what a real home should be.

We will gladly tell you all about any house in this book and will show you how easy it is to own a home on our Easy Payment Plan. Write us. An Information Blank has been placed in the back of this book for your convenience.

Be sure to read about our Ready-Cut System on pages 10 and 11, and how this system will save about one-half of your carpenter labor.

Information Blank on Page 141

Save Your Rent Money

Give the Kiddies a Chance

Get Close to Nature

Have Real Friends and Neighbors

Be Independent in Old Age

Our EASY *Payment* PLAN *makes it* POSSIBLE
WHY PAY RENT?

Page from the Sears, Roebuck catalog selling kit homes, 1928 (LIBRARY OF CONGRESS)

Further reading

Hendrickson, Robert. *The Grand Emporiums: An Illustrated History of America's Great Department Stores.* New York: Stein & Day, 1979.

Katz, Donald R. *The Big Store: The Inside Crisis and Revolution at Sears.* New York: Viking, 1987.

Mahoney, Tom, and Leonard Sloane. *The Great Merchants.* New York: Harper & Row, 1966.

Worthy, James C. *Shaping an American Institution: Robert E. Wood and Sears, Roebuck.* Urbana: University of Illinois Press, 1984.

Securities Act of 1933 The first federal securities REGULATION was passed in March 1933 in response to congressional hearings into stock market practices. The act required corporate issuers of new securities to register the issue with the (then) FEDERAL TRADE COMMISSION. After the Securities Exchange Act was passed in 1934, jurisdiction for new issues passed to the newly created Securities and Exchange Commission (SEC).

Before the act was passed, the only protection against the sale of fraudulent securities was blue-sky laws. The first blue-sky law was passed in Kansas in 1911 as a reaction to unscrupulous stock salesmen selling sham securities. Other states then began to pass their own laws, especially since no comparable federal regulations existed. About two-thirds of them had similar laws on the books by 1920.

The laws were a product of the Progressive Era, when the rural, agricultural states of the Midwest and far West looked askance at Wall Street and financiers in general. Many stock promoters would sell worthless stock in these states to unsuspecting investors. After the Securities Act of 1933 was passed, the federal government assumed the prominent role in controlling the sale of securities interstate, but the local laws remained. The act was first referred to as the federal blue-sky law. As part of the process of selling new corporate securities, investment bankers refer to the process of registering with the individual states as "blue-skying." Most of the blue-sky laws remain in effect today.

Historically, the laws were the first to attempt to control the securities markets in the absence of federal law. At the same time, several states in the Midwest also enacted legislation to control insurance sold within their jurisdictions, partly in response to scandals occurring in the New York insurance market before 1910. Although most of the blue-sky laws could restrict only the securities sold within a state's borders, they were a clear attempt to protect citizens from the sort of fraudulent securities dealing in which only the "blue sky" was being sold to unsuspecting investors rather than securities of any tangible value. When combined with other attempts to protect investors and savers in some states from the sale of bogus insurance policies, they remained the cornerstone of what regulation did exist in the United States prior to the passing of New Deal legislation.

With the passing of the Securities Act, standard procedures were adopted. Before new issues of corporate securities could be sold, a registration statement had to be filed with the SEC, which required a company to fully disclose its financial position. In addition, a prospectus had to be prepared making all relevant details of the company's business and finances available to the public. Failure to disclose relevant information, or the dissemination of deliberately misleading information, or fraud were proscribed and accompanied by penalties, both for the issuing company and its investment bankers and auditors.

In addition to domestic corporate securities, the issues of foreign companies and governments were also included in response to problems encountered after the 1929 crash, when many foreign bonds defaulted on their interest to American investors. Many were found to have been issued with minimal information provided by either the borrowers themselves or their investment bankers. As a result of the act, due diligence was given a legal basis, meaning that a company must be properly vetted before it enters the marketplace for public securities.

A significant requirement of the act was publication of a tombstone ad after a new securities issue has been sold. A tombstone ad is a type of financial advertising that lists in a box advertisement the basic details of a new issue of stock or bond. "Tombstone" derives from the language used in the ads, which are usually printed in the newspapers after the securities mentioned have been sold, that is, after the deal has been completed. The ads require all issuers of corporate securities to follow certain procedures when first selling them to the public. The tombstone ad is one of the last steps in the process.

In addition to the basic details of the new issue, tombstone ads also list the underwriters in a new securities deal. Those at the very top of the list are the major bankers to the deal, while those below are ordinary underwriters, members of the syndicate arranged especially for the deal itself. The top left spot in the list is for the manager that arranged the transaction with the issuer of the securities. Keeping track of tombstone ads, especially in determining which investment bank arranged the deal, is a major preoccupation on Wall Street, where prowess in underwriting is closely monitored.

Tombstone ads are also required when municipal securities are sold and are also used in certain types of banking transactions, especially for large loans that are syndicated among participating banks. In the past, securities regulators have closely studied tombstone ads over a period of time to detect patterns among investment bankers, mostly to determine whether syndicates are formed for the occasion or whether they contain the same underwriters over the years.

One of the areas affected by the new law was initial public offerings, or IPOs—the sale of shares in a company for the first time. Previously, companies' capital was held in private hands. The sale of an IPO allows companies to grow and also to limit the liabilities of the individual owners. Traditionally, new issues of stock are sold by investment bankers, who charge a fee to the companies for their services.

IPOs usually grow exponentially in strong STOCK MARKETS, when investors search for new companies and ideas. They are distinct, however, from venture capital—money provided by investors to help a company develop its products or services. The money usually is provided on a private basis for a limited period of time, after which the company normally is expected to sell stock. The investors' return can be measured by the amount they take away from the company versus their original investment. Venture capital is the riskiest investment ordinarily made in a company but also the one with the highest potential return. If the investment should fail at an early stage, there is little outlet for investors other than to find other buyers at lower prices. Nevertheless, venture capital plays a significant role in helping many companies establish themselves early in their development.

The Securities Act helped revolutionize Wall Street, establishing regulatory control over the new issues process for the first time. It also helped establish uniform accounting (GENERALLY ACCEPTED ACCOUNTING PRINCIPLES) standards used for financial reporting. It marked the beginning of greater transparency in the corporate securities markets, in which all financial statements are assumed to contain all the relevant information that is known about a company when it files.

See also FINANCIAL ACCOUNTING STANDARDS BOARD; INVESTMENT BANKING; SARBANES-OXLEY ACT.

Further reading
Carosso, Vincent. *Investment Banking in America: A History.* Cambridge, Mass.: Harvard University Press, 1970.
Elliott, John M. *The Annotated Blue Sky Laws of the United States.* Cincinnati: W. H. Anderson Co., 1919.
Federal Bar Association, Securities Law Committee. *Federal Securities Laws: Legislative History, 1933–1982.* Washington, D.C.: Bureau of National Affairs, 1983.
Jennings, Richard W., ed. *Securities Regulation, 8th ed.* New York: Foundation Press, 1998.

Securities and Exchange Commission   See SECURITIES EXCHANGE ACT OF 1934.

Securities Exchange Act of 1934   Passed the year following the milestone banking and securities acts of 1933, this act was designed to provide federal regulation of the organized stock exchanges for the first time. Previously, the exchanges had regulated themselves, and their practices were subject only to state securities laws.

The act provided a regulator for the new issues market for corporate securities, in addition to the self-regulation practiced by the various stock exchanges. It created the Securities and Exchange Commission (SEC), the regulator of the exchanges that would also oversee the registration procedures outlined in the SECURITIES ACT OF 1933, assuming the authority for new issues registration from the FEDERAL TRADE COMMISSION. All organized securities exchanges in the country were required to register with the new SEC— with the exception of the over-the-counter market, which was not considered to be an organized exchange with a central location. Stock exchange procedures were also made uniform, and strict rules were written to control stock market practices such as short selling.

The SEC consists of five members. Joseph P. KENNEDY was the first chairman, and James Landis, Ferdinand Pecora, George Matthews, and Robert Healy were the other original commissioners. The first commissioners spent most of their time organizing the SEC's agenda and making sure that Wall Street accepted its first national regulator. Subsequent commissions have played a strong role in enforcing the securities laws and prosecuting those accused of insider trading and other securities infractions.

The new law also gave the FEDERAL RESERVE the right to set margin requirements for stock market investors. Previously, margin requirements were set by the brokers themselves, who often extended their customers too much credit, contributing to the Crash of 1929. Since margin money was often loaned to the brokers by banks, the ability to regulate that form of bank lending naturally fell to the Fed as the regulator of the nation's credit.

Over the years the SEC's effectiveness has ranged from weak to very strong. It has constantly attempted to adapt its rules to the needs of the marketplace so as not to become an ineffective regulator. One of its most important changes occurred in the 1980s, when it adopted Rule 415b, also known as the shelf registration rule. This refers to the process of registering new corporate securities with the SEC, which bypasses the traditional procedures outlined in the Securities Act of 1933. According to the 1933 act, new securities could not be sold until 20 days after registration in order for the potential new issue to be vetted properly by the SEC. During that waiting period, underwriters were able to form syndicates in order to sell the securities once they were approved for sale.

The 20-day cooling-off period was proving to be too slow for new issues to reach market. In response, the SEC began a new procedure under Rule 415b called shelf registration. A company could preregister its potential issues with the SEC, which would then put the registration "on the shelf." When a company wanted to get to market quickly, it would present its interim financial statements to the SEC and would then be allowed to proceed to market immediately rather than wait. The procedure quickened access to the new issues market and allowed companies to take advantage of conducive market conditions.

The rule also helped many companies use new defenses against the hostile takeover, which was becoming common in the 1980s. Companies would register new issues of bonds and preferred stocks and then issue them quickly if a hostile takeover was detected. The resulting leverage from the new issue would help ward off unwanted corporate raiders. The quick access to market provided by Rule 415b proved advantageous for corporate defenses as well as more traditional capital raising activities.

Although a Wall Street practice confined to the new issue of securities, Rule 415b was seen as a part of the DEREGULATION trend that affected many industries in the 1980s and 1990s. It was especially significant on Wall Street, since the securities industry is one of the most regulated industries in the country and changes in SEC practices and procedures traditionally came very slowly.

In the wake of the trading scandals of the early 2000s, the SEC became more of an activist agency than in the past. During the tenure of Arthur Levitt, named by President Clinton to be chairman, the agency took strong stands on accounting practices and small investor fraud but was often drowned out by the clamor created by the bull market that finally collapsed in 2000. After Harvey Pitt resigned, the commission began a series of active investigations headed by William Donaldson.

Along with the Securities Act of 1933, the Securities Exchange Act provides the cornerstone of securities regulation in the United States. The 1933 act regulates the primary market for securities, while the 1934 act regulates the secondary market for registered securities.

See also NATIONAL ASSOCIATION OF SECURITIES DEALERS; SARBANES-OXLEY ACT; STOCK MARKETS.

Further reading

Auerbach, Joseph, and Samuel L. Hayes. *Investment Banking and Diligence: What Price Deregulation?* Boston: Harvard Business School Press, 1986.

Federal Bar Association, Securities Law Committee. *Federal Securities Laws: Legislative History, 1933–1982.* Washington, D.C.: Bureau of National Affairs, 1983.

Meyer, Charles H. *The Securities Exchange Act of 1934 Analyzed and Explained.* New York: Francis Emory Fitch, 1934.

Seligman, Joel. *The Transformation of Wall Street: A History of the Securities and Exchange Commission and Modern Corporate Finance.* Boston: Houghton Mifflin, 1982.

Seligman & Co., J. & W.   Investment banking house founded by Joseph Seligman (1819–80) in Lancaster, Pennsylvania, originally as a dry goods and general merchandise store. Seligman immigrated to the United States from his native Germany in 1837 and went to work for Asa Packer, who manufactured canal boats. After working for Packer for a short period, he saved enough money to bring two of his brothers to the United States and with them opened the general merchandise store in Lancaster in 1841.

Shortly thereafter, the store moved to Selma, Alabama, where it remained until the firm opened a branch in New York City in 1846. By the beginning of the Civil War, the firm had changed its business to general merchant banking and in 1864 fully converted to a banking business, as did several other Jewish-American merchant houses, including Lehman Brothers. The firm was aided greatly by the Seligmans' friendship with Ulysses S. Grant, who they had met while he was a lieutenant in the peacetime army. They did a thriving business supplying the army with merchandise but were also impressed by the success of Jay COOKE in selling war bonds to the public. As a result, they used their European connections to begin selling bonds, and the business began to shift.

After the war, the firm began to underwrite securities in gas companies and RAILROADS. They also provided financial support for Mary Todd Lincoln after her husband was assassinated. Several of the brothers also posted bond for Jay GOULD when he was jailed for his activities at the ERIE RAILROAD in 1868. A tutor hired by Joseph Seligman to teach his children—Horatio Alger—used the family as his model for hard work and success, and Alger's stories of young men working their way to success in America became some of the best-selling books of the century.

The firm enjoyed its greatest success between the 1890s and the 1920s. It participated in all major Wall Street financings, including the reorganization of GENERAL MOTORS during the 1910s, when it was led by William C. Durant. The Seligmans remained firmly in the INVESTMENT BANKING business through the 1920s, when they began to offer MUTUAL FUNDS in addition to their other banking services at the suggestion of a nonfamily partner, Francis Randolph. The firm offered its first, called the Tri-Continental Corp., a year before the Crash of 1929, and it was a resounding success. After 1929, the firm moved closer to the funds business and further from investment banking and finally became known as an investment company, offering mutual funds rather than investment banking.

See also KUHN LOEB & CO.

Further reading

Geisst, Charles R. *The Last Partnerships: Inside the Great Wall Street Money Dynasties.* New York: McGraw-Hill, 2001.

Muir, Ross, and Carl J. White. *Over the Long-Term: The Story of J. & W. Seligman & Co.* New York: privately published, 1964.

sewing machine See SINGER SEWING CO.

Sherman Act First ANTITRUST legislation passed by Congress, in 1890. Senator John Sherman of Ohio proposed the statute that bears his name, but the people most responsible for the bill that finally emerged were Senators George Edmunds of Vermont, James George of Mississippi, and George Hoar of Massachusetts. The most important provisions of the Sherman Act condemned contracts, combinations, and conspiracies in restraint of trade, and also condemned monopolization.

Nominally, the two provisions were intended to federalize state common law in regard to trade restraints, thus enabling courts to reach firms such as Standard Oil Co., which operated in many states. But judicial interpretation of the Sherman Act soon abandoned common law principles, beginning with the Supreme Court's 1897 conclusion in the Trans-Missouri Railroad case that the act reached "every" restraint of trade,

and not merely unreasonable restraints. By the 1920s the modern structure of antitrust law was largely developed, with the simple CARTEL condemned automatically, more complex joint ventures involving coordination of production condemned only if unreasonable, and anticompetitive conduct by dominant firms condemned only in the presence of economic power plus one or more anticompetitive acts.

Much of the recent scholarly debate about the Sherman Act has concerned its ideology, intended beneficiaries, and economic consequences. Beginning in the 1960s some scholars argued that Congress's goal in passing the Sherman Act was to encourage economic efficiency from low-cost production and competitive markets. Others argued that Congress was really concerned about high prices and wished to protect consumers from being gouged. But the most persuasive arguments are that Congress was mainly concerned with protecting small businesses from aggressive competition and innovation by larger firms, perhaps at the expense of high consumer prices. Standard Oil and the sugar trust, frequently named as villains in the legislative history, had both produced dramatically declining prices during the 1890s—hardly suggesting that Congress was obsessed with high prices.

Scholarly interpretation of the antitrust laws has fallen into three different camps, or "schools." On the political left, the Columbia School advocated an antitrust policy sensitive to antitrust's common law origins, solicitous of small business and relatively noneconomic in its approach. This view was prominent from the late New Deal through the 1950s but is clearly in eclipse today. On the right is the Chicago School, whose views were developed by Chicago School economists in the 1950s and 1960s, practically applied to antitrust policy by Richard A. Posner in the 1970s, and popularized by Robert H. Bork. Chicago School adherents believe that markets are extremely robust, that consumers are well informed, and that government intervention rarely benefits consumers in the long run. They favor a minimalist antitrust policy focusing on collusion and MERGERS that create monopolies. In the middle is the Harvard School, championed by Edward Chamberlain in the 1930s, Joe S. Bain in the 1950s, and Phillip E. Areeda and Donald F. Turner in the 1970s and 1980s. In common with the Chicago School, the Harvard School employs sophisticated economic methodologies, but the economics is more complex, inclined to take strategic behavior and game theory more seriously, and doubts that markets are quite as robust as the Chicago School makes them out to be. As a result, it finds more room for intervention than the Chicago School does, but considerably less room than the Columbia School.

See also CLAYTON ACT; ROBINSON-PATMAN ACT.

Further reading

Bork, Robert H. *The Antitrust Paradox: A Policy at War With Itself.* Rev. ed. New York: Basic Book, 1993.

Hovenkamp, Herbert. *Enterprise and American Law: 1836–1937.* Cambridge, Mass.: Harvard University Press, 1991.

Neale, A. D. *The Antitrust Laws of the United States of America: A Study of Competition Enforced by Law.* New York: Cambridge University Press, 1960.

Herbert Hovenkamp

shipbuilding industry Shipbuilding is one of the oldest manufacturing industries in the United States, and the nearly constant competition with foreign producers provides many insights into American business history. Technology has been dominant throughout and defines the three major periods in the evolution of shipbuilding.

The first oceangoing ship built in the United States dates to 1631. The abundance of excellent timbers close to the seacoast fostered the establishment of many small shipyards throughout New England, with a notable concentration in Maine. Other shipyards later appeared in the Delaware River Valley and in Chesapeake Bay, until a total of 125 existed by the end of the colonial period. To build warships, the Royal Navy established naval shipyards at Portsmouth (now in New Hampshire) and at the fine harbor of what later became Norfolk Navy Yard. This last yard marked the southern limit of the shipbuilding industry. Although ship repair facilities came to the U.S. South by the end of the 19th century, no major shipyards appeared there until the 20th century.

During the colonial period, the abundance of low-priced lumber meant that building ships in America, in spite of higher wages for workers, cost 30 to 50 percent less than in Britain. One-third of British tonnage came from the colonies, and American-built ships were present in all the major trade routes of the British Empire. The quality of American ships, however, was not always satisfactory, and the largest and finest vessels came from Britain.

Independence from Britain in 1783 brought challenges to a new republic that was no longer enjoying the benefits of imperial protection. In what became a permanent characteristic of U.S. policy, the government tried to foster shipping and shipbuilding simultaneously. In 1789, the U.S. Congress approved a ship registry that limited the U.S. flag to ships built in the United States; this law was intended to protect domestic shipbuilding from foreign competition. Congress increasingly restricted the participation of foreign ships in the "coastwise" trade (among U.S. ports); after 1817, only vessels flying the U.S. flag and built in domestic shipyards could carry cargo and passengers in the coastwise trade. These two protectionist measures have remained the foundation of maritime policy and have guaranteed markets to both shipping companies and domestic shipyards. In reality, the low price of U.S. wooden ships made the laws unnecessary.

More effective than U.S. laws were the foreign Navigation Acts. To protect their own shipbuilding industries, Britain and other foreign countries prohibited or hindered the purchase of U.S.-built ships. Thus, the only market left for domestic shipbuilders was U.S. shipping, which enjoyed its greatest period of expansion and prosperity from independence until the 1850s.

Maine became the most important shipbuilding state. The Boston yards remained very active, but the rest of New England declined. First the Hudson River and then the ERIE CANAL brought lumber from inland forests to New York City, which became a new shipbuilding center after 1830. Throughout the age of wood, shipyards remained small personal ventures, without any large organization; changes in location to take advantage of nearness to timber stands were not unheard of. In a distinct category were the large U.S. Navy shipyards. The U.S. Navy had taken over the old shipyards of the Royal Navy at Portsmouth and Norfolk and eventually established new yards at Philadelphia and New York. In the early decades of the 19th century the naval shipyards moved from ship repair to the construction of warships, a tradition of building that lasted until 1967.

The great shipbuilding boom of 1847–57 was the climax of the age of wood and sail. New shipyards appeared, while existing yards labored under a backlog of orders. Shipbuilders strove to design and produce the best and fastest wooden ships in the world. For the North Atlantic trade, shipbuilders launched packet ships to carry cotton and to return from Europe with passengers and manufactured goods. Less profitable but more spectacular were the famous clipper ships. In response to the California gold rush of 1848–49, shipbuilders constructed the long and narrow clippers with their towering masts to achieve the maximum speed. The financial Panic of 1857 ended the 11-year boom. Even during the boom years, the price of lumber had been steadily climbing, and scarcity had forced builders to employ inferior woods. Labor costs had been rising, too, while shipyards remained undercapitalized and lacked the equipment available in British yards that were rapidly converting to a new technology.

The shipbuilding boom of 1847–57 had disguised the stagnation in the industry. Shipbuilders refused to experiment with the steam engine. The U.S. Navy did realize that warships needed to have steam power, and thus only naval shipyards fitted steam engines to wooden vessels. The Civil War (1861–65) gave one last boost to the construction of wooden ships, but the shipbuilders did not use their wartime profits to fuel a gradual transition to iron and steam, even though the classic naval battle between the *Monitor* and the *Merrimack* had already shown that armor plating and steam engines were indispensable for warships. Britain, meanwhile, had taken the lead in replacing wood first with iron and later with steel in the 1880s. The compound engine and then the triple-expansion engine had made steam power competitive with sailing ships. Britain was producing a large number of economical steamships that would dominate the trade routes of the world after the Civil War.

The end of the Civil War dried up new ship orders, yet wooden shipbuilding continued in the United States until the early 20th century, declining at a steady tempo. Few shipbuilders of the age of wood made the transition to steam, the Cramp yards being the only notable exception. The new shipyards that emerged in the 1870s grew out of machine and engine shops. Labor costs remained higher than in Britain, and steel cost more than in Britain because of the monopoly practices of the U.S. STEEL INDUSTRY. Depending on the vessel type, shipbuilding prices were 25 to 50 percent higher in the United States than in Britain. Ship orders came primarily from the coastwise trade, which expanded after the Spanish-American War of 1898 to include the islands of Hawaii and Puerto Rico. The discovery of large oil fields in Texas created a demand for U.S.-built tankers to carry oil to the Northeast.

The expansion begun by the U.S. Navy in the late 1870s provided the single most important customer for domestic shipyards. Although the U.S. Navy wanted to rely exclusively on its own yards, private owners, most notably John Roach, lobbied aggressively to obtain navy contracts. Roach's shipyard became the largest in the United States, but its owner's bankruptcy in 1885 passed the leadership to the Cramp shipyard.

The latter struggled to survive but in its weak financial position could not prevent New York Shipbuilding from becoming the most prominent U.S. shipyard by the turn of the century. In spite of its name, New York Shipbuilding was in the Philadelphia area, near the Cramp and Roach yards. Like the other yards, New York Shipbuilding also obtained contracts from foreign navies such as Argentina's. Unlike with merchant ships, U.S. yards were able to reduce the price differential for warships, sometimes to only 10 percent more than British yards.

From the Civil War to World War I, foreign ships, usually built in British yards, carried almost all the foreign trade of the United States. The outbreak of World War I in Europe in 1914 created an acute shipping shortage, and high freight rates easily covered the higher prices of U.S.-built ships. The domestic yards were swamped with orders and had a backlog of many years. Another shipbuilding boom, reminiscent of that during the Civil War, had begun, but builders could not produce ships fast enough to end the crisis. Cries for government intervention and support were insistent. The opposition to government ownership of commercial ships delayed the congressional creation of the U.S. Shipping Board until September 1916, and even then little activity took place. Only on April 17, 1917—after the U.S. declaration of war on Germany on April 6—did the U.S. Shipping Board establish the Emergency Fleet Corporation to build and to operate merchant ships. The new corporation opened government yards to build ships. The most famous was the Hog Island yard in Philadelphia, which pioneered mass-production techniques to build ships in series.

World War I ended unexpectedly in November 1918, when the construction program was barely underway. Most ships of the program entered service after the war had ended and produced a glut in tonnage throughout the world. After 1920, shipbuilding slowly slipped into a depression as the new yards of World War I closed and the old yards dramatically shrank.

The greatest shock came in 1927, when the by now venerable Cramp shipyard ceased operations. Even with timely naval contracts, New York Shipbuilding struggled to survive. The Great Depression paralyzed the surviving shipyards, and not until the naval rearmament program of the late 1930s did shipbuilding start to revive.

The outbreak of World War II in Europe in 1939 brought another wartime shipbuilding boom. Just as during previous wars, the United States now hurriedly rushed to create a shipbuilding capacity. After U.S. entry into the war in December 1941, the United States Maritime Commission (the successor to the U.S. Shipping Board) took full control of shipbuilding. Besides supporting the enlargement of existing shipyards, the Maritime Commission offered lucrative contracts to lure businessmen into opening shipyards. As during World War I, the Maritime Commission built merchant ships in series, most notably the Liberty and the Victory types. The commission also built many warships and military craft, but navy yards constructed most of the large warships. Again, as after World War I, the end of the war in 1945 left world shipping glutted with surplus tonnage.

The surplus ships were much more numerous than after World War I and depressed world shipbuilding for more than a decade. U.S. shipbuilding again was in crisis. Surplus ships invaded even the shrinking coastwise trade, which had lost to pipelines the profitable tanker route between Texas and the Northeast. Government funding ("construction differential subsidies") helped land orders for U.S.-flag vessels in the foreign trade, but increasingly ferocious competition checked the expansion of U.S. shipping companies. The Maritime Administration, the successor of the United States Maritime Commission, made one last attempt to save both shipbuilding and shipping. In coordination with the individual shipping companies, the Maritime Administration designed and financed the Mariner class of fast merchant vessels. Produced

A floating dry dock in Louisiana, 1903 (LIBRARY OF CONGRESS)

in series in the 1950s, the Mariners were the last major commercial success of U.S. shipyards.

Since the 1880s, steel has remained the basic material for shipbuilding, and in the 1920s the diesel began to replace the steam engine in world shipping. The United States resisted this trend and instead shifted to the steam turbine, which powered the Mariners but was costly to operate. The appearance of containers in the 1960s marked an urgent need to build a new type of ship. The Maritime Administration, the shipyards, and the shipping companies failed to devise a comprehensive response to the new technological environment. The export of oil from Alaska to the continental United States provided a substitute for the lost Texas trade; otherwise, coastwise shipping continued to decline and virtually disappeared among U.S. continental ports.

As the U.S.-flag fleet in the foreign trade dwindled, the U.S. Navy increasingly took on the principal role in keeping the private shipyards alive. In 1967, the navy assigned all future ship orders to private builders and kept its own yards as a reserve in case of emergency. The end in 1981 of the subsidy for building in private U.S. yards left them at the mercy of naval construction. The program to build a 600-ship navy, which started in 1981, did bring a sorely needed respite to the beleaguered shipbuilding industry.

But the 600-ship program was the last gasp of the cold war; as it and the 1980s faded away, U.S. shipyards were left with little work to do. Of 23 major shipyards in 1985, almost a dozen had folded or were in BANKRUPTCY by 1990. A major loss was the bankruptcy of Todd Shipyards, with installations in three cities. Repeatedly referred to as a dying industry, shipbuilding in the United States, one of the oldest manufacturing industries, faces bleak prospects in the 21st century.

See also KAISER, HENRY J.

Further reading

De La Pedraja, René. *The Rise and Decline of U.S. Merchant Shipping in the Twentieth Century.* New York: Twayne, 1992.

Heinrich, Thomas R. *Ships for the Seven Seas: Philadelphia Shipbuilding in the Age of Industrial Capitalism.* Baltimore: Johns Hopkins University Press, 1997.

Whitehurst, Clinton H., Jr. *The U.S. Shipbuilding Industry: Past, Present, and Future.* Annapolis, Md.: Naval Institute Press, 1986.

René De La Pedraja

shipping industry The transportation of goods and passengers aboard oceangoing ships has been fundamental to the economic expansion of the United States. Two stages constitute the history of shipping in the United States.

The merchants owned and controlled the cargo and the ships during the first 200 years of U.S. shipping history. In the colonial period the modest economy of the agrarian society required little specialization. Thus, shipping formed an intrinsic part of mercantile activities. Using small ships, merchants handled the trade of the many towns along the East Coast. The merchants owned the merchandise they sold at each town and bought a town's commodities for shipment either to other colonial cities or to Britain.

No large investment was necessary because of the low price of U.S.-built ships. The abundance of seamen at low wages and the relatively simple technology of the small wooden sailing vessels made entry into shipping easy for merchants. Residents in the ports often bought "shares" in a merchant's ship and thus spread the risks. As the colonial economy grew, British merchants came to provide a major part of the capital invested in ships.

Independence from Britain did not change the fundamental structure of U.S. shipping. Britain excluded U.S. shipping from all its possessions, but alternate opportunities, such as the formerly forbidden Asia trade, readily appeared. The long period of European warfare from 1789 to 1815, although disruptive, did provide ample profits for U.S. shipping. After 1815, the construction of roads and canals began to expand the hinterland of each major city on the U.S. coast, and the growth of the economy increased the volume of cargo and the number of ships. The moment was rapidly approaching when entrepreneurs could specialize in carrying the cargo of merchants and producers.

The westward territorial expansion of the United States and the opening of new regions to agricultural settlement vastly increased the cargo pouring into the growing cities of New York, Boston, Philadelphia, and Baltimore. No longer did the economy of the United States hug the shore line. The construction of the first railroad lines provided feeders to bring even more goods into the port cities. Many owners of merchandise preferred to export abroad themselves, without having to go through merchant middlemen. Shipowners had traditionally been eager to carry the goods of other persons, but only if extra space was available on the ship. Merchants who dispatched cargo irregularly or in small lots did not want to make the large outlay of buying and maintaining a ship. The demand was rising for a scheduled service offering to carry anyone's goods across the sea.

The Reciprocity Treaty of 1815 opened British ports to U.S. ships without discrimination and made possible the establishment of the Black Ball

Line in 1818. The Black Ball Line, the first successful packet service in the North Atlantic, emphasized dependable departure dates for its sailing vessels from New York City. Eastbound, the voyage to Liverpool averaged 24 days depending on weather and wind. On the westbound trip, the adverse winds made for a longer voyage on the average of 38 days, with a range from 17 to 55 days. In a break with the centuries-old tradition of carrying mainly the owner's cargo, the Black Ball Line existed primarily to carry the merchandise of others. Merchants or producers now knew that at New York City (and later at other ports) ships were waiting and willing to take merchandise to Europe. In addition, as ships became more plentiful, owners of large amounts of cargo now began to enjoy the new option of renting ("chartering") a ship ("tramp vessel") for a single voyage or for a longer period.

As the shipping function separated itself from trading after 1830, the owners of cargo ("shippers") could now concentrate on trading or producing while leaving transportation to specialists. Charging a fee to carry cargo or passengers became the fundamental activity of world shipping. The success of the Black Ball Line encouraged imitators, starting with the Red Star Line in 1822 and many foreign competitors afterward. To lure passengers and cargo, the new shipping companies offered new routes, increased the frequency of departures, and sought faster crossing times. The craze for speed culminated in the deployment of the fast clipper ships, whose small carrying capacity limited their profitability to periods of acute demand, such as during the California Gold Rush of 1848–49.

The years from 1830 to 1857 marked the golden age of U.S. shipping, which reached a dominance, prestige, and profitability never again seen. In spite of the improvements to the wooden sailing ship, the variability of the winds still prevented the on-schedule delivery of merchandise to both sides of the North Atlantic. Shipping awaited the appearance of a new technology to achieve a superior level of performance.

The introduction of the steam engine and steel started a new stage in world history but also had the unfortunate effect of crippling U.S. shipping. U.S. shipyards continued to experiment with ingenious designs for wood and sail vessels, whose production continued into the early years of the 20th century. Long before then, shipping supremacy had passed from the United States to Britain, whose corporations dominated the world's sea lanes for almost a hundred years. The large capital requirements of steel steamships gave the British a decided advantage over U.S. competitors who struggled to find investors. The British government provided steamship subsidies for decades, while the U.S. government only haltingly and sparingly offered subsidies. The price of ships, until then the greatest comparative advantage of U.S. shipping, became in the age of steel and steam the most serious disadvantage. The price of steel steamships was between 25 to 50 percent higher in the United States than in Britain, and to try to overcome this hurdle, shipping companies constantly pleaded for permission to register foreign-built ships under the U.S. flag. The struggle for "free ships," as they were known, raged until 1914, when, under the pressure of war in Europe, the U.S. Congress temporarily agreed as an emergency measure to register foreign ships in the United States.

As the struggle for "free ships" dragged on after the Civil War, U.S. shipowners quietly shifted to foreign flags, usually as the final step toward abandoning ocean transportation. As the ships built during the Civil War became obsolete, U.S. shipowners invested their capital and their talents into profitable ventures on land. Entire routes, such as those in the North Atlantic, became the preserves of European (mostly British) steamship companies. In contrast to the marked decline of the fleet in the foreign trade, coastwise shipping continued its steady rise in importance. In 1820, the tonnage in the coastwise fleet for the first time exceeded that in foreign trade and continued to rise afterward. Without any foreign competition, the wooden sailing vessels in the coastwise trade gradually gave way to modern steamships built in domestic shipyards. As coastwise service extended to the South, several companies scheduled calls in Latin American ports, particularly in Cuba and in Mexico, as part of their regular service.

The only truly successful U.S.-flag steamship company prior to 1914 was the Pacific Mail Steamship Company. Established in 1848 to unite California with the East Coast, Pacific Mail began a transpacific service in 1867. The slower pace of technological change in the vast Pacific Ocean gave the company time to adopt the new steel steamers. By a reliance on Chinese crews the company helped offset the higher price of U.S.-built ships. Extremely diligent management exploited every opportunity to expand, and Pacific Mail's successful career continued after 1893, when the Southern Pacific Railroad bought the company. In contrast to the often hectic career of Pacific Mail, "proprietary companies" (those that owned the cargo and the ships) relied on dependable foreign-flag ships (usually British) for their transportation needs. The proprietary companies were the linear descendants of the merchants who had owned the cargo aboard their wooden sailing ships. For complex and changing reasons, proprietary companies, such as petroleum companies or the UNITED FRUIT COMPANY, have preferred to own and to operate fleets of ships or tankers for their own cargo.

The critical shipping shortage at the outbreak of World War I found the United States without an adequate fleet. Allowing foreign ships to register under the U.S. flag in 1914 provided inadequate relief, and in 1916 Congress created the U.S. Shipping Board to remedy the shortage of vessels. After U.S. entry into the war in April 1917, shipping fell under full governmental control, and the Shipping Board gave all shipowners orders on where to employ their vessels. This total governmental control ended when peace returned at the end of 1918, but the shipbuilding program of the Shipping Board continued for several more years. The resulting glut of ships

gave the Shipping Board the opportunity to assign the surplus ships on almost giveaway terms to new operators. Many new shipping companies, such as Lykes Brothers and United States Lines, appeared on routes previously not served by U.S.-flag vessels.

The wartime construction program had given U.S. shipping the boost indispensable for competition in the world routes. But by the late 1930s, as the surplus ships became old, U.S. shipping again was in decline. The outbreak of World War II in 1939 started another shipping revival. After U.S. entry into the war in 1941, the government created the War Shipping Administration to control all U.S. ships, in a manner similar to what the Shipping Board had done in World War I. Another crash shipbuilding program, just as in World War I, had a decisive impact on U.S. shipping. So many were the surplus ships after 1945 that the U.S. government sold them not only to U.S. firms but also to foreign countries, thus partially offsetting the benefits to U.S. shipping companies. As foreign competition from low-wage operators became intense in the 1950s, the Maritime Administration teamed up with individual companies to design and to finance the Mariner class of merchant vessels. The Mariners, with their high speed, were a major commercial success and temporarily halted the decline of U.S. shipping companies, already completely dependent on operating subsidies to remain in business.

The effective partnership between government and the private sector for the Mariners was not repeated in the much more crucial transition to containers and diesel engines. The spread of diesel engines had begun worldwide in the 1920s, but the United States had resisted that tendency. Because of their smaller size and lower operating costs, the diesels were superior to steam engines in merchant ships. The appearance of containerships in the early 1960s made obsolete almost all existing merchant ships, but not all U.S. shipping companies grasped this obvious truth. The subsidies were no longer enough to offset the blunder of a tardy and partial transition to containerships. The long delay in the adoption of diesels also worsened the financial weakness of U.S. shipping companies. The high capital investment in new containerships required large cargo volumes to make them profitable and made consolidation of the smaller firms inevitable. What did not have to be inevitable was the almost complete disappearance of U.S. shipping companies during the last quarter of the 20th century, sometimes in sudden bankruptcies, such as that of United States Lines in 1986. Military cargo, traditionally limited to U.S.-flag shipping, allowed some small companies to eke out a survival.

Coastwise trade remained the backbone of U.S.-flag operators, but competition from RAILROADS, trucks, and airplanes largely eliminated the coastwise trade in the continental United States. The coastwise trade remained important only on the routes for Alaska and for the island portions of the United States, such as Hawaii and Puerto Rico. U.S. shipping, which once played such a fundamental role in the expansion of the United States, was no longer a vital force in the economy and faced very poor prospects at the start of the 21st century.

Steamship loading hides in New Orleans, Louisiana, 1903 (LIBRARY OF CONGRESS)

Further reading

Albion, Robert G. *The Rise of the Port of New York: 1815–1860.* New York: Scribner's, 1939.

De La Pedraja, René. *The Rise and Decline of U.S. Merchant Shipping in the Twentieth Century.* New York: Twayne, 1992.

———. *A Historical Dictionary of the U.S. Merchant Marine and Shipping Industry.* Westport, Conn.: Greenwood Press, 1994.

Hutchins, John G. B. *The American Maritime Industries and Public Policy, 1789–1914.* Cambridge, Mass.: Harvard University Press, 1941.

René De La Pedraja

short selling   See STOCK MARKETS.

Siebert, Muriel (1932–   ) *financial executive* Muriel Siebert was born in Cleveland, Ohio, in 1932, the daughter of a dentist. She attended Case Western Reserve University to study accounting but dropped out after her father died from cancer in 1954. Despite her lack of a degree, she packed all her belongings into an old car, relocated to New York City, and began looking for work as a securities analyst. At length she was employed by the firm Bache and Company and encountered numerous instances of sexism and anti-Semitism on the job. She especially resented that fact that male coworkers often received 50 to 100 percent more for the same work she performed. Determined to succeed, Siebert left Bache in 1957 and spent the next decade working efficiently at a number of Wall Street firms. Despite obvious talent, she remained banned from investment clubs due to gender discrimination, although in 1960 she became a partner in a brokerage firm. By 1967 Siebert was successful as an analyst and sought to do what no woman had ever done previously—buy a seat on the NEW YORK STOCK EXCHANGE. This all-male institution vigorously resisted the move, and several months lapsed before Siebert found an institution that would

loan her the $445,000 for her seat. Nonetheless, on December 28, 1967, she became Wall Street's first female floor broker, breaking a male monopoly that had lasted since 1792. Two years later, she followed up this success by establishing her own brokerage, Muriel Siebert and Company, which remains the only female-owned and operated brokerage firm on Wall Street. Despite ongoing discrimination from colleagues and businesses, Siebert performed as efficiently as possible and accumulated a small fortune. In May 1975, she was among the first companies to advertise discount stocks to the public—an act that outraged many contemporaries at the time. Since then stock advertisements and discount commissions have become standard fare.

Siebert's conspicuous success prompted New York governor Hugh Carey to appoint her to the post of state banking commissioner in 1979—another first for a woman. More surprisingly, Carey, a Democrat, appointed Siebert, a lifelong Republican, to the task. At that time many banks across the country were facing insolvency, and Siebert imposed her usual no-nonsense approach to fiscal and accounting discipline on a bewildering array of banks, credit unions, and savings and loan associations. Amazingly, after five years not a single bank failed—a bravura performance considering how perilous the New York monetary system had become. In 1982 Siebert sought to expand her celebrity by entering politics, and she ran for the U.S. Senate from New York, finishing a strong second in the primary. Afterward she took her firm out of a trust fund and resumed the chair of Muriel Siebert and Company.

The decade of the 1980s proved tumultuous, but Siebert's good performance enabled her to stave off several buyout offers, and by 1985, she proved solvent enough to acquire two of the firms in question. By that time she had also become closely identified with numerous civic and philanthropic concerns, especially the National Woman's Forum for successful business women. In 1990, she founded the Siebert Philanthropic Foundation, which uses her own assets to give to charitable purposes. And, mindful of her own experience in the business world, Siebert also established the Women's Entrepreneurial Foundation to assist female-owned small businesses. Muriel Siebert and Company continued as one of Wall Street's premier brokerage firms, so in 1996 she took the company public as the Siebert Financial Corporation with additional offices in Los Angeles, California, and Boca Raton, Florida. Politics remain an area of interest, so she maintains and funds the WISH List, intending to support Republican women candidates nationwide. She remains highly sought after as a speaker at such prestigious business schools as Harvard and New York University and is the recipient of numerous awards and citations from around the world. Siebert, however, shrugs off her celebrity status and contentedly plies the treacherous waters of the stock market well past her retirement age. Her reputation as a legendary and successful maverick of Wall Street is secure.

Further reading

Benn, Alec. *The Unseen Wall Street of 1969–1975 and Its Significance for Today.* Westport, Conn.: Quorum Books, 2000.
Geisst, Charles R. *100 Years of Wall Street.* New York: McGraw-Hill, 2000.
Herera, Sue. *Women of the Street: Making It on Wall Street—the World's Toughest Business.* New York: Wiley, 1997.
Siebert, Muriel. *Changing the Rules: Adventures of a Wall Street Maverick.* New York: Free Press, 2002.

John C. Fredriksen

Singer Sewing Co. Founded by I. M. Singer (1811–75), the company became the largest and best-known manufacturer of sewing machines in the world. Borrowing $40, Singer founded his company in 1851, selling an improved version of a machine that had been used for stitching boots. A previous machine developed by Orson C.

Phelps of Boston was already being manufactured under license from John A. Lerow. The machine was not very practical, operating on a circular motion. After examining the machine, Singer decided that the job could be done better by a needle that moved up and down in a more efficient manner.

In order to offset the relatively high purchase price of $75, Singer introduced the first installment payment plan. The company was incorporated as the Singer Manufacturing Company in 1853 in New York City. The machines became an immediate hit and became even more popular after the 1855 Paris World's Fair, where the machine won a first prize. When the Civil War began, Singer was producing more than 3,000 units per year. By 1875, when he died, output had reached 250,000 units per year and five years later topped 500,000.

His successor, Inslee Hopper, opened a manufacturing facility in Scotland in 1867 to meet increasing worldwide demand, making Singer one of the first multinational companies. The company had already opened offices in Scotland and Germany. In 1880, an Edison-developed electric motor was added to the machines, making them motor driven, although it took nine more years to develop practically. By 1903, sales exceeded a million units annually.

In 1908, the company opened the Singer Building on Broadway in New York. At 47 stories, it was one of the tallest SKYSCRAPERS in the city.

In 1958, the company reached $500 million in annual sales. By 1970, annual sales reached $2 billion, and the company was at the height of its power. By the late 1970s, however, the firm was losing money as demographics changed and sewing at home became less popular. Beginning in 1975, the company, under new management, began an aggressive diversification into the aerospace business, manufacturing flight simulators and defense equipment, and the Singer Sewing Machine Co. was spun off as a separate entity. Other products produced included appliances and television sets that were sold worldwide. Despite its financial setbacks, the company still held about 30 percent of the market for sewing machines worldwide.

Another series of financial setbacks led the company to file for Chapter 11 bankruptcy protection in 2000, and the NYSE suspended trading of its stock. The post-bankruptcy Singer has reduced operations to half its former size. The company remains the best-known and largest maker of sewing machines in the world, with exposure in more than 100 countries.

Further reading

Bissell, Don C. *The First Conglomerate.* Brunswick, Maine: Audenreed Press, 1999.

Brandon, Ruth. *A Capitalist Romance: Singer and the Sewing Machine.* New York: Lippincott, 1977.

skyscrapers A uniquely American style of architecture seeking to expand a building's capacities by adding height rather than breadth. Skyscrapers abandoned the European style of office building in favor of a building that reached upward and was built around a steel frame. They began being erected in the late 19th century in Chicago and New York and depended for practicality upon the invention of the safety elevator by Elisha Graves Otis.

Otis's first electric elevator was introduced in 1889, supplanting the steam-operated elevator introduced in the late 1850s. It coincided with the opening of the 160-foot-high Tower Building, the first New York skyscraper, at 50 Broadway. The early tall buildings used a steel frame designed by Andrew CARNEGIE as their basic component. Three years earlier, a nine-story building, the Home Insurance Building, had been opened in Chicago. Many more tall buildings would be built in New York, which became the home of the skyscraper, in part due to the firm bedrock that supports Manhattan.

Other skyscrapers of various design were opened in succeeding years. The Flatiron Build-

Empire State Building at night, 1937 (LIBRARY OF CONGRESS)

ing (285 feet) was opened in 1902, the Singer Building in 1908 (612 feet), the Metropolitan Life Building (700 feet) in 1909, and the Woolworth Building (792 feet) in 1913. The Woolworth Building held the distinction of being the world's tallest building until the 1920s, when it was surpassed by the Bank of Manhattan Building on Wall Street (927 feet). When the Chrysler Building was built in midtown Manhattan a few years later, it was short of the Bank of Manhattan by two feet, until a steel spire was added to the Chrysler, allowing it to claim the distinction as the tallest.

The most famous American skyscraper, the Empire State Building, was built in 1930 and 1931 and opened on May 1, 1931. Its developers were Al Smith, the former governor of New York, and John J. RASKOB, a former DuPont and General Motors executive. The building, at 1,250 feet, was built in 15 to 16 months by approximately 3,000 workers. When it opened, the 1920s boom was over, and the Great Depression had begun. For the first 10 years of its life, the building was referred to as the Empty State Building because of a lack of tenants. During World War II, the RECONSTRUCTION FINANCE CORP. took an interest in renting part of it, underlining how slowly occupancy rates rose during its first 15 years.

The Empire State was eventually surpassed by the twin towers of the World Trade Center in lower Manhattan in the 1970s. They, in turn, were surpassed by the Sears Tower in Chicago as the country's tallest building at 1,454 feet. The Sears Tower retains that distinction.

Skyscrapers are an original American contribution to architecture and have been built as a testament to the strength and unlimited reach of business. In all cases, they have been sponsored by corporations, with the exception of the World Trade Center, which was built and operated by the Port Authority of New York and New Jersey and was originally conceived to revive New York's position as the center of international trade. The original skyscrapers in particular were built by industrialists to showcase the success of their companies

See also SINGER SEWING CO.; WOOLWORTH, FRANK WINFIELD.

Further reading
Bascomb, Neal. *Higher: A Historic Race to the Sky and the Making of a City.* New York: Doubleday, 2003.
Landau, Sarah Bradford, and Carl W. Condit. *The Rise of the New York Skyscraper, 1865–1913.* New Haven, Conn.: Yale University Press, 1996.
Macauley, David. *Unbuilding.* Boston: Houghton Mifflin, 1980.
Sabbagh, Karl. *Skyscraper: The Making of a Building.* New York: Viking, 1990.

slavery Slavery is an economic phenomenon. Throughout history, slavery has existed where it has been economically worthwhile to those in power. The principal modern example is the U.S. South. Nearly 4 million slaves worth close to $4 billion lived there just before the Civil War. Masters enjoyed rates of return on slaves comparable to those on other assets; sea captains, cotton consumers, slave traders, banks and insurance companies, and industrial enterprises benefited from slavery as well. In fact, U.S. slavery was one of the most sophisticated and encompassing economic institutions of the antebellum era.

Not long after Columbus sailed for the New World, French and Spanish explorers brought personal slaves with them on various expeditions. But a far greater percentage of slaves arrived in chains in crowded, sweltering cargo holds, with the first arriving in Virginia in 1619 aboard a Dutch vessel.

Commanders of slave ships and their financial backers made fortunes from the Atlantic trade. Transporting slaves was a major industry in the 17th and 18th centuries, with the Royal African Company a principal player for five decades. David Galenson's study of the company uncovered a picture of closely connected competitive markets in Africa and America that responded quickly to economic incentives. Despite its size, the company was hardly a monopoly. Hordes of small ship captains found the trade worthwhile, with prospective rates of return of 9 to 10 percent, comparable to returns on alternative ventures.

Other interests also profited. European banks and merchant houses enjoyed substantial profits as they helped develop the New World plantation system through complicated credit and insurance mechanisms. Well-placed African dealers also benefited. In sickening cycles, early Sudanic tribes sold slaves for horses, then used horses to obtain more slaves. Later tribes similarly traded slaves for guns, then used guns to hunt more captives. Early New England industry—cotton textiles, shipbuilding, and the like—had strong connections to the slave trade as well. Among the beneficiaries were the Brown, Cabot, and Faneuil families.

From 1500 to 1900, approximately 12 million Africans were forced westward, with about 10 million completing the journey across the Atlantic. Yet very few ended up in the British colonies and the young American republic. By 1808, when the transatlantic slave trade to the United States officially ended, only about 6 percent of African slaves landing in the New World had come to North America.

Colonial slavery started slowly, particularly in the North. By 1775, fewer than 10 percent of the half-million slaves in the thirteen colonies resided in the North, working mostly in agriculture. Scholars have speculated as to why, without coming to a definite conclusion. Some surmise that indentured servants were fundamentally better suited to the northern climate, crops, and tasks at hand; some claim that antislavery sentiment provides the explanation.

Throughout colonial and antebellum history, slaves lived primarily in the South. They constituted less than a 10th of the South's population in 1680 but grew to a third by 1790. After the American Revolution, the southern slave population exploded, reaching about 1.1 million in 1810 and more than 3.9 million in 1860. Despite their numbers, slaves typically made up a minority of the local population. Most southerners owned no slaves, and most slaves lived in small groups rather than on large plantations.

How did the U.S. slave population increase nearly fourfold between 1810 and 1860, given the demise of the transatlantic trade? They experienced an exceptional rate of natural increase due to relatively high birth rates and relatively low mortality rates. Unlike elsewhere in the New World, the South did not require a constant infusion of immigrants to keep its slave population intact. In fact, by 1825, 36 percent of the slaves in the Western Hemisphere lived in the United States.

Market prices for slaves reflected their substantial economic value. Price evidence comes from censuses, probate records, plantation and slave-trader accounts, and proceedings of slave auctions. These data reveal that prime field hands sold for $400 to 600 in 1800, $1,300 to $1,500 in 1850, and up to $3,000 just before Fort Sumter fell. Even adjusting for inflation, slave prices rose significantly in the six decades before secession. Slavery remained a thriving business on the eve of the Civil War: By one estimate, average slave prices by 1890 would have increased more than 50 percent over their 1860 levels. No wonder the South rose in armed resistance to protect its enormous investment.

Slave markets existed across the antebellum South. Private auctions, estate sales, and professional traders facilitated easy exchange. Established dealers such as Franklin and Armfield in Virginia, Woolfolk, Saunders, and Overly in Maryland, and Nathan Bedford Forrest in Tennessee prospered alongside itinerant traders who operated in a few counties, buying slaves for cash from their owners, then moving them overland in shackles to the lower South. More than a million slaves were taken across state lines between 1790 and 1860, with many more moving within states. Some of these slaves went with their owners; some were sold to new owners. In his monumental study, Michael Tadman found that slaves who lived in the upper South faced a significant chance of being sold for profit. Along with slave sale markets came farseeing methods for coping with risk, such as warranties of title, fitness, and merchantability.

The prices paid for slaves reflected two economic factors: the characteristics of the slave and the conditions of the market. Important individual features included age, sex, childbearing capacity for females, physical condition, temperament, and skill level. In addition, the supply of slaves, the demand for products produced by slaves, and seasonal factors helped determine market conditions and therefore prices.

Prices followed a life-cycle pattern. Infant slaves sold for a positive price because masters expected them to live long enough to make the initial costs of raising them worthwhile. Prices rose through puberty as productivity and experience increased. In 19th-century New Orleans, for example, prices peaked at about age 22 for females and age 25 for males. Girls cost more than boys up to their mid-teens. The genders then switched places in terms of value. After the peak age, prices declined slowly for a time, then fell off rapidly as the aging process caused productivity to fall. Compared to full-grown men, women were worth 80 to 90 percent as much. One characteristic in particular set some females apart—their ability to bear children. Fertile females commanded a premium. The mother-child link also proved important for pricing in a different way: People sometimes paid more for intact families.

Skills, physical traits, mental capabilities, and other qualities also helped determine a slave's price. Skilled workers sold for premiums of 40 to 55 percent, whereas crippled and chronically ill slaves sold for deep discounts. Slaves who proved troublesome—runaways, thieves, layabouts, drunks, slow learners, and the like—also sold for lower prices. Taller slaves cost more, perhaps because height acted as a proxy for healthiness. In New Orleans, light-skinned females (who were relatively more popular as concubines) sold for a 5 percent premium.

Prices fluctuated with market conditions as well as with individual characteristics. U.S. slave prices fell around 1800 as the Haitian Revolution sparked the movement of slaves into the southern states. Less than a decade later, prices climbed when the international slave trade was banned, cutting off legal external supplies. Interestingly, many southern slaveholders supported closing the Atlantic trade. The resulting reduction in supply drove up prices of slaves already living in the United States and, hence, their masters' wealth. U.S. slaves had high enough fertility rates and low enough mortality rates to reproduce themselves, so southerners did not worry about having too few slaves to go around.

Demand helped determine prices as well. The demand for slaves derived in part from the demand for commodities and services that slaves provided. Changes in slave occupations and variability in prices for slave-produced goods therefore created movements in slave prices. For instance, as slaves replaced increasingly expensive indentured servants in the New World, slave prices went up. In the period 1748–75, slave prices in British America rose nearly 30 percent. As cotton prices fell in the 1840s, southern slave prices also fell. But as the demand for cotton and tobacco grew after 1850, slave prices increased as well.

Differences in demand across regions led to transitional regional price differences, which in turn meant large movements of slaves. Yet because planters experienced greater stability among their workforce when entire plantations moved, 84 percent of slaves were taken to the lower South in this way rather than being sold piecemeal.

Demand sometimes had to do with the time of year a sale took place. For example, slave prices in the New Orleans market were 10 to 20 percent higher in January than in September. September was a busy time of year for plantation owners, and the opportunity cost of their time was relatively high. Consequently, prices had to be relatively low for them to be willing to travel to New Orleans during harvest time.

One additional demand factor loomed large in determining slave prices—the expectation of continued legal slavery. As the Civil War progressed, prices dropped dramatically because people could not be sure that slavery would survive. In New Orleans, prime male slaves sold on average for $1,381 in 1861 and for $1,116 in 1862. Burgeoning inflation meant that real prices fell considerably more. By war's end, slaves sold for a small fraction of their 1860 price.

That slavery was profitable seems almost obvious. Yet scholars have argued furiously about this matter. On one side stand antebellum writers such as Hinton Rowan Helper and Frederick Law Olmstead, many abolitionists, early researchers such as Ulrich Phillips and Charles Ramsdell, and contemporary scholars such as

Eugene Genovese, who speculated that American slavery was unprofitable, inefficient, and incompatible with urban life. On the other side are those who contend that slavery was profitable and efficient relative to free labor and that slavery suited cities as well as farms. These researchers stress the similarity between slave markets and markets for other sorts of capital.

The battle has largely been won by the latter group. They have shown that much like other businessmen, slaveowners responded to market—signals adjusting crop mixes, reallocating slaves to more profitable tasks, hiring out idle slaves, and selling slaves for profit. One well-known instance shows that contemporaneous free labor thought urban slavery worked far too well: Employees of the Tredegar Iron Works in Richmond, Virginia, went out on their first strike in 1847 to protest the use of slave labor there.

Carrying the banner of the "slavery was profitable" camp is Nobel laureate Robert Fogel. Perhaps the most controversial book ever written about American slavery is his *Time on the Cross,* coauthored by Stanley Engerman. These men were among the first to use modern statistical methods, high-speed computers, and large datasets to answer a series of empirical questions about the economics of slavery. Building on earlier work by Alfred Conrad and John Meyer, Fogel and Engerman used data from probate and plantation records, invoices from the New Orleans slave-sale market, coastwise manifests for shipped slaves, and manuscript census schedules to find profit levels and rates of return. Despite criticism (notably a series of articles collected as *Reckoning with Slavery*), *Time on the Cross* and Fogel's subsequent *Without Consent or Contract* have solidified the economic view of slavery. Even Eugene Genovese, long an ardent proponent of the belief that southern planters held slaves for prestige value, finally acknowledged that slavery probably was a profitable enterprise.

Among Fogel and Engerman's findings are these: Antebellum southern farms were 35 per-

cent more efficient overall than northern ones. Moreover, slavery generated a rate of economic growth in the U.S. South comparable to that of many European countries. Fogel and Engerman also discovered that because slaves constituted a considerable portion of individual wealth, masters fed and treated their slaves reasonably well. Although some evidence indicates that infant slaves suffered much worse conditions than their freeborn counterparts, juvenile and adult slaves lived in conditions similar to—and sometimes better than—those enjoyed by many free laborers of the same period.

One potent piece of evidence supporting the notion that slavery provided pecuniary benefits is this: Slavery replaced other labor when it became relatively cheaper. In the colonies, for example, indentured servitude was common. As the demand for skilled servants (and therefore their wages) rose in England, the cost of indentured servants went up in the colonies. At the same time, second-generation slaves became more productive than their forebears because they spoke English and did not have to adjust to life in a strange new world. Consequently, the balance of labor shifted away from indentured servitude and toward slavery. Georgia offers a compelling example. Its original 1732 charter prohibited ownership of black slaves. Yet by 1750 the trustees of the new colony had to relax the prohibition because Georgia growers simply could not compete with producers elsewhere who used lower-cost slave labor.

The value of slaves arose in part from the value of labor generally in the antebellum United States. Scarce factors of production will command economic rent, and labor was by far the scarcest available input in America. But a large part of the reward to owning and working slaves resulted from innovative labor practices. Certainly, the use of the "gang" system in antebellum agriculture contributed to profits. In the gang system, groups of slaves performed synchronized tasks under the watchful overseer's eye, much like parts of a single machine. Masters found that treating people like machinery paid off handsomely.

Slaveowners experimented with various other methods to increase productivity. For example, they developed an elaborate scheme of "hand ratings" in order to improve the match between the slave worker and the job. Hand ratings categorized slaves by age and sex and rated their productivity relative to that of a prime male field hand. Masters also capitalized on the native intelligence of slaves by using them as agents to receive goods, keep books, and the like.

Masters offered positive incentives to make slaves work more efficiently. Slaves—in contrast to free workers—often had Sundays off. Slaves could sometimes earn bonuses in cash or in goods, or quit early if they finished tasks quickly. Some masters allowed slaves to keep part of the harvest or to work their own small plots. In places, slaves could sell their own crops. To prevent stealing, however, many masters limited the products that slaves could raise and sell, confining them to corn or brown cotton, for example. In antebellum Louisiana, slaves even had under their control a sum of money called a *peculium*. This served as a sort of working capital, enabling slaves to establish thriving businesses that often benefited their masters as well. Yet these practices may have helped lead to the downfall of slavery, for they gave slaves a taste of freedom that left them longing for more.

Masters profited from reproduction as well as production. Southern planters encouraged slaves to have large families because U.S. slaves lived long enough to generate more revenue than cost over their lifetimes. But researchers have found little evidence of slave breeding; instead, masters encouraged slaves to live in nuclear or extended families for stability. Lest anyone think sentimentality triumphed on the southern plantation, let them recall the willingness of most masters to sell if the bottom line was big enough.

One element contributing to profitability was the slave's African heritage. Africans, more than indigenous Americans, were accustomed to the discipline of agricultural practices and knew metalworking. Some scholars surmise that Africans, in contrast to Europeans, could better withstand tropical diseases and, unlike Native Americans, also had some exposure to the European disease pool.

Perhaps the most distinctive feature of African slaves, however, was their skin color. Because they looked different from their masters, their movements were easy to monitor. Denying slaves education, property ownership, contractual rights, and other things enjoyed by those in power was simple: One needed only to look at people to ascertain their likely status. Using color was a low-cost way of distinguishing slaves from free persons. For this reason, the colonial practices that freed slaves who converted to Christianity quickly faded away. Deciphering true religious beliefs was far more difficult than establishing skin color.

Among those who profited from slavery were men who worked as slave catchers and received

A 1780s broadside advertising a slave auction (LIBRARY OF CONGRESS)

fees for returning escaped slaves to their masters. However, because skin color was the principal identifying mark, free blacks also faced the horrifying possibility of capture and sale.

Slavery never generated superprofits, because people always had the option of putting their money elsewhere. Nevertheless, investment in slaves offered a rate of return—about 10 percent—that was comparable to returns on other assets. Slaveowners, slave sellers, and slave catchers were not the only ones to reap rewards, however. So did cotton consumers, who enjoyed low prices, and Northern entrepreneurs who helped finance plantation operations. As antebellum editor James de Bow put it, without slavery "ships would rot at [the New York] docks; grass would grow in Wall Street and Broadway, and the glory of New York . . . would be numbered with the things of the past." Even today evidence is being found in the archives of present financial firms that had dealings in slavery. In 2005, Bank One, now a division of J. P. Morgan Chase, acknowledged that two of its predecessor banks—Citizens Bank and Canal Bank in Louisiana—accepted approximately 13,000 enslaved individuals as collateral on loans and took ownership of approximately 1,250 of them when the plantation owners defaulted on the loans.

So slavery was profitable. Was it an efficient way of organizing the workforce? On this question, considerable controversy remains. Slavery might well have profited masters, but only because they exploited their chattel. What is more, slavery could have locked people into a method of production and way of life that might later have proven burdensome.

Fogel and Engerman claimed that slaves kept about 90 percent of what they produced. Because these scholars also found that agricultural slavery produced relatively more output for a given set of inputs, they argued that slaves actually may have shared in the overall benefits resulting from the gang system. Other scholars contend that slaves in fact kept less than half of what they pro-

duced and that slavery, while profitable, certainly was not efficient.

Gavin Wright called attention as well to the difference between the short run and the long run. He noted that slaves accounted for a very large percentage of most masters' portfolios of assets. Although slavery might have seemed an efficient means of production at a point in time, it tied masters to a certain system of labor, which might not have adapted quickly to changed economic circumstances. This argument has some merit. Although the South's growth rate compared favorably with that of the North in the antebellum period, a considerable portion of wealth was held in the hands of planters. Consequently, commercial and service industries lagged in the South. The region also had far less rail transportation than the North. Yet many plantations used the most advanced technologies of the day, and certain innovative commercial and insurance practices appeared first in transactions involving slaves. Slaveowners led in using new inventions, such as the circular saw. What is more, although the South fell behind the North and Great Britain in its level of manufacturing, it compared favorably to other advanced countries of the time. In sum, no clear consensus emerges as to whether the antebellum South created a standard of living comparable to that of the North or, if it did, whether it could have sustained it.

And what of the standard of life for slaves themselves? In terms of material conditions, diet, and treatment, southern slaves may have fared as well in many ways as the poorest class of free citizens. Yet the root of slavery is coercion. By its very nature, slavery involves involuntary transactions. Slaves are property, whereas free laborers are persons who make choices (at times constrained, of course) about the sort of work they do and the number of hours they work.

The behavior of former slaves after abolition clearly reveals that they cared strongly about the manner of their work and valued their nonwork time more highly than their masters did. Even the most benevolent former masters in the U.S. South found it impossible to entice their former chattels back into gang work, even with large wage premiums. Nor could they persuade women back into the labor force: Many female ex-slaves simply chose to stay at home. In the end, perhaps, slavery is an economic phenomenon only because slave societies fail to account for the incalculable costs borne by the slaves themselves.

See also COTTON INDUSTRY.

Further reading

Aitken, Hugh, ed. *Did Slavery Pay? Readings in the Economics of Black Slavery in the United States.* Boston: Houghton Mifflin, 1971.

Barzel, Yoram. "An Economic Analysis of Slavery." *Journal of Law and Economics* 21, no. 1 (1977): 87–110.

David, Paul A., Herbert G. Gutman, Richard Sutch, Peter Temin, and Gavin Wright. *Reckoning with Slavery: A Critical Study in the Quantitative History of American Negro Slavery.* New York: Oxford University Press, 1976.

Fogel, Robert W. *Without Consent or Contract.* New York: Norton, 1989.

Fogel, Robert W., and Stanley L. Engerman. *Time on the Cross: The Economics of American Negro Slavery.* New York: Little, Brown, 1974.

Galenson, David W. *Traders, Planters, and Slaves: Market Behavior in Early English America.* New York: Cambridge University Press, 1986

Ransom, Roger L., and Richard Sutch. *One Kind of Freedom: The Economic Consequences of Emancipation.* New York: Cambridge University Press, 1977.

Wright, Gavin. *The Political Economy of the Cotton South: Households, Markets, and Wealth in the Nineteenth Century.* New York: Norton, 1978.

Jenny Wahl

Sloan, Alfred (1875–1966) *auto executive*

Born in New Haven, Connecticut, Sloan studied electrical engineering at MIT and graduated in 1895 before going to work for the Hyatt Roller Bearing Co. in Newark, New Jersey. The company had great promise because of the importance of roller bearings to the young automobile industry. In 1897, his father invested $5,000 in the company, and Sloan became its president. While still a young man, he became acquainted with most of the motor industry's giants, such as Walter CHRYSLER, Henry FORD, and William C. DURANT, since the company, of which he was chief executive, supplied parts to the automobile industry.

He sold the company to Durant during the First World War, and it was reorganized as United Motors with Sloan as president. United was purchased by GENERAL MOTORS in 1918, and Sloan eventually became a vice president of the automobile manufacturer. When GM ran into financial difficulties in 1920 with Durant at the helm of the company, it was reorganized by Pierre DuPont and John RASKOB, both of whom were major investors with the assistance of J. P. Morgan & Company. Pierre DuPont became the new president of the company, and Sloan became operating vice president. Sloan became chief executive of the company in 1923, after he had undertaken a study of the operations of GM under DuPont, which quickly became the model used to change the company. Later, it also became a classic business school case study.

Despite the changes made in the company due to the study, Sloan's major achievements at GM centered around marketing. In his first year as president, he doubled GM's manufacturing capacity. He made the credit arm of GM, the General Motors Acceptance Corp., more prominent in the company as it helped to finance consumer sales by providing consumer credit. He was also responsible for introducing the annual model changes that afterward characterized the industry in order to stimulate more sales. This was in distinction to Ford's Model T, which had not changed substantially since it was first introduced. The strategy worked well during the Depression, especially since GM reported a profit every year during the 1930s, although it did lay off workers in order to do so.

Sloan gave up the presidency of the company in 1937 after a confrontation with the United Auto Workers over working conditions and pay. A sit-down strike lasted for many months before Sloan was persuaded to bargain with the union by Franklin D. Roosevelt. After the incident, he became chairman of the company.

Sloan retired from GM in 1956. In the 1950s, a GM executive boasted with pride that "what's good for GM is good for America," attesting to the success his methods had achieved. Most of the company's success was attributed to Sloan and his management techniques that left the company as the largest producer of automobiles in the country, replacing Ford. It also became the world's largest corporation. His philanthropic interests included the Sloan-Kettering Institute in New York and the Sloan Foundation. He died in 1966.

Further reading
Farber, David R. *Sloan Rules: Alfred P. Sloan and the Triumph of General Motors.* Chicago: University of Chicago Press, 2002.

Seltzer, Lawrence H. *A Financial History of the American Automobile Industry.* Boston: Houghton Mifflin, 1928.

Sloan, Alfred P. *My Years with General Motors.* New York: Doubleday, 1964.

———. *Adventures of a White Collar Man.* New York: Doubleday, Doran, 1941.

Small Business Administration (SBA) The Small Business Administration is a federal agency established in 1953 to help firms that are "independently owned and operated." The SBA's definition of "small" varies by industry but generally includes firms with fewer than 500 employees. Agency services include direct loans and loan guarantees, venture capital, management assistance, disaster loans, and procurement preferences for small and minority-owned enterprises.

The SBA was an orphan of the Reconstruction Finance Corporation (RFC), a large lending agency created during the Great Depression to spur economic recovery. President Dwight D. Eisenhower made elimination of the RFC one of his top priorities. Congress, however, insisted on creating the SBA to retain a source of credit for small business. It also transferred disaster lending from the RFC and procurement operations from the Small Defense Plants Administration, an agency that helped small manufacturers secure contracts during the Korean War. The Small Business Administration was the first peacetime agency to represent all types of small business. Originally authorized for only two years, Congress made the SBA permanent in 1958.

With strong congressional backing, the Small Business Administration grew rapidly. In 1958, Congress authorized SBA loans for Small Business Investment Companies (SBICs), privately-owned firms that provide venture capital to businesses with growth potential. To leverage its resources and reduce losses associated with direct lending, the SBA increasingly relied on loan guarantees issued to banks making loans to small businesses. In fiscal year 2000, total loan authorizations (including SBICs) hit a record $15 billion.

The Small Business Administration's nonlending programs are less well known. In 1964, the agency established the Service Corps of Retired Executives (SCORE). Retirees offer free management advice to small business owners who request it. The SBA also has the power to set aside government contracts for small firms, thus excluding larger businesses from competing. Set-aside contracts are negotiated (given to an individual firm) or opened to bidding by small businesses. They make up half of all government contracts awarded to small firms. The SBA's Office of Advocacy (established 1974) defends small business interests before congressional committees and federal regulatory agencies. This advocacy role has grown in response to criticism that government regulation is burdensome to small business.

The SBA was a pioneer in race-based affirmative action. In 1964, SBA administrator Eugene Foley persuaded Congress to include Economic Opportunity Loans (EOLs) in the enabling legislation for the War on Poverty. EOLs were available to low-income entrepreneurs regardless of race, but the urban riots of the mid-1960s transformed the program into a de facto preference for minorities. EOLs failed to lift the disadvantaged out of poverty and left many worse off when their businesses folded. Congress cut the program in the 1980s but revived a similar "micro loan" program after the Rodney King riots of 1992.

President Richard Nixon (1969–74) boosted the SBA's minority enterprise programs by advocating "black capitalism," a term that embraced nonwhite minorities, including African Americans, Hispanics, Native Americans, and Asian Americans. The SBA used its authority under Section 8(a) of the Small Business Act to set aside no-bid contracts for "socially and economically disadvantaged" business owners, a euphemism for minorities. Section 8(a) set-asides were enormously controversial as critics charged "reverse discrimination" against white business owners. Since the 1970s, periodic scandals have erupted as journalists and prosecutors uncovered widespread corruption, particularly the fraudulent use of minority "fronts" by white business owners. Two scandals involving SBA minority enterprise programs—Wedtech and Whitewater—embarrassed the presidential administrations of Ronald Reagan and William Clinton, respectively. Nevertheless, Section 8(a) has withstood court challenges. Moreover, 8(a) group eligibility criteria, first developed in 1980, have become the standard for other agencies' affirmative action programs.

Controversy has followed the SBA since its inception. Critics of the Small Business Administration charged that its definition of "small" departed from the public conception of "Mom and Pop." In 1967, for example, the SBA awarded the American Motors Corporation procurement preferences because it was "small" within its industry. Opponents of affirmative action attacked the agency's racial preferences. Fiscal conservatives—including Ronald Reagan, who tried to abolish the SBA in 1985 and 1986—disputed the need for federal assistance to small business. Nevertheless, the Small Business Administration has historically enjoyed broad bipartisan support in Congress, undoubtedly reflecting public esteem for small business.

See also RECONSTRUCTION FINANCE CORP.

Further reading

Bean, Jonathan J. *Beyond the Broker State: Federal Policies Toward Small Business, 1936–1961.* Chapel Hill: University of North Carolina Press, 1996.

———. *Big Government and Affirmative Action: The Scandalous History of the Small Business Administration.* Lexington: University Press of Kentucky, 2001.

Dwyer, Christopher. *The Small Business Administration.* New York: Chelsea House Publishers, 1991.

Jonathan J. Bean

Specie Resumption Act   See GOLD STANDARD.

sports industry   Professional sports represent a large and growing industry in the United States. Combined ticket sales for all professional sports, including those as diverse as football, golf, and auto racing, exceeded $15 billion in 2000, with another $10 billion spent on-site for parking, concessions, and merchandise. Factoring in media revenues, sporting goods, licensed apparel, and advertising, the size of the industry easily exceeds $50 billion per year.

Furthermore, sports affect society in a way that goes beyond simple economics. Championship matches can attract television audiences in the hundreds of millions. Entire cities or countries rejoice or despair upon the outcome of a single game. In 1969, Honduras and El Salvador even fought a short-lived "Football War," sparked by tensions surrounding soccer matches played between the two countries.

The sports industry can be broken down between "participatory sports," in which individuals actively take part in athletic contests, and "spectator sports," in which individuals watch athletes compete. As incomes have risen substantially over the past century, so too have both participatory and spectator sports as people have had both higher incomes to pay for these activities and an increased availability of leisure time.

Spectator sports can be further broken down into "professional sports," in which the contestants are paid, and "amateur sports," in which the athletes are unpaid. Amateur sports have a long history. Many ancient sports such as archery, horseback riding, and wrestling can be seen as offshoots of military or fitness training. However, other activities can be seen more directly as entertainment. Organized ball games were played in ancient Egypt, the Greeks created the now famous Olympic Games in 776 B.C., and Native Americans played handball in the Mayan empire and a forerunner of lacrosse in what is now the northeastern portion of the United States. While contestants in these games may have been rewarded by government or religious leaders or the spectators themselves for their athletic performance, the rise of the truly professional athlete did not begin until the late 1800s.

The first sport in the United States to give rise to fully professional athletes was baseball. Following codification of the rules of the sport in 1845 by Alexander Cartwright, baseball grew in popularity both as a spectator and participatory sport. While some players on certain teams received compensation for their play, it was not until 1869 that the Cincinnati Red Stockings formed the first team comprised entirely of professional players. Their success on the field led other teams to adopt their strategy, and by 1871 the National Association was formed with nine teams, including the Boston Braves, the forerunner of today's Atlanta Braves.

The first two decades of professional baseball saw a proliferation of teams and leagues. The National Association collapsed four years after its formation and was replaced in 1876 by the modern National League (NL). Other upstart leagues included the American Association in 1882, the Union Association in 1884, and the Players League in 1890. Competition drove each of these rival leagues out of business and led to consolidation of the four strongest teams of the American Association into the National League in 1890.

The biggest challenge to the established National League came in 1901 with the formation of the American League (AL), which raided many of the top players from the "senior circuit." Agreements between the leagues to honor the other league's player contracts allowed them to peacefully coexist and led to the creation in 1903 of the World Series, pitting the champions from each league against each other. The popularity of Major League Baseball (MLB), the moniker for the united American and National Leagues, has risen steadily since its formation, as has the level of cooperation between the leagues, with the formation of the All-Star Game in 1933, the first amateur draft in 1965, and ultimately with interleague play in 1997.

While competition from rival leagues has lessened since its early days, at least three rival leagues have served to fundamentally change the nature of professional baseball. In 1914, the Federal League was formed to challenge Major League Baseball and took the novel approach of suing the established leagues for antitrust violations. Sports leagues present an unusual problem to antitrust experts since for a game to take place, the two competitors must agree to play each other, and in order for a sports league to run smoothly, a great deal of cooperation between teams, who are nominally competitors, must occur. The Federal League was driven out of business, but in *Federal Base Ball Club of Baltimore, Inc. v. National League of Professional Base Ball Clubs et al., 259 U.S. 200 (1922),* the Supreme Court ruled that baseball did not qualify as interstate commerce, as the interstate travel was a "mere incident, not the essential thing." Since the federal antitrust statutes apply only to interstate commerce, as opposed to "purely state affairs," this ruling established the infamous "antitrust exemption" enjoyed by MLB since that time.

Rival leagues also led MLB to expand its national footprint. Prior to 1950, no Major League Baseball teams existed west of St. Louis or south of Washington, D.C., and no team had moved to a new market since the early days of the AL/NL merger. While the 1950s witnessed the first franchise moves since 1903, with the Boston Braves heading to Milwaukee, the Philadelphia Athletics moving to Kansas City, and the Brooklyn Dodgers and New York Giants leaving for the West Coast, the league remained at 16 teams, the same as immediately after the 1901 merger. In 1959, the formation of the Continental League was announced. This eight-team league was designed to expand top-level professional baseball to eight new cities, primarily in the West and South, and to eventually join the AL and NL in Major League Baseball. While the plan for the Continental League never came to fruition, it is generally accepted that MLB expansion in the 1960s from 16 to 24 teams was a direct response to this proposed league. Indeed, by 1971, Major League Baseball had come to five of the eight cities proposed by the Continental League either through expansion or relocation. Additional rounds of expansion in 1977, 1993, and 1998 added two teams each year, bringing the total to 30 teams in the United States and Canada. Unlike the other "big four" sports, franchise relocation has been exceedingly rare in MLB since 1970, due in part to MLB's antitrust exemption, which gave owners the power to prohibit any team's move.

For the first 80 years of professional baseball, African Americans were prohibited from playing in the Major Leagues. Instead, talented black athletes played in the Negro Leagues, which competed concurrently with MLB. In 1947, team owner Branch Rickey signed Negro Leagues star Jackie Robinson to MLB's Brooklyn Dodgers. The success of Robinson and other black players on the field led all MLB teams eventually to integrate; faced with the loss of their best players to MLB, the Negro Leagues largely disappeared by the late 1950s.

Until the 1970s, MLB, like most other sports leagues, operated with a "reserve clause" for its players. The reserve clause bound each player to the team for which he originally signed a contract. The team owned the exclusive rights to the services of that player for the player's entire career unless they released the player or traded the contract to another team. Players wishing for the right to negotiate their own contracts with other teams challenged this system on numerous occasions, culminating with the case of *Curt Flood v. Bowie Kuhn,* the commissioner of MLB, in 1972. While Flood lost his case when the Supreme Court cited the precedent of the 1922 Federal Base Ball decision, his efforts led MLB to adopt a system of arbitration and FREE AGENCY for veteran players. The tension between owners and players did not end with this change, however, as MLB would witness numerous periods of labor strife, including strikes that resulted in the cancellation of numerous games in 1981 and 1994–95.

Most recently MLB, like many other sports, has entered a period in which media revenues have become increasingly important, and a concerted effort has been made to replace aging stadiums with newer facilities, often financed at significant taxpayer expense and designed to provide more amenities and enhance revenue through the sale of luxury box seats.

Football, like many modern sports, has its origins in ancient games. The game was popular enough in the British Isles by the 14th and 15th centuries that Kings Edward III of England and James I of Scotland passed laws to suppress the sport, as it was a distraction from military exercises. As the rules for football became codified in the early 19th century, two versions of the game emerged: rugby football, named after Rugby

School, where its rules were drawn up, in which carrying the ball with the hands was permitted, and association football, also known as soccer from an abbreviation of "association," in which handling the ball was not allowed. The modern game of American football derived from the rugby rules.

The first formally organized game of what would become American football was played between rival universities Princeton and Rutgers in 1869. Collegiate athletes were, and continue to this day to be, amateur players who receive no direct compensation for their performance, although they may receive subsidized tuition for their participation on college teams.

Professional play did not come about until the 1890s, when former Yale All-America guard William (Pudge) Heffelfinger became the first professional football player by accepting $500 from the Allegheny Athletic Association to play in a game against the Pittsburgh Athletic Club in 1892. Five years later, the Latrobe Athletic Association football team became the first club to field an entirely professional lineup. While many professional clubs formed in the first 30 years of professional football, no significant league arose to organize the sport until the creation of the American Professional Football Association in 1920, which brought together in a single organization 10 existing clubs, including the Chicago Cardinals and Decatur Staleys, today's Arizona Cardinals and Chicago Bears, respectively. In 1922, the league changed its name to the National Football League (NFL).

The first 15 years of the league witnessed a great deal of team turnover. Between 1920 and 1935, more than 50 teams played at least one season in the NFL, 43 of them folding or relocating by the end of that era. The teams with the most solid financial bases realized that their own profitability depended on the financial success of the other teams in the league and therefore adopted what became the strongest system of revenue sharing among the "big four" sports leagues. Home teams shared 40 percent of game day rev-

enue with the visiting team, and all broadcast media revenue was evenly shared among all teams in the league. Initial media revenues were small, following the experimental broadcast of the first televised NFL game in 1939, but this revenue stream grew consistently for the next six decades, reaching a record high in 1998 for an eight-year, $17.6-billion national television deal.

As in baseball, rival leagues surfaced periodically to challenge the NFL's dominance, which often resulted in MERGERS or acquisitions. In 1950, the NFL absorbed three franchises of the All-America Football Conference, formed four years earlier. Similarly, the American Football Conference, a 1960 start-up, merged with the NFL in 1966, leading to the first Super Bowl in January 1967. A notable exception to this trend was the case of the United States Football League (USFL). For three seasons from 1982 through 1985, the USFL challenged the NFL for players, fans, and media attention and filed an antitrust suit against the established league. In July of 1986, a month before the league was to begin its first fall season, the USFL won its suit against the NFL but was awarded just one dollar in damages. Faced with mounting debts, the league folded soon after. The NFL has faced less labor strife than other leagues but did suffer strikes in both 1982 and 1985.

Basketball was invented in Springfield, Massachusetts, by James Naismith in 1891 as an alternative indoor winter sport to gymnastics. Like football, basketball was widely played at the collegiate level long before professional leagues became well established. Numerous professional leagues were formed in the first half of the 20th century, including the National Basketball League (NBL) and American Basketball League, but none established itself as a major league until the formation of the 11-team Basketball Association of America (BAA) in 1946. This new league merged with the existing NBL in 1949 and changed its name to the National Basketball Association (NBA). As with the NFL, the early years of the league involved significant instability. By 1954, only eight of the original 23 teams from the NBL and BAA remained, and four of those were to relocate over the next six years.

Like other sports, the NBA faced competition from rival leagues, most notably the American Basketball Association (ABA), which was formed in 1967. The ABA competed somewhat successfully with the NBA for nine years, attracting many of the top stars such as Julius "Dr. J." Erving. Ultimately the league folded in 1976, with the NBA agreeing to accept four of the top ABA franchises.

Perhaps more than any other team sport, basketball has derived its popularity from a small handful of elite players. While the NBA steadily expanded from eight teams in 1954 to 22 teams by 1976 and developed popular players such as Bill Russell and Wilt Chamberlain, the league suffered from the combination of a lack of competitive balance (the Boston Celtics won 11 of 13 league titles between 1956 and 1969) and a reputation as a haven for drug-using athletes. The league began its turnaround in 1979 with the signing of Earvin "Magic" Johnson by the Los Angeles Lakers and Larry Bird by the Boston Celtics. Their rivalry throughout the 1980s as well as the later success of six-time NBA champion Michael Jordan lifted the NBA to record financial success.

Hockey, the smallest of the "big four" sports, is unique in that Canadian teams have had a profound influence on the development of the game in North America. Five Canadian-based teams formed the National Hockey League in 1917 as a reorganization of an existing league. American teams were added to the league in the 1920s, and by 1946, the NHL consisted of the Boston Bruins, Chicago Blackhawks, Detroit Red Wings, Montreal Canadians, New York Rangers, and Toronto Maple Leafs, also known as the "Original Six." The number of teams in the league increased through major expansion in 1967 and through a merger with the rival World Hockey Association in 1979. The 1990s and 2000s saw an increasing number of European players, as the league estab-

lished itself as the world's top hockey league, and the introduction of the NHL into nontraditional markets in the southern and western United States through expansion and the relocation of franchises from Canada and the Northeast.

Other team sports have achieved more limited financial success in North American, including soccer, the most popular team sport in Europe and Latin America. As with other sports, numerous minor professional leagues formed with fleeting success. In 1967, the North American Soccer League (NASL) was formed. The league flourished briefly and signed many well-known international stars, including the Brazilian great, Pele. Overexpansion, a lack of competitive balance, and dearth of home-grown American stars led to the league's demise by 1984. Following their success in hosting the World Cup in 1994, soccer boosters tried again with the formation of Major League Soccer in 1996. Although the league remains in business through 2004, the owners lost in excess of $250 million in the first eight years of the league. Other upstart sports such as lacrosse, arena football, team volleyball, and indoor soccer have realized only minor financial success.

Professionalism is not limited to team sports. Indeed, boxing rivals baseball as the first sport to give rise to the truly professional athlete, and among the first professional sports icons were boxers, such as "Gentleman" Jim Corbett of the 1890s. Historically, huge numbers of fans attended championship bouts. The 1926 Jack Dempsey–Gene Tunney fight attracted a record 145,000 spectators to Chicago's Soldier Field and was heard by an estimated 50 million by radio, the largest radio audience in history to that point. Despite the popularity of such boxing notables as Joe Louis and Muhammad Ali, the sport's popularity began to wane in the second half of the 20th century due to its violent nature, a reputation for corruption and gambling, and a lack of promotional organization.

Tennis and golf have risen over this time period to replace boxing. While competitive tennis has been played since at least the era of the first

Wimbledon championship in 1877, the first professional tennis was played in 1926, when Suzanne Lenglen was paid $50,000 by a promoter to make a professional exhibition tour of the United States. While professional tours and tennis leagues existed for the next 40 years, the age of professional tennis truly arrived in 1968, when the major tournaments such as Wimbledon and the U.S. Open began to accept professional players.

Similarly, golf had a long history as a recreational sport before giving rise to professional players. Indeed, amateur players such as the American Bobby Jones regularly won major tournaments until the 1930s. The Professional Golfers Association (PGA) was formed in 1916 but represented primarily club pros who worked as instructors rather than tournament players who earned their living through prize winnings. The post–World War II period gave way to the first generation of highly successful professional golfers as average PGA tournament prizes rose to more than $10,000 for the first time. Not until Arnold Palmer reached the mark in 1968 did any golfer's career prize earnings exceed $1 million. The increased popularity of the game both as a participatory and a spectator sport, as well as the recent phenomenal attraction of Tiger Woods, has led to huge increases in tournament prizes and player earnings. By the 2000s, top players regularly earned well over $1 million each season in prize money as well as multiples of this in sponsorship earnings. Tiger Woods's $100 million contract signed with Nike in 2000 was the largest endorsement contract in any sport in history and put Woods among the world's highest paid athletes.

Professional athletes also compete, although generally to lesser public appeal and monetary reward, in distance running, track and field, bowling, bicycle racing, beach volleyball, figure skating, downhill skiing, and extreme sports—among other activities.

With the exception of a few notable performers such as multisport star Babe Didrikson Zaharias and figure skater Sonja Henie, professional sports has been historically dominated by men. However, due in part to changing societal norms as well as enforcement of Title IX, which mandated equal athletic opportunities for women at publicly funded educational institutions, female participation in interscholastic sports increased 10-fold at the high school level and five fold at the collegiate level between 1971 and 2002. Growth in women's sports participation has led to some strides in promoting professional sports for women athletes. American success in the 1999 Women's World Cup of soccer led to large crowds and significant media attention as well as a short-lived professional women's league. The Women's National Basketball Association (WNBA) has also attracted modest crowds, although the league remains dependent on subsidies from its parent, the NBA. The Ladies Professional Golfers Association (LPGA) also maintains a successful tour, although with prizes that typically average roughly one-quarter those of the men's PGA tour.

Only in tennis have women achieved a measure of parity with men. Beginning in 1973 with the famous "Battle of the Sexes" in which top female player Billie Jean King defeated the aging former Wimbledon champion Bobby Riggs in the most-watched tennis match in history, tournament purses have steadily risen for women so that, at least at the U.S. and Australian Opens, purses are similar for both sides of the bracket.

Further reading

Fort, Rodney. *Sports Economics*. Englewood, N.J.: Prentice Hall, 2003.

Rader, Benjamin G. *American Sports: From the Age of Folk Games to the Age of Televised Sports*, 5th ed. New York: Pearson Education, 2003.

Riess, Steven A. *Major Problems in American Sport History*. Boston: Houghton Mifflin, 1997.

Victor Matheson

Staggers Rail Act (1980) Legislation passed to deregulate the RAILROADS in order to allow them to compete more freely with other forms of freight traffic. Since the creation of the interstate highway system, beginning in the 1950s, truck haulage had become more popular than railway shipping, and the industry began to lose its appeal as a shipper.

Previous regulations from Washington had curtailed the railroads' ability to flexibly price their rates, causing them to lose money and become outdated. As a result, the act centered around establishing reasonable rates and allowing railroad management to be in charge of the roads rather than regulators. The regulations passed against the railroads 50 years earlier were aiding in the decline of the industry, along with the rise of shipping by truck and by airplane.

Specifically, the Staggers Act allowed railroads to price routes and services differently, reflecting the demand for them rather than using a predetermined formula. It also allowed them to enter into confidential contracts with shippers. The power of the INTERSTATE COMMERCE COMMISSION (later succeeded by the Surface Transportation Board) was also expanded to exempt some rail traffic from REGULATION. It also allowed the railroads greater flexibility when closing unused rail lines or selling them.

As a result of the act, railroad freight revenues began to rise after 1980, and the railroads' financial performance improved. Before it was passed, approximately 25 percent of the nation's rail freight was being carried on bankrupt railroads. Equally, train accidents and employee related injuries declined, and capital expenditures increased. Since the Interstate Commerce Commission (ICC) was created in the 19th century, the railroads had complained about its inflexibility when determining rates. The Staggers Act was passed, somewhat belatedly, to remedy the situation. The ICC itself passed out of existence in 1996, succeeded by the Surface Transportation Board.

The Staggers Act is one of the major pieces of deregulatory legislation passed in the last 20 years of the 20th century. It recognized that rail transportation was losing serious ground to trucking as a major method of freight transportation in the United States.

See also DEREGULATION.

Further reading
Dooley, Frank J., and William E. Thoms. *Railroad Law a Decade after Deregulation.* Westport, Conn.: Greenwood Press, 1994.
United States General Accounting Office. *Railroad Regulation: Economic and Financial Impacts of the Staggers Rail Act of 1980: Report to Congressional Requesters.* Washington, D.C.: U.S. General Accounting Office, 1990.

steel industry In the United States, this industry owes its existence to the invention of the Bessemer process. Before Henry Bessemer's discovery in 1858, steel could be made only in small batches. By blowing air through pig iron to manipulate the amount of impurities, steelmakers could make large amounts of this useful metal, chemically related to iron but much stronger. The engineer Alexander Holley perfected practical Bessemer steelmaking when he designed the Edgar Thomson Steel Works in Pittsburgh, Pennsylvania, for Andrew CARNEGIE's firm in 1875. Because of this technological advantage and its championship of other innovations, Carnegie Steel grew to dominate the industry by out-producing and underselling its competitors. The lockout at Carnegie's Homestead mill in 1892 came to symbolize the declining importance of skilled workers during the industrialization of this and many other industries.

Steel was a vital component of American industrialization. Steel rails produced in the 1870s and 1880s made the railroad boom in the trans-Mississippi west possible. Beginning in the 1880s, steelmakers built large structural shapes that formed the skeletons of large city buildings and pieces of bridges. Later, abundant steel made the spread of automobiles possible. Firms in this industry made steel for screws and razors,

The Carnegie Steel Plant, Homestead, Pennsylvania, 1905 (LIBRARY OF CONGRESS)

stretched steel into wire, molded it into nails, and coated it with tin and sold it as roofing material. In short, the presence of the steel industry was a necessary precursor for many other industries.

J. P. Morgan bought out Carnegie in 1901 and merged Carnegie Steel with his own holdings to form the U.S. STEEL CORP., history's first billion-dollar company. Although U.S. Steel dominated the market for a wide range of steel products, it did not use its power to drive the competition out of business. Instead, it set its prices annually and let other companies gain market share at its expense by charging lower prices. This is why the corporation survived an antitrust suit against it, settled in 1920. Along these same lines, U.S. Steel's first president, Elbert GARY, formed the

American Iron and Steel Institute (AISI) in 1909 to encourage good relations within the industry and prevent destructive competition.

American steelmakers continued to work closely together during the Great Depression under the auspices of the AISI and the National Industrial Recovery Act. In the late 1930s, however, labor relations drove a wedge between U.S. Steel and its largest competitors. Faced with an organizing drive by the Steel Workers Organizing Committee, U.S. Steel recognized the union without a fight in 1937 so that labor strife would not interrupt the company's returning prosperity. Bethlehem Steel, Republic Steel, and other large firms refused to go along until forced to do so by the government during World War II. By the end of the war, an industry that had been almost entirely nonunion since 1892 faced one of the strongest unions in America.

Bad labor relations were one of several reasons for the industry's downfall after World War II. The steel industry faced five nationwide strikes between 1946 and 1959. Each one contributed to a greater wage and benefit bill that made American steel expensive in comparison to foreign competition. The industry was also slow to innovate during the postwar period, holding on to old technologies when firms in other countries had built more-productive mills using recent innovations. Because of foreign competition, American steel companies closed plants and laid off workers by the thousands during the 1970s and 1980s in an effort to remain profitable in a new economic environment. Many of the towns where these plants were located, such as Youngstown, Ohio, and Homestead, Pennsylvania, have yet to fully recover.

Recently a new kind of steel company has emerged in the United States. Minimills are erected by small firms that recycle scrap steel by melting it down in electric furnaces. The resulting product is less expensive than new steel and competitive with foreign steel because these companies tend to ship only to local markets and tend to operate on a nonunion basis. At present, minimills produce approximately one-third of the steel made in the United States and represent the only new capacity in the market since the 1960s.

See also MORGAN, JOHN PIERPONT; SCHWAB, CHARLES M.

Further reading

Hogan, William T. *Economic History of the Iron and Steel Industry in the United States.* 5 vols. Lexington, Mass.: Lexington Books, 1971.

Misa, Thomas. *A Nation of Steel: The Making of Modern America.* Baltimore: Johns Hopkins University Press, 1995.

Tiffany, Paul. *The Decline of the American Steel Industry: How Management, Labor, and Government Went Wrong.* New York: Oxford University Press, 1988.

Jonathan Rees

Stetson, John B. (1830–1906) *hat manufacturer* Born in Orange, New Jersey, Stetson had little formal education and suffered from various ailments in his youth. As a result, he traveled West in an attempt to restore his health. While traveling to Pike's Peak, he designed a shelter tent from a design he had learned from his father, a master hat maker, and later designed a hat in the same manner, made of felt. He sold the hat to a local cattle driver in Central City, Colorado, for $5 and began a tradition of hat making that made him famous.

Returning to the East, he used $100 to establish himself in Philadelphia in 1865 in rented quarters and slowly began designing a hat based on his original design. He originally called it "Boss of the Plains," intending that it would protect the wearer from the elements. The hat became known as the "ten-gallon" hat, and its popularity quickly outstripped his ability to manufacture them. Building upon his early success, he formed the John B. Stetson Company, and it soon became the largest manufacturer of hats in the world.

His hats were worn by many western personalities, including General George Custer, and soon became identified with the American cowboy and the West. The traveling shows of people such as Buffalo Bill Cody and Annie Oakley also made the hat popular and provided much advertising for the design. Although the company manufactured many other styles, the Stetson hat became the symbol of the company and, like the Colt revolver, made its originator a household name forever linked with the West and frontier life. Although he is most often associated with the ten-gallon hat, Stetson made dozens of styles of hats for various occasions, both formal and informal.

Stetson was a generous contributor throughout his life to Baptist causes. He endowed the DeLand University in Florida, and in 1889, it changed its name to Stetson University. The company continues as a successful hatmaker and today is headquartered in St. Joseph, Missouri.

Its hats are bought for both practical and nostalgic reasons since the ten-gallon hat has come to be a long-lasting symbol of the American West.

Further reading
Christian, Mary B. *Hats off to John B. Stetson.* New York: Macmillan, 1992.
Snyder, Jeffrey B. *Stetson Hats and the John B. Stetson Company, 1865—1970.* Philadelphia: Schiffer Publishing, 2000.

Stevens, John (1749–1838) *inventor and engineer* Born in New York City, Stevens graduated from Kings College (today Columbia University) in 1768. His father was a ship owner and merchant who had extensive land holdings in New Jersey. After graduating from college, he spent three years studying law but never practiced. Stevens would later serve as treasurer of New Jersey during the Revolutionary War and collected money for the Continental Army in New Jersey.

Around 1788 he became interested in the development of a steamboat, and he immersed himself in the design of boilers and a steam engine. He was also instrumental in launching the first U.S. patent office, chartered by Congress in 1790. He was one of the first recipients of a patent from the bureau, for a boiler and a steam engine. In 1797, he joined with Robert LIVINGSTON and Nicholas Roosevelt in developing a steamboat that could provide ferry service in and around New York Harbor. Despite a partnership agreement between them, Livingston took up the ambassadorship to France in 1801 and afterward allied himself with Robert FULTON in operating steamboats around New York Harbor and on the Hudson River. Livingston obtained the exclusive rights to operate a steamboat service in and around New York, a monopoly that eventually was overturned in the case of *Gibbons v. Ogden.* Robert Fulton began steamboat service to Albany, and the two services omitted Stevens, who instead sent his latest boat to Philadelphia, becoming the world's first ocean-going steamboat. The boat, the *Phoenix*, began a regular service between Trenton and Philadelphia.

Before the War of 1812, Stevens turned his attention to applying the steam engine to railways. He helped persuade the New Jersey state legislature to create a state railway line in 1815, and eight years later he was commissioned by the Pennsylvania legislature to build one for that state. The state did not have ample resources to make the venture successful, however, and Stevens turned to developing an experimental steam locomotive that he ran on his estate in Hoboken, New Jersey. It was the first American attempt at steam locomotion.

Stevens was also ahead of his time by proposing several other engineering innovations that would take some years to reach fruition. He proposed an elevated rail system for New York City, a tunnel under the Hudson River, and armored naval ships to replace those made of wood. One of his sons, Robert Stevens, invented the T-rail, the standard form of railroad track used throughout the world. Another son, Edwin, helped develop ironclad battleships for the navy. When he died in 1838, Edwin's will provided for an engineering institute to be founded in Hoboken bearing the family name, which today is the Stevens Institute of Technology.

See also VANDERBILT, CORNELIUS.

Further reading
Morrison, John H. *History of American Steam Navigation.* New York: Stephen Daye Press, 1958.
Turnbull, Archibald Douglas. *John Stevens: An American Record.* New York: Century, 1928.

Stewart, Martha (1941–) *entertainment executive* Martha Kostyra was born in Jersey City, New Jersey, on August 3, 1941, the daughter of a pharmaceutical salesman. At an early age she displayed aptitude for cooking and gardening, traits that carried over into her adult life. Kostyra attended Barnard College in New York City and supported herself by modeling. After graduating in 1963 with a degree in art, she married a Yale law student, Andrew Stewart. Stewart then settled into the lifestyle of a young wife and mother until she grew restless and began looking for moneymaking ventures. In 1968, she became a stock broker on Wall Street, amassed a small fortune, and bought an old house in Westport, Connecticut. After spending several years renovating it, Stewart—who loved to cook—turned her attention to the gourmet catering business in 1976. She proved phenomenally successful and by 1979 employed a full-time staff with an annual budget of $1 million. She also began acquiring a national reputation by authoring articles on food in the *New York Times* and columns in various magazines. The turning point in her career happened in 1980, when she was approached by Crown Publishing to write about recipes and decor. The resulting book, *Martha Stewart's Entertaining,* was an overnight success that sold 600,000 copies and rendered her a nationally recognized authority on homemaking.

Stewart followed up on her publishing success by releasing a score of equally successful titles on gardening, fashion, and interior decorating. She was also contracted to appear in various television shows and videos. Stewart became such a household icon that in 1987 she signed on as an official spokesperson for the K-Mart chain of retail stores. In this capacity she was allowed to design and market her own line of signature towels, sheets, and other domestic impedimenta under the K-Mart label. However, the toll of too many hours of work resulted in her divorce in 1990. Divested of household concerns, Stewart devoted her considerable energies into establishing her own commercial empire. In 1990, she commenced publishing *Martha Stewart Living,* a glossy bimonthly magazine, through the auspices of Time-Warner, Inc. Its circulation peaked at 2.1 million subscribers by 1997 and also gave rise to a weekly syndicated television program with an audience of 5 million viewers.

By 1997, Stewart was well positioned to officially proffer herself as America's "diva of domesticity" through the establishment of Martha Stewart Living Omnimedia. She was both chairperson and the company's leading trademark. This was a large, multifaceted corporation promoting Stewart's products, advice, and—above all—her carefully guarded reputation as an exacting perfectionist. It is estimated that revenues from her line of K-Mart products, media programming, personal Web site, and publications approached the $1-billion mark, establishing Stewart as the most successful female entrepreneur in history. She clearly reveled in her role as America's most recognizable symbol of both good taste and the good life. However, her reputation was sullied in 2002 when the government accused her of insider trading on Wall Street—a potential felony. Government prosecutors maintain that Stewart—acting on the advice of her broker—illegally sold off several thousand shares of ImClone, a failing biochemical interest, before their value declined. Stewart vigorously and vociferously denied all allegations and professed her innocence. But in June 2003, the government announced its intention to prosecute Stewart on felony charges. Such bad publicity exerted a negative impact on her business empire, and she was summarily dropped as a K-Mart spokesperson. In March 2004, a jury found Stewart guilty, and she was sentenced to five months in prison and five months in home confinement, along with having to pay a $30,000 fine. As a result of the guilty conviction, Viacom pulled *Martha Stewart Living* from its television lineup. That same month Stewart resigned from the board of Martha Stewart Omnimedia. In October 2004 Stewart reported to a minimum security prison to serve her five-month sentence. An additional five months of home confinement ended in August 2005. Her current projects include two new television series.

Further reading

Bryon, Christopher. *Martha, Inc.: The Incredible Story of Martha Stewart Living Omnimedia.* New York: Wiley, 2002.

Connor, Tom, and Jim Downey. *Martha, Really and Cruelly: My True Life Story.* Kansas City, Mo.: Andrews McMeel, 2003.

Meachum, Virginia. *Martha Stewart, Successful Busi-nesswoman.* Springfield, N.J.: Enslow Publishers, 1998.

John C. Fredriksen

stock markets Markets where the shares of existing companies are traded. In the United States, there are two types of stock market: organized exchanges with central locations such as the NEW YORK STOCK EXCHANGE (NYSE), and over-the-counter markets such as the NATIONAL ASSOCIATION OF SECURITIES DEALERS Automated Quotations (NASDAQ) system, a market where stocks trade on a centrally linked computer system between dealers. Technically, centrally located markets are called exchanges, while the NASDAQ, due to its widespread character, is referred to as a market only.

The New York Stock Exchange is the country's oldest market, dating to an agreement made among traders in 1792. It was not until 1817, when the market moved indoors and renamed itself the New York Stock and Exchange Board, that it began to take on a structure that would be recognized today. One of the most significant developments of the 19th century was the introduction of the TICKER TAPE to instantly report trades as they were made, greatly adding to information flow.

The second-largest exchange, the AMERICAN STOCK EXCHANGE, began in 1953, after changing its name from the New York Curb Exchange. Until 1921, the curb had been an outdoor market, conducted around the intersection of Broad and Wall Streets in lower Manhattan. Other exchanges also developed in Philadelphia, Los Angeles, Boston, and Chicago and were referred to as REGIONAL STOCK EXCHANGES. They all adopted the same sort of selling system used by the NYSE—namely, a specialist system for auctioning stocks.

In a specialist system, one floor trader is designated as the specialist and devotes his time to maintaining a market price for the stock(s)

under his aegis. Other traders on the floor of the exchange trade with him for their customers. The "book" of that stock's prices is constantly maintained by the specialist, who is charged with maintaining orderly trading in the stock. In the NASDAQ environment, a central location is not possible, but various dealers around the country are designated as "market makers." They are responsible for making and maintaining prices in those stocks and are linked by a central computer, which, in effect, is the market.

Stock market performance traditionally has been viewed as either a bull or bear market. The term bull market is given to strong performing financial markets, in which prices continue in an upward trend. Although the exact origin of the term is not known, it is generally assumed to refer to the running of bulls, whereby investors tend to follow each other in bidding prices up, especially in the stock market. Certain periods in stock exchange history have been characterized as bull markets, while others, in which prices tend to fall and stay depressed for relatively long periods of time, are referred to as bear markets.

Since World War I, bull markets have occurred in the 1920s, 1950s, and 1960s when the stock indexes all rose substantially. After the inflationary period of the 1970s and early 1980s, another bull market began in 1982 and continued well into the late 1990s, interrupted by a market drop in 1987. In many cases, the markets ended with major scandals on Wall Street, acting as preludes to the bear markets that followed. Both terms still form a strong part of market folklore and are commonly cited in the press, although advances in stock price reporting and the rapid transmission of news allow more technical analysis of the trends that the terms represent.

Bear markets usually follow periods of strength in market indexes and lead to lower asset prices. As a result, previous market highs usually are not reached again for a relatively long period of time. Traditionally, in a bear market, prices fall about 20 percent from their previous levels, affecting investor confidence and the number of new stock issues coming to market as well. The term *bear* derives from traders of the 19th century who were said to be bears because they "tore" open the markets by clawing at them through short-selling, or selling stocks they did not own hoping that the prices would drop so that they could purchase them at a lower price. Increased short-selling forced prices down and caused the markets to lose confidence, leading to prolonged periods of depressed prices and slow economic activity.

Since the Civil War, bear markets have been evident in 1869, 1873, 1893, 1907 and the period following the stock market crash in 1929, when prices remained depressed until the end of World War II in 1945. Recently the late 1970s and early 1980s as well as the period following the stock market collapse in 1987, were also considered bear markets. After the Internet bubble of the late 1990s collapsed, the stock markets again entered a bear phase, fueled by a drop in corporate earnings, accounting scandals, and several Wall Street scandals. Today the phenomenon is no longer primarily the product of short-selling or wild market speculation by unregulated traders but is indicative of the aftermath of a rapid increase in prices whereby high stock valuations cannot be maintained in the face of falling profitability or productivity.

The markets changed dramatically when the Securities Exchange Act was passed in 1934. The new law enabled the Securities and Exchange Commission (SEC) to enforce more equitable practices on the exchanges, eliminating many abuses of the past. One of the most notable was the prohibition against insider trading, the term given to someone who sells securities using information obtained from someone in a company who is in possession of financial or other important information not available to the general public. Gains made from such trades are illegal and subject the trader to penalties and prosecution. The SEC rules are intended to make the process of trading securities as transparent as possible, meaning that no one should have access to information at the expense of others.

Several subsequent SEC rules changed the way the markets did business. One of the most fundamental involved margin trading. Margin trading is the practice of buying securities or commodity futures contracts with borrowed money. The term means the amount of money loaned against the purchase. Margin is extended to investors by brokers, although the amount that can be loaned in the securities markets is governed by the FEDERAL RESERVE, by authority given to it in the SECURITIES EXCHANGE ACT OF 1934.

Before the Fed was given the authority to set margin rates, brokers had sole discretion to determine how much a customer could borrow. In some cases, they would loan up to 90 percent of a security's value. In many stock market falls, margin played a large role since, if customers were unable to make up the losses incurred by a loss in value, the securities in their accounts could be automatically sold to prevent further loss. The fall in the stock index during the Crash of 1929 was exacerbated by forced margin selling. As a result, the matter of setting margin rates was given to the central bank rather than continuing to be discretionary on the part of brokers.

Since 1974, margin has been set at 50 percent, although it has ranged as high as 100 percent in 1946 and 90 percent in 1958 and 1962. The rate has been increased when the Federal Reserve wanted to limit the amount of speculation in the stock market, although margin was not raised during the 1990s stock market bubble. At the time, some brokerages did raise the margins they required on certain speculative stocks. They are allowed to do so by NYSE and NASDAQ regulations, since all exchanges may impose margin requirements of their own as long as they do not conflict with those set by regulators.

The amount of money loaned by brokers for margin trading is often studied to determine how much speculation is occurring in the various markets. During the stock market rises in the 1920s, late 1950s, 1960s, 1987, and again in the late 1990s, margin levels rose substantially as speculation increased dramatically in the markets.

Another widespread practice in the markets that was substantially changed by the SEC was the matter of short-selling. In the securities markets, short-selling occurs when a trader sells a stock he does not own with the intention of buying it at a later date at a lower price. The difference between the prices is his profit. In order to sell short, the securities must be borrowed from another investor who loans them for the occasion. When the purchase eventually is made, the bought securities are returned to the lender and the transaction is complete.

On the stock exchanges, short-selling has existed almost from the beginning of the exchanges, and selling short was often associated with bears, those investors who believed a stock's price was going to fall and wanted to profit. Before the Civil War, short-selling was best exemplified by the activities of Jacob Little and Daniel Drew, two notorious bears who made a living by forcing down the price of stocks.

After the Crash of 1929, a great deal of short-selling occurred on the stock exchanges as traders took advantage of falling prices, eliciting criticism from many quarters. As a result, the practice was regulated by the Securities Exchange Act of 1934, which made it illegal to short on a downtick, that is, to sell a stock as prices were constantly falling. The futures exchanges also implemented their own procedures that controlled the process to an extent.

One of the regulators' greatest contributions to the integrity of the stock markets has been defining insider trading. The term insider trading also applies to employees and officers of a company who may have access to this sort of information. Usually, this is referred to as "insider activity." Occasionally, when these employees sell stock in their company, they are required to report the transaction to the SEC, and it becomes a matter of public record and is published in the financial pages of the major financial newspapers.

In response to a Wall Street crisis beginning in the late 1960s, Congress acted to preserve the integrity of the marketplace. The Securities Investor Protection Corp. (SIPC) was a government sponsored private company created by the Securities Investor Protection Act of 1970. The corporation acts as an insurance company protecting securities held in customer accounts at broker/dealers registered with the Securities Exchange Commission. The insurance protects the securities themselves, not their market value.

The law creating SIPC was passed in response to a Wall Street crisis that began in the late 1960s. Increased volume on the stock markets created a backlog at many securities firms, which were unable to keep abreast of the buy and sell transactions. Subsequently, many orders were improperly recorded or not recorded at all, and many others were the subject of fraud and theft. Several dozen securities houses were forced to close their doors as a result, and several major Wall Street houses absorbed the accounts of customers at the failed firms. Congress then passed the act in order to ensure the integrity of trading on the exchanges and to reassure customers that the securities in their accounts were safe.

The SIPC was the securities market's version of deposit insurance as originally provided to bank depositors by the FEDERAL DEPOSIT INSURANCE CORPORATION. Accounts were insured to protect cash and securities held in them but not the market value of the securities themselves. The fund helped restore the integrity of Wall Street after one of its worst internal crises and led to rapid computerization at securities firms, vital to their survival as market volume continued to increase from year to year. In the 1980s and 1990s, SIPC insurance became as common as deposit insurance at banks and must be displayed by member firms on their advertisements.

The markets taken as a whole have increased both in volume and the number of stocks traded over the years. Both the NYSE and the NASDAQ now regularly record days of 1 billion shares traded or more. Since the market collapse of 1987, the NYSE has implemented a circuit breaker that effectively halts trading temporarily if the market index should fall precipitously. The smaller regional exchanges have lost volume and business to the larger exchanges, which have had more money to invest for increasingly expensive computers and communications equipment. The NASDAQ and the Amex merged in 1998, bringing the two types of marketplace under one umbrella. The merger did not prove successful, however, and the American Stock Exchange was sold to a private investor group in 2003.

In the late 1990s, another type of market came into existence. Several ECNs, or electronic communication networks, began trading stocks after the other markets closed. These are virtual trading markets where business may be done only by computer over a Web site. These markets are still in an early stage of development.

Further reading

Cowing, Cedric. *Populists, Plungers, and Progressives: A Social History of Stock and Commodity Speculation.* Princeton, N.J.: Princeton University Press, 1965.

Geisst, Charles R. *Wall Street: A History.* New York: Oxford University Press, 1997.

Sobel, Robert. *NYSE: A History of the New York Stock Exchange, 1935–1975.* New York: Weybright & Talley, 1975.

Strong, Benjamin (1872–1928) *banker and central banker* Strong was born in Fishkill-on-Hudson, New York. At age 19, he began working for a private New York bank, later switching to a trust company. Joining the J. P. Morgan & Company-affiliated Bankers Trust Company as secretary in 1904, Strong rose rapidly and became its president in 1914. The Panic of 1907 convinced Strong of the imperative need to implement national monetary reform and to establish a U.S. central bank empowered to manage the currency and to promote American financing of the country's foreign trade. With other prominent New York bankers he lobbied for this objective, from 1910 working with prominent senators and congressmen to pass the requisite legislation, which eventually resulted in the 1913 Federal Reserve Act.

Despite serious reservations regarding the decentralized nature of the Federal Reserve System thereby established and what he considered its excessive exposure to undesirable political influence, in 1914 the pragmatic Strong became first governor of the New York Federal Reserve Bank, remaining so until his death. Under his dominant leadership the New York institution swiftly attained the unofficial status of primus inter pares among the system's 12 regional banks, usually overshadowing the supposedly preeminent Washington-based board of governors. Staunchly pro-Allied in World War I, Strong backed credit and loan policies that effectively facilitated British and French access to U.S. funds to finance their war effort against Germany.

Wartime correspondence he opened with the Bank of England and Banque de France betokened the prominence international activities quickly assumed in Strong's vision of the Federal Reserve System. In the 1920s, Strong worked closely with Governor Montagu Norman of the Bank of England to implement a systematic currency stabilization program embracing most major European countries, backed by loans from private American bankers and, on occasion, Federal Reserve credits; efforts both men believed vital to the postwar restoration of prosperity. In the mid-1920s, Strong acquiesced in Great Britain's return to gold at an overly high rate against the dollar, to facilitate which he deliberately left U.S. interest rates substantially lower than their British counterparts. Some, though by no means all, economic historians later argued that his policies helped to precipitate not just Britain's subsequent economic difficulties, but also the United States' speculative boom and succeeding slump of the mid- to late 1920s, thereby impelling the Great Depression.

Strong's death in 1928 deprived the Federal Reserve System of its most forceful figure just as the coming economic crisis began to gather strength. The absence of equally decisive leadership during the Great Depression was one factor behind mid-1930s banking legislation designed to strengthen the central Federal Reserve Board vis-à-vis the regional banks.

See also FEDERAL RESERVE.

Further reading

Chandler, Lester V. *Benjamin Strong, Central Banker.* Washington, D.C.: Brookings Institution, 1958.

Wueschner, Silvano A. *Charting Twentieth-Century Monetary Policy: Herbert Hoover and Benjamin Strong, 1917–1927.* Westport, Conn.: Greenwood Press, 1999.

Priscilla Roberts

Sutter's Mill   The name John Augustus Sutter (1803–80) became synonymous in the pre–Civil War era with the vast wealth and opportunity associated with the California gold rush. Ironically, Sutter suffered great losses due to the discovery of gold on his property near Sacramento. A pioneer, Sutter obtained possession of great tracts of land only to see them slip away through his own carelessness and bad judgment and the dishonesty of others. While never destitute, he spent his later years trying to recoup at least a fraction of his lost wealth.

Before coming to the United States, Sutter was a Swiss citizen and served in the Swiss army. Leaving behind a wife and three children, he ventured to the United States in 1834. After stops in other parts of the country, he finally arrived in Mexican California at San Francisco by ship in July 1839. With the help of Indians, he established the fortified colony of New Helvetia at the junction of the American and Sacramento Rivers. Sutter acquired a large estate through a land grant from Governor Micheltorena in 1845. The establishment of U.S. rule over California brought even greater wealth to Sutter. Curiously, his prospects dimmed when James Marshall, a millwright and Sutter's partner, found evidence of gold on Sutter's property in January 1848. Ambivalent from the start about the discovery, Sutter intended to keep the whole matter a secret, at least for the time being. However, the temptation to share information about the strike was too great. Sutter was torn between his commitment to agriculture and the allure of the precious mineral. By May 1848, reports of the gold strike had spread widely, and Sutter discovered his gristmill workers had left their jobs to search for gold. The hapless Sutter, meanwhile, had little success finding gold and even less success keeping what he did find.

As stories of his great wealth spread, Sutter became the target of multitudes of sharpers. Many of the people who flocked to the area pillaged his property and possessions. The hungry simply slaughtered his cattle, his crops were overrun, and virtually anything that could be carted away disappeared. In the fall of 1848 Sutter's son August arrived, but he was no more of a match for swindlers than his father. With virtually no established law enforcement, the Sutters were left to their own highly inadequate devices. Squatters evaded the Sutters' attempts to run them off and killed livestock as they pleased. In the midst of this chaos, Sutter served as a delegate to the state constitutional convention, after which he offered himself as a candidate for governor. He finished third in the election, garnering just over 2,000 votes. His wife and remaining offspring arrived soon after the gubernatorial election and were disappointed that Sutter had lost. By the mid-1850s, Sutter had been stripped of most of his land. Always a boaster, he bragged even about the great extent of his losses.

Sutter gained at least some status in February 1853, when the California legislature made him a major general in the California militia. While performing the honorary duties of this office, his property continued to be taken from him, and judicial decisions failed to uphold his land claims. His economic troubles, while probably not the cause, certainly contributed to his consumption of alcohol. Sutter's economic decline continued into the 1860s, and in 1864, the state legislature established a fund of $15,000 to be paid to him in monthly amounts of $250 for five years. The final blow came in 1865, when a disgruntled vagrant set fire to Hock Farm, Sutter's home. Sutter and his wife lost nearly all their possessions.

Five months after the fire, Sutter and his wife sailed for the East, never to return to California. With the assistance of Colonel William H. Russell, Sutter endeavored to gain reimbursement for his losses, alleging that an ineffective court system in 1848 and 1849 had failed to protect his property from illegal encroachments. Pursuant to this, Sutter and his wife, Anna, went to Washington, D.C., in December 1865. The Senate Claims Committee, while rejecting the basis for the claim, nevertheless recommended that Sutter be awarded funds from the sale of property to which he had once established ownership. However, Congress took no action. Sutter continued to push his claim during subsequent congressional sessions. When not suffering from bouts of rheumatism, Sutter enjoyed Washington social life and actively pursued the support of legislators. Many noted Americans, including General William Tecumseh Sherman and Mark Twain, assisted Sutter by writing letters on his behalf to Congress.

At the conclusion of the 1870–71 session, Sutter, tiring of life in Washington hotels, moved to Lititz, Pennsylvania, where he lived comfortably. He continued to receive the California allowance, which was renewed for an additional four years. He received other small annuities, and his son August also offered assistance. In 1876, when Sutter was 76 years old, historian Hubert H. Bancroft came to Lititz to question him about his California experiences. Bancroft noticed that Sutter was wearing a ring made from the first gold discovered in California that fateful winter of 1848. The historian was not kind to Sutter in his account of California history. Bancroft saw the old man as a minor figure who deserved little credit for the development of the state and merited little sympathy for his personal downfall. Sutter, health permitting, took part in reunions of the Associated Pioneers of the Territorial Days of California and was elected president at the 1878 meeting. In 1879, Sutter was so

racked with rheumatism that he could not attend the Associated Pioneers meeting. To add to his misery, Congress once more declined to act on his claim.

Hope arose once again the following year as Senator Daniel Voorhees sponsored a joint resolution to grant Sutter $50,000. After initial high hopes, the measure fell victim to an early adjournment in an election year. Hearing the news, Sutter fell into a deep depression and died in a Washington, D.C., hotel.

See also MINING INDUSTRY.

Further reading
Brands, H. W. *The Age of Gold: The California Gold Rush and the New American Dream.* New York: Doubleday, 2002.
Dillon, Richard. *Fool's Gold: The Decline and Fall of Captain John Sutter of California.* New York: Coward-McCann, 1967.

Glenn Utter

swap market   A large, over-the-counter market developed in the late 1970s and early 1980s, conducted between commercial and investment banks and (mostly) corporate customers. Customers trade swaps with dealers, which agree to exchange cash flows, currencies, or commodity-based payments with the customers for a specific period of time. The swap contracts are irrevocable and cannot be sold to a third party, being similar in this respect to a forward contract. Swaps are the latest development in the derivatives markets, which also include options and futures trading.

Swaps became popular products offered by banks after the debt crisis in the developing countries in the 1980s. Banks realized that offering swap trading abilities for their customers did not require additional capital and that they could trade them in a relatively unregulated atmosphere. As a result, swap trading among banks and their customers exploded.

Swap trading quickly developed into one of the largest financial markets in the 20th century, partly due to the way swaps are counted. When two parties swap interest payments on $100 million, it is the principal amount that is counted rather than the actual amount of money that changes hands. This tends to make the market appear larger than it really is because the principal amounts outstanding rapidly reached the $1 trillion level in the early 1990s and continued to grow. But the market is still substantial by most measures and widely used by corporate treasurers as well as others to manage their cash flows and hedge liabilities. Those liabilities are recorded by the banks as off-balance sheet, or contingent, liabilities and have become the subject of concern among regulators because the market is essentially unregulated and private— the record of a swap is private and is not normally made public.

Swap agreements played a pivotal role in the BANKRUPTCY of Orange County, California, and in financial difficulties in other municipalities in the early and mid-1990s. Many of these municipalities entered into intricate swap arrangements with swap dealers unaware of the risks they faced. Some entered into the arrangements on their own, while others joined a pool of swap investments run by larger municipalities. Orange County ran one of these pool arrangements before it collapsed.

Swaps are overseen by the International Swap and Derivatives Association (ISDA), a trade group. Within the last 10 years there has been substantial movement to adequately account for them on balance sheets according to GENERALLY ACCEPTED ACCOUNTING STANDARDS. The private nature of swaps can present problems to regulators who often attempt to discover the liabilities of a firm or government entity only to find that swap arrangements can be difficult to detect. ENRON CORPORATION is a case in point.

See also FUTURES MARKETS, INVESTMENT BANKING.

Further reading

Flavell, Richard. *Swaps and Other Instruments*. New York: John Wiley & Sons, 2002.

Joiron, Philippe. *Big Bets Gone Bad: Derivatives and Bankruptcy in Orange County*. San Diego: Academic Press, 1995.

T

Taft-Hartley Act Labor legislation passed by Congress in 1947, officially called the Labor-Management Relations Act. Sponsored by Senator Robert Alphonso Taft of Ohio and Representative Fred Allan Hartley of New Jersey, the act amended many provisions of the earlier NATIONAL LABOR RELATIONS ACT of 1935, or Wagner Act, a law that regulated the labor relations of businesses engaged in interstate commerce.

The act enlarged the powers of the National Labor Relations Board and required either unions or employers to file notice of any intent to terminate a collective bargaining agreement, and also give notice to government mediation services. For its part, the federal government was given the power to obtain an injunction if negotiations broke down between parties and if it judged that the strike endangered public health or safety.

The government was empowered to obtain an 80-day injunction against any strike that it determined to be a threat to national health or safety. The act also prohibited jurisdictional strikes between two unions over which should act as the bargaining agent for employees and secondary boycotts against an already organized company doing business with another company that a union was trying to organize. In addition, the law did not extend protection to workers on wildcat strikes, outlawed the closed shop, and permitted the union shop only if a majority of the employees agreed. In addition, the law prohibited union officials from being Communists.

Originally, President Harry Truman vetoed the act, but nevertheless it has stood the test of time. John L. LEWIS also initially opposed it. Generally, its most popular and often used power was the government's ability to call for a cooling-off period if negotiations failed and a strike was scheduled. Use of the law declined in the 1980s and 1990s as the labor movement itself became less powerful in calling strikes and work actions.

Further reading

Lee, R. Alton. *Truman & Taft Hartley: A Question of Mandate* Lexington: University Press of Kentucky, 1966.

Millis, Harry, and Emily Clark Brown. *From the Wagner Act to Taft-Hartley: A Study of National Labor Policy and Labor Relations*. Chicago: University of Chicago Press, 1961.

tariffs   Taxes imposed on the import of foreign goods. Traditionally, they have been enacted to protect segments of the domestic economy from foreign competition or to raise revenues. Tariffs have existed in one form or other since the late 18th century. The power to enact tariffs is found in the Constitution and is invested solely in the federal government, not the states.

Congress raised tariffs in 1828 in order to protect the New England manufacturing industry, triggering a constitutional crisis. When tariffs again were raised in 1832, the South Carolina assembly declared them null and void, fearing they would lead to retaliation against American agricultural exports. This led to a states' rights confrontation between South Carolina and the administration of Andrew Jackson. Higher tariffs were also enacted during the Civil War and remained in effect until World War I. They were raised again in the 1920s by Republicans, mainly through the Fordney-McCumber tariff and the HAWLEY-SMOOT TARIFF ACT. The latter especially allowed the president to impose tariffs on imports of foreign goods that had a price advantage over those produced domestically, thereby eliminating any such advantage. Both tariffs contributed to the depression of the 1930s. After Franklin D. Roosevelt was elected president, the Reciprocal Trade Agreements Act of 1934 was passed, enabling the president to negotiate lower tariffs with the country's major trading partners.

After World War II, 23 of the leading industrial nations signed the General Agreement on Tariffs and Trade (GATT). The agreement called for trading nations to act multilaterally rather than unilaterally when considering tariffs. It was analogous to the agreement signed at Bretton Woods, New Hampshire, which required signatory nations to the International Monetary Fund to act multilaterally when considering currency devaluation or revaluation. After 1995, the GATT was incorporated into the World Trade Organization (WTO). In the 1960s, Congress passed the Trade Expansion Act, which prompted GATT to reduce tariffs on heavy equipment and machin-ery and chemicals and led to a favorable U.S. trade balance in the years that followed.

Also in the 1960s, Congress passed the Interest Equalization Act (IET), one of the few tariffs ever assessed against intangibles such as foreign securities issued in the United States. Similar to the Hawley-Smoot tariff, it allowed the executive branch to impose a tariff that would dissuade investors from purchasing foreign securities issued in the United States if they presented an advantage over American securities.

In the 1970s, the United States engaged in a series of voluntary agreements whereby foreign competitors agreed to limit their exports to the United States. The Japanese agreement to limit export of automobiles to the United States in 1981 was one example of this policy. In 1988, Congress passed the Omnibus Trade and Competitiveness Act, which gave the president powers to regulate trade, including voluntary quotas, subsidies to domestic exporters, and voluntary restraints. In the same year, the United States and Canada created the NORTH AMERICAN FREE TRADE AGREEMENT (NAFTA), which Mexico joined in 1994, forming the world's largest geographical free-trade zone.

Further reading

Dobson, John M. *Two Centuries of Tariffs: The Background and Emergence of the U.S. International Trade Commission.* Washington, D.C.: U.S. International Trade Commission, 1976.

Eckes, Alfred E. *Opening America's Market: U.S. Foreign Trade Policy Since 1776.* Chapel Hill: University of North Carolina Press, 1995.

Taussig, F. W. *Tariff History of the United States.* New York: Capricorn Books, 1964.

Wolman, Paul. *Most Favored Nation: The Republican Revisionists and U.S. Tariff Policy, 1897–1912.* Chapel Hill: University of North Carolina Press, 1992.

Tax Reform Act (1986)   A major overhaul of the INCOME TAX code passed during the administration of Ronald Reagan. The act had three main parts: simplification of the tax code, a reduction in tax rates, and the elimination of special treatment for capital gains. The law was the first attempt in decades to make tax more equitable, to level the playing field for both corporations and individuals.

By simplifying the tax code, fewer exemptions were allowed, in theory broadening the tax base. Those laws that remained were simplified to make them more understandable. More specifically, the top tax rate on individuals was reduced from 50 percent to 28 percent. The marginal rates for less wealthy taxpayers were also reduced. The law also changed depreciation schedules and eliminated tax credits on depreciable assets. Importantly, for individuals the deduction for contributing to an individual retirement account (IRA) was eliminated for those in the high marginal tax brackets. Also, tax shelter benefits were eliminated from real estate investments.

The act also changed deductions for interest payments on individual tax returns. Deductions were limited to interest expenses paid on mortgages on primary and secondary homes. Deductions paid on consumer interest not attached to mortgage payments, such as credit card interest, were eliminated. The law also affected the tax exclusion traditionally associated with some municipal bonds, and caused major changes in the municipal bond market as a result. Municipal bonds now had to meet an acid test to determine the use of funds raised. If they could not clearly be shown as being for the use of a municipality, they could not be classified as municipal bonds. Equally, some forms of interest rate arbitrage previously allowed municipalities that raised municipal bonds and then sought higher yielding TREASURY BONDS, were closed.

Since the act was passed, changes have been made that increase the top earned income tax rate and reinstate a preferential rate for capital gains and losses. When the act was passed, it was hoped that it would simplify tax laws and fairness. But subsequent events, such as the continuing federal budget deficit in the early 1990s and the bull market that followed, necessitated changes that could not be foreseen in the mid-1980s. However, the act remains a significant attempt to overhaul the tax laws in the name of simplicity and fairness.

Further reading
Birnbaum, Jeffrey, and Alan Murray. *Showdown at Gucci Gulch: Lawmakers, Lobbyists, and the Unlikely Triumph of Tax Reform*. New York: Random House, 1987.
Slemrod, Joel, ed. *Do Taxes Matter?: The Impact of the Tax Reform Act of 1986*. Boston: MIT Press, 1991.

Taylor, Frederick Winslow (1856–1915) *management consultant* Often called the father of scientific management, Taylor was born in Germantown, Pennsylvania. He enrolled at Phillips Exeter Academy in New Hampshire prior to taking the admissions examination for Harvard; he planned to become a lawyer. Passing the admissions examination with honors, 18-year-old Frederick experienced eyesight problems and instead chose to pursue a personal interest by going to work as a machinist apprentice. He joined a firm in Philadelphia, Ferrel and Jones, that manufactured steam-pumps. He eventually graduated in engineering from Stevens Institute of Technology in 1883.

Following the American Civil War, industrialization in the United States grew rapidly with a proliferation of factories, the involvement of large numbers of workers, and the use of new machinery and equipment. Taylor, now an assistant foreman at Midvale Steel in Philadelphia, became interested in how people worked. This led him to closely observe workers' use of motion and time as they interacted with machinery, materials, and workplace arrangements during production. Studying and recording his observations, Taylor analyzed work in a new way and established methodologies to improve worker and factory productivity. He believed that both owners and workers should share in these advances. Taylor rose from foreman in 1880 to become Midvale Steel's chief engineer by 1887.

He left Midvale steel in 1894. Awarded a gold medal at the Paris Exposition of 1900 and holding more than a hundred patents, he was named president of the American Society of Mechanical Engineers in 1906; Henry Gantt and Frank and Lillian Gilbreth were among his followers. Taylor was awarded an honorary doctorate from the University of Pennsylvania that same year, and his methods were widely introduced into factories and offices throughout the world. He published numerous articles in the *Proceedings of the American Society of Mechanical Engineers* and authored four books, *The Principles of Scientific Management,* and *Shop Management,* both in 1911, *Concrete Costs* with S. E. Thompson in 1912, and *Scientific Management,* edited by C. B. Thompson, in 1914.

Further reading

Copley, Frank B. *Frederick W. Taylor: Father of Scientific Management.* New York: Harpers, 1923.
Kanigel, R. *The One Best Way: Frederick Winslow Taylor and the Enigma of Efficiency.* New York: Viking, 1997.
Noble, David. *Forces of Production: A Social History of Industrial Automation.* New York: Knopf, 1984.

Lawrence P. Huggins

telecommunications industry American telecommunications began with the mid-19th-century TELEGRAPH, was extended with undersea telegraph cables after the Civil War, and grew further with the telephone and new modes of transmission (microwave, satellite, fiber optic, and wireless) in the late 20th century. By the early 2000s, the industry was expanding into a host of other technologies, having become a vital sector of the economy. The technology-based business consists of both manufacturing and service (long distance, local, wireless) sectors, with many aspects regulated by federal and state governments.

Telecommunications began with the successful innovation of Samuel Morse's telegraph system in 1844. For three years, the U.S. Post Office ran the pioneering Washington to Baltimore line, deciding in 1847 to sell it to private interests because of its expense and relative lack of use (in part, as the two cities were too close and already had good rail connections). By that time other private telegraph companies had developed (the first connected New York and Philadelphia) and were rapidly growing. For decades thereafter postal officials regularly sought congressional authority to regain control of the industry, but to no avail.

Telegraph expansion paralleled and aided the growth of the nation's network of RAILROADS. The latter provided a prepared right of way, while the former offered vital communication links for the often single-track networks that moved people and goods. The first coast-to-coast telegraph line was opened in 1862 (seven years before rail links extended that far) and immediately made money, demonstrating the value of telecommunications over great distances.

WESTERN UNION, the first telecommunications monopoly, was formed as a regional alliance of several smaller firms in 1856 and rapidly expanded, often following railway lines. Just a year later the six largest telegraph companies developed a CARTEL, dividing up the country and business among themselves. The Civil War demonstrated the value of telegraph links (the Union was far better equipped than the Confederacy) and drove up rates and company profits. Western Union took over some 15,000 miles of government-built lines at the end of the war and became by far the largest company in the field.

Telegraph systems initially served only land routes, as it was presumed impossible to lay lines underwater. After experiments running insulated telegraph lines under lakes and across rivers, in 1858 an American-led consortium laid the first cable connecting Britain and the United States, only to see it fail in a few months. The Civil War intervened, and after a failed attempt to lay a cable in 1865, success came in 1866; soon others were added. The Pacific was not crossed until 1902 because of the great distances involved. Availability of global telegraphy rapidly changed the face of business and government affairs. The ability to "instantly" communicate had great (and generally positive) impact on diplomacy, business affairs, and other aspects of daily life.

The equipment needs of an expanding telegraph industry (as well as those of lighting, power, and transport) helped create an electrical manufacturing industry. The first electrical companies rapidly demonstrated the importance of continuing research to develop patents as the chief means of controlling innovation. Western Electric was begun in 1869 as the manufacturing subsidiary of Western Union but was sold to the fledgling Bell System in the early 1880s. The first association of electrical engineers appeared in 1884. Westinghouse, based on important air-brake patents, was founded the same year, while GENERAL ELECTRIC combined two older firms (one of them Thomas Edison's) in 1892. Together they soon dominated the electrical industry, all the more so after agreeing to pool (share) many of their patents in 1896, with two-thirds of the business going to GE and a third to Westinghouse.

This condition of an established telegraph industry and rising electrical manufacturing businesses formed the context for the telephone. Though many others had tried, the telephone was largely the creation of Alexander Graham BELL, who received his first patent in March 1876. Early development of the telephone was fraught with technical and financial problems. Business and government users of the telegraph preferred its ability to cover great distance and record a message, not trusting the new voice-only means of communication. Western Union was offered a chance to buy Bell's patent rights in 1877, but the telegraph giant saw little value in the telephone and turned down the chance, forcing Bell's backers to develop their own system. Patent battles between Bell's backers and other firms and inventors were litigated for years, nearly always resulting in Bell victories.

Restricted by crude technology to providing local service (initial iron wires rarely extended 100 miles), telephone service developed slowly before the Bell patents expired in 1893. Initial Bell business strategy focused on licensing use of its patents and selling equipment to companies building systems in cities and towns, largely to serve business and the wealthy. The first telephone switchboard was placed in service in New Haven, Connecticut, in early 1878, and demonstrated its greater efficiency over individual lines between each customer. The first use of telephone numbers and directories of telephone users appeared about the same time. Telephone exchanges (using many switchboards) appeared about two decades later.

A Kansas City undertaker, concerned that telephone operators were sending business to his competitors, developed the first mechanically automated telephone switch in 1891. The first automated switches began to appear around the turn of the century in major cities—and would be used in smaller communities for decades. Copper telephone lines were placed in use between Boston and New York, extending telephone service to 300 miles. Transcontinental telephone service became possible only around 1915 by use of amplifiers based on Lee De Forest's "Audion" vacuum tube.

As Bell's basic telephone patents expired in and after 1893, hundreds of competing firms entered the business. Soon known as the "Independents" (meaning independent of the expanding Bell System), most offered lower prices but were poorly capitalized and fell into Bell System (by now AMERICAN TELEPHONE & TELEGRAPH) hands. While many cities featured competing telephone systems, these steadily disappeared, in part because, after 1900, AT&T refused to interconnect its growing network with competitors. In 1909 Western Union was taken over by the rapidly growing AT&T, raising federal antitrust concerns.

Government regulation of telecommunication developed very slowly. Based on the COM-MERCE CLAUSE (Article I, Section 8) of the Constitution, which gave Congress the right to regulate business between and among the states, the Post Roads Act of 1866 offered telegraph companies the right to extend their lines along public rights-of-way in turn for allowing the government priority use of their facilities. Two decades later, Congress created the INTERSTATE COMMERCE COMMISSION (the first independent regulatory agency), which in the 1910 Mann-Elkins Act was assigned some rather weak directives to regulate the price of telegraph and telephone service.

On the state level, REGULATION of telecommunications (as well as power and transport) grew out of the Progressive political movement, appearing first in 1907 in both Wisconsin and New York. The first state public utility commissions resulted, an idea that slowly spread to other

William Howard Taft on the telephone, ca. 1904
(LIBRARY OF CONGRESS)

states. Such commissions regulated telegraph and telephone carrier rates and service within the borders of their states.

Passage of the Sherman antitrust law in 1893 provided a strong federal tool to break up industry cartels. In 1913, AT&T was threatened with such a suit if it did not modify its expansive business strategy of taking over independent companies, as well as spinning off ownership of Western Electric. The company agreed to both, essentially accepting limited government regulatory oversight in return for government recognition of its dominant role within the telephone business. Regulators and AT&T executives alike spoke of the "natural monopoly" of telephone service as being the most efficient way to extend service to the most users.

For a brief period during the U.S. involvement in World War I (1917–18), Congress gave the post office what it had long sought—administrative control over telegraph (Western Union) and telephone (AT&T) operations, while the U.S. Navy supervised wireless. Debate raged in 1919 over whether to continue such government operation (a standard practice in most other nations at the time), and both the navy and post office lobbied hard for it, but Congress decided to return the carriers to their private owners. At no time since has the U.S. government operated commercial services, even temporarily.

Only with the formation of the FEDERAL COM-MUNICATIONS COMMISSION (FCC) in 1934 was a firm basis established for comprehensive regulation of interstate telegraph and telephone service. After an intensive study of the country's communication companies and their finances, Congress established the new commission with, for the first time, extensive federal powers to regulate prices and conditions of service by telecommunication common carriers. From 1936 to 1939, the FCC intensively investigated the telephone industry, recommending many changes in AT&T operation and government regulation. By this time, the unified Bell System of local companies and long distance facilities was largely synonymous with the telephone industry. Using some of the FCC findings, in 1949 the Justice Department brought suit to break up AT&T, a case that never went to trial and was settled with a 1956 consent decree that changed little.

Improved technology would begin to change the face of telecommunications after 1945. Paced by wartime needs and spending, Bell Labs and other researchers produced coaxial cable and microwave links that were first used commercially in the years after the war. No longer was it necessary to build an expensive telecommunication network using copper wires. Microwave links required the use of many antenna towers— and a license to use the high-frequency spectrum—but this was less expensive than a traditional wired network. Coaxial cable offered the broadband capacity needed to transmit thousands of telephone calls or full-motion video. Developed largely by AT&T, coax made possible the linking of the initial television networks after 1948 and, perhaps ironically in terms of the eventual cable competition, the means to distribute cable television service. In 1956, AT&T spearheaded the laying of the first transatlantic telephone cable (TAT-1).

Even more fundamental was the rise of solid-state electronics. Development of the transistor at Bell Labs in 1947, followed by the silicon chip in 1959, led to the era of modern electronics. Telecommunication equipment of all kinds could now be made smaller and more cheaply—and would last longer. Combined with analog and then digital computers, electronics was rapidly revolutionized.

Development of satellite communication was first hinted at in a 1945 article by Arthur C. Clarke in which he postulated a geostationary orbit 22,300 miles high that would keep a satellite above the same part of Earth. Pushed by the cold war missile race, the world's first artificial satellite came just 12 years later as the Soviet Union launched *Sputnik* into a low Earth orbit in October 1957. Early military satellite communications followed the same low-orbit path until

the first commercial geostationary satellites appeared in the 1970s. Construction and launch expense limited satellite links.

Pushed in large part by these technical advances, a shift to telecommunications DEREGULATION began slowly, first with the federal courts and the FCC, finally expanding to more fundamental change by Congress. The idea of limiting and then rolling back federal (and later state) regulatory power originated from these expanding technological choices (that allowed more than one company to participate), tight government budgets, changing ideology, and the realization that government could no longer "do it all."

Deregulation began slowly, with no sense of any overall plan. In its Hush-a-phone (1956) and Carterfone (1968) cases, the courts and the FCC began to open up access by non–common carrier firms to the telecommunications equipment market, while the FCC's Above 890 (1959) and MCI (1969) decisions likewise began a very limited provision of telecommunication services on other than a regulated common carrier basis. The FCC's Specialized Common Carrier (1971) and related Domestic Communications Satellite, or "Domsat," (1972) decisions more fundamentally established competition rather than regulation as the most efficient means of expanding use of telecommunication technologies. Armed with such active FCC support, MCI (and eventually other firms) became an increasingly aggressive competitor to AT&T, beginning to offer consumer telephone service in 1975. Western Union launched the country's first Domsat, *Westar I,* in 1974; many others soon followed from several different firms. By the mid- to late 1970s, deregulation and the encouragement of competitive entry by new companies was becoming the standard FCC approach to telecommunications policy.

AT&T strongly resisted these changes, arguing that one company could more efficiently provide varied services to all users. However, it rapidly became apparent that for a truly competitive market to be established, no single player could dominate. AT&T's anticompetitive approach became a target. After a 10-year legal antitrust battle (the third time the federal government had sought to break up AT&T), the Bell System was broken up at the beginning of 1984 under the conditions of a consent decree issued by a U.S. district court. The local operating companies—about three-quarters of the unified system—were divested (spun off) to eventually become seven (later reduced to four) regional holding companies. The decision to break up AT&T was based on the conception of a domestic telecommunications market bifurcated into monopoly (local service) and competitive (long distance and manufacturing) sectors. Such a division promised to prevent illegal cross-subsidy between monopoly and competitive services, such as AT&T had engaged in for years. After the breakup, the new regional firms thrived, while AT&T began a slow decline amid management confusion and growing competition. In 1995, the company underwent a self-imposed breakup, shedding its manufacturing and much of its research functions into separate companies.

The height of U.S. deregulation was reached with the Telecommunications Act of 1996, with which Congress established conditions to create a fully competitive marketplace as the chief goal for the telecommunications sector. The fundamental changes, outlined in the law and detailed in many subsequent related FCC administrative rule makings, defined the conditions under which new competitors would face entrenched service providers, especially the monopoly local telephone carriers and cable television systems. How to successfully interconnect the various carriers—and at what cost—is a hugely complex technical and economic undertaking and was progressing in the early 2000s more slowly than many had expected or hoped. Likewise, the push to develop an effective policy of "universal service" whereby every household in the country is connected with all others has primarily been a matter of economics and politics rather than technology. By the early 2000s, only about 6 percent of the nation's households were not con-nected. The 1996 act provided a basic scheme to underwrite installation and service costs for such households, building on schemes that had been developed in many states over the previous two decades.

Digital technology first appeared in American telecommunications with AT&T's introduction of its T1 Carrier System in 1962. A T1 line offered far more capacity and a cleaner (less noisy) signal. Soon digital telephone switches appeared, allowing for more flexible network design and operation. But the most sweeping change came with the installation of fiber-optic cables to carry voice, data, and video signals. The huge carrying capacity of fiber—constantly raised with further technical improvements—finally placed telecommunication networks well ahead of projected growth (and planted the seeds for disaster in the early 2000s).

Wireless telecommunications developed slowly for decades after World War II, limited by poor analog technology and very limited capacity—no more than 250 subscribers per market, only 10 percent of whom could use their portable telephones at a time. Bell Labs developed the notion of "cellular" systems allowing for frequency reuse (and thus far greater capacity) and developed it through the 1970s. The FCC approved operation of an analog cellular mobile telephone system in 1982, sparking a new growth sector. The arrival of all-digital personal communication systems in the 1990s led to even more rapid expansion as prices fell, such that about half of the population used one by the early 2000s. Promises of 3G (third-generation) services and a continually growing demand led telecommunication carriers to bid billions for access to the needed spectrum when the FCC held auctions.

The INTERNET, based on government networks dating back to 1969, became a widely used public network in 1995. Development of the World Wide Web and the graphic user interface making it possible opened up a wealth of expanding information resources and growing public acceptance. By the early 2000s, more than half of American households were connected to the Internet, a slowly growing number of them linked by broadband connections. Projections of Internet growth sparked bullish plans for the underlying telecommunication services and manufacturing that made the Web possible. Many of those projections were wide of the reality.

Telecommunications was generally a growth industry in the postwar years. As the "dot-com" industry boom cooled and then collapsed after 2000, however, telecommunications was dragged down with it. The key problem was overcapacity—too many channels and too few users. Fiberoptic links had been hugely overbuilt in the competitive frenzy of the 1990s. The country was served by six national wireless networks when half that number would better serve existing and projected demand. Broadband services (that would encourage greater network use) were slow to develop because industry lacked the funds to innovate, and the public seemed unmoved by various offerings.

The overbuilding had been driven by easily available investment funds. As the industry slowed in 2001, investment dried up, and stock prices began to plummet. The result was a credit squeeze that forced virtually all telecommunication carriers and manufacturers to lay off workers. A few went further and, facing Wall Street pressure to report constantly rising earnings, perpetrated outright fraud. First Global Crossing and then WORLDCOM fell into BANKRUPTCY, wiping out jobs and investments of shareholders. Other companies—especially Lucent and Nortel—teetered on the edge of financial failure. Competitive local exchange carriers, often thinly capitalized to begin with, nearly all collapsed, setting back development of local competition. Long-distance companies all showed sharp revenue declines as local monopoly telephone carriers received permission to provide inter-exchange service to their customers. Of the six national wireless carriers, only the two largest (Verizon and Cingular) were making a profit by 2003.

Part of the cause for the crisis in telecommunications was a collapse of policy oversight. Neither the FCC nor the state public utility commissions applied brakes or even expressed caution at the overbuilding of facilities beyond all projections of use for decades to come. Countless new players had been encouraged by the promise of the 1996 Telecommunications Act and were done in by the realities of a relentless market only slowly changing from regulated monopoly to free competition. Though the industry was by 2002–03 in its worst financial crisis in the entire history of the FCC, the agency said little and did less to change the bleak outlook. Indeed, many argued that the commission's spreading use of spectrum auctions made things worse as carriers spent far more than market conditions would suggest to be wise, thus damaging their overall financial strength.

That the industry's financial fortunes (if not all of its players) would revive was assured—telecommunication is too vital for it to fail or disappear. As use (driven especially by spreading broadband access to Internet services) rises, excess capacity will be taken up, and investment will return. The question is how soon this will take place.

See also RADIO CORPORATION OF AMERICA; SARNOFF, DAVID.

Further reading

Brock, Gerald W. *The Telecommunications Industry: The Dynamics of Market Structure.* Cambridge, Mass.: Harvard University Press, 1981.

LeBow, Irwin. *Information Highways and Byways: From the Telegraph to the 21st Century.* New York: IEEE Press, 1995.

Oslin, George P. *The Story of Telecommunications.* Macon, Ga.: Mercer University Press, 1992.

Spar, Debora L. *Ruling the Waves: Cycles of Discovery, Chaos, and Wealth from the Compass to the Internet.* New York: Harcourt, 2001.

Winston, Brian. *Media Technology and Society: A History from the Telegraph to the Internet.* London: Routledge, 1998.

Christopher H. Sterling

telegraph By strict definition, a telegraph is any means, beyond the reach of normal conversation, for transmitting information at a distance. From time immemorial coded signals have been sent using sound over short distances and light over longer. Optical telegraphy has exploited smoke signals, mirrors, beacons, and, in systems reaching their highest development in France in the first half of the 19th century, semaphores.

The Chappe semaphore system eventually drove a network with 5,000 kilometers of lines, most radiating from Paris. The system was never effectively used at night, and fog or heat inversion during the day could disrupt its operation. Nevertheless, within the limits of its bandwidth and atmospheric conditions, the technology worked, and there were serious discussions before the U.S. Congress in the 1830s of building a line from New York to New Orleans using French technology. Samuel F. B. MORSE, working on an alternate technology, lobbied against this proposal.

During the 18th century, a number of individuals had experimented with sending static electricity over wires to cause pith balls to move at a distance or to create bubbles in chemical solutions. But static electricity is high voltage and low amperage, is vulnerable, like the Chappe system, to atmospheric disturbance, and drops off in strength quickly over distances. Progress in producing and storing low-voltage high-amperage electricity by Volta, and the development of a working electromagnet by Faraday and Henry, provided the scientific underpinnings of Morse's technology.

Using a $30,000 subvention from Congress, Morse built a demonstration project from Washington to Baltimore and successfully inaugurated it in 1844. The telegraph reached San Francisco in 1861, and a permanent transatlantic link was established in 1866. Software also mattered. Morse code survives to this day, although the Telex and TWX systems of the mid-20th century used the 5-bit Baudot code (from which the modern term *baud* derives). ASCII, the 7-bit American Standard Code for Information Interchange, was introduced in 1966 and underlies 21st-century e-mail, fax, and Internet communication.

During its heyday, the electromagnetic telegraph had an impact in two major areas: military and diplomatic command and control, and the commercial transmission of high-value, time-sensitive information. Commercial uses were most highly developed in the United States, where the telegraph was used for command and control in large business organizations, and for transmittal of high-value time-sensitive information in the newspaper and financial services industries.

See also FIELD, CYRUS W.

Further reading
Coe, Lewis. *The Telegraph: A History of Morse's Invention and Its Predecessors in the United States*. New York: McFarland & Company, 2003.

Alexander J. Field

television industry Today television is a dynamic industry that is constantly evolving. There are more than 1,200 television stations on the air generating almost $53 billion in television and cable advertising. At least 98 percent of American households have a television receiver, more than 76 percent of these households have multiple sets, and 68 percent subscribe to cable television. There are more television sets in the United States than there are bathtubs.

The evolution of television began more than 100 years ago, and it was not the invention of a single individual. The evolution of theory and application was mixed with fierce competitiveness as inventors and corporations recognized the technology as potentially profitable.

In 1873, Englishmen Joseph May and Willoughby Smith discovered that light falling on photosensitive elements produced a small amount of energy. G. R. Cary, in 1887, developed a proposal paralleling systems of the human eye. Not far from Cary's work in Boston, Alexander

D. E. Replogle giving the first public demonstration of talking moving pictures being transmitted over radio from the studios of the Jenkins Television Corp., Jersey City, New Jersey, 1927 (LIBRARY OF CONGRESS)

Graham BELL first tried to use light in the transmission of the human voice. Bell's experiments produced a system that was a forerunner to the facsimile. It was the French who first used the principle of "scanning," and scientist Maurice Leblanc who developed the scanning system to improve picture quality. In 1883, a German scientist, Paul Nipkow, developed the mechanical scanning device. The idea of scanning produced several mechanical apparatuses, some of which hung around until the mid-1940s.

The inventors primarily responsible for the 20th-century system were John Logie Baird, Charles Francis Jenkins, Philo Taylor Farnsworth, and Vladimir Kosma Zworykin. In the early 1920s Baird and Jenkins, working with mechanical systems, set the stage for electronic television.

According to George Shiers, the first public demonstration of television was conducted by John Logie Baird of Great Britain. The demonstration, conducted in March 1925, was held at Selfridge's Oxford Street department store. He named his apparatus the "televisor." His work almost became the English standard, but it was turned aside by the British government in favor of an electronic scanning system.

Charles Francis Jenkins was not far behind Baird in his television experimentation. Jenkins was an independent inventor and known in the United States as founder of the Society of Motion Picture Engineers (today, the Society of Motion Picture and Television Engineers, or SMPTE). In the early 1920s Jenkins was experimenting with what he called "Prismatic Rings." These were rotating disks similar to Baird's. Jenkins referred to his work as "radio photographs, radio movies and radio vision." Jenkins's first public demonstration came just three months after Baird's, in June 1925. Jenkins arranged for an influential gathering of visitors from the Washington, D.C., area to witness the event in his laboratory on Connecticut Avenue. The result produced glowing reviews in the press.

As technology began to increase the prospect of profitability, interest grew among developers and major corporations. Zworykin left Westinghouse for RCA because of the promise of financial backing. Zworykin did not join RCA until 1929, but RCA was active in research and did take out licenses for three experimental stations. Among Farnsworth's first experiments was the transmission of a dollar sign. The market crash of 1929 and its aftermath made financing a difficult task. Still, there were those who wanted to "cash in" on this new gadget called television. GENERAL ELECTRIC, with Ernst F. W. Alexanderson as chief television engineer, experimented with a mechanical scanning system. AT&T was experimenting under the leadership of Herbert E. Ives, a Bell Laboratories scientist. Philco started its own television work in 1928, but activities were modest until Farnsworth was hired in 1931 and put a station on the air for them. The Allen Du Mont Laboratories were organized in 1931. Peter Goldmark was the chief scientist for the COLUMBIA BROADCASTING SYSTEM (CBS). He did not have the early start of some of the corporations, but CBS had an experimental station on the air in New York. By 1937 Goldmark had color television on the drawing board.

Farnsworth's story is a fascinating one. He first drew an electronic schematic for his high school chemistry teacher. That drawing was later a turning point in a patent suit between RCA and Farnsworth Television. It was September 7, 1927, when Farnsworth produced his first electronic television picture. The picture was a single vertical line. By 1929, he had the only working electronic television system in the world. Experiments

grew from a line to a triangle and a dollar sign, and the "smoke' within the laboratory was the first motion seen. Then photographs were added. In 1929, his wife, Elma "Pem" Gardner-Farnsworth, was the subject of demonstrations, making her the first woman to ever appear on television. The first electronic television broadcast transmission, outside of the laboratory, was in the summer of 1930, when Farnsworth was broadcasting between the Green Street Laboratory and the San Francisco Merchant's Exchange Building. Farnsworth's greatest triumph was the world's first general public demonstration of the electronic television system, on August 25, 1934, at the Franklin Institute in Philadelphia. This demonstration continued for several weeks as vaudeville skits and athletes paraded before the camera tossing a few balls and swinging tennis rackets. Drawing a great deal of attention were the night shots of the moon. The competition between Farnsworth and RCA was, as described by Farnsworth's wife, Elma, a "David and Goliath" confrontation. In this situation Goliath lost the patent case but won the free-enterprise war for corporate dominance of television.

Vladimir Zworykin was in charge of RCA's television development. He was a Russian immigrant who was first employed by Westinghouse but moved to RCA when the company showed greater interest in developing a television system. The backing of Sarnoff and RCA provided Zworykin with a strong foundation for his work through the difficult years of the Depression and World War II. Zworykin had convinced Sarnoff that he could complete television in two years and for $100,000. He visited the labs of both Baird and Farnsworth. Because Zworykin and Farnsworth were both working with electronic scanning systems, they later found themselves embroiled in patent-interference cases. Zworykin's work was demonstrated at the 1939 New York World's Fair; with the force of RCA behind him, he became the most powerful innovator in the history of television.

Television evolved as AM radio began to mature, and headlines in the popular press were touting the marvels of a number of new inventions: the televisor, the telephone, the phonograph, and radio. Television was the latecomer, trying to obtain a position on the Roaring Twenties prosperity bandwagon. All of this was to television's advantage; the new technologies were at least somewhat related and provided significant financing for television's development.

The Federal Communication Commission's (FCC) slow pace resulted in considerable frustration among developers. They criticized the commission for being slow to establish television picture quality and color television standards. Those ready to manufacture and distribute television were stymied while others were given the opportunity to catch up. Farnsworth, for example, at the end of the 1930s had won the patent-interference case with RCA, thus forcing RCA to agree to Farnsworth's terms in the acquisition of his patents. However, this was also a success for RCA: With access to Farnsworth's patents, RCA was again ready to push forward toward standardization with the FCC. Not only did RCA have the system prepared for commercial operation, it had also been competitively successful in persuading the Radio Manufacturer Association to adopt its standards for production manufacturing.

World War II halted the development of television. As American participation in the war approached, the companies switched their emphasis from consumer development to defense manufacturing. At the end of the war there was renewed enthusiasm, corporations were ready to launch a national system, and local radio stations were ready to put local-market television stations on the air.

In 1948, the FCC realized that its frequency-allocation system for television was insufficient; taking note of other pressing issues, such as educational allocations, UHF, and color television, the FCC issued its "freeze." The order, coming September 20, 1948, again stalled further expansion of television while the FCC considered allo-cation issues. This was a brief boon to existing stations as they operated without competition, but frustrating to those who anxiously awaited FCC decisions before they could go on the air.

Of all the major corporations, CBS gained the most from this hiatus, including a competitive equilibrium with RCA. Although the decisions to be rendered from the freeze were primarily those of allocation, the issue of color television was also of importance. The CBS engineers had put forward a color-reproduction system, just as RCA was beginning to place monochrome receivers on the market. However, because of the incompatibility of the CBS color system with RCA's monochrome sets, CBS reasoned that with RCA black-and-white sets already in the marketplace, its color system would be precluded. The CBS strategy was to acquire FCC approval for its color system, thus blocking RCA's sale of receivers. This approach resulted in a second battle for broadcast standards—color standard versus black and white. Although CBS played the role of underdog, RCA already had the support of the manufacturers, and its public relations and manufacturing machinery were in place. Eventually, the FCC approved CBS's color system (October 1950), and then later rescinded its order approving the RCA system (December 1953). Although CBS had lost the initial battle for adoption of a color system, it did gain the time it needed to become competitive with RCA once the standards were announced. The technological and regulatory foundations for television had thus been laid.

The FCC's freeze was lifted on April 11, 1952, after nearly four years of frustration and contentious debate. The Sixth Report and Order led to the establishment of standards that form the foundation of the system we have today. The spectrum space was allocated for commercial television, with special channels set aside for educational telecasting. The number of VHF (very high frequency) channels allocated to most cities was increased (channels 2–13), and the FCC opened an additional 70 UHF (ultrahigh frequency) channels for commercial licensing. Individual allocations were made on a city-by-city basis, providing both VHF and UHF assignments. World War II and the freeze were major turning points in television's history. The industry was now on its way, with somewhat of a firm footing and business operational patterns in place as well. The issues of technological development, financing, and REGULATION were for the most part resolved. Programming for a growing audience was the next challenge.

Television had a significant advantage in the development of its programming—existing radio programs and local radio stations. The business of radio set the pattern of operation for television, both locally and nationally. Radio networks became radio-TV networks. Television's personnel were largely trained in radio. Radio stations became combined AM-TV, then AM-TV-FM operations as radio stations took out television licenses and provided financial support for both the early networks and individual stations. The local operational patterns of radio were adapted and superimposed on early television stations. Many radio pioneers were also television pioneers.

In the case of many local TV stations those on the air first had a distinct advantage in developing a strong affiliate relationship, a talent base, film resources, and live local programming. The actual expansion of the broadcast program schedule usually coincided with efforts to promote the sale of television sets. Local bars invested in sets to broadcast sporting events and to lure potential male viewers. A sometimes disproportionate number of first-day broadcasts from around the country featured wrestling or professional boxing matches surrounded, of course, by a lot of talk and ceremony. Sports grew from these local beginnings to national telecasts of football, baseball, and even bowling.

In most markets today, television news accounts for a substantial element of the station income. News began to be financially successful at a local level during the 1960s. WABC was later instrumental in developing a format that spread

to local stations throughout the nation—"action news." It was known by different titles—"Eyewitness News," "Action News," "Happy Talk"—but introduced a faster-paced, localized format to the audience. Critics today call it tabloid and often blame social science and research consultants for its spread. However, this local development has today become a major program genre.

The 1960s and 1970s marked television's accommodation and adjustment to changing technology and competition. It was the beginning of a number of trends that transferred the power base from the national networks to local stations and increased competition for the growing diversity of channels. Technology and DEREGULATION placed emphasis on the marketplace—a marketplace both local and national. The technology of recording, satellite, electronic news gathering (ENG), and electronic field production (EFP) helped pass control from the network to the local stations. Heretofore the local stations had been dependent upon the network to cover a nationally breaking news story. The local stations acquired their visual material from the network via the evening news and material fed to the station as delayed electronic feeds (DEFs). Today, the local station, via satellite and ENG/EFP technology, can cover a story no matter where it occurs. Local stations today use their elaborate production facilities not only to produce news, but also to create material for syndication. The talk shows, "produced in the facilities of . . .," are delivered via satellite rather than through a network. In effect, a multitude of alternative networks were being established contractually. Broadcast networks, syndication networks, cable, and satellite networks all link local program distributors to an audience.

Competition marks the chief characteristic of today's television. Cable delivery of television signals reached 68 percent of all U.S. households in 2002. And while broadcast television still boasted a 99 percent household penetration rate, cable, video cassette, digital video disks, and satellite-delivered programming all are eating away at the traditional network and local station rating base. New technology has provided more viewing choices. High-definition television, the home theater, and the convergence of the computer with video technology are just beginning to inch into market shares. The winner in these races will ultimately be the viewers as they are presented with more choices, programming on demand, and a more efficient, quality technology.

See also SARNOFF, DAVID.

Further reading

Abramson, Albert. *Electronic Motion Pictures*. 1955. Reprint, New York: Arno, 1974.

———. *The History of Television, 1880–1941*. Jefferson, N.C.: McFarland, 1987.

———. *The History of Television, 1942–2000*. Jefferson, N.C.: McFarland, 2003.

Bilby, Kenneth. *The General: David Sarnoff and the Rise of the Communications Industry*. New York: Harper & Row, 1985.

Murray, Michael D., and Donald G. Godfrey. *Television in America: Local Station History from across the Nation*. Ames: Iowa State University Press, 1997.

Donald G. Godfrey

Tennessee Valley Authority (TVA)   Government owned power authority established by Congress in May 1933 in order to develop the resources of, and provide electricity for, the Tennessee River Valley. The TVA became one of several organizations referred to as GOVERNMENT-SPONSORED ENTERPRISES.

The authority was designed to embrace government-sponsored power projects that had never been completed. The Wilson Dam at Muscle Shoals, Alabama, was partially built during World War I to develop both power and nitrates but was never finished. When private interests, led by Henry FORD, offered to buy the property from the government at discount prices, advocates of public power companies lobbied heavily for government intervention.

The price of electric power varied greatly during the 1920s and 1930s, depending upon geographical location and the type of ownership of the actual power plants. Power produced by public enterprises was generally cheaper than that provided by private companies. Senator George NORRIS was an outspoken critic of many of the privately owned power companies and finally helped persuade the new Roosevelt administration to create the TVA in order to keep the power generation facilities out of private hands.

The TVA originally had three directors: Harcourt Morgan, David Lilienthal, and Arthur Morgan. In the 1930s, the company helped redevelop the multistate area by replanting depleted forests, developing fertilizers, and improving crop yields. Electricity supplied by its dams and generators helped improve the quality of life for the inhabitants. Electricity provided by the TVA, measured in cents per kilowatt hour, proved to be the cheapest in the country after the agency became fully operational. In the 1940s, during World War II, the company embarked on a massive power generation plan. By the end of the decade, it had become the largest supplier of electricity in the country.

In the 1950s, the TVA was granted congressional approval to issue bonds in its own name in order to finance its capital investment projects. It continued to build power plants and by the 1960s was the lowest priced supplier of wholesale electric power. By the late 1990s, it was ranked as the third-cheapest supplier of electric power. It remains a government-sponsored enterprise, although its debt instruments are sold to the investing public.

See also NEW DEAL.

Further reading

Conkin, Paul, and Erwin Hargrove. *TVA: Fifty Years of Grass Roots Democracy*. Urbana: University of Illinois Press, 1984.

Hubbard, Preston J. *Origins of the TVA: The Muscle Shoals Controversy, 1920–1932*. New York: Norton, 1961.

ticker tape   Thin paper tape, mounted in roll form, upon which was printed data on trades on the NEW YORK STOCK EXCHANGE (NYSE). Beginning in the 1870s, two entirely separate telegraph networks served the financial services industry. The first was a point-to-point system connecting branch brokerage offices with the floor of the exchange. Over these wires, customers sent orders to trade and received confirmation of execution. The second was a broadcast system. After execution of each trade, details were broadcast to brokerages and other subscribers, where the data were received over a specialized printer known as a stock ticker.

A ticker was first introduced in 1867, and was dramatically improved upon over the next two years by Thomas A. EDISON. The device printed

Stock ticker tape machine (MUSEUM OF AMERICAN FINANCIAL HISTORY)

out a stock symbol, how many shares of that stock were traded and at what price, producing a linear barrage of information whose form is familiar to this day, even though individuals now watch it at the bottom of their television screen or on their computers. Prior to the introduction of the computer and streaming prices, "reading" the ticker tape was a Wall Street art practiced by those who would trade stocks based upon how they interpreted prices coming across the tape.

These two networks enabled million-share days as early as 1886, giving rise to a technological regime that tested its limits in October of 1929, when on one day more than 16 million shares were traded, a level not reached again until 1968. In that year the regime basically broke down and was replaced with one that today routinely accommodates trading volumes two orders of magnitude higher. The tape also became consolidated in the 1970s as part of a stock market reform aimed at providing the prices of all traded stocks on a consolidated tape, not just those of the NYSE and the AMERICAN STOCK EXCHANGE.

Dropped out the windows of New York skyscrapers, used ticker tape has assumed an important place in celebratory American iconography, serving as a distinctive visual flourish when the nation's financial capital honored national heroes, such as Charles Lindbergh after his transatlantic flight and John Glenn after he orbited the Earth.

See also STOCK MARKETS.

Further reading
Field, Alexander J. "The Telegraphic Transmission of Financial Asset Prices and Orders to Trade: Implications for Economic Growth." *Research in Economic History* 18 (1998): 145–184.

Alexander J. Field

Time Warner   An entertainment and communications company formed by the merger between America Online (AOL) and Time Warner Communications in 2001. The merger was the largest ever recorded and combined an Internet company founded in the 1980s with an older, established publishing and broadcasting company that was a mainstay of the entertainment industry.

The older of the two companies was Time Warner, originally founded by Henry Robinson Luce (1898–1967). Born in China to missionaries, Luce was educated at Yale before entering the publishing business. He and Briton Hadden founded *Time* magazine in 1923, and it became the basis for a successful publishing empire. *Fortune* was founded in 1930 and became a leading business magazine. A year later, a radio program, *The March of Time,* was begun and continued until 1953. Luce also developed *Life* magazine as a weekly, beginning in 1936. It ceased publication but resumed in 1978 as a monthly. Other notable periodicals included *House & Home* (1952) and *Sports Illustrated* (1954).

In addition, the company published more than 30 other magazines and owned recording companies and book publishers. It also was the second-largest provider of cable TV operations, including Home Box Office and CNN.

AOL had earned a different reputation. It was founded in 1983 as an Internet provider and game company and had witnessed spectacular growth under the aegis of Steve Case, who joined the company soon after its inception and became CEO in 1993. By the late 1990s, when it began adding advertising to its Web pages, AOL had 26 million paying subscribers and was the world's preeminent on-line service. Although its tangible assets were much smaller than those of Time Warner, its stock market valuation was more than twice that of the older company. The original deal was valued at $156 billion, offered by AOL for Time Warner stock and was the largest stock transaction ever proposed.

Only a year after the deal was announced, the value had dropped to $103.5 billion when it was finally approved by the FEDERAL COMMUNICATIONS COMMISSION, the regulatory agency charged with approving telecommunications MERGERS. The new company was the largest entertainment company in the world. Shortly after the merger, it suffered the worst earnings loss in corporate history, experiencing a $100 billion loss in 2002 as a result of new accounting rules put in place before its merger was complete.

The company's performance after the merger did not measure up to expectations, and talks were begun to divest some of its holdings, including separating the two companies again in order to raise the stock price and restore investor confidence. Finally, the name AOL was dropped from the logo, and the company became known as Time Warner.

See also INTERNET.

Further reading

Clurman, Richard M. *To the End of Time: The Seduction and Conquest of a Media Empire.* New York: Simon & Schuster, 1992.

Klein, Alec. *Stealing Time: Steve Case, Jerry Levin, and the Collapse of AOL Time Warner.* New York: Simon & Schuster, 2003.

Swanberg, W. A. *Luce and His Empire.* New York: Scribner, 1972.

Swisher, Kara. *AOL.com.* New York: Crown Publishers, 1999.

Treasury bonds   Fully marketable long-term debt of the U.S. Treasury, issued almost immediately after adoption of the Constitution in 1789 to consolidate the debt of the former colonies. They have been issued with varying degrees of frequency ever since. Bonds are different from Treasury bills, which are issued for periods of less than one year.

In the 1790s, the bonds were sold on the early stock exchanges. During the War of 1812, the Treasury employed a small syndicate of wealthy merchants, including John Jacob ASTOR and Stephen GIRARD, to help distribute bonds, but the merchants exacted such a high price for their efforts that the Treasury was criticized for being too lax in monitoring debt sales. Similar criticisms arose during the Mexican War, when bonds were sold again and private bankers were used to distribute the bonds. Congressional critics maintained that they were benefiting at the Treasury's expense.

When the Civil War began, the Treasury again needed to raise funds and employed Jay Cooke & Co. to distribute the bonds nationwide. Despite Cooke's success at relatively thin margins of profit, criticism again arose, but the Treasury had no effective mechanism for distributing bonds other than employing private bankers. Throughout the 19th century, the method of employing private bankers to sell bonds to the public remained the same. Several private banking houses, notably J. P. Morgan & Company and J. & W. Seligman & Company, made substantial profits and reputations aiding the Treasury in its funding needs.

During World War I, the Treasury sold its massive Liberty loans (bonds) to the public directly, avoiding bankers and the costs associated with employing them. The same method was used during World War II as well, when the borrowing requirement ballooned to the largest in history. During the war, Treasury bonds could also be purchased by banks with deposits, allowing the banks to avoid reserve requirements. The provision was lifted once the war was over.

After the war, the Treasury began auctioning its new issues to its recognized primary dealers on a best bid basis, again avoiding underwriting costs. As the federal debt became larger, the auctions became the most cost effective method of raising funds that the Treasury had ever employed. Dealers in Treasury bonds wee not paid an underwriting fee but profited only on the difference between auction price and the price at which the bonds could be sold to investors.

The amount of bonds that can be issued by the Treasury is subject to congressional debt limitation. In 1977, Congress authorized the Treasury to issue a 30-year bond as its maximum maturity and in 1983 allowed the FEDERAL RESERVE to authorize stripping coupons off of Treasury bonds to create STRIP (Separate Trad-

ing Receipts of Interest and Principal), or zero coupon bonds. The maturities on these bonds often are changed according to Treasury funding needs. During the Clinton administration, the Treasury indicated that it was shortening the maturities of bonds issued, but deficits would later require the 30-year Treasury bond to be revived.

In the 1990s, the Treasury began issuing Treasury Inflation Protected Securities, or TIPS. This was the first time that the Congress allowed the Treasury to index bonds to inflation, a practice common in some other industrialized countries.

See also COOKE, JAY; MORGAN, JOHN PIERPONT; SALOMON BROTHERS; SELIGMAN & CO., J. & W.

Further reading
Fisher, Lawrence, and James H. Lorie. *A Half Century of Returns on Stocks and Bonds.* Chicago: University of Chicago Press, 1977.
Geisst, Charles R. *Wall Street: A History.* New York: Oxford University Press, 1997.

Turner, Ted (1938–) *media executive* Robert Edward (Ted) Turner was born in Cincinnati, Ohio, on November 19, 1938, the son of a former Mississippi cotton farmer. In 1947, he accompanied his family south to Savannah, Georgia, where his father acquired a billboard advertising business. Turner, displaying a trademark rebelliousness, dropped out of college and briefly enrolled in the Coast Guard. In 1963, he joined his father's firm just as it approached insolvency. The two Turners skirmished repeatedly about keeping the company, and he was aghast when his father committed suicide. Forced into the role of executive officer at 24, he quickly turned the company around by dint of hard work and imaginative promotions. By 1970, Turner, against the advice of friends and authorities, decided to enter the media business by acquiring a bankrupt Atlanta broadcasting station. Again, he surprised the pundits by turning a profit through creative programming: old movies and television shows, leavened throughout with sports broadcasts. Turner amassed a small fortune in the process, and by 1976, he was able to purchase the Atlanta Braves and the Atlanta Hawks, two local athletic teams. His ownership enabled him to ingeniously broadcast games without paying broadcast rights.

But mere success would not placate this restless, visionary entrepreneur. Wishing to expand his viewing franchise on a national basis, in 1975 he built one of the first ground stations capable of using new satellite communications. This, in turn, gave rise to the first superstation, modestly christened WTBS for "Turner Broadcast System." It was another bold venture that succeeded against expectations, and within three years it was beaming messages into 2 million homes across the nation. Turner nonetheless remained unsatisfied, and he turned to developing a personal project: a 24-hour cable news network providing live coverage of breaking events. When CNN premiered in 1980 the experts scoffed, but within two decades it was carried in almost 80 million households. Its success subsequently occasioned the new Headline News Network, which proffered succinct news summaries every half-hour. Both efforts reconfirmed Turner's reputation as a mercurial and farsighted media genius. Five years later Turner decided he was strong enough to compete with the media giants, although he failed in his attempt to take over CBS. Undeterred, he then acquired the entire film library of MGM/UA in 1986, whose repertoire included some of the most famous movies of all time, for $1.6 billion. Charges then surfaced that the amount was vastly overinflated; in fact, Turner was close to BANKRUPTCY for several years and had to be bailed out by a consortium of cable TV companies. But within three years he was enabled to start a second cable network, TNT, whose sole purpose was to showcase the classic films in his possession. This was another solid success for Turner, although he was roundly criticized by the Hollywood film establishment for colorizing classic black and white movies. Ruffled feathers notwithstanding, his

boldness and risk-taking reaped considerable dividends for the owner.

Turner, a stormy, tempestuous personality, enjoyed a spate of failed marriages before settling down with movie star and political activist Jane Fonda in 1991. This seemed to exert a calming effect on his personal life and his business ambitions, for in 1995 he sold TBS to TIME WARNER, Inc., for $7.5 billion. The move created the world's largest media conglomerate, with literally thousands of films, cartoons, and other media assets in its inventory. Moreover, Turner willingly served in a subordinate position as vice chairman of the cable division. And, having amassed a mountain of wealth, he embraced the cause of philanthropy and pledged $1 billion to the United Nations—the largest such donation in history. He then typically challenged others so disposed to be as generous. Whatever his motives, the outspoken Turner remains a media legend and one of the most influential entrepreneurs in broadcast history.

See also TELEVISION INDUSTRY.

Further reading
Bibb, Porter. *It Ain't as Easy as It Looks: Ted Turner's Amazing Story.* New York: Crown Publishers, 1993.
Goldberg, Robert, and Gerald J. Goldberg. *Citizen Turner: The Wild Rise of an American Tycoon.* New York: Harcourt Brace, 1995.
Turner, Ted. *Ted Turner Speaks: Insights from the World's Greatest Maverick.* New York: John Wiley & Sons, 1999.

John C. Fredriksen

turnpikes   Roadways built mostly in the eastern states at the end of the 18th and in the early 19th centuries, designed to provide roads suitable for commerce and travel. Before the turnpikes, no roads existed linking most cities and towns, and these roadways were the first attempt to link major centers in the country. Because of a convergence of other factors, mainly the development of canals and the RAILROADS, turnpikes were of limited use by the 1840s.

The first turnpike built in the United States by a private company, the Lancaster Turnpike, was also the country's first hard-surface roadway, linking Lancaster, Pennsylvania, to Philadelphia in 1792. Previously, turnpikes were built by states and were usually unpaved roads that were the beginnings of the American infrastructure. Virginia authorized a turnpike run by the state in 1785. But the high costs and the potential for lucrative tolls led many private companies to be formed to build the roads. Most of the turnpikes were built by 1825, and many of the original routes are still in existence, such as the Boston Post Road from New York City to Boston and the Albany Post Road from New York City to Albany.

Many of the turnpike companies became the first publicly held corporations in the country, selling stock to pay the expense of building the roads. The turnpikes held exclusive right to the territories they crossed and also held the right of eminent domain so that they could be built without obstruction. But the rapidly developing canal and shipping industries provided fierce and cheaper competition for the turnpikes. Even the paved roadways were uneven, often being paved with wood planks or other materials that were of rough quality.

Often it was cheaper to ship goods in a roundabout manner rather than use the turnpikes because of their expensive tolls. Despite the fact that turnpikes were often the shortest distance between two points, the tolls charged by their builders proved prohibitive to shippers, many of whom would use circuitous routes taking more time because shipping by water routes was still cheaper. The turnpikes that eventually failed financially were taken over by their respective states.

Canals also fulfilled a function that turnpikes were incapable of filling. They allowed large quantities of goods and commodities packed on barges to cover long distances relatively cheaply. The ERIE CANAL allowed shippers to transport goods from the Great Lakes to New York City and beyond relatively quickly. The turnpikes were, by contrast, slower and less reliable. As a result, turnpike development slowed considerably once the canals became established.

See also CONESTOGA WAGON; INTERSTATE HIGHWAY ACT.

Further reading

Faris, John T. *Old Roads out of Philadelphia*. Philadelphia: Lippincott, 1917.

Holbrook, Stewart H. *The Old Post Road: The Story of the Boston Post Road*. New York: McGraw-Hill, 1962.

Wood, Frederick J. *The Turnpikes of New England*. Boston: Marshall Jones Co., 1919.

typewriter   After the introduction of movable type in the Middle Ages, the typewriter was one of the most important developments in print. Because of its slow introduction, it was not until the 19th century that the typewriter became well developed and used in business on a regular basis. It was, however, the single most important invention for business communications until the advent of the personal computer.

The concept of a typewriter had existed for several centuries before Christopher Sholes, Carlos Glidden, and Samuel Soule patented the first machine in 1867. The machine was designed primarily by Sholes. They sold the rights to an investment group, which in turn sold them to Remington & Sons, the firearms manufacturer, which produced the Sholes and Glidden Typewriter in 1873. The machine did not employ the same sort of keyboard that typewriters employ today. It wrote capital letters only on what is called the QWERTYUIOP keyboard. The original machine produced an "up-strike" design, in which the key strikes upward when pressed. The technique meant that the typist could not see what was being typed and was referred to as the "blind writer."

In order to avoid jamming of the keys, the machine was designed with this unusual keyboard so that the most commonly used letter keys would not jam. But the invention did not enjoy instant success. Initially, it sold only about 1,000 units per year and cost $125. Five years later, Remington designed its Number 2 machine, which had many improvements over the original model, including upper and lower case letters using a shift key. It still took almost 10 years for the Number 2 to become popular, but when it did, the machine became a staple in the American office.

Many other attempts were made both in the United State and abroad at perfecting the machine. The Caligraph Number 1 was the second typewriter to appear in the United States, in 1880. Its Number 2 model had a larger keyboard featuring both lower and upper cases rather than the shift key used by Remington. In 1884, Hammond used a type-shuttle design that had a curved keyboard with its own unique key arrangement. Hammond type-shuttles were made in numerous different typefaces and languages. It also produced the Varityper, a standard office type-setting machine that was the forerunner of today's computer-based keyboards. Blickensderfer introduced its "scientific" keyboard in 1893 and used yet another typing mechanism known as a type-wheel. It also produced the first electric model in 1902 using the same principles as the IBM Selectric, which came on the market more than 40 years later.

Although many rivals challenged Remington, none seriously threatened it until the introduction of the first "visible" typewriter by Underwood. Its Number 1 machine, designed by German inventor Franz Xavier Wagner, was considered to be the first modern typewriter. Its front-strike design finally made the type fully visible to the typist. Other models followed, including the Number 5, which sold millions over its 30-year life.

During World War II, INTERNATIONAL BUSINESS MACHINES introduced the Selectric model, an

Woman seated at an Underwood typewriter, ca. 1918 (LIBRARY OF CONGRESS)

electric version that finally revolutionized office procedures based upon the old Blickensderfer model. It quickly dominated the office machine segment of the market, while Smith Corona introduced machines for personal and office use. The typewriter began to be replaced by the personal computer in the 1980s, since the PC was faster and also used the same keyboard design.

See also OFFICE MACHINES.

Further reading

Beeching, Wilfred A. *Century of the Typewriter.* London: Heineman, 1974.

Bliven, Bruce. *The Wonderful Writing Machine: The Fascinating Story of the Typewriter from its Earliest Beginnings to the Present.* New York: Random House, 1954.

U

Union Pacific Railroad The railroad company that helped build the transcontinental link connecting the East and West Coasts in 1869. Impetus for creation of the company was given by Congress in the Pacific Railroad Act of 1862, which authorized the building of a rail line by private carriers that would connect both coasts. Throughout its early history, the company was plagued by scandal as well as engineering success.

The company that completed the massive building job was founded by Oakes Ames, Oliver Ames, and Thomas Durant. They invested some of their personal fortunes into an effort that was floundering until they became involved. They were charged with building the eastern link of the rail connection westward from Nebraska while the Central Pacific Railroad built the western link eastward from California. Both companies took over the job from earlier companies that had started building lines but never completed them. The building took six years and occupied more than 20,000 men, mostly immigrants from Europe and China. It became the most daunting engineering and construction project yet undertaken in the United States.

One river, the Weber, had to be crossed 31 times. The two lines were connected at Promontory Point, Utah Territory, on May 10, 1869. The original trip from New York to San Francisco took 10 days.

After the work was complete, the Crédit Mobilier scandal erupted concerning the financing of the railway. In 1872, it was revealed that the construction firm that built the road, named after a French finance company and bank, had embezzled millions of dollars of government-provided funds, raising the cost of construction substantially. The result left the Union Pacific heavily in debt, and it was forced into BANKRUPTCY in 1893, during a depression that also forced many other RAILROADS and businesses to close. Jay GOULD controlled the railroad until 1892, when he died, passing ownership to his son George. The company was resurrected as the Union Pacific Railroad Company by E. H. HARRIMAN, who owned the Illinois Central at the time; others invested $110 million in the railroad in 1897, and it became a viable company again.

In 1901, the railroad bought the stock of the Southern Pacific and merged it with its own operations. After Harriman's death, UP was forced to relinquish the Southern Pacific by the U.S. Supreme Court in 1913.

In the 1920s and 1930s, the railroad began to diversify its holdings, first by opening the Sun Valley resort in Idaho in 1936 and then by moving into the trucking business. It also premiered the "City of Salina," a high-speed diesel train that featured luxury dining and touring cars. In 1969, the Union Pacific Corporation was formed as a HOLDING COMPANY, and the railroad became one of its holdings. By 1971, the company effectively was out of the passenger business and concentrated exclusively on freight.

In 1980, the Union Pacific, Missouri Pacific, and Western Pacific railroads filed merger applications with the INTERSTATE COMMERCE COMMISSION, and the consolidation was approved two years later. It also purchased other railroad companies, including the Chicago & North Western, which was completely absorbed in 1995. The company recorded $1 billion in revenues in 1999.

Further reading

Ambrose, Stephen E. *Nothing Like It in the World: The Men Who Built the Transcontinental Railroad, 1863–1869.* New York: Simon & Schuster, 2000.

Bain, David H. *Empire Express: Building the First Continental Railroad.* New York: Viking, 1999.

Davis, John P. *The Union Pacific Railway: A Study in Railway Politics, History, and Economics.* Chicago: S. C. Griggs, 1894.

Klein, Maury. *Union Pacific: Birth of a Railroad, 1862–1893.* New York: Doubleday, 1987.

United Automobile Workers (UAW)

Founded in the mid-1930s, the UAW challenged managerial prerogatives in automobile factories and would become one of the most powerful labor unions in the United States. The UAW was, in a way, a byproduct of mass production techniques pioneered by Henry FORD in the 1910s. By striving to make jobs simple and deskilled, Ford and other promoters of highly efficient production inadvertently helped create an enormous number of potential recruits to the industrial unions that formed during the Great Depression. During the Depression, auto production plummeted from 5.3 million cars in 1929 to 1.3 million in 1932. Likewise, the number of autoworkers dropped during the same period from 450,000 to 250,000. Employment totals varied throughout the 1930s, however, and were actually on the upswing in 1936, when the UAW began to gain momentum.

The UAW held its first convention in 1935 in Detroit as part of the American Federation of Labor (AFL), which consisted mainly of craft unions for skilled workers. Historically, the AFL had not been enthusiastic about organizing the masses of unskilled production workers, who were mainly first- and second-generation European immigrants and rural internal migrants from the Midwest, the upper South, and Canada. UAW activists envisioned a union that encompassed all automobile workers, skilled and unskilled, but there was much competition in the early years for the allegiance of the work force. Many skilled workers remained reluctant to make common cause with unskilled employees, and there were disagreements about whether autoworker unions should be limited to individual companies or should represent all workers in the industry.

The most important factors in the rise of the UAW were the living and working conditions of unskilled autoworkers. Surprisingly, wages were not the workers' main concern. Instead, the arbitrary and often punitive power of foremen figured most prominently in workers' complaints. Foremen controlled hiring, firing, transfers, layoffs, rehiring, and even bathroom breaks. More than anything else, workers wanted job security, with hiring, layoffs, and transfers determined by seniority rights independent of a foreman's whims. Workers also wanted input into the speed and content of their particular jobs. In response to extremely difficult market conditions during the Great Depression, automakers had increased the speed of production on assembly lines and had demanded that workers meet higher production quotas. From the workers' perspective, this quest for greater productivity had increased stress, fatigue, and the potential for injury to unacceptable levels. Workers wanted to be treated like human beings, not like purchased labor, but if they were to gain redress for any of these grievances they would have to impinge on what had traditionally been management's domain.

Adding to the complexity of the situation, a number of the UAW's most effective organizers, such as Wyndham Mortimer and Bob Travis, were members of the Communist Party, which from 1936 to 1939 adopted a strategy of working with non-Communist, progressive constituencies in American political life. By virtually all accounts these Communist organizers worked tirelessly in the interests of autoworkers, and there is little evidence to suggest that many of these workers desired the overthrow of power relations in the workplace or in the larger society. Nevertheless, the presence of Communists in the UAW helped auto companies and other antiunion forces argue that the union was un-American and was not acting in the best interests of its potential members.

The UAW, however, including Communists, argued in response that they had federal law on their side. In 1935, President Roosevelt had signed the NATIONAL LABOR RELATIONS ACT (NLRA, also called the Wagner Act after its chief sponsor, Senator Robert Wagner from New York), which guaranteed the right of workers to organize into unions without interference from employers. But few employers obeyed the law. Certain that the NLRA would be declared unconstitutional by the Supreme Court, major automakers continued to fire anyone suspected of harboring union sympathies. In response, the UAW embraced a strategy, the "sit-down" strike, designed to fight lawbreaking with lawbreaking. By sitting down in factories and refusing to leave until demands were met, workers violated trespassing laws but also prevented management

from using its regular arsenal of strike breaking tactics. It was impossible to maintain production with strike breakers when plants were occupied—physically attacking sit-down strikers would likely result in enormous damage to machinery.

Led by Mortimer and Travis, the UAW used this tactic effectively in Flint, Michigan, during the winter of 1936–37. At least 80 percent of Flint citizens relied on GENERAL MOTORS for their livelihoods, but until the sit-down strike, which began on December 30, 1936, only a few workers had been willing to risk their jobs and associate openly with the UAW. By February 11, 1937, however, after groups of committed workers successfully shut down production of Chevrolet and GM suffered significant loss of profits and market share, the corporation was forced to recognize the union. Immediately, thousands of GM employees shook off their fear and joined the UAW.

Within weeks, Chrysler capitulated to unionization with only mild resistance, while Ford continued to fire thousands of workers annually for union activity. Indeed, in 1937 Ford security personnel administered a bloody beating to four UAW officials, including future UAW president Walter REUTHER, outside the River Rouge Plant in Dearborn, Michigan. Despite widely publicized photographs of the attack, Ford violated the National Labor Relations Act with impunity until 1941, when it was finally forced to recognize the union. The UAW also worked, with mixed success, to organize employees at the hundreds of parts suppliers, largely in the Midwest, that were vital to the auto industry.

The UAW's first contracts with GM and Chrysler were slender and not very specific, guaranteeing mainly that the union would be the sole bargaining agent for employees, that seniority would determine layoffs and rehiring, and that multistep grievance procedures would be used to resolve disagreements. It remained to be seen whether any of these provisions would help resolve workers' grievances. Having a voice at all, however, was enough to increase dues-paying membership in the UAW to 220,000 by September 1936. That number rose to 375,000 by August 1937.

Within a year, however, the UAW barely existed. Auto production slumped from 4 million in 1937 to 2 million in 1938. The auto work force, hence union membership, dropped accordingly. By mid-1938, the UAW had only 90,000 dues-paying members, and by early 1939, only 500 members in good standing remained in Flint. Bitter disagreements within the UAW leadership, often about the role of Communists, also weakened the union, while automakers cracked down on workers who, unwilling to wait for grievance procedures to run their course, engaged in unauthorized "wildcat" strikes. To many, it looked like the union might disappear.

World War II saved the UAW. Long before the Japanese attack on Pearl Harbor, wartime production had begun to revive the nation's economy. The war economy eventually created virtually full employment and allowed the UAW to reassert itself as the sole bargaining agent for autoworkers. By mid-1940, the UAW had contracts covering more than 410,000 workers. UAW membership surpassed 1 million by 1945, including large numbers of women and African Americans who entered the industrial work force during the war, as well as many workers in the aerospace and farm implement industries.

During the war, UAW leadership emphasized the patriotism of its 250,000 members serving in the armed forces and its production workers turning out war materiel. At the federal government's urging, the union signed a no-strike pledge for the duration of the war in return for the automatic check-off of union dues and a "maintenance of membership" clause designed to guarantee a strong union presence in defense plants. UAW leaders also argued that since the government placed ceilings on workers' wages, it should also limit corporate profits and businessmen's salaries. Although union officials were never convinced that businessmen and corporations sacrificed equally with labor, the UAW supported the continuation of a government-business-labor partnership in organizing the American economy after the war. UAW leaders hoped to avoid any postwar recession, like the one that followed World War I, and they hoped that the labor movement would have a formal, permanent voice in postwar economic affairs.

Those dreams did not materialize. Auto companies strongly opposed postwar government control of the economy, especially in partnership with the labor movement, and in the emerging cold war any plan with even a hint of central planning had little chance of survival. The UAW's GM director, Walter Reuther, launched a showdown with GM in late 1945, demanding a 30 percent wage increase to compensate for wartime inflation while challenging GM not to raise the prices of its automobiles and to open its financial records if the corporation claimed that it could not afford to do so. In this strike, GM held the line against having to share financial information with the union and escaped with having to pay far less than the 30 percent wage increase. All the UAW could hope to gain in the future, it seemed, was increased wages and benefits from automakers.

In the postwar boom, this often seemed possible. Profits in the auto industry soared, and wages rose dramatically. In addition, in the early postwar years GM offered an Annual Improvement Factor (AIF) and an annual Cost of Living Allowance (COLA) to allow workers' incomes to rise with productivity and not be eroded by inflation. Ford and Chrysler followed suit. During the 1950s, the UAW negotiated health benefits for its members, as well as Supplemental Unemployment Benefits that protected workers against financial ruin during layoffs and increased the incentive for companies to maintain high employment. The UAW sought federally funded pensions, unemployment insurance, and health benefits. The union thought the Big Three would support this expanded federal role because government responsibility would substantially reduce the automakers' financial commitments. GM, Ford, and Chrysler, however, feared an increasing role for government in the economy and supported company-paid benefits instead. This private commitment would vex managements in later decades when large numbers of autoworkers retired under UAW contracts and continued to expect their benefits. (In 2003 contract negotiations, for example, the UAW bargained for about 300,000 active autoworkers and more than 500,000 retirees.)

In order to bargain with large auto companies and monitor the expanding details of contracts, the UAW became highly centralized, depending more on skilled attorneys than shop-floor activists. Coupled with the influx of new employees after the war who had no experience working without a union and might have taken their working conditions for granted, the crusading, reforming spirit of the early UAW seemed to wane. A number of union critics argued that the UAW too often appeared to side with management in opposition to the interests of its members.

Still, throughout the 1960s the union appeared to have achieved many of its early goals—workers had far more job security than in the 1930s, they had some input over the speed and content of their jobs (although line speed and safety grievances increased in the 1960s), and they were buffered from the wildest swings of the economy. But that was true only for those whose jobs continued to exist. Automation in the 1950s eliminated thousands of jobs, mainly the dirtiest and hardest positions that had generally been relegated to African Americans. Moreover, plant relocations began in the 1950s, moving many auto jobs away from Detroit and to the suburbs, to rural areas in the Midwest, and to the South. Union membership remained between 1.1 and 1.5 million until the late 1960s, but in future decades the union's inability to control the placement of factories would decimate its membership, just like job losses had devastated the city of Detroit.

In addition to plant relocation, foreign competition began making inroads into the U.S. auto market. As early as 1959, foreign cars constituted 10 percent of domestic sales. European and Japanese competition would intensify after the oil crises of 1973 and 1979, when the large, "gas guzzling" cars produced by GM, Ford, and Chrysler fell out of favor. By 1980, Detroit factories were producing only half of what they had in the mid-1970s, and the UAW accepted wage concessions to help survive the crisis. Working with management, however, did not guarantee any favors in the future. Eventually, the UAW lost members as American auto companies transferred much work to new factories outside the United States, often in Mexico. Meanwhile, foreign car companies began building factories in the United States and managed to stave off organizing efforts by the UAW, generally by offering UAW-style wages and benefits to their workforces. Although some argue that the UAW priced the labor of its members out of the global auto manufacturing market, it is unclear what the long-term ramifications will be from the decline in unionized manufacturing jobs in the United States. After all, by increasing the purchasing power of its members, the UAW was central to post-WWII American economic prosperity.

Further reading
Asher, Robert, and Ronald Edsforth, eds. *Autowork*. Albany: State University of New York Press, 1995.
Barnard, John. *American Vanguard: The United Auto Workers during the Reuther Years, 1935–1970*. Detroit: Wayne State University Press, 2003.
Boyle, Kevin. *The UAW and the Heyday of American Liberalism, 1945–1968*. Ithaca, N.Y.: Cornell University Press, 1995.
Chinoy, Ely. *Automobile Workers and the American Dream*. 2nd ed. Urbana: University of Illinois Press, 1992.
Serrin, William. *The Company and the Union*. New York: Knopf, 1970.

Daniel J. Clark

United Fruit Company   Boston-based banana producing and marketing company. In 1870, Captain Lorenzo Dow Baker made an experimental import with bananas he bought in Jamaica for a shilling and sold in Jersey City for $2 a bunch. After this success, Baker joined Bostonian entrepreneur Andrew Preston and created the Boston Fruit Company. This company owned a large fleet of steamships that, with time, became the largest private fleet in the world—the Great White Fleet.

In 1899, another Bostonian entrepreneur, Minor C. Keith, approached Preston and Baker and proposed to merge their company with his business. Keith had built railways in Central America and Colombia, owned lands in those countries, and was also involved in the banana export business. They agreed, and on March 30, 1899, the United Fruit Company was born.

The new company had Preston as president and Keith as vice president. Keith had his railroad network and plantations in Central America, plus the market in the U.S. Southeast, and Preston grew bananas in the West Indies, ran the Great White Fleet, and sold to the U.S. Northeast. As the company grew, Keith continued with his railroad projects in Central America.

United Fruit needed to assure a steady output of bananas to its consumer market in the United States. This was a difficult task because bananas, contrary to other goods, rot quickly. Given that they could not be produced in the consumer markets, the company developed an impressive production and distribution network between the tropical lands in the Caribbean and the United States. This included plantations (with health and housing infrastructure), railways, ports, telegraph lines, and steamships.

In 1900, United Fruit owned 212,394 acres of land, while in 1954 it owned 603,111 acres scattered in Central America and the Caribbean. The company also established the Fruit Dispatch Company, a subsidiary in charge of distributing bananas in the United States. United Fruit was a major shareholder of the Hamburg Line, a German shipping company, and also bought 85 percent of the shares of the British banana import and shipping company Elders & Fyffes, with which United Fruit assured itself a privileged

position in the British market. By 1928, United Fruit had bought 99 percent of Elders & Fyffes shares. In 1913, the company also created the Tropical Radio and Telegraph Company to keep in constant communication with its ships and plantations. Finally, United Fruit quickly eliminated its smaller competitors such as the Atlantic Fruit Company and Cuyamel Fruit Company.

The company's expansion was facilitated by a business-friendly environment in Central America. Before World War II, United Fruit counted on dictatorships that repressed labor unionism and gave generous concessions in terms of land grants and tax incentives. In some of these countries, United Fruit was the major employer, was the largest investor in infrastructure, and was permitted the international marketing of the country's main export. Countries such as Guatemala, Panama, and Honduras depended on bananas for more than 60 percent of their total exports. Because of this, the local governments encouraged the company's operations in their national territories.

After World War II, the company faced serious threats that obliged it to change its internal structure from a producing company to a marketing one. The rise of nationalistic governments and stronger labor unionism in Latin America made its investments in the region riskier. In 1954, when Guatemalan president Jacobo Arbenz attempted to expropriate some of the company's lands, the Honduran banana workers went on the biggest strike in that country's history, and the U.S. government sued the company for failing to comply with antitrust legislation. These events made United Fruit's shareholders think that land ownership in Central America increased the company's risks, so in the 1960s the company gradually got rid of its plantations and RAILROADS and concentrated its efforts in the international marketing of bananas.

With demand for bananas decreasing in the U.S. market after the 1950s, United Fruit diversified its operations to processed food in the 1960s. This transformation went further when the company merged with AMK Corporation and created a food conglomerate in 1970 called United Brands Company. In 1989, this conglomerate changed its name to Chiquita Brands International, Inc.

Further reading

Adams, Frederick U. *The Conquest of the Tropics: The Story of the Creative Enterprises Conducted by the United Fruit Company.* Garden City, N.Y.: Doubleday Page, 1914.
May, Stacy, and Galo Plaza. *United States Business Performance Abroad: The Case Study of the United Fruit Company in Latin America.* Washington, D.C.: National Planning Association, 1958.

Marcelo Bucheli

United Mine Workers of America America's mid-19th-century coal industry depended heavily on skillful immigrant colliers from the British Isles. Proud of their mining knowledge and skills, these British immigrants also brought a tradition of craft associations and proved to be a motivating force behind the formation of miners' unions in the United States. The first British miners thought of themselves as craftsmen with a role equal to that of owners, but the growth of modern capitalism had intensified the separation between capital and labor. Labor constituted the major expense of mine operations, and, consequently, owners tended to reduce wages in an effort to remain competitive in the volatile coal market. Potential union leaders soon realized the need to abandon the craft association ideology for industrial unionism. Mine operators, embroiled in a fiercely competitive market and fearful that unionization might limit their ability to survive, developed methods of resistance that characterized the industry's antiunion efforts well into the 20th century: operator associations, private police, "blacklisting" of unionists, and legal actions based on the right to control and manage private property.

Despite intense operator resistance, miners experienced an expanding collective consciousness during the 1880s. Yet rivalry continued among two associations, the National Federation of Miners and Mine Laborers and the National Trades Assembly No. 135 of the Knights of Labor. Attempting to end dual unionism, the two groups met at Columbus, Ohio, in 1888 and organized the National Progressive Union of Miners and Mine Laborers (NPU). But rivalry continued, and in January of 1890, again in Columbus, a conference reorganized the NPU into the United Mine Workers of America (UMWA), with an American Federation of Labor industrial union charter.

The new union hoped to resolve such issues as fluctuating wages, payment in company scrip, and private police forces that regulated everyday life, but also realized the need to assist operators in stabilizing a highly competitive market. Coal suffered from overproduction and intense price competition between regions. Wages constituted about 70 percent of production costs, and miners often suffered from market instability. Unfortunately, the economic downturn of the early 1890s led to wage cuts and strikes that nearly bankrupted the fledgling UMWA.

Union efforts rebounded with fiscal recovery and led to the first major success. In 1898, operators of the Central Competitive Field (western Pennsylvania, Ohio, Indiana, and Illinois) met jointly with the union and signed the Central Competitive Agreement. This "Interstate Agreement" gave miners an eight-hour day and standard wage rate, and the victory helped the UMWA expand membership from 33,000 in 1898 to a quarter-million in 1903. With this success, union president John Mitchell next decided to organize the anthracite coalfields of western Pennsylvania; the subsequent 1902 strike precipitated a national crisis. A five-month deadlock led to shortages and higher coal prices, resulting in President Theodore Roosevelt's first-ever federal intervention in coal's labor conflicts.

The 1902 anthracite strike opened the market for "smokeless" bituminous coal from nonunion areas. Mining expanded rapidly outside the

Central Competitive Field, and operators in the newly opened areas embraced severe antiunion measures. In the first two decades of the 20th century, UMWA strength and resources proved unequal to private police and operator use of state-vested authority. This was particularly true in West Virginia and Colorado and led to the killing of unarmed workers in episodes at Holly Grove and Ludlow. Attempts at unionization produced two major mine "wars" in West Virginia, but the UMWA still failed to make progress outside the Central Competitive Field.

Workers patriotically honored a "no-strike" pledge during the production upswing of World War I. Federal mobilization efforts had standardized wages and addressed some worker grievances under the Washington Agreement. Officials declared the compact binding until 1920, but miners complained about increased operator profits while inflation devoured wages. Postwar employers immediately attempted to protect profit increases by maintaining fixed wages, invalidating union recognition, and abolishing the right of collective bargaining. Owners refused to negotiate, and a widespread strike crippled the industry in 1919. Miners vehemently complained that national authorities had abandoned forcing companies to abide by coal prices or labor rules, but instead were using wartime legalities to impose a comprehensive injunction on workers. Colliers ignored the injunction despite claims that Bolsheviks financed the strike, and President Woodrow Wilson ordered a temporary 14 percent wage increase and appointed an investigative Bituminous Coal Commission to direct a final settlement.

Unionism held the promise of stabilizing the industry by encouraging corresponding operator associations, but these groups varied in purpose—some to facilitate bargaining with the UMWA, others to prevent unionization. With the latter increasing in the 1920s, the UMWA entered a period of decline. Overproduction, cutthroat competition, and the development of other fuel sources blended with expanding antiunionism to make the miners' union ineffective by the end of the decade.

John L. LEWIS, the most famous UMWA president, assumed leadership during this period. Elected in 1920, Lewis pledged to accept no reduction of past union gains and, in the Jacksonville Agreement of 1924, convinced the Central Field producers to maintain the base wage rate. These high wages encouraged the growth of nonunion mines elsewhere, which placed the Central Field at a competitive disadvantage. Federal attempts at stabilization failed when postwar operator unity declined, and entrepreneurs revived resistance to governmental interference. When Lewis rejected wage concessions, operators nullified the 1924 agreement and began a largely successful open-shop campaign.

The shrinking UMWA seemed powerless in an overdeveloped coal industry. Coal companies, particularly in the South, continued to control workers through traditional methods, and governmental actions bolstered these antiunion efforts. Federal troops arrived to suppress major strikes, and court injunctions impeded organizing campaigns. Reckless competition intensified in an industry roughly divided between the northern fields and southern Appalachia.

In this era of union decline, Lewis ignored UMWA ethics and moved aggressively to centralize power in the international office. From the outset, the UMWA had based its administration on democratic principles. Local chapters elected delegates who voiced the concerns and opinions of rank-and-file members at district and national conventions. Lewis made himself a virtual autocrat as he intimidated, discredited, and purged dissenters. He hoped that a similar autocracy might develop among the coal operators and result in industry-wide contract bargaining and a standardized wage scale.

Lewis's domineering practices, the long period of RECESSION, and company antiunion methods contributed to a resurgence of organizational spirit in the 1930s. Rank-and-file militancy manifested itself in 1931 and 1932, when the upstart National Miners Union led strikes in Kentucky, Pennsylvania, and Ohio, and wildcat walkouts occurred in southern Illinois. Lewis capitalized on the new militancy to both solidify his leadership and expand the union. In June 1933, Section 7(a) of the National Industrial Recovery Act further fueled the movement, and the UMWA quickly organized more than 90 percent of the coalfields, including the historically violent antiunion operations of West Virginia.

Unionization of the notoriously antiunion captive mines, those who sold only to a parent company in such industries as steel, provided a needed victory. Organizing the STEEL INDUSTRY could protect these newly established locals, and Lewis again recognized labor's militancy and advocated the organization of mass production industries. When the AFL ignored the movement, Lewis established the Congress of Industrial Organizations (CIO) in 1938. UMWA human and financial resources supported the efforts that brought unionization to thousands of the nation's mass production laborers. The UMWA left the CIO when Lewis fulfilled his pledge to resign from the CIO presidency if Roosevelt won reelection in 1940.

Coal boomed during World War II, but Lewis ignored the wartime no-strike pledges of other labor leaders. Two strikes won significant gains but damaged the public image of organized labor. After the war, the UMWA demanded an end to the often substandard health care associated with "company" medical services. Thousands of miners lay disabled, and postwar strikes won a welfare and retirement fund financed by tonnage royalties. In time, the funds paid benefits to millions of miners and their families and subsidized the building of 10 miners' hospitals in the mid-1950s.

Postwar technological innovations enabled coal's customers to turn to other fuels. Lewis had long believed that mechanization coupled with comprehensive unionization provided a solution for the unstable market; labor organization equalized wages, and increased tonnage might competitively eliminate less-efficient operations.

By 1950, the Bituminous Coal Operators Association (BCOA) concurred and settled a new contract that established nationwide bargaining and promoted automation. Subsequent technological unemployment reduced the number of miners from 416,000 to 130,000 by the mid-1960s.

A significant era of labor history ended when Lewis resigned the presidency in 1960, passing the reigns of leadership to the ill and elderly Thomas Kennedy. W. A. (Tony) Boyle actually controlled the union during Kennedy's short administration. Boyle assumed the presidency in 1963 and attempted to wield the power established by Lewis, but Boyle had neither the personality nor political skills of Lewis. America had entered an era of grassroots movements motivated by a distrust of vested authority, and Boyle's tactics and a perceived disregard for miners aroused serious rank-and-file disapproval. Boyle tried to continue the Lewis-established BCOA-UMWA partnership, but unemployment, company flexibility in layoffs, and tendencies to cut financial support to widows and disabled miners energized a trend to revive union democracy. Boyle's company-friendly attitude at the Farmington, West Virginia, mine disaster in 1968 seemed to validate suspicions of corruption. Grassroots reformers lobbied for the federal Coal Mine Health and Safety Act of 1969 as well as black lung compensation.

Joseph A. (Jock) Yablonski represented the reformers in an unsuccessful attempt to oust Boyle in 1969. A few weeks later, rumors of election corruption escalated when assassins murdered Yablonski and his family. Reform efforts intensified, and dissenters formally organized as the Miners for Democracy (MFD) in 1972. A federal court convicted Boyle of illegal political contributions, and a judge abrogated the 1969 election. Arnold Miller of the MFD won the presidency in 1972 on a pledge to restore union democracy. In 1974, Boyle received a murder conviction for ordering the Yablonski killings.

Miller's administration fell short of reform expectations. The militant spirit of the era and a return to local union autonomy contributed to a rash of wildcat strikes in the 1970s. Miners lost faith in Miller, particularly after the 111-day 1977–78 contract strike. An oversupplied market gave coal consumers the upper hand in disputes, and conservative president Sam Church attempted to reestablish the industry-labor accord of the later Lewis years. An expansion of nonunion mining and use of western strip-mined coal had weakened UMWA bargaining power, but miners felt betrayed by the Church administration's 1981 contract proposal. In 1982, intelligent miner-turned-lawyer Richard Trumka accused the union leadership of reactionary policies, and he won election to the presidency.

Trumka's administration returned miners' faith in their leadership and restored order to the union's democratic process. A more sophisticated approach broke from tradition with innovations such as selective strikes and programs to raise public awareness of labor issues. This became particularly important in 1989, when the Pittston Company withdrew from the BCOA. Increasing health costs and the rising number of retirees led Pittston to rescind its obligation to the funds, and the resulting 10-month strike witnessed the adoption of new labor tactics such as mass civil disobedience. Facing a determined corporate effort, right-to-work law, and replacement workers, the union nurtured a community-based resistance that garnered an acceptable contract.

In 1989, the UMWA reentered the AFL-CIO, and in 1995 Trumka became secretary-treasurer of that organization. Today the president of the 110,000-member UMWA is Cecil Roberts, whose strategies and coordination contributed much to the successful campaign against Pittston. While the union continues to represent the interests of American coal miners, it has also entered the arena of international labor issues.

Further reading

Fox, Maier B. *United We Stand: The United Mine Workers of America, 1890–1990*. Washington, D.C.: United Mine Workers of America, 1990.

Laslett, John H. M., ed. *The United Mine Workers of America: A Model of Industrial Solidarity?* University Park: Pennsylvania State University Press, 1996.

Seltzer, Curtis. *Fire in the Hole: Miners and Managers in the American Coal Industry*. Lexington: University Press of Kentucky, 1985.

Paul H. Rakes

U.S. Steel Corp.   A company created by J. P. Morgan and Elbert Gary after Morgan acquired Carnegie Steel for almost $500 million in 1901. Carnegie Steel was merged with the Federated Steel Co., founded in 1898, and several other companies to form the largest company in the world. It was the first company with a balance sheet valued at more than $1 billion, and its initial market capitalization stood at $1.4 billion. When it was first formed, the company was responsible for an explosive rally on Wall Street, followed by a sharp drop in the market index.

Immediately after being founded, the company accounted for almost two-thirds of U.S. steel production. Its first president was Charles M. Schwab, who left after two years to run Bethlehem Steel. Despite its size and potential for market domination, the company was loosely run and did not dominate the market as originally feared. The company boasted 170 subsidiaries and net earnings in its first year of operation of $108 million. It employed more than 160,000 workers. When first formed it accounted for 62 percent of domestically produced steel, but the numbers began to fall, to 52 percent during World War I and 46 percent in the 1920s.

U.S. Steel was sued by the government for antitrust violations in 1912. The case was not settled until 1920, when the Supreme Court ruled that U.S. Steel no longer had a monopoly. The war years were among some of its most profitable. Free of antitrust problems, the company prospered in the 1920s as it had during World War I. Along with other "smokestack" stocks, "Big Steel" became known as one of the country's "wheelhorse" industries, being emblematic of American industrial production. During the stock market crash of 1929, New York Stock

Exchange president Richard Whitney entered an order for U.S. Steel in an attempt to stabilize the market in the face of sell orders, symbolizing its importance to the market. It remained the country's largest producer of steel until the 1950s, when foreign competition began to emerge from Europe and the Far East. Competition from alternative products, such as plastics, also reduced demand for steel products, and the American share of worldwide steel production fell by 50 percent by the late 1950s.

The company took a major step toward diversification in 1982, when it acquired Marathon Oil Co. Several years later it also acquired Texas Oil and Gas and then changed its name to the USX Corporation. It also became the target of several corporate takeover specialists who viewed its parts as worth more than the whole. The company returned to profitability in the 1980s and was restructured again in 1991, spinning off two publicly traded companies, the USX-US Steel and USX-Marathon companies. It also bought some eastern European operations after the fall of Soviet communism in order to expand its operations internationally. In 2001, USX shareholders voted to spin off the steel making unit into a freestanding company known, once again, as United States Steel Corporation.

See also MORGAN, JOHN PIERPONT; STEEL INDUSTRY; WHITNEY, RICHARD.

Further reading

Broude, Henry. *Steel Decisions and the National Economy.* New Haven, Conn.: Yale University Press, 1963.

Urofsky, Melvin I. *Big Steel and the Wilson Administration.* Columbus: Ohio State University Press, 1969.

Warren, Kenneth. *Big Steel: The First Century of the United States Steel Corporation, 1901–2001.* Pittsburgh: University of Pittsburgh Press, 2001.

utilities   Name traditionally associated with companies that provide electricity and water. Traditionally, utility companies have been referred to as public utilities, even if they were organized as corporate stock companies. Other utilities have been owned and operated by government authorities, usually municipal or, in one case, by a federal government agency.

Although companies providing water are included within the category, the term *utilities* is usually associated with companies that provide electricity. The first company in the United States to provide electricity was the Edison Electric Co. in New York City, originally owned by Thomas EDISON. With financial assistance from J. P. Morgan & Co., Edison Electric began producing electricity in lower Manhattan. Although early attempts were made at consolidating the industry, electricity was provided by many companies in the 19th century. The fragmented nature of the early industry gave way to larger utility companies that began to form in the early 1900s, financed by Wall Street. The GENERAL ELECTRIC CO., the successor to Edison Electric, was one example.

In the 1920s, consolidation of the electric producing industry intensified when large industrial holding companies were formed, which in turn owned the smaller generating units. Disputes arose in states where there was a mix of ownership. Some states had their electricity provided by private, independently owned companies in some areas and by municipally owned companies in other areas. As a result, charges for electricity varied greatly. The debate over the ownership of electric companies became one of the major public policy issues of the 1920s. By the latter part of the decade, several larger utility holding companies controlled almost 50 percent of electrical production in United States. Some of the better known among them were Samuel Insull's Midwest Utilities and the United Corporation, controlled by J. P. Morgan Jr.

During the 1930s, the debate continued, and the U.S. government created the TENNESSEE VALLEY AUTHORITY in 1933. The massive utility company was the outcome of a government-inspired electric power facility built at Muscle Shoals, Alabama, during World War I. The large HOLDING COMPANY provided hydroelectric power for rural areas in the South. It was one of the rare instances in which the government entered the industrial sector to provide a service usually

Edison electric plant, Detroit, Michigan, ca. 1900 (Library of Congress)

delivered on the local level and has been cited as one of the accomplishments of the New Deal.

As a result of the debate over ownership of utilities and the relationship of Wall Street with many of the holding companies, Congress passed the Public Utility Holding Company Act in 1935. The law required utilities to seek permission from the Securities and Exchange Commission before issuing new securities and also limited holding companies to owning only one power generating company—known at the time as the death sentence provision because it effectively ended many utilities empires. This provision effectively limited the size of holding companies and put the power generating capacity within a state or region in the hands of one company. Utilities within the states were also subject to the various state power commissions for rate increases and pricing.

The utilities industry was partially deregulated in 1992, when the Energy Policy Act was passed by Congress, allowing utilities to deregulate sales and opening the door for cheaper wholesale rates and potentially cheaper rates for consumers. The states also began to deregulate in their own right, although the price of electricity still varied from state to state, much as it had in the earlier part of the century.

See also Insull, Samuel; Morgan, John Pierpont, Jr.

Further reading

Jacobson, Charles David. *Ties that Bind: Economic and Political Dilemmas of Urban Utility Networks, 1800–1990.* Pittsburgh: University of Pittsburgh Press, 2001.

Ramsay, M. L. *Pyramids of Power: The Story of Roosevelt, Insull and the Utility Wars.* Indianapolis: Bobbs-Merrill, 1937.

Schap, David. *Municipal Ownership in the Electric Utility Industry.* Westport, Conn.: Praeger, 1986.

V

Vail, Theodore N. (1845–1920) *telephone executive* Born in Minerva, Ohio, Vail became the prime force behind the creation of the AMERICAN TELEPHONE & TELEGRAPH CO. (AT&T) and the first general manager of the telephone system in the United States. After moving to New Jersey with his family at age two, he graduated from the Morristown Academy and then went to work in a drugstore, which was also a TELEGRAPH office. He quickly learned to operate a telegraph and then found a job working for the WESTERN UNION TELEGRAPH CO. in New York City.

Vail's family moved to Iowa in 1866, and he accompanied them and began a career with Union Pacific's railway postal service. During his tenure with the service, he established the first mail-only train service and eventually became superintendent of the railway mail service in 1876. During his time with the postal service, he became acquainted with Gardiner Green Hubbard, who was in the process of forming Bell Telephone Associates with other businessmen; in 1878, Vail was lured away to run the Bell Telephone Co. as general manager. Under his auspices, the company developed a long-distance service from Boston to Providence, Rhode Island.

Vail also presided over the formation of Western Electric Co., the arm of Bell that manufactured telephone equipment. He retired from the company in 1887 after coming into conflict with the board of directors, which did not want to expand the company as quickly as he did.

After retiring from the telephone company, Vail embarked on business ventures in Argentina, helping finance and develop electric and power projects in Cordoba and Buenos Aires. He was persuaded to return to the telephone company after it was consolidated as the American Telephone & Telegraph Co. in 1907 with the financial backing of J. P. Morgan. Vail believed that competition was wasteful and proceeded to strengthen the company. He moved the company headquarters from Boston to New York and quickly moved to unite all of the Bell companies around the country by personally becoming acquainted with their presidents. He developed a strong affiliation with the Western Union Telegraph Company in 1909, although antitrust action caused them to separate four years later. In 1914, AT&T introduced the first coast-to-coast long-distance service, and Vail had the distinction of placing the first call from Boston to

455

San Francisco. During the war, the service was so successful that Congress effectively granted AT&T a virtual monopoly over telecommunications. Vail joined the company's board of directors in 1919, when he retired from the operating unit of the company. He died in New York in 1920.

See also BELL, ALEXANDER GRAHAM.

Further reading

Boettinger, H. M. *Telephone Book: Bell, Watson, Vail and American Life, 1876–1983*. New York: Stearn Publishers, 1983.

Garnet, Robert W. *The Telephone Enterprise: The Evolution of the Bell System's Horizontal Structure*. Baltimore: Johns Hopkins University Press, 1985.

Paine, Albert W. *In One Man's Life*. 1921. Reprint, Murietta, Calif.: New Library Press, 2003.

Vanderbilt, Cornelius (1794–1877) *shipping and railroad entrepreneur* Born in Staten Island, New York, to Dutch parents, Vanderbilt left school early to establish his own ferry service from Staten Island to Manhattan. Using $100 borrowed from his parents, he bought a small boat and began ferrying customers to lower Manhattan. He established his reputation for toughness and reliability during the War of 1812 by working long hours. He was soon able to expand his fleet of small sailing boats and became one of New York's best-known ferrymen, acquiring the nickname of "Commodore" that became his hallmark. By 1817, his fleet covered much of the East Coast, from Boston to Charleston.

Recognizing that sailing ships had a limited future after the introduction of steamships, Vanderbilt sold his fleet and went to work for another ferry operator, Thomas Gibbons, who operated a service between Philadelphia and New York City. The ferry service itself ran between New York and New Brunswick, New Jersey, with the balance of the trip conducted by coach. The New York legislature previously had granted a monopoly to Robert FULTON and Robert LIVINGSTON to operate a steamship ferry in New York harbor, and they in turn licensed Aaron Ogden of New Jersey to operate a ferry between New Jersey and New York. Gibbons and Vanderbilt challenged the service, and Vanderbilt took great delight in encroaching on their territory and taking paying customers to New Brunswick. Finally, the monopoly was attacked in court by Gibbons. After losing the case in the lower courts, Gibbons appealed to the Supreme Court, where the landmark case of *Gibbons v. Ogden* was decided in his favor.

Vanderbilt entered the steamship business in 1829 and entered the same market, New York to Philadelphia. Shortly afterward, he started a service up the Hudson River. He was so successful on the route that he was eventually bought out by a competitor, as he had been on the Philadelphia route as well. He then opened a service to New England and became one of the dominant forces in East Coast shipping. When the Gold Rush

Cornelius Vanderbilt (LIBRARY OF CONGRESS)

began in California in 1849, he contemplated a service between New York and California, crossing Central America through Nicaragua. He was unable to solve the logistics involved, but his problems were solved when he was again bought out by his competition. He then opened a transatlantic service that was successful until the Civil War broke out.

During the Civil War, he turned his attention to RAILROADS. He bought an operating interest in the New York & Harlem Railroad in New York. When acquiring control, he also learned the techniques of stock market manipulation that many of the early railroad entrepreneurs employed to gain control of a company's stock. He improved the railroad substantially and then acquired the Hudson River Railroad as well. In 1867, he also took control of the New York Central Railroad, which operated between Albany and Buffalo. His holdings stretched from lower Manhattan to Buffalo. He then launched an attempt to take over the ERIE RAILROAD, which extended from Buffalo to Chicago. At the time, the Erie was controlled by Jay GOULD and Jim FISK, who were not about to relinquish control to Vanderbilt. What followed became known as the "Erie War."

Vanderbilt began accumulating shares in the railroad. The two directors of Erie responded by issuing more stock in the company, effectively taking Vanderbilt's money while denying him a controlling interest. He threatened them with legal action, and Gould and Fisk decamped quickly to New Jersey with a large horde of the railroad's cash. Vanderbilt eventually gave up the battle, again for a million-dollar settlement in his favor.

In addition to acquiring railroads, Vanderbilt built the original Grand Central Station in New York City during the depression of 1873, winning him accolades for public service during a difficult period. He died in 1877, leaving the bulk of his $100-million fortune to his son, William Henry Vanderbilt, who continued his father's railroading interests.

See also COMMERCE CLAUSE.

Further reading
Croffut, William. *The Vanderbilts and the Story of Their Fortune.* New York: Belford, Clarke, 1886.
Lane, Wheaton J. *Commodore Vanderbilt: An Epic of the Steam Age.* New York: Knopf, 1942.

Veblen, Thorstein (1857–1929) *economist and social theorist*   Born in Wisconsin on the family farm, Veblen was the son of Norwegian immigrants who came to the United States in 1847. He graduated from Carleton College in three years and moved to Baltimore to do graduate work in philosophy at Johns Hopkins. Three years later, he enrolled at Yale, where he earned a Ph.D. in 1884. He then started a peripatetic career that began with a long period of unemployment before he enrolled at Cornell in 1891 to study economics.

His first substantial job came in 1892, when he taught political economy at the University of Chicago, recently founded by John D. Rockefeller. He remained on the staff until 1906, during which time he published his most famous book, *The Theory of the Leisure Class* (1899). In the book, he adopted a neoclassical view of how humans attained leisure and coined the phrase for which he is best remembered—"conspicuous consumption." According to Veblen, those with the most leisure time indulge in consumption beyond their basic needs and desires as part of an anthropological desire to gain attention. This form of attention-getting was a primal force in life, no different from the urge to mating or self-preservation. He used August Belmont II as his model, since both he and his father, August Belmont, were known for their indulgences.

Veblen also wrote *The Theory of Business Enterprise* (1904) and taught at several other universities after leaving Chicago. He subsequently taught at Stanford and the University of Missouri and was a founding member of the New School for Social Research in 1918. He wrote several books during and after World War I, among them *The Instinct of Workmanship and the State of*

Industrial Arts (1914), *The Vested Interests and the Common Man* (1919), and *Absentee Ownership and Business Enterprise in Recent Times* (1923). He also served on the Food Administration during World War I and taught at the New School for Social Research until his retirement in 1926. He died in California in 1929.

Despite his other writings, Veblen is best remembered in business for coining the term *conspicuous consumption,* which along with other terms like ROBBER BARONS, has become standard usage in American language.

See also BELMONT, AUGUST; BELMONT, AUGUST, II.

Further reading

Dorfman, Joseph. *Thorstein Veblen and His America.* New York: Viking, 1966.

Edgell, Stephen. *Veblen in Perspective: His Life and Thought.* New York: M. E. Sharpe, 2001.

Volcker, Paul (1927–) *chairman of the Federal Reserve Board*   Paul Volcker was born in Cape May, New Jersey, on September 5, 1927, the son of a city manager who had saved the city of Teaneck, New Jersey, from insolvency. His father's disciplined approach to finance greatly influenced Volcker. He himself proved adept at economics; in 1949, he graduated with honors from Princeton University and two years later earned his master's degree from Harvard University. After a year of postgraduate work at the London School of Economics on a Rotary fellowship, Volcker joined the Federal Reserve Bank of New York in 1952. Five years of working for the government ensued, then Volcker left in 1957 to join CHASE MANHATTAN BANK as a financial economist. In 1962 he briefly served with the U.S. Treasury Department as a financial analysis director, and the following year he functioned as undersecretary for monetary affairs. In 1965, Volcker resumed relations with the private sector as vice president of planning at Chase Manhattan, although he subsequently returned to the Treasury four years later as undersecretary of mone-

tary affairs. He departed again in 1974 to become a senior fellow in the School of Public and International Affairs at Princeton; within a year he was tapped to serve as president of the Federal Reserve Bank of New York. Over the next four years the garrulous, cigar-chomping Volcker acquitted himself with distinction at this, the most important bank within the FEDERAL RESERVE system, and his success did not go unnoticed by the political establishment. In August 1979, he was nominated by President Jimmy Carter to serve as chairman of the Federal Reserve Board, an essential position within the government.

Volcker assumed office at a difficult time in American financial history. Carter's handling of the economy resulted in double-digit inflation, while the value of the dollar spiraled downward. Volcker, as head of the Federal Open Market Committee (FOMC), decided to invoke draconian measures to rein inflation back. Instead of controlling interest rates by allowing higher money growth supply rates, the Fed did the opposite: It clamped down by imposing strict money supply growth targets. This policy resulted in extremely high interest rates of 21 percent by December 1980, which triggered the worst RECESSION in 40 years. Unemployment skyrocketed to 10.7 percent in 1982, which jeopardized the mid-term congressional elections of a new president, Ronald Reagan, but Volcker proved adamant. Though vilified by the press as heartless and amid clamoring for his recall by Congress, he maintained his tight-fisted control of the money supply until inflation bottomed out at 4 percent. Many in political circles questioned the sagacity of his policies and whether the price of taming inflation was too high. Nonetheless, in August 1983 President Reagan reappointed Volcker to another four-year term as Fed chairman.

Throughout his second tenure in office, Volcker confronted problems inherent in the DEREGULATION of the financial industry. This brought on sudden and unexpected shifts in the growth supply of money, which threatened to spur inflation, but the Fed maintained a watchful eye and regulated such growth carefully when possible. He also incurred criticism from the banking industry for insisting that the Federal Reserve was obliged by its very nature to closely monitor banks on a daily basis, even in an age of deregulation. Despite an air of uncertainty, Volcker silenced his detractors by keeping inflation in check and by ushering in a period of sustained economic growth—the so-called Reagan revolution. By the time he left office in 1987, he was hailed as among the most influential chairmen of the Federal Reserve in American history. His replacement was the equally gifted Alan GREENSPAN. Since leaving the public sector, Volcker has served as a consultant to the World Bank and as chairman of the National Commission on the Public Service. He remains chairman of the investment banking firm James D. Wolfson.

Further reading

Greider, William. *Secrets of the Temple: How the Federal Reserve Runs the Country.* New York: Simon & Schuster, 1987.

Neikirk, William. *Volcker: Portrait of the Moneyman.* New York: Congdon & Weed, 1987.

Timberlake, Richard H. *Monetary Policy in the United States: An Intellectual and Institutional History.* Chicago: University of Chicago Press, 1993.

Volcker, Paul, and Toyoo Gyohten. *Changing Fortunes: The World's Money and the Threat to American Leadership.* New York: Times Books, 1992.

John C. Fredriksen

Volstead Act   The National Prohibition Act, commonly referred to by the name of its author, Andrew J. Volstead, was the statute enacted in 1919 to enforce Prohibition, imposed by the Eighteenth Amendment to the U.S. Constitution. (Volstead represented a Minnesota district in the House of Representatives, 1903–23.) Constitutional Prohibition, which went into effect in January 1920, forbade the manufacture, distribution, and sale of alcoholic beverages and was thus an important measure of America's determination at the time to exercise public power over objectionable business behaviors. The Volstead Act borrowed from previous state statutes; in general, federal policy relied on local enforcement. However, the law provided for action by federal officials when state and local law enforcement officers were unable or unwilling to enforce Prohibition.

The Volstead Act, like the Prohibition policy it enforced, was controversial. The law placed responsibility for enforcing Prohibition in the Department of the Treasury, not the Justice Department, because Treasury was experienced with taxing alcoholic beverages. Thus, responsibility was placed in the hands of elected and appointed officials, not civil servants chosen by merit. Eventually, after the election of Herbert Hoover in 1928, Congress changed the law to place responsibility under the Justice Department and in the hands of professional law enforcement officers.

The law narrowly defined an intoxicating beverage as one containing more than 0.5 percent alcohol by volume, effectively forbidding the sale of all beer. This strict standard outraged brewers, some of whom had expected Prohibition to exclude their products. Throughout the period of Prohibition, this standard was controversial, with powerful efforts mounted to legalize the businesses of making and selling light beers and wines.

In April 1933, after the inauguration of Franklin D. Roosevelt as president, Congress modified the law so as to allow breweries to operate even before the repeal of the Eighteenth Amendment in December of that year. Finally, the statute had failed to outlaw the possession of alcoholic beverages, especially disappointing some Prohibition advocates, most notably Wayne B. Wheeler, in charge of the legal department of the Anti-Saloon League of America. Thus, under Prohibition, private owners of alcoholic beverages purchased before the imposition of Prohibition continued legally to consume them. What the statute forbade was their manufacture, distribution, or sale; it was in that sense an antibusiness measure.

Alcohol was still manufactured during the period of Prohibition. The Volstead Act permitted sales for medicinal and sacramental purposes. Most important, there were important industrial markets for alcohol in the CHEMICAL INDUSTRY. The Volstead Act thus permitted the continued distillation of industrial alcohol and its withdrawal under government supervision for use by the chemical industry.

Further reading

Hamm, Richard F. *Shaping the Eighteenth Amendment: Temperance Reform, Legal Culture, and the Polity, 1880–1920.* Chapel Hill: University of North Carolina Press, 1995.

Kerr, K. Austin. *Organized for Prohibition: A New History of the Anti-Saloon League.* New Haven, Conn.: Yale University Press, 1985.

Austin Kerr

W

wage and price controls Restraints placed by the federal government on increases in wages and prices (usually) during wartime. In order to keep inflation from rising during times of crisis, the government can dictate the amount of percentage gain for both wages and prices, if any. The theory behind the controls is that if wages are contained then the demand for goods and services will be kept in check. Similarly, if prices are contained, then consumers will not rush to purchase goods and services in anticipation of even higher prices in the future, also keeping percentage gains in check.

Wage and price controls were instituted by the Roosevelt administration during World War II. The Office of Price Administration (OPA) was established in order to monitor prices and began imposing limits on price increases on most commodities in 1942. The prices of commodities that year became the ceiling for most commodities until further notice. It also extended limits on residential rents and then on retail prices. The OPA also had the power to ration scarce goods and soon imposed limits on automobiles, tires, meats, coffee, and oil, among other commodities. Many commodity futures exchanges were forced to curtail business in these commodities because speculation in them was not permitted. The controls were phased out after the war, and the OPA was dismantled in 1947.

A second attempt was made at wage and price controls in 1971, when President Richard Nixon announced a series of measures designed to keep inflation in check. Inflation was rising because of the effects of the Vietnam War and unstable foreign exchange market conditions. As a result, the administration announced in August of that year a package designed to check inflation. Included were temporary restraints on prices and wage contract increases. The results were somewhat positive, although there was much criticism for using a wartime precedent, designed for emergencies, when war had not been declared.

One of the most important and overlooked parts of the package was the administration's decision to unilaterally devalue the dollar, effectively ending the BRETTON WOODS SYSTEM of fixed parity exchange rates. The decision was not in keeping with the Bretton Woods agreement since it was a unilateral devaluation. The devaluation part of the package proved to be the longest-standing result of the wage and price controls since all of the other measures were temporary and soon rescinded.

Further reading

Campbell, Colin Dearborn, ed. *Wage-Price Controls in World War II, United States and Germany.* Washington, D.C.: American Enterprise Institute, 1971.

Rockoff, Hugh. *Drastic Measure: A History of Wage and Price Controls in the United States.* Cambridge: Cambridge University Press, 1984.

Walton, Sam (1918–1992) *retailer* The founder of Wal-Mart stores, Walton was born in Kingfisher, Oklahoma. He attended the University of Missouri and served in the military during World War II. After leaving the service, he purchased a Ben Franklin variety store in Arkansas in 1945 with borrowed money and began a long retailing career that lasted until his death.

The venture was so successful that the leaseholder of the store forced Walton to relinquish it. He returned to Arkansas and purchased another store, called Walton's Five & Dime, located in Bentonville. It opened in 1950 and became the first in his long string of successes. Within 10 years, he owned 15 stores. The chain was renamed Wal-Mart in 1962 and began employing management techniques that would make Walton famous. Wal-Mart became one of the first retail discounters, selling on small margins. All of his stores were opened in small towns in rural settings, and until 1970 he funded them with retained earnings.

In 1970, the chain went public, raising more capital for expansion. By 1980, there were 276 stores in the company. Although the stores remained mostly in low population density areas, Walton adopted technology so that inventory could be closely controlled by a satellite-based system that linked all of the stores with his headquarters in Bentonville, Arkansas.

After going public, Walton employed an employee profit-sharing plan that became very popular with his employees. By 1985, Walton was proclaimed the richest man in America, and by 1991 sales were soaring as a result of his management practices. The market capitalization of the company was more than $25 billion in 1990. Walton died in Little Rock in 1992, but the practices he instituted outlived him, and the company continued to grow.

By the end of the 1990s, the number of stores had risen to more than 3,000, located in eight countries. The stock was added to the DOW JONES INDUSTRIAL AVERAGE in 1997 as Wal-Mart passed Sears as the largest retailer in the country. By the end of the 1990s, the company was the largest private sector employer in the world, with more than 1.3 million employees.

In 2000, it passed annual sales of $165 billion. Wal-Mart began opening more stores overseas, in Latin America, and in Mexico in the 2000s. The store chain became the source of controversy as it was revealed that it paid some of its workers the minimum wage with no additional benefits. The impact of the store's relentless expansion and its effect on local communities was debated in academic and trade circles as it became clear that Wal-Mart's impact was raising the same sort of fears that surfaced in the 1920s with the first expansion of CHAIN STORES on a widespread basis.

See also K-MART; SEARS, ROEBUCK & CO.; WARD, AARON MONTGOMERY.

Further reading

Ortega, Bob. *In Sam We Trust: The Untold Story of Sam Walton and How Wal-Mart Is Devouring America.* New York: Times Books, 1998.

Tedlow, Richard S. *Giants of Enterprise: Seven Business Innovators and the Empires They Built.* New York: HarperBusiness, 2001.

Trimble, Vance. *Sam Walton: Founder of Wal-Mart.* New York: Dutton, 1990.

Vance, Sandra Stringer, and Roy Vernon Scott. *Wal-Mart: A History of Sam Walton's Retail Phenomenon.* New York: Twayne, 1994.

Walton, Sam. *Sam Walton: Made in America.* New York: Doubleday, 1992.

The front of a Wal-Mart store (WAL-MART)

Wanamaker, John (1838–1922) *merchant and businessman* Born in Philadelphia, Wanamaker left school with only a grammar school education at age 13 and went to work as a delivery boy, eventually finding a job in the retail clothing business several years later. After deteriorating health, he took a trip to the American West to recover. Upon his return, he took a position as secretary of the Philadelphia YMCA.

In 1861, he used his meager savings to open Brown & Wanamaker, a men's clothing store in Philadelphia, with his brother-in-law. The store opened just as the ready-to-wear clothing industry began to grow larger. In 1869, a year after Brown died, Wanamaker opened a more upmarket clothier called John Wanamaker & Co. He expanded into dry goods in 1875 and two years later created the forerunner of the modern department store by opening a number of specialty shops around his flagship store. The store was originally called the Depot but in 1885 changed its name to Wanamaker's.

Wanamaker constantly strived for innovation in his retailing endeavors. In 1876, he established a mail order business and also opened a restaurant in one of his stores. Two years later, his first store powered by electricity was opened, and in 1882 he installed a soda fountain and elevators. He also opened a Downstairs Store in one of his stores, a bargain basement selling at discount prices.

In 1896, he purchased a New York store and expanded his offerings and operations from Philadelphia. Wanamaker's stores were the first to include such specialty areas as Ford dealerships. He also had the world's largest pipe organ installed in a Philadelphia store to entertain shoppers. He was one of the first retailers to use advertising and hired the first department store copywriter in 1880. Although a keen advocate of advertising, he staunchly refused to open his stores on Sundays. He also is well remembered for an observation concerning advertising, which has endured: "Half my advertising is wasted, I just don't know which half."

Wanamaker also implemented employee benefit programs, including training programs for his clerks. These programs evolved into the John Wanamaker Commercial Institute, one of the early training schools for business and commerce. He also was a strong advocate of fringe benefits for employees, including vacations, life insurance, and pensions. He also instituted one of the first telephone ordering systems for shoppers.

Later in his life he became involved in political activities and served as postmaster general under Benjamin Harrison after raising significant funds for his presidential campaign in 1888. His death was a major event in Philadelphia, and his funeral attracted many of Pennsylvania's politicians and notables.

See also CHAIN STORES; K-MART; SEARS, ROEBUCK & CO.; WALTON, SAM; WARD, AARON MONTGOMERY.

Further reading

Appel, Joseph. *Business Biography of John Wanamaker.* New York: Macmillan, 1930.

Burt, Olive W. *John Wanamaker.* New York: Bobbs-Merrill, 1962.

Ershowitz, Herbert. *John Wanamaker: Philadelphia Merchant.* New York: Da Capo Press, 1999.

Mahoney, Tom, and Leonard Sloane. *The Great Merchants.* New York: Harper & Row, 1966.

Ward, Aaron Montgomery (1843–1913)

retailer Born in Chatham, New Jersey, Ward left school at age 14 to work in the dry goods business in the Midwest when his family moved to Michigan. His first jobs were making barrels and as a day laborer. At age 19, he worked in a general store, rising to become its manager. He left the job to work in a Marshall Field store before going to work for a dry goods wholesaler in St. Louis.

While working in St. Louis, he recognized the problems faced by farmers who, because of isolation, could not shop for consumer goods effectively. As a result, he opened a retail mail-order house in 1872, which bought dry goods from manufacturers directly and offered them for sale by catalog, eliminating the middleman. The business proved popular very quickly, especially among farmers, at whom it was targeted.

Ward's first venture began in Chicago with a one-page catalog. It quickly proved successful in part because he instituted a liberal returns policy. The mail-order concept also coincided with the rise of the Grange movement, advocating better conditions for farmers, and succeeded as a result. The catalog expanded from year to year, and by 1888 annual sales exceeded $1 million. Along with Sears, Roebuck, Ward became one of the founders of mail-order sales in the United States. The catalog became a staple in both rural and urban homes for years and epitomized the innovative nature of American retailing. The mail-order business in general was aided greatly with the introduction of rural free delivery by the U.S. postmaster general in 1895.

In the early 1900s, more than 3 million catalogs were circulated annually, and each catalog weighed approximately four pounds. Ward retired from active management of the company in 1901, although he remained as its titular president. In 1926, the company began opening Montgomery Ward retail stores and by 1929 had opened more than 530. But the expansion occurred haphazardly. More than 400 stores were operating at a deficit, and the company lost almost $9 million. A new chief executive, Sewell Avery, was installed in 1931 to turn the operation around. Within seven years, sales reached $475 million, a rise of $300 million since Avery took over.

In one of the most successful store promotions, a company copywriter created a character named Rudolph the Red Nosed Reindeer for a Christmas sales promotion. A storybook was created, which reached 6 million copies in circulation by 1946. The promotion became a prototype for others to follow, copied by many stores and entertainment companies.

Upon his death, most of Ward's fortune was bequeathed to charities. A sizable portion was also left by his wife to Northwestern University, which established medical and dental schools with the money. The Ward catalog was discontinued in 1985. After steadily losing market share in the 1990s, the stores finally closed in 2000 after changing hands several times.

See also CHAIN STORES; FIELD, MARSHALL; K-MART; WALTON, SAM; WANAMAKER, JOHN.

Further reading
Baker, Nina Brown. *Big Catalogue: The Life of Aaron Montgomery Ward.* New York: Harcourt Brace, 1956.

Mahoney, Tom, and Leonard Sloane. *The Great Merchants.* New York: Harper & Row, 1966.

Watson, Thomas A. (1854–1934) *telephone pioneer and businessman*   Watson was born in Salem, Massachusetts, over a livery stable where his father worked. He left school at 14, became a crockery salesman for $5 per week, but also began taking commercial courses in Boston. Suffering from an eye malaise, he took a job in an electrical machine shop when he was 18 rather than pursue a career in which intense reading was required. It was in the machine shop that he began developing techniques that later would make him a pioneer in the development of the telephone.

While working in the machine shop, Watson met Alexander Graham BELL, a lecturer at Boston University, in 1874. After becoming acquainted, Bell explained his idea for a harmonic telegraph to him, and Watson set about developing modifications for the device. Within a short time, they were collaborating on Bell's idea for a telephone, and Watson became the first person to ever hear a phone message when Bell called him over a short line in their laboratory: "Mr. Watson, come here, I want you."

In 1876, they participated in the first two-way telephone conversation between Boston and Cambridgeport, Massachusetts. After the device was patented, Watson was given a financial interest in Bell's new invention and became the first research and technical head of Bell Telephone Company. However, he left the company long before the telephone became well developed and before the intense competition for service that began when many of the company's patents started to expire in the 1890s.

Watson received more than 60 patents relating to the telephone, but in 1881 he resigned to begin designing ships and engines and produced several battleships for the U.S. Navy after 1896. In 1901, his company was incorporated as the Fore River Ship & Engine Company. During his post-Bell period, he also pursued other intellectual interests. He studied geology at the Lowell Institute with his wife, and they both then entered the Massachusetts Institute of Technology as students. He retired from business in 1904 and devoted himself to geology, literature, and European travel, his lifelong interests. He died in Florida in 1934. He is remembered as the technical and mechanical brains behind many of the Bell Company's technological achievements.

Further reading
Boettinger, H. M. *The Telephone Book: Bell, Watson, Vail & American Life, 1876–1983.* New York: Stearn Publishers, 1983.

Watson, Thomas A. *Exploring Life.* New York: D. Appleton, 1926.

Watson, Thomas J. (1874–1956) *computer manufacturer* Thomas John Watson was born in East Campbell, New York, on February 17, 1874, the son of a lumberman. Rather than pursue a legal career at his father's behest, he briefly attended the Elmira School of Commerce but quit before graduating to become a salesman. After fulfilling various odd jobs Watson joined National Cash Register (NCR) in 1898 and gradually moved up the company ladder. Long one of the firm's most successful salesmen, in 1912 he and others were implicated by the government in an illegal scheme to monopolize the cash register business, but he was never prosecuted. Watson left NCR in 1913 and became president of the Computer Tabulating Recording Company in Elmira, New York. Through adroit leadership he turned the ailing firm around and began acquiring other businesses. In 1917, he bought out International Business Machines, Ltd., adopted its name, and in 1923 formally established the IBM Corporation in Delaware. Despite his lack of a college degree, Watson displayed an amazing aptitude for strategic planning and marketing. And, because he insisted on leasing machines instead of selling them outright, he ensured a steady cash flow over the years. Part of his success lay with thoroughly training his sales personnel to impart that they were selling a service, not simply machines. Moreover, salesmen were expected to fix and install any company products they sold to further ensure customer loyalty. Within a few years IBM became the world's greatest innovator in terms of new punch card technology, powered calculators, and electric TYPEWRITERS: As early as 1941, Watson owned more than 1,400 patents on a wide-ranging variety of business devices.

What set Watson apart from contemporaries was his philosophy toward corporate life. Workers were held to a strict dress code and expected to inculcate virtues of loyalty and devotion to the firm. In exchange, IBM paid them higher-than-average wages, offered them stock options, and pioneered the practice of fringe benefits such as paid retirement. This give and take was adroitly balanced, so IBM never experienced a period of labor unrest or union organizing. Watson also demonstrated keen insight as to worker psychology. An excellent motivator, he invariably decorated company offices with signs such as "THINK" to drive home the corporate notion of innovation—and workers' personal responsibility for it. Watson was also a firm believer in plowing back a certain percentage of profits into ongoing research and development projects to maintain his competitive edge. All told, the IBM management style was a unique blend of paternalism, obedience, and imagination in equal measures. It gave the company unmatched intellectual vitality and rendered it one of the most influential companies in business history. In fact, Watson's near domination of the business machine market made him the subject of several antitrust lawsuits; the company was never convicted of any wrongdoing beyond being highly successful.

American entry into World War II created a burgeoning new demand for IBM machinery, and

Thomas J. Watson (LIBRARY OF CONGRESS)

Watson received government funding to create the first electronic computer at Harvard. This was a technological breakthrough of the first magnitude, and IBM wasted no time in creating versions compatible for business purposes by 1953. Thus, Watson played a large role in the rise of office automation, which revolutionized the way the world did business. Furthermore, he maintained the company's traditional supremacy over competitors through aggressive marketing worldwide and by offering the first software packages; this way the same machine could be programmed for multiple applications. Watson became renowned for putting in 16-hour work days, but he also generously donated money and time to charity and the arts. When he died in New York City on July 19, 1956, Watson had orchestrated the rise of one of the largest and most profitable corporations. Moreover, the management techniques he originated set standards for the newly emerging corporate culture and were widely emulated across the globe. But his greatest contribution was in setting the stage for the new information age, which reached its greatest expression in the personal desktop computer.

See also COMPUTER INDUSTRY.

Further reading

Maney, Kevin M. *The Maverick and His Machine: Thomas Watson, Sr., and the Making of IBM.* New York: John Wiley & Sons, 2003.

Simmons, W. W. *Inside IBM: The Watson Years, a Personal Memoir.* Bryn Mawr, Pa.: Dorrance, 1988.

Sobel, Robert. *Thomas Watson, Sr.: IBM and the Computer Revolution.* Washington, D.C.: BeardBooks, 2000.

Tedlow, Richard S. *The Watson Dynasty: The Fiery Reign and Troubled Legacy of IBM's Father and Son.* New York: Harper Business, 2003.

Watson, Thomas J. *Father, Son, & Co.: My Life at IBM and Beyond.* New York: Bantam Books, 2000.

John C. Fredriksen

Weill, Sanford (1933–   ) *banker and securities executive*   Weill was born in 1933 in New York City and lived in Brooklyn before attending military school and Cornell University. After graduating, he found a clerical job on Wall Street and shortly decided to make a career as a broker. He got his start in 1958, when I. W. "Tubby" Burnham gave him a job at Burnham & Co., a brokerage founded in 1935. The same firm would later give Michael Milken his first job on the street. Weill started ambitiously and within several years began his own brokerage, leasing space from Burnham. His small firm grew rapidly, and he spied his first opportunity to expand in the wake of the backoffice crisis that plagued Wall Street in the early 1970s.

In 1970, Weill purchased Hayden Stone, a retail broker, adopted its name, and eventually became its CEO three years later. The acquisition began a pattern for the company and the ambitious Weill. After purchasing another firm in 1974, the name was again changed to Shearson Hayden Stone. In 1979, it became significantly larger by buying the ailing small investment bank Loeb Rhoades & Co., becoming Shearson Loeb Rhoades. After purchasing more than a dozen small- and medium-size firms, Weill sold Shearson to American Express in 1981, remaining with the firm as a senior executive but not as president.

Despite assuming the presidency in 1983, Weill quit American Express in 1985. A year later, he became CEO of Commercial Credit Corp., a consumer credit company. He then employed a familiar tactic and began a series of MERGERS using the company as his acquisitions vehicle. In 1988, he acquired another financial services company, Primerica, which owned the old-line securities house Smith Barney. He then purchased Shearson back from American Express and also acquired the Travelers Insurance Company. He purchased the jewel in his Wall Street crown by acquiring investment bank SALOMON BROTHERS in 1997 for $9 billion.

Weill engineered the largest Wall Street merger when he agreed to merge Travelers with

CITIBANK in 1998. A merger between an insurance company, investment bank, and commercial bank was forbidden by the BANKING ACT OF 1933, but the deal was allowed to proceed because of the DEREGULATION trend occurring at the time. The merger was allowed by the FEDERAL RESERVE with the provision that it adhere to both the BANK HOLDING COMPANY ACT and the Banking Act within two years. In 1999, Congress passed the FINANCIAL SERVICES MODERNIZATION ACT, doing away with many of the strictures found in the Banking Act, and the merger was allowed to stand. Weill and John Reed of Citicorp shared CEO duties until Reed retired, leaving Weill in charge.

Weill resigned from the chief executive post at Citigroup at the end of 2003, remaining as chairman. He also is noted for his philanthropy, especially to the Cornell University Medical School located in Manhattan, and to numerous other cultural institutions in New York City.

See also INVESTMENT BANKING.

Further reading

Langley, Monica. *Tearing Down the Walls: How Sandy Weill Fought His Way to the Top of the Financial World . . . and Then Nearly Lost It All.* New York: Free Press, 2002.

Stone, Amey, and Mike Brewster. *The King of Capital: Sandy Weill and the Making of Citigroup.* New York: John Wiley & Sons, 2002.

Welch, John F. (1935–) *businessman*

Better known as Jack, John F. Welch was born in Salem. Massachusetts, and earned a degree in chemical engineering from the University of Massachusetts in 1957 and a Ph.D. from the University of Illinois in 1960, also in chemical engineering. After leaving graduate school, he took a job with GENERAL ELECTRIC CO. Over the course of his career at GE, he would become one of the world's best-known executives, presiding over a period of exponential growth for the company.

Welch rose through the ranks at GE, becoming a vice president in 1972, senior vice president in 1977, and the eighth chairman of the company and chief executive officer in 1981, succeeding Reginald Jones. His rapid rise was attributed to his dislike of bureaucracy and rigid organizational structures, favoring instead a looser learning environment for his staff and management, with employees at all levels communicating with each other in an environment permeated with information flow and ideas.

Welch also expanded the company through a series of aggressive acquisitions and divestments. In the four years following being named chairman and CEO, Welch presided over the acquisition of more than 300 businesses and the divestment of dozens of others in order to diversify the company's operations. By 1986, GE had more than 300,000 employees and annual sales of $28 billion. In 1985, GE made its most notable acquisition by purchasing RCA for $6.28 billion, enabling the one-time manufacturer of light bulbs and electrical equipment to enter broadcasting. A year later, it also purchased investment bank KIDDER PEABODY in an effort to expand its financial services. GE Capital was already one of the largest providers of nonbank financial services but lacked an investment banking division.

In addition to acquisitions, Welch was known for trimming operations and using fewer employees than his predecessors, earning him the sobriquet "Neutron Jack." But the stock market applauded his efforts, and the company value steadily rose. Welch retired from the company in 2001 after serving 20 years. His extremely generous retirement package drew intense criticism from shareholders, and he agreed to relinquish parts of it in order to quell the criticism. But he is best remembered for presiding over General Electric during the period of its most rapid growth. During his tenure, the company's market capitalization rose from $12 billion to more than $280 billion, and it became the world's most highly valued company.

See also CONGLOMERATES; YOUNG, OWEN D.

Further reading

Slater, Robert. *The GE Fieldbook: Jack Welch's Plan for Corporate Revolution*. New York: McGraw-Hill, 1999.

———. *The New GE: How Jack Welch Revived an American Institution*. New York: McGraw-Hill, 1992.

Welch, Jack. *Jack: Straight from the Gut*. New York: Warner Books, 2001.

Wells Fargo   A diversified financial services company that provides banking, mortgage, consumer credit, investment, corporate funding, and international finance throughout the United States and abroad. It serves 20 million households through 5,400 offices, staffed by 120,00 employees, while Wells Fargo's on-line offerings dominate cyberspace. Its banking covers 23 states with 3,000 branches and 7,000 automated teller machines.

In 1848, the cry of "Gold!" reverberated from California around the world. Four years later, on March 18, 1852, New Yorkers Henry Wells and William George Fargo organized Wells, Fargo & Co. to offer innovative banking, express, and letter delivery on the Pacific coast. Reliability, honesty, and good management allowed their firm to shine during an 1855 financial panic that crushed California's two largest banks.

Wells Fargo became a universal business agent demanding fair treatment for all. It delivered express packages by the fastest means of transportation available, and small businesses especially patronized Wells Fargo's Letter Express, which consistently beat government mail delivery. Pleased customers entrusted so much bullion to it that from 1858 until 1900 Wells Fargo compiled western mining statistics from British Columbia through Mexico.

In 1858, Wells Fargo helped inaugurate the Overland Mail Company, whose stagecoaches sped letters and passengers across the Southwest in 24 days, three-fourths the time by steamship. In 1861, the first year of the Civil War, Wells Fargo ran the western end of the Pony Express and the Overland Mail coaches on a central route through Salt Lake City. Through the 1860s, additional gold rushes expanded Wells Fargo's banking from California, New York, and Boston into Oregon, British Columbia, Nevada, Utah, and Idaho. By the late 19th century, banking services contributed one-third of Wells Fargo & Company's earnings; since 1871, Wells Fargo has paid regular dividends.

In 1866, Wells Fargo added Ben Holladay's stage lines to its own and ran stagecoaches between California and Nebraska railheads and north into Idaho and Montana. Though stagecoaching led to heavy losses, it cemented Wells Fargo's claim to service all land west of the Missouri River and gave the company a timeless logo. But the future lay with the iron horse. In 1869, the Central Pacific Railroad gained control of Wells Fargo, and the express went nationwide on iron rails. In the early 1880s, contracts with RAILROADS brought Wells Fargo into the interior of Mexico and in 1888 across the continent to New York. In 1918, Wells Fargo operated 10,000 express offices nationwide, but a government-sponsored wartime consolidation of this business left Wells Fargo only with a bank in San Francisco.

A 1905 merger with the Nevada National Bank (1875) became the first of many to double Wells Fargo's size. Isaias W. Hellman ran the combined Wells Fargo Nevada National Bank, seeking strength and quality over size. In 1924, Hellman's Union Trust Company, California's first (1893), joined Wells Fargo, and through the 1930s and 1940s, it practiced correspondent banking that was highly valued. A new consumer economy emerged after World War II, and in 1960 Wells Fargo entered branch banking grandly through a merger with American Trust Company (1854). A 1967 foray into southern California made Wells Fargo a statewide bank.

The 1980s, under Carl Reichardt, saw banking deregulation, automated teller machines, 24-hour customer telephone service, and longer branch hours. A 1986 marriage with Crocker

Bank (1870) again doubled Wells Fargo's size. Customer convenience grew with supermarket banks in 1990 and the pioneering of on-line banking in 1995. The next year, Wells Fargo acquired First Interstate Bank, which grew from Transamerica Corporation, A. P. Gianinni's 1928 HOLDING COMPANY.

November 1, 1998, brought new opportunity when Wells Fargo joined Norwest; Wells Fargo founder William George Fargo in 1872 had helped organize the Northwestern National Bank of Minneapolis. A 1929 holding company formed to block Gianinni's expansion into Minnesota laid the foundation for Norwest's aggressive, but decentralized, interstate growth in the 1990s. It proved visionary in other financial markets, too. In 1969 Norwest acquired Iowa Securities Company (1906) of Waterloo, which offered home mortgages, and in 1982 added Dial Finance Corporation (1897) of Des Moines. Under CEO Dick Kovacevich, adaptable Wells Fargo celebrated its sesquicentennial in 2002.

See also COMMERCIAL BANKING; CONESTOGA WAGON.

Further reading

Chandler, Robert J. "Integrity Amid Tumult: Wells, Fargo & Co's Gold Rush Banking." *California History* 70 (Fall 1991): 258–277.

Fradkin, Philip L. *Stagecoach: Wells Fargo and the American West.* New York: Simon & Schuster, 2001.

Loomis, Noel M. *Wells Fargo.* New York: Bramhall House, 1968

Robert J. Chandler

Western Union Telegraph Co.

A communications company founded in 1851 as the New York & Mississippi Valley Printing Telegraph Co. Using the TELEGRAPH developed by Samuel MORSE, the company provided coded messages sent along an electrical wire that were decoded and delivered to customers when they reached their destination. Originally, the company had less than 600 miles of cable and used a device for sending messages developed by Royal House, and based upon the Morse code. The lines transmitting messages were developed by Morse and substantially improved by Ezra Cornell, who developed the glass-coated lines strung from telegraph poles that became common.

Over the next five years, the company began to acquire other similar companies and incorporate them into its network. In 1856, it changed its name to the Western Union Telegraph Co. Its first major project was to string a telegraph line from Missouri to California—a project that most considered foolish and too risky. However, under the guidance of one of its agents, Edward Creighton, the project was completed in only 112 days when the wires from east and west were joined at Salt Lake City on October 24, 1861. The effect on the federal government was immediate, and it adopted the telegraph as its official form of long-distance communication, replacing the Pony Express.

Other developments quickly followed. The company began using the transatlantic cable laid by Cyrus Field. The cable proved unreliable and Western Union sought its own route through Alaska and Siberia to Europe. Field's subsequent cables proved more successful, and the transatlantic cables again were used. One valuable benefit did accrue to the United States from the Alaskan-Siberian idea. In its early stages, the Russian government offered to sell Alaska to the United States. The United States quickly accepted the offer and granted Western Union access to many railroad and post lines as a result.

The company moved its offices to New York City in 1866 from Rochester and quickly entered financial communications by developing the TICKER TAPE, which revolutionized the STOCK MARKETS. It also developed the idea of wiring funds from one office to another, acting as something of a bank funds transfer agent in the absence of a nationwide banking system. It also began its own time service, which helped standardize time around the country before time zones were established. The company became so large that its stock was one of the 12 original Dow Jones Industrials. It also developed the telex, which became a standard method of communication in finance and with news agencies until the 1980s.

In the 20th century, the company pioneered transmissions of pictures via the transatlantic cable and widespread use of the radiotelegraph, which helped marine navigation considerably. Its Mailgram services introduced next-day delivery service, an idea that would later be employed successfully by the nationwide delivery services. It also became active in satellite communications and in the mid-1970s was the first company to have a commercial satellite in space. In 1987, the company was restructured, and in 1990 it divested itself of its satellites. More recently, the company has concentrated on financial services and other forms of priority messaging.

See also FIELD, CYRUS.

Further reading

Dorf, Philip. *The Builder: The Biography of Ezra Cornell.* New York: Macmillan, 1952.
Gabler, Edwin. *The American Telegraphy A Social History 1860–1900.* New Brunswick, N.J.: Rutgers University Press, 1988.

Westinghouse, George, Jr. (1846–1914) *inventor* Born in Central Bridge, New York, Westinghouse's father was a manufacturer of farm equipment. At age 15, he ran away from home to join the Union Army but returned at his parents' request and went back to school. He attended Union College for a short time before returning to work at his father's machine shop. During this time he developed a rotary steam engine and a device that was able to replace derailed railway cars. But it was while on a railroad trip in 1866 that he got the inspiration for his most famous invention.

While riding on a train, he recognized that existing braking systems were not capable of stopping a train adequately. Early train brakes were often inadequate and caused as many deaths as accidents. As a result, he returned home and designed the first air braking system for railway cars. The system used compressed air and would revolutionize railway travel. He patented the device at age 22 and founded the Westinghouse Air Brake Co. Building upon his success, he next founded the Union Switch and Signal Co., a company that used his own designs and those of others to improve railroad signaling and switching. In 1881, he perfected the automatic block signal, which helped alert train engineers to track blockages. Within 10 years, from 1880 to 1890, he patented more than 130 inventions, all mechanical devices ranging from air brakes to electrical apparatuses and steam turbines.

At the age of 40, he started the Westinghouse Electric Co., a pioneer in alternating current (AC), developed as an alternative to direct current (DC). He purchased an English patent, and his company began developing AC motors in order to transmit high-tension current. One of his projects was the development of an electric chair using alternating current, putting him in competition with Thomas EDISON, who was the best-known advocate of DC. In 1893, he won the contract to supply electricity to the Columbian Exposition. After that time AC began to win the battle with DC and would become the most widely used electrical transmission system in the country. He then signed mutually agreeable licenses with the GENERAL ELECTRIC CO., and the two began sharing patents and technology. He also helped in the development of hydroelectric power at Niagara Falls in 1896. Westinghouse became one of the largest companies in the country by 1900, employing more than 50,000 people.

Westinghouse lost control of Westinghouse Electric in 1907 because of financial problems but retained control of his other companies. The company became a leader in railroad electrification and then began moving into consumer products in the 1920s. Its main competitor was the General Electric Company. After World War II, the company produced electrical turbines for the UTILITIES industry but began losing market share to GE after some of its turbines proved defective. The same problem occurred again when engines it supplied to the San Francisco Bay Area Rapid Transit Company proved defective.

During his lifetime, Westinghouse held more than 360 patents, not all of which were in electricity. He held one for a telephone switching system, and his ideas also were used to harness the energy produced by Niagara Falls. The first radio station in the country, KDKA in Pittsburgh, was a Westinghouse station, and his company went on to become a major producer of electrical appliances and atomic-powered submarines and ships.

Further reading

Henry, Thomas. *George Westinghouse.* New York: G. P. Putnam's Sons, 1960.

Passer, Harold C. *The Electrical Manufacturers, 1875–1900: A Study in Competition, Entrepreneurship, Technical Change, and Economic Growth.* Cambridge, Mass.: Harvard University Press, 1953.

Prout, Henry G. *Life of George Westinghouse.* New York: American Society of Mechanical Engineers, 1921.

Weyerhaeuser, Frederick (1834–1914) *timber executive*

Born in Niedersaulheim, Germany, Weyerhaeuser immigrated to the United States in 1848 with his mother and sister. Originally, he became a day laborer in Pennsylvania before moving to Illinois, where he worked as a supplier of lumber and grain for the Rock Island and Pacific Railroad. Working his way up the ladder at the Rock Island, he saved enough money to buy a sawmill and a lumberyard after the Panic of 1857 and then began acquiring additional sawmills. During the Civil War, he began buying timberland in Wisconsin and then began buying more land in the West.

After the war, his company participated in the Mississippi River Boom and Logging Company, a monopoly of lumber interests along the river. Weyerhaeuser became friendly with railroad baron James J. HILL when he moved to Minnesota in 1891, and eventually his company bought 900,000 acres from the Northern Pacific Railroad for $5.4 million and started the Weyerhaeuser Company near Tacoma, Washington, in 1900. The company became the largest timber and lumber company in the United States at the time and built what were considered to be the finest sawmill facilities ever seen in the Unites States.

Throughout his career in the LUMBER INDUSTRY, Weyerhaeuser constantly advocated conservation and protecting nature. He was the largest owner of timberland in the United States and was considered one of the country's wealthiest men, although he avoided the public spotlight. He died at the outbreak of World War I.

During the 1930s, the company began selling wood pulp and began specializing in reforestation and management of timberlands. After World War II, it began expanding into other building products. The company went public in 1963 and began diversifying in order to protect itself from the vicissitudes of the lumber business. In 1983, it purchased the GNA Corp. and diversified further into financial services and annuities. In the late 1980s and early 1990s, the company returned to its traditional strengths by selling off some of its previous acquisitions and extended its operations into Georgia by purchasing almost 200,000 acres of Georgia forestland. In 1995, it began expanding its operations outside the United States.

Weyerhaeuser, along with the Georgia-Pacific Corp., remains one of the largest owners of timberland in the United States, owning more than 5 million acres in the Northwest and Georgia. It also holds rights to almost 20 million acres in Canada. It is one of the largest producers of building products and wood derivative products in the United States and also maintains a sizable presence in financial services.

Further reading

Hidy, Ralph, Frank E. Hill, and Allan Nevins. *Timber & Men: The Weyerhaeuser Story.* New York: Macmillan, 1963.

Sensil, Joni. *Traditions through the Trees: Weyerhaeuser's First 100 Years.* Seattle: Documentary Book Publishers Corporation, 1999.

Wharton School   The business school of the University of Pennsylvania, Wharton was established in 1881 through a $100,000 gift from Joseph Wharton (1826–1909), an industrialist who later donated more money to ensure the school's success. Wharton wrote the university asking it to create a business school to prepare young men for the rigors of the industrial economy. It was the first collegiate school of business and initially awarded only undergraduate degrees. The Wharton School named its first business professor two years later.

The school awarded its first degrees to women in 1908. A year later, it began offering courses in advertising and salesmanship, originally offered in the merchandising department, the original name for marketing. The courses were in recognition of the inroads made by marketing in selling all sorts of goods before World War I. The new discipline was instrumental in the rapid growth of CHAIN STORES and retailing, which exploded in popularity and numbers in the 1920s after World War I was over and the American consumer had more disposable income.

An MBA degree was added in 1921, but unlike the example set by the HARVARD BUSINESS SCHOOL, the case study method was eschewed in favor of students specializing in a particular area and writing a thesis on a chosen topic of interest. In the 1920s, Wharton also became the leading center for insurance study and research, helping to lift jobs in the life insurance industry onto a level with many other professions.

After World War II, the school opened a center for the study of finance, becoming one of the leading centers in the country in financial research. The popularity of postgraduate degrees in the 1960s made the school better known for its MBA than its undergraduate degrees, although undergraduate education remained a fixture at the school. By the 1970s, it was recognized as one of the top three business schools in the country, offering a range of specializations not found in most schools. In 1988, it became the first American business school to establish representative offices overseas, marking the beginning of overseas affiliations for the top American schools in general and recognition of the increasingly global nature of business education. In 2000, it opened a permanent branch in San Francisco, dubbed Wharton West, and later forged an alliance with INSEAD, the French business school also with overseas branches.

Further reading

Sass, Steven A. *The Pragmatic Imagination: A History of the Wharton School*. Philadelphia: University of Pennsylvania Press, 1982.

Whitney, Eli (1765–1825) *inventor*   Whitney was the inventor of the cotton gin. Born in Westboro, Massachusetts, the son of a farmer, he originally stayed at home and tinkered with various mechanical devices before deciding to go to college at age 24. He graduated from Yale in 1792 after having taught school for five years in order to afford the tuition. After graduation, while on a trip to Georgia, he recognized the need for a machine that was able to separate cotton from its seed. He quickly developed the cotton gin, or jenny, within a year of graduating from college. A patent was granted for the device in 1794, and he began producing the machines in a factory in New Haven, Connecticut.

Originally, Whitney and his partner, Phineas Miller, decided to process cotton for a royalty rather than sell the machines to farmers but were soon faced with the problem of imitations that allowed farmers to avoid the royalty payments. As a result, he filed many lawsuits against imitators who were producing similar machines copied from his. His patent was confirmed in 1807 but expired in 1812, and he failed to profit from his invention, which by that time was already in widespread use.

His invention quickly revolutionized agricultural production in the South, where the separation of seed from cotton had previously been done by hand. But legal problems and a fire at his factory slowed production to a trickle, and then Congress refused to renew his patent when it expired. However, since 1798 he had been involved with manufacturing muskets for the army. He devised a method whereby the parts for rifles became standard rather than being individually produced by a gunsmith. As a result, the army could use standard produced rifles, at a great cost savings and with greater efficiency. It was then possible to assemble a musket from the parts he produced rather than to build each one individually. He obtained a contract to produce rifles during the War of 1812, although his success was only modest. In such a manner he became the father of MASS PRODUCTION, although his legacy centers almost entirely on the invention of the cotton gin.

Whitney is the best example of the sort of inventiveness that Alexander HAMILTON envisaged would make the United States independent of Great Britain after the Revolution, in what was still a mercantilist economy. The cotton gin was one of the first true American industrial inventions that would help shape the COTTON INDUSTRY. It revolutionized cotton production in the South and greatly aided American exports, while the concepts Whitney employed in making muskets helped turn the country into a strong manufacturing economy in the decades ahead.

Further reading
Green, Constance. *Eli Whitney and the Birth of American Technology.* Boston: Little, Brown, 1956.

Hays, Wilma Pitchford. *Eli Whitney and the Machine Age.* New York: Franklin Watts, 1954.

Howard, Robert West. *Eli Whitney.* Chicago: Follett Publishing Co., 1966.

Mirsky, Jeanette, and Allan Nevins. *The World of Eli Whitney.* New York: Macmillan, 1952.

Whitney, Richard (1888–1974) *stockbroker*

Born in Massachusetts, Whitney was descended from immigrants who arrived in the 1630s. His father was a well-known Boston banker. Richard graduated from Groton and Harvard and went to New York, becoming a member of the NEW YORK STOCK EXCHANGE (NYSE) in 1912. He became a broker for J. P. Morgan & Co., where his brother George was a partner. He assumed command of his father's investment banking business and renamed it Richard Whitney & Co.

Whitney became a member of the NYSE board in 1919 and became a spokesman for the exchange during the decade that followed, when he became one of the NYSE's best-known figures. He achieved nationwide notoriety in 1929 during the crash. At J. P. Morgan's behest, he entered the exchange floor as the market was falling and entered an order above the market for 10,000 shares of U.S. Steel, designed to demonstrate bankers' support for the market. At the time, he was acting president of the exchange. He also entered other orders personally during the few days in which a bankers' consortium continued to supply funds to the market. But his actions were in vain as the index dropped and did not recover. Whitney's actions and his other pronouncements during the 1920s and early 1930s earned him membership in the "Old Guard," those dedicated to maintaining the status quo on the NYSE.

During Senate hearings following the crash in 1932 and 1933, he staunchly defended the NYSE against outside criticism, especially over the issue of short-selling, which many critics blamed for further drops in the market index. As criticism of the NYSE and Wall Street increased in the mid-1930s, Whitney decided not to run again for the presidency of the exchange. He became heavily involved in speculative adventures in the 1930s, borrowing heavily to support his investments. In 1938, it was revealed that he had been embezzling funds from the Gratuity Fund of the NYSE, a fund designed to aid older exchange members and had then embezzled more money from accounts at his own firm to cover them up. He was indicted shortly thereafter, convicted of fraud, and sentenced to five to 10 years imprisonment. He subsequently was incarcerated at Sing Sing, becoming the first and only NYSE president to serve a prison term. Upon his release, he moved to Massachusetts and dropped out of public view.

Whitney's time as president of the NYSE was pivotal in the history of finance because it marked a turning point in the REGULATION of INVESTMENT BANKING and the exchanges. When the Securities Exchange Act was passed in 1934, it marked a decided shift from the Old Guard to a new, regulated environment.

See also MORGAN, JOHN PIERPONT, JR.; SECURITIES EXCHANGE ACT OF 1934.

Further reading

Pecora, Ferdinand. *Wall Street under Oath: The Story of Our Modern Moneychangers.* New York: Simon & Schuster, 1939.

Winfrey, Oprah (1954–) *television personality* Oprah Gail Winfrey was born in Kosciusko, Mississippi, on January 29, 1954, the illegitimate daughter of two farmworkers. She acquired her name by default; originally intended to be called by the biblical moniker Orpah, it was misspelled Oprah and stuck. Raised by her grandmother, a strict disciplinarian, she exhibited a gift for oratory at an early age. However, at six she relocated with her mother to a ghetto in Milwaukee, Wisconsin, and became a teenage delinquent. Winfrey was then allowed to move in with her father in Nashville, Tennessee, which changed her life. He was another strict disciplinarian who gave her guidance, made her read, and let her practice public speaking in church. Winfrey flourished under the new regimen, and she became an honors student in high school. While attending Tennessee State University on a scholarship, she displayed a talent for television broadcast news and was hired at WTVF-TV as a part-time news announcer. Winfrey subsequently graduated in 1976 and took a full-time announcing position with WJZ-TV in Baltimore. Within months she began giving local news updates during the nationally televised *Good Morning, America* pro-

gram, which gave her additional exposure. Winfrey made such a good impression on superiors that within a year she was tapped to cohost the morning show *Baltimore Is Talking.* Her smooth delivery and penchant for empathy continually pushed her up the broadcast ladder until January 1984, when she transferred to the important Chicago market to host *A.M. Chicago.* Winfrey, using her considerable broadcast instincts, revamped the format from traditional women's issues to contemporary and more controversial ones, and began pulling ahead of the vaunted *Phil Donahue Show.* Consequently, in September 1985 Winfrey expanded her program to a one-hour format as *The Oprah Winfrey Show.*

Few media pundits could have anticipated the following events. Winfrey's show completely capitalized on the host's powers of empathy with other women and her willingness to tackle controversial subjects such as rape and child abuse. For maximum effectiveness, she opted against using prepared scripts and interacted smoothly and spontaneously with her audience. As Winfrey's ratings soared, she was tapped by producer Quincy Jones to appear in the Steven Spielberg movie *The Color Purple* in 1986, to rave reviews. Her newfound celebrity only pushed her ratings higher, and in August 1986 Winfrey founded her own production company, Harpo (Oprah spelled backward). She thus became the first African-American woman to produce her own programming and only the third woman, after Mary Pickford and Lucille Ball, to own a production company. By this time *The Oprah Winfrey Show* was also America's most highly rated talk show, with a viewing audience of 22 million.

In addition to her televised activities, Winfrey has also sponsored a number of television dramas focusing on the African-American community and produced them through her company. As a victim of child abuse herself, she offered vocal support for federal child protection legislation to track convicted child abusers. In September 1996 her career took a particular turn when she declared her intention to "get the country reading" and founded the Oprah Book Club. Here she would tout recent fiction, self-help, or inspirational titles, most of which went on to become overnight best sellers. Winfrey was widely sought after for her endorsements, but the demand proved so overwhelming that she modified her book club philosophy in 2002, only recommending literature drawn from the classics, until 2005, when she once again included contemporary works. From her modest beginnings, Winfrey's climb to fame has seldom been matched in the entertainment industry. By dint of intelligence, drive, and sheer personality, she carved out a niche for herself in the highly competitive world of talk show television and emerged as one of the highest-paid entertainers in history, with an estimated annual income of $40 million. "I don't think of myself as a poor, deprived ghetto girl who made good," Winfrey maintains. "I think of myself as somebody who from an early age knew she was responsible for herself—and I had to make good."

Further reading

Illouz, Eva. *Oprah Winfrey and the Glamour of Misery: An Essay on Popular Culture.* New York: Columbia University Press, 2003.

Mair, George. *Oprah Winfrey: The Real Story.* Secaucus, N.J.: Carol Publishing Group, 1998.

Wilson, Sherryl. *Oprah, Celebrity, and Formations of Self.* New York: Palgrave Macmillan, 2003.

John C. Fredriksen

women in American business   In 1975, historian Caroline Bird wrote, "If you believe what you read in history books, the prosperity of America is strictly man made." Bird's *Enterprising Women* was the first serious study of women in business in a generation and a harbinger of what has become a sustained exploration of women and gender in American business history. While research in this field is ongoing, a number of general trends are becoming clear. Whereas men took the reins of power in the railroad, steel, mining,

and construction industries, women clustered in trades and industries that required less capital and whose products and services tended to be for women or for household use (retail trade, health care, the beauty and fashion industries, and more recently in finance and real estate). In contrast to men's independent decision making, women generally calculated business decisions against the conflicting claims of family duty. Further, custom and law opened doors to training, education, and capital for men that remained closed to women until the very recent past. As a result, businesswomen devised innovative personnel, managerial, and financial strategies that satisfied their family responsibilities and legal disabilities. They pioneered organizational and managerial practices that infused an ethic of public service into the definition of business success. They met gendered proscriptions against going into business with new prescriptions that valued "independent womanhood" as a mark of female success.

The study of women in American business is pushing historians to move beyond narrow considerations of leadership to reexamine the forces driving economic change. The expansion of 19th-century commercial agriculture becomes more comprehensible as historians recognize the household as a business enterprise in the family economies of rural America. The success of mass production technologies in the early 20th century becomes more understandable as scholars consider the way gendered appeals stimulated a mass consumer demand. The continuing importance of small business amid the explosion of global markets in the late 20th century takes on a new significance as investigators examine changes in family and community life.

Six months after proclaiming independence, the Continental Congress contracted with Mary Katherine Goddard (1738–1816) to print the first signed copy of the Declaration of Independence. Goddard, publisher of Baltimore's leading newspaper, the *Maryland Journal,* was a logical choice for this important and dangerous job. Like many women of her time, Goddard learned this traditionally male craft as an assistant in the family business, in this case her brother William's various printing enterprises. It was Goddard's fate, however, to have a brother whose attention quickly moved from one venture to another. In each case, Katherine Goddard and, until her death, her mother, Sarah Goddard, stepped into the breach and ran the printing business when William moved on. Thus, when Katherine Goddard took over management of her brother's latest venture in Baltimore in 1774, she had more than 10 years of experience in the printing business. She quickly established her own credentials by coming out from behind her brother's shadow and printing her own name as publisher on the *Maryland Journal*'s masthead. By the time Goddard received the contract to print the Declaration of Independence, she had established her newspaper's reputation in the highly charged atmosphere of revolutionary America, was serving as the first female postmaster in colonial America, and had begun her own financially successful bookbinding and bookselling business.

While Mary Katherine Goddard was more successful than most, she was not unique. Rather, Goddard acted within a well-established colonial tradition of female entrepreneurship, a tradition that grew out of the necessities of the colonial family economy. Whether engaged in farming, trade, or craft, American colonists worked within family enterprises whose success depended on the labor of all family members. The colonial woman's title of "good wife" or "helpmeet" clearly reflected her important role in the family enterprise. The colonial farmer knew that commercial success required not only his and his sons' labor in the fields, but also his wife and daughters' field labor at critical times of the year. The colonial shopkeeper and craftsman depended on female family members to meet customers and suppliers, care for stock, and, as in Goddard's case, acquire expertise at various stages of his craft (which launched a small number of women into a range of traditionally male crafts, including printing, glassblowing, black-

smithing, and upholstery). In the event of a husband's prolonged absence these women gained the authority to manage the business as "deputy husbands."

The colonial woman, however, did not simply work as an assistant. She frequently developed her own petty business, which formed part of the overall family enterprise or, if single or widowed, was the family enterprise. Rural women produced home manufactures (of cheese, yarn, woven cloth, clothing, baskets, feather beds, and other necessities) to barter in local markets for the food, household goods, and in some cases cash that they and their family did not produce. Urban women engaged in an even wider range of business activities, specializing in retail shopkeeping, brewing and tavernkeeping, running boardinghouses, and dressmaking. While the historical record is not entirely clear, some historians have estimated that as many as half of all retailers in 18th-century colonial cities were women. These merchants supplied their customers with both locally produced and imported goods, specializing in dry goods, food, and alcoholic beverages. In the 1750s, for example, Mahetabel Hylton, a widowed merchant in colonial New York, advertised "a large assortment of European and East India Goods" plus cordage, earthenware, pepper, snuff, bar iron, gunpowder, shot pipes, candles, and Madeira wine. About 50 years earlier another widowed merchant, Helena Rombouts, reported to the New York customs house that she was exporting hundreds of deer and racoon skins to London and importing more than 2,600 gallons of West Indian rum. Records suggest that women ran 40 percent of Boston's taverns in 1690.

Whether active in women's crafts or home manufactures or competing with men in shopkeeping or printing, colonial businesswomen operated within legal constraints that were unique to their sex. British common law classified women as either *femme sole* (woman alone) or *femme covert* (woman covered). The *femme sole* could own and sell property, make contracts, sue and be sued, and will property to others. A woman acquired *femme sole* status only if she reached majority age (commonly 21 years) and remained unmarried. Prior to this and after marriage she was *femme covert,* subsumed under the legal identity first of her father and then of her husband. Thus, most women never acquired *femme sole* status, or did so for only a very few years. The vast majority of colonial women lived as *femme covert,* a legal status that prohibited them from owning property, making contracts, suing and being sued, or willing property to others. This legal invisibility meant that married women could not perform the most basic functions necessary to establish or expand a business (borrowing money, selling property, enforcing contracts). Whereas many colonial husbands could rely on their wife's dowry to build or expand their business, as did Benjamin Franklin and George Washington, few colonial women had a legal right even to their own dowry. As a consequence women frequently entered business (or at least appeared in the historical record) at an older age than men, often as a result of widowhood. Widows gained most of the rights of the *femme sole.* However, colonial inheritance laws, which granted a widow use rights only in one-third of her deceased husband's estate, meant that widows generally did not have full legal control over properties they inherited. Thus, they could not sell or will away, and often could not acquire credit against, those properties.

Women in the short-lived Dutch colony of New Amsterdam were the exception to this general picture, an exception that demonstrates the impact of these legal disabilities. Dutch law, in contrast to British common law, recognized women's rights in property. Thus, merchant Margaret Hardenbroeck continued in local trade during her yearlong first marriage. Widowed in 1661, Margaret inherited full title to a 50 percent share of her husband's estate and used it to buy two ships for the transatlantic trade. Although she married a wealthy trader the following year, Margaret Hardenbroeck Philipse continued in the lucrative transatlantic trade, often traveling with her trading ships until 1690.

Few colonial businesswomen were as successful as Goddard or Hardenbroeck. Lack of access to education and capital, combined with time-consuming household and family duties, placed severe restraints on what most women could hope to achieve. Rather than measuring women's business success by the wealth or power they amassed, we might do better to measure success against the alternative of failure. Businesswomen often eked out a poor living that managed, through dint of hard work and perseverance, to keep them and their children off the poor rolls. Rachel Draper, widowed with two small children in the years leading up to the American Revolution, typified the colonial businesswoman. Draper held licenses to run a small tavern, probably out of her Philadelphia home, and take in boarders. Although she was apparently too poor to appear on the tax rolls, Draper did succeed in providing an independent living for herself and her children.

Family duty, rather than a desire for profits, drove Elizabeth Hobbs Keckley (1818–1907) into the dressmaking business. Born into SLAVERY, Keckley began sewing fine women's dresses after she persuaded her impoverished owner to send her, rather than her aging mother, out to work in the homes of strangers. Keckley's labors soon provided enough money to support a household of 17 people, masters and slaves. In 1855, a wealthy client loaned her $1,200 to buy freedom for herself and her son. Keckley quickly headed north, establishing dressmaking businesses in New York, Baltimore, and, finally, Washington, D.C. Keckley's business thrived in Washington, where her skill made her the most popular dressmaker in the nation's capital. By the eve of the Civil War, Keckley employed more than 20 assistants in a large dressmaking shop. In addition to providing a comfortable living for herself and her son, Keckley committed a portion of her profits to philanthropic work, organizing the Contraband Relief Association and founding the Home for Destitute Women and Children. Mary Todd Lincoln hired Keckley as her personal dressmaker and soon came to rely on Keckley as her close friend and confidante. Keckley's decision to write an autobiography, *Behind the Scenes or Thirty Years a Slave and Four Years in the White House,* led to the collapse of her business. The story revealed details of the Lincoln family life that led Mary Lincoln to end their friendship and many African Americans to accuse Keckley of disloyalty to Lincoln the liberator. Keckley spent her final days in the Home for Destitute Women and Children.

Like Keckley, most women entered business in order to provide for themselves and their children. Similarly, most 19th-century businesswomen engaged in activities tied to household products or skills. According to one estimate, two-thirds of women in business at that time were proprietors of dressmaking, mantua-making, seamstress, or millinery operations. The second-largest number of businesswomen ran boardinghouses, restaurants, and, particularly in western states, brothels. In addition to these large clusters, businesswomen established themselves in a wide variety of trades and services that catered to daily needs. In Albany, New York, mid-19th-century businesswomen owned and managed bookstores, shoe shops, groceries, ornamental hair shops, and manufactories. Although women in small towns were the most likely to become entrepreneurs, rural women's petty businesses provisioned much of the nation. Throughout the antebellum period, for example, women produced and marketed the vast majority of milk, cheese, and butter consumed by Americans. One historian attributes increased butter production during this era to farmwomen's inventiveness and adaptation of existing processes and tools. In addition to food production, women's businesses could be important venues of food distribution. Free black women in the South engaged in retail trade in even larger numbers than did free black men, peddling a wide variety of foodstuffs from carts or small stands to a largely white clientele. While busi-

nessmen clearly outnumbered businesswomen, the significance of entrepreneurship in women's lives is suggested by the fact that in the Midwest in 1870, women in business outnumbered women factory workers by 4,000 and that there were as many women engaged in business as in teaching.

A small but influential group of female reformers introduced a new element into 19th-century business formation, a development that historian Virginia Drachman has called "profit in the service of women." Education reformers led by Emma Willard, Mary Lyon, and Catherine Beecher conceptualized their new curriculum for women as a new "product." In place of traditional finishing schools intended to prepare women for genteel domesticity, these education reformers built female academies that offered an academic secondary education that prepared young women for careers in teaching. Their successful, although often short-lived, efforts to open female academies across the country introduced a new kind of business into the American landscape. Unable to tap into the loans and credit available to hopeful businessmen, these educational entrepreneurs also innovated new strategies for raising capital. In 1821, Emma Willard, founder of Troy Female Seminary, convinced city officials in Troy, New York, to invest public monies in her enterprise. More typically, these businesswomen embarked on speaking tours that served both as advertisements for their educational ideas and as organizing forums for fund raising. In addition to collecting funds through paid admissions to their lectures, educational entrepreneurs used their speaking tours to organize associations of paid subscribers who, they hoped, would provide the long-term financial stability their schools needed.

Ellen Demorest, who invented paper dress patterns and, along with her husband, created a fashion empire in the mid-19th century, connected profits with service as well. In the 1850s, Demorest integrated African-American women on her production floor. Two decades later, she and businesswoman Susan King cofounded the Woman's Tea Company with the express purpose of making profits while creating business opportunities for other women; the Woman's Tea Company employed only sales*women*.

Although Demorest and King were able to use personal fortunes to finance their international trading company, the fact that most female academies closed their doors within 10 years reflected both the instability of 19th-century business ventures in general and the particularly precarious financial situation faced by most female entrepreneurs. While women's access to credit remained extremely limited, changes in women's legal status made it possible for a growing number of women to enter the business arena. The first significant change came with the post-Revolution codification of laws that abolished primogeniture. This democratic change created a system of inheritance law that allowed women, as well as all sons, to inherit real property. Further changes in women's legal status grew out of women's concerted demands for property rights. The first women's rights movement, dating from the Seneca Falls Convention in 1848, established women's property rights as one of its most important demands. Decades of campaigning brought some relief by the end of the 19th century. In most cases this took the form of extending the rights of *femme sole* status to married women. Between 1830 and the 1880s, every state passed laws that granted some form of property rights to married women. Depending on the state this included the right of married women to negotiate contracts, to buy, sell, or mortgage property, or to control their own earnings. Some states, recognizing the volatility of the American economy, protected a married woman's property from being seized to pay off her husband's debts.

While providing new rights to married women, 19th-century laws continued to limit women's access to property in significant ways. For example, in the mid-19th century, fewer than half the states allowed women to serve as executors of wills, a right that would be recognized nationwide only in the late 20th century. Many states refused widows access to their husband's personal property. Alongside this general trend, regional variations meant that particular groups of women faced different sets of legal freedoms and barriers. For example, women living in the Mexican cession lands (ceded to the United States following the Mexican-American War) continued to enjoy rights based on existing community property laws, which recognized that husbands and wives had equal shares in marital property. On the other hand, some southern states imposed legal restrictions intended to limit free black women's ability to engage in the retail trades on which so many depended. This included, for example, prohibitions against selling such items as beer, fruit, cakes, or candy.

Operating businesses that catered to local markets, often serving a female clientele that did not control its own resources, and bucking the emerging Victorian ideal that defined women's sphere as the home, few women in the 19th century could acquire the skills or resources that would have allowed them to compete at the cutting edge of the newly industrializing economy. However, scattered evidence suggests that 19th-century businesswomen were somewhat less likely to be living on the edge of destitution than were their colonial counterparts. One study found that between 1850 and 1880, businesswomen in the Midwest reported personal assets averaging $500, the equivalent of a year's income for a wage-earner. Some women did even better, achieving remarkable success. Among these were Martha Coston (ca. 1826–ca. 1902). Widowed at 21 and with three small children, her husband's inability to perfect an idea for night flares had left his pyrotechnic laboratory in precarious financial condition. Within a few years, Coston succeeded where her husband had failed, inventing colored night flares that, after intensive lobbying, were purchased by the U.S. Navy. Coston Night Signals were widely credited with ensuring Union victories during the Civil War; as Coston continually improved on her original design, they became standard safety equipment on boats and ships well into the 20th century.

Born to struggling tenant farmers in Canada, Florence Nightingale Graham (1878–1966) decided to leave home and seek her fortune when she was 30 years old. After joining her brother in New York, Graham moved through a series of jobs before settling in as cashier at Eleanor Adair's beauty parlor. There, Graham eventually worked her way up to a position as a "treatment girl." Soon, she and a fellow worker decided to try the business on their own. Within a short time Graham bought out her partner, redecorated the shop, and assumed a name that seemed more befitting to the upscale clientele she hoped to attract, Elizabeth Arden. Over the course of the next 30 years, Arden would employ chemists to develop a widening line of beauty products, open salons across the United States and in Europe, introduce beauty products into elite department stores, and redefine American ideas about beauty and cosmetics. By the mid-1930s, Arden's cosmetics empire included 26 salons worldwide, employed 1,000 people, and grossed more than $8 million a year.

It does seem clear that despite their small numbers, businesswomen were active creators of the modern corporate system. In fact, recognizing the empires built by businesswomen such as Elizabeth Arden and Helena Rubenstein in cosmetics, Madame C. J. Walker in hair care products, and Ida Rosenthal, creator of Maidenform, in fashion, corrects a mistaken impression that modern corporations existed primarily in heavy industry. These women's significance extended beyond their ability to amass fortunes; by 1930, cosmetics was the 10th-largest industry in the United States. In many respects, it was pioneering businesswomen of this era who ensured that MASS PRODUCTION and mass consumption permeated deeply into all corners of the expanding economy.

While women engaged in big business confronted the same kinds of financing, organizational, and marketing issues that faced big business men, more research is needed to better understand the extent to which their solutions may have differed from men's. Two differences, however, are striking. Reinventing the practice of "profits in the service of women," the most successful African-American businesswomen owed their fortunes to business practices designed to promote racial uplift. Annie Turnbo Malone, founder of Poro hair care products in St. Louis, designed a sales strategy that offered African-American women dignified work and an opportunity to build their own customer base. One of her sales agents, Sarah Breedlove, demonstrated the full potential of this business strategy. Breedlove was working as a washerwoman when Malone recruited her to be a sales agent around 1902. By 1905, Breedlove had decided to strike out on her own. Like Arden, she added style to her product by renaming herself Madame C. J. Walker; when her business grew sufficiently to employ sales agents, Walker adopted Malone's policy of grooming them as independent businesswomen rather than as company employees. By the time of her death in 1919, 25,000 Walker agents sold her products nationwide. Walker had joined the ranks of the wealthiest Americans and was living in a mansion on the Hudson River.

Another striking characteristic, evident among the most successful businesswomen of the 19th century as well, was the tendency to bring their husbands (or sons) into the business as full partners. Ida Rosenthal handled the business side of Maidenform, while her husband served as the creative partner. An opposite division of labor characterized Ellen Demorest's successful partnership in the 19th century; Demorest was the creative and fashion genius, while her husband innovated marketing practices that spread Demorest fashions into homes nationwide. This practice of female-directed partnerships stands in contrast to the pattern that developed within male-directed corporations, where men's success was measured, at least in part, by the separation of their work from the domestic and philanthropic concerns of their wives.

Few businessmen or businesswomen, of course, could aspire to this level of success. In fact, as the scale of business operations grew, managerial bureaucracies replaced individual entrepreneurs as the driving force in American business. Women, however, were largely excluded from this expanding arena. Women, who were presumed to be dependent, submissive, and domestic, seemed inherently unfit for the demands of executive management. Nevertheless, a small number of women did find positions in the expanding corporate bureaucracies. According to one estimate, on the eve of World War II women constituted about 10 percent of all middle managers. Significantly, many of these women entered management by capitalizing on the very gender ideas that defined women as unfit for business management. The first group of women to enter the ranks of corporate management pioneered the field of labor relations. Originally called welfare secretaries and later welfare managers, these women (and male colleagues in similar positions) offered a solution to the destructive confrontations between workers and employers at the end of the 19th and beginning of the 20th centuries. Women such as Gertrude Beeks at INTERNATIONAL HARVESTER, Elizabeth Briscoe at DuPont, and Mary B. Gilson at Joseph Feiss & Sons, called for a new kind of labor management, modeled on the harmonious Victorian family. Welfare managers promoted managerial qualities that combined feminine compassion, self-sacrifice, and cooperation with masculine discipline, rationality, and perseverance. Although the corporate welfare system failed to solve class conflict, welfare managers were responsible for introducing labor relations as a permanent management responsibility and were instrumental in defining the modern managerial ethos.

In addition to labor management, some businesswomen found positions as heads of departments that catered specifically to women. The largest group of these worked in middle manage-ment positions as department store buyers. According to one estimate, 40 percent of buyers in the mid-1920s were women. Buyers needed a keen sense of fashion as well as an ability to manage a largely female sales force. Another small door opened as bank and insurance companies hired women to head new "women's departments" created to attract a growing female clientele.

As their numbers grew, businesswomen began to form organizations to support their involvement in a world clearly dominated by men. In the 1910s and 1920s, businesswomen established general associations that welcomed women from an array of business sectors (National Federation of Business and Professional Women's Club), as well as special associations for women active in a common profession (Association of Banking Women). These clubs organized social as well as political activities, and many published newsletters. The BPW's *Independent Woman,* one of the largest circulating women's magazines of the early 20th century, helped to define the New Woman of the 1920s, addressing its readers as professionals seeking personal independence and offering advice about balancing career and marriage. When the public mood shifted during the Great Depression, the magazine devoted increasing space to home and fashion.

Women's entry into these new business arenas is particularly remarkable given the fact that their legal status had changed very little and, in one respect, could be considered to have become more restrictive. With few exceptions, the *femme sole* rights acquired by the 1880s remained intact but were not expanded; also, women's limited property ownership meant that access to credit remained extremely limited. Access to higher education, expanding until more than 40 percent of all college students in the 1930s were women, also remained restrictive. Most of the new university schools of business, for example, did not accept women. During the early decades of the century, social reformers successfully introduced state and local legislation to protect women workers. Although protective legislation affected wage-earners only, it did reinforce patriarchal ideas about women's frailty and domesticity. At the same time, most businesswomen and their organizations were active in the women's suffrage campaigns. While its impact was not immediate, businesswomen understood that they could use the suffrage issue to protect and further their interests. Equally important, suffrage work demonstrated their ability and their claim to act as independent women in the public arena.

As a girl Debbi Sivyer (1956–   ) liked to bake cookies, especially chocolate chip cookies. As a young wife Debbi Sivyer Fields baked cookies for her husband's business clients. However, neither her husband nor his clients showed much enthusiasm when Fields decided to turn her domestic talents into a profit-making enterprise. Driven by a desire to make something of herself, Fields defied their skepticism and applied for a business loan. Persistence and free product samples finally persuaded one banker to make the $50,000 start-up loan. Further defying normal business practice, Fields decided to locate her cookie store in a shopping mall. Mrs. Fields Chocolate Chippery opened in 1977, ringing up $75 in sales the first day. At the end of the first year Mrs. Fields Cookies had grossed $250,000. By the time she was 25 Debbi Sivyer Fields had turned her favorite pastime into a multimillion-dollar business. Her success opened the door to other mall-based specialty food shops. In 1990, Mrs. Fields Cookies operated almost 500 stores in 50 countries. Its founder and president was actively managing the company and raising five daughters. Fields sold her company in the early 1990s for $100 million.

Fields typifies both the continuity and change that characterized women in American business at the end of the 20th century. As in the past, most female entrepreneurs offered products or services connected to women's needs or domestic skills. A mid-1950s survey conducted by the Federation of Business and Professional Women (BPW) found that almost 33 percent of respondents owned retail firms. Another 35 percent

Woman working on an airplane engine during World War II (LIBRARY OF CONGRESS)

owned companies in female-related areas of personal services, education, hotels, and restaurants. Almost 40 years later, the U.S. Census Bureau reported that the largest proportion of women-owned businesses, 55 percent, was engaged in personal services, with retail trade accounting for the second-largest concentration, 17 percent. As in the past, most women's businesses remained quite small. Only 15 percent of women-owned firms in 1997 had paid employees, and 30 percent reported annual receipts of less than $5,000. The small scale of women's businesses reflected, in part, ongoing differences in men's and women's access to credit and loans. Businesswomen were significantly more likely than men to finance their enterprises using personal savings, CREDIT CARDS, or family loans. Reports in the mid-1990s found that more than 50 percent of all women-owned businesses used credit cards as a source of business financing, compared to less than 20 percent of all small businesses that relied on credit card financing. Although credit cards provided access to a new source of personal capital, women's dependence on personal and family resources to finance their business ventures continued a pattern that stretched back over two centuries.

Yet the business landscape did change in significant ways. Certain trends evident in the early 20th century had profoundly affected women's business opportunities by the end of the century. Dressmakers and milliners, who made up the largest number of businesswomen in the mid-19th century, accounted for one-half of 1 percent of the women-owned businesses reported to the BPW in the mid-1950s. Farmwomen's petty trade in cheese, eggs, and garden vegetables gave way during this period to industrial-scale production and wholesaling. By the end of the 20th century, farmwomen were much more likely to be working in town for wages than selling their own farm products. At the same time, businesswomen began to gain footholds in traditionally male-exclusive business sectors, including construction, manufacturing, and financial services. Women-owned firms grew from less than 2 percent of all construction companies in 1977 to almost 6 percent in 1987. During the same decade, women's ownership of manufacturing firms more than tripled, from 7 percent to 21 percent. Businesswomen's movement into finance, insurance, and real estate was even more substantial; by 1990 women owned more than 35 percent of the firms in these sectors, up from less than 5 percent in the 1970s.

Notably, these traditionally female sectors achieved new importance in the consumer-based postwar economy. Rather than functioning at the margins of the economy as in the past, women's businesses have become concentrated in core sectors of the American economy. Equally noteworthy, women-owned businesses were at the leading edge of the postwar expansion of the small business sector. In 1977, women owned 7 percent of all business firms in the United States. A decade later, that number had grown to 30 percent, and by the end of the century 8 million female entrepreneurs owned almost 40 percent of American business firms. Of these, 13 percent, more than 1 million enterprises, were owned by

women of color. The Foundation for Women Business Owners (FWBO) reported that during the last decade of the century the number of women-owned businesses grew at almost twice the national rate of business growth. At the end of the century, women-owned businesses employed almost 20 million workers, more than 25 percent of the American workforce. At the same time, businesswomen continued to innovate management and business practices that combined service with profit making. In the mid-1990s, the FWBO reported that women-owned businesses were much more likely than the average business to offer flex-time schedules, job sharing, and tuition reimbursement. Almost 85 percent of women-owned businesses offered one or more of these benefits. For reasons that are not yet clear, female entrepreneurs seem to be navigating the difficulties of small business ownership more successfully than men. A 1995 Dun and Bradstreet study found that women-owned firms were more likely to stay in business for three or more years than was the average business firm.

These gains in business ownership must be balanced against the emergence of corporate management as the primary form of business leadership in the late 20th century. In many respects, corporate officers have replaced the individual entrepreneur of the previous century as the prototypical businessperson. Census records show that an increasing number of women moved into upper levels of business leadership in the last quarter of the 20th century, accounting for more than 5 percent of such positions in the mid-1970s and holding more than 12 percent of executive, administrative, and managerial positions by the mid-1990s. Among the most successful of these women are chief executive officers Carleton Fiorino at Hewlett Packard Company, Andrea Jung at Avon Products, Anne Mulcahy at Xerox, Patricia Russo at Lucent Technologies, and Meg Whitman at e-Bay Technologies.

Although this represents substantial change, there is much evidence that a "glass ceiling" continues to limit women's access to executive leadership. The glass ceiling reflects a combination of challenges, including ongoing questions about women's dual commitments to career and family and a tendency to denigrate women for the kind of assertiveness that would be praised in male executives. In addition, women who move onto the lower rungs of management often find that they cannot reach the highest executive offices. The clerical, public relations, marketing, and labor relations positions through which most women move into management, classified as "staff positions," are generally excluded from the promotional ladder leading to executive leadership, which draws from "line positions." The research institution Catalyst reported that women held only 6.2 percent of line officer positions in 2000. Thus, despite decades of progress, only six women served as CEOs of Fortune 500 companies in 2004.

Changes in women's legal and educational status at the end of the 20th century contributed to this mixed picture. In the 1960s and 1970s, feminists challenged legal assumptions that had remained unchanged for most of the century. Although few of those challenges were directly related to business, they did affect women's access to training, credit, and promotion. The Equal Pay Act (1963) and Title VII of the Civil Rights Act (1964) dramatically altered women's employment status, requiring equal pay for equal work and outlawing discrimination in employment and in unions on the basis of sex. Directed primarily at the problems faced by wage-earning women, these laws were equally applicable to women in management. The increased numbers of women executives, administrators, and managers during the last quarter-century is attributable, at least in part, to the principle of nondiscrimination established by these laws. These were not the only laws affecting women's ability to move into corporate management. Title IX of the Higher Education Amendments (1972), best known for its impact on women's sports, required equal access to all higher education programs and activities, including all academic and professional programs. While most female students continued to cluster in health care, education, English, and the arts, Title IX's nondiscriminatory requirements opened the doors to nontraditional fields of study, including business. Business-minded women quickly took advantage of the opportunity. The proportion of women earning master of business administration (MBA) degrees increased fivefold, from 6 percent to more than 30 percent, between the mid-1970s and the mid-1980s. Despite this preparation for business leadership and laws banning discrimination, women continue to be grossly underrepresented at top levels of corporate management.

In addition to expanding women's access to corporate management, a number of administrative and legislative actions increased opportunities for business ownership. Among these were executive orders issued by Presidents Lyndon Johnson and Richard Nixon, first requiring nondiscrimination in granting federal contracts and later requiring affirmative action to grant federal contracts to women- and minority-owned businesses (1967, 1970). These opened the door for women-owned businesses to compete in the expanding arena of government contracting. Perhaps more significantly, the Equal Credit Opportunity Act (1974) outlawed sex-based discrimination in lending. While the primary purpose of this law was to ensure women's access to consumer credit, it had the additional effect of opening the door to business credit. As with legislation banning discrimination on the basis of sex in employment and education, the legal right to equal treatment has not automatically resulted in equal access. In the mid-1990s, for example, the SMALL BUSINESS ADMINISTRATION, which should have been a resource for the thousands of small women-owned businesses, admitted that it had been discriminating against women- and minority-business applicants.

As they navigated the expanding opportunities and continued limitations of the late 20th century, businesswomen increasingly turned to each other for information and support. A new generation of businesswomen reenergized older businesswomen's organizations, such as the Business and Professional Women's Clubs, founded new organizations, including the National Foundation for Women Business Owners and the National Association for Female Executives, and established research institutions, such as Catalyst, to study women in business. In addition, businesswomen increasingly integrated traditionally male-exclusive business organizations, including chambers of commerce.

Further reading

Drachman, Virginia G. *Enterprising Women: 250 Years of American Business.* Chapel Hill: University of North Carolina Press, 2002.

Kwolek-Folland, Angel. *Incorporating Women: A History of Women and Business in the United States.* New York: Twayne Publishers, 1998.

Mandell, Nikki. *The Corporation as Family: The Gendering of Corporate Welfare, 1890–1930.* Chapel Hill: University of North Carolina Press, 2002.

Yeager, Mary, ed. *Women in Business.* Northhampton, Mass.: E. Elgar Publisher, 1999.

Nikki Mandell

Woolworth, Frank Winfield (1852–1919) *retailer* The founder of the Woolworth chain of "five and dime" stores was born in Rodman in upstate New York and spent his teens working at menial jobs in dry goods stores. He studied briefly at a local business college. When he was 21, after several unsuccessful stints as a salesman and clerk in variety stores, he persuaded the manager of a store he was working in to place slightly damaged goods on a special counter and sell them for 5 cents. The idea became immediately popular, and he soon opened his own store in 1879 in Utica selling a variety of items all priced at 5 cents.

The first store failed, but Woolworth persisted, opening another in Lancaster, Pennsylvania, offering items for up to 10 cents. He called the store Woolworth's Five and Ten Cents Store. After it succeeded, he began opening others in Pennsylvania and New York. He bought stores from competitors, consolidating them into his own operation. By 1900, he operated almost 60 stores with sales exceeding $5 million. Stores were added in England in 1909, with sales from all sources at almost $110 million. In 1912, all the stores and those acquired in the intervening years were merged into the F. W. Woolworth Co., and the company was incorporated.

In 1913, he built one of New York City's earliest SKYSCRAPERS—the Woolworth Building—that made his name even more famous. It was nicknamed the "Cathedral of Commerce" and cost almost $14 million to build. Woolworth paid for the building out of his personal funds.

The success made Woolworth one of America's best-known retailers. The company arguably was the best known of the "five and dime" retailers. The stock was added to the Dow Jones 30 Industrial Average in 1924 and remained in the index until 1997. The stores were so popular in Britain that the name was assumed to be English and the company a local one. But success was clouded to an extent by Woolworth's treatment of his employees. He was not known as an enlightened employer. He treated his female employees poorly and often dismissed them quickly when business was not good. The poor treatment often made news headlines. Woolworth died in 1919 on Long Island at a time when his empire totaled more than 1,000 stores and his personal estate was estimated at $65 million.

In later years, the company expanded its operations into other areas. It purchased the retailer and shoemaker G. R. Kinney Corp. in 1963. But competition from more diversified stores such as Wal-Mart finally took its toll. The last of Woolworth's retail stores was closed in 1997, and the name of the company changed to the Venator Group.

See also CHAIN STORES; K-MART; SEARS, ROEBUCK, & CO.; WANAMAKER, JOHN; WARD, AARON MONTGOMERY.

Further reading

Baker, Nina Brown. *Nickels and Dimes: The Story of F. W. Woolworth.* New York: Harcourt Brace, 1954.

Plunkett-Powell, Karen. *Remembering Woolworth's: A Nostalgic History of the World's Most Famous Five-And-Dime.* New York: St. Martin's Press, 1999.

Winkler, John K. *Five & Ten: The Fabulous Life of F. W. Woolworth.* New York: Bantam Books, 1957.

Works Progress Administration (WPA)   A federal agency organized during the first administration of Franklin D. Roosevelt in 1936. The WPA was created by executive order after the Emergency Relief Appropriation of 1935. The appropriation of $5 billion gave $1.39 billion to the WPA, which in turn attempted to provide public works projects using the unemployed. The WPA was clearly a make-work agency that existed alongside the Public Works Administration, designed to get people off the public dole and working again.

The agency was put under the direction of Harry Hopkins. The agency provided an average weekly pay of $55, an amount designed to provide a subsistence wage to its recipients. The administration did not want the WPA to compete with private industry and therefore kept its wages low. It was intended only to provide some relief and dignity to the unemployed and was not meant to substitute government employment for higher wages in the private sector. As a result, some workers collected more from the public dole than they did from a WPA job. The agency was highly politicized from the beginning.

Unlike the PWA, the WPA did not undertake giant engineering projects but contented itself with smaller building projects such as building schools, playgrounds, bridges, streets and roads, parks, and airfields, among others. It also allocated funds for unemployed professionals and created federal projects for the arts, music, theater, and writers. The writers' project provided work for many writers later to become famous, including Saul Bellow, John Cheever, and Ralph

Poster for the Works Progress Administration (LIBRARY OF CONGRESS)

Ellison. The arts project produced murals by Mexican artist Diego Rivera that were highly criticized at the time because of the graphic nature of the work. The music project became the basis for symphony orchestras established in several cities after World War II.

The agency was subsequently named the Works Projects Administration and continued to provide support until World War II, when it was terminated. It remained controversial during the 1930s but stood as an example of government intervention in the private sector during times of economic crisis; although it was overshadowed by the PWA, it did manage to employ more than 8 million people on 1.4 million projects in 3,000 counties across the country.

See also NATIONAL RECOVERY ADMINISTRATION; NEW DEAL.

Further reading

MacMahon, Arthur, John D. Millett, and Gladys Ogden. 1941. Reprint, *The Administration of Federal Work Relief*. New York: Da Capo Press, 1971.

McDonald, William F. *Federal Relief Administration and the Arts: The Origins and Administrative History of the Arts Projects of the Works Progress Administration*. Columbus: Ohio State University Press, 1969.

McElvaine, Robert S. *The Great Depression*. New York: Times Books, 1984.

WorldCom   A telecommunications company founded in a motel restaurant in Mississippi in 1983 by Bernard Ebbers (1941–   ) and a group of local businessmen, the same year that AMERICAN TELEPHONE & TELEGRAPH (AT&T) agreed to be dissolved. WORLDCOM purchased wholesale long-distance service from AT&T and resold it, mostly to the small business community. AT&T's monopoly over long distance had been challenged in the 1970s by MCI Corp., and the venerable company agreed to a settlement with the Justice Department allowing for its breakup in the same year that WorldCom was founded.

Through a series of acquisitions, Ebbers built the company into a major long-distance provider. WorldCom adopted an acquisitions strategy that centered on buying other companies rather than developing them from the start. The company acquired 68 phone companies after 1983, following its original model of offering services mostly to small businesses. Ebbers then branched into the local markets with the $12 billion acquisition of MFS Communications in 1996.

WorldCom stock soared on these prospects, and Ebbers was presented with an opportunity to expand even further. The company that was the prize acquisition target was MCI, better known than WorldCom but cheaper in market price. Another competitor was GTE, which made an all-cash bid for MCI worth $28 billion. WorldCom prevailed, however, with an all-stock bid valued at $37 billion, a Wall Street record at the time. The sheer size of the all-stock deal required outside financing, and WorldCom issued an additional 760 million shares to pay for it, with MCI shareholders receiving 1.2439 shares of new stock for each share they held. BT (British Telecom) also received $51 in cash for each of the MCI shares it held as compensation.

MCI WorldCom was a giant in the TELECOMMUNICATIONS INDUSTRY, with combined revenue of $30 billion and operations in 65 countries, including 75,000 employees and 22 million customers. Regulators in Europe and the United States insisted on certain divestitures, including Internet service, so that the new company would not have an undue influence in emerging communications. But the telecommunications market was already proving soft, and the deal did not provide the revenues originally anticipated.

In 2002, the company revealed massive accounting irregularities and was forced to file for BANKRUPTCY, the largest of its kind at the time. Ebbers was charged with looting the company for personal gain, and the company operated under the protection of a bankruptcy court until it could reorganize itself. The company continued but dropped WorldCom from its logo, and it reverted to MCI in order to dissociate itself from the scandal and forge ahead.

Further reading

Jeter, Lynne W. *Disconnected: Deceit and Betrayal at WorldCom*. New York: John Wiley & Sons, 2003.

Kahaner, Larry. *On the Line: The Men of MCI Who Took on AT&T, Risked Everything, and Won*. New York: Warner Books, 1986.

Y

yankee peddlers Name given to itinerant salesmen of dry goods and household items who sold their goods by wagon in both urban and rural areas in the 18th and 19th centuries. There are even records of peddlers plying their wares in New England in the 17th century, although the activity was frowned upon before the country began to expand. Once the value of peddlers became recognized, especially in the South and in hard-to-access rural areas, criticism of them abated, although they were constantly accused of cheating their customers or worse.

Typically, peddlers would take a wagonload of goods on consignment and travel distances to sell them. They often borrowed the money to buy a consignment. The money they borrowed is thought to be the source of the term "working capital," since it was for relatively short periods of time and would be paid back to the lender in full once the peddlers returned from their travels. The difference between the cost of the goods and the sale price was the peddler's profit, although it sometimes took a considerable time to realize because the distances traveled could be extensive. Some peddlers traveled up and down the eastern seaboard, while others traveled into the frontier areas of the West. The name "damn Yankees" is thought to have originated with peddlers before the Civil War, since it was northerners who made up most of the peddling population that sold goods in the South.

Many well-known merchants and traders began their careers as itinerant salesmen, including William Filene, who later opened a famous Boston department store once described by Louis BRANDEIS; Daniel DREW, who became infamous on Wall Street as a stock trader and manipulator; Stephen GIRARD, the Philadelphia banker; Benedict Arnold; and William A. Rockefeller, father of John D. Rockefeller. The peddlers specialized in selling more than just housewares and over the years offered all sorts of goods and services to their customers. Often, they also offered simple credit to their better customers, providing the first sort of consumer credit offered in the United States, similar to the type later offered by stores directly to customers.

Once much of the hinterland had been settled and rural areas gained in population, the peddlers often gave up their traveling and became proprietors of country stores to serve the local population. They were the original retailers in the country before the advent of better communications and travel. The inaccessibility of many parts of rural America persisted well beyond the time of the Yankee peddlers, however, and became the basis for the mail-order catalog business developed in the 19th century by Sears, Roebuck and Montgomery Ward.

Further reading

Dolan, J. R. *The Yankee Peddlers of Early America.* New York: Clarkson Potter, 1964.

Harris, Leon. *Merchant Princes.* New York: Harper & Row, 1979.

Hendrickson, Robert. *The Grand Emporiums: The Illustrated History of America's Great Department Stores.* New York: Stein & Day, 1979.

Young, Owen D. (1874–1962) *businessman*
Born on a farm in Van Hornesville, New York, Young was educated at local schools and graduated from St. Lawrence University in 1894. He then attended Boston University's law school and joined a Boston law firm after graduation in 1896. He became a litigator at a firm headed by Charles H. Taylor and was made a partner in 1907. He specialized in law relating to UTILITIES companies. One of his cases brought him to the attention of Charles A. Coffin, the first president of the GENERAL ELECTRIC CO. In 1913, Coffin offered him a job as general counsel to the company, which he promptly accepted. In 1922, when Coffin retired, Young succeeded him as chairman.

Young served on two government conferences under different administrations. He served on Woodrow Wilson's National Industrial Conference in 1919 and 1920 and on Warren Harding's Unemployment Conference in 1921. In 1919, he helped create the RADIO CORPORATION OF AMERICA at the request of the government in order to combat threatened foreign control of the nascent American RADIO INDUSTRY. At issue was technology that the government feared would fall into the hands of the Marconi Wireless Telegraph Company, a British firm, and would allow Britain to become preeminent in radio technology. Young arranged to have RCA buy technology from GE, AMERICAN TELEPHONE & TELEGRAPH, the UNITED FRUIT COMPANY, GENERAL MOTORS, and Westinghouse so that it could assume the role as the leading radio technology company in the world. He became chairman of its board in 1922 and served until 1929, during which time he also helped establish the National Broadcasting Company.

When the courts forced a separation of GE and RCA, Young remained with GE while maintaining ties with RCA and David SARNOFF, who ran RCA. Along with a strong contingent of American bankers, he also served on the committee working on German war reparations in 1924, which produced the Dawes report. Five years later, a similar group produced the Young plan, a revised reparations program that also helped establish the Bank for International Settlements.

After World War II, Governor Thomas Dewey of New York appointed him to a state commission that created the state university system in New York. Throughout his career, he displayed strong skills as a negotiator and a mediator that made him much sought after as a leader of disparate groups. He was named *Time* magazine's Man of the Year in 1930. He retired as chairman of GE in 1939. He was widely praised as an industrial leader who recognized the importance of public service and international affairs.

Further reading

Case, Josephine, and Everett Case. *Owen D. Young and American Enterprise: A Biography.* Boston: David R. Godine, 1982.

Tarnell, Ida. *Owen D. Young: A New Type of Industrial Leader.* New York: Macmillan, 1932.

CHRONOLOGY

1670
• Hudson's Bay Co. chartered by British Crown

1784
• Bank of New York founded

1790
• U.S. Patent Office created

1791
• First Bank of the United States founded

1792
• Buttonwood Agreement signed, forms early stock exchange in New York
• Lancaster Turnpike opened in Pennsylvania

1793
• cotton gin invented

1800
• Congress passes first U.S. bankruptcy law

1802
• DuPont de Nemours & Co. founded

1807
• first steamboat, the *Clermont,* begins service in New York on Hudson River

1817
• Second Bank of the United States founded (rechartered)

1824
• *Gibbons v. Ogden* Supreme Court decision

1825
• Erie Canal completed

1836
• Colt Firearms Co. founded

1837
• stock market crash (or panic)

1840
• mechanical reaper produced by Cyrus McCormick

1844
• Samuel Morse successfully demonstrates the first telegraph

1847
• John Deere & Co. founded

1848
• Chicago Board of Trade founded
• gold discovered at Sutter's Mill, California

1851
• Singer Sewing Co. founded
• Western Union Telegraph Co. founded

1852
• Wells Fargo organized

1857
• stock market crash (or panic)

1858
• first transatlantic cable laid

1859
- Great Atlantic & Pacific Tea Co. founded

1864
- Congress passes National Bank Act

1867
- first ticker tape introduced
- first typewriter patented

1869
- east-west railroad link completed at Promontory, Utah
- John Wanamaker & Co. opens

1872
- Montgomery Ward opens first mail-order house

1876
- Alexander Graham Bell receives patent for telephone

1878
- Bell Telephone Company formed
- General Electric Company founded as Edison Electric

1879
- F. W. Woolworth opens first store

1880
- B. F. Goodrich Co. founded

1881
- Wharton School established at University of Pennsylvania

1884
- W. Duke Sons & Co. opened in New York City
- Westinghouse Electric founded

1886
- Coca-Cola founded
- Sears, Roebuck founded

1888
- George Eastman produces first Kodak camera

1889
- *Wall Street Journal* founded

1890
- Congress passes Sherman Antitrust Act
- J. P. Morgan & Co. founded after death of Junius S. Morgan

1892
- strike at Homestead Steel plant of Carnegie Steel
- U.S. Rubber Company founded

1893
- J. P. Morgan assists Treasury in raising gold

1896
- first Dow Jones Industrial Average appears
- IBM Corp. formed as the Tabulating Machine Co.

1900
- National Negro Business League convenes for first time
- Weyerhaeuser Co. founded

1901
- United States Steel Corp. formed

1903
- Ford Motor Co. founded
- Wright brothers make their first flight at Kitty Hawk, North Carolina

1904
- Bank of America founded in California as the Bank of Italy

1908
- General Motors Corp. founded
- Harvard Business School established

1911
- Supreme Court orders breakup of Standard Oil and American Tobacco

1913
- Congress passes Federal Reserve Act
- Congress creates first permanent income tax

1914
- Clayton Act passed
- Federal Trade Commission created
- New York Stock Exchange and other exchanges closed
- Panama Canal opened

1915
- Carrier Air Conditioning Co. founded

1916
- William Boeing starts his company

1919
- Congress passes Volstead Act
- Radio Corp. of America founded as a subsidiary of General Electric

1921
- Chrysler Corporation founded

1923
- Alfred Sloan becomes chief executive of General Motors
- Walt Disney founds cartoon studio in Hollywood

1925
- Congress passes the Air Mail Act of 1925, allowing the government to hire private air carriers to deliver the mail

1927
- Congress passes McFadden Act

1928
- Columbia Broadcasting System founded

1929
- stock market crashes (October)

1930
- Congress passes Hawley-Smoot Tariff

1931
- United Airlines incorporated

1932
- Congress creates Reconstruction Finance Corp.
- Congress creates the Federal Home Loan Bank Board

1933
- Banking (Glass-Steagall) Act passed
- Securities Act passed
- Congress creates Tennessee Valley Authority
- Volstead Act repealed

1934
- Congress passes National Labor Relations Act
- Federal Communications Commission formed
- Congress passes Gold Reserve Act
- Securities Exchange Act passed

1935
- Eccles Act strengthens Federal Reserve powers
- NIRA declared unconstitutional
- Public Utility Holding Company Act passed

1937
- Congress creates the NASD

1938
- Civil Aeronautics Act releases the airlines from the control of the U.S. Post Office Department and establishes the Civil Aeronautics Board as the airlines regulating agency

1944
- Bretton Woods agreement signed

1947
- Congress passes Taft-Hartley Act

1950
- first Walton store opened as Walton's Five & Dime

1955
- the AFL merges with the CIO

1964
- first Visa card appears

1971
• United States cuts fixed gold content of dollar

1972
• foreign exchange rates begin floating; Bretton Woods system collapses

1974
• Microsoft Corp. founded

1975
• Wall Street adopts negotiable commission structure

1978
• Congress passes Airline Deregulation Act

1979
• Federal Reserve changes U.S. monetary policy

1980
• Depository Institutions Deregulation and Monetary Control Act passed

1982
• Congress passes Depository Institutions Act

1984
• AT&T monopoly broken up; regional Bell companies become independent

1986
• Congress passes Tax Reform Act

1987
• stock market records largest drop in history

1989
• savings and loan crisis
• Congress creates Financial Institutions Reform, Recovery and Enforcement Act
• Internet organized as World Wide Web

1990
• Drexel Burnham collapses

1991
• Pan Am Airways declares bankruptcy

• Eastern Airlines shuts down all flight operations

1993
• Orange County, California, bankrupt because of derivatives transactions

1994
• interstate banking permitted by Congress
• NAFTA becomes effective

1997
• Boeing merges with McDonnell Douglas Corporation, making it the largest aerospace firm in the world

1998
• Long-Term Capital Management collapses
• Travelers Insurance and Citibank merge

1999
• Financial Services Modernization Act passed

2000
• Chase Manhattan and J. P. Morgan merge

2001
• stock market collapses after 9/11 attack
• AOL merges with Time Warner
• Enron Corp. collapses
• American Airlines acquires TWA, making American the largest U.S. commercial airline

2002
• Congress passes Sarbanes-Oxley Act
• United Airlines declares bankruptcy
• WorldCom files for bankruptcy protection

2004
• New York Attorney General Eliot Spitzer brings civil action against mutual funds and the insurance industry

2005
• New York Stock Exchange and NASDAQ announce plans to merge with electronic trading networks

SELECTED PRIMARY DOCUMENTS

1. Hudson's Bay Company Charter, 1670
2. Alexander Hamilton, *Report on the Subject of Manufactures*, 1791
3. Constitution of the American Federation of Labor, 1886
4. Interstate Commerce Act, 1887
5. Andrew Carnegie, "Wealth," 1889
6. Sherman Antitrust Act, 1890
7. Pure Food and Drug Act, 1906
8. *Standard Oil Company of New Jersey et al. v. United States*, 1911
9. Clayton Antitrust Act, 1914
10. Franklin D. Roosevelt, "Forgotten Man" Radio Speech, 1932
11. Securities Exchange Act, 1934
12. National Labor Relations Act, 1935
13. Dwight D. Eisenhower's "Military-Industrial Complex" Address, 1961
14. Ronald Reagan's Address to the Nation on the Economy, 1981
15. *United States v. Microsoft*, 2000

1. HUDSON'S BAY COMPANY CHARTER, 1670

Royal charter for incorporating the Hudson's Bay Company, granted on May 2, 1670, by England's King Charles II. It gave this English fur-trading company wide proprietary rights to territory surrounding "Hudson's Bay" and to all lands drained by rivers flowing into it. The charter allowed the company to make laws for the "lands aforesaid" and to send warships and armed men "into any of their (the company's) plantations, forts, factories, or places of trade aforesaid, for the security and defense of the same." Two Frenchmen who founded the company—Pierre Esprit Radisson and Medard Chouart (Sieur des Groseilliers)—had been unable to interest French authorities in the fur-trading route through Hudson Bay and had turned to Prince Rupert, a cousin of Charles II, who secured the charter. The company eventually maintained trading posts throughout Canada and a few forts on U.S. soil; it still exists, but without its original monopolistic, territorial, and administrative rights.

---⚬✦⚬---

THE ROYAL CHARTER FOR INCORPORATING THE HUDSON'S BAY COMPANY, A.D. 1670

Charles the Second By the grace of God King of England Scotland France and Ireland defender of the faith &c To All to whome these presentes shall come greeting Whereas Our Deare and entirely Beloved Cousin Prince Rupert Count Palatyne of the Rhyne Duke of Bavaria and Cumberland &c Christopher Duke of Albemarle William Earle of Craven Henry Lord Arlington Anthony Lord Ashley Sir John Robinson and Sir Robert Vyner Knightes and Baronettes Sir Peter Colliton Baronett Sir Edward Hungerford Knight of the Bath Sir Paul Neele Knight Sir John Griffith and Sir Phillipp Carteret Knightes James

495

Hayes John Kirke Francis Millington William Prettyman John Fenn Esquires and John Portman Cittizen and Goldsmith of London have at theire owne great cost and charge undertaken an Expedicion for Hudsons Bay in the North west part of America for the discovery of a new Passage into the South Sea and for the finding some Trade for Furrs Mineralls and other considerable Commodityes and by such theire undertakeing have already made such discoveryes as doe encourage them to proceed further in pursuance of theire said designe by meanes whereof there may probably arise very great advantage to us and our Kingdome And whereas the said undertakers for theire further encouragement in the said designe have humbly besought us to Incorporate them and grant unto them and theire successors the sole Trade and Commerce of all those Seas Streightes Bayes Rivers Lakes Creekes and Soundes in whatsoever Latitude they shall bee that lye within the entrance of the Streightes commonly called Hudsons Streightes together with all the Landes Countryes and Territoryes upon the Coastes and Confynes of the Seas Streightes Bayes Lakes Rivers Creekes and Soundes aforesaid which are not now actually possessed by any of our Subjectes or by the Subjectes of any other Christian Prince or State Now know yee that Wee being desirous to promote all Endeavours tending to the publique good of our people and to encourage the said undertakeing have of our especiall grace certaine knowledge and meere mocion Given granted ratifyed and confirmed And by these Presentes for us our heires and Successors doe give grant ratifie and confirme unto our said Cousin Prince Rupert Christopher Duke of Albemarle William Earle of Craven Henry Lord Arlington Anthony Lord Ashley Sir John Robinson Sir Robert Vyner Sir Peter Colleton Sir Edward Hungerford Sir Paul Neile Sir John Griffith and Sir Phillipp Carterett James Hayes John Kirke Francis Millington William Prettyman John Fenn and John Portman That they and such others as shall bee admitted into the said Society as is hereafter expressed

shall bee one Body Corporate and Politique in deed and in name by the name of the Governor and Company of Adventures of England tradeing into Hudsons Bay and them by the name of the Governor and Company of Adventurers of England tradeing into Hudsons Bay one Body Corporate and Politique in deede and in name really and fully for ever for us our heirs and successors Wee doe make ordeyne constitute establish confirme and declare by these Presentes and that by the same name of Governor & Company of Adventurers of England Tradeing into Hudsons Bay they shall have perpetuall succession And that they and theire successors by the name of the Governor and Company of Adventurers of England tradeing into Hudsons Bay bee and at all tymes hereafter shall bee persons able and capable in Law to have purchase receive possesse enjoy and reteyne Landes Rentes priviledges libertyes Jurisdiccions Franchyses and hereditamentes of what kinde nature and quality soever they bee to them and theire Successors And alsoe to give grant demise alien assigne and dispose Landes Tenementes and hereditamentes and to doe and execute all and singuler other thinges by the same name that to them shall or may apperteyne to doe And that they and theire Successors by the name of the Governor and Company of Adventurers of England Tradeing into Hudsons Bay may pleade and bee impleaded answeare and bee answeared defend and bee defended in whatsoever Courtes and places before whatsoever Judges and Justices and other persons and Officers in all and singuler Accions Pleas Suitts Quarrells causes and demandes whatsoever of whatsoever kinde nature or sort in such manner and forme as any other our Liege people of this our Realme of England being persons able and capable in Lawe may or can have purchase receive possesse enjoy reteyne give grant demise alien assigne dispose pleade and bee defended doe permitt and execute And that the said Governor and Company of Adventurers of England Tradeing into Hudsons Bay and theire successors may have a Common Seale to serve for all the causes and busnesses of them and theire Successors and that itt shall and my bee lawful to the said Governor and Company and theire Successors the same Seall from tyme to tyme at theire will and pleasure to breake change and to make a new or alter as to them shall seeme expedient And further Wee will And by these presentes for us our Heires and successors Wee doe ordeyne that there shall bee from henceforth one of the same Company to bee elected and appointed in such forme as hereafter in these presentes is expressed which shall be called The Governor of the said Company And that the said Governor and Company shall or may elect seaven of theire number in such forme as hereafter in these presentes is expressed which shall bee called the Comittee of the said Company which Comittee of seaven or any three of them together with the Governor or Deputy Governor of the said Company for the tyme being shall have the direccion of the Voyages of and for the said Company and the Provision of the Shipping and Merchandizes thereunto belonging and alsoe the sale of all merchandizes Goodes and other thinges returned in all or any the Voyages or Shippes of or for the said Company and the mannageing and handleing of all other busness affaires and thinges belonging to the said Company And Wee will ordeyne and Grant by these presentes for us our heires and successors unto the said Governor and Company and theire successors that they the said Governor and Company and theire successors shall from henceforth for ever bee ruled ordered and governed according to such manner and forme as is hereafter in these presentes expressed and not otherwise And that they shall have hold reteyne and enjoy the Grantes Libertyes Priviledges Jurisdiccions and Immunityes only hereafter in these presentes granted and expressed and noe other And for the better execucion of our will and Grant in this behalfe Wee have assigned nominated constituted and made And by these presentes for us our heires and successors Wee doe assigne nominate constitute and make our said Cousin Prince

Rupert to bee the first and present Governor of the said Company and to continue in the said Office from the date of these presentes untill the tenth of November then next following if hee the said Prince Rupert shall soe long live and soe untill a new Governor bee chosen by the said Company in forme hereafter expressed And alsoe Wee have assigned nominated and appointed And by these presentes for us our heires and Successors Wee doe assigne nominate and constitute the said Sir John Robinson Sir Robert Vyner Sir Peter Colleton James Hayes John Kirke Francis Millington and John Portman to bee the seaven first and present Committees of the said Company from the date of these presentes untill the said tenth Day of November then alsoe next following and soe untill new Committees shall bee chosen in forme hereafter expressed And further Wee will and grant by these presentes for us our heires and Successors unto the said Governor and Company and theire successors that itt shall and may bee lawfull to and for the said Governor and Company for the tyme being or the greater part of them present at any publique Assembly commonly called the Court Generall to bee holden for the said Company the Governor of the said Company being alwayes one from tyme to tyme to elect nominate and appoint one of the said Company to bee Deputy to the said Governor which Deputy shall take a corporall Oath before the Governor and three or more of the Committee of the said Company for the tyme being well truely and faithfully to execute his said Office of Deputy to the Governor of the said Company and after his Oath soe taken shall and may from tyme to tyme in the absence of the said Governor exercize and execute the Office of Governor of the said Company in such sort as the said Governor ought to doe And further Wee will and Grant and by these presentes for us our heires and Successors unto the said Governor and Company of Adventurers of England tradeing into Hudsons Bay and theire Successors That they or the greater part of them whereof the Governor for the Tyme being or his Deputy to bee one from tyme to tyme and at all tymes hereafter shall and may have authority and power yearely and every yeare betweene the first and last day of November to assemble and meete together in some convenient place to bee appointed from tyme to tyme by the Governor or in his absence by the Deputy of the said Governor for the tyme being And that they being soe assembled itt shall and may bee lawfull to and for the said Governor or Deputy of the said Governor and the said Company for the tyme being or the greater part of them which then shall happen to bee present whereof the Governor of the said Company or his Deputy for the tyme being to bee one to elect and nominate one of the said Company which shall be Governor of the same Company for one whole yeare then next following which person being soe elected and nominated to bee Governor of the said Company as is aforesaid before hee bee admitted to the Execucion of the said Office shall take a Corporall Oath before the last Governour being his Predecessor or his Deputy and any three or more of the Committee of the said Company for the tyme being that hee shall from tyme to tyme well and truely execute the Office of Governour of the said Company in all things concerneing the same and that Ymediately after the same Oath soe taken hee shall and may execute and use the said Office of Governor of the said Company for one whole yeare from thence next following and in like sort Wee will and grant that aswell every one of the above named to bee of the said Company or fellowship as all other hereafter to bee admitted or free of the said Company shall take a Corporall Oath before the Governor of the said Company or his Deputy for the tyme being to such effect as by the said Governor and Company or the greater part of them in any publick Court to bee held for the said Company shall bee in reasonable and legall manner sett down and devised before they shall bee allowed or admitted to Trade or traffique as a freeman of the said Company And further Wee will and grant by these presentes for us our heires and successors unto the said Governor

and Company and theire successors that the said Governor or Deputy Governor and the rest of the said Company and theire successors for the tyme being or the greater part of them whereof the Governor or the Deputy Governor from tyme to tyme to bee one shall and may from tyme to tyme and at all tymes hereafter have power and authority yearely and every yeare betweene the first and last day of November to assemble and meete together in some convenient place from tyme to tyme to be appointed by the said Governour of the said Company or in his absence by his Deputy and that they being soe assembled itt shall and may bee lawfull to and for the said Governor or his Deputy and the Company for the tyme being or the greater part of them which then shall happen to bee present whereof the Governor of the said Company or his Deputy for the tyme being to bee one to elect and nominate seaven of the said Company which shall bee a Committee of the said Company for one whole yeare from thence next ensueing which persons being soe elected and nominated to bee a Committee of the said Company as aforesaid before they bee admitted to the execucion of theire Office shall take a Corporall Oath before the Governor or his Deputy and any three or more of the said Committee of the said Company being theire last Predecessors that they and every of them shall well and faithfully performe theire said Office and Committees in all things concerneing the same And that imediately after the said Oath soe taken they shall and may execute and use theire said Office of Committees of the said Company for one whole yeare from thence next following And moreover Our will and pleasure is And by these presentes for us our heires and successors Wee doe grant unto the said Governor and Company and theire successors that when and as often as itt shall happen the Governor or Deputy overnor of the said Company for the tyme being at any tyme within one yeare after that hee shall bee nominated elected and sworne to the Office of the Governor of the said Company as is aforesaid to dye or to bee removed from the said Office which Governor or Deputy Governor not demeaneing himselfe well in his said Office Wee will to bee removeable at the Pleasure of the rest of the said Company or the greater part of them which shall bee present at theire publick assemblies commonly called theire Generall Courtes holden for the said Company that then and soe often itt shall and may be lawfull to and for the Residue of the said Company for the tyme being or the greater part of them within convenient tyme after the death or removeing of any such Governor or Deputy Governor to assemble themselves in such convenient place as they shall thinke fitt for the election of the Governor or Deputy Governor of the said Company and that the said Company or the greater part of them being then and there present shall and may then and there before theire departure from the said place elect and nominate one other of the said Company to bee Governour or Deputy Governor for the said Company in the place and stead of him that soe dyed or was removed which person being soe elected and nominated to the Office of Governor or Deputy Governor of the said Company shall have and exercize the said Office for and dureing the residue of the said yeare takeing first a Corporall Oath as is aforesaid for the due execucion thereof And this to bee done from tyme to tyme soe often as the case shall soe require And also Our Will and Pleasure is and by these presentes for us our heires and successors Wee doe grant unto the said Governor and Company that when and as often as itt shall happen any person or persons of the Committee of the said Company for the tyme being at any tyme within one yeare next after that they or any of them shall bee nominated elected and sworne to the Office of Commitee of the said Company as is aforesaid to dye or to be removed from the said Office which Committees not demeaneing themselves well in theire said Office Wee will to be removeable at the pleasure of the said Governor and Company or the greater part of them whereof the Governor of the said Company for the tyme being or his Deputy to bee

one that then and soe often itt shall and may bee lawfull to and for the said Governor and the rest of the Company for the tyme being or the greater part of them whereof the Governor for the tyme being or his Deputy to bee one within convenient tyme after the death or removeing of any of the said Committee to assemble themselves in such convenient place as is or shall bee usuall and accustomed for the eleccion of the Governor of the said Company or where else the Governor of the said Company for the tyme being or his Deputy shall appoint And that the said Governor and Company or the greater part of them whereof the Governor for the tyme being or his Deputy to bee one being then and there present shall and may then and there before theire Departure from the said place elect and nominate one or more of the said Company to bee of the Committee of the said Company in the place and stead of him or them that soe died or were or was soe removed which person or persons soe elected and nominated to the Office of Committee of the said Company shall have and exercize the said Office for and dureing the residue of the said yeare takeing first a Corporall Oath as is aforesaid for the due execucion thereof and this to bee done from tyme to tyme soe often as the case shall require And to the end the said Governor and Company of Adventurers of England Tradeing into Hudsons Bay may bee encouraged to undertake and effectually to prosecute the said designe of our more especial grace certaine knowledge and meere Mocion Wee have given granted and confirmed And by these presentes for us our heires and successors doe give grant and confirme unto the said Governor and Company and theire successors the sole Trade and Commerce of all those Seas Streightes Bayes Rivers Lakes Creekes and Soundes in whatsoever Latitude they shall bee that lie within the entrance of the Streightes commonly called Hudsons Streightes together with all the Landes and Territoryes upon the Countryes Coastes and confynes of the Seas Bayes Lakes Rivers Creekes and Soundes aforesaid that are not already actually possessed by or granted to any of our Subjectes or possessed by the Subjectes of any other Christian Prince or State with the Fishing of all Sortes of Fish Whales Sturgions and all other Royall Fishes in the Seas Bayes Isletes and Rivers within the premisses and the Fish therein taken together with the Royalty of the Sea upon the Coastes within the Lymittes aforesaid and all Mynes Royall aswell discovered as not discovered of Gold Silver Gemms and pretious Stones to bee found or discovered within the Territoryes Lymittes and Places aforesaid And that the said Land bee from henceforth reckoned and reputed as one of our Plantacions or Colonyes in America called *Ruperts Land* And further Wee doe by these presentes for us our heires and successors make create and constitute the said Governor and Company for the tyme being and theire successors the true and absolute Lordes and Proprietors of the same Territory lymittes and places aforesaid And of all other the premisses saving always the faith Allegiance and Soveraigne Dominion due to us our heires and successors for the same To have hold possesse and enjoy the said Territory lymittes and places and all and singuler other the premisses hereby granted as aforesaid with theire and every of their Rightes Members Jurisdictions Prerogatives Royaltyes and Appurtenances whatsoever to them the said Governor and Company and theire Successors forever to bee holden of us our heires and successors as of our Mannor of East Greenwich in our Country of Kent in free and common Soccage and not in Capite or by Knightes Service yeilding and paying yearely to us our heires and Successors for the same two Elkcs and two Black beavers whensoever and as often as Wee our heires and successors shall happen to enter into the said Countryes Territoryes and Regions hereby granted And further our will and pleasure is And by these presentes for us our heires and successors Wee doe grant unto the said Governor and Company and to theire successors that itt shall and may be lawfull to and for the said Governor and Company and theire successors from tyme to tyme to assemble themselves for or about any the matters causes affaires or businesses of the said Trade in any place or places for the same convenient within our Dominions or elsewhere and there to hold Court for the said Company and the affaires thereof And that alsoe itt shall and may bee lawfull to and for them and the greater part of them being soe assembled and that shall then and there bee present in any such place or places whereof the Governor or his Deputy for the tyme being to bee one to make ordeyne and constitute such and soe many reasonable Lawes Constitucions Orders and Ordinances as to them or the grater part of them being then and there present shall seeme necessary and convenient for the good Government of the said Company and of all Governors of Colonyes Fortes and Plantacions Factors Masters Mariners and other Officers employed or to bee employed in any of the Territoryes and Landes aforesaid and in any of theire Voyages and for the better advancement and contynuance of the said Trade or Traffick and Plantacions and the same Lawes Constitucions Orders and Ordinances soe made to putt in use ad execute accordingly and at theire pleasure to revoke and alter the same or any of them as the occasion shall require And that the said Governor and Company soe often as they shall make ordeyne or establish any such Lawes Constitucions Orders and Ordinances in such forme as aforesaid shall and may lawfully impose ordeyne limitt and provide such paines penaltyes and punishmentes upon all Offenders contrary to such Lawes Constitucions Orders and Ordinances or any of them as to the said Governor and Company for the tyme being or the greater part of them then and there being present the said Governor or his Deputy being always one shall seeme necessary requisite or convenient for the observacion of the same Lawes Constitucions Orders and Ordinances And the same Fynes and Amerciamentes shall and may by theire Officers and Servantes from tyme to tyme to bee appointed for that purpose levy take and have to the use of the said Governor and Company and theire successors without the impediment of us our heires or successors or of any the Officers or Ministers of us our heires or successors and without any accompt therefore to us our heires or successors to bee made All and singuler which Lawes Constitucions Orders and Ordinances soe as aforesaid to bee made Wee will to bee duely observed and kept under the paines and penaltyes therein to bee conteyned soe always as the said Lawes Constitucions Orders and Ordinances Fynes and Amerciamentes bee reasonable and not contrary or repugnant but as neare as may bee agreeable to the Lawes Statutes or Customes of this our Realme And furthermore of our ample and abundant grace certaine knowledge and meere mocion Wee have granted and by these presentes for us our heires and successors doe grant unto the said Governor and Company and theire Successors That they and theire Successors and theire Factory Servantes and Agentes for them and on their behalfe and not otherwise shall for ever hereafter have use and enjoy not only the whole Entire and only Trade and Traffick and the whole entire and only liberty use and priviledge of tradeing and Trafficking to and from the Territory Lymittes and places aforesaid but alsoe the whole and entire Trade and Trafficke to and from all Havens Bayes Creekes Rivers Lakes and Seas into which they shall find entrance or passage by water or Land out of the Territoryes Lymittes or places aforesaid and to and with all the Natives and People Inhabitting or which shall inhabit within the Territoryes Lymittes and places aforesaid and to and with all other Nacions Inhabitting any the Coaste adjacent to the said Territoryes Lymittes and places which are not already possessed as aforesaid or whereof the sole liberty or priviledge of Trade and Trafficke is not granted to any other of our Subjectes And Wee of our further Royall favour And of our more espciall grace certaine knowledge and meere Mocion have granted and by these presentes for us our heires and Successors doe grant to the said Governor and Company and to theire Successors That neither the said Territoryes Lymittes and places hereby Granted as aforesaid nor any part thereof nor the islandes Havens Portes Cittyes

Townes or places thereof or therein conteyned shall bee visited frequented or haunted by any of the Subjects of us our heires or successors contrary to the true meaneing of these presentes and by vertue of our Prerogative Royall which wee will not have in that behalfe argued or brought into Question Wee Streightly Charge Command and prohibitt for us our heires and Successors all the subjectes of us our heires and Successors of what degree or Quality soever they bee that none of them directly or indirectly doe visit haunt frequent or Trade Trafficke or Adventure by way of Merchandize into or from any the said Territoryes Lymittes or Places hereby granted or any or either of them other then the said Governor and Company and such perticuler persons as now bee or hereafter shall bee of that Company theire Agentes Factors and Assignes unlesse itt bee by the Lycence and agreement of the said Governor and Company in writing first had and obteyned under theire Common Seale to bee granted upon paine that every such person or persons that shall Trade or Trafficke into or from any the Countryes Territoryes or Lymittes aforesaid other then the said Governor and Company and theire Successors shall incurr our Indignacion and the forfeiture and the losse of the Goodes Merchandizes and other thinges whatsoever which soe shall bee brought into this Realme of England or any the Dominions of the same contrary to our said Prohibicion or the purport or true meaneing of these presentes for which the said Governor and Company shall finde take and seize in other places out of our Dominions where the said Company theire Agentes Factors or Ministers shall Trade Traffick inhabitt by vertue of these our Letters Patente As alsoe the Shipp and Shippes with the Furniture thereof wherein such goodes Merchandizes and other thinges shall bee brought or found the one halfe of all the said Forfeitures to bee to us our heires and successors and the other halfe thereof Wee doe by these Presentes cleerely and wholly for us our heires and Successors Give and Grant unto the said Governor and Company and theire Successors And further all and every the said Offenders for theire said contempt to suffer such other punishment as to us our heires or Successors for soe high a contempt shall seeme meete and convenient and not to bee in any wise delivered until they and every of them shall become bound unto the said Governor for the tyme being in the summe of one thousand Poundes at the least of noe tyme then after to Trade or Traffick into any of the said places Seas Streightes Bayes Portes Havens or Territoryes aforesaid contrary to our Expresse Commandment in that behalfe herein sett downe and published And further of our more especiall grace Wee have condiscended and granted And by these presentes for us our heires and Successor doe grant unto the said Governor and Company and theire successors That Wee our heires and Successors will not Grant liberty lycence or power to any person or persons whatsoever contrary to the tenour of these our Letters Patente to Trade trafficke or inhabit unto or upon any the Territoryes lymittes or places afore specifyed contrary to the true meaneing of these presentes without the consent of the said Governor and Company or the most part of them And of our more abundant grace and favour to the said Governor and Company Wee doe hereby declare our will and pleasure to bee that if it shall soe happen that any of the persons free or to bee free of the said Company of Adventurers of England Tradeing into Hudsons Bay who shall before the goeing forth of any Shipp or Shippes appointed for A Voyage or otherwise promise or agree by Writeing under his or theire handes to adventure any summe or Sumes of money towardes the furnishing any provision or maintainance of any voyage or voyages sett forth or to bee sett forth or intended or meant to bee sett forth by the said Governor and Company or the more part of them present at any Publick Assembly commonly called theire Generall Court shall not within the Space of twenty Dayes next after Warneing given to him or them by the said Governor or Company or theire knowne Officer or Minister bring in and deliver to the Treasurer or Treasurers appointed for the Company such summes of money as shall have beene expressed and sett

downe in writeing by the said Person or Persons subscribed with the name of the said Adventurer or Adventurers that then and at all Tymes after itt shall and may bee lawfull to and for the said Governor and Company or the more part of them present whereof the said Governor or his Deputy to bee one at any of theire Generall Courtes or Generall Assemblyes to remove and disfranchise him or them and every such person and persons at their wills and pleasures and hee or they soe removed and disfranchised not to bee permitted to trade into the Countryes Territoryes and Lymittes aforesaid or any part thereof nor to have any Adventure or Stock goeing or remaineing with or amongst the said Company without the speciall lycence of the said Governor and Company or the more part of them present at any Generall Court first had and obteyned in that behalfe Any thing before in these presentes to the contrary thereof in any wise notwithstanding And Our Will and Pleasure is And hereby wee doe alsoe ordeyne that itt shall and may bee lawfull to and for the said Governor and Company or the greater part of them whereof the Governor for the tyme being or his Deputy to bee one to admitt into and to bee of the said Company all such Servantes or Factors of or for the said Company and all such others as to them or the most part of them present at any Court held for the said Company the Governor or his Deputy being one shall bee thought fitt and agreeable with the Orders and Ordinances made and to bee made for the Government of the said Company And further Our will and pleasure is And by these presentes for us our heires and Successors Wee doe grant unto the said Governor and Company and to theire Successors that itt shall and may bee lawfull in all Eleccions and Bye-Lawes to bee made by the Generall Court of the Adventurers of the said Company that every person shall have a number of votes according to his Stock that is to say for every hundred poundes by him subscribed or brought into the present Stock one vote and that any of these that have Subscribed lesse then one hundred poundes may joyne theire respective summes to make upp one hundred poundes and have one vote joyntly for the same and not otherwise And further of our speciall grace certaine knowledge and meere mocion Wee doe for us our heires and successors grant to and with the said Governor and Company of Adventurers of England Tradeing into Hudsons Bay that all Landes Islandes Territoryes Plantacions Fortes Fortificacions Factoryes or Colonyes where the said Companyes Factoryes and Trade are or shall bee within any the Portes and places afore lymitted shall bee ymediately and from henceforth under the power and command of the said Governor and Company theire Successors and Assignes Saving the faith and Allegiance due to bee performed to us our heires and successors as aforesaid and that the said Governor and Company shall have liberty full Power and authority to appoint the establish Governors and all other Officers to governe them And that the Governor and his Councill of the severall and respective places where the said Company shall have Plantacions Fortes Factoryes Colonyes or Places of Trade within any the Countryes Landes or Territoryes hereby granted may have power to judge all persons belonging to the said Governor and Company or that shall live under them in all Causes whether Civill or Criminall according to the Lawes of this Kingdome and to execute Justice accordingly And in case any crime or misdemeanor shall bee committed in any of the said Companyes Plantacions Fortes Factoryes or Places of Trade within the Lymittes aforesaid where Judicature cannot bee executed for want of a Governor and Councill there then in such case itt shall and may bee lawfull for the chiefe Factor of that place and his Councill to transmitt the party together with the offence to such other Plantacion Factory or Fort where there shall bee a Governor and Councill where Justice may bee executed or into his Kingdome of England as shall bee thought most convenient there to receive such punishment as the nature of his offence shall deserve And Moreover Our will and pleasure is And by these presentes for us our heires and Successors Wee doe give and grant unto the said Governor and Company

and theire Successors free Liberty and Lycence in case they conceive it necessary to send either Shippes of War Men or Amunicion unto any theire Plantacions Fortes Factoryes or Places of Trade aforesaid for the security and defence of the same and to choose Commanders and Officers over them and to give them power and authority by Commission under theire Common Seale or otherwise to continue or make peace or Warre with any Prince or People whatsoever that are not Christians in any places where the said Company shall have any Plantacions Fortes or Factoryes or adjacent thereunto as shall bee most for the advantage and benefit of the said Governor and Company and of theire Trade and alsoe to right and recompence themselves upon the Goodes Estates or people of those partes by whome the said Governor and Company shall susteyne any injury losse or dammage or upon any other People whatsoever that shall any way contrary to the intent of these presentes interrupt wrong or injure them in theire said Trade within the said places Territoryes and Lymittes granted by this Charter and that itt shall and may bee lawfull to and for the said Governor and Company and theire Successors from tyme to tyme and at all tymes from henceforth to Erect and build such Castles Fortifications Fortes Garrisons Colonyes or Plantacions Townes or Villages in any partes or places within the Lymittes and Boundes granted before in these presentes unto the said Governor and Company as they in theire Discrecions shall thinke fitt and requisite and for the supply of such as shall be needeful and convenient to keepe and bee in the same to send out of this Kingdome to the said Castles Fortes Fortifications Garrisons Colonyes Plantacions Townes or Villages all Kindes of Cloathing Provision of Victuales Ammunicion and Implementes necessary for such purpose paying the Dutyes and Customes for the same As alsoe to transport and carry over such number of Men being willing thereunto or not prohibited as they shall thinke fitt and alsoe to governe them in such legall and reasonable manner as the said Governor and Company shall thinke best and to inflict punishment for misdemeanors or impose such Fynes upon them for breach of theire Orders as in these Presentes are formerly expressed And further Our will and pleasure is And by these presentes for us our heires and Successors Wee doe grant unto the said Governor and Company and to theire Successors full Power and lawfull authority to seize upon the Persons of all such English or any other our Subjectes, which shall saile into Hudsons Bay or Inhabit in any of the Countryes Islandes or Territoryes hereby Granted to the said Governor and Company without theire leave and Licence in that Behalfe first had and obteyned or that shall contemne or disobey theire Orders and send them to England and that all and every Person or Persons being our Subjectes any wayes Imployed by the said Governor and Company within any the Partes places and Lymittes aforesaid shall bee lyable unto and suffer such punnishment for any Offences by them committed in the Partes aforesaid as the President and Councill for the said Governor and Company there shall thinke fitt and the meritt of the offence shall require as aforesaid And in case any Person or Persons being convicted and Sentenced by the President and Councill of the said Governor and Company in the Countryes Landes or Lymittes aforesaid theire Factors or Agentes there for any Offence by them done shall appeale from the same That then and in such Case itt shall and may be lawfull to and for the said President and Councill Factors or Agentes to seize upon him or them and to carry him or them home Prisoners into England to the said Governor and Company there to receive such condigne punnishment as his Cause shall require and the Law of this Nacion allow of and for the better discovery of abuses and injuryes to bee done unto the said Governor and Company or theire Successors by any Servant by them to bee imployed in the said Voyages and Plantacions itt shall and may be lawfull to and for the said Governor and Company and theire respective Presidentes Chiefe Agent or Governor in the partes aforesaid to examine upon Oath all Factors Masters Pursers Supra

Cargoes Commanders of Castles Fortes Forticacions Plantacions or Colonyes or other Persons touching or concerneing any matter or thing in which by Law or usage an Oath may bee administered soe as the said Oath and the matter therein conteyned bee not repugnant but agreeable to the Lawes of this Realme And Wee doe hereby streightly charge and Command all and singuler our Admiralls Vice- Admiralls Justices Mayors Sheriffs Constables Baryliffes and all and singuler other our Officers Ministers Liege Men and Subjectes whatsoever to bee ayding favouring helping and assisting to the said Governor and Company and to theire Successors and to theire Deputyes Officers Factors Servantes Assignes and Ministers and every of them in execueting and enjoying the premisses as well on Land as on Sea from tyme to tyme when any of you shall thereunto bee required any Statute Act Ordinance Proviso Proclamation or restraint heretofore had made sett forth ordeyned or provided or any other matter cause or thing whatsoever to the contrary in any wise notwithstanding In witness whereof wee have caused these our Letters to bee made Patentes Witness Ourselves at Westminster the second day of May in the two and twentieth yeare of our Raigne

By Writt of Privy Seale
Pigott

Source:
Charters, Statutes, Orders in Council & C, Relating to the Hudson Bay Company. London: Hudson's Bay Co., 1957.

2. ALEXANDER HAMILTON, *REPORT ON THE SUBJECT OF MANUFACTURES, 1791*

Report submitted by U.S. secretary of the Treasury Alexander Hamilton to Congress on December 5, 1791, proposing federal aid to infant industries through protective tariffs. It responded to an argument put forth most notably by Thomas Jefferson that "Agriculture is the most beneficial and pro-

ductive *object of human industry." Hamilton argued that the national welfare required the federal government to encourage manufacturing in order to increase productivity as well as the national income and provide a dependable home market for agriculture. Hamilton's views were influenced by Adam Smith's* Wealth of Nations *(1776), but he rejected Smith's laissez-faire view that the state must not direct economic processes. Of note are Hamilton's reliance on his own previous arguments favoring a national bank and establishment of a public debt. Also of note, considering more recent values, are his favoring immigration and also the employment of women (as being less costly than men) and children, even "of tender age." Congress took no action on the report, the only time a report of his failed. However, it later fueled arguments on both sides of the protection question.*

———————— ⌒⟩⟨⟨⟩⌒ ————————

To the Speaker of the House of Representatives

The Secretary of the Treasury in obedience to the order of ye House of Representatives, of the 15th day of January 1790, has applied his attention, at as early a period as his other duties would permit, to the subject of Manufactures; and particularly to the means of promoting such as will tend to render the United States, independent on foreign nations, for military and other essential supplies. And he there [upon] respectfully submits the following Report.

The expediency of encouraging manufactures in the United States, which was not long since deemed very questionable, appears at this time to be pretty generally admitted. The embarrassments, which have obstructed the progress of our external trade, have led to serious reflections on the necessity of enlarging the sphere of our domestic commerce: the restrictive regulations, which in foreign markets abridge the vent of the increasing surplus of our Agriculture produce, serve to beget an earnest desire, that a more extensive demand for that surplus may be created at home: And the complete success, which has rewarded manufacturing enterprise, in some valuable branches, conspiring with the promis-

ing symptoms, which attend some less mature essays, in others, justify a hope, that the obstacles to the growth of this species of industry are less formidable than they were apprehended to be; and that it is not difficult to find, in its further extension; a full indemnification for any external disadvantages, which are or may be experienced, as well as an accession of resources, favourable to national independence and safety.

*   *   *

It is now proper to proceed a step further, and to enumerate the principal circumstances, from which it may be inferred—That manufacturing establishments not only occasion a positive augmentation of the Produce and Revenue of the Society, but that they contribute essentially to rendering them greater than they could possibly be, without such establishments. These circumstances are—

1. The division of Labour
2. An extension of the use of Machinery.
3. Additional employment to classes of the community not ordinarily engaged in the business.
4. The promoting of emigration from foreign Countries.
5. The furnishing greater scope for the diversity of talents and dispositions which discriminate men from each other.
6. The affording a more ample and various field for enterprize.
7. The creating in some instances a new, and securing in all, a more certain and steady demand for the surplus produce of the soil.

Each of these circumstances has a considerable influence upon the total mass of industrious effort in a community. Together, they add to it a degree of energy and effect, which are not easily conceived. Some comments upon each of them, in the order in which they have been stated, may serve to explain their importance.

I. As to the Division of Labour

It has justly been observed, that there is scarcely any thing of greater moment in the oeconomy of a nation, than the proper division of labour. The separation of occupations causes each to be carried to a much greater perfection, than it could possible acquire, if they were blended. This arises principally from three circumstances.

1st—The greater skill and dexterity naturally resulting from a constant and undivided application to a single object. . . . 2nd. The oeconomy of time—by avoiding the loss of it, incident to a frequent transition from one operation to another of a different nature. . . . 3rd. An extension of the use of Machinery. A man occupied on a single object will have it more in his power, and will be more naturally led to exert his imagination in devising methods to facilitate and abridge labour, than if he were perplexed by a variety of independent and dissimilar operations. . . . And from these causes united, the mere separation of the occupation of the cultivator, from that of the Artificer, has the effect of augmenting the productive powers of labour, and with them, the total mass of the produce or revenue of a Country. In this single view of the subject, therefore, the utility of Artificers or Manufacturers, towards promoting an increase of productive industry, is apparent.

II. As to an extension of the use of Machinery a point which though partly anticipated requires to be placed in one or two additional lights.

The employment of Machinery forms an item of great importance in the general mass of national industry. 'Tis an artificial force brought in aid of the natural force of man; and, to all the purposes of labour, is an increase of hands; an accession of strength, unincumbered too by the expence of maintaining the laborer. May it not therefore be fairly inferred, that those occupations, which give greatest scope to the use of this auxiliary, contribute most to the general Stock of industrious effort, and, in consequence, to the general product of industry?

. . . The substitution of foreign for domestic manufactures is a transfer to foreign nations of the advantages accruing from the employment of Machinery, in the modes in which it is capable of being employed, with most utility and to the greatest extent.

The Cotton Mill invented in England, within the last twenty years, is a signal illustration of the general proposition, which has been just advanced. In consequence of it, all the different processes for spining Cotton are performed by means of Machines, which are put in motion by water. . . . And it is an advantage of great moment that the operations of this mill continue with convenience, during the night, as well as through the day. The prodigious affect of such a Machine is easily conceived. To this invention is to be attributed essentially the immense progress, which has been so suddenly made in Great Britain in the various fabrics of Cotton.

III. As to the additional employment of classes of the community, not ordinarily engaged in the particular business.

This is not among the least valuable of the means, by which manufacturing institutions contribute to augment the general stock of industry and production. In places where those institutions prevail, besides the persons regularly engaged in them, they afford occasional and extra employment to industrious individuals and families, who are willing to devote the leisure resulting from the intermissions of their ordinary pursuits to collateral labours, as a resource of multiplying their acquisitions of [their] enjoyments. The husbandman himself experiences a new source of profit and support from the encreased industry of his wife and daughters; invited and stimulated by the demands of the neighboring manufactories.

. . . There is another of a nature allied to it [and] of a similar tendency. This is—the employment of persons who would otherwise be idle (and in many cases a burthen on the community), . . . In general, women and Children are rendered more useful and the latter more early useful by manufacturing establishments, than they would otherwise be. Of the number of persons employed in the Cotton Manufactories of Great Britain, it is computed that 4/7 nearly are women and children; of whom the greatest proportion are children and many of them of a very tender age.

And thus it appears to be one of the attributes of manufactures, and one of no small consequence, to give occasion to the exertion of a greater quantity of Industry, even by the same number of persons, where they happen to prevail, than would exist, if there were no such establishment.

IV. As to the promoting of emigration from foreign Countries. . . . Manufacturers, who listening to the powerful invitations of a better price for their fabrics, or their labour, of greater cheapness of provisions and raw materials, of an exemption from the chief part of the taxes burthens and restraints, which they endure in the old world, of greater personal independence and consequence, under the operation of a more equal government, and of what is far more precious than mere religious toleration—a perfect equality of religious privileges; would probably flock from Europe to the United States to pursue their own trades or professions, if they were once made sensible of the advantages they would enjoy, and were inspired with an assurance of encouragement and employment, will, with difficulty, be induced to transplant themselves, with a view to becoming Cultivators of Land.

*   *   *

V. As to the furnishing greater scope for the diversity of talents and dispositions, which discriminate men from each other.

. . . The results of human exertion may be immensely increased by diversifying its objects. When all the different kinds of industry obtain in a community, each individual can find his proper element, and can call into activity the whole vigour of his nature. And the community is benefitted by the services of its respective members, in the manner, in which each can serve it with most effect.

If there be anything in a remark often to be met with—namely that there is, in the genius of the people of this country, a peculiar aptitude for mechanic improvements, it would operate as a forcible reason for giving opportunities to the exercise of that species of talent, by the propagation of manufactures.

VI. As to the affording a more ample and various field for enterprise.

. . . To cherish and stimulate the activity of the human mind, by multiplying the objects of enterprise, is not among the least considerable of the expedients, by which the wealth of a nation may be promoted. Even things in themselves not positively advantageous, sometimes become so, by their tendency to provoke exertion. Every new scene, which is opened to the busy nature of man to rouse and exert itself, is the addition of a new energy to the general stock of effort.

The spirit of enterprise, useful and prolific as it is, must necessarily be contracted or expanded in proportion to the simplicity or variety of the occupations and productions, which are to be found in a Society. It must be less in a nation of mere cultivators, than in a nation of cultivators and merchants; less in a nation of cultivators, and merchants, than in a nation of cultivators, artificers and merchants.

VII. As to the creating, in some instances, a new, and securing in all a more certain and steady demand, for the surplus produce of the soil.

This is . . . a principal mean, by which the establishment of manufactures contributes to an augmentation of the produce or revenue of a country, and has an immediate and direct relation to the prosperity of Agriculture.

It is evident, that the exertions of the husbandman will be steady or fluctuating, vigorous or feeble, in proportion to the steadiness or fluctuation, adequateness, or inadequateness of the markets on which he must depend.... For the purpose of this vent, a domestic market is greatly to be preferred to a foreign one; because it is in the nature of things, far more to be relied upon.

It is a primary object of the policy of nations, to be able to supply themselves with subsistence from their own soils; and manufacturing nations, as far as circumstances permit, endeavor to procure, from the same source, the raw materials necessary for their own fabrics. . .

* * *

But it is also a consequence of the policy, which has been noted, that the foreign demand for the products of Agricultural Countries, is, in a great degree, rather casual and occasional, than certain or constant . . . .

* * *

It merits particular observation, that the multiplication of manufactories not only furnishes a Market for those articles, which have been accustomed to be produced in abundance, in a country; but it likewise creates a demand for such as were either unknown or produced in inconsiderable quantities. The bowels as well as the surface of the earth are ransacked for articles which were before neglected. Animals, Plants and Minerals acquire an utility and value, which were before unexplored.

The foregoing considerations seem sufficient to establish, as general propositions, That it is the interest of nations to diversify the industrious pursuits of the individuals, who compose them—That the establishment of manufactures is calculated not only to increase the general stock of useful and productive labour; but even to improve the state of Agriculture in particular; certainly to advance the interests of those who are engaged in it. There are other views, that will be hereafter taken of the subject, which, it is conceived, will serve to confirm these inferences.

* * *

. . . The United States are to a certain extent in the situation of a country precluded from foreign Commerce. They can indeed, without difficulty obtain from abroad the manufactured supplies, of which they are in want; but they experience numerous and very injurious impediments to the emission and vent of their own commodities. Nor is this the case in reference to a single foreign nation only. The regulations of several countries, with which we have the most extensive intercourse, throw serious obstructions in the way of the principal staples of the United States.

In such a position of things, the United States cannot exchange with Europe on equal terms; and the want of reciprocity would render them the victim of a system, which should induce them to confine their views to Agriculture and refrain from Manufactures. A constant and encreasing necessity, on their part, for the commodities of Europe, and only a partial and occasional demand for their own, in return, could not but expose them to a state of impoverishment, compared with the opulence to which their political and natural advantages authorise them to aspire.

. . . Tis for the United States to consider by what means they can render themselves least dependent, on the combinations, right or wrong of foreign policy.

It is no small consolation, that already the measures which have embarrassed our Trade, have accelerated internal improvements, which upon the whole have bettered our affairs. To diversify and extend these improvements is the surest and safest method of indemnifying ourselves for any inconveniences, which those or similar measures have a tendency to beget. If Europe will not take from us the products of our soil, upon terms consistent with our interest, the natural remedy is to contract as fast as possible our wants of her.

* * *

The supposed want of Capital for the prosecution of manufactures in the United States is the most indefinite of the objections which are usually opposed to it.

It is very difficult to pronounce any thing precise concerning the real extent of the monied capital of a Country, and still more concerning the proportion which it bears to the objects that invite the employment of Capital. It is not less difficult to pronounce how far the effect of any given quantity of money, as capital, or in other words, as a medium for circulating the industry and property of a nation, may be increased by the very circumstance of the additional motion, which is given to it by new objects of employment. That effect, like the momentum of descending bodies, may not improperly be represented, as in a compound ratio to mass and velocity. It seems pretty certain, that a given sum of money, in a situation, in which the quick impulses of commercial activity were little felt, would appear inadequate to the circulation of as great a quantity of industry and property, as in one, in which their full influence was experienced.

It is not obvious, why the same objection might not as well be made to external commerce as to manufactures; since it is manifest that our immense tracts of land occupied and unoccupied are capable of giving employment to more capital than is actually bestowed upon them. It is certain, that the United States offer a vast field for the advantageous employment of Capital; but it does not follow, that there will not be found, in one way or another, a sufficient fund for the successful prosecution of any species of industry which is likely to prove truly beneficial.

The following considerations are of a nature to remove all inquietude on the score of want of Capital.

The introduction of Banks, as has been shewn on another occasion has a powerful tendency to extend the active Capital of a Country. Experience of the Utility of these Institutions is multiplying them in the United States. It is probable that they will be established wherever they can exist with advantage; and wherever, they can be supported, if administered with prudence, they will add new energies to all pecuniary operations.

The aid of foreign Capital may safely, and, with considerable latitude be taken into calculation. Its instrumentality has been experienced in our external commerce; and it has begun to be felt in various other modes. Not only our funds, but our Agriculture and other internal improvements have been animated by it. It has already in a few instances extended even to our manufactures.

It is a well known fact, that there are parts of Europe, which have more Capital, than profitable domestic objects of employment. Hence, among other proofs, the large loans continually furnished, to foreign states. And it is equally certain that the capital of other parts may find more profitable employment in the United States, than at home. . . . Both these Causes operate to produce a transfer of foreign capital to the United States. 'Tis certain, that various objects in this country hold out advantages, which are with difficulty to be equalled elsewhere; and under the increasingly favorable impressions, which are entertained of our government, the attractions will become more and More strong. These impressions will prove a rich mine of prosperity to the Country, if they are confirmed and strengthened by the progress of our affairs. And to secure this advantage, little more is now necessary, than to foster industry, and cultivate order and tranquility, at home and abroad.

*   *   *

And whatever be the objects which originally attract foreign Capital, when once introduced, it may be directed towards any purpose of beneficial exertion, which is desired. And to detain it among us, there can be no expedient so effectual as to enlarge the sphere, within which it may be usefully employed: Though induced merely with views to speculations in the funds, it may afterwards be rendered subservient to the Interests of Agriculture, Commerce & Manufactures.

*   *   *

But while there are Circumstances sufficiently strong to authorise a considerable degree of reliance on the aid of foreign Capital towards the attainment of the object in view, it is satisfactory to have good grounds of assurance, that there are domestic resources of themselves adequate to it. It happens, that there is a species of Capital actually existing within the United States, which relieves from all inquietude on the score of want of Capital—This is the funded Debt.

*   *   *

To all the arguments which are brought to evince the impracticability of success in manufacturing establishments in the United States, it might have been a sufficient answer to have referred to the experience of what has been already done. It is certain that several important branches have grown up and flourished with a rapidity which surprises: affording an encouraging assurance of success in future attempts: of these it may not be improper to enumerate the most considerable.

I. of Skins. Tanned and tawed leather dressed skins, shoes, boots and Slippers, harness and sadlery of all kinds. Portmanteau's and trunks, leather breeches, gloves, muffs and tippets, parchment and Glue.

II. of Iron. Barr and Sheet Iron, Steel, Nailrods & Nails, implements of husbandry, Stoves, pots and other household utensils, the steel and Iron work of carriages and for Shipbuilding, Anchors, scale beams and Weights & Various tools of Artificers, arms of different kinds; though the manufacture of these last has of late diminished for want of demand.

III. of Wood. Ships, Cabinet Wares and Turnery, Wool and Cotton cards and other Machinery for manufactures and husbandry, Mathematical instruments, Coopers wares of every kind.

IV. of flax & Hemp. Cables, sail-cloth, Cordage, twine and packthread.

V. Bricks and coarse tiles & Potters Wares.

VI. Ardent Spirits, and malt liquors.

VII. Writing and printing Paper, sheathing and wrapping Paper, pasteboards, fillers or press papers, paper hangings.

VIII. Hats of furr and Wool and of mixtures of both, Womens Stuff and Silk shoes.

IX. Refined Sugars.

X. Oils of Animals and seeds; Soap, Spermaceti and Tallow Candles

XI. Copper and brass wares, particularly utensils for distillers, Sugar refiners and brewers, And—Irons and other Articles for household Use, philosophical apparatus

XII. Tin Wares, for most purposes of Ordinary use.

XIII. Carriages of all kinds

XIV. Snuff, chewing & smoking Tobacco.

XV. Starch and Hairpowder.

XVI. Lampblack and other painters colours,

XVII. Gunpowder

Besides manufactories of these articles which are carried on as regular Trades, and have attained to a considerable degree of maturity, there is a vast scene of household manufacturing, which contributes more largely to the supply of the Community, than could be imagined; without having made it an object of particular enquiry. This observation is the pleasing result of the investigation, to which the subject of the report has led, and is applicable as well to the Southern as to the middle and Northern States; great quantities of coarse cloths, coatings, serges, and flannels, linsey Woolseys, hosiery of Wool, cotton & thread, coarse fustians, jeans and Muslins, check(ed) and striped cotton and linen goods, bed ticks, Coverlets and Counterpanes, Tow linens, coarse shirtings, sheetings, toweling and table linen, and various mixtures of wool and cotton, and of Cotton & flax are made in the household way, and in many instances to an extent not only sufficient for the supply of the families in which they are made, but for sale, and (even in some cases) for exportation. It is computed in a number of districts that 2/3 3/4 and even 4/5 of all the clothing of the Inhabitants are made by themselves. The importance of so great a progress, as appears to have been made in family Manufactures, within a few years, both in a moral and political view, renders the fact highly interesting.

Neither does the above enumeration comprehend all the articles, that are manufactured as regular Trades. Many other occur, which are equally well established, but which not being of equal importance have been omitted. And there are many attempts stills in their Infancy, which though attended with very favorable appearances, could not have been properly comprized in an enumeration of manufactories, already established. There are other articles also of great importance, which tho' strictly speaking manufactures are omitted, as being immediately connected with husbandry: such are flour, pot & pearl ash, Pitch, tar, turpentine and the like.

There remains to be noticed an objection to the encouragement of manufactures, of a nature different from those which question the probability of success. This is derived from its supposed tendency to give a monopoly of advantages to particular classes at the expence of the rest of the community, who, it is affirmed, would be able to procure the requisite supplies of manufactured articles on better terms from foreigners, than from our own Citizens, and who it is alledged, are reduced to a necessity of paying an enhanced price for whatever they want, by every measure, which obstructs the free competition of foreign commodities.

*   *   *

It is not an unreasonable supposition, that measures, which serve to abridge the free competition of foreign But though it were true, that the immediate and certain effect of regulations controuling the competition of foreign with domestic fabrics was an increase of price, it is universally true, that the contrary is the ultimate effect with every successful manufacture. When a domestic manufacture has attained to perfection, and has engaged in the prosecution of it a competent number of Persons, it invariably becomes cheaper. Being free from the heavy charges, which attend the importation of foreign commodities, it can be afforded, and accordingly seldom or never fails to be sold Cheaper, in process of time, than was the foreign Article for which it is a substitute. The internal competition, which takes place, soon does away every thing like Monopoly, and by degrees reduces the price of the Article to the minimum of a reasonable profit on the Capital employed. This accords with the reason of the thing and with experience.

Whence it follows, that it is the interest of a community with a view to eventual and permanent oeconomy, to encourage the growth of manufactures. In a national view, a temporary enhancement of price must always be well compensated by a permanent reduction of it.

*   *   *

There seems to be a moral certainty, that the trade of a country which is both manufacturing and Agricultural will be more lucrative and prosperous, than that of a Country, which is, merely Agricultural. . . .

Another circumstance which gives a superiority of commercial advantages to states, that manufacture as well as cultivate, consists in the more numerous attractions, which a more diversified market offers to foreign Customers, and greater scope, which it affords to mercantile enterprise. It is a position of indisputable truth in Commerce, depending too on very obvious reasons, that the greatest resort will ever be to those marts where commodities, while equally abundant, are most various. . . .

. . . Two important inferences are to be drawn, one, that there is always a higher probability of a favorable balance of Trade, in regard to countries in which manufactures founded on the basis of a thriving Agriculture flourish, than in regard to those, which are confined wholly or almost wholly to Agriculture; the other (which is also a consequence of the first) that countries of the former description are likely to possess more pecuniary wealth, or money, than those of the latter.

*   *   *

Not only the wealth; but the independence and security of a Country, appear to be materially connected with the prosperity of manufactures. Every nation, with a view to those great objects, ought to endeavour to possess within itself all the essentials of national supply. These comprise the means of Subsistence habitation clothing and defence.

The possession of these is necessary to the perfection of the body politic, to the safety as well as to the welfare of the society; the want of either, is the want of an important organ of political life and Motion; and in the various crises which await a state, it must severely feel the effects of any such deficiency. The extreme embarrassments of the United States during the late War, from an incapacity of supplying themselves, are still matter of keen recollection: A future war might be expected again to exemplify the mischiefs and dangers of a situation, to which that incapacity is still in too great a degree applicable, unless changed by timely and vigorous exertion. To effect this change as fast as shall be prudent, merits all the attention and all the Zeal of our Public Councils; 'tis the next great work to be accomplished.

*   *   *

One more point of view only remains in which to Consider the expediency of encouraging manufacturers in the United states.

It is not uncommon to meet with an opinion that though the promoting of manufactures may be the interest of a part of the Union, it is contrary to that of another part. The Northern & southern regions are sometimes represented as having adverse interest in this respect. Those are called Manufacturing, these Agricultural states; and a species of opposition is imagined to subsist between the Manufacturing and Agricultural interests.

This idea of an opposition between those two interest is the common error of the early periods of every country. . . . But it is nevertheless a maxim well established by experience, and generally acknowledged, where there has been sufficient experience, that the aggregate prosperity of manufactures, and the aggregate prosperity of Agriculture are intimately connected. . . .

*   *   *

. . . If the Northern and middle states should be the principal scenes of such establishments, they would immediately benefit the more southern, by creating a demand for productions; some of which they have in common with the other states, and others of which are either peculiar to them, or more abundant, or of better quality, than elsewhere. These productions, principally are Timber, flax, Hemp, Cotton, Wool, raw silk, Indigo, iron, lead, furs, hides, skins and coals. Of these articles Cotton & Indigo are peculiar to the southern states; as are hitherto Lead & Coal. Flax and Hemp are or may be raised in greater

abundance there, than in the More Northern states; and the Wool of Virginia is said to be of better quality than that of any other state: a Circumstance rendered the more probable by the reflection that Virginia embraces the same latitudes with the finest Wool Countries of Europe. The Climate of the south is also better adapted to the production of silk.

The extensive cultivation of Cotton can perhaps hardly be expected, but from the previous establishment of domestic Manufactories of the Article; and the surest encouragement and vent, for the others, would result from similar establishments in respect to them.

*   *   *

In order to a better judgment of the Means proper to be resorted to by the United states, it will be of use to Advert to those which have been employed with success in other Countries. The principal of these are.

I Protecting duties—or duties on those foreign articles which are the rivals of the domestic ones, intended to be encouraged. . . . They enable the National Manufacturers to undersell all their foreign Competitors. . . .

II Prohibitions of rival articles or duties equivalent to prohibitions. . . . In general it is only fit to be employed when a manufacture, has made such a progress and is in so many hands as to insure a due competition, and an adequate supply on reasonable terms. Of duties equivalent to prohibitions, there are examples in the Laws of the United States, and there are other Cases to which the principle may be advantageously extended, but they are not numerous.

*   *   *

VIII The encouragement of new inventions and discoveries, at home, and of the introduction into the United States of such as may have been made in other countries; particularly those, which relate to machinery.

This is among the most useful and unexceptionable of the aids, which can be given to manufactures. The usual means of that encouragement are pecuniary rewards, and, for a time, exclusive privileges. The first must be employed, according to the occasion, and the utility of the invention, or discovery: For the last, so far as respects "authors and inventors" provision has been made by Law. But it is desirable in regard to improvements and secrets of extraordinary value, to be able to extend the same benefit to Introducers, as well as Authors and Inventors; a policy which has been practiced with advantage in other countries. Here, however, as in some other cases, there is cause to regret, that the competency of the authority of the National Government to the good, which might be done, is not without a question. Many aids might be given to industry; many internal improvements of primary magnitude might be promoted, by an authority operating throughout the Union, which cannot be effected, as well, if at all, by an authority confined within the limits of a single state.

*   *   *

IX Judicious regulations for the inspection of manufactured commodities. This is not among the least important of the means, by which the prosperity of manufactures may be promoted. It is indeed in many cases one of the most essential. Contributing to prevent frauds upon consumers at home and exporters to foreign countries—to improve the quality & preserve the character of the national manufactures, it cannot fail to aid the expeditious and advantageous Sale of them, and to serve as a guard against successful competition from other quarters. . . .

X The facilitating of pecuniary remittances from place to place is a point of considerable moment to trade in general, and to manufactures in particular; by rendering more easy the purchase of raw materials and provisions and the payment for manufactured supplies. A general circulation of Bank paper, which is to be expected from the institution lately established will be a most valuable mean to this end. But much good would also accrue from some additional provisions respecting inland bills of exchange. If those drawn in one state payable in another were made negotiable, everywhere, and interest and damages allowed in case of protest, it would greatly promote negotiations between the Citizens of different states, by rendering them more secure; and, with it the convenience and advantage of the Merchants and manufacturers of each.

XI The facilitating of the transportation of commodities. Improvements favoring this object intimately concern all the domestic interests of a community; but they may without impropriety be mentioned as having an important relation to manufactures. . . .

There can certainly be no object, more worthy of the cares of the local administrations; and it were to be wished, that there was no doubt of the power of the national Government to lend its direct aid, on a comprehensive plan.... "Good roads, canals, and navigable rivers, by diminishing the expence of carriage, put the remote parts of a country more nearly upon a level with those in the neighborhood of the town. They are upon that account the greatest of all improvements. They encourage the cultivation of the remote, which must always be the most extensive circle of the country. . . .

*   *   *

All the additional duties which shall be laid . . . will yield a considerable surplus.

This surplus will serve.

First. To constitute a fund for paying the bounties which shall have been decreed.

Secondly. To constitute a fund for the operations of a Board, to be established, for promoting Arts, Agriculture, Manufactures and Commerce . . .

*   *   *

In countries where there is great private wealth much may be effected by the voluntary contributions of patriotic individuals, but in a community situated like that of the United States, the public purse must supply the deficiency of private resource. In what can it be so useful as in prompting and improving the efforts of industry?

All which is humbly submitted.

Source:

Harold C. Syrett, ed. *The Papers of Alexander Hamilton.* New York: Columbia University Press, 1961-87.

3. CONSTITUTION OF THE AMERICAN FEDERATION OF LABOR, 1886

Charter of organization for the American Federation of Labor (AFL), the association of trade unions formed in December 1886 at a national labor convention in Columbus, Ohio. Delegates of the Federation of Organized Trades and Labor Unions and other labor groups, representing virtually the whole American trade union movement, assembled at Columbus in hopes of organizing all skilled craft unions under a single aegis. They founded the AFL as a permanent federation of trade unions, and elected Samuel Gompers its first president, a post he held every year except one until 1924. The constitution spelled out the AFL's structure and principles. It pledged strict recognition of each trade's autonomy and established the national or international union as the new federation's basic organizational unit. A membership tax was to be levied to raise money to assist striking workers and fund AFL legislative initiatives. The executive council, responsible for administering affairs at the national level, was charged with settling jurisdictional disputes, lobbying for legislation, investigating strikes and lockouts, and influencing public opinion.

PREAMBLE

Whereas, A struggle is going on in all the nations of the civilized world, between the oppressors and the oppressed of all countries, a struggle between the capitalist and the laborer, which grows in intensity from year to year, and will work disastrous results to the toiling millions, if they are not combined for mutual protection and benefit.

It therefore behooves the representatives of the Trades and Labor Unions of America, in Convention, assembled, to adopt such measures and disseminate such principles among the mechanics and laborers of our country as will permanently unite them, to secure the recognition of the rights to which they are justly entitled.

We therefore declare ourselves in favor of the formation of a thorough Federation, embracing every Trade and Labor Organization in America.

CONSTITUTION

Article I—Name

Section 1. This association shall be known as "The American Federation of Labor," and shall consist of such Trades and Labor Unions as shall conform to its rules and regulations.

Article II—Objects

Section 1. The objects of this Federation shall be the encouragement and formation of local Trades and Labor Unions, and the closer Federation of such societies through the organization of Central Trades and Labor Unions in every city, and the further combination of such bodies into state, territorial, or provincial organizations, to secure legislation in the interests of the working masses.

Sec. 2. The establishment of National and International Trades Unions, based upon a strict recognition of the autonomy of each trade, and the promotion and advancement of such bodies.

Sec. 3. An American Federation of all National and International Trades Unions, to aid and assist each other; and, furthermore, to secure National Legislation in the interests of the working people, and influence public opinion, by peaceful and legal methods, in favor of Organized Labor.

Sec. 4. To aid and encourage the labor press of America.

Article III—Convention

Section 1. The convention of the Federation shall be held annually, on the second Tuesday of December, at such place as the delegates have selected at the preceding Convention.

Article IV—Representation

Section 1. The basis of representation in the convention shall be: From National or International Unions, for less than four thousand members, one delegate; four thousand or more, two delegates; eight thousand or more, three delegates; sixteen thousand or more, four delegates; thirty-two thousand or more, five delegates; and so on; and from each Local or District Trades Union, not connected with, or having a National or International head, affiliated with this Federation, one delegate.

Sec. 2. No organization which has seceded from any Local, National or International or organization, shall be allowed a representation or recognition in this Federation.

Article V—Officers

Section 1. The officers of the Federation shall consist of a President, two Vice-Presidents, a Secretary, and a Treasurer, to be elected by the Convention.

Sec. 2. At the opening of the Convention the President shall take the chair and call the Convention to order, and preside until his successor is elected.

Sec. 3. The following Committee, consisting of three members each, shall be appointed by the President: 1st, Credentials; 2d, Rules and Order of Business; 3d, Resolutions; 4th, Finance; 5th, Report of Executive Council.

Sec. 4. Should a vacancy in any office occur between the annual meetings of the Convention, such vacancies shall be filled by the President of the Federation, by and with consent of the Executive Council. When a vacancy occurs in the office of President, the Vice-Presidents shall succeed in their respective order.

Sec. 5. The President and Secretary shall be members of the succeeding Convention in case they are not delegates, but without vote.

Article VI—Executive Council

Section 1. The Officers shall be an Executive Council with power to watch legislative measures directly affecting the interests of working people, and to initiate, whenever necessary, such legislative action as the Convention may direct.

Sec. 2. The Executive Council shall use every possible means to organize new National or International Trades Unions, and to organize local Trades Unions and connect them with the Federation, until such time as there are a sufficient number to form a National or International Union, when it shall be the duty of the President of the Federation to see that such organization is formed.

Sec. 3. While we recognize the right of each trade to manage its own affairs, it shall be the duty of the Executive Council to secure the unification of all labor organizations, so far as to assist each other in any justifiable boycott, and with voluntary financial help in the event of a strike or lock-out, when duly approved by the Executive Council.

Sec. 4. When a strike has been approved by the Executive Council, the particulars of the difficulty, even if it be a lock-out, shall be explained in a circular issued by the President of the Federation to the unions affiliated therewith. It shall then be the duty of all affiliated societies to urge their Local Unions and members to make liberal financial donations in aid of the working people involved.

Article VII—Revenue

Section 1. The revenue of the Federation shall be derived from International, National, District and Local organizations, which shall pay into the treasury of the Federation a per capita tax of one-half cent per month for each member in good standing, the same to be payable monthly to the Treasurer of the Federation.

Sec. 2. Delegates shall not be entitled to a seat in this Federation, unless the per capita tax of their organization is paid in full.

Sec. 3. Any organization, affiliated with this Federation, not paying its per capita tax on or before the 15th of each month, shall be notified of the fact by the President of the Federation, and if at the end of three months it is still in arrears, it shall be suspended from membership in the Federation, and can only be reinstated by vote of the Convention.

Sec. 4. Each society affiliated with this Federation, shall make a monthly report of its standing and progress to the President of the Federation.

Sec. 5. It shall be the duty of the President to attend to all correspondence, publish a monthly journal, and travel, with consent of the Executive Council, wherever required in the interest of the Federation. His salary shall be $1,000 per year, payable monthly, with mileage and expenses.

Sec. 6. Whenever the revenue of the Federation shall warrant such action, the Executive Council shall authorize the sending out of Trades Union speakers, from place to place, in the interests of the Federation.

Sec. 7. The funds of the Federation shall be banked monthly by three Trustees, who shall be selected by the Executive Council. The said Trustees shall be residents of the same city with the Treasurer. No money shall be paid out only in conformity with the rules laid down by the Executive Council.

Sec. 8. It shall be the duty of the Secretary to attend to such business as may be decided by the Executive Council.

Sec. 9. The accounts of the year shall be closed fourteen days prior to the assembling of the Convention, and a balance sheet, duly certified, shall be presented to the same.

Sec. 10. The remuneration for the loss of time by the executive council shall be at the rate of $3.000 per diem; traveling and incidental expenses to be also defrayed.

Article VIII—Miscellaneous

Section 1. In all questions not covered by this Constitution, the Executive Council shall have power to make rules to govern the same, and shall report accordingly to the Federation.

Sec. 2. Charters for the Federation shall be granted by the President of the Federation, by and with the consent of the Executive Council, to all National and International, and Local bodies affiliated with this Federation.

Sec. 3. Any seven wage workers of good character, an favorable to Trades Unions, and not members of any body affiliated with this Federation, who will subscribe to this Constitution, shall have the power to form a local body, to be known as a "Federal Labor Union," and they shall hold regular meetings for the purpose of strengthening and advancing the Trades Union movement, and shall have the power to make their own rules in conformity with this Constitution, and shall be granted a local charter by the President of this Federation, provided the request for a charter be endorsed by the nearest Local or National Trades Union officials connected with this Federation.

Sec. 4. The charter fee for affiliated bodies shall be $5.00, payable to the Treasurer of the Federation.

Sec. 5. Where there are one or more Local Unions in any city, belonging to a National or International Union, affiliated with this Federation, it shall be their duty to organize a Trades Assembly or Central Labor Union, or join such body, if already in existence.

Article IX—Amendments

Section 1. This Constitution can be amended or altered only at a regular session of the Convention, and to do so, it shall require a two-thirds vote of the delegates, and must be ratified within six weeks thereafter, by a majority vote of the members of the societies composing this Federation.

Sec. 2. This Constitution shall go into effect March 1st, 1887.

Source:

Report of the Sixth Annual Session of the Federation of Organized Trades and Labor Unions of the United States and Canada. Official Archives of the American Federation of Labor and Congress of Individual Organizations, Silver Spring, MD.

4. INTERSTATE COMMERCE ACT, 1887

Federal law that established the Interstate Commerce Commission (ICC), the first federal administrative agency. The act, introduced by Illinois senator Shelby M. Cullom and enacted on February 4, 1887, came as the result of public outcry over railroad abuses. The act applied only to railroads traveling through two or more states and provided that all railroad charges be "reasonable and just." It prohibited pooling arrangements, rebates, drawbacks, and other discriminatory rates, and it made the practice of charging more for a short haul than a long haul illegal. The ICC, charged with regulating railroad management, had the power to subpoena witnesses and documents and to require annual reports. The commission was strengthened by later legislation.

———————————⟨✖⟩———————————

Be it enacted by the Senate and House of Representatives of the United States of America in Congress assembled, That the provisions of this act shall apply to any common carrier or carriers engaged in the transportation of passengers or property wholly by railroad, or partly by railroad and partly by water when both are used, under a common control, management, or arrangement, for a continuous carriage or shipment, from one State or Territory of the United States, or the District of Columbia, to any other State or Territory of the United States, or the District of Columbia, or from any place in the United States to an adjacent foreign country, or from any place in the United States through a foreign country to any other place in the United States, and also to the transportation in like manner of property shipped from any place in the United States to a foreign country and carried from such place to a port of trans-shipment, or shipped from a foreign country to any place in the United States and carried to such place from a port of entry either in the United States or an adjacent foreign country: Provided, however, That the provisions of this act shall not apply to the transportation of passengers or property, or to the receiving, delivering, storage, or handling of property, wholly within one State, and not shipped to or from a foreign country from or to any State or Territory as aforesaid.

The term "railroad" as used in this act shall include all bridges and ferries used or operated in connection with any railroad, and also all the road in use by any corporation operating a railroad, whether owned or operated under a contract, agreement, or lease; and the term "transportation" shall include all instrumentalities of shipment or carriage.

All charges made for any service rendered or to be rendered in the transportation of passengers or property as aforesaid, or in connection therewith, or for the receiving, delivering, storage, or handling of such property, shall be reasonable and just; and every unjust and unreasonable charge for such service is prohibited and declared to be unlawful.

Sec. 2. That if any common carrier subject to the provisions of this act shall, directly or indirectly, by any special rate, rebate, drawback, or other device, charge, demand, collect, or receive from any person or persons a greater or less compensation for any service rendered, or to be rendered, in the transportation of passengers or property, subject to the provisions of this act, than it charges, demands, collects, or receives from any other person or persons for doing for him or them a like and contemporaneous service in the transportation of a like kind of traffic under substantially similar circumstances and conditions, such common carrier shall be deemed guilty of unjust discrimination, which is hereby prohibited and declared to be unlawful.

Sec. 3. That it shall be unlawful for any common carrier subject to the provisions of this act to make or give any undue or unreasonable preference or advantage to any particular person, company, firm, corporation, or locality, or any particular description of traffic, in any respect whatsoever, or to subject any particular person, company, firm, corporation, or locality, or any particular description of traffic, to any undue or unreasonable prejudice or disadvantage in any respect whatsoever.

Every common carrier subject to the provisions of this act shall according to their respective powers, afford all reasonable, proper, and equal facilities for the interchange of traffic between their respective lines, and for the receiving, forwarding, and delivering of passengers and property to and from their several lines and those connection therewith, and shall not discriminate in their rates and charges between such connecting lines; but this shall not be construed as requiring any such common carrier to give the use of its tracks or terminal facilities to another carrier engaged in like business.

Sec. 4. That it shall be unlawful for any common carrier subject to the provisions of this act to charge or receive any greater compensation in the aggregate for the transportation of passengers or of like kind of property, under substantially similar circumstances and conditions, for a shorter than for a longer distance over the same line, in the same direction, the shorter being included within the longer distance; but this shall not be construed as authorizing any common carrier within the terms of this act to charge and receive as great compensation for a shorter as for a longer distance: Provided, however, That upon application to the Commission appointed under the provisions of this act, such common carrier may, in special cases, after investigation by the Commission, be authorized to charge less for longer than for shorter distances for the transportation of passengers or property; and the Commission may from time to time prescribe the extent to which such designated common carrier may be relieved from the operation of this section of this act.

Sec. 5. That it shall be unlawful for any common carrier subject to the provisions of this act to enter into any contract, agreement, or combination with any other common carrier or carriers for the pooling of freights of different and competing railroads, or to divide between them the aggregate or net proceeds of the earnings of such railroads, or any portion thereof; and in any case of an agreement for the pooling of freights as aforesaid, each day of its continuance shall be deemed a separate offense.

Sec. 6. That every common carrier subject to the provisions of this act shall print and keep for public inspection schedules showing the rates and fares and charges for the transportation of passengers and property which any such com-

mon carrier has established and which are in force at the time upon its railroad, as defined by the first section of this act. The schedules printed as aforesaid by any such common carrier shall plainly state the places upon its railroad between which property and passengers will be carried, and shall contain the classification of freight in force upon such railroad, and shall also state separately the terminal charges and any rules or regulations which in any wise change, affect, or determine any part or the aggregate of such aforesaid rates and fares and charges. Such schedules shall be plainly printed in large type, of at least the size of ordinary pica, and copies for the use of the public shall be kept in every depot or station upon any such railroad, in such places and in such form that they can be conveniently inspected.

*   *   *

Every common carrier subject to the provisions of this act shall file with the Commission hereinafter provided for copies of its schedules of rates, fares, and charges which have been established and published in compliance with the requirements of this section, and shall promptly notify said Commission of all changes made in the same. Every such common carrier shall also file with said Commission copies of all contracts, agreements, or arrangements with other common carriers in relation to any traffic affected by the provisions of this act to which it may be a party. And in cases where passengers and freight pass over continuous lines or routes operated by more than one common carrier, and the several common carriers operating such lines or routes establish joint tariffs of rates or fares or charges for such continuous lines or routes, copies of such joint tariffs shall also, in like manner, be filed with said Commission. Such joint rates, fares, and charges on such continuous lines so filed as aforesaid shall be made public by such common carriers when directed by said Commission. . . .

If any such common carrier shall neglect or refuse to file or publish its schedules or tariffs of rates, fares, and charges as provided in this section, or any part of the same, such common carrier shall, in addition to other penalties herein prescribed, be subject to a writ of mandamus. . .and failure to comply with its requirements shall be punishable as and for a contempt; and the said Commissioners, as complainants, may also apply, in any such circuit of the United States, for a writ of injunction against such common carrier, to restrain such common carrier from receiving or transporting property among the several States and Territories of the United States. . . .

Sec. 7. That it shall be unlawful for any common carrier subject to the provisions of this act to enter into any combination, contract, or agreement, expressed or implied, to prevent, by change of time schedule, carriage in different cars, or by other means or devices, the carriage of freights from being continuous from the place of shipment to the place of destination; and no break of bulk, stoppage, or interruption made by such common carrier shall prevent the carriage of freights from being and being treated as one continuous carriage from the place of shipment to the place of destination, unless such break, stoppage, or interruption was made in good faith for some necessary purpose, and without any intent to avoid or unnecessarily interrupt such continuous carriage or to evade any of the provisions of this act.

Sec. 8. That in case any common carrier subject to the provisions of this act shall do, cause to be done, or permit to be done any act, matter, or thing in this act prohibited or declared to be unlawful, or shall omit to do any act, matter, or thing in this act required to be done, such common carrier shall be liable to the person or persons injured thereby for the full amount of damages sustained in consequence of any such violation of the provisions of this act, together with a reasonable counsel or attorney's fee, to be fixed by the court in every case of recovery, which attorney's fee shall be taxed and collected as part of the costs in the case.

Sec. 10. That any common carrier subject to the provisions of this act, or, whenever such common carrier is a corporation, any director or

officer thereof, or any receiver, trustee, lessee, agent, or person acting for or employed by such corporation, who, alone or with any other corporation, company, person, or party, shall willfully do or cause to be done, or shall willingly suffer or permit to be done, any act, matter, or thing in this act prohibited or declared to be unlawful . . . shall be deemed guilty of a misdemeanor, and shall . . . be subject to a fine of not to exceed five thousand dollars for each offense.

Sec. 11. That a Commission is hereby created and established to be known as the Inter-State Commerce Commission, which shall be composed of five Commissioners, who shall be appointed by the President, by and with the advice and consent of the Senate. . . . Any Commissioner may be removed by the President for inefficiency, neglect of duty, or malfeasance in office. Not more than three of the Commissioners shall be appointed from the same political party. No person in the employ of or holding any official relation to any common carrier subject to the provisions of this act, or owning stock or bonds thereof, or who is in any manner pecuniarily interested therein, shall enter upon the duties of or hold such office. Said Commissioners shall not engage in any other business, vocation, or employment. No vacancy in the Commission shall impair the right of the remaining Commissioners to exercise all the powers of the Commission.

Sec. 12. That the Commission hereby created shall have authority to inquire into the management of the business of all common carriers subject to the provisions of this act . . . and shall have the right to obtain from such common carriers full and complete information necessary to enable the Commission to perform the duties and carry out the objects for which it was created; and for the purposes of this act the Commission shall have power to require the attendance and testimony of witnesses and the production of all books, papers, tariffs, contracts, agreements, and documents relating to any matter under investigation, and to that end may invoke the aid of any court of the United States in requiring the attendance and testimony of witnesses and the production of books, papers, and documents under the provisions of this section.

Sec. 13. That any person, firm, corporation, or association, or any mercantile, agricultural, or manufacturing society, or any body politic or municipal organization complaining of anything done or omitted to be done by any common carrier subject to the provisions of this act in contravention of the provisions thereof, may apply to said Commission by petition. . . .

Said Commission shall in like manner investigate any complaint forwarded by the railroad commissioner or railroad commission of any State or Territory . . . and may institute any inquiry on its own motion in the same manner and to the same effect as though complaint had been made.

* * *

Sec. 16. That whenever any common carrier, as defined in and subject to the provisions of this act, shall violate or refuse or neglect to obey any lawful order or requirement of the Commission in this act named, it shall be the duty of the Commission, and lawful for any company or person interested in such order or requirement, to apply, in a summary way, by petition . . . and the said court shall have power to hear and determine the matter. . . .

* * *

Sec. 20. That the Commission is hereby authorized to require annual reports from all common carriers subject to the provisions of this act. . . .

Sec. 21. That the Commission shall, on or before the first day of December in each year, make a report to the Secretary of the Interior, which shall be by him transmitted to Congress. . . . This report shall contain such information and data collected by the Commission as may be considered of value in the determination of questions connected with the regulation of commerce, together with such recommendations as to additional legislation relating thereto as the Commission may deem necessary.

Sec. 22. That nothing in this act shall apply to the carriage, storage, or handling of property free or at reduced rates for the United States, State, or municipal governments, or for charitable purposes, or to or from fairs and expositions for exhibition thereat, or the issuance of mileage, excursion, or commutation passenger tickets; nothing in this act shall be construed to prohibit any common carrier from giving reduced rates to ministers of religion; nothing in this act shall be construed to prevent railroads from giving free carriage to their own officers and employees, or to prevent the principal officers of any railroad company or companies from exchanging passes or tickets with other railroad companies for their officers and employees; and nothing in this act contained shall in any way abridge or alter the remedies now existing at common law or by statute, but the provisions of this act are in addition to such remedies: Provided, That no pending litigation shall in any way be affected by this act.

* * *

Approved, February 4, 1887.

Source:
Statutes at Large, vol. 25, pp. 379–387.

5. Andrew Carnegie, "Wealth," 1889

Essay, sometimes called "The Gospel of Wealth," written by American industrialist and philanthropist Andrew Carnegie and published in the North American Review *in June 1889; he defended laissez-faire capitalism and also argued that rich men must use their surplus wealth to benefit the community. After claiming that competition and inequality of wealth are the inevitable costs of material development, Carnegie enunciated the duties of the rich man: to live modestly, to provide moderately for his dependents, and to administer all surplus revenues as trust funds, which he must administer to advance the general welfare of the community. The millionaire should be the "trustee for the poor." Carnegie* *followed this philosophy in his own life, donating some $350 million to various social, educational, and cultural causes, especially public libraries, many of which are still in regular use.*

———————————— ⬥ ————————————

The problem of our age is the proper administration of wealth, so that the ties of brotherhood may still bind together the rich and poor in harmonious relationship. The conditions of human life have not only been changed, but revolutionized, within the past few hundred years. In former days there was little difference between the dwelling, dress, food, and environment of the chief and those of his retainers. The Indians are to-day where civilized man then was. When visiting the Sioux, I was led to the wigwam of the chief. It was just like the others in external appearance, and even within the difference was trifling between it and those of the poorest of his braves. The contrast between the palace of the millionaire and the cottage of the laborer with us to-day measures the change which has come with civilization.

This change, however, is not to be deplored, but welcomed as highly beneficial. It is well, nay, essential for the progress of the race, that the houses of some should be homes for all that is highest and best in literature and the arts, and for all the refinements of civilization, rather than that none should be so. Much better this great irregularity than universal squalor. Without wealth there can be no Maecenas. The "good old times" were not good old times. Neither master nor servant was as well situated then as to-day. A relapse to old conditions would be disastrous to both—not the least so to him who serves—and would sweep away civilization with it. But whether the change be for good or ill, it is upon us, beyond our power to alter, and therefore to be accepted and made the best of. It is a waste of time to criticize the inevitable.

It is easy to see how the change has come. One illustration will serve for almost every phase of the cause. In the manufacture of products we have the whole story. It applies to all combinations of human industry, as stimulated and enlarged by the inventions of this scientific age. Formerly articles were manufactured at the domestic hearth or in small shops which formed part of the household. The master and his apprentices worked side by side, the latter living with the master, and therefore subject to the same conditions. When these apprentices rose to be masters, there was little or no change in their mode of life, and they, in turn, educated in the same routine succeeding apprentices. There was, substantially, social equality, and even political equality, for those engaged in industrial pursuits had then little or no political voice in the State.

But the inevitable result of such a mode of manufacture was crude articles at high prices. To-day the world obtains commodities of excellent quality at prices which even the generation preceding this would have deemed incredible. In the commercial world similar causes have produced similar results, and the race is benefited thereby. The poor enjoy what the rich could not before afford. What were the luxuries have become the necessaries of life. The laborer has now more comforts than the farmer had a few generations ago. The farmer has more luxuries than the landlord had, and is more richly clad and better housed. The landlord has books and pictures rarer, and appointments more artistic, than the King could then obtain.

The price we pay for this salutary change is, no doubt, great. We assemble thousands of operatives in the factory, in the mine, and in the counting-house, of whom the employer can know little or nothing, and to whom the employer is little better than a myth. All intercourse between them is at an end. Rigid Castes are formed, and, as usual, mutual ignorance breeds mutual distrust. Each Caste is without sympathy for the other, and ready to credit anything disparaging in regard to it. Under the law of competition, the employer of thousands is forced into the strictest economies, among which the rates paid to labor figure prominently, and often there is friction between the employer and the employed, between capital and labor, between rich and poor. Human society loses homogeneity.

The price which society pays for the law of competition, like the price it pays for cheap comforts and luxuries, is also great; but the advantages of this law are also greater still, for it is to this law that we owe our wonderful material development, which brings improved conditions in its train. But, whether the law is benign or not, we must say of it, as we say of the change in the conditions of men to which we have referred: It is here, we cannot evade it; no substitutes for it have been found; and while the law may be sometimes hard for the individual, it is best for the race, because it insures the survival of the fittest in every department. We accept and welcome, therefore, as conditions to which we must accommodate ourselves, great inequality of environment, the concentration of business, industrial and commercial, in the hands of a few, and the law of competition between these, as being not only beneficial, but essential for the future progress of the race. Having accepted these, it follows that there must be great scope for the exercise of special ability in the merchant and in the manufacturer who has to conduct affairs upon a great scale. That this talent for organization and management is rare among men is proved by the fact that it invariably secures for its possessor enormous rewards, no matter where or under what laws or conditions. The experienced in affairs always rate the Man whose services can be obtained as a partner as not only the first consideration, but such as to render the question of his capital scarcely worth considering, for such men soon create capital; while, without the special talent required, capital soon takes wings. Such men become interested in forms or corporations using millions; and estimating only simple interest to be made upon the capital invested, it is inevitable that their income must exceed their expenditures, and that they must accumulate wealth. Nor is there any middle ground which such men can occupy, because the great manufacturing or commercial concern which does not earn at least interest upon its capital

soon becomes bankrupt. It must either go forward or fall behind: to stand still is impossible. It is a condition essential for its successful operation that it should be thus far profitable, and even that, in addition to interest on capital, it should make profit. It is a law, as certain as any of the others named, that men possessed of this peculiar talent for affairs, under the free play of economic forces, must, of necessity, soon be in receipt of more revenue than can be judiciously expended upon themselves; and this law is as beneficial for the race as the others.

Objections to the foundations upon which society is based are not in order, because the condition of the race is better with these than it has been with any others which have been tried. Of the effect of any new substitutes proposed we cannot be sure. The Socialist or Anarchist who seeks to overturn present conditions is to be regarded as attacking the foundation upon which civilization itself rests, for civilization took its start from the day that the capable, industrious workman said to his incompetent and lazy fellow, "If thou dost not sow, thou shalt not reap," and thus ended primitive Communism by separating the drones from the bees. One who studies this subject will soon be brought face to face with the conclusion that upon the sacredness of property civilization itself depends—the right of the laborer to his hundred dollars in the savings bank, and equally the legal right of the millionaire to his millions. To those who propose to substitute Communism for this intense Individualism the answer, therefore, is: The race has tried that. All progress from that barbarous day to the present time has resulted from its displacement. Not evil, but good, has come to the race from the accumulation of wealth by those who have the ability and energy that produce it.

But even if we admit for a moment that it might be better for the race to discard its present foundation, Individualism, that it is a nobler ideal that man should labor, not for himself alone, but in and for a brotherhood of his fellows, and share with them all in common, realizing Swedenborg's idea of Heaven, where, as he says, the angels derive their happiness, not from laboring for self, but for each other—even admit all this, and a sufficient answer is, This is not evolution, but revolution. It necessitates the changing of human nature itself—a work of aeons, even if it were good to change it, which we cannot know. It is not practicable in our day or in our age. Even if desirable theoretically, it belongs to another and long-succeeding sociological stratum. Our duty is with what is practicable now; with the next step possible in our day and generation. It is criminal to waste our energies in endeavoring to uproot, when all we can profitably or possibly accomplish is to bend the universal tree of humanity a little in the direction most favorable to the production of good fruit under existing circumstances. We might as well urge the destruction of the highest existing type of man because he failed to reach our ideal as to favor the destruction of Individualism, Private Property, the Law of Accumulation of Wealth, and the Law of Competition; for these are the highest results of human experience, the soil in which society so far has produced the best fruit. Unequally or unjustly, perhaps, as these laws sometimes operate, and imperfect as they appear to the Idealist, they are, nevertheless, like the highest type of man, the best and most valuable of all that humanity has yet accomplished.

We start, then, with a condition of affairs under which the best interests of the race are promoted, but which inevitably gives wealth to the few. Thus far, accepting conditions as they exist, the situation can be surveyed and pronounced good. The question then arises—and, if the foregoing be correct, it is the only question with which we have to deal—What is the proper mode of administering wealth after the laws upon which civilization is founded have thrown it into the hands of the few? And it is of this great question that I believe I offer the true solution. It will be understood that *fortunes* are here spoken of, not moderate sums saved by many years of effort, the returns from which are required for the comfortable maintenance and education of families. This is not *wealth*, but only *competence,* which it should be the aim of all to acquire.

There are but three modes in which surplus wealth can be disposed of. It can be left to the families of the decedents; or it can be bequeathed for public purposes; or, finally, it can be administered during their lives by its possessors. Under the first and second modes most of the wealth of the world that has reached the few has hitherto been applied. Let us in turn consider each of these modes. The first is the most injudicious. In monarchical countries, the estates and the greatest portion of the wealth are left to the first son, that the vanity of the parent may be gratified by the thought that his name and title are to descend to succeeding generations unimpaired. The condition of this class in Europe to-day teaches the futility of such hopes or ambitions. The successors have become impoverished through their follies or from the fall in the value of land. Even in Great Britain the strict law of entail has been found inadequate to maintain the status of an hereditary class. Its soil is rapidly passing into the hands of the stranger. Under republican institutions the division of property among the children is much fairer, but the question which forces itself upon thoughtful men in all lands is: Why should men leave great fortunes to their children? If this is done from affection, is it not misguided affection? Observation teaches that, generally speaking, it is not well for the children that they should be so burdened. Neither is it well for the state. Beyond providing for the wife and daughters moderate sources of income, and very moderate allowances indeed, if any, for the sons, men may well hesitate, for it is no longer questionable that great sums bequeathed oftener work more for the injury than for the good of the recipients. Wise men will soon conclude that, for the best interests of the members of their families and of the state, such bequests are an improper use of their means.

It is not suggested that men who have failed to educate their sons to earn a livelihood shall cast them adrift in poverty. If any man has seen fit to rear his sons with a view to their living idle lives, or, what is highly commendable, has instilled in them the sentiment that they are in a position to labor for public ends without reference to pecuniary considerations, then, of course, the duty of the parent is to see that such are provided for *in moderation*. There are instances of millionaires' sons unspoiled by wealth, who, being rich, still perform great services in the community. Such are the very salt of the earth, as valuable as, unfortunately, they are rare; still it is not the exception, but the rule, that men must regard; and, looking at the usual result of enormous sums conferred upon legatees, the thoughtful man must shortly say, "I would as soon leave to my son a curse as the almighty dollar," and admit to himself that it is not the welfare of the children, but family pride, which inspires these enormous legacies.

As to the second mode, that of leaving wealth at death for public uses, it may be said that this is only a means for the disposal of wealth, provided a man is content to wait until he is dead before it becomes of much good in the world. Knowledge of the results of legacies bequeathed is not calculated to inspire the brightest hopes of much posthumous good being accomplished. The cases are not few in which the real object sought by the testator is not attained, nor are they few in which his real wishes are thwarted. In many cases the bequests are so used as to become only monuments of his folly. It is well to remember that it requires the exercise of not less ability than that which acquired the wealth to use it so as to be really beneficial to the community. Besides this, it may fairly be said that no man is to be extolled for doing what he cannot help doing, nor is he to be thanked by the community to which he only leaves wealth at death. Men who leave vast sums in this way may fairly be thought men who would not have left it at all, had they been able to take it with them. The memories of such cannot be held in grateful remembrance, for there is no grace in their gifts. It is not to be wondered at that such bequests seem so generally to lack the blessing.

The growing disposition to tax more and more heavily large estates left at death is a cheering indication of the growth of a salutary change in public opinion. The State of Pennsylvania now takes—subject to some exceptions—one-tenth of the property left by its citizens. The budget presented in the British Parliament the other day proposes to increase the death-duties; and, most significant of all, the new tax is to be a graduated one. Of all forms of taxation, this seems the wisest. Men who continue hoarding great sums all their lives, the proper use of which for public ends would work good to the community, should be made to feel that the community, in the form of the state, cannot thus be deprived of its proper share. By taxing estates heavily at death the state marks its condemnation of the selfish millionaire's unworthy life.

It is desirable that nations should go much further in this direction. Indeed, it is difficult to set bounds to the share of a rich man's estate which should go at his death to the public through the agency of the state, and by all means such taxes should be graduated, beginning at nothing upon moderate sums to dependents, and increasing rapidly as the amounts swell, until of the millionaire's hoard, as of Shylock's, at least:

" . . . The other half Comes to the privy coffer of the state."

This policy would work powerfully to induce the rich man to attend to the administration of wealth during his life, which is the end that society should always have in view, as being that by far most fruitful for the people. Nor need it be feared that this policy would sap the root of enterprise and render men less anxious to accumulate, for to the class whose ambition it is to leave great fortunes and be talked about after their death, it will attract even more attention, and, indeed, be a somewhat nobler ambition to have enormous sums paid over to the state from their fortunes.

There remains, then, only one mode of using great fortunes; but in this we have the true antidote for the temporary unequal distribution of wealth, the reconciliation of the rich and the poor—a reign of harmony—another ideal, differing, indeed, from that of the Communist in requiring only the further evolution of existing conditions, not the total overthrow of our civilization. It is founded upon the present most intense individualism, and the race is prepared to put it in practice by degrees whenever it pleases. Under its sway we shall have an ideal state, in which the surplus wealth of the few will become, in the best sense, the property of the many, because administered for the common good; and this wealth, passing through the hands of the few, can be made a much more potent force for the elevation of our race than if it had been distributed in small sums to the people themselves. Even the poorest can be made to see this, and to agree that great sums gathered by some of their fellow-citizens and spent for public purposes, from which the masses reap the principal benefit, are more valuable to them than if scattered among them through the course of many years in trifling amounts.

If we consider what results flow from the Cooper Institute, for instance, to the best portion of the race in New York not possessed of means, and compare these with those which would have arisen for the good of the masses from an equal sum distributed by Mr. Cooper in his lifetime in the form of wages, which is the highest form of distribution, being for work done and not for charity, we can form some estimate of the possibilities for the improvement of the race which lie embedded in the present law of the accumulation of wealth. Much of this sum, if distributed in small quantities among the people, would have been wasted in the indulgence of appetite, some of it in excess; and it may be doubted whether even the part put to the best use, that of adding to the comforts of the home, would have yielded results for the race, as a race, at all comparable to those which are flowing and are to flow from the Cooper Institute from generation to generation. Let the advocate of violent or radical change ponder well this thought.

We might even go so far as to take another instance, that of Mr. Tilden's bequest of five millions of dollars for a free library in the city of New York; but in referring to this one cannot help saying involuntarily, How much better if Mr. Tilden had devoted the last years of his own life to the proper administration of this immense sum; in which case neither legal contest nor any other cause of delay could have interfered with his aims. But let us assume that Mr. Tilden's millions finally become the means of giving to this city a noble public library, where the treasures of the world contained in books will be open to all forever, without money and without price. Considering the good of that part of the race which congregates in and around Manhattan Island, would its permanent benefit have been better promoted had these millions been allowed to circulate in small sums through the hands of the masses? Even the most strenuous advocate of Communism must entertain a doubt upon this subject. Most of those who think will probably entertain no doubt whatever.

Poor and restricted are our opportunities in this life; narrow our horizon; our best work most imperfect; but rich men should be thankful for one inestimable boon. They have it in their power during their lives to busy themselves in organizing benefactions from which the masses of their fellows will derive lasting advantage, and thus dignify their own lives. The highest life is probably to be reached, not by such imitation of the life of Christ as Count Tolstoi gives us, but, while animated by Christ's spirit, by recognizing the changed conditions of this age, and adopting modes of expressing this spirit suitable to the changed conditions under which we live; still laboring for the good of our fellows, which was the essence of his life and teaching, but laboring in a different manner.

This, then, is held to be the duty of the man of Wealth: First, to set an example of modest, unostentatious living, shunning display or extravagance; to provide moderately for the legitimate wants of those dependent upon him; and after doing so to consider all surplus revenues which come to him simply as trust funds, which he is called upon to administer, and strictly bound as a matter of duty to administer in the manner which, in his judgment, is best calculated to produce the most beneficial results for the community—the man of wealth thus becoming the mere agent and trustee for his poorer brethren, bringing to their service his superior wisdom, experience, and ability to administer, doing for them better than they would or could do for themselves.

We are met here with the difficulty of determining what are moderate sums to leave to members of the family; what is modest, unostentatious living; what is the test of extravagance. There must be different standards for different conditions. The answer is that it is as impossible to name exact amounts or actions as it is to define good manners, good taste, or the rules of propriety; but, nevertheless, these are verities, well known although undefinable. Public sentiment is quick to know and to feel what offends these. So in the case of wealth. The rule in regard to good taste in the dress of men or women applies here. Whatever makes one conspicuous offends the canon. If any family be chiefly known for display, for extravagance in home, table, equipage, for enormous sums ostentatiously spent in any form upon itself—if these be its chief distinctions, we have no difficulty in estimating its nature or culture. So likewise in regard to the use or abuse of its surplus wealth, or to generous, free-handed cooperation in good public uses, or to unabated efforts to accumulate and hoard to the last, whether they administer or bequeath. The verdict rests with the best and most enlightened public sentiment. The community will surely judge, and its judgments will not often be wrong.

The best uses to which surplus wealth can be put have already been indicated. Those who would administer wisely must, indeed, be wise, for one of the serious obstacles to the improvement of our race is indiscriminate charity. It were

better for mankind that the millions of the rich were thrown into the sea than so spent as to encourage the slothful, the drunken, the unworthy. Of every thousand dollars spent in so called charity to-day, it is probable that $950 is unwisely spent; so spent, indeed, as to produce the very evils which it proposes to mitigate or cure. A well-known writer of philosophic books admitted the other day that he had given a quarter of a dollar to a man who approached him as he was coming to visit the house of his friend. He knew nothing of the habits of this beggar, knew not the use that would be made of this money, although he had every reason to suspect that it would be spent improperly. This man professed to be a disciple of Herbert Spencer; yet the quarter-dollar given that night will probably work more injury than all the money which its thoughtless donor will ever be able to give in true charity will do good. He only gratified his own feelings, saved himself from annoyance—and this was probably one of the most selfish and very worst actions of his life, for in all respects he is most worthy.

In bestowing charity, the main consideration should be to help those who will help themselves; to provide part of the means by which those who desire to improve may do so; to give those who desire to rise the aids by which they may rise; to assist, but rarely or never to do all. Neither the individual nor the race is improved by alms-giving. Those worthy of assistance, except in rare cases, seldom require assistance; the really valuable men of the race never do, except in cases of accident or sudden change. Every one has, of course, cases of individuals brought to his own knowledge where temporary assistance can do genuine good, and these he will not overlook. But the amount which can be wisely given by the individual for individuals is necessarily limited by his lack of knowledge of the circumstances connected with each. He is the only true reformer who is as careful and as anxious not to aid the unworthy as he is to aid the worthy, and, perhaps, even more so, for in alms-giving more injury is probably done by rewarding vice than by relieving virtue.

The rich man is thus almost restricted to following the examples of Peter Cooper, Enoch Pratt of Baltimore, Mr. Pratt of Brooklyn, Senator Stanford, and others, who know that the best means of benefiting the community is to place within its reach the ladders upon which the aspiring can rise—parks, and means of recreation, by which men are helped in body and mind; works of art, certain to give pleasure and improve the public taste, and public institutions of various kinds, which will improve the general condition of the people—in this manner returning their surplus wealth to the mass of their fellows in the forms best calculated to do them lasting good.

Thus is the problem of Rich and Poor to be solved. The laws of accumulation will be left free; the laws of distribution free. Individualism will continue, but the millionaire will be but a trustee for the poor; intrusted for a season with a great part of the increased wealth of the community, but administering it for the community far better than it could or would have done for itself. The best minds will thus have reached a stage in the development of the race in which it is clearly seen that there is no mode of disposing of surplus wealth creditable to thoughtful and earnest men into whose hands it flows save by using it year by year for the general good. This day already dawns. But a little while, and although, without incurring the pity of their fellows, men may die sharers in great business enterprises from which their capital cannot be or has not been withdrawn, and is left chiefly at death for public uses; yet the man who dies leaving behind him millions of available wealth, which was his to administer during life, will pass away "unwept, unhonored, and unsung," no matter to what uses he leaves the dross which he cannot take with him. Of such as these the public verdict will then be: "The man who dies thus rich dies disgraced."

Such, in my opinion, is the true Gospel concerning Wealth, obedience to which is destined some day to solve the problem of the Rich and the Poor, and to bring "Peace on earth, among men Good-Will."

Source:
John Scott, ed. *Living Documents in American History*. New York: Washington Square Press, 1964–68.

6. SHERMAN ANTITRUST ACT, 1890

First federal U.S. legislation to regulate trusts, enacted on July 2, 1890. Introduced by Republican senator John Sherman, it declared illegal "every contract, combination in the form of trust or otherwise, or conspiracy, in restraint of trade or commerce among the several States, or with foreign nations." The legislation, based on Congress's constitutional power to regulate interstate commerce, grew out of public dissatisfaction with the abuses of business trusts and corporations controlling various commodities. While at first, Supreme Court decisions condemned labor rather than business practices, the act was used successfully in President Theodore Roosevelt's "trust-busting" campaigns and in later actions. The law was strengthened and clarified by the Clayton Antitrust Act of 1914.

An Act
To protect trade and commerce against unlawful restraints and monopolies.

Be it enacted by the Senate and House of Representatives of the United States of America in Congress assembled,

Sec. 1. Every contract, combination in the form of trust or otherwise, or conspiracy, in restraint of trade or commerce among the several States, or with foreign nations, is hereby declared to be illegal. Every person who shall make any such contract or engage in any such combination or conspiracy, shall be deemed guilty of a misdemeanor, and, on conviction thereof, shall be punished by fine not exceeding five thousand dollars, or by imprisonment not exceeding one year, or by both said punishments, in the discretion of the court.

Sec. 2. Every person who shall monopolize, or attempt to monopolize, or combine or conspire with any other person or persons, to monopolize any part of the trade or commerce among the several States, or with foreign nations, shall be deemed guilty of a misdemeanor, and, on conviction thereof, shall be punished by fine not exceeding five thousand dollars, or by imprisonment not exceeding one year, or by both said punishments, in the discretion of the court.

Sec. 3. Every contract, combination in form of trust or otherwise, or conspiracy, in restraint of trade or commerce in any Territory of the United States or of the District of Columbia, or in restraint of trade or commerce between any such Territory and another, or between any such Territory or Territories and any State or States or the District of Columbia, or with foreign nations, or between the District of Columbia and any State or States or foreign nations, is hereby declared illegal. Every person who shall make any such contract or engage in any such combination or conspiracy, shall be deemed guilty of a misdemeanor, and, on conviction thereof, shall be punished by fine not exceeding five thousand dollars, or by imprisonment not exceeding one year, or by both said punishments, in the discretion of the court.

Sec. 4. The several circuit courts of the United States are hereby invested with jurisdiction to prevent and restrain violations of this act; and it shall be the duty of the several district attorneys of the United States, in their respective districts, under the direction of the Attorney-General, to institute proceedings in equity to prevent and restrain such violations. Such proceedings may be by way of petition setting forth the case and praying that such violation shall be enjoined or otherwise prohibited. When the parties complained of shall have been duly notified of such petition the court shall proceed, as soon as may be, to the hearing and determination of the case; and pending such petition and before final decree, the court may at any time make such temporary restraining order or prohibition as shall be deemed just in the premises.

Sec. 5. Whenever it shall appear to the court before which any proceeding under section four of this act may be pending, that the ends of justice require that other parties should be brought before the court, the court may cause them to be summoned, whether they reside in the district in which the court is held or not; and subpoenas to that end may be served in any district by the marshal thereof.

Sec. 6. Any property owned under any contract or by any combination, or pursuant to any conspiracy (and being the subject thereof) mentioned in section one of this act, and being in the course of transportation from one State to another, or to a foreign country, shall be forfeited to the United States, and may be seized and condemned by like proceedings as those provided by law for the forfeiture, seizure, and condemnation of property imported into the United States contrary to law.

Sec. 7. Any person who shall be injured in his business or property by any other person or corporation by reason of anything forbidden or declared to be unlawful by this act, may sue therefor in any circuit court of the United States in the district in which the defendant resides or is found, without respect to the amount in controversy, and shall recover three fold the damages by him sustained, and the costs of suit, including a reasonable attorney's fee.

Sec. 8. That the word "person," or "persons," wherever used in this act shall be deemed to include corporations and associations existing under or authorized by the laws of either the United States, the laws of any of the Territories, the laws of any State, or the laws of any foreign country.

Source:
Statutes at Large, vol. 26, pp. 209–210.

7. Pure Food and Drug Act, 1906

Federal legislation enacted on June 30, 1906, prohibiting the manufacture, sale, or transportation of adulterated or fraudulently labeled foods and drugs shipped in foreign or interstate commerce. Among the items prohibited were confectionery that contained dangerous colorings or flavorings, food composed of filthy or decomposed animal matter, food containing poisonous ingredients, and food adulterated to conceal inferior goods. Labels of proprietary medicines were required to indicate the percentages of narcotics, stimulants, or other potentially harmful ingredients.

The same day, Congress enacted the Meat Inspection Act, giving the U.S. secretary of agriculture the power to inspect meat and condemn products that are "unsound, unhealthful, unwholesome, or otherwise unfit for human food." The act was intended to correct unsanitary and dangerous practices in the meat-packing industry, such as resulted in the "embalmed beef" scandal, when soldiers in the Spanish-American War (1898) were fed tainted meat. The act allowed for federal inspection of all companies.

Although President Theodore Roosevelt and others had previously backed pure food and drug legislation, the impetus for these acts came from the publication of Upton Sinclair's The Jungle *the same year. Sinclair, a socialist, meant his exposé of conditions in the meat-packing industry to highlight the exploitation of immigrant workers like his book's protagonist. Instead, the public focused on the sections describing the processing of diseased cattle and the fate of workers who fell unreclaimed into open vats "till but the bones of them had gone out to the world as Durham's Pure Leaf Lard."*

The 1906 Pure Food and Drug Act was superseded by the Food and Drug Act of June 24, 1938. It prohibited the sale of foods dangerous to health as well as foods, drugs, and cosmetics packaged in insanitary or contaminated containers. It required manufacturers of foods, drugs, and cosmetics to list their ingredients on the labels. It also prohibited the sale of "poisonous" or "deleterious" substances and broadened the definitions of "adulteration" and "misbranding." The Food and Drug Administration was authorized to enforce the act, and inspection stations were established in several large cities. Three months earlier, in the Wheeler-Lea Act, sponsored by Senator Burton K. Wheeler of Montana and Representative Clarence F. Lea of California, individuals and agencies were prohibited from presenting false or misleading statements about "food, drugs, diagnostic and therapeutic devices, and cosmetics" in interstate media. This statute gave the Federal Trade Commission control over such advertising and gave the Food and Drug Administration authority over questions of misbranding.

An Act

For preventing the manufacture, sale, or transportation of adulterated or misbranded or poisonous or deleterious foods, drugs, medicines, and liquors, and for regulating traffic therein, and for other purposes.

Be it enacted by the Senate and House of Representatives of the United States of America in Congress assembled, That is shall be unlawful for any article of food or drug which is adulterated or misbranded, within the meaning of this Act; and any person who shall violate any of the provisions of this section shall be guilty of a misdemeanor, and for each offense shall, upon conviction thereof, be fined not to exceed five hundred dollars or shall be sentenced to one year's imprisonment, or both such fine and imprisonment, in the discretion of the court, and for each subsequent offense and conviction thereof shall be fined not less than one thousand dollars or sentenced to one year's imprisonment, or both such fine and imprisonment, in the discretion of the court.

Sec. 2. That the introduction into any State or Territory or the District of Columbia from any other State or Territory or the District of Columbia, or from any foreign country, or shipment to any foreign country of any article of food or drugs which is adulterated or misbranded, within the meaning of this Act, is hereby prohibited; and any person who shall ship or deliver for shipment from any State or Territory or the District of Columbia to any other State or Territory or the District of Columbia, or to a foreign country, or who shall receive in any State or Territory or the District of Columbia from any other State or Territory or the District of Columbia, or foreign country, and having so received, shall deliver, in original unbroken packages, for pay or otherwise, or offer to deliver to any other person, any such article so adulterated or misbranded within the meaning of this Act, or any person who shall sell or offer for sale in the District of Columbia or the Territories of the United States any such adulterated or misbranded foods or drugs, or export or offer to export the same to any foreign country, shall be guilty of a misdemeanor, and for such offense be fined not exceeding two hundred dollars for the first offense, and upon conviction for each subsequent offense not exceeding three hundred dollars or be imprisoned not exceeding one year, or both, in the discretion of the court: *Provided,* That no article shall be deemed misbranded or adulterated within the provisions of this Act when intended for except to any foreign country and prepared or packed according to the specifications or directions of the foreign purchaser when no substance is used in the preparation or packing thereof in conflict with the laws of the foreign country to which said article is intended to be shipped; but if said article shall be in fact sold or offered for sale for domestic use or consumption, then this proviso shall not exempt said article from the operation of any of the other provisions of this Act.

Sec. 3. That the Secretary of the Treasury, the Secretary of Agriculture, and the Secretary of Commerce and Labor shall make uniform rules and regulations for carrying out the provisions of this Act, including the collection and examination of specimens of foods and drugs manufactured or offered for sale in the District of

Columbia, or in any Territory of the United States, or which shall be offered for sale in unbroken packages in any State other than that in which they shall have been respectively manufactured or produced, or which shall be received from any foreign country, or intended for shipment to any foreign country, or which may be submitted for examination by the chief health, food, or drug officer of any State, Territory, or the District of Columbia, or at any domestic or foreign port through which such product is offered for interstate commerce, or for export or import between the United States and any foreign port or country.

Sec. 4. That the examinations of specimens of foods and drugs shall be made in the Bureau of Chemistry of the Department of Agriculture, or under the direction and supervision of such Bureau, for the purpose of determining from such examinations whether such articles are adulterated or misbranded within the meaning of this Act; and if it shall appear from any such examination that any of such specimens is adulterated or misbranded within the meaning of this Act, the Secretary of Agriculture shall cause notice thereof to be given to the party from whom such sample was obtained. Any party so notified shall be given an opportunity to be heard, under such rules and regulations as may be prescribed as aforesaid, and if it appears that any of the provisions of this Act have been violated by such party, then the Secretary of Agriculture shall at once certify the facts to the proper United States district attorney, with a copy of the results of the analysis or the examination of such article duly authenticated by the analyst or officer making such examination, under the oath of such officer. After judgment of the court, notice shall be given by publication in such manner as may be prescribed by the rules and regulations aforesaid.

Sec. 5. That it shall be the duty of each district attorney to whom the Secretary of Agriculture shall report any violation of this Act, or to whom any health or food or drug officer or agent of any State, Territory, or the District of Columbia shall present satisfactory evidence of any such violation, to cause appropriate proceedings to be commenced and prosecuted in the proper courts of the United States, without delay, for the enforcement of the penalties as in such case herein provided.

Sec. 6. That the term "drug," as used in this Act, shall include all medicines and preparations recognized in the United States Pharmacopoeia or National Formulary for internal or external use, and any substance or mixture of substances intended to be used for the cure, mitigation, or prevention of disease of either man or other animals. The term "food," as used herein, shall include all articles used for food, drink, confectionery, or condiment by man or other animals, whether simple, mixed, or compound.

Sec. 7. That for the purposes of this Act an article shall be deemed to be adulterated:

In case of drugs:

First. If, when a drug is sold under or by a name recognized in the United States Pharmacopoeia or National Formulary, it differs from the standard of strength, quality, or purity, as determined by the test laid down in the United States Pharmacopoeia or National Formulary official at the time of investigation: *Provided,* That no drug defined in the United States Pharmacopoeia or National Formulary shall be deemed to be adulterated under this provision if the standard of strength, quality, or purity be plainly stated upon the bottle, box, or other container thereof although the standard may differ from that determined by the test laid down in the United States Pharmacopoeia or National Formulary.

Second. If its strength or purity fall below the professed standard or quality under which it is sold.

In the case of confectionery:

If it contain terra alba, barytes, talc, chrome yellow, or other mineral substance or poisonous color or flavor, or other ingredient deleterious or detrimental to health, or any vinous, malt or spirituous liquor or compound or narcotic drug.

In the case of food:

First. If any substance has been mixed and packed with it so as to reduce or lower or injuriously affect its quality or strength.

Second. If any substance has been substituted wholly or in part for the article.

Third. If any valuable constituent of the article has been wholly or in part abstracted.

Fourth. If it be mixed, colored, powdered, coated, or stained in a manner whereby damage or inferiority is concealed.

Fifth. If it contain any added poisonous or other added deleterious ingredient which may render such article injurious to health: *Provided,* That when in the preparation of food products for shipment they are preserved by any external application applied in such manner that the preservative is necessarily removed mechanically, or by maceration in water, or otherwise, and directions for the removal of said preservative shall be printed on the covering or the package, the provisions of this Act shall be construed as applying only when said products are ready for consumption.

Sixth. If it consists in whole or in part of a filthy, decomposed, or putrid animal or vegetable substance, or any portion of an animal unfit for food, whether manufactured or not, or if it is the product of a diseased animal, or one that has died otherwise than by slaughter.

Sec. 8. That the term, "misbranded," as used herein, shall apply to all drugs, or articles of food, or articles which enter into the composition of food, the package or label of which shall bear any statement, design, or device regarding such article, or the ingredients or substances contained therein which shall be false or misleading in any particular, and to any food or drug product which is falsely branded as to the State, Territory, or country in which it is manufactured or produced.

That for the purposes of this Act an article shall also be deemed to be misbranded:

In case of drugs:

First. If it be an imitation of or offered for sale under the name of another article.

Second. If the contents of the package as originally put up shall have been removed, in whole or in part, and other contents shall have been placed in such package, or if the package fail to bear a statement on the label of the quantity or proportion of any alcohol, morphine, opium, cocaine, heroin, alpha or beta eucaine, chloroform, cannabis indica, chloral hydrate, or acetanilide, or any derivative or preparation of any such substances contained therein.

In the case of food:

First. If it be an imitation of or offered for sale under the distinctive name of another article.

Second. If it be labeled or branded so as to deceive or mislead the purchaser, or purport to be a foreign product when not so, or if the contents of the package as originally put up shall have been removed in whole or in part and other contents shall have been placed in such package, or if it fail to bear a statement on the label of the quantity or proportion of any morphine, opium, cocaine, heroin, alpha or beta eucaine, chloroform, cannabis indica, chloral hydrate, or acetanilide, or any derivative or preparation of any such substances contained therein.

Third. If in package form, and the contents are stated in terms of weight or measure, they are not plainly and correctly stated on the outside of the package.

Fourth. If the package containing it or its label shall bear any statement, design, or device regarding the ingredients or the substances contained therein, which statement, design, or device shall be false or misleading in any particular: *Provided*, That an article of food which does not contain any added poisonous or deleterious ingredients shall not be deemed to be adulterated or misbranded in the following cases:

First. In the case of mixtures or compounds which may be now or from time to time hereafter known as articles of food, under their own distinctive names, and not an imitation of or offered for sale under the distinctive name of another article, if the name be accompanied on the same label or brand with a statement of the place where said article has been manufactured or produced.

Second. In the case of articles labeled, branded, or tagged so as to plainly indicate that they are compounds, imitations, or blends, and the word "compound," "imitation," or "blend," as the case may be, is plainly stated on the package in which it is offered for sale: *Provided*, That the term blend as used herein shall be construed to mean a mixture of like substances, not excluding harmless coloring or flavoring ingredients used for the purpose of coloring and flavoring only: *And provided further*, That nothing in this Act shall be construed as requiring or compelling proprietors or manufacturers of proprietary foods which contain no unwholesome added ingredient to disclose their trade formulas, except in so far as the provisions of this Act may require to secure freedom from adulteration or misbranding.

Sec. 9. That no dealer shall be prosecuted under the provisions of this Act when he can establish a guaranty signed by the wholesaler, jobber, manufacturer, or other party residing in the United States, from whom he purchases such articles, to the effect that the same is not adulterated or misbranded within the meaning of this Act, designating it. Said guaranty, to afford protection, shall contain the name and address of the party or parties making the sale of such articles to such dealer, and in such case said party or parties shall be amenable to the prosecutions, fines, and other penalties which would attach, in due course, to the dealer under the provisions of this Act.

Sec. 10. That any article of food, drug, or liquor that is adulterated or misbranded within the meaning of this Act, and is being transported from one State, Territory, District, or insular possession to another for sale, or, having been transported, remains unloaded, unsold, or in original unbroken packages, or if it be sold or offered for sale in the District of Columbia or the Territories, or insular possessions of the United States, or if it be imported from a foreign country for sale, or if it is intended for export to a foreign country, shall be liable to be proceeded against in any district court of the United States within the district where the same is found, and seized for confiscation by a process of libel for condemnation. And if such article is condemned as being adulterated or misbranded, or of a poisonous or deleterious character, within the meaning of this Act, the same shall be disposed of by destruction or sale, as the said court may direct, and the proceeds thereof, if sold, less the legal costs and charges, shall be paid into the Treasury of the United States, but such goods shall not be sold in any jurisdiction contrary to the provisions of this Act or the laws of that jurisdiction: *Provided, however*, That upon the payment of the costs of such libel proceedings and the execution and delivery of a good and sufficient bond to the effect that such articles shall not be sold or otherwise disposed of contrary to the provisions of this Act, or the laws of any State, Territory, District, or insular possession, the court may by order direct that such articles be delivered to the owner thereof. The proceedings of such libel cases shall conform, as near as may be, to the proceedings in admiralty, except that either party may demand trial by jury of any issue of fact joined in any such case, and all such proceedings shall be at the suit of and in the name of the United States.

Sec. 11. The Secretary of the Treasury shall deliver to the Secretary of Agriculture, upon his request from time to time, samples of foods and drugs which are being imported into the United States or offered for import, giving notice thereof to the owner or consignee, who may appear before the Secretary of Agriculture, and have the right to introduce testimony, and if it appear from the examination of such samples that any article of food or drug offered to be imported into the United States is adulterated or misbranded within the meaning of this Act, or is otherwise dangerous to the health of the people of the United States, or is of a kind forbidden entry into, or forbidden to be sold or restricted in sale in the country in which it is made or from which

it is exported, or is otherwise falsely labeled in any respect, the said article shall be refused admission, and the Secretary of the Treasury shall refuse delivery to the consignee and shall cause the destruction of any goods refused delivery which shall not be exported by the consignee within three months from the date of notice of such refusal under such regulations as the Secretary of the Treasury may prescribe: *Provided*, That the Secretary of the Treasury may deliver to the consignee such goods pending examination and decision in the matter on execution of a penal bond for the amount of the full invoice value of such goods, together with the duty thereon, and on refusal to return such goods for any cause to the custody of the Secretary of the Treasury, when demanded, for the purpose of excluding them from the country, or for any other purpose, said consignee shall forfeit the full amount of the bond: *And provided further*, That all charges for storage, cartage, and labor on goods which are refused admission or delivery shall be paid by the owner or consignee, and in default of such payment shall constitute a lien against any future importation made by such owner or consignee.

Sec. 12. That the term "Territory" as used in this Act shall include the insular possessions of the United States. The word "person" as used in this Act shall be construed to import both the plural and the singular, as the case demands, and shall include corporations, companies, societies and associations. When construing and enforcing the provisions of this Act, the act, omission, or failure of any officer, agent, or other person acting for or employed by any corporation, company, society, or association, within the scope of his employment or office, shall in every case be also deemed to be the act, omission, or failure of such corporation, company, society, or association as well as that of the person.

Sec. 13. That this Act shall be in force and effect from and after the first day of January, nineteen hundred and seven.

Source:
Statutes at Large, vol. 34, pp. 768–772.

8. *STANDARD OIL COMPANY OF NEW JERSEY ET AL. V. UNITED STATES*, 1911

U.S. Supreme Court decision issued on May 15, 1911, upholding the dissolution of the Standard Oil Company, a powerful monopolistic trust, on the grounds that it represented an "unreasonable" restraint of trade under the Sherman Antitrust Act. The decision resulted from a lawsuit initiated by the federal government in 1906, charging Standard Oil and others with conspiring to restrain trade and commerce in petroleum and related products. The Supreme Court, in upholding a 1909 U.S. circuit court ruling that the company had to divest itself of numerous subsidiaries, declared that the Sherman Antitrust Act should be applied according to the "rule of reason."

As Justice White points out, the case file was exceptionally voluminous and the allegations unusually complicated. However, its prosecution was then, and continues to be, a landmark event. The excerpts here include Justice White's use of history to come to his decision.

───────────── ✦ ─────────────

Chief Justice White delivered the opinion of the court:

The Standard Oil Company of New Jersey and thirty-three other corporations, John D. Rockefeller, William Rockefeller, and five other individual defendants, prosecute this appeal to reverse a decree of the court below. Such decree was entered upon a bill filed by the United States under authority of Section 4 of the act of July 2, 1890 known as the anti-trust act. . . . The record is inordinately voluminous, consisting of twenty-three volumes of printed matter, aggregating about 12,000 pages, containing a vast amount of confusing and conflicting testimony relating to innumerable, complex, and varied business

transactions, extending over a period of nearly forty years. In an effort to pave the way to reach the subjects which we are called upon to consider, we propose at the outset, following the order of the bill, to give the merest possible outline of its contents, to summarize the answer, to indicate the course of the trial, and point out briefly the decision below rendered.

The bill and exhibits, covering 170 pages of the printed record, was filed on November 15, 1906. Corporations known as Standard Oil Company of New Jersey, Standard Oil Company of California, Standard Oil Company of Indiana, Standard Oil Company of Iowa, Standard Oil Company of Kansas, Standard Oil Company of Kentucky, Standard Oil Company of Nebraska, Standard Oil Company of New York, Standard Oil Company of Ohio, and sixty-two other corporations and partnerships, as also seven individuals, were named as defendants. The bill was divided into thirty numbered sections, and sought relief upon the theory that the various defendants were engaged in conspiring "to restrain the trade and commerce in petroleum, commonly called 'crude oil,' in refined oil, and in the other products of petroleum, among the several states and territories of the United States and the District of Columbia and with foreign nations, and to monopolize the said commerce." The conspiracy was alleged to have been formed in or about the year 1870 by three of the individual defendants, viz.: John D. Rockefeller, William Rockefeller, and Henry M. Flagler. The detailed averments concerning the alleged conspiracy were arranged with reference to three periods, the first from 1870 to 1882, the second from 1882 to 1899, and the third from 1899 to the time of the filing of the bill.

[Discussions of the bill and jurisdiction are omitted]

We are thus brought face to face with the merits of the controversy.

Both as to the law and as to the facts, the opposing contentions pressed in the argument are numerous, and in all their aspects are so irreconcilable that it is difficult to reduce them to some fundamental generalization, which, by being disposed of, would decide them all. For instance, as to the law. While both sides agree that the determination of the controversy rests upon the correct construction and application of the 1st and 2d sections of the anti-trust act, yet the views as to the meaning of the act are as wide apart as the poles, since there is no real point of agreement on any view of the act. And this also is the case as to the scope and effect of authorities relied upon, even although in some instances one and the same authority is asserted to be controlling.

So also is it as to the facts. Thus, on the one hand, with relentless pertinacity and minuteness of analysis, it is insisted that the facts establish that the assailed combination took its birth in a purpose to unlawfully acquire wealth by oppressing the public and destroying the just rights of others, and that its entire career exemplifies an inexorable carrying out of such wrongful intents, since, it is asserted, the pathway of the combination from the beginning to the time of the filing of the bill is marked with constant proofs of wrong inflicted upon the public, and is strewn with the wrecks resulting from crushing out, without regard to law, the individual rights of others. Indeed, so conclusive, it is urged, is the proof on these subjects, that it is asserted that the existence of the principal corporate defendant—the Standard Oil Company of New Jersey—with the vast accumulation of property which it owns or controls, because of its infinite potency for harm and the dangerous example which its continued existence affords, is an open and enduring menace to all freedom of trade, and is a byword and reproach to modern economic methods. On the other hand, in a powerful analysis of the facts, it is insisted that they demonstrate that the origin and development of the vast business which the defendants control was but the result of lawful competitive methods, guided by economic genius of the highest order, sustained by courage, by a keen insight into commercial situations, resulting in the

acquisition of great wealth, but at the same time serving to stimulate and increase production, to widely extend the distribution of the products of petroleum at a cost largely below that which would have otherwise prevailed, thus proving to be at one and the same time a benefaction to the general public as well as of enormous advantage to individuals. It is not denied that in the enormous volume of proof contained in the record in the period of almost a lifetime, to which that proof is addressed, there may be found acts of wrongdoing, but the insistence is that they were rather the exception than the rule, and in most cases were either the result of too great individual zeal in the keen rivalries of business, or of the methods and habits of dealing which, even if wrong, were commonly practised at the time. And to discover and state the truth concerning these contentions both arguments call for the analysis and weighing, as we have said at the outset, of a jungle of conflicting testimony covering a period of forty years—a duty difficult to rightly perform, and, even if satisfactorily accomplished, almost impossible to state with any reasonable regard to brevity.

Duly appreciating the situation just stated, it is certain that only one point of concord between the parties is discernible, which is, that the controversy in every aspect is controlled by a correct conception of the meaning of the 1st and 2d sections of the anti-trust act. We shall therefor–departing from what otherwise would be the natural order of analysis–make this one point of harmony the initial basis of our examination of the contentions.... When we have done this, we shall then approach the facts....

First. The text of the act and its meaning.

We quote the text of the 1st and 2d sections of the act, as follows:

"Section 1. Every contract, combination in the form of trust or otherwise, or conspiracy, in restraint of trade or commerce among the several states or with foreign nations, is hereby declared to be illegal. Every person how shall make any such contract, or engaged in any such combination or conspiracy, shall be deemed guilty of a misde-meanor, and, on conviction thereof, shall be pun-ished by fine not exceeding $5,000, or by imprisonment not exceeding one year, or by both said punishments, in the discretion of the court.

"Sec. 2. Every person who shall monopolize, or attempt to monopolize, or combine or con-spire with any other person or persons to monopolize, any part of the trade or commerce among the several states, or with foreign nations, shall be deemed guilty of a misdemeanor, and, on conviction thereof, shall be punished by fine not exceeding $5,000, or by imprisonment not exceeding one year, or by both said punishments, in the discretion of the court." [26 Stat. at L. 209, chap. 647, U.S. Comp. Stat. 1901, p. 3200.]

The debates show that doubt as to whether there was a common law of the United States which governed the subject in the absence of leg-islation was among the influences leading to the passage of the act. They conclusively show, how-ever, that the main cause which led to the legis-lation was the thought that it was required by the economic condition of the times; that is, the vast accumulation of wealth in the hands of corpora-tions and individuals, the enormous develop-ment of corporate organization, the facility for combination which such organization afforded, the fact that the facility was being used, and that combinations known as trusts were being multi-plied, and the widespread impression that their power had been and would be exerted to oppress individual and injure the public generally. Although debates may not be used as a mean for interpreting a statute, that rule, in the nature of things, is not violated by resorting to debates as a means of ascertaining the environment at the time of the enactment of a particular law; that is, the history of the period when it was adopted.

*   *   *

The evils which led to the public outcry against monopolies [in England] and to the final denial of the power to make them may be thus sum-marily stated: (1) The power which the monop-oly gave to the one who enjoyed it, to fix the price and thereby injure the public; (2) The power which it engendered of enabling a limita-tion on production; and (3) The danger of dete-rioration in quality of the monopolized article which it was deemed was the inevitable resultant of the monopolistic control over its production and sale. . . .

*   *   *

And by operation of the mental process which led to considering as a monopoly acts which, although they did not constitute a monopoly, were thought to produce some of its baneful effects, so also because of the impediment or bur-den to the due course of trade which they pro-duced, such acts came to be referred to as in restraint of trade. . . .

Generalizing these considerations, the situ-ation is this: 1. That by the common law, monopolies were unlawful because of their restriction upon individual freedom of contract and their injury to the public. 2. That as to nec-essaries of life, the freedom of the individual to deal was restricted where the nature and charac-ter of the dealing was such as to engender the presumption of intent to bring about at least one of the injuries which it was deemed would result from monopoly—that is, an undue enhancement of price. 3. That to protect the freedom of contract of the individual, not only in his own interest, but principally in the inter-est of the common weal, a contract of an indi-vidual by which he put an unreasonable restraint upon himself as to carrying on his trade or business was void. And that at common law the evils consequent upon. . . those things to be treated as coming within monopoly and sometimes to be called monopoly, and the same considerations caused monopoly, because of its operation and effect, to be brought within and spoken of generally as impeding the due course of, or being in restraint of, trade.

*   *   *

In this country also the acts from which it was deemed there resulted a part, if not all, of the injurious consequences ascribed to monopoly, came to be referred to as a monopoly itself. In other words, here as had been the case in England, practical common sense caused attention to be concentrated not upon the theoretically correct name to be given to the condition or acts which gave rise to a harmful result, but to the result itself and to the remedying of the evils which it produced. . . .

It is also true that while the principles concerning contracts in restraint of trade, that is, voluntary restraint put by a person on his right to pursue his calling, hence only operating subjectively, came generally to be recognized in accordance with the English rule, it came moreover to pass that contracts or acts which it was considered had a monopolistic tendency, especially those which were thought to unduly diminish competition and hence to enhance prices–in other words, to monopolize–came also in a generic sense to be spoken of and treated as they had been in England, as restricting the due course of trade, and therefore as being in restraint of trade.

*   *   *

In view of the common law and the law in this country as to restraint of trade, which we have reviewed, and the illuminating effect which that history must have under the rule to which we have referred, we think it results:

a. That the context manifests that the statute was drawn in the light of the existing practical conception of the law of restraint of trade. . . .

b. That in view of the many new forms of contracts and combinations which were being evolved from existing economic conditions, it was deemed essential by an all-embracing enumeration to make sure that no form of contract or combination by which an undue restraint of interstate or foreign commerce was brought about could save such restraint from condemnation. . . . .

c. . . . Thus not specifying, but indubitably contemplating and requiring a standard, it follows that it was intended that the standard of reason which had been applied at the common law

and in this country in dealing with subjects of the character embraced by the statute was intended to be the measure used for the purpose of determining whether, in a given case, a particular act had or had not brought about the wrong against which the statute provided.

And a consideration of the text of the 2d section serves to establish that it was intended to supplement the 1st, and to make sure that by no possible guise could the public policy embodied in the 1st section be frustrated or evaded. . . . By reference to the terms of Section 8 it is certain that the word "person" clearly implies a corporation as well as an individual.

*   *   *

Undoubtedly, the words "to monopolize" and "monopolize," as used in the section, reach every act bringing about the prohibited results. . . .

Second. The contentions of the parties as to the meaning of the statute, and the decisions of this court relied upon concerning those contentions. [Omitted]

Third. The facts and the application of the statute to them.

Beyond dispute the proofs establish substantially as alleged in the bill the following facts:

1. The creation of the Standard Oil Company of Ohio.

2. The organization of the Standard Oil Trust of 1882, and also a previous one of 1879, not referred to in the bill, and the proceedings in the supreme court of Ohio, culminating in a decree based upon the finding that the company was unlawfully a party to that trust; the transfer by the trustees of stocks in certain of the companies; the contempt proceedings; and, finally, the increase of the capital of the Standard Oil Company of New Jersey and the acquisition by that company of the shares of the stock of the other corporations in exchange for its certificates.

The vast amount of property and the possibilities of far-reaching control which resulted from the facts last stated are shown by the statement which we have previously annexed concerning the parties to the trust agreement of

1882, and the corporations whose stock was held by the trustees under the trust, and which came therefore to be held by the New Jersey corporation. But these statements do not with accuracy convey an appreciation of the situation as it existed at the time of the entry of the decree below, since, during the more than ten years which elapsed between the acquiring by the New Jersey corporation of the stock and other property which was formerly held by the trustees under the trust agreement, the situation, of course, had somewhat changed—a change which, when analyzed in the light of the proof, we think establishes that the result of enlarging the capital stock of the New Jersey company and giving it the vast power to which we have referred produced its normal consequences; that is, it gave to the corporation, despite enormous dividends and despite the dropping out of certain corporations enumerated in the decree of the court below, an enlarged and more perfect sway and control over the trade and commerce in petroleum and its products. . . .

Giving to the facts just stated the weight which it was deemed they were entitled to, in the light afforded by the proof of other cognate facts and circumstances, the court below held that the acts and dealings established by the proof operated to destroy the "potentiality of competition" which otherwise would have existed to such an extent as to cause the transfer of stock which were made to the New Jersey Corporation and the control which resulted over the many and various subsidiary corporations to be a combination or conspiracy in restraint of trade, in violation of the 1st section of the act, but also to be an attempt to monopolize and monopolization bringing about a perennial violation of the 2d section.

We see no cause to doubt the correctness of these conclusions, considering the subject from every aspect; that is, both in view of the facts established by the record and the necessary operation and effect of the law as we have construed it upon the inferences deducible from the facts, for the following reasons:

a. Because the unification of power and control over petroleum and its products which was the inevitable result of the combining in the New Jersey corporation by the increase of its stock and the transfer to it of the stocks of so many other corporations, aggregating so vast a capital, gives rise, in and of itself, in the absence of countervailing circumstances, to say the least, to the prima facie presumption of intent and purpose to maintain the dominancy over the oil industry, not as a result of normal methods of industrial development, but by new means of combination which were resorted to in order that greater power might be added than would otherwise have arisen had normal methods been followed, the whole with the purpose of excluding others from the trade, and thus centralizing in the combination of a perpetual control of the movements of petroleum and its products in the channels of interstate commerce.

b. Because the prima facie presumption of intent to restrain trade, to monopolize and to bring about monopolization, resulting from the act of expanding the stock of the New Jersey corporation and vesting it with such vast control of the oil industry, is made conclusive by considering (1) the conduct of the persons or corporations who were mainly instrumental in bringing about the extension of power in the New Jersey corporation before the consummation of the result and prior to the formation of that trust agreements of 1879 and 1882; (2) by considering the proof as to what was done under those agreements and the acts which immediately preceded the vesting of power in the New Jersey corporation, as well as by weighing the modes in which the power vested in that corporation has been exerted and the results which have arisen from it.

*   *   *

Fourth, The remedy to be administered.

*   *   *

As penalties which are not authorized by law may not be inflicted by judicial authority, it follows that to meet the situation with which we are confronted the application of remedies two-fold in character becomes essential: 1st. To forbid the doing in the future of acts like those which we have found to have been done in the past which would be violative of the statute. 2d. The exertion of such measure of relief as will effectually dissolve the combination found to exist in violation of the statute, and thus neutralize the extension and continually operating force which the possession of the power unlawfully obtained has brought and will continue to bring about.

In applying remedies for this purpose, however, the fact must not be overlooked that injury to the public by the prevention of an undue restraint on, or the monopolization of, trade or commerce, is the foundation upon which the prohibitions of the statute rest, and moreover that one of the fundamental purposes of the statute is to protect, not to destroy, rights of property.

Let us, then, as a means of accurately determining what relief we are to afford, first come to consider what relief was afforded by the court below, in order to fix how far it is necessary to take from or add to that relief, to the end that the prohibitions of the statute may have complete and operative force.

. . . Section 5 of the decree forbade the New Jersey corporation from in any form or manner exercising any ownership or exerting any power directly or indirectly in virtue of its apparent title to the stocks of the subsidiary corporations, and prohibited those subsidiary corporations from paying any dividends to the New Jersey corporations, or doing any act which would recognize further power in that company, except to the extent that it was necessary to enable that company to transfer the stock. So far as the owners of the stock of the subsidiary corporations and the corporations themselves were concerned after the stock had been transferred, Section 6 of the decree enjoined them from in any way conspiring or combining to violate the act, or to monopolize or attempt to monopolize in virtue of their ownership of the stock transferred

to them, and prohibited all agreements between the subsidiary corporations or other stockholders in the future, tending to produce or bring about further violations of the act.

By Section 7, pending the accomplishment of the dissolution of the combination by the transfer of stock, and until it was consummated, the defendants . . . were enjoined from engaging in or carrying on interstate commerce. . . . So far as the decree held that the ownership of the stock of the New Jersey corporation constituted a combination in violation of the 1st section and an attempt to create a monopoly or to monopolize under the 2d section, and commanded the dissolution of the combination, the decree was clearly appropriate. And this also is true of Section 5 of the decree, which restrained both the New Jersey corporation and the subsidiary corporations from doing anything which would recognize or give effect to further ownership in the New Jersey corporation of the stocks which were ordered to be retransferred.

* * *

Our conclusion is that the decree below was right and should be affirmed, except as to the minor matters concerning which we have indicated the decree should be modified. Our order will therefore be one of affirmance, with directions, however, to modify the decree in accordance with this opinion. The court below to retain jurisdiction to the extent necessary to compel compliance in every respect with its decree.

And it is so ordered.

Source:
Supreme Court Reporter, vol. 31, pp. 502–534.

9. Clayton Antitrust Act, 1914

Federal legislation enacted on October 15, 1914, that supplemented the Sherman Antitrust Act and outlawed specific practices that would "substantially lessen competition or tend to create a monopoly in any line of commerce." It prohibited exclusive sales contracts, discrimination in prices among different producers, interlocking directorates in large corporations engaged in the same business, rebates, and the acquisition of stock by one company in another. Labor unions and agricultural cooperatives were exempted from the act on the grounds that "the labor of a human being is not a commodity or article of commerce." As a result, the Clayton Act sought to overcome impediments to collective action by labor, such as the 1908 U.S. Supreme Court decision Loewe v. Lawlor *(208 U.S. 274). In this case, the first applying the Sherman Antitrust Act against organized labor, the Court held that a union boycott constituted a conspiracy in restraint of trade.*

An Act

An Act To supplement existing laws against unlawful restraints and monopolies, and for other purposes.

Be it enacted by the Senate and House of Representatives of the United States of America in Congress assembled, That "antitrust laws," as used herein, includes the Act entitled "An Act to protect trade and commerce against unlawful restraints and monopolies," approved July second, eighteen hundred and ninety; sections seventy-three to seventy-seven, inclusive, of an Act entitled "An Act to reduce taxation, to provide revenue for the Government, and for other purposes," of August twenty-seventh, eighteen hundred and ninety-four; and Act entitled "An Act to amend sections seventy-three and seventy-six of the Act of August twenty-seventh, eighteen hundred and ninety-four, entitled 'An Act to reduce taxation, to provide revenue for the Government, and for other purposes,'" approved February twelfth, nineteen hundred and thirteen, and also this Act.

"Commerce," as used herein, means trade or commerce among the several States and with foreign nations, or between the District of Columbia or any Territory of the United States and any State, Territory, or foreign nation, or between any insular possessions or other places under the jurisdiction of the United States, or between any such possession or place and any State or Territory of the United States or the District of Columbia or any foreign nation, or within the District of Columbia or any Territory or any insular possession or other place under the jurisdiction of the United States: *Provided,* That nothing in this Act contained shall apply to the Philippine Islands.

The word "person" or "persons" wherever used in this Act shall be deemed to include corporations and associations existing under or authorized by the laws of either the United States, the laws of any of the Territories, the laws of any State, or the laws of any foreign country.

Sec. 2. That it shall be unlawful for any person engaged in commerce, in the course of such commerce, either directly or indirectly to discriminate in price between different purchasers of commodities, which commodities are sold for use, consumption, or resale within the United States or any Territory thereof or the District of Columbia or any insular possession or other place under the jurisdiction of the United States, where the effect of such discrimination may be to substantially lessen competition or tend to create a monopoly in any line of commerce: *Provided,* That nothing herein contained shall prevent discrimination in price between purchasers of commodities on account of differences in the grade, quality, or quantity of the commodity sold, or that makes only due allowance for difference in the cost of selling or transportation, or discrimination in price in the same or different communities made in good faith to meet competition: *And provided further,* That nothing herein contained shall prevent persons engaged in selling goods, wares, or merchandise in commerce from selecting their own customers in bona fide transactions and not in restraint of trade.

Sec. 3. That it shall be unlawful for any person engaged in commerce, in the course of such commerce, to lease or make a sale or contract for sale of goods, wares, merchandise, machinery, supplies or other commodities, whether patented or unpatented, for use, consumption or resale within the United States or and Territory thereof or the District of Columbia or any insular possession or other place under the jurisdiction of the United States, or fix a price charged therefor, or discount from, or rebate upon, such price, or the condition, agreement or understanding that the lessee or purchaser thereof shall not use or deal in the goods wares, merchandise, machinery, supplies or other commodities of a competitor or competitors of the lessor or seller, where the effect of such lease, sale, or contract for sale or such condition, agreement or understanding may be to substantially lessen competition or tend to create a monopoly in any line of commerce.

Sec. 4. That any person who shall be injured in his business or property by reason of anything forbidden in the antitrust laws may sue therefor in any district court of the United States in the district in which the defendant resides or is found or has an agent, without respect to the amount in controversy, and shall recover threefold the damages by him sustained, and the cost of suit, including a reasonable attorney's fee.

Sec. 5. That a final judgment or decree hereafter rendered in any criminal prosecution or in any suit or proceeding in equity brought by or on behalf of the United States under the antitrust laws to the effect that a defendant has violated said laws shall be prima facie evidence against such defendant in any suit or proceeding brought by any other party against such defendant under said laws as to all matters respecting which said judgment or decree would be an estoppel as between the parties thereto: *Provided,* This section shall not apply to consent judgments or decrees entered before any testimony has been taken: *Provided further,* This section shall not apply to consent judgments or decrees rendered in criminal proceedings or suits in equity, now pending, in which the taking of testimony has been commenced but has not been concluded, provided such judgments or decrees are rendered before any further testimony is taken.

Whenever any suit or proceeding in equity or criminal prosecution is instituted by the United States to prevent, restrain or punish violations of any of the antitrust laws, to running of the statute of limitations in respect of each and every private right of action arising under said laws and based in whole or in part on any matter complained of in said suit or proceeding shall be suspended during the pendency thereof.

Sec. 6. That the labor of a human being is not a commodity or article of commerce. Nothing contained in the antitrust laws shall be construed to forbid the existence and operation of labor, agricultural, or horticultural organizations, instituted for the purposes of mutual help, and not having capital stock of conducted for profit, or to forbid or restrain individual members of such organizations from lawfully carrying out the legitimate objects thereof; nor shall such organizations, or the members thereof, be held or construed to be illegal combinations or conspiracies in restraint of trade, under the antitrust law.

Sec. 7. That no corporation engaged in commerce shall acquire, directly or indirectly, the whole or any part of the stock or other share capital of another corporation engaged also in commerce, where the effect of such acquisition may be to substantially lessen competition between the corporation whose stock is so acquired and the corporation making the acquisition, or to restrain such commerce in any section or community, or tend to create a monopoly of any line of commerce.

No corporation shall acquire, directly or indirectly, the whole or any part of the stock or other share capital of two or more corporations engaged in commerce where the effect of such acquisition, or the use of such stock by the voting or granting of proxies or otherwise, may be to substantially lessen competition between such corporations, or any of them, whose stock or other share capital is so acquired, or to restrain such commerce in any section or community, or tend to create a monopoly of any line of commerce.

This section shall not apply to corporations purchasing such stock solely for investment and not using the same by voting or otherwise to bring about, or in attempting to bring about, the substantial lessening of competition. Nor shall anything contained in this section prevent a corporation engaged in commerce from causing the formation of subsidiary corporations for the actual carrying on of their immediate lawful business, or the natural and legitimate branches or extensions thereof, or from owning and holding all or a part of the stock of such subsidiary corporations, when the effect of such formation is not to substantially lessen competition.

Nor shall anything herein contained be construed to prohibit any common carrier subject to the laws to regulate commerce from aiding in the construction of branches or short lines so located as to become feeders to the main line of the company so aiding in such construction or from acquiring or owning all or any part of the stock of such branch lines, nor to prevent any such common carrier from acquiring and owning all or any part of the stock of a branch or short line constructed by an independent company where there is no substantial competition between the company owning the branch line so constructed and the company owning the main line acquiring the property or an interest therein, nor to prevent such common carrier from extending any of its lines through the medium of the acquisition of stock or otherwise of any other such common carrier where there is no substantial competition between the company extending its lines and the company whose stock, property, or an interest therein is so acquired.

Nothing contained in this section shall be held to affect or impair any right heretofore legally acquired: *Provided,* That nothing in this section shall be held or construed to authorize or make lawful anything heretofore prohibited or made illegal by the antitrust laws, nor to exempt any person from the penal provisions thereof or the civil remedies therein provided.

Sec. 8. That from and after two years from the date of the approval of this Act no person shall at the same time be a director or other officer or employee of more than one bank, banking association or trust company, organized or operating under the laws of the United States, either of which has deposits, capital, surplus, and undivided profits aggregating more than $5,000,000; and no private banker or person who is a director in any bank or trust company, organized and operating under the laws of a State, having deposits, capital, surplus, and undivided profits aggregating more than $5,000,000 shall be eligible to be a director in any bank or banking association organized or operating under the laws of the United States. The eligibility of a director, officer, or employee under the foregoing provisions shall be determined by the average amount of deposits, capital, surplus, and undivided profits as shown in the official statements of such bank, banking association, or trust company filed provided by law during the fiscal year next preceding the date set for the annual election of directors, and when a director, officer, or employee has been elected or selected in accordance with the provisions of this Act it shall be lawful for him to continue as such for one year thereafter under said election or employment.

No bank, banking association or trust company, organized or operating under the laws of the United States, in any city or incorporated town or village of more than two hundred thousand inhabitants, as shown by the last preceding decennial census of the United States, shall have as a director or other officer or employee any private banker or any director or other officer or employee of any other bank, banking association or trust company located in the same place: *Provided,* That nothing in this section shall apply to mutual savings banks not having a capital stock represented by shares: *Provided further,* That a director or other officer or employee of such bank, banking association or trust company may be a director or other officer or employee of not more than one other bank or trust company organized under the laws of the United States or any State where the entire capital stock of one is owned by stockholders in the other: *And provided further,* That nothing contained in this section shall forbid a director of class A of a Federal reserve bank, as defined in the Federal Reserve Act, from being an officer or director or both an officer and director in one member bank.

That from and after two years from the date of approval of this Act no person at the same time shall be a director in any two or more corporations, any one of which has capital, surplus, and undivided profits aggregating more than $1,000,000, engaged in whole or in part in commerce, other than banks, banking associations, trust companies and common carriers subject to the Act to regulate commerce, approved February fourth, eighteen hundred and eighty-seven, if such corporations are or shall have been theretofore, by virtue of their business and location of operation, competitors, so that the elimination of competition by agreement between them would constitute a violation of any of the provisions of any of the antitrust laws. The eligibility of a director under the foregoing provision shall be determined by the aggregate amount of capital, surplus, and undivided profits, exclusive of dividends declared but not paid to stockholders, at the end of the fiscal year of said corporation next preceding the election of directors, and when a director has been elected in accordance with the provisions of this Act it shall be lawful for him to continue as such for one year thereafter.

When any person elected or chosen as a director or officer or selected as an employee of any bank or other corporation subject to the provisions of this Act is eligible at the time of his election or selection to act for such bank or other corporation in such capacity his eligibility to act in such capacity shall not be affected and he shall not become or be deemed amenable to any of the provisions hereof by reason of any change in the affairs of such bank or other corporation from whatsoever cause, whether specifically excepted by any of the provisions hereof or not, until the expiration of one year from the date of his election or employment.

Sec. 9. Every president, director, officer or manager of any firm, association or corporation engaged in commerce as a common carrier, who embezzles, steals, abstracts or willfully misapplies, or willfully permits to be misapplied, any of the moneys, funds, credits, securities, property or assets of such firm, association or corporation, arising or accruing from, or used in, such commerce, in whole or in part, or willfully or knowingly converts the same to his own use or to the use of another, shall be deemed guilty of a felony and upon conviction shall be fined not less than $500 or confined in the penitentiary not less than one year nor more than ten years, or both, in the discretion of the court.

Prosecutions hereunder may be in the district court of the United States for the district wherein the offense may have been committed.

That nothing in this section shall be held to take away or impair the jurisdiction of the courts of the several States under the laws thereof; and a judgment of conviction or acquittal on the merits under the laws of any State shall be a bar to any prosecution hereunder for the same act or acts.

Sec. 10. That after two years from the approval of this Act no common carrier engaged in commerce shall have any dealings in securities, supplies or other articles of commerce, or shall make or have any contracts for construction or maintenance of any kind, to the amount of more than $50,000, in the aggregate, in any one year, with another corporation, firm, partnership or association when the said common carrier shall have upon its board of directors or as its president, manager or as its purchasing or selling officer, or agent in the particular transaction, any person who is at the same time a director, manager, or purchasing or selling officer of, or who has any substantial interest in, such other corporation, firm, partnership or association, unless and except such purchases shall be made from, or such dealings shall be with, the bidder whose bid is the most favorable to such common carrier, to be ascertained by competitive bidding under regulations to be prescribed by rule or otherwise by the Interstate Commerce Commission. No bid shall be received unless the name and address of the bidder or the names and addresses of the officers, directors and general managers thereof, if the bidder be a corporation, or of the members, if it be a partnership or firm, be given with the bid.

Any person who shall, directly or indirectly, do or attempt to do anything to prevent anyone from bidding or shall do any act to prevent free and fair competition among the bidders or those desiring to bid shall be punished as prescribed in this section in the case of an officer or director.

Every such common carrier having any such transactions or making any such purchases shall within thirty days after making the same file with the Interstate Commerce Commission a full and detailed statement of the transaction showing the manner of the competitive bidding, who were the bidders, and the names and addresses of the directors and officers of the corporations and the members of the firm or partnership bidding; and whenever the said commission shall, after investigation or hearing, have reason to believe that the law has been violated in and about the said purchases or transactions it shall transmit all papers and documents and its own views or findings regarding the transaction to the Attorney General.

If any common carrier shall violate this section it shall be fined not exceeding $25,000; and every such director, agent, manager or officer thereof who shall have knowingly voted for or directed the act constituting such violation or who shall have aided or abetted in such violation shall be deemed guilty of a misdemeanor and shall be fined not exceeding $5,000, or confined in jail not exceeding one year, or both, in the discretion of the court.

Sec. 11. That authority to enforce compliance with sections two, three, seven and eight of this Act by the persons respectively subject thereto is hereby vested: in the Interstate Commerce Commission where applicable to common carriers, in the Federal Reserve Board where applicable to banks, banking associations and trust companies, and in the Federal Trade Commission where applicable to all other character of commerce, to be exercised as follows:

Whenever the commission or board vested with jurisdiction thereof shall have reason to believe that any person is violating or has violated any of the provisions of sections two, three, seven and eight of this Act, it shall issue and serve upon such person a complaint stating its charges in that respect, and containing a notice of a hearing upon a day and at a place therein fixed at least thirty days after the service of said compliant. The person so complained of shall have the right to appear at the place and time so fixed and show cause why an order should not be entered by the commission or board requiring such person to cease and desist from the violation of the law so charged in said complaint. Any person may make application, and upon good cause shown may be allowed by the commission or board, to intervene and appear in said proceeding by counsel or in person. The testimony in any such proceeding shall be reduced to writing and filed in the office of the commission or board. If upon such hearing the commission or board, as the case may be, shall be of the opinion that any of the provisions of said section have been or are being violated, it shall make a report in writing in which it shall state its findings as to the facts, and shall issue and cause to be served on such person an order requiring such person to cease and desist from such violations, and divest itself of the stock held or rid itself of the directors chosen contrary to the provisions of sections seven and eight of this Act, if any there be, in the manner and within the time fixed by said order. Until a transcript of the record in such hearing shall have been filed in a circuit court of appeals of the United States, as hereinafter provided, the commission or board may at any time, upon such notice and in such manner as it shall deem proper, modify or set aside, in whole or in part, any report or any order made or issued by it under this section.

If such person fails or neglects to obey such order of the commission or board while the same is in effect, the commission or board may apply to the circuit court of appeals of the United States, within any circuit where the violation complained of was or is being committed or where such person resides or carries on business, for the enforcement of its order, and shall certify and file with its application a transcript of the entire record in the proceeding, including all the testimony taken and the report and order of the commission or board. Upon such filing of the application and transcript the court shall cause notice thereof to be served upon such person and thereupon shall have jurisdiction of the proceeding and of the question determined therein, and shall have power to make and enter upon the pleadings, testimony, and proceedings set forth in such transcript a decree affirming, modifying, or setting aside the order of the commission or board. The findings of the commission or board as to the facts, if supported by testimony, shall be conclusive. If either party shall apply to the court for leave to adduce additional evidence, and shall show to the satisfaction of the court that such additional evidence is material and that there were reasonable grounds for the failure to adduce such evidence in the proceeding before the commission or board, the court may order such additional evidence to be taken before the commission or board and to be adduced upon the hearing in such manner and upon such terms and conditions as to the court may seem proper. The commission or board may modify its findings as to the facts, or make new findings, by reason of the additional evidence so taken, and it shall file such modified or new findings, which, if supported by testimony, shall be conclusive, and its recommendation, if any, for the modification or setting aside of its original order, with the return of such additional evidence. The judgment and decree of the court shall be final, except that the same shall be subject to review by the Supreme Court upon certiorari as provided in section two hundred and forty of the Judicial Code.

Any party required by such order of the commission or board to cease and desist from a violation charged may obtain a review of such order in said circuit of appeals by filing in the court a written petition praying that the order of the commission or board be set aside. A copy of such petition shall be forthwith served upon the commission or board, and thereupon the commission or board forthwith shall certify and file in the court a transcript of the record as hereinbefore provided. Upon the filing of the transcript the court shall have the same jurisdiction to affirm, set aside, or modify the order of the commission or board as in the case of an application by the commission or board for the enforcement of its order, and the findings of the commission or board as to the facts, if supported by testimony, shall in like manner be conclusive.

The jurisdiction of the circuit court of appeals of the United States to enforce, set aside, or modify orders of the commission or board shall be exclusive.

Such proceedings in the circuit court of appeals shall be given precedence over other cases pending therein, and shall be in every way expedited. No order of the commission or board or the judgment of the court to enforce the same shall in any wise relieve or absolve any person from any liability under the antitrust Acts.

Complaints, orders, and other processes of the commission or board under this section may be served by anyone duly authorized by the commission or board, either (a) by delivering a copy thereof to the person to be served, or to a member of the partnership to be served, or to the president, secretary, or other executive officer or a director of the corporation to be served; or (b) by leaving a copy thereof at the principal office or place of business of such person; or (c) by registering and mailing a copy thereof addressed to such person at his principal office or place of business. The verified return by the person so serving said complaint, order, or other process setting forth the manner of said service shall be proof of the same, and the return post-office receipt for said complaint, order, or other process registered and mailed as aforesaid shall be proof of the service of the same.

Sec. 12. That any suit, action, or proceeding under the antitrust laws against a corporation may be brought not only in the judicial district whereof it is an inhabitant, but also in any district wherein it may be found or transacts business; and all process in such cases may be served in the district of which it is an inhabitant, or wherever it may be found.

Sec. 13. That in any suit, action, or proceeding brought by or on behalf of the United States subpoenas for witnesses who are required to attend a court of the United States in any judicial district in any case, civil or criminal, arising under the antitrust laws may run into any other district: *Provided,* That in civil cases no writ of subpoena shall issue for witnesses living out of the district in which the court is held at a greater distance than one hundred miles from the place of holding the same without the permission of the trial court being first had upon proper application and cause shown.

Sec. 14. That whenever a corporation shall violate any of the penal provisions of the antitrust laws, such violation shall be deemed to be also that of the individual directors, officers, or agents of such corporation who shall have authorized, ordered, or done any of the acts constituting in whole or in part such violation, and such violation shall be deemed a misdemeanor, and upon conviction therefor of any such director, officer, or agent he shall be punished by a fine of not exceeding $5,000 or by imprisonment for not exceeding one year, or by both, in the discretion of the court.

Sec. 15. That the several district courts of the United States are hereby invested with jurisdiction to prevent and restrain violations of this Act, and it shall be the duty of the several district attorneys of the United States, in their respective districts, under the direction of the Attorney General, to institute proceedings in equity to prevent and restrain such violations. Such proceedings may be by way of petition setting forth the case and praying that such violation shall be enjoined or otherwise prohibited. When the parties complained of shall have been duly notified of such petition, the court shall proceed, as soon as may be, to the hearing and determination of the case; and pending such petition, and before final decree, the court may at any time make such temporary restraining order or prohibition as shall be deemed just in the premises. Whenever it shall appear to the court before which any such proceeding may be pending that the ends of justice require that other parties should be brought before the court, the court may cause them to be summoned, whether they reside in the district in which the court is held or not, and subpoenas to that end may be served in any district by the marshal thereof.

Sec. 16. That any person, firm, corporation, or association shall be entitled to sue for and have injunctive relief, in any court of the United States having jurisdiction over the parties, against threatened loss or damage by a violation of the antitrust laws, including sections two, three, seven and eight of this Act, when and under the same conditions and principles as injunctive relief against threatened conduct that will cause loss or damage is granted by courts of equity, under the rules governing such proceedings, and upon the execution of proper bond against damages for an injunction improvidently granted and a showing that the danger of irreparable loss or damage is immediate, a preliminary injunction may issue: *Provided,* That nothing herein contained shall be construed to entitle any person, firm, corporation, or association, except the United States, to bring suit in equity for injunctive relief against any common carrier subject to the provisions of the Act to regulate commerce, approved February fourth, eighteen hundred and eighty-seven, in respect of any matter subject to the regulation, supervision, or other jurisdiction of the Interstate Commerce Commission.

Sec. 17. That no preliminary injunction shall be issued without notice to the opposite party.

No temporary restraining order shall be granted without notice to the opposite party unless it shall clearly appear from specific facts shown by affidavit or by the verified bill that immediate and irreparable injury, loss, or damage will result to the applicant before notice can be served and a hearing had thereon. Every such temporary restraining order shall be indorsed with the date and hour of issuance, shall be forthwith filed in the clerk's office and entered of record, shall define the injury and state why it is irreparable and why the order was granted without notice, and shall by its terms expire within such time after entry, not to exceed ten days, as the court or judge may fix, unless within the time so fixed the order is extended for a like period for good cause shown, and the reasons for such extension shall be entered of record. In case a temporary restraining order shall be granted without notice in the contingency specified, the matter of the issuance of a preliminary injunction shall be set down for a hearing at the earliest possible time and shall take precedence of all matters except older matters of the same character; and when the same comes up for hearing the party obtaining the temporary restraining order shall proceed with the application for a preliminary injunction, and if he does not do so the court shall dissolve the temporary restraining order. Upon two days' notice to the party obtaining such temporary restraining order the opposite party may appear and move the dissolution or modification of the order, and in that event the court or judge shall proceed to hear and determine the motion as expeditiously as the ends of justice may require.

Section two hundred and sixty-three of an Act entitled "An Act to codify, revise, and amend the laws relating to the judiciary," approved March third, nineteen hundred and eleven, is hereby repealed.

Nothing in this section contained shall be deemed to alter, repeal, or amend section two hundred and sixty-six of an Act entitled "An Act to codify, revise, and amend the laws relating to the judiciary," approved March third, nineteen hundred and eleven.

Sec. 18. That, except as otherwise provided in section 16 of this Act, no restraining order or

interlocutory order of injunction shall issue, except upon the giving of security by the applicant in such sum as the court or judge may deem proper, conditioned upon the payment of such costs and damages as may be incurred or suffered by any party who may be found to have been wrongfully enjoined or restrained thereby.

Sec. 19. That every order of injunction or restraining order shall set forth the reasons for the issuance of the same, shall be specific in terms, and shall describe in reasonable detail, and not by reference to the bill of complaint or other document, the act or acts sought to be restrained, and shall be binding only upon the parties to the suit, their officers, agents, servants, employees, and attorneys, or those in active concert or participating with them, and who shall, by personal service or otherwise, have received actual notice of the same.

Sec. 20. That no restraining order or injunction shall be granted by any court of the United States, or a judge or the judges thereof, in any case between an employer and employees, or between employers and employees, or between employees, or between persons employed and persons seeking employment, involving, or growing out of, a dispute concerning terms or conditions of employment, unless necessary to prevent irreparable injury to property, or to a property right, of the party making the application, for which injury there is no adequate remedy at law, and such property or property right must be described with particularity in the application, which must be in writing and sworn to by the applicant or by his agent or attorney.

And no such restraining order or injunction shall prohibit any person or persons, whether singly or in concert, from terminating any relation of employment, or from ceasing to perform any work or labor, or from recommending, advising, or persuading others by peaceful means so to do; or from attending at any place where any such person or persons may lawfully be, for the purpose of peacefully obtaining or communicating information, or from peacefully persuading any person to work or to abstain from working; or from ceasing to patronize or to employ any party to such dispute, or from recommending, advising, or persuading others by peaceful and lawful means so to do; or from paying or giving to, or withholding from, any person engaged in such dispute, any strike benefits or other moneys or things of value; or from peaceably assembling in a lawful manner, and for lawful purposes; or from doing any act or thing which might lawfully be done in the absence of such dispute by any party thereto; nor shall any of the acts specified in this paragraph be considered or held to be violations of any law of the United States.

Sec. 21. That any person who shall willfully disobey any lawful writ, process, order, rule, decree, or command of any district court of the United States or any court of the District of Columbia by doing any act or thing therein, or thereby forbidden to be done by him, if the act or thing so done by him be of such character as to constitute also a criminal offense under any statute of the United States, or under the laws of any State in which the act was committed, shall be proceeded against for his said contempt as hereinafter provided.

Sec. 22. That whenever it shall be made to appear to any district court of judge thereof, or to any judge therein sitting, by the return of a proper officer on lawful process, or upon the affidavit of some credible person, or by information filed by any district attorney, that there is reasonable ground to believe that any person has been guilty of such contempt, the court or judge thereof, or any judge therein sitting, may issue a rule requiring the said person so charged to show cause upon a day certain why he should not be punished therefor, which rule, together with a copy of the affidavit or information, shall be served upon the person charged, with sufficient promptness to enable him to prepare for and make return to the order at the time fixed therein. If upon or by such return, in the judgment of the court, the alleged contempt be not sufficiently purged, a trial shall be directed at a time and place fixed by the court:

Provided, however, That if the accused, being a natural person, fail or refuse to make return to the rule to show cause, an attachment may issue against his person to compel an answer, and in case of his continued failure or refusal, or if for any reason it be impracticable to dispose of the matter on the return day, he may be required to give reasonable bail for his attendance at the trial and his submission to the final judgment of the court. Where the accused is a body corporate, an attachment for the sequestration of its property may be issued upon like refusal or failure to answer.

In all cases within the purview of this Act such trial may be by the court, or, upon demand of the accused, by a jury; in which latter event the court may impanel a jury from the jurors then in attendance, or the court or the judge thereof in chambers may cause a sufficient number of jurors to be selected and summoned, as provided by law, to attend at the time and place of trial, at which time a jury shall be selected and impaneled as upon a trial for misdemeanor; and such trial shall conform, as near as may be, to the practice in criminal cases prosecuted by indictment or upon information.

If the accused be found guilty, judgment shall be entered accordingly, prescribing the punishment, either by fine or imprisonment, or both, in the discretion of the court. Such fine shall be paid to the United States or to the complainant or other party injured by the act constituting the contempt, or may, where more than one is so damaged, be divided or apportioned among them as the court may direct, but in no case shall the fine to be paid to the United States exceed, in case the accused is a natural person, the sum of $1,000, nor shall such imprisonment exceed the term of six months: *Provided,* That in any case the court or a judge thereof may, for good cause shown, by affidavit or proof taken in open court or before such judge and filed with the papers in the case, dispense with the rule to show cause, and may issue an attachment for the arrest of the person charged with contempt; in which event such person, when arrested, shall be brought before such court or a judge thereof without unnecessary delay and shall be admitted to bail in a reasonable penalty for his appearance to answer to the charge or for trial for the contempt; and thereafter the proceedings shall be the same as provided herein in case the rule had issued in the first instance.

Sec. 23. That the evidence taken upon the trial of any persons so accused may be preserved by bill of exceptions, and any judgment of conviction may be reviewed upon writ of error in all respects as now provided by law in criminal cases, and may be affirmed, reversed, or modified as justice may require. Upon the granting of such writ of error, execution of judgment shall be stayed, and the accused, if thereby sentenced to imprisonment, shall be admitted to bail in such reasonable sum as may be required by the court, or by any justice, or any judge of any district court of the United States or any court of the District of Columbia.

Sec. 24. That nothing herein contained shall be construed to relate to contempts committed in the presence of the court, or so near thereto as to obstruct the administration of justice, nor to contempts committed in disobedience of any lawful writ, process, order, rule, decree, or command entered in any suit or action brought or prosecuted in the name of, or on behalf of, the United States, but the same, and all other cases of contempt not specifically embraced within section twenty-one of this Act, may be punished in conformity to the usages at law and in equity now prevailing.

Sec. 25. That no proceeding for contempt shall be instituted against any person unless begun within one year from the date of the act complained of; nor shall any such proceeding be a bar to any criminal prosecution for the same act or acts; but nothing herein contained shall affect any proceedings in contempt pending at the time of the passage of this Act.

Sec. 26. If any clause, sentence, paragraph, or part of this Act shall, for any reason, be adjudged by any court of competent jurisdiction to be invalid, such judgment shall not affect, impair, or invalidate the remainder thereof, but shall be confined in its operation to the clause, sentence, paragraph, or part thereof directly involved in the controversy in which such judgment shall have been rendered.

Source:
Statutes at Large, vol. 38, pp. 730–740.

10. FRANKLIN D. ROOSEVELT, "FORGOTTEN MAN" RADIO SPEECH, 1932

National radio address delivered by Franklin D. Roosevelt, then Democratic governor of New York, on April 7, 1932, in which he argued that hope for national economic recovery from the Great Depression resided with the ordinary farmer and industrial worker—"the forgotten man at the bottom of the economic pyramid." Roosevelt spoke from Albany under the auspices of the Democratic National Committee. An emerging presidential candidate, he used the speech to present his alternative to the Republican Hoover administration's economic reform effort. Roosevelt likened the nation's economic crisis in 1932 to the grave emergency America faced in 1917 as it entered World War I. Just as America had mobilized economically for war from "bottom to top," he asserted, so it now must do to survive the Depression. An economic reform program, he said, must rest upon the "forgotten man," who represented the indispensable unit of economic power. Roosevelt advocated federal measures to restore the farmer's purchasing power, provide mortgage relief to small banks and home owners, and lower tariffs to promote export markets for American goods.

Although I understand that I am talking under the auspices of the Democratic National Committee, I do not want to limit myself to politics. I do not want to feel that I am addressing an audience of Democrats, nor that I speak merely as a Democrat myself. The present condition for our national affairs is too serious to be viewed through partisan eyes for partisan purposes.

Fifteen years ago my public duty called me to an active part in a great national emergency—the World War. Success then was due to a leadership whose vision carried beyond the timorous and futile gesture of sending a tiny army of 150,000 trained soldiers and the regular Navy to the aid of our Allies.

The generalship of that moment conceived of a whole nation mobilized for war, economic, industrial, social and military resources gathered into a vast unit, capable of and actually in the process of throwing into the scales 10,000,000 men equipped with physical needs and sustained by the realization that behind them were the united efforts of 110,000,000 human beings. It was a great plan because it was built from bottom to top and not from top to bottom.

In my calm judgment, the nation faces today a more grave emergency than in 1917.

It is said that Napoleon lost the Battle of Waterloo because he forgot his infantry. He staked too much upon the more spectacular but less substantial cavalry.

The present Administration in Washington provides a close parallel. It has either forgotten or it does not want to remember the infantry of our economic army.

These unhappy times call for the building of plans that rest upon the forgotten, the unorganized but the indispensable units of economic power, for plans like those of 1917 that build from the bottom up and not from the top down, that put their faith once more in the forgotten man at the bottom of the economic pyramid.

Obviously, these few minutes tonight permit no opportunity to lay down the ten or a dozen closely related objectives of a plan to meet our present emergency, but I can draw a few essentials, a beginning, in fact, of a planned program.

It is the habit of the unthinking to turn in times like this to the illusions of economic magic. People suggest that huge expenditures of public funds by the Federal Government and by State and local governments will completely solve the unemployment problem. But it is clear that even if we could raise many billions of dollars and find definitely useful public works to spend these billions on, even all that money would not give employment to the 7,000,000 or 10,000,000 people who are out of work.

Let us admit frankly that it would be only a stopgap. A real economic cure must go to the killing of bacteria in the system rather than to the treatment of external symptoms.

How much do the shallow thinkers realize, for example, that approximately one-half of our population, fifty or sixty million people, earn their living by farming or in small towns where existence immediately depends on farms. They have today lost their purchasing power. Why? They are receiving for farm products less than the cost to them of growing these farm products.

The result of this loss of purchasing power is that many other millions of people engaged in industry in the cities cannot sell industrial products to the farming half of the nation. This brings home to every city worker that his own employment is directly tied up with the farmer's dollar. No nation can long continue half bankrupt. Main Street, Broadway, the mills, the mines will close if half of the buyers are broke.

I cannot escape the conclusion that one of the essentials of a national program of restoration must be to restore purchasing power to the farming half of the country. Without this the wheels of railroads and of factories will not turn.

Closely associated with this first objective is the problem of keeping the home-owner and the farm-owner where he is, without being dispossessed through the foreclosure of his mortgage.

His relationship to the great banks of Chicago and New York is pretty remote. The two billion dollar fund which President Hoover and the Congress have put at the disposal of the big banks, the railroads and the corporations of the nation is not for him.

His is a relationship to his little local bank or local loan company. It is a sad fact that even though the local lender in many cases does not want to evict the farmer or homeowner by foreclosure proceedings, he is forced to do so in order to keep his bank or company solvent. Here should be an objective of government itself, to provide at least as much assistance to the little fellow as it is now giving to the large banks and corporations. That is another example of building from the bottom up.

One other objective closely related to the problem of selling American products is to provide a tariff policy based upon economic common sense rather than upon politics—hot air—pull.

This country during the past few years, culminating with the Hawley-Smoot Tariff of 1929, has compelled the world to build tariff fences so high that world trade is decreasing to the vanishing point. The value of goods internationally exchanged is today less than half of what it was three or four years ago.

Every man and woman who gives any thought to the subject knows that if our factories run even 80 per cent of capability they will turn out more products than we as a nation can possibly use ourselves.

The answer is that if they are to run on 80 per cent of capacity we must sell some goods abroad. How can we do that if the outside nations cannot pay us in cash—and we know by sad experience that they cannot do that. The only way they can pay us is in their own goods or raw materials, but this foolish tariff of ours makes that impossible.

What we must do is this: To revise our tariff on the basis of a reciprocal exchange of goods, allowing other nations to buy and to pay for our goods by sending us such of their goods as will not seriously throw any of our industries out of balance, and, incidentally, making impossible in this county the continuance of pure monopolies

which cause us to pay excessive prices for many of the necessities of life.

Such objectives as these three—restoring farmers' buying power, relief to the small banks and homeowners and a reconstructed tariff policy—these are only a part of ten or a dozen vital factors.

But they seem to be beyond the concern of a National Administration which can think in terms only of the top of the social and economic structure. They have sought temporary relief from the top down rather than permanent relief from the bottom up. They have totally failed to plan ahead in a comprehensive way. They have waited until something has cracked and then at the last moment have sought to prevent total collapse.

It is high time to get back to fundamentals. It is high time to admit with courage that we are in the midst of an emergency at least equal to that of war. Let us mobilize to meet it.

Source:

Landmark Documents in American History, Facts On File, Inc.

11. SECURITIES EXCHANGE ACT, 1934

Federal legislation enacted on June 6, 1934, that established the Securities and Exchange Commission (SEC) to regulate American stock exchanges and to enforce the U.S. Securities Act enacted May 27, 1933. The latter act was designed to ensure full disclosure to purchasers of all stocks and bonds offered for public sale (with the exception of certain government bonds, railroad securities, and securities of some nonprofit institutions). The securities were to be registered with the U.S. Federal Trade Commission, and such registration had to include accurate and complete financial and other relevant information, as well as a prospectus. The prospectus was required to be given to every potential investor. The act imposed stiff penalties for the sale of misrepresented or unregistered securities.

The SEC, consisting of five members appointed by the president and approved by the Senate, was authorized to license stock exchanges and regulate securities trading. To prevent unfair and deceptive practices, the act required that current information about corporations whose securities were traded be made available to investors and that each security traded be registered with the SEC. The Federal Reserve Board was authorized to regulate margin requirements in securities trading so as to reduce speculation. Roosevelt appointed financier and speculator Joseph P. Kennedy, father of the future president, as the SEC's first chair, because "he knew the tricks of the trade."

Congress designed both acts to curb the problems that led to the stock market crash of 1929. While recessions occurred periodically after the 1930s, the country did not suffer a major depression again in the 20th century. However, a number of securities regulations were modified or abrogated during the prosperity of the 1990s. By taking advantage of loopholes the changes had opened, and through downright corruption, corporate executives contributed to a severe downturn in the stock markets of the first years of the 21st century.

An Act

To provide for the regulation of securities exchanges and of over-the-counter markets operating in interstate and foreign commerce and through the mails, to prevent inequitable and unfair practices on such exchanges and markets, and for other purposes.

Be it enacted by the Senate and House of Representatives of the United States of America in Congress assembled,

Title I—Regulation of Securities Exchanges
Short Title

Section 1. This Act may be cited as the "Securities Exchange Act of 1934."

Necessity for Regulation as Provided in This Title

Sec. 2. For the reasons hereinafter enumerated, transactions in securities as commonly conducted upon securities exchanges and over-the-counter markets are affected with a national public interest which makes it necessary to provide for regulation and control of such transactions and of practices and matters related thereto, including transactions by officers, directors, and principal security holders, to require appropriate reports, and to impose requirements necessary to make such regulation and control reasonably complete and effective, in order to protect interstate commerce, the national credit, the Federal taxing power, to protect and make more effective the national banking system and Federal Reserve System, and to insure the maintenance of fair and honest markets in such transactions:

(1) Such transactions (a) are carried on in large volume by the public generally and in large part originate outside the States in which the exchanges and over-the-counter markets are located and/or are effected by means of the mails and instrumentalities of interstate commerce; (b) constitute an important part of the current of interstate commerce; (c) involve in large part the securities of issuers engaged in interstate commerce; (d) involve the use of credit, directly affect the financing of trade, industry, and transportation in interstate commerce, and directly affect and influence the volume of interstate commerce; and affect the national credit.

(2) The prices established and offered in such transactions are generally disseminated and quoted throughout the United States and foreign countries and constitute a basis for determining and establishing the prices at which securities are bought and sold, the amount of certain taxes owing to the United States and to the several States by owners, buyers, and sellers of securities, and the value of collateral for bank loans.

(3) Frequently the prices of securities on such exchanges and markets are susceptible to manipulation and control, and the dissemination of such prices gives rise to excessive speculation, resulting in sudden and unreasonable fluctuations in the prices of securities which (a) cause

alternately unreasonable expansion and unreasonable contraction of the volume of credit available for trade, transportation, and industry in interstate commerce, (b) hinder the proper appraisal of the value of securities and thus prevent a fair calculation of taxes owing to the United States and to the several States by owners, buyers, and sellers of securities, and (c) prevent the fair valuation of collateral for bank loans and/or obstruct the effective operation of the national banking system and Federal Reserve System.

(4) National emergencies, which produce widespread unemployment and the dislocation of trade, transportation, and industry, and which burden interstate commerce and adversely affect the general welfare, are precipitated, intensified, and prolonged by manipulation and sudden and unreasonable fluctuations of security prices and by excessive speculation on such exchanges and markets, and to meet such emergencies the Federal Government is put to such great expense as to burden the national credit.

Source:
United States Statutes at Large, vol. 48, pp. 881–909.

12. NATIONAL LABOR RELATIONS ACT, 1935

New Deal legislation, enacted on July 5, 1935, that created the National Labor Relations Board (NLRB) and guaranteed workers the right to organize and to bargain collectively through their chosen representatives. It represented a major landmark in the history of the labor movement.

Previously, in an act of March 23, 1932, Congress forbade the use of federal court injunctions to preserve antiunion employment contracts or to restrain strikes, boycotts, or picketing, except where such strikes affected the public safety. Sponsored by Senator George W. Norris of Nebraska and Representative Fiorello LaGuardia of New York, it protected workers' rights to join a union by prohibiting

"yellow dog" contracts (agreements by which employers required their workers not to join unions and not to participate in any strike against the employers).

The National Labor Relations Act was also sponsored by Senator Wagner joined by Representative William P. Connery Jr. of Massachusetts. It authorized the NLRB to investigate complaints, issue cease-and-desist orders against unfair labor practices in interstate commerce, protect the right to collective bargaining, and arbitrate labor disputes. It prohibited employers from interfering with workers' rights to organize or to join independent unions, from promoting company unions, from discriminating in employment because of union membership, from punishing employees who file charges or testify under the act, and from refusing to negotiate with an elected union.

Its constitutionality was upheld 5-4 on April 12, 1937 in NLRB v. Jones and Laughlin Steel Corporation (301 U.S. 1).

An Act
To diminish the causes of labor disputes burdening or obstructing interstate and foreign commerce, to create a National Labor Relations Board, and for other purposes.

Be it enacted by the Senate and House of Representatives of the United States of America in Congress assembled,

Findings and Policy
Section 1. The denial by employers of the right of employees to organize and the refusal by employers to accept the procedure of collective bargaining lead to strikes and other forms of industrial strife or unrest, which have the intent or the necessary effect of burdening or obstructing commerce by (a) impairing the efficiency, safety, or operation of the instrumentalities of commerce; (b) occurring in the current of commerce; (c) materially affecting, restraining, or controlling the flow of raw materials or manufactured or processed goods from or into the

channels of commerce, or the prices of such materials or goods in commerce; or (d) causing diminution of employment and wages in such volume as substantially to impair or disrupt the market for goods flowing from or into the channels of commerce.

The inequality of bargaining power between employees who do not possess full freedom of association or actual liberty of contract, and employers who are organized in the corporate or other forms of ownership association substantially burdens and affects the flow of commerce, and tends to aggravate recurrent business depressions, by depressing wage rates and the purchasing power of wage earners in industry and by preventing the stabilization of competitive wage rates and working conditions within and between industries.

Experience has proved that protection by law of the right of employees to organize and bargain collectively safeguards commerce from injury, impairment, or interruption, and promotes the flow of commerce by removing certain recognized sources of industrial strife and unrest, by encouraging practices fundamental to the friendly adjustment of industrial disputes arising out of differences as to wages, hours, or other working conditions, and by restoring equality of bargaining power between employers and employees.

It is hereby declared to be the policy of the United States to eliminate the causes of certain substantial obstructions to the free flow of commerce and to mitigate and eliminate these obstructions when they have occurred by encouraging the practice and procedure of collective bargaining and by protecting the exercise by workers of full freedom of association, self-organization, and designation of representatives of their own choosing, for the purpose of negotiating the terms and conditions of their employment or other mutual aid or protection...

Rights of Employees

Sec. 7. Employees shall have the right to self-organization, to form, join, or assist labor organizations, to bargain collectively through representatives of their own choosing, and to engage in concerted activities, for the purpose of collective bargaining or other mutual aid or protection.

Sec. 8. It shall be an unfair labor practice for an employer—

(1) To interfere with, restrain, or coerce employees in the exercise of the rights guaranteed in section 7.

(2) To dominate or interfere with the formation or administration of any labor organization or contribute financial or other support to it: *Provided,* That subject to rules and regulations made and published by the Board pursuant to section 6(a), an employer shall not be prohibited from permitting employees to confer with him during working hours without loss of time or pay.

(3) By discrimination in regard to hire or tenure of employment or any term or condition of employment to encourage or discourage membership in any labor organization: *Provided,* That nothing in this Act, or in the National Industrial Recovery Act (U.S.C., Supp. VII, title 15, secs. 701-712), as amended from time to time, or in any code or agreement approved or prescribed thereunder, or in any other statute of the United States, shall preclude an employer from making an agreement with a labor organization (not established, maintained, or assisted by any action defined in this Act as an unfair labor practice) to require as a condition of employment membership therein, if such labor organization is the representative of the employees as provided in section 9(a), in the appropriate collective bargaining unit covered by such agreement when made.

(4) To discharge or otherwise discriminate against an employee because he has filed charges or given testimony under this Act.

(5) To refuse to bargain collectively with the representatives of his employees, subject to the provisions of Section 9(a).

Source:
Statutes at Large, Vol. 48, pp. 449–457.

13. Dwight D. Eisenhower's "Military-Industrial Complex" Address, 1961

Address to the American public delivered by U.S. president Dwight D. "Ike" Eisenhower on January 17, 1961, as he prepared to leave office. Eisenhower pointed out the dangers not only of the ruthless, hostile communist ideology but also of the military establishment and arms industry built to combat communism's global ambitions. He warned against "the acquisition of unwarranted influence, whether sought or unsought, by the military-industrial complex," whose enormous power, if not properly meshed with peaceful methods and goals, could threaten American liberties and the democratic process. He also warned that centralized research could inhibit intellectual curiosity and that public policy could become "the captive of the scientific-technological elite." He urged the nation not to plunder tomorrow's resources for today's comforts and argued that disarmament must be a continuing imperative.

My fellow Americans:

Three days from now, after half a century in the service of our country, I shall lay down the responsibilities of office as, in traditional and solemn ceremony, the authority of the Presidency is vested in my successor.

This evening I come to you with a message of leave-taking and farewell, and to share a few final thoughts with you, my countrymen.

Like every other citizen, I wish the new President, and all who will labor with him, God-speed. I pray that the coming years will be blessed with peace and prosperity for all. Our people expect their President and the Congress to find essential agreement on issues of great moment, the wise resolution of which will better shape the future of the Nation. My own relations with the Congress, which began on a remote and tenuous basis when, long ago, a member of the Senate appointed me to West Point, have since ranged to the intimate during the war and immediate post-war period, and, finally, to the mutually interdependent during these past eight years.

In this final relationship, the Congress and the Administration have, on most vital issues, cooperated well, to serve the national good rather than mere partisanship, and so have assured that the business of the Nation should go forward. So, my official relationship with the Congress ends in a feeling, on my part, of gratitude that we have been able to do so much together.

II.

We now stand ten years past the midpoint of a century that has witnessed four major wars among great nations. Three of these involved our own country. Despite these holocausts America is today the strongest, the most influential and most productive nation in the world. Understandably proud of this pre-eminence, we yet realize that America's leadership and prestige depend, not merely upon our unmatched material progress, riches and military strength, but on how we use our power in the interests of world peace and human betterment.

III.

Throughout America's adventure in free government, our basic purposes have been to keep the peace; to foster progress in human achievement, and to enhance liberty, dignity and integrity among people and among nations. To strive for less would be unworthy of a free and religious people. Any failure traceable to arrogance, or our lack of comprehension or readiness to sacrifice would inflict upon us grievous hurt both at home and abroad.

Progress toward these noble goals is persistently threatened by the conflict now engulfing the world. It commands our whole attention, absorbs our very beings. We face a hostile ideology—global in scope, atheistic in character, ruthless in purpose, and insidious in method. Unhappily the danger it poses promises to be of indefinite duration. To meet it successfully, there is called for, not so much the emotional and transitory sacrifices of crisis, but rather those which enable us to carry forward steadily, surely, and without complaint the burdens of a prolonged and complex struggle—with liberty the stake. Only thus shall we remain, despite every provocation, on our charted course toward permanent peace and human betterment.

Crises there will continue to be. In meeting them, whether foreign or domestic, great or small, there is a recurring temptation to feel that some spectacular and costly action could become the miraculous solution to all current difficulties. A huge increase in newer elements of our defense; development of unrealistic programs to cure every ill in agriculture; a dramatic expansion in basic and applied research—these and many other possibilities, each possibly promising in itself, may be suggested as the only way to the road we wish to travel.

But each proposal must be weighed in the light of a broader consideration: the need to maintain balance in and among national programs—balance between the private and the public economy, balance between cost and hoped for advantage—balance between the clearly necessary and the comfortably desirable; balance between our essential requirements as a nation and the duties imposed by the nation upon the individual; balance between actions of the moment and the national welfare of the future. Good judgment seeks balance and progress; lack of it eventually finds imbalance and frustration.

The record of many decades stands as proof that our people and their government have, in the main, understood these truths and have responded to them well, in the face of stress and threat. But threats, new in kind or degree, constantly arise. I mention two only.

IV.

A vital element in keeping the peace is our military establishment. Our arms must be mighty, ready for instant action, so that no potential aggressor may be tempted to risk his own destruction.

Our military organization today bears little relation to that known by any of my predecessors in peacetime, or indeed by the fighting men of World War II or Korea. Until the latest of our world conflicts, the United States had no armaments industry. American makers of plowshares could, with time and as required, make swords as well. But now we can no longer risk emergency improvisation of national defense; we have been compelled to create a permanent armaments industry of vast proportions. Added to this, three and a half million men and women are directly engaged in the defense establishment. We annually spend on military security more than the net income of all United States corporations.

This conjunction of an immense military establishment and a large arms industry is new in the American experience. The total influence—economic, political, even spiritual—is felt in every city, every State house, every office of the Federal government. We recognize the imperative need for this development. Yet we must not fail to comprehend its grave implications. Our toil, resources and livelihood are all involved; so is the very structure of our society.

In the councils of government, we must guard against the acquisition of unwarranted influence, whether sought or unsought, by the military-industrial complex. The potential for the disastrous rise of misplaced power exists and will persist.

We must never let the weight of this combination endanger our liberties or democratic processes. We should take nothing for granted. Only an alert and knowledgeable citizenry can compel the proper meshing of the huge industrial and military machinery of defense with our peaceful methods and goals, so that security and liberty may prosper together. Akin to, and largely responsible for the sweeping changes in our industrial-military posture, has been the technological revolution during recent decades.

In this revolution, research has become central; it also becomes more formalized, complex, and costly. A steadily increasing share is conducted for, by, or at the direction of, the Federal government.

Today, the solitary inventor, tinkering in his shop, has been over-shadowed by task forces of scientists in laboratories and testing fields. In the same fashion, the free university, historically the fountainhead of free ideas and scientific discovery, has experienced a revolution in the conduct of research. Partly because of the huge costs involved, a government contract becomes virtually a substitute for intellectual curiosity. For every old blackboard there are now hundreds of new electronic computers.

The prospect of domination of the nation's scholars by Federal employment, project allocations, and the power of money is ever present—and is gravely to be regarded. Yet, in holding scientific research and discovery in respect, as we should, we must also be alert to the equal and opposite danger that public policy could itself become the captive of a scientific-technological elite.

It is the task of statesmanship to mold, to balance, and to integrate these and other forces, new and old, within the principles of our democratic system—ever aiming toward the supreme goals of our free society.

V.

Another factor in maintaining balance involves the element of time. As we peer into society's future, we—you and I, and our government—must avoid the impulse to live only for today, plundering, for our own ease and convenience, the precious resources of tomorrow. We cannot mortgage the material assets of our grandchildren without risking the loss also of their political and spiritual heritage. We want democracy to survive for all generations to come, not to become the insolvent phantom of tomorrow.

VI.

Down the long lane of the history yet to be written America knows that this world of ours, ever growing smaller, must avoid becoming a community of dreadful fear and hate, and be instead, a proud confederation of mutual trust and respect.

Such a confederation must be one of equals. The weakest must come to the conference table with the same confidence as do we, protected as we are by our moral, economic, and military strength. That table, though scarred by many past frustrations, cannot be abandoned for the certain agony of the battlefield.

Disarmament, with mutual honor and confidence, is a continuing imperative. Together we must learn how to compose differences, not with arms, but with intellect and decent purpose. Because this need is so sharp and apparent I confess that I lay down my official responsibilities in this field with a definite sense of disappointment. As one who has witnessed the horror and the lingering sadness of war—as one who knows that another war could utterly destroy this civilization which has been so slowly and painfully built over thousands of years—I wish I could say tonight that a lasting peace is in sight. Happily, I can say that war has been avoided. Steady progress toward our ultimate goal has been made. But, so much remains to be done. As a private citizen, I shall never cease to do what little I can to help the world advance along that road.

VII.

So—in this my last good night to you as your President—I thank you for the many opportunities you have given me for public service in war and peace. I trust that in that service you find some things worthy; as for the rest of it, I know you will find ways to improve performance in the future.

You and I—my fellow citizens—need to be strong in our faith that all nations, under God, will reach the goal of peace with justice. May we be ever unswerving in devotion to principle, confident but humble with power, diligent in pursuit of the Nation's great goals. To all the peoples of the world, I once more give expression to America's prayerful and continuing aspiration:

We pray that peoples of all faiths, all races, all nations, may have their great human needs satisfied; that those now denied opportunity shall come to enjoy it to the full; that all who yearn for freedom may experience its spiritual blessings; that those who have freedom will understand, also, its heavy responsibilities; that all who are insensitive to the needs of others will learn charity; that the scourges of poverty, disease and ignorance will be made to disappear from the earth, and that, in the goodness of time, all peoples will come to live together in a peace guaranteed by the binding force of mutual respect and love.

Source:

Public Papers of the Presidents, Dwight D. Eisenhower, 1960, pp. 1,035–1,040.

14. RONALD REAGAN'S ADDRESS TO THE NATION ON THE ECONOMY, 1981

President Ronald Reagan gave his first broadcast address to the nation on February 5, 1981. His topic was the state of the economy. He warned that the nation was facing its "worst economic mess since the Great Depression," and he urged the adoption of his economic program. He called for tax cuts to stimulate investment and for reduced government spending to cut inflation and unemployment. He asked Congress and business and labor groups to cooperate with his efforts. Reagan used a number of visual aids to illustrate his remarks, including charts with red and blue lines to indicate tax and spending trends, as well as a crumpled dollar bill (which he held in one hand) and a quarter, a dime, and a penny (which he held in the other) to demonstrate how the 1960 value of a dollar had fallen to 36 cents.

───────── ⟨∞⟩ ─────────

Good evening.

I'm speaking to you tonight to give you a report on the state of our Nation's economy. I regret to say that we're in the worst economic mess since the Great Depression.

A few days ago I was presented with a report I'd asked for, a comprehensive audit, if you will, of our economic condition. You won't like it. I didn't like it. But we have to face the truth and then go to work to turn things around. And make no mistake about it, we can turn them around.

I'm not going to subject you to the jumble of charts, figures, and economic jargon of that audit, but rather will try to explain where we are, how we got there, and how we can get back. First, however, let me just give a few "attention getters" from the audit.

The Federal budget is out of control, and we face runaway deficits of almost $480 billion for this budget year that ends September 30th. That deficit is larger than the entire Federal budget in 1957, and so is the almost $80 billion we will pay in interest this year on the national debt.

Twenty years ago, in 1960, our Federal Government payroll was less than $13 billion. Today it is $75 billion. During these 20 years our population has only increased by 23.3 percent. The Federal budget has gone up 528 percent.

Now, we've just had 2 years of back-to-back double-digit inflation—13.3 percent in 1979, 12.4 percent last year. The last time this happened was in World War I.

In 1960 mortgage interest rates averaged about 6 percent. They're 2 1/2 times as high now, 15.4 percent.

The percentage of your earnings the Federal Government took in taxes in 1960 has almost doubled.

And finally there are 7 million Americans caught up in the personal indignity and human tragedy of unemployment. If they stood in a line, allowing 3 feet for each person, the line would reach from the coast of Maine to California.

Well, so much for the audit itself. Let me try to put this in personal terms. Here is a dollar such as you earned, spent, or saved in 1960. And here is a quarter, a dime, and a penny—36 cents. That's what this 1960 dollar is worth today. And if the present world inflation rate should continue 3 more years, that dollar of 1960 will be worth a quarter. What initiative is there to save? And if we don't save we're short of the investment capital needed for business and industry expansion. Workers in Japan and West Germany save several times the percentage of their income than Americans do.

What's happened to that American dream of owning a home? Only 10 years ago a family could buy a home, and the monthly payment averaged little more than a quarter—27 cents out of each dollar earned. Today, it takes 42 cents out of every dollar of income. So, fewer than 1 out of 11 families can afford to buy their first new home.

Regulations adopted by government with the best of intentions have added $666 to the cost of an automobile. It is estimated that together regulations of every kind, on shopkeepers, farmers, and major industries, add $100 billion or more to the cost of the goods and services we buy. And then another $20 billion is spent by government handling the paperwork created by those regulations.

I'm sure you're getting the idea that the audit presented to me found government policies of the last few decades responsible for our economic troubles. We forgot or just overlooked the fact that government—any government—has a built-in tendency to grow. Now, we all had a hand in looking to government for benefits as if government had some source of revenue other than our earnings. Many if not most of the things we thought of or that government offered to us seemed attractive.

In the years following the Second World War it was easy, for a while at least, to overlook the price tag. Our income more than doubled in the 25 years after the war. We increased our take-home pay in those 25 years by more than we had amassed in all the preceding 150 years put together. Yes, there was some inflation, 1 or 1 1/2 percent a year. That didn't bother us. But if we look back at those golden years, we recall that even then voices had been raised, warning that inflation, like radioactivity, was cumulative and that once started it could get out of control.

Some government programs seemed so worthwhile that borrowing to fund them didn't

bother us. By 1960 our national debt stood at $284 billion. Congress in 1971 decided to put a ceiling of $400 billion on our ability to borrow. Today the debt is $934 billion. So-called temporary increases or extensions in the debt ceiling have been allowed 21 times in these 10 years, and now I've been forced to ask for another increase in the debt ceiling or the government will be unable to function past the middle of February—and I've only been here 16 days. Before we reach the day when we can reduce the debt ceiling, we may in spite of our best efforts see a national debt in excess of a trillion dollars. Now, this is a figure that's literally beyond our comprehension.

We know now that inflation results from all that deficit spending. Government has only two ways of getting money other than raising taxes. It can go into the money market and borrow, competing with its own citizens and driving up interest rates, which it has done, or it can print money, and it's done that. Both methods are inflationary.

We're victims of language. The very word "inflation" leads us to think of it as just high prices. Then, of course, we resent the person who puts on the price tags, forgetting that he or she is also a victim of inflation. Inflation is not just high prices; it's a reduction in the value of our money. When the money supply is increased but the goods and services available for buying are not, we have too much money chasing too few goods. Wars are usually accompanied by inflation. Everyone is working or fighting, but production is of weapons and munitions, not things we can buy and use.

Now, one way out would be to raise taxes so that government need not borrow or print money. But in all these years of government growth, we've reached, indeed surpassed, the limit of our people's tolerance or ability to bear an increase in the tax burden. Prior to World War II, taxes were such that on the average we only had to work just a little over 1 month each year to pay our total Federal, State, and local tax bill. Today we have to work 4 months to pay that bill.

Some say shift the tax burden to business and industry, but business doesn't pay taxes. Oh, don't get the wrong idea. Business is being taxed, so much so that we're being priced out of the world market. But business must pass its costs of operations—and that includes taxes—on to the customer in the price of the product. Only people pay taxes, all the taxes. Government just uses business in a kind of sneaky way to help collect the taxes. They're hidden in the price; we aren't aware of how much tax we actually pay.

Today this once great industrial giant of ours has the lowest rate of gain in productivity of virtually all the industrial nations with whom we must compete in the world market. We can't even hold our own market here in America against foreign automobiles, steel, and a number of other products. Japanese production of automobiles is almost twice as great per worker as it is in America. Japanese steelworkers outproduce their American counterparts by about 25 percent.

Now, this isn't because they're better workers. I'll match the American working man or woman against anyone in the world. But we have to give them the tools and equipment that workers in the other industrial nations have.

We invented the assembly line and mass production, but punitive tax policies and excessive and unnecessary regulations plus government borrowing have stifled our ability to update plant and equipment. When capital investment is made, it's too often for some unproductive alterations demanded by government to meet various of its regulations. Excessive taxation of individuals has robbed us of incentive and made overtime unprofitable.

We once produced about 40 percent of the world's steel. We now produce 19 percent. We were once the greatest producer of automobiles, producing more than all the rest of the world combined. That is no longer true, and in addition, the "Big Three," the major auto companies in our land, have sustained tremendous losses in the past year and have been forced to lay off thousands of workers.

All of you who are working know that even with cost-of-living pay raises, you can't keep up with inflation. In our progressive tax system, as you increase the number of dollars you earn, you find yourself moved up into higher tax brackets, paying a higher tax rate just for trying to hold our own. The result? Your standard of living is going down.

Over the past decades we've talked of curtailing government spending so that we can then lower the tax burden. Sometimes we've even taken a run at doing that. But there were always those who told us that taxes couldn't be cut until spending was reduced. Well, you know, we can lecture our children about extravagance until we run out of voice and breath. Or we can cure their extravagance by simply reducing their allowance.

It's time to recognize that we've come to a turning point. We're threatened with an economic calamity of tremendous proportions, and the old business-as-usual treatment can't save us. Together, we must chart a different course.

We must increase productivity. That means making it possible for industry to modernize and make use of the technology which we ourselves invented. That means putting Americans back to work. And that means above all bringing government spending back within government revenues, which is the only way, together with increased productivity, that we can reduce and, yes, eliminate inflation.

In the past we've tried to fight inflation one year and then, with unemployment increased, turn the next year to fighting unemployment with more deficit spending as a pump primer. So, again, up goes inflation. It hasn't worked. We don't have to choose between inflation and unemployment—they go hand in hand. It's time to try something different, and that's what we're going to do.

I've already placed a freeze on hiring replacements for those who retire or leave government service. I've ordered a cut in government travel, the number of consultants to the government, and the buying of office equipment and other items. I've put a freeze on pending regulations and set up a task force under Vice President Bush to review regulations with an eye toward getting rid of as many as possible. I have decontrolled oil, which should result in more domestic production and less dependence on foreign oil. And I'm eliminating that ineffective Council on Wage and Price Stability.

But it will take more, much more. And we must realize there is no quick fix. At the same time, however, we cannot delay in implementing an economic program aimed at both reducing tax rates to stimulate productivity and reducing the growth in government spending to reduce unemployment and inflation.

On February 18th, I will present in detail an economic program to Congress embodying the features I've just stated. It will propose budget cuts in virtually every department of government. It is my belief that these actual budget cuts will only be part of the savings. As our Cabinet Secretaries take charge of their departments, they will search out areas of waste, extravagance, and costly overhead which could yield additional and substantial reductions.

Now, at the same time we're doing this, we must go forward with a tax relief package. I shall ask for a 10-percent reduction across the board in personal income tax rates for each of the next 3 years. Proposals will also be submitted for accelerated depreciation allowances for business to provide necessary capital so as to create jobs.

Now, here again, in saying this, I know that language, as I said earlier, can get in the way of a clear understanding of what our program is intended to do. Budget cuts can sound as if we're going to reduce total government spending to a lower level than was spent the year before. Well, this is not the case. The budgets will increase as our population increases, and each year we'll see spending increases to match that growth. Government revenues will increase as the economy grows, but the burden will be lighter for each individual, because the economic base will have been expanded by reason of the reduced rates.

Now, let me show you a chart that I've had drawn to illustrate how this can be.

Here you see two trend lines. The bottom line shows the increase in tax revenues. The red line on top is the increase in government spending. Both lines turn upward, reflecting the giant tax increase already built into the system for this year 1981, and the increases in spending built into the '81 and '82 budgets and on into the future. As you can see, the spending line rises at a steeper slant than the revenue line. And that gap between those lines illustrates the increasing deficits we've been running, including this year's $80 billion deficit.

Now, in the second chart, the lines represent the positive effects when Congress accepts our economic program. Both lines continue to rise, allowing for necessary growth, but the gap narrows as spending cuts continue over the next few years until finally the two lines come together, meaning a balanced budget.

I am confident that my administration can achieve that. At that point tax revenues, in spite of rate reductions, will be increasing faster than spending, which means we can look forward to further reductions in the tax rates.

Now, in all of this we will, of course, work closely with the Federal Reserve System toward the objective of a stable monetary policy.

Our spending cuts will not be at the expense of the truly needy. We will, however, seek to eliminate benefits to those who are not really qualified by reason of need.

As I've said before, on February 18th I will present this economic package of budget reductions and tax reform to a joint session of Congress and to you in full detail.

Our basic system is sound. We can, with compassion, continue to meet our responsibility to those who, through no fault of their own, need our help. We can meet fully the other legitimate responsibilities of government. We cannot continue any longer our wasteful ways at the expense of the workers of this land or of our children.

Since 1960 our government has spent $5.1 trillion. Our debt has grown by $648 billion. Prices have exploded by 178 percent. How much better off are we for all that? Well, we all know we're very much worse off. When we measure how harshly these years of inflation, lower productivity, and uncontrolled government growth have affected our lives, we know we must act and act now. We must not be timid. We will restore the freedom of all men and women to excel and to create. We will unleash the energy and genius of the American people, traits which have never failed us.

To the Congress of the United States, I extend my hand in cooperation, and I believe we can go forward in a bipartisan manner. I've found a real willingness to cooperate on the part of Democrats and members of my own party.

To my colleagues in the executive branch of government and to all Federal employees, I ask that we work in the spirit of service.

I urge those great institutions in America, business and labor, to be guided by the national interest, and I'm confident they will. The only special interest that we will serve is the interest of all the people.

We can create the incentives which take advantage of the genius of our economic system—a system, as Walter Lippmann observed more than 40 years ago, which for the first time in history gave men "a way of producing wealth in which the good fortune of others multiplied their own."

Our aim is to increase our national wealth so all will have more, not just redistribute what we already have which is just a sharing of scarcity. We can begin to reward hard work and risk-taking, by forcing this Government to live within its means.

Over the years we've let negative economic forces run out of control. We stalled the judgment day, but we no longer have that luxury. We're out of time.

And to you, my fellow citizens, let us join in a new determination to rebuild the foundation of our society, to work together, to act responsibly. Let us do so with the most profound respect for that which must be preserved as well as with sensitive understanding and compassion for those who must be protected.

We can leave our children with an unrepayable massive debt and a shattered economy, or we can leave them liberty in a land where every individual has the opportunity to be whatever God intended us to be. All it takes is a little common sense and recognition of our own ability. Together we can forge a new beginning for America.

Thank you, and good night.

Source:
Ronald Reagan Presidential Library, Simi Valley, California, p. 79–83.

15. *United States v. Microsoft,* 2000

Findings of Judge Thomas Penfield Jackson of the U.S. District Court for the District of Columbia stating that the Microsoft Corporation violated U.S. antitrust laws. Antitrust laws protect consumers against unfair business practices such as price-fixing and monopolizing markets. According to sections one and two of the Sherman Antitrust Act (15 U.S.C.), it is illegal to restrain and to monopolize trade.

Microsoft, founded by Bill Gates and Paul Allen in 1975, is a manufacturer and licenser of computer software based in Redmond, Washington. Microsoft's Windows operating system controls over 90 percent of the personal computer (PC) software market. In May 1998, the U.S. Department of Justice, along with 18 states and the District of Columbia, filed suit against the company for engaging in unfair business practices. In his decision, Judge Jackson determined that Microsoft was a monopoly that actively sought to suppress competition in order to maintain its own substantial share of the software market. Two threats to Microsoft's dominance were Netscape, a browser, or type of software that enables a PC user to access the Internet, and Sun Microsys-

tems, Inc. (Sun), which makes the Java programming language. Jackson charged that Microsoft attempted to crush Netscape to ensure that its own browser, Internet Explorer, would be the predominant software available to consumers. He also found that Microsoft, having determined that software written in Java would become profitable, sought to ensure that any such software would depend upon Microsoft's technologies, rather than Sun's.

Microsoft appealed the decision, but after a U.S. appeals court confirmed Jackson's decision in April 2000, the company was ordered to break into two parts as punishment for violating antitrust laws. This decision was overturned on appeal in June 2001. Federal prosecutors and Microsoft attorneys then began working on a settlement, and in November 2001 the Department of Justice and nine states accepted the proposed settlement. However, another nine states and the District of Columbia rejected the settlement and continued to pursue litigation against the software giant. In November 2002, after Microsoft began to incorporate features into its software that would allow for freer competition, U.S. District Judge Colleen Kollar-Kotelly ruled to accept a revised settlement that loosened Microsoft's hold on the software markets, but allowed the company to remain intact. While this victory was welcome news, the company continues to have legal troubles. In addition to the state-led monopoly cases, Sun Microsystems and AOL Time Warner's Netscape unit have filed private antitrust suits, and a European commission has launched an investigation into Microsoft's efforts to stifle overseas competition in the computer-server and media-player markets. Below is an excerpt of Judge Jackson's decision.

VII.
The Effect on Consumers of Microsoft's Efforts to Protect the Applications Barrier to Entry

408. The debut of Internet Explorer and its rapid improvement gave Netscape an incentive to improve Navigator's quality at a competitive rate. The inclusion of Internet Explorer with Windows at no separate charge increased general familiarity with the Internet and reduced the cost to the public of gaining access to it, at least in part because it compelled Netscape to stop charging for Navigator. These actions thus contributed to improving the quality of Web browsing software, lowering its cost, and increasing its availability, thereby benefitting consumers.

409. To the detriment of consumers, however, Microsoft has done much more than develop innovative browsing software of commendable quality and offer it bundled with Windows at no additional charge. As has been shown, Microsoft also engaged in a concerted series of actions designed to protect the applications barrier to entry, and hence its monopoly power, from a variety of middleware threats, including Netscape's Web browser and Sun's implementation of Java. Many of these actions have harmed consumers in ways that are immediate and easily discernible. They have also caused less direct, but nevertheless serious and far-reaching, consumer harm by distorting competition.

410. By refusing to offer those OEMs who requested it a version of Windows without Web browsing software, and by preventing OEMs from removing Internet Explorer—or even the most obvious means of invoking it—prior to shipment, Microsoft forced OEMs to ignore consumer demand for a browserless version of Windows. The same actions forced OEMs either to ignore consumer preferences for Navigator or to give them a Hobson's choice of both browser products at the cost of increased confusion, degraded system performance, and restricted memory. By ensuring that Internet Explorer would launch in certain circumstances in Windows 98 even if Navigator were set as the default, and even if the consumer had removed all conspicuous means of invoking Internet Explorer, Microsoft created confusion and frustration for consumers, and increased technical support costs for business customers. Those Windows purchasers who did not want browsing software—businesses, or parents and teachers, for example, concerned with the potential for irresponsible Web browsing on PC systems—not only had

to undertake the effort necessary to remove the visible means of invoking Internet Explorer and then contend with the fact that Internet Explorer would nevertheless launch in certain cases; they also had to (assuming they needed new, non-browsing features not available in earlier versions of Windows) content themselves with a PC system that ran slower and provided less available memory than if the newest version of Windows came without browsing software.

By constraining the freedom of OEMs to implement certain software programs in the Windows boot sequence, Microsoft foreclosed an opportunity for OEMs to make Windows PC systems less confusing and more user-friendly, as consumers desired. By taking the actions listed above, and by enticing firms into exclusivity arrangements with valuable inducements that only Microsoft could offer and that the firms reasonably believed they could not do without, Microsoft forced those consumers who otherwise would have elected Navigator as their browser to either pay a substantial price (in the forms of downloading, installation, confusion, degraded system performance, and diminished memory capacity) or content themselves with Internet Explorer.

Finally, by pressuring Intel to drop the development of platform-level NSP software, and otherwise to cut back on its software development efforts, Microsoft deprived consumers of software innovation that they very well may have found valuable, had the innovation been allowed to reach the marketplace. None of these actions had pro-competitive justifications.

411. Many of the tactics that Microsoft has employed have also harmed consumers indirectly by unjustifiably distorting competition. The actions that Microsoft took against Navigator hobbled a form of innovation that had shown the potential to depress the applications barrier to entry sufficiently to enable other firms to compete effectively against Microsoft in the market for Intel-compatible PC operating systems. That competition would have conduced to consumer choice and nurtured innovation. The campaign against Navigator also retarded widespread acceptance of Sun's Java implementation.

This campaign, together with actions that Microsoft took with the sole purpose of making it difficult for developers to write Java applications with technologies that would allow them to be ported between Windows and other platforms, impeded another form of innovation that bore the potential to diminish the applications barrier to entry. There is insufficient evidence to find that, absent Microsoft's actions, Navigator and Java already would have ignited genuine competition in the market for Intel-compatible PC operating systems. It is clear, however, that Microsoft has retarded, and perhaps altogether extinguished, the process by which these two middleware technologies could have facilitated the introduction of competition into an important market.

412. Most harmful of all is the message that Microsoft's actions have conveyed to every enterprise with the potential to innovate in the computer industry. Through its conduct toward Netscape, IBM, Compaq, Intel, and others, Microsoft has demonstrated that it will use its prodigious market power and immense profits to harm any firm that insists on pursuing initiatives that could intensify competition against one of Microsoft's core products. Microsoft's past success in hurting such companies and stifling innovation deters investment in technologies and businesses that exhibit the potential to threaten Microsoft. The ultimate result is that some innovations that would truly benefit consumers never occur for the sole reason that they do not coincide with Microsoft's self-interest.

Thomas Penfield Jackson
U.S. District Judge
Date: November 5, 1999

GENERAL BIBLIOGRAPHY

Baskin, Jonathan B., and Paul J. Miranti. *A History of Corporate Finance*. New York: Cambridge University Press, 1997.

Bernstein, Peter L. *The Power of Gold: The History of an Obsession*. New York: John Wiley, 2000.

Blackford, Mansel G. *A History of Small Business in America*. 2nd ed. Chapel Hill: University of North Carolina Press, 2003.

Bodenhorn, Howard. *A History of Banking in Antebellum America*. New York: Cambridge University Press, 2000.

Brooks, Thomas R. *Toil and Trouble: A History of American Labor*. 2nd ed. New York: Delacorte Press, 1971.

Brownlee, W. Elliot. *Federal Taxation in America: A Short History*. New York: Cambridge University Press, 1996.

Calder, Lendol. *Financing the American Dream: A Cultural History of Consumer Credit*. Princeton, N.J.: Princeton University Press, 1999.

Campbell-Kelly, Martin. *From Airline Reservations to Sonic the Hedgehog: A History of the Software Industry*. Cambridge, Mass.: MIT Press, 2003.

Campbell-Kelly, Martin, and William Aspray. *Computer: A History of the Information Machine*. New York: Basic Books, 1996.

Chandler, Alfred, and James W. Cortada. *A Nation Transformed by Information: How Information Has Shaped the United States from Colonial Times to the Present*. New York: Oxford University Press, 2000.

Chandler, Alfred D., Jr. *The Visible Hand: The Managerial Revolution in American Business*. Cambridge, Mass.: Harvard University Press, 1977.

Chernow, Ron. *The House of Morgan: An American Banking Dynasty and the Rise of Modern Corporate Finance*. New York: Simon & Schuster, 1990.

Clark, Robert Louis, Lee A. Craig, and Jack W. Wilson. *A History of Public Sector Pensions in the United States*. Philadelphia: University of Pennsylvania Press, 2003.

Eckes, Alfred E. *Opening America's Market: U.S. Foreign Trade Policy Since 1776*. Chapel Hill: University of North Carolina Press, 1995.

Fogel, Robert W. *Railroads and American Economic Growth*. Baltimore: Johns Hopkins University Press, 1964.

Fox, Stephen R. *The Mirror Makers: A History of American Advertising and Its Creators*. Urbana: University of Illinois Press, 1997.

Friedman, Milton, and Anna Schwartz. *A Monetary History of the United States*. Princeton, N.J.: Princeton University Press, 1963.

Galenson, Walter. *The American Labor Movement, 1955–1995*. Westport, Conn.: Greenwood Press, 1996.

Geisst, Charles R. *Monopolies in America: Empire Builders and Their Enemies from Jay Gould to Bill Gates*. New York: Oxford University Press, 2000.

———. *Wheels of Fortune: The History of Speculation from Scandal to Respectability*. New York: John Wiley & Sons, 2002.

———. *Deals of the Century: Wall Street, Mergers, and the Making of Modern America*. Hoboken, N.J.: John Wiley & Sons, 2003.

———. *Wall Street: A History*. Rev. ed. New York: Oxford University Press, 2004.

Goodrum, Charles A., and Helen Dalrymple. *Advertising in America: The First 200 Years*. New York: Harry N. Abrams, 1990.

Groner, Alex. *The American Heritage History of American Business and Industry*. New York: American Heritage Publishing Co., 1972.

Hendrickson, Robert. *The Grand Emporiums: An Illustrated History of America's Great Department Stores*. New York: Stein & Day, 1979.

Irwin, Douglas A. *Against the Tide: An Intellectual History of Free Trade*. Princeton, N.J.: Princeton University Press, 1996.

Jonnes, Jill. *Empires of Light: Edison, Tesla, Westinghouse, and the Race to Electrify the World*. New York: Random House, 2003.

Kaplan, Edward S. *American Trade Policy, 1923–1995*. Westport, Conn.: Greenwood Press, 1996.

Kindleberger, Charles Poor. *Manias, Panics, and Crashes: A History of Financial Crises*. 4th ed. New York: Wiley, 2000.

Klein, Maury. *Unfinished Business: The Railroad in American Life*. Hanover, N.H.: University Press of New England, 1994.

Krooss, Herman, ed. *Documentary History of Banking and Currency in the United States*. 4 vols. New York: Chelsea House, 1983.

Kwolek-Folland, Angel. *Incorporating Women: A History of Women and Business in the United States*. New York: Twayne Publishers, 1998.

Lears, T. J. Jackson. *Fables of Abundance: A Cultural History of Advertising in America*. New York: Basic Books; 1994.

Lemann, Nicholas. *The Promised Land: The Great Black Migration and How It Changed America*. New York: Macmillan, 1991.

Loeb, Stephen E., and Paul J. Miranti. *The Institute of Accounts: Nineteenth Century Origins of Accounting Professionalism in the United States*. London: Routledge, 2004.

Marchand, Roland. *Creating the Corporate Soul: The Rise of Public Relations and Corporate Imagery in American Big Business*. Berkeley: University of California Press, 1998.

Markham, Jerry W. *A Financial History of the United States*. Armonk, N.Y.: M. E. Sharpe, 2002.

McCraw, Thomas K. *American Business, 1920–2000: How It Worked*. Wheeling, Ill.: Harlan Davidson, 2000.

———. *Prophets of Regulation*. Cambridge, Mass.: Harvard University Press, 1984.

McMaster, Susan E. *The Telecommunications Industry*. Westport, Conn.: Greenwood Press, 2002.

Means, Howard B. *Money and Power: The History of Business*. New York: John Wiley, 2001.

Meltzer, Allan H. *A History of the Federal Reserve, 1913–1951*. Chicago: University of Chicago Press, 2003.

Misa, Thomas. *A Nation of Steel: The Making of Modern America*. Baltimore: Johns Hopkins University Press, 1995.

Morrison, Steven, and Clifford Winston. *The Evolution of the Airline Industry*. Washington, D.C.: Brookings Institution, 1995.

Myers, Gustavus. *History of the Great American Fortunes*. 3 vols. Chicago: Charles H. Kerr & Co., 1911.

Norris, Floyd, and Christine Bocklemann. *The New York Times Century of Business*. New York: McGraw-Hill, 1999.

Norris, James D. *Advertising and the Transformation of American Society, 1865–1920*. New York: Greenwood Press, 1990.

Previts, Gary John, and Barbara Dubis Merino. *A History of Accountancy in the United States: The Cultural Significance of Accounting*. Columbus: Ohio State University Press, 1998.

Rayback, Joseph G. *History of American Labor*. New York: Free Press, 1966.

Seligman, Joel. *The Transformation of Wall Street: A History of the Securities and Exchange Commission and Modern Corporate Finance*. Boston: Houghton Mifflin, 1982.

Shippen, Katherine. *Andrew Carnegie and the Age of Steel* New York: Random House, 1964.

Skeel, David A. *Debt's Dominion: A History of Bankruptcy Law in America*. Princeton, N.J.: Princeton University Press, 2001.

Smith, Robert Michael. *From Blackjacks to Briefcases: A History of Commercialized Strikebreaking and Unionbusting in the United States*. Athens: Ohio University Press, 2003.

Sobel, Robert. *The Age of Giant Corporations: A Microeconomic History of American Business, 1914–1992*. 3rd ed. Westport, Conn.: Greenwood Press, 1993.

Sullivan, George. *By Chance a Winner: The History of Lotteries*. New York: Dodd, Mead, 1972.

Tedlow, Richard S. *New and Improved: The Story of Mass Marketing in America*. New York: Basic Books, 1998.

Walker, Juliet E. K. *The History of Black Business in America: Capitalism, Race, Entrepreneurship.* New York: Prentice Hall, 1998.

Weisman, Steven R. *The Great Tax Wars from Lincoln to Wilson: The Fierce Battles over Money and Power That Transformed the Nation.* New York: Simon & Schuster, 2002.

Wilkins, Mira. *A History of Foreign Investment in the United States to 1914.* Cambridge, Mass.: Harvard University Press, 1989.

Yergin, Daniel. *The Prize: The Epic Quest for Oil, Money, and Power.* New York: Simon & Schuster, 1991.

INDEX

Boldface page numbers indicate primary discussions or documents. *Italicized* page numbers indicate photographs or illustrations.

A

A&P. *See* Great Atlantic & Pacific Tea Co. (A&P)
ABC. *See* American Broadcasting Company (ABC)
abolition 400–401
accounting x, xi, 113, 316, 372
Accounting Principles Board (APB) 160, 182
accounting research bulletins (ARBs) 182
acquisitions, holding companies and 199
"action news" 434
Adams, Charles F. 180, 290
Adams, Henry 290
Advanced Micro Devices 98
Advanced Research Projects Agency 223
advertising industry **1–9**
    agencies 2–3, 5–7
    American Express and 15
    in business history x
    Coca-Cola and 83, *83*
    coffee industry and 85–86
    CBS and 88
    FTC and 157
    history of xi
    Macy's and 259
    Cyrus McCormick and 263
    National Advertising Review Board (NARB) 53–54
    newspaper industry and 304–305

pharmaceutical industry 335, *335*
    radio industry 351
    Charles Revson 362
    slavery and *399*
    television industry 430
    J. Walter Thompson and 231–232
    Time Warner and 437
    Ted Turner and 438–439
    John Wanamaker and 464
    Wharton School and 473
    Wheeler-Lea Act and 529
Advocacy, Office of, SBA 402
Aerial Experiment Association 50–51
aerospace industry 13, 446, 494
Aetna Insurance Company 282
affirmative action 403, 485
AFL. *See* American Federation of Labor (AFL)
AFL-CIO 19, 265, 361–362, 452, 493
African Americans
    advertising agencies of 7
    business organizations of 297–298
    capitalism and 297–298, 403
    freed slaves 400
    Elizabeth Hobbs Keckley 479
    National Negro Business League **297–298**, 492

newspapers owned by 302
    George M. Pullman 343
    PWA 343
    slavery 399
    sports industry 405
    UAW 446
    Oprah Winfrey 475
agribusiness 150
Agricultural Adjustment Acts 144, 148
Agricultural Adjustment Agency (AAA) 300
agricultural cooperatives 540
Agricultural Credit Act 143
agriculture 144, 148, 150. *See also* farming
air braking system 471
air conditioning 65
Airline Deregulation Act 11–12, 494
airline industry **9–12**, 118, 325, 494. *See also* individual airlines
Air Mail Act 10, 493
air mail service 9–10, 57, 324
airplane industry **12–14**, 181, 391, *483*
alcoholic beverages, prohibition of 459–460
Aldrin, Mildred 131
Alexanderson, Ernst F. W. 432
Alger, Horatio 382
Allen, Paul 562
Allen & Co., S. & M. 80–81
Allstate Insurance Company 377

alternating current (AC) 471
AM (amplitude modulation) 353
amateur sports 404
Amazon.com 224
A.M. Chicago (television program) 475
American Airlines 494
American Association of Pharmaceutical Chemists 337
American Basketball Association (ABA) 407
American Broadcasting Company (ABC) 62
American Express Company **14–16**, 467
American Federation of Labor (AFL) **16–19**. *See also* AFL-CIO
    Samuel Gompers and 187
    John L. Lewis and 248
    George Meany and 265
    UAW 444
    UMWA 449
American Flint Glass Workers Union 320
American Fur Company 26–27
American Institute of Certified Public Accountants (AICPA) 160, 182
American International Corporation 79–80
American Iron and Steel Institute (AISI) 410
American Jockey Club 52

American League (AL) 404
American Liberty League 356
American Medical Association
    218
American Motors Corporation
    77, 403
American National Standards
    Institute 262
American Professional
    Football Association 406
American Railway Express
    Company 15
American Railway Union 114,
    343
American Record Corporation
    352
American Society of
    Composers, Authors and
    Publishers 351–352
American Society of
    Mechanical Engineers 423
American Society of
    Newspaper Editors 305
American Standard Code for
    Information Interchange
    (ASCII) 430
American Steel and Wire Co.
    178
American Stock Exchange
    (AMEX) 20, 295, 319, 359,
    414, 417
American system of
    manufacture 208
American Telephone &
    Telegraph Co. (AT&T)
    20–22
    antitrust cases against
        25–26
    Alexander Graham Bell
        and 50
    breakup of 494
    deregulation 118
    FCC and 151
    J. P. Morgan and 280
    Kidder Peabody & Co.
        238
    radio industry 348–351
    RCA 346
    telecommunications
        industry 425–428
    television industry 432
    Theodore N. Vail 455
    WorldCom and 488
    Owen D. Young 490
American Tobacco Co. 22–23,
    24, 126, 251, 492
American Trust Company 469
American Way of Life 278
America OnLine (AOL)
    436–437, 494

Ameritech 21
Ames, Oakes 443
Ames, Oliver 443
AMEX. See American Stock
    Exchange (AMEX)
Amgen 339
AMK Corporation 448–449
ammonia, synthetic 70
Amoco 366
Amtrak. See National Railroad
    Passenger Corp. (Amtrak)
amusement parks 120
Anderson, Harland 97
Andrews, Samuel 365
Andruss, Leonard 115
animation 119–120
Annual Improvement Factor
    (AIF) 446
anthracite strike 449
antibiotics 71, 338
anticompetitive conduct 383,
    427–428
anti-Semitism 30, 58, 67, 166,
    375, 392
Antitrust Division, U.S.
    Department of Justice 24,
    26, 156, 179–180
antitrust laws 383, 562. See
    also Clayton Antitrust Act;
    Robinson-Patman Act;
    Sherman Antitrust Act
antitrust suits 23–26
    against AT&T 22
    against cartels 66
    against conglomerates
        101–102
    FTC and 156
    Industrial Revolution and
        209
    against Microsoft 99,
        179–180
    Morgan Stanley & Co.
        and 283
    in motion picture industry
        286, 288
    in petroleum industry
        364–365, 534
    in sports industry
        404–406
    in steel industry 178,
        410, 452
    suspension of 298
    treble damages plus fees
        82
antiunionism 449–450
antiwar movement 362
AOL. See America OnLine
    (AOL)
AOL Time Warner 563. See
    also Time Warner

AP. See Associated Press of
    New York (AP)
apothecaries 334
Apple Computer Company
    98, 179, 221, 229–230
Araskog, Rand 180
Arbenz, Jacobo 448
arbitrage 56
arbitration, in sports industry
    405
Areeda, Phillip E. 341, 384
Armour, Philip 266
Army, U.S. 274
Arnold, Benedict 489
Aroostook War 253
ARPANET 99, 223
Arthur Andersen & Co. 136
artificial farming 150
artists, and WPA 487
assembly line production
    30–31, 125, 166–167, 263
Associated Pioneers of the
    Territorial Days of California
    419
Associated Press of New York
    (AP) 302
Astor, John Jacob 26–27, 122,
    185, 437
Astoria 26–27
Atabrine 337
athletes, professional 171–173
Atlantic cable 158
Atlantic Richfield Company
    365–366
AT&T. See American
    Telephone & Telegraph Co.
    (AT&T)
August Belmont & Co. 51–52,
    367
autocracy, of UMWA 450–451
automated telephone switch
    425
automatic block signal 471
automatic teller machines 80
automation 447, 451
automobile insurance
    215–216
automotive industry 27–37.
    See also Iacocca, Lee; specific
    auto manufacturers; United
    Automobile Workers (UAW)
    annual model changes
        401
    and chain stores 66
    Chrysler Windsor club
        coupé 77
    electric car 28
    Ford Crown Victoria 32
    Interstate Highway Act
        226

Henry J. Kaiser and 235
mass production in 262
Ralph Nader and 293
petroleum industry and
    330
quality gap 33–34
rubber industry 367
Alfred Sloan 401
steel industry 409
Tin Lizzes 168
Avery, Sewell 465
aviation 14
Avis 180

B
Babbitt (Lewis) 291
Babson, Roger Ward 35–36
Babson's Reports 35
Bache and Company 392
backlogs, stock market 416
backward integration 266
Baekeland, Leo 70
Bain, Joe S. 384
Baird, John L. 431
Bakelite 70
Baker, George F. 36–37, 197
Baker, James 194
Baker, Lorenzo D. 447
balance of trade 73, 141–142
Baldridge, Malcolm 260
Ballistic Research Laboratory
    95
Baltimore & Ohio Railway
    104, 354
Baltimore Is Talking (television
    program) 475
bananas 447–448
Bancroft, Hubert H. 419
Bankers Trust Company 417
bank failures 45, 47, 91, 264
Bank for International
    Settlements 490
Bank Holding Company Act
    37–38, 162–163, 199
Banking Act (1933) (Glass-
    Steagall Act) 38–39
    Bank of United States and
        45
    Brown Brothers Harriman
        60
    Chase Manhattan Bank
        and 67
    commercial banking and
        91
    FDIC 152
    Financial Services
        Modernization Act 162
    investment banking and
        228
    McFadden Act 264

Morgan Stanley & Co.
    and 282
    National City Company
        80
    passage of 493
Banking Act (1935) 134
banking industry. *See also*
    panics; *specific banks*
    George F. Baker **36–37**
    banknote circulation 40
    crashes **108**
    crisis of 1980s 152
    deregulation 118
    failures 45, 47, 91, 264
    Joseph P. Kennedy and
        236
    reforms 45
    Paul Volcker 459
    Wells Fargo 469
banking laws 224–225, 246
Bank Insurance Fund (BIF)
    152, 161
banknotes **39–41**, 90
Bank of America **41–42**, 492
Bank of England 39–40, 282
Bank of Italy 492
Bank of Manhattan 394
Bank of New York x, **42–43**,
    90, 125, 491
Bank of North America 90,
    284
Bank of Scotland 39–40
Bank of Stephen Girard 185
Bank of the United States
    (BUS) **43–45**, 54, *55*, 178,
    263, 491
Bank of United States **45–46**
Bank One 400
bankruptcy **46–47**, 126, 429,
    488, 491. *See also specific
    companies*
bargain basement 464
Baring Brothers **47–48**, 119,
    366–367
Barney, Charles D. 104
Barron, Clarence W. 48, 122
Barron's 48
barter 200
Baruch, Bernard Mannes
    48–49, 230–231
baseball 171–173, 404–405
basketball 406–407
Basketball Association of
    America (BAA) 406–407
basket currency 140–141
battlefield reporters 303
"Battle of the Sexes" 408
Baudot code 430
bear markets 108, 414–415
bear raids 74

beauty shops 362
Beecher, Catherine 479
beef production 266
Beeks, Gertrude 482
*Behind the Scenes or Thirty
    Years a Slave and Four Years
    in the White House* (Keckley)
    479
Bell, Alexander Graham
    49–51
    telecommunications
        industry and 21, 348,
        425
    telephone patent 492
    television industry
        430–431
    Thomas A. Watson 465
Bellamy, Edward 108
Bellow, Saul 487
Bell System 425–428
Bell Telephone Company *21*,
    21–22, 50, 455, 465, 492
Belmont, August 47, **51–52**,
    367
Belmont, August, II *52*, 367,
    457
Belmont Stakes 51–52
Bennett, James G. 302
Bergstresser, Charles 305
Berkshire-Hathaway 62
Bernbach, Bill 6–7
Berners-Lee, Tim 99, 224
Berry, Marcellus Fleming
    14–15
Bessemer, Henry 105, 211,
    409
Bethlehem Steel 236, 376, 410
Better Business Bureaus
    53–54
B. F. Goodrich Company 188,
    367, 492
bicycle tires 367
Biddle, Nicholas 44, **54–55**
Big Five, motion picture
    industry 287–288
Big Four, meat packing
    industry 266–268
bigotry, AFL and 17–18
Big Three, automotive
    industry 31–34
Big Three, meat packing
    industry 269
billboard advertisements 8
Bill of Rights 301
Biltmore Agreement 352
Bingham mine, Utah 277–278
Biogen 339
Biograph 285–286
biotechnology 69, 339
Bird, Caroline 476

Bird, Larry 407
Bituminous Coal Commission
    450
bituminous coal mining
    449–450
Bituminous Coal Operators
    Association 451
Black, Fischer 55–56
Black Ball Line 388–389
black capitalism 297–298,
    403
Black Friday 163, 189
black lung compensation 451
Black-Scholes model **55–56**,
    319–320
Blickensderfer typewriters
    441
"blind writer" typewriters 440
blockbusters, motion picture
    industry 289
blood products 337–338
Blue Cross 218
Blue Shield 218
blue-sky laws 379
*Board of Trade of City of
    Chicago v. Christie Grain &
    Stock Company* 61
Boeing, William E. 56–57,
    493
Boeing Co. *11*, 13–14, **56–57**,
    131, *324–325*, 494
bonded debt, issuance of 112
bonds. *See also* Treasury bonds
    federal 43
    indexed to inflation 438
    junk 116, 124, 153, **231**
    original-issue discount
        231
    valuations 119
    war 103–104, 112, 382
book publishers 437
boot and shoe industry
    208–209
Border Environment
    Cooperation Commission,
    NAFTA 311
Bork, Robert H. 383
Borman, Frank 132
Boston 300, 358–359
Boston Bruins 407
Boston Celtics 407
Boston Fruit Company 448
Boston Newsletter 300
Boulder Dam 235
boutique companies 6, 289
boxed beef 268–269
boxing 407
boycotts, union 540
Boyle, W. A. (Tony) 451
Bradshaw, Thornton 347

Bradstreet, John M. 110
Bradstreet Agency 110
Brady, Nicholas 119
branch banking 469
branch houses, meat packing
    industry 266–268
branch system of retailing 377
Brandeis, Louis D. **57–58**
brand-name campaigns 3
Breakers (Palm Beach, Florida)
    164
Bretton Woods system **58–59**
    collapse of 494
    Marriner S. Eccles and
        134
    foreign exchange market
        169
    gold standard 187
    Hawley-Smoot Tariff Act
        198
    John M. Keynes and 238
    Richard M. Nixon and
        461–462
    signing of agreement 493
bribery, of foreign businesses
    168
Briscoe, Elizabeth 482
Bristol Laboratories 338
Britain
    navigation laws of 207
    overseas investments of
        47–48
    shipbuilding industry
        385
    shipping industry
        388–389
    women and common law
        477–478
British Petroleum 334
broadband services 429
broadcasting industry
    General Electric Co. 181
    licenses 151
    and newspaper industry
        305
    television industry and
        434
    Oprah Winfrey **475–476**
Brooklyn Dodgers 405
Brown, Alexander 60
Brown & Wanamaker 463
Brown Brothers Harriman **60**
Browning, John 88
BT (British Telecom) 488
bucket shops **60–61**, 74–75
Buffett, Warren **61–62**, 371
Buick, David 29
Buick Motor Company 29,
    128, 183
bullion standard 186–187

bull markets 283, 414
Bureau of Mines (BOM) 276
Burnett, Leo 6
Burnham & Co. 467
Burns, Arthur 193
Burr, Aaron 195–196
Burrell, Berkeley G. 297–298
Burroughs Corporation 314
Bush, George H. W. 311
Bush, George W. 194, 197, 294
Business, A Profession (Brandeis) 58
business school programs 197, 261, 473, 492
business statistics x–xi
business unionism 18
Butterfield, John 14
Buttonwood Agreement 126, 308, 491

C

Cable News Network (CNN) 439
cable television 8, 430, 434, 437, 439
Cadillac Motor Company 128
caffeine consumption 86
California gold rush 274–276, 385, 418–419
call centers 317
cameras 132
Campbell, John 300
Canada 34, 311
Canadian Pacific Railroad 198
Canal Bank 400
canals
    Cape Cod 52
    Erie 137
    farming and 145
    Industrial Revolution and 209–210
    Panama 323–324, 493
    railroads and 354
    turnpikes 439–440
Candler, Asa 82
Canons of Journalism 305
Cape Cod Canal 52
capitalism
    black 297–298, 403
    Eugene V. Debs on 114–115
    managerial xi, 106, 260–261
    UMWA 449
capital requirements, for savings and loans 161
Carey, Hugh 392
Carnegie, Andrew 63–64
    H. C. Frick Coke Company 173

Industrial Revolution and 211
    public libraries 521
    robber barons 363
    Thomas A. Scott 376
    skyscrapers 394
    steel industry 409
    "Wealth" 520–527
Carnegie, McCandless & Co. 63
Carnegie Endowment 64
Carnegie Institute of Technology 64
Carnegie Steel
    Henry C. Frick and 173
    Homestead steelworks 64, 173, 375, 409, 492
    J. P. Morgan and 64, 280
    Charles M. Schwab 375
    U.S. Steel Corp. 452
Carothers, Wallace 71
Carrier, Willis H. 65
Carrier Air Conditioning Company 493
Carrier Engineering Corporation 65
cartels 14, 65–66, 69, 383, 424
Carter, Jimmy 265, 458
cartoons 120
Cartwright, Alexander 404
Cary, G. R. 430
Case, Steve 437
case studies 197, 401
"cash and carry" concept 191
casualty insurance 213
Catalyst 485
CBS. *See* Columbia Broadcasting System (CBS)
Celler-Kefauver Act 101
cellophane 128
cell phones 318, 428
Celluloid 70
cellulose 70
censorship boards 288
Census Bureau, U.S. 95, 218
Central America 448
central bank. *See* national central bank
Central Competitive Agreement, UMWA 449
Central Competitive Field, UMWA 449–450
centralization, union 447, 450
Central Pacific Railroad 354, 443, 469
Central Trust Company of Illinois 113
certificates of deposit 39–40
chain stores 66–67, 85, 326–327, 364, 462, 473

Chamberlain, Edward 384
Chambers, John 78
Champion v. Ames 252
Chandler Act 46
Chappe semaphore system 430
Charles H. Merrill & Co. 271
Charles Pratt & Co. 329
Chase Manhattan Bank 67–68, 458, 494
Chase National Bank 38, 67
Chavez, Cesar 150
Cheever, John 487
Chemical Banking Corporation 68
chemical industry 68–74, 73, 121, 460
Chesapeake & Ohio Railroad 138
Chevrolet Motor Company 30–31
Chevron 333–334, 365–366
chewing tobacco 251
Chicago 61, 253, 266, 358–359
Chicago, Burlington & Quincy line 198
Chicago Blackhawks 407
Chicago Board of Trade (CBOT) 74–75, 175, 491
Chicago Board Options Exchange 56, 75, 319
Chicago Edison Company 212–213
Chicago Tribune 263
child labor 298, 505
China 26–27, 39
Chiquita Brands International, Inc. 449
Chouart, Medard 495
Chrysler, Walter Percy 31, 75–76
Chrysler Building 76, 394
Chrysler Corp. 76–78
    in automotive industry 31–32, 34
    Clarence Dillon and 119
    founding of 493
    Lee Iacocca and 203
    UAW 445–446
Church, Sam 452
cigarettes 211, 251
Cincinnati 265–266, 358–359
Cincinnati Red Stockings 404
cinématographe 285
CIO. *See* Congress of Industrial Organizations (CIO)
circuit breaker 416
Cisco Corporation 78, 99
Citibank (Citigroup) 78–80, 162, 371, 467–468, 494

Citizens Bank 400
Civil Aeronautics Act 493
Civil Aeronautics Authority (CAA) 10
Civil Aeronautics Board 493
civil class actions 345–346
civil disobedience, UMWA 452
Civil Rights movement 7, 362, 485
Civil War
    banknote circulation 40
    August Belmont 51
    Chicago Board of Trade 74–75
    coffee industry 84
    Colt Firearms 88
    commercial banking 90
    James Fisk Jr. 162
    Benjamin F. Goodrich 188
    greenbacks 192–193
    income tax 204–205
    life insurance 217
    newspaper industry 302
    pharmaceutical industry 335
    Treasury bonds 438
    war bonds 103–104
Civil Works Administration 343
Clark, Enoch 80–81
Clark, Howard 15
Clark, Maurice 364–365
Clark Dodge & Co. 80–81, 239
Clarke, Arthur C. 427
Clark-McNary Act 254
class action lawsuits 103
Clayton Antitrust Act 81–82, 539–549
    antitrust laws 24
    E. I. DuPont de Nemours & Co. 128
    Samuel Gompers on 187
    passage of 493
    predatory pricing 341
clear-cutting 256
Clermont (steamship) 249
Cleveland, Grover 304, 343
Cleveland Press (newspaper) 304
Clinton, DeWitt 137
Clinton, William J. (Bill) 26, 118, 194, 311, 403
clipper ships 385, 389
close-relationship banking 375
CNN. *See* Cable News Network (CNN)
Coal Mine Health and Safety Act 451

coal mining industry 274, 449–451
coal oil 329
coastwise trade 384–386, 389–391
Coates, George A. 351
coaxial cable 427
Coburn, Irving W. 320
Coca-Cola Co. 82–83, 492
Code of Fair Competition for the Motion Picture Industry 288
coffee industry 83–86
Coffin, Charles A. 181, 490
Cohen, Benjamin 342
cold war 99, 272, 388, 446
Coldwater Road Cart Company 128
Coldwell Banker 377
Colgate, William 86–87
Colgate University 87
collective bargaining 421, 450, 553
college athletics 406
collusive trade practices 288
Colombia 323
colonial period
    family enterprises 477
    farming 144
    imports and exports of 207–209
    inheritance laws 478
    mining industry 273
    newspapers 301
    shipbuilding industry 384
    shipping industry 388
    slavery 396
Color Purple, The (film) 475
color-reproduction system 433
Colt Firearms 87–88, 491
Columbia Broadcasting System (CBS) 88–89
    founding of 493
    radio industry 88, 351–353
    David Sarnoff 373
    television industry 432–433
Columbian Exposition 471
Columbia Phonograph Broadcasting System (CPBS-UIB) 352
Columbia Phonograph Corporation 352
Columbia Trust Company 236
Columbia University, School of Journalism 303
commerce clause 89–90, 326, 426

commercial banking 38–39, 67, 90–92
Commercial Credit Corporation 467
commercial paper 92–93, 108, 112, 186
commissions, discount 392
Committee for Industrial Organization (CIO) 248. See also Congress of Industrial Organizations (CIO)
Committee on Accounting Procedures (CAP) 160, 182
commodities trading 74–75, 93–94, 175–176, 245, 319
Commonwealth Edison Company 133, 213
communication. See also telecommunications industry
    advertising and mass 4
    all-weather 210
    computer-based 223–224
    electronic communication networks 417
    laser 50
    Samuel F. B. Morse and 284
    typewriters 440–441
Communications Act (1934) 349
communications industry 436–437
communism 16–17, 421, 445–446, 555
communities of interest 196–197
community credit needs 94
Community Reinvestment Act (CRA) 94, 162
competition 101, 156, 241, 341, 366, 455. See also specific industries
composite currency 140–141
computer chips 316–317
computer designers 229–230
computer industry 95–100
    convergence with telecommunications 318
    credit cards and 108
    mainframes 316
    office machines 316
    RCA 347
    stock market and 416
    Thomas J. Watson 466
Computing Tabulating Recording Company (C-T-R) 219, 466
Comstock Lode 275

Concept of a Corporation, The (Drucker) 124
Conestoga wagon 100–101
confidential contracts 409
conflicts of interest 372
conglomerates 101–102. See also cartels; trusts
    antitrust laws and 24–25
    food 85–86
    Harold S. Geneen and 180
    General Electric Co. 181
    growth of 270
    holding companies and 199
    in military-industrial complex 272
    in motion picture industry 289
    United Fruit Company 449
    Congress, U.S. 310
Congress of Industrial Organizations (CIO) 18–19, 248, 265, 451. See also AFL-CIO
Connery, William P., Jr. 553
Connolly Hot Oil Act 331
Conoco 128, 333
Conrad, Alfred 398
Consolidated Rail Corporation (Conrail) 139–140, 356
consolidation trend 269–270
"conspicuous consumption" 457–458
Constitution, U.S.
    Bill of Rights 301
    on bills of credit 40
    commerce clause 89–90, 426
    Constitutional Convention 249, 325
    Eighteenth Amendment 459
    First Amendment 301
    patents and trademarks 325–326
    Sixteenth Amendment 205
Constitutional Convention 249, 325
Constitution of the American Federation of Labor 514–516
construction equipment manufacturers 222
consumer credit x, 42, 92–93, 374, 401, 489
Consumer Federation of America 103
consumerism x, 157, 293–294

Consumer Leasing Act 157
consumer movement 4, 7, 53, 102–103, 232
Consumer Product Safety Commission 103, 156
Consumer Reports (magazine) 102
consumption taxes 205
containerships 387, 390–391
Continental Congress 249, 283
Continental Gas and Electric Company 133
Continental Illinois Bank 152
Continental League 405
continuity script 287
continuous process production 330
Contraband Relief Association 478
Contract Air Mail (CAM) 10
Control Data Corporation (CDC) 97
Cooke, Jay 81, 103–104
Cooley, Wadsworth, and Company 158
Coolidge, Calvin 113, 272
Cooper, Peter 104–105, 157
Cooper Union 105
copper mining industry 276
copywriters, in advertising 3, 465
Corcoran, Thomas 342
Corliss, Charles 242
Cornell, Ezra 470
corn harvester 146
corporate radio 350
corporate raiders 381
corporations 105–107
    bureaucracies of 482
    credit-rating agencies and 112
    holding companies 342
    income tax 205–206
    managerial capitalism and 261
    Ralph Nader and 294
    Thomas J. Watson on culture of 466–467
    women and 485
correspondent banking 469
corruption 18, 168–169, 345–346, 451, 552. See also fraud; scandals
Cosby, William 301
cosmetics 362–363
Cost of Living Allowance (COLA) 446
cotton industry 107–108, 145, 397, 473–474, 491
Council of Better Business Bureaus (CBBB) 53–54

Council of Economic Advisors 193
counterfeiting 40–41, 338
Court of Appeals for the Federal Circuit Court (CAFC) 326
craft unions 18, 449, 514. *See also* labor organizations
Craigie, Andrew 334
Cramp shipyard 385–386
crashes 108. *See also* panics; stock markets
Cray Research 97
credit
    and bankruptcy 46
    community needs 94
    consumer x, 42, 92–93, 374, 401, 489
    for United States 42
    women's access to 482
credit cards 108–109
    American Express 15
    commercial paper and 92–93
    Discover 377
    savings and loans 374
Crédit Mobilier scandal 354, 443
credit-rating agencies 109–112
credit-reporting agencies 109–110
Creighton, Edward 470
criminal enterprises 345–346
Crocker Bank 469–470
Crown Publishing 413
crude oil. *See* petroleum industry
crude rubber 368
Crystal Palace Exhibition 208
Cullom, Shelby M. 516
currencies
    composite 140–141
    devaluation of 58–59
    exchange crisis xi
    floating 169
    foreign exchange market 169
    fraud 296
    national 295–296
    stabilization program 417
    U.S. dollar 187, 461–462
Curt Flood v. Bowie Kuhn 405
cut-off saw 254
cyanide heap-leaching gold mines 278

D
Daimler-Benz 34, 77
Dallas Federal Reserve Bank 311

data processing 218–221, 314
Davis, Richard H. 303
Davison, Henry 242
Dawes, Charles G. 113–114
Dawes Report 113
Day, Benjamin 302
Dean Witter & Co. 283, 377
Dearborn Independent (newspaper) 166
Debs, Eugene V. 114–115, 343
debt instrument, short-term 92–93
debtors, individual 47
decaffeinated coffee 85
decentralization, in rubber industry 368–369
decision tree 56
Declaration of Independence 249, 283, 476–477
Deere, Charles H. 115–116
Deere, John 115–116
Deering, Charles 222
defense contracts 201, 272. *See also* U.S. Department of Defense
De Forest, Lee 349
DeLand University 411
Delaware, Lackawanna & Western Railroad 139
delayed electronic feeds (DEFs) 434
de Lesseps, Ferdinand 323
Democratic National Committee 51, 244, 356
Demorest, Ellen 479
Dempsey, Jack 407
Department of Agriculture, U.S. 337
Department of Commerce, U.S. 10, 325
Department of Defense, U.S. (DoD)
    Boeing Co. and 57
    and computer industry 95–96, 99, 219
    Internet 318
    military-industrial complex and 272–273
Department of Interior, U.S. 275
Department of Justice, U.S.
    Antitrust Division 24, 26, 156, 179–180
    antitrust suit against Microsoft 563
    Morgan Stanley & Co. and 282–283
    Volstead Act 459
Department of Labor, U.S. 293

Department of Transportation, U.S. 225
Department of the Treasury, U.S.
    Jay Cooke and 104
    William Duer and 125–126
    Federal National Mortgage Association (FNMA) 153
    Federal Reserve 155
    Albert Gallatin as secretary 177–178
    Jay Gould and 189
    greenbacks 192–193
    Alexander Hamilton 42, 195
    J. P. Morgan and 279, 492
    Office of Thrift Supervision 161
    Prohibition 459
    RFC and 358
    Treasury bonds 437–438
    Paul Volcker 458
department stores 209–210, 259, 326–327, 336, 463, 482
deposit insurance 45, 361, 416. *See also* Depository Institutions Act; Federal Deposit Insurance Corporation (FDIC)
Depository Institutions Act 116–117, 231, 374, 494
Depository Institutions Deregulation and Monetary Control Act (DIDMCA) 39, 91, 117, 494
depression. *See* Great Depression
deregulation 117–119
    of airline industry 494
    antitrust activity and 26
    of banking industry 38, 469
    of financial services 116, 458–459
    of holding companies 199
    in 1970s to 1990s xii
    of railroads 356
    Securities Exchange Act of 1934 382
    of telecommunications industry 427–428
    of television industry 434
    of transportation industry 225
    of utilities 454
derivatives markets 56, 319, 419–420

Des Moines Register and Tribune (newspaper) 307
Detroit Automobile Company 167
Detroit Red Wings 407
Dewey, Thomas 490
Dichter, Ernest 5–6
Dickson, W. K. L. 285–286
Dictaphones 136
dictatorships 448
DIDMCA. *See* Depository Institutions Deregulation and Monetary Control Act (DIDMCA)
diesel engines 139, 387, 390, 444
Digital Equipment Corporation (DEC) 97
digital technology 354, 428
Dillon Read & Co. 76, 119
Diners Club 15, 108
direct investment 170
disarmament 555
disaster lending 402
discount commissions 392
discount rate 155
Discover credit card 377
discrimination 17–18, 225, 246, 364
disk operating system (DOS) 98, 179
Disney, Walt 119–121, 493
Disneyland (television series) 120
distribution, motion picture industry 289
diversification 180, 188, 326–327, 393–394, 452, 468
Dodge, Edward 81
Dodge Brothers' Motor Co. 76, 119
dollar, U.S. 59, 140–141, 169, 187, 461–462
Domestic Communications Satellite (Domsat) 427
Donaldson, William 382
Dort, J. Dallas 29, 128
dot-com industry 99, 224, 429
Dot system, NYSE 308
Douglas (aircraft manufacturer) 13
Douglass, Benjamin 110
Douglass, Frederick 302
Dow, Charles H. 121–122, 305
Dow Chemical Company 70–71, 72, 121
Dow Jones & Co. 48, 305
Dow Jones Industrial Average 121–122, 181, 305, 377, 492

Doyle Dane Bernbach 6–7
Drake, Edwin L. 328
Draper, Rachel 478
dream factories 287
dressmaking business 478
Drew, Daniel **122–123**, 138, 162, 188, 416, 489
Drew, Robinson, & Co. 122
Drew University 123
Drexel, Anthony J. **123**
Drexel, Francis M. 123
Drexel, Katherine 123
Drexel & Co. 281
Drexel Burnham 494
Drexel Burnham Lambert 116, **123–124**, 231, 346
Drexel Morgan & Co. 60, 279
Drexel University 123
drought of 1931 148
Drucker, Peter **124–125**
drug manufacturers. *See* pharmaceutical industry
Drug Price Competition and Patent Term Restoration Act 338
drug stores 326–327
dry dock, floating *387*
Dubinsky, David 18–19
due diligence 379
Duer, William 46, **125–126**, 308
Duff & Phelps Credit Rating Agency 111
Duke, James Buchanan 23, **126–127**, 211
Duke, Sons & Co., W. 23, 126, 492
Duke, Washington 22–23
Duke Endowment 126–127
Duke Power Company 126
Duke University 126–127
Dun, Robert G. 110
Dun & Bradstreet 111
DuPont, Alfred I. 127
DuPont, Pierre S. 127–128, 356, 401
DuPont, Thomas C. 127
DuPont Company 261, 356
DuPont de Nemours & Co., E. I. 69, 71, **127–128**, 356, 491
Duquesne Steel Company 173
Durant, Thomas 443
Durant, William Crapo 29–31, **128–129**, 182–183, 356, 401
Durant-Dort Carriage Company 183
Dutch wagon 100

duties of the rich man 520–527
dyestuffs, synthetic 69

E

Eagleton Iron Works 343–344
E. A. Pierce & Co. 271
Eastern Airlines **131–132**, 494
Eastman, George **132–133**, *286*, 492
Eastman Kodak Company 132–133, 243
East Texas Field 331–333
Eaton, Cyrus **133–134**, 235
Ebbers, Bernard 488
e-businesses 136
Eccles, Marriner S. **134–135**
Eccles Act 493
Eccles-Browning Affiliated Banks 134
Eckert, J. Presper 95, 219
Eckert-Mauchly Computer Corporation 95
e-commerce firms 99
Economic Consequences of the Peace, The (Keynes) 237
economic depression. *See* Great Depression
Economic Opportunity Loans 403
Economic Recovery Act 206
economic reform 549–551, 558
economics
    industrialization and laissez-faire theory 241
    Nobel Prize in 56
    Phillips curve 339–340
    of slavery 396–401
    of sports industry 403
    supply-side 206
economy
    colonial period 207
    development of American 47–48
    Samuel Gompers on 187
    Interstate Highway Act and 226
    shipping industry and 388
    sustained growth 459
    UAW and 447
    Thorstein Veblen on 457–458
    wartime 446
Edgar Thomson Steel Works 375, 409
Edison, Thomas A. **135–136**
    automotive industry 29
    Alexander Graham Bell and 50

Industrial Revolution and 212
    Samuel Insull and 212
    with motion picture camera *286*
    in motion picture industry 285
    ticker tape 436
Edison Electric Co. 181, 453, 454, 492
Edison Illuminating Company 165
Edmunds, George 383
Edsel automobile 168
education 260, 433, 479, 482
EEC. *See* European Economic Community (EEC)
E. I. DuPont de Nemours & Co. 69, 71, **127–128**, 491
Eisenhower, Dwight D. 226, 272, 402, **555–558**
Eisner, Michael 120, 230
Elders & Fyffes 448
electric chairs 135
electricity trading markets 136
electric power. *See also specific companies;* utilities industry
    automobiles 28
    hydroelectric generation 126, 453–454, 471
    Industrial Revolution and 212
    lightbulbs 135
    mining industry and 277
    Singer Sewing Co. 393
    Tennessee Valley Authority 435
    transmission systems 471
    utilities 453
    Theodore N. Vail 455
    Wanamaker's 463
electromagnetic telegraph 284, 430
electronic chemicals 69
electronic communication networks (ECNs) 417
Electronic Data Systems (EDS) 183
electronic field production (EFP) 434
electronic media 348, 431–432. *See also* radio industry; television
electronic networks (ETNs) 309
electronic news gathering (ENG) 434

Electronic Numerical Integrator and Computer (ENIAC) 95
elevated rail system 412
elevators 394
Ellison, Ralph 487
e-mail 223–224, 318–319
"embalmed beef" scandal 529
Embargo Act 207, 214
embezzlement 474
Emergency Fleet Corporation 386
Emergency Relief Appropriation 487
eminent domain 440
Empire State Building 76, 356, 394, *397*
employee benefits
    at Eastman Kodak Company 133
    employee stock ownership plans 327–328
    Henry Ford and 166
    at IBM 466
    pension funds 327–328
    Walter P. Reuther and 361
    UAW and 444, 446–447
    UMWA and 451
    Sam Walton and 462
    John Wanamaker and 464
    in women-owned businesses 484
Employee Retirement Income Security Act (ERISA) 327–328
employee stock ownership plans (ESOPS) 327–328
Employment Act of 1946 154–155
End of Economic Man, The (Drucker) 124
energy. *See* electric power; utilities industry
Energy Policy Act 342, 454
Engerman, Stanley 398
Engineering Research Associates 96
engineers, in mining industry 276
Enron Corporation xi, **136–137**, 372, 420, 494
Enterprising Women (Bird) 476
entertainment industry 412–413, 436–437, 476
entrepreneurship, women and 477, 479–480
environmental issues 74, 121, 278, 311

Equal Credit Opportunity Act 485
Equal Pay Act 485
Equitable Life Assurance Company 174, 280
Erie Canal 137, 440, 491
Erie-Lackawanna Railroad (EL) 139
Erie Railroad Company 122, 137–140, 188–189, 354, 457
Erie War 138, 163, 354, 457
Esch-Cummins Transportation Act 225
Esso 70–71, 332–334, 365
EU. See European Union (EU)
euro xi, 140–141, 169
European Economic Community (EEC) 140
European Monetary Union 140
European System of Central Banks 140
European Union (EU) 169
exchange rates 58, 140
exchanges. See stock markets
exchange-traded derivatives markets 56
exclusive service territory 342
executive compensation 56
Eximbank. See Export-Import Bank of the United States 141–142
export credits 141
Export-Import Bank of the United States 141–142
exports 207, 477
express cartel 14
express money order 14
express package delivery 469
Exxon Corporation 332–334, 365
Exxon/Mobil 334, 366
eyewitness radio news 353

F
facsimile 431
factory system 212, 261–262, 277, 423
Fairchild Semiconductor 98
family enterprises 477
family values, in advertising 6
Fannie Mae. See Federal National Mortgage Association
Faraday and Henry 430
Fargo, William G. 14, 469
Farmall tractor 222
Farm Credit System 143–144, 190
farmers 354–356, 464

Farmer's Advance 263
farm implements industry
advertising industry and 2
corn harvester 146
John Deere and 115–116
farming mechanization and 148
International Harvester Company 221–222
Cyrus McCormick and 262–263
UAW and 446
Eli Whitney and 473
farming 144–151, 249
Farnsworth, Philo T. 431–433
Farwell, Field, and Company 158
fashion 479
FCC. See Federal Communications Commission (FCC)
FDIC. See Federal Deposit Insurance Corporation (FDIC)
Federal Agricultural Mortgage Corporation (Farmer Mac) 144, 190
Federal-Aid Highway Act 226
Federal Aviation Agency/ Administration (FAA) 11
Federal Base Ball Club of Baltimore, Inc. v. National League of Professional Base Ball Clubs et al. 404–405
Federal Communications Commission (FCC) 151, 307, 347, 426–429, 433, 493
Federal Courts Improvements Act 326
federal debt 43, 177, 505. See also Treasury bonds
federal deposit insurance 45, 361, 416. See also Depository Institutions Act
Federal Deposit Insurance Corporation (FDIC) 38–39, 151–152, 161
Federal Deposit Insurance Corporation Improvement Act (FDICIA) 152
Federal Farm Loan Board 143, 272
federal funds rate 155
Federal Home Loan Bank Board 152–153, 161, 374, 493
Federal Home Loan Bank System 190

Federal Home Loan Mortgage Corporation (Freddie Mac) 153–154, 190–191
Federal Housing Administration 152–153
federal insurance 213
Federalist, The (Hamilton, Jay, and Madison) 195
Federalist Papers 301
Federalist Party 195
federal land banks 143
Federal League 404
Federal Loan Agency 358
Federal National Mortgage Association 153–154, 190–191
Federal Open Market Committee 154–155, 458
Federal Power Act 342
Federal Reserve (Fed) 154–156
  Bank Holding Company Act and 37–38
  banknotes and 39
  commercial banking 91–92
  commercial paper and 92–93
  Commodity Futures Trading Commission 176
  DIDMCA and 117
  Financial Services Modernization Act 162
  monetary policy changes by 494
  Jacob Schiff and 240
  Securities Exchange Act 381
  stock markets 415
Federal Reserve Act 41, 417, 493
Federal Reserve Bank of New York 45–46, 250, 417, 458
Federal Reserve banks 154
Federal Reserve Board 193–194, 250, 272, 417, 458, 552
Federal Savings and Loan Insurance Corporation (FSLIC) 152, 161, 361
Federal Trade Commission (FTC) 24, 26, 156–157, 493, 529
Federated Department Stores 260
Federated Steel Co. 452
Federation of Business and Professional Women (BPW) 483

Federation of Organized Trades and Labor Unions of the United States and Canada (FOTLU) 16–17, 187
federation of trade unions 514
female academies 479
feminist movement 7
femme covert (woman covered) 477–478
femme sole (woman alone) 477–478, 482
ferry service 456
Fessenden, Reginald A. 349
fiber-optics 50, 428–429
Field, Cyrus W. 157–159, 470
Field, David D. 157
Field, Marshall 158–159
Field, Stephen J. 157
Field, Palmer, and Leitner 158
Fields, Debbie Sivyer 483
Filene, William 489
Film Booking Offices of America 236
film industry. See motion picture industry
finance, history of ix
Financial Accounting Foundation 160
Financial Accounting Standards Advisory Council (FASAC) 160
Financial Accounting Standards Board (FASB) 159–160, 182
financial advertising 380
financial futures and options 75
financial holding companies 162
Financial Institutions Reform, Recovery, and Enforcement Act (FIRREA) 116, 153, 160–161, 360–361, 374, 494
financial journalism 48
Financial Modernization Act 228
financial research 473
Financial Services Modernization Act 94, 161–162, 468, 494
financial supermarkets 162
financing 92–93, 483
Finding Nemo (film) 230
Finley, Charles 172
Fiorino, Carleton 484
firearms 87–88, 491
fire insurance 214–215
Firemen's Magazine (Debs) 114

Fireside Chats 352
FIRREA. *See* Financial
    Institutions Reform,
    Recovery, and Enforcement
    Act (FIRREA)
First Global Crossing 429
First Interstate Bank 470
First National Bank of New
    York
First National City Bank 38,
    79–80
First National City Bank
    (National City Bank) 80
First Security Corporation
    134
Fish, Stuyvesant 196–197
Fisk, James, Jr. (Jim) **162**
    in cartoon 139
    Daniel Drew 122
    Erie War 138
    Jay Gould and 188–189
    railroads 354
    Cornelius Vanderbilt 457
Fisk, Belden & Co. 162
Fitch Ratings 112
five and dime stores 239, 486
5-20s (Treasury bonds) 104,
    193
fixed parity system 58–59
fixed-rate commissions 359
flag and shipping fleet 387,
    390–391
Flagler, Henry M. **163–164**,
    365
Flatiron Building 394
Flint (Michigan) 445
Flint, Charles 219
floating currencies 169
floating exchange rates 59
"floats" 15
Flood, Curt 172
floor traders 414
Florida 164
Florida East Coast Railroad
    163–164
flour milling 208
FM (frequency modulation)
    353
Fogel, Robert 398
Foley, Eugene 403
Fonda, Jane 439
Food and Drug Administration
    337, 529
Food and Drug Law (1906)
    336–337
Food, Drug and Cosmetic Act
    (1938) 337–339, 529
football 405–406
Forbes, Bertie C. 164
Forbes, Malcolm **164–166**
Forbes Magazine 164

Ford, Edsel 166
Ford, Henry **165–167**
    automotive industry
        29–31
    Bernard M. Baruch and
        49
    Industrial Revolution and
        211
    mass production 262
    Tennessee Valley
        Authority 435
    UAW 444
Ford, Henry, II 32, 167, 203
Ford, William C., Jr. 168
Ford Crown Victoria 32
Ford Foundation 166–167
Ford Motor Company
    167–168
    automotive industry 29,
        32
    William C. Durant and
        128–129
    Henry Ford and 166–167
    founding of 492
    Lee Iacocca and 203
    Walter P. Reuther 361
    UAW 445–446
Ford Motor Credit 167
Fordney-McCumber tariff 422
foreclosures, farms 148
foreign banks 367
foreign capital xii
foreign competition 33–34,
    411, 447, 452
foreign correspondent
    networks 79–80
Foreign Corrupt Practices Act
    168–169
Foreign Credit Insurance
    Association 141
foreign exchange market 59,
    141, **169–170**, 198, 494
foreign investments xii,
    170–171
foreign markets 291
foreign oil 332
foreign ships 386, 389–390
Fore River Ship & Engine
    Company 465
forest management 254–256
forest products industry. *See*
    lumber industry
Forest Service, U.S. 256
forfeiture of property 345–346
"Forgotten Man" (Roosevelt)
    549–551
Fortune (magazine) 437
Fortune 500 291
49ers 274
forward integration 266, 268
forward market 169

Foundation for Women
    Business Owners 484
401k plans 328
franchise relocation 405
franchise system, in bottling
    and distribution 83
"francking privileges" 300
Franklin, Benjamin 300
Franklin, James 300
fraud 40–41, 296, 338,
    340–341, 403, 429, 474. *See
    also* corruption; scandals
free agency **171–173**, 405
Free Banking Era 40
free blacks 400
freedom of the press 300–301
free laborers 398–399
freeze order 433
freight transport 100–101,
    208, 409
French Revolution 249
French Thomson 347
frequency-allocation system
    433
Frick, Henry Clay 64,
    173–174
Frick Museum 174
Fruit Dispatch Company 448
Frye, Gene 268
FTC. *See* Federal Trade
    Commission (FTC)
fuel oil 332
full disclosure 551
Fulton, Robert **174–175**, 249,
    456
funds clearance system 40–43
fur trade 26–27, 199–200
futures markets 61, 74–75,
    93, **175–176**, 319, 416
F. W. Woolworth Co. 486,
    492

G

Gale, Leonard 284
Gallatin, Albert **177–178**
games of chance 251–252
gang system, in slavery
    398–401
Gannett Newspapers 304, 307
Gardner-Farnsworth, Elma
    "Pem" 432
Garn–St. Germain Act **116**
Gary (Indiana) 178
Gary, Elbert H. **178**, 375–376,
    410, 452
gasoline 330–333
Gates, Bill **179–180**, 230, 562
Gay, Edwin F. 197
GE. *See* General Electric Co.
    (GE)
GE Capital 181

Geneen, Harold S. **180–181**,
    244
Genentech 339
General Agreement on Tariffs
    and Trade (GATT) 422
General Electric Co. (GE) **181**
    Thomas A. Edison
        135–136
    founded as Edison
        Electric 492
    Samuel Insull and 212
    J. P. Morgan and 280
    Kidder Peabody & Co.
        239
    radio industry 349–351
    RCA 346–347
    David Sarnoff 373
    telecommunications
        industry 425
    television industry 432
    utilities 453
    John F. Welch 468
    George Westinghouse Jr.
        471
    Owen D. Young 490
General Foods 85–86
general interest newspapers
    304
generally accepted accounting
    principles (GAAP) xi, 159,
    181–182, 380, 420
General Motors Acceptance
    Corp. 183, 401
General Motors Corp. (GM)
    in automotive industry
        29–30, 32
    in chronology 492–493
    Walter Percy Chrysler and
        75–76
    consumer movement 103
    Peter Drucker and 124,
        128–129, **182–183**
    Pierre S. DuPont and 128
    J. & W. Seligman & Co.
        382
    managerial capitalism and
        261
    Ralph Nader investigation
        293
    John J. Raskob 356
    Alfred Sloan 401
    UAW 445–446
    Owen D. Young 490
*General Shipping and
    Commercial List*
    (newspaper) 305
*General Theory of Money,
    Interest and Prices, The*
    (Keynes) 237–238
generic pharmaceuticals 338
Genovese, Eugene 398

Geological Survey, U.S. 276
George, James 383
Georgia 398
Germany 69, 337
Gerstner, Louis 221
Getty, J. Paul **183–185**
Giannini, A. P. 41–42
Gibbons, Thomas 174, 456
Gibbons v. Ogden 89–90, 412, 456, 491
Gilman, George 191
Gilson, Mary B. 482
Girard, Stephen **185**, 437, 489
glass ceiling 484–485
glass manufacturers 320–321
Glass-Steagall Act. *See* Banking Act (1933) (Glass-Steagall Act)
Glidden, Carlos 440
globalization xii
    of agriculture 150
    in coffee industry 85–86
    of media culture 290
    of mining industry 278
    multinational
      corporations and
      291–292
    telecommunications
      industry 425
    Wharton School 473
    of world's market 118
global outsourcing 100
Glucksman, Lewis 246
GM. *See* General Motors Corp. (GM)
GNA Corporation 472
Goddard, Mary Katherine 476–477
Goddard, Sarah 477
Goethals, George W. 323
Goizueta, Roberto 83
gold 188–189, 323
gold corner 163
Golden Rule Store 326
Gold Indicator Company 135
Goldman, Marcus 92
Goldman Sachs & Co. 92, **185–186**, 245, 250, 377
Goldmark, Peter 432
gold mining 278
Gold Reserve Act 187, 493
gold rushes 244, 274–276, 385, 418–419, 456–457
gold standard 169, **186–187**, 193, 494
golf 407–408
Gompers, Samuel 16–17, **187–188**, 514
Goodrich, Benjamin Franklin **188**

Goodyear Tire & Rubber Company 119, 133
Gore, Al 294
"Gospel of Wealth." *See* "Wealth"
Gould, George 443
Gould, Jay **188–190**
    Daniel Drew 122
    Erie War 138
    Cyrus W. Field and 158
    James Fisk Jr. and 163
    railroads 354
    robber barons 363
    Thomas A. Scott 376
    Union Pacific Railroad 443
    Cornelius Vanderbilt 457
government assistance 198–199
government-business-labor partnerships 446
government guarantees, implied 190
Government National Mortgage Association (Ginnie Mae) 153–154, 190
government-owned utilities 453–454
government spending 558
government-sponsored enterprises (GSEs) 153–154, **190–191**, 435
government subsidies 150, 190–191
grading of meat 268
Graham, Benjamin 61
Graham, Katherine Meyer 272
Grain Futures Act 93, 175
Gramm-Leach-Bliley Act 94, 161–162
Grand Central Station 457
Grange movement 355, 464
Grant, Ulysses S. 189, 382
Grasselli, Eugene 69
Great American Tea Company 191
Great Atlantic & Pacific Tea Co. (A&P) 85, **191–192**, 364, 492
Great Depression
    automotive industry and 31
    in business history x, xi
    Deere & Co. 116
    Export-Import Bank of the United States 141–142
    farming and 148
    Federal Reserve and 154
    J. Paul Getty and 184

    government-sponsored enterprises and 190
    income tax and 205
    logging industry and 256
    motion picture industry and 288
    NRA 298
    pension funds and 327
    PWA 342
    radio industry 352
    recession 357
    and regulation 118, 360
    RFC and 113
    Franklin D. Roosevelt on 549–551
    shipbuilding industry 386
    Benjamin Strong 417
    tariffs and 198, 422
    UAW 444
Great Erie War 138, 163, 354, 457
Greater Seminole Field 331
Great Inflation 155–156
Great Northern Railroad 198, 255
Great Society programs 362
Great White Fleet 448
Greeley, Horace 302
Greeley, William 256
Green, William 17–19
greenbacks **192–193**
Greenbacks (political party) 205
greenmail 270
Green Party 294
Greenspan, Alan 155, **193–194**
G. R. Kinney Corp. 486
grocers, and coffee industry 83–84
gross domestic product x
growth-by-acquisition strategy 78
GR-S (government rubber-styrene) 368
guided missile systems 57
Gulf Oil and Refining 330–332
gunpowder 127

H
Hadden, Briton 437
Haitian Revolution 397
Halsey Stuart & Co. 134
Hamburg Line 448
Hamilton, Alexander **195–196**
    Bank of New York 90
    Bank of New York charter 42

    Bank of the United States 43–44
    Albert Gallatin and 177
    Robert R. Livingston and 249
    Report on the Subject of Manufactures (1791) **504–514**
    William Duer and 125–126
Hamilton, Andrew 301
Hammond typewriters 441
hand calculators 316
handguns 87–88
handkerchief trick 122
hand ratings, in slavery 399
Hanover Trust Company 341
Hardenbroeck, Margaret 478
Harding, Warren 490
hard rock mining 274, 276, 278
hardwood lumber production 257
Harkness, William 365
Harpo 475
Harriman, Edward H. **196–197**, 198, 375, 443
Harriman, William A. 196
Harriman Ripley & Co. 60
Harris, Benjamin 300
Harrison, Benjamin 464
Hartford, George H. 191
Hartford, John 191
Hartford Fire Insurance Company 180
Hartley, Fred A. 421
Hart-Scott-Rodino Act 157
Harvard Graduate School of Business **197**, 261, 492
Hawley, Willis 197
Hawley-Smoot Tariff Act 141, **197–198**, 422, 493
Hayden, Stone and Company 236, 467
Hayek, Friedrich 237
hazardous waste 278
H. C. Frick Coke Co. 173
Headline News Network 439
health care benefits 451
health insurance 213, 217–218
health maintenance organizations (HMOs) 235
Healy, Robert 381
Hearst, William Randolph 303, *304*
hedge funds 250, 292
Heffelfinger, William (Pudge) 406
Hellman, Isaias W. 469

Hellman's Union Trust
    Company 469
Henie, Sonja 408
Henry, Joseph 284, 430
Henry Ford Company
    166–167. *See also* Ford
    Motor Company
Hepburn Act 225, 356
Herrold, Charles D. 350
Hertz, Heinrich 348
Hewlett-Packard 229
hidden options 56
Hidden Persuaders, The
    (Packard) 6
Hill, James J. **198–199**, 472
Hillman, Sidney 18–19
*History of Erie and Other
    Essays* (Adams and Adams)
    290
*History of the Great American
    Fortunes, A* (Myers) 290,
    363
*History of the Standard Oil
    Company* (Tarbell) 290
Hitler, Adolf 184
H. K. Mulford Company 336
Hoar, George 383
hockey 407
Hoechst Company 121
Hog Island shipyard 386
hog slaughtering 267
holding companies **199**
    diversified 101–102
    General Motors as 30
    James J. Hill and 198
    public utility 342
    trusts as forerunner of 23
    Union Pacific Railroad
        444
Hollerith, Herman 95, 218,
    315
Holley, Alexander 409
Hollywood 286–290
Holman, Currier 268
Home for Destitute Women
    and Children 478–479
Home Insurance Building 394
home mortgages 152–153,
    190, 374
home offices 318
Home Owner's Loan
    Association 152–153
Homestead Act 146–147
Homestead steelworks 64,
    173, 375, 409, 492
Hoover, Herbert 197–198,
    272, 357–358
Hopkins, Harry 342–343, 487
Hopper, Inslee 393
horizontal integration 289
horizontal mergers 270

horse racing 51–52
hostile takeovers 270, 328,
    381
hot-air ballooning 165
House of Morgan 279, 282.
    See also J. P. Morgan & Co.
    (House of Morgan)
House of Rothschild 47,
    51–52, **366–367**
House Un-American Activities
    Committee 288. *See also*
    communism
Howe, Mather & Co. 282
Hubbard, Gardiner G. 455
Hudson River Railroad 457
Hudson River Rubber
    Company
Hudson's Bay Company
    199–200, 491, **495–504**
Hughes, Howard, Jr. **200–201**
Humble Oil and Refining 331
Humphrey-Durham
    Amendment 338
Hunt, H. I. 331
Hunter, Jim "Catfish" 172
Hussey, Obed 262
Hutzler, Morton 371
Hyatt Roller Bearing Company
    401
hydraulic mining 275
hydroelectric power 126,
    453–454, 471
hypertext markup language
    (HTML) 99

I

Iacocca, Lee 77, 168, **203–204**
IBM Corporation *See*
    International Business
    Machines (IBM
    Corporation)
ICC. *See* Interstate Commerce
    Commission (ICC)
Ickes, Harold 342–343
Idaho Silver Valley 277–278
I. G. Farben 69, 71
Illinois Central Railroad 196
illuminants 328–329
immigrants
    in business history xii
    Alexander Hamilton on
        505
    Industrial Revolution and
        208
    Charles Ponzi and 341
    George M. Pullman and
        343
    UAW and 444
    UMWA and 449
    Union Pacific Railroad
        and 443

Immunex 339
imports 207, 422
income tax xii, **204–206**,
    422–423, 493
indentured servants 396–398
independent producers,
    motion picture industry
    289
Independent Woman
    (magazine) 482
index funds 20
indies, motion picture
    industry 289
indigo 145
indirect investment 170
industrialization 241, 409,
    423
industrial life insurance 217
Industrial Revolution in the
    United States 1–3, 145–146,
    206–212, 207
industrial unionism 449. *See
    also* labor organizations
Industrial Workers of the
    World (IWW) 17
industries, U.S. 209, *210*, 211,
    395
inflation 358, 458
inflation-unemployment trade-
    off 339–340
Information Processing
    Techniques Office (IPTO) 99
information technology (IT)
    100
infrastructure 208, 366–367
Ingram, Orrin H. 253
initial public offering (IPO)
    186, 380
innovations
    in advertising industry 6,
        232–233
    in automotive industry
        32, 166, 183
    in business practices 484
    in farming 146–147
    in glass manufacture
        320–321
    in lumber industry 255
    in management 183, 484
    in manufacture 209
    in newspaper industry
        303
    in pharmaceutical
        industry 336
    in retail 159, 463–464
    in steel industry 211
insider trading 124, 413,
    415–416
installment payment plan 393
Insull, Samuel 133, 135,
    212–213, 453

insurance industry **213–218**,
    280, 379, 494
integrated circuit (IC) 96
integration 479
Intel 98
interchangeable parts
    208–209
intercontinental ballistic
    missiles 57
intercontinental widebody
    airliner 13
interest
    DIDMCA and 117
    rate ceilings 39
    rate pegs 91, 154
    savings and loans 374
    Benjamin Strong 417
    Tax Reform Act 423
Interest Equalization Act (IET)
    422
interlocking directorates. *See*
    Clayton Antitrust Act
Intermarket Trading System
    (ITS) 359
International Bank for
    Reconstruction and
    Development. *See* World
    Bank 59
international banking 42
International Banking
    Corporation 79–80
International Business
    Machines (IBM
    Corporation) **218–221**
    antitrust cases against
        25–26
    Bill Gates and 179
    computer industry 95–98
    founded as Tabulating
        Machine Co. 492
    Malcolm Baldrige
        National Quality Award
        260
    office machines and 315,
        441
    Thomas J. Watson 466
international currency
    stabilization program 417
international exchange
    standard 59
International Harvester
    Company **221–223**, 263,
    280
International Monetary Fund
    (IMF) 58–59, 198
International Monetary Market
    75
international monetary system
    141, 169
International Motor Vehicle
    Program 33

International News Service 304
International Swap and Derivatives Association 420
International Telephone & Telegraph 180
Internet 223–224
    and banknotes 41
    browsers 99, 224, 318
    organized as World Wide Web 494
    routing equipment 78
    stock market bubble 415
    telecommunications industry 428–429
    Time Warner 437
Internet-based business xi
Internet Explorer 224, 563
Internet Service Providers (ISPs) 223
interpretive journalism 305–307
interstate banking 90–91, 224–225, 264, 494
Interstate Branching Act 224–225, 264
interstate commerce 89–90, 405
Interstate Commerce Act 279, 516–520
Interstate Commerce Commission (ICC) 225–226
    commerce clause and 90
    deregulation and 118
    railroads and 138, 147, 355–356
    Staggers Rail Act 409
    telecommunications industry 426
Interstate Highway Act 226, 356
interstate highway system 227, 268, 332
Interstate Oil Compact 331–332
inventory control, Wal-Mart 462
investigative journalism 290–291, 363–364
Investment Advisors Act 292
Investment Bankers Association 228
investment banking 226–228
    Banking Act of 1933 38
    August Belmont 51
    August Belmont II and 52
    Jay Cooke 103–104
    Drexel Burnham Lambert 123–124
    Cyrus Eaton and 133

General Electric Co. and 181
Goldman Sachs & Co. 185–186
House of Rothschild 366–367
J. & W. Seligman & Co. 382–383
Kidder Peabody & Co. 238–239
Kuhn Loeb & Co. 240
Lazard Freres 243–244
Lehman Brothers and 245–246
mergers and 269
Morgan Stanley & Co. and 282–283
Salomon Brothers 371
investment trusts 186
ironclad battleships 412
iron industry 208, 211
ITT Corporation 244, 246
ITT Financial Services 180
Ives, Herbert E. 432

J

Jackson, Andrew 44, 54–55, 55, 301, 422
Jackson, Thomas P. 562–564
Jacksonville Agreement 450
Jacobs Pharmacy (Atlanta) 82
James Fisk (steamboat) 163
J. & W. Seligman & Co. 382–383, 438
Japan, foreign investment of 170
Japanese carmakers 33–34, 203
Java programming language 563
Jay, John 195, 249
Jay Cooke & Co. 81, 103–104, 123, 193, 228, 438
Jazz Singer, The (film) 288
J. C. Penney & Co. 326–327
Jefferson, Thomas 44, 127, 249, 273, 325, 504–505
Jenkins, Charles F. 431–432
Jenkins Television Corporation 431
jet airliners 13
jet propulsion 10
jet service 325
J. H. Hobbs, Brockunier, and Company 320
Jobs, Steve 229–230
John A. Brown & Co. 60
John B. Stetson Company 411–412
John Deere & Co. 491

Johnson, Earvin "Magic" 407
Johnson, Hugh Samuel 230–231, 298
John Wanamaker & Co. 463, 492
John Wanamaker Commercial Institute 464
joint ventures 383
Jones, Edward 121, 305
Jones, Jesse 358
Jordan, Michael 407
Josephson, Matthew 291, 363
journalism 48, 290–291, 303, 305–307, 363–364
Journal of Commerce (newspaper) 305
J. Paul Getty Museum 184
J. P. Morgan & Co. (House of Morgan). See also Morgan, John Pierpont
    August Belmont and 51
    Drexel & Co. 124
    Erie Railroad Company 138
    founding of 492
    Glass-Steagall Act and 38
    Kidder Peabody & Co. 238
    Thomas W. Lamont and 242
    merger with Chase Manhattan 68, 494
    J. P. Morgan Jr. and 281
    Morgan Stanley & Co. 282
    Alfred Sloan 401
    Treasury bonds 438
    utilities 453
    Richard Whitney 474
J. P. Morgan Chase 68, 400
J. S. Morgan & Co. of London 123, 281–282
Judson, Arthur 352
Jung, Andrea 484
Jungle, The (Sinclair) 291, 529
junk bonds 116, 124, 153, 231
J. Walter Thompson 4, 231–233
JWT Group, Inc. 233

K

Kaiser, Henry J. 235–236
Kaiser Permanente Medical Care Program 235
Kaiser Steel 235
kaizen, principle of 34
Karmazin, Mel 89
KDKA Pittsburgh 350, 472
Keckley, Elizabeth H. 478
Keith, Minor C. 448

Kelley, Florence 102
Kelso, Louis 327–328
Kennedy, Joseph P. 236–237, 381, 552
Kennedy, Thomas 451
Kerkorian, Kirk 203
kerosene 329
Kerr-McGee 333
Keynes, John Maynard 237–238, 360
Keynesianism 206
Keys, Clement 131
Keystone Bridge Company 63, 376
Keystone Telegraph Co. 63
Kidder, Henry 238
Kidder Peabody & Co. 47, 81, 181, 238–239, 468
Kiernan News Agency 305
kinetoscope 285
King, Billie Jean 408
King, Susan 480
Kings College (Columbia University) 237, 303
Kinney Corp., G. R. 486
kit homes 378
K-Mart 239–240, 377, 413
Knight-Ridder newspapers 304
Knights of Labor, UMWA 449
Kodak 132, 492
Kollar-Kotelly, Colleen 563
Korean War 13
Kostyra, Martha. See Stewart, Martha
Kovacevich, Dick 470
Kresge, Sebastien S. 239
Kuhn Loeb & Co. 240, 246, 375

L

labor. See also farming; labor organizations; labor relations
    migrant 150
    movement 102, 114–115
    value of 385, 398
Labor Management Relations Act 421
labor organizations. See also specific labor organizations
    Civil War 18–19
    corruption in 18, 451
    democracy in 450–452
    Eastern Airlines and 132
    farmworkers' unions 150
    Ford Motor Company and 167
    Samuel Gompers and 187–188
    John L. Lewis and 248

local autonomy in 452
lumber industry and 256
George Meany and
    264–265
mergers of 19, 361–362
multinational
    corporations and
    291–292
NAFTA and 311
organizers 445
pure and simple 17–18
Walter P. Reuther and
    362
rubber industry 368
United Fruit Company
    448
labor relations. *See also* strikes
Lee Iacocca and 203
International Harvester
    Company 222
Peter Drucker on 125
George M. Pullman 343
sports industry 406
steel industry 410–411
women in 482
Lachman, Charles 362
Ladies Professional Golfers
    Association (LPGA) 408
LaGuardia, Fiorello 553
laissez-faire **241–242**,
    520–527
Lamont, Thomas W. **242**
Lamont, Corliss & Company
    242
Lancaster Turnpike 440, 491
Land, Edwin H. **243**
land, timbered 472
land development 235
land grants 418
Landis, James 381
land speculation 126, 341
Land-Wheelwright
    Laboratories 243
Lanham Act 326
Lansdowne, Helen 232
laptop computers 318
laser communication 50
Latrobe Athletic Association
    406
Lavoisier, Antoine 127
Lay, Kenneth 136
Lazard Freres **243–244**
Lea, Clarence F. 529
Lead Leasing Act 273
lead mining 273–274, 276
League of Nations 113
lean production 33–34
Leblanc, Maurice 431
lecture tours 479
Lederle Antitoxin Laboratories
    336

Lee, Ivy L. **244–245**
Lehman Brothers 186, 240,
    245–246, 377
Leitner, Levi Z. 159
Leland, Henry M. 29–30
Lenglen, Suzanne 408
Leo Burnett Co. 6
Lerow, John A. 393
leverage 61
leveraged buyout (LBO) 270,
    328
Levitt, Arthur 382
Levitt & Sons 246
Levittown 226, **246–247**
Lewis, John L. 18–19, **248**,
    450–451
Lewis, Sinclair 291
Libbey, Edward D. 320–321
Libbey-Owens Sheet Glass
    Company 320
Liberty loans 371, **438**
life insurance 213, 216–217
Life (magazine) 437
Lilienthal, David 435
Lincoln, Abraham 343
Lincoln, Mary Todd 479
Lincoln Highway 226
Lincoln Motor Company 167
Lippman, Walter 307
lipsticks 362
liquidity policies, National
    City Bank 79
Little, Jacob 416
Little Three, motion picture
    industry 287–288
livestock buyers 266
Livingston, Robert R. 174,
    248–250, 412, 456
L., J., & S. Joseph 367
Lloyd, William D. 290
Loan Guarantee Act 77
loans to developing countries
    91–92
local operating companies,
    telecommunications
    industry 428
local television stations 434
Lockheed 13
lode mining 275
Loeb, Solomon 240
Loewe v. Lawlor 540
London School of Economics
    237
Long, George S. 256
Long, Huey 206
long-playing (LP) record 88
Long-Term Capital
    Management 250, 494
Looking Backward (Bellamy)
    108
Lorenzo, Frank 132

Lorillard & Company, P[ierre].
    251
Los Angeles 358–359
Los Angeles Lakers 407
lotteries **251–252**
Louisiana Purchase 177, 249,
    273
Louisiana State Lottery 252
Lovestone, Jay 19
Lowell, Francis 208
lumber industry 208,
    252–257, 385, 472
Lydia Pinkham Company 335
Lyle, Irving 65
Lynch, Edmond 271
Lyon, Mary 479

M

Maastricht Treaty 140
*Machine That Changed the
    World, The* (International
    Motor Vehicle Program) 33
machine tool techniques 261
MacIntyre, Malcolm 131
MacNamara, Robert S. 203
Macy, Rowland H. **259–260**
Made Beaver (MB) 200
Madison, James 44, 195
magazines 2, 232, 437
magnesium, extraction from
    seawater 121
mail delivery 226, 464, 469.
    See also air mail service
Mailgram 471
mail-order sales 326, 377,
    464
Maine 253
Maine (battleship) 303–304
Major League Baseball
    171–173, 404–405
Major League Soccer 407
makeup 362–363
Malcolm Baldrige National
    Quality Award **260**
Maloney Act 295, 298
management buyout 270
management practices
    Peter Drucker and
        124–125
    Frederick W. Taylor 423
    Sam Walton 462
    Thomas J. Watson
        466–467
    John F. Welch 468
management theory x, xi
managerial bureaucracies,
    women and 482
managerial capitalism xi, 106,
    260–261
Manhattan Company 67
Manhattan Project 71–72

Mann-Elkins Act (1910) 356,
    426
*Manual of Railroads in the
    United States* (Poor) 112
manufacturing industry
    Alexander Hamilton on
        504–514
    Industrial Revolution and
        206–212
    Malcolm Baldrige
        National Quality Award
        260
    office machines 314
    pharmaceutical industry
        334–335
    plant relocations 447
    shipbuilding 384–388
maquiladora industry 311
March of Time, The (radio
    program) 437
Marconi, Guglielmo 348, 350
Marconi Company 373
margin trading 381, 415, 552
marine insurance 213–214
Mariner merchant vessels
    386–387, 390
Maritime Administration
    386–387, 390
Maritime Commission, U.S.
    236, 386
maritime technology 349
market baskets 20
marketing programs 15, 259,
    339, 362, 401, 473
marketing tools 9
market research 3, 232–233
Marshall, Charles 334
Marshall, Christopher, Jr. 334
Marshall, James 418
Marshall, John 89–90, 263
Marshall Field and Company
    158
Martha Stewart Living
    Omnimedia 413
martial law 331
Maryland Journal 476–477
Mason, David T. 256
Massachusetts Spy (newspaper)
    301
mass communications,
    advertising and 4
mass distribution 209–210
Massengill 337
mass extraction, mining
    industry 276, 278
mass housing 246
mass-market newspapers 303
mass production **261–262**
    in automotive industry
        30–31
    of bottles 320

mass production (*continued*)
George Eastman and 133
shipbuilding industry
386
UAW 444
UMWA 451
Eli Whitney 474
MasterCard 108
master of business
administration (MBA) 485
Mather, Cotton 300
Mather, Increase 300
Matthews, George 381
Mauchly, John 95, 219
Maxwell, James C. 348
Maxwell-Briscoe Company 76
Maxwell Motor Co. 76
May, Joseph 430
McCarran-Ferguson Act
(1945) 215
McCarthy, Joseph 307
McCormick, Cyrus 262–263,
491
McCormick, Cyrus, Jr. 222
McCrory, J. G. 239
McCulloch v. Maryland
263–264
McDonnell Douglas
Corporation 13–14, 494
McFadden, Louis T. 264, 272
McFadden Act 39, 91,
224–225, **264**, 493
MCI 22, 427, 488
McNamara, Robert 167
Meag Inspection Act 529
Meany, George 19, **264–265**
meat packing industry
265–269, 293, 529
mechanical reaper 262–263,
491
mechanization 107, 147, 320,
451
media 120, 307, 405, 438–439
Medicaid 218
Medicare 218
medicines. *See* pharmaceutical
industry
Mercantile Agency 110
mercantilism 241, 388
merchandise catalog
companies 377–379
merchandise tie-ins 120
merchant banking 367, 382
merchant ships 386, 388
Mercury automobile 167
mergers **269–271**. *See also
specific companies*
in advertising industry 7
of agricultural equipment
companies 221–222

in airplane industry
13–14
AMEX and NASDAQ 20
in automotive industry
77
in banking industry
42–43, 67–68, 225, 228
in chemical industry 74
Clayton Antitrust Act and
82
conglomerates and
101–102
of labor unions 19,
361–362
in manufacturing 209
in newspaper industry
304
of NYSE and NASDAQ
494. *See also* antitrust
in petroleum industry
333–334
in pharmaceutical
industry 339
in railroad industry 139,
356, 444
of regional stock
exchanges 359
under Republican
administrations 24
in retail industry 240
in sports industry 406
trends and regulation 360
*United States v. E.C. Knight
& Co.* 90
Sanford Weill 467–468
mergers and acquisitions. *See
also specific companies*
Drexel Burnham Lambert
124
investment banking and
228
J. P. Morgan and 280
managerial capitalism and
261
specialists in 119, 240,
244
Wells Fargo 469–470
Meriwether, John W. 250
Merrill, Charles **271**
Merrill Lynch & Co. 271
Merton, Robert C. 55–56, 250
Metropolitan Elevated
Railroad 344
Metropolitan Life Building
216, 394
Mexican War 437–438
Mexico 311
Meyer, Andre 244
Meyer, Eugene **271–272**
Meyer, John 398
MFS Communications 488

MGM/UA 439
Michelin 368
Michigan 29
Mickey Mouse 120
microchip 98
microprocessors 98
Microsoft Corporation 26, 98,
179–180, 221, 494
Microsoft Network (MSN)
224
microwave links 427
Middle East 332
Midvale Steel 423–424
Midwest Utilities 453
migrant laborers 150
military. *See also* Department
of Defense, U.S. (DoD)
contracts 201, 272
patents and trademarks
325
pension funds 327
shipping industry and
391
military-industrial complex
272–273
"Military-Industrial Complex"
address (Eisenhower)
555–558
Milken, Michael 123–124,
231, 346
Miller, Arnold 451
Miller, Marvin 171
Miller, Phineas 473
Miners for Democracy 451
mine wars 450
minicomputers 97, 220–221,
316
minimills, steel industry 411
mining industry **273–279**
Mining Law 275
minority enterprise programs
403
Minuteman missile program
57
misbranding 529
Mississippi River Boom and
Logging Company 472
Mississippi Valley, upper 273
Mitchell, Charles E. 79–80
Mitchell, John 449
Mobil Corporation 332–333,
366
Model A 167
Model C seaplane 57
Model T 29–30, 166–168, 262
Modern Business Enterprise
(MBE) 209–210, 212
monetary policy, U.S. 494
money brokers 371
money market 92–93
money order, express 14

money supply, control of 458
"money trust" 37, 58, 91, 238,
280
monopolies 428, 456, 562
Monsanto 70
Montgomery Ward 492
Montreal Canadians 407
Moody's Investors Service 111
Moore, Gordon 98
Moore's Law 98
Morgan, Arthur 435
Morgan, Harcourt 435
Morgan, Henry S. 282
Morgan, John Pierpont
279–281
George F. Baker and 37
Louis D. Brandeis and 58
Andrew Carnegie and 64
central bank
establishment 55
Anthony J. Drexel and
123
Thomas Edison and
135–136
Henry C. Frick and
173–174
Elbert H. Gary 178
James J. Hill and 198
Thomas W. Lamont and
242
robber barons 363
Charles M. Schwab 375
steel industry 410
Treasury Department and
492
U.S. Steel Corp. 106, 452
Morgan, John Pierpont, Jr.
(Jack) 119, **281–282**, 453
Morgan, Junius Spencer 279,
282, 492
Morgan Stanley & Co. 281,
282–283
Morgenthau, Henry 205
Morrill Land Grant Act 147
Morris, Robert 90, **283–284**
Morse, Samuel F. B. **284–285**,
348, 430, 491
Morse Code 284, 430, 470
mortgage-backed securities
371
mortgages 152–153, 190, 374
Mortimer, Wyndham 445
motion picture industry 135,
285–290
motivational research (MR)
5–6
Motor Carrier Act 225
motor vehicle industry. *See*
automotive industry
movies. *See* motion picture
industry

movie stars, as cultural phenomenon 287
moving assembly line 30–31, 125, 166–167, 263
Mrs. Fields Cookies 483
muckrakers 102, **290–291**, 363
Mulcahy, Anne 484
Mullins, David W. 250
multinational corporations **291–292**
multinational enterprises 393
municipal bonds 263, 423
municipal securities 380
Munn v. Illinois 89, 355
Murdock, J. J. 236
Muriel Siebert and Company 392
Murray, Phillip 18–19
Murrow, Edward R. 353
Muscle Shoals power plant 166, 310, 435
music 353, 487
muskets 261, 474
Mustang automobile 168, 203
mutual companies 214, 374
mutual funds **292**, 310, 383, 494
Myers, Gustavus 290, 363

N

Nader, Ralph 32–33, 53, 103, **293–294**
NAFTA. *See* North American Free Trade Agreement (NAFTA)
nail polish 362
Naismith, James 406
Nally, Edward 346
Napoleonic Wars 214
NASDAQ. *See* National Association of Securities Dealers Automated Quotations (NASDAQ)
National Academy of Design 284
National Association (sports industry) 404
National Association of Broadcasters 351–352
National Association of Securities Dealers Automated Quotations (NASDAQ) 20, 295, *414*, 416–417, 494
National Bank Act 90, **295–296**, 492
National Banking Act (1863) 41
National Bank of New York 177
National Bankruptcy Commission 47

National Basketball Association (NBA) 406–407
National Basketball League (NBL) 406–407
National Broadcasting Company (NBC) 346–347, 351, 353, 373, 490
National Bureau of Economic Research 357–358
National Business League 297–298
National Cash Register (NCR) 219, 314, *315*, 466
national central bank
    Bank of the United States 43–44
    Nicholas Biddle and 54–55
    Alexander Hamilton on 505
    recession and lack of 357
    stock markets 415
    Benjamin Strong and 417
    Frank A. Vanderlip and 79–80
National City Bank 38, 79–80
National Consumers' League 102
national currencies 140–141, 295–296
national debt 43, 177, 505. *See also* Treasury bonds
national defense system 226
National Do Not Call Registry 157
National Federation of Business and Professional Women's Club (BPW) 482
National Federation of Miners 449
National Football League (NFL) 406
National Hockey League (NHL) 407
National Industrial Recovery Act (NIRA)
    consumer movement 102
    declared unconstitutional 493
    Hugh Samuel Johnson and 231
    New Deal 299
    NRA 295, 298
    petroleum industry and 331
    PWA 342
    rubber industry 368
    UMWA 451
National Labor Relations Act (NLRA) **296–297**, 421, 445, 493, **553–554**

National Labor Relations Board (NLRB) 296–297, 421, 553
National League (NL) 171, 404
National Market System 359
National Miners Union 451
national monetary reform 417
National Negro Business League **297–298**, 492
National Progressive Union of Miners and Mine Laborers (NPU) 449
National Prohibition Act. *See* Volstead Act
National Railroad Passenger Corp. (Amtrak) 356
national railroad strike 355
National Recovery Administration (NRA) 288, **298–299**, 299
National Woman's Forum 392
natural gas 73, 332
"natural monopoly" 426
natural rubber 368
Naval Consulting Board 136
naval ships, armored 412
naval shipyards 384
Navigation Acts, foreign 384
Navistar International Transportation Corporation 222
Navy, U.S. 385, 387, 426
Nazis 124
NBC. *See* National Broadcasting Company (NBC)
Needham, James 308
negotiable commission structure 494
Negro Leagues 405
Netscape 224, 562–563
network broadcasting 351
Nevada National Bank 469
New Deal **299–300**
    Louis D. Brandeis and 58
    consumer movement and 102
    farming and 147
    government-sponsored enterprises and 190
    Hugh Samuel Johnson and 231
    John M. Keynes and 238
    model of regulation 360
    National Association of Securities Dealers (NASD) 294–295
    National Labor Relations Act (NLRA) and 296–297

George W. Norris and 310
PWA 342
regulation and 118
Tennessee Valley Authority 453–454
New England Courant, The (newspaper) 300
New England Glass Company 320
New Helvetia 418
Newhouse Newspapers 304
new issues market 381
Newport (Rhode Island) 251
news broadcasts 434
New School for Social Research 457
news organizations 352–353
newspaper industry 1–2, **300–308**, 352
Newspaper Preservation Act 307
New United Motor Manufacturing, Inc. (NUMMI) 33
New York 253
New York Academy of Music 51
New York & Erie Railway Company 137–138
New York & Harlem Railroad 457
New York & Mississippi Valley Printing Telegraph Co. 470
New York Cash Exchange (NYCE) 68
New York Central Railroad 457
New York City 3, 8
New York Coffee Exchange 84
New York Curb Exchange 414
New York Daily News 305
New York Evening Post (newspaper) 242
New York Herald (newspaper) 302
New York, Lake Erie & Western Railroad 138
New York Mercantile Exchange (NYMEX) 333
New York Morning Journal (newspaper) 303
New York Rangers 407
New York Shipbuilding 386
New York State banking commission 392
New York State Barge Canal System 137
New York State Federation of Labor 264

New York Stock Exchange
(NYSE) **308–310**
AMEX and 20
Bernard M. Baruch and
49
Better Business Bureaus
53
closure of 493
NASDAQ merger with
494
record keeping by x
regional stock exchanges
359
Muriel Siebert 392
stock markets 414, 416
ticker tape 436
Richard Whitney 474
New York Sun (newspaper)
302
New York Times (newspaper)
302, 305, *306*
New York Tribune (newspaper)
302
New York Weekly Journal 301
New York World (newspaper)
189, 303
NeXT 229–230
Nicaragua 323
Nickelodeons 285
Nike 408
Nipkow, Paul 431
Nixon, Richard M.
antitrust activity 25
conglomerates and 102
devaluation of dollar 59
Alan Greenspan and 193
ITT Financial Services
and 180
George Meany and 265
SBA 403
wage and price controls
461
N. M. Rothschild & Sons 367
Nobel, Alfred 69
Nobel Prizes 56, 113
no-bid contracts 403
Noble, Orange 329–330
no-fault insurance 216
nondiscrimination, in federal
contracts 485
Norris, Frank 291
Norris, George W. **310–311**,
435, 553
North American Free Trade
Agreement (NAFTA) 34,
294, **311–312**, 422, 494
North American Land
Company 284
North American Soccer League
(NASL) 407

Northern Pacific Railroad 198
Northern Securities Company
198
Northrup 13–14
North Star (newspaper) 302
North West Company 26–27,
199–200
Northwestern University 465
Norton, Edwin 84–85
Norwest 470
no-strike pledges 446, 450
NOW (negotiated orders of
withdrawal) accounts 117
NRA. *See* National Recovery
Administration (NRA)
numeric data, analysis of 314
Nye Committee 281
nylon 71
Nynex *21*
NYSE. *See* New York Stock
Exchange (NYSE)

O

Oakland Athletics 172
Oakland Motor Car Company
30
ocean-going steamboat 412
Ochs, Adolph S. 305
Octopus, The (Norris) 291
OECD Convention on
Combating Bribery of
Foreign Public Officials in
International Business
Transactions 168
office machines 95–96, 219,
313–319, 467
offshore exploration 333
Ogden, Aaron 456
Ogilvy & Mather 6
oil industry. *See* petroleum
industry
Oil Producing and Exporting
Countries 332–333
Old Age, Survivors, Disability
and Hospital Insurance
Program. *See* Social Security
Olds 30
oligopoly structure, in motion
picture industry 287–289
Olsen, Kenneth 97
Olympic Games 404
Omnibus Trade and
Competitiveness Act 422
one-bank holding companies
38
one-newspaper towns 307
on-line computer services
223
OPEC (Organization of
Petroleum Exporting
Countries) 33, 66

open-hearth process of steel
making 376
open market operations 155
"open outcry" system 175
open-pit mining 277–278
open-shop campaigns 450
open-source systems 98
operating systems 98, 179,
220–221, 562
Oprah Book Club 476
Oprah Winfrey Show, The
(television program) 475
optical telegraphy 430
options markets 20, 56, 176,
319–320
Orange County, California
420, 494
organic farming 150
organized crime 345–346
organized labor x, 296–297,
355–356, 421. *See also* labor
organizations
original-issue discount bonds
231
Ostend Manifesto 51
Oswald the Rabbit 120
Other People's Money
(Brandeis) 58
Otis, Elisha G. 394
Otis & Company 133
Outcault, R. F. 303
overcapacity,
telecommunications
industry 429
Overland Mail Company 469
overproduction
coal mining industry 450
farming 147–148, 150
logging industry 256
lumber industry 255
over-the-counter markets 56,
93, 295, 319, 414
Owens, Michael J. **320–321**
Oxford Provident Building
Association 374
Oxley, Mike 372

P

Pacific Exchanges 359
Pacific Mail Steamship
Company 390
Pacific Railroad Act of 1862
443
Pacific Telesis Group *21*
Pacific Western 184
package delivery, express 469
Packard, Vance 6, 103
packet ships 385, 389
packet-switched network 223
Paine Webber 239
Paley, William S. 88, 373

Palmer, Arnold 408
Palmer, Potter 158
Panama Canal **323–324**, 493
Pan American Airways
324–325, 494
panics 126, 154, 308, 357–358.
See also crashes
Panic of 1837 44, 491
Panic of 1857 188, 282,
385, 491
Panic of 1873 138, 173
Panic of 1893 138, 355
Panic of 1901 271
Panic of 1907 280, 417
paper money 39, 192–193
Paramount 287
Paris Peace Conference 242
Paris World's Fair 393
Parke Davis & Co. 336
Parker, George 245
Parker & Lee 244
Parrish, David 185
partnerships 105–106
Patent Act 325–326
Patent and Trademark Office
325
patent claims, in mining 275
patent medicines 2, 335–337
Patent Office, U.S. 412, 491
patents **325–326**
cross-licensed 346
drug 337
lawsuits 432
pooled 349, 425
U.S. Patent Office 412,
491
Pathé Frères Cinema 271
Patman, Wright 364
Patrons of Husbandry
(Grange) 147
pattern bargaining process
31
Patterson, John 219
Patterson, Joseph 305
Paul v. Virginia 215
PayPal 41
Peabody, Francis 238
Peabody, George 282
Peabody, Oliver 238
Pecora, Ferdinand 381
peddlers, yankee **489–490**
Peek, George 230–231
pegged interest rates 91, 154
Pemberton, John S. 82
penicillin 338
Penn Central Railroad default
112
Penney & Co., J. C. **326–327**
Pennsylvania 177, 253, 329
Pennsylvania Gazette
(newspaper) 300

Pennsylvania Railroad 63, 244, 354–355, 375–377
Pennsylvania Rock Oil Company 328
Penny Benny 327
penny press 2, 302. *See also* newspaper industry
Pension Benefits Guaranty Board 327
pension funds **327–328**
People's Party 147
Pepper, George 264
perfumes 87, 363
Perkins, George W. 222
Permian Basin 331
personal computers 98, *100,* 179–180, 221, 316–317
personal rivalries, between industrialists 76
Peterson, Peter G. 246
petrochemical industry 68–70, 72–74, 332–333
petroleum industry **328–334.** *See also specific companies*
  antitrust suits 364–365
  continuous process production 330
  crude oil prices 73
  domestic reservoirs 330–332, 385
  exports 387
  J. Paul Getty and 183–184
  oil well in Oklahoma *330*
  price volatility 333
  production deficits 332
  refineries 211, 329, 331–334
Pfizer 338
pharmaceutical industry **334–339**
Pharmaceutical Research and Manufacturers of America (PhRMA) 337
pharmatechnology 69
Phelps, Orson C. 393
Phibro Salomon 371
Philadelphia 358–359
philanthropy 364. *See also specific individuals*
Philco 432
Philipse, Margaret Hardenbroeck
Phillip Morris 85–86
Phillips, A. W. 339
Phillips curve **339–340**
Phillips Petroleum 333
Phoenix (steamboat) 412
phonographs 50, 135
photography 132, 232, 302
Photophone 50, 287

physicians 335
Pierce, Franklin 51
Pike's Opera House 163
pipelines 332
pistols 88
Pit, The (Norris) 291
Pitcairn, Harold 131
Pittston Company 452
PIXAR 229–230
planned obsolescence 103
planned towns 226, 246–247, 343
plantations 145, 395, 448
plant relocations 447
plastics 69–70, 121
Players League 171
P. Lorillard & Company 251
plows 115
point-of-sale (POS) systems 314
poison pill defenses 270
Polaroid Corporation 243
political campaigns, advertising in 5–6
Pollock v. Farmers' Loan & Trust Company 205
polystyrene 71
polyvinyl chloride (PVC) 71
Pony Express 469
Ponzi, Charles 48, **340–341**
Poor's Publishing Company 112
Populists 205, 363
pork-packing industry 265–266, 267, 269
portfolio insurance 176
portfolio investment 170
Portland General Electric Corporation 136
Posner, Richard A. 383
postal money orders 14
Postal Office, U.S. (department)
  Air Mail Act 493
  express cartel and 14–15
  inauguration of airline industry 9–10
  postmasters and newspaper industry 300
  railroads 356
  telecommunications industry 424, 426
Post Roads Act 426
Potomac railroad yards *355*
Power & Weightman 334
prairie schooner 101
precious metals trading 93
predatory pricing policies 82, **341**, 365
prescription drugs 338–339

presidential election of 2000 294
Preston, Andrew 448
Price Administration, Office of 461
price discrimination 225, 364
price expectations, and Phillips curve 340
price rigging 354, 365
price supports 150
price volatility, petroleum industry 329
pricing based on demand 409
primus inter pares 417
prismatic rings 431–432
private label products 191
privatization, of Fannie Mae 153–154
prizefight broadcast 373
processed food 448
process management movement 317–318
product distribution 364
Production Code Administration, dissolution of 289
productivity, UAW 445
productivity analyses 423
professional athletes 404, 406, 408
Professional Golfers Association (PGA) 408
professional managers xi, 260–261
professional sports. *See* sports industry
profiteers 279, 283, 310
profit motives, in newspaper industry 300
programming
  computer 97, 563
  radio industry 351–353
  television industry 434–435
program trading 176
Progressive Era
  consumer movement 102
  Edward H. Harriman and 196–197
  and laissez-faire economic theory 241
  muckrakers 290
  regulation 359–360
  robber barons 363
  Securities Act of 1933 379
  telecommunications industry 426
Prohibition 82, 459–460
Project Outreach 297–298
promotional ladder 485
promotion options, in advertising 9

property boom x
property insurance 213
property rights 482
proprietary companies 390
prospectuses 551
protectionist measures 384. *See also* tariffs
Prudhoe Bay Field 332–333
Public Accounting Oversight Board 372
Public Company Accounting Reform and Investor Protection Act 372
public domain 144–145
public finance 206
Publick Occurrences both Forreign and Domestick (newspaper) 300
public libraries 521
publicly held corporations 440
public relations x, 244–245
public service, women and 476
public utilities. *See* utilities
Public Utilities Regulatory Policies Act 342
public utility commissions 426, 429
Public Utility Holding Company Act (PUHCA) 199, 213, **342**, 454, 493
Public Works Administration (PWA) **342–343**
public works projects 226, 235
Publishers Financial Bureau 35
Pugwash Conference 134
Pujo Committee hearings 280
Pullman, George M. **343–344**
Pullman strike 114, 343
pulp industry 254
punch-card equipment 218–219, 314–315
Pure Food and Drug Act (1906) 53, 85, 335, **529–534**
puts and calls 319
PWA. *See* Public Works Administration (PWA)
Pyne, Percy 79

Q
Quadricycle 166
Quill, Shirley 18
QWERTYUIOP keyboard 440

R
Racketeer Influenced and Corrupt Organizations Act (RICO) **345–346**

racketeering 18
radial tires 368
Radio Act 349
Radio Corporation of America
   (RCA) **346–347**
   founding of 493
   motion picture industry
      and 287
   radio industry 350–353
   David Sarnoff 373
   television industry
      432–433
   John F. Welch 468
   Owen D. Young 490
radio industry **348–354**
   advertising industry and
      4, 232–233
   General Electric Co. 181
   networks and television
      industry 434
   David Sarnoff 373
   sports industry 407
   George Westinghouse Jr.
      472
   Owen D. Young 490
Radio-Keith-Orpheum
   Corporation 236
Radio Manufacturer
   Association 433
radio telegraphy 348, 471
Radisson, Pierre Esprit 495
railroads **354–356**. *See also
   specific companies*
   air braking system 471
   canals and 137
   coffee industry and 84
   Jay Cooke and 104
   Peter Cooper and 104
   deregulation of 118, 409
   Dow Jones averages 122
   east-west railroad link
      492
   electrification of 471
   elevated systems 412
   farming and 145–146
   financing 375
   Edward H. Harriman and
      196–197
   James J. Hill and 198–199
   ICC and 225
   Industrial Revolution and
      209–210, 212
   Interstate Commerce Act
      516–520
   investment banking and
      228
   lumber industry and 256
   mail service 455
   managerial capitalism and
      261

meat packing industry
   266
J. P. Morgan and 279
newspaper industry and
   303
Panama Canal and 323
pharmaceutical industry
   335
George M. Pullman 343
regulation of 89–90, 359
John D. Rockefeller 365
Thomas A. Scott 376–377
shipping industry 388,
   391
steel industry 409
stocks 122
telecommunications
   industry 424
turnpikes 439–440
United Fruit Company
   448
Cornelius Vanderbilt 457
Wells Fargo 469
Randolph, Francis 383
Raskob, John J. 76, **356–357**,
   394–395, 401
Raymond, Henry J. 302
Raytheon 180
RCA. *See* Radio Corporation of
   America (RCA)
Read, William 119
ready-to-wear clothing
   industry 463
Reagan, Ronald
   Address to the Nation on
      the Economy (1981)
      556–562
   deregulation 26, 117–118
   and Japanese auto
      manufacturers
      170–171
   SBA 403
   Tax Reform Act 422–423
   Paul Volcker 458–459
real estate loans 374
reason-why copy 3
rebates, in railroad industry
   225
recessions **357–358**
   commercial banking and
      92
   James Fisk Jr. and 163
   junk bonds and 231
   of 1980s 155
   John D. Rockefeller 365
   Paul Volcker 458
Reciprocal Trade Agreements
   Act 422
Reciprocity Treaty (1815)
   388

Reconstruction Finance Corp.
   358
   creation of 493
   Empire State Building
      395
   government-sponsored
      enterprises 190
   Great Depression and 113
   New Deal 299–300
   SBA 402
Reconstruction South 147
recording companies 437
record keeping x–xi
records, long-playing (LP) 88
Red Line Agreement (1928)
   332
Red Star Line 389
Reeves, Rosser 5–6
Reference Book (Dun)
   110–111
refineries 211, 329, 331–334
reformers, women as 479
refrigeration 266
Regional Bell Operating
   Companies 22
regional stock exchanges
   358–359, 414, 417
regulation xii, **359–360**
   of advertising 7
   of chemical industry 74
   of futures markets 93
   of holding companies
      199
   in 19th century 117–118
   NYSE and 310
   pharmaceutical industry
      336–337
   radio industry 352–354
   of railroads 355, 409
   of savings and loans
      160–161, 374
   swap market 420
   telecommunications
      industry 426–427
   of utility industry 342
   of Wall Street 381–382
Regulation Q 116–117
Reichardt, Carl 469
relocation of manufacturing
   plants 447
Remington, Frederic 303
Remington & Sons 440–441
Remington Rand 96, 219
Replogle, D. E. *431*
Report on Manfactures, The
   (Hamilton) 195
Republic Steel Corporation
   133, 410
required reserve ratio 155
research industry 337–338,
   346–347

reserve clauses, in sports
   industry 171–172, 405
residential mortgages
   152–153, 190, 374
Resolution Trust Corporation
   161, **360–361**
Resor, Stanley 232
retail operations
   discounters 462
   Marshall Field 159
   Hudson's Bay Company
      200
   revolution of 1920s 191
   Sears, Roebuck & Co.
      377
   Wharton School and 473
   women and 477
   Frank W. Woolworth
      486
   yankee peddlers 489
retirement packages 468
returns policy 464
Reuther, Victor 18
Reuther, Walter P. 19, 265,
   361–362, 445–446
revenue sharing 406
Revlon Company 362
Revolutionary War 40, 207,
   283–284, 334
revolvers 87–88
Revson, Charles **362–363**
RFC. *See* Reconstruction
   Finance Corp. (RFC)
Richard Whitney & Co. 474
Rickenbacker, Edward 131
Rickey, Branch 405
RICO. *See* Racketeer
   Influenced and Corrupt
   Organizations Act (RICO)
Riegle Community
   Development and
   Regulatory Improvement
   Act 94
Riegle-Neal Interstate Banking
   and Branching Efficiency
   Act 224
Riggs, Bobby 408
rivalries between industrialists
   76
Rivera, Diego 487
RKO Pictures 271, 287
Roach, John 385
Roach shipyard 385–386
roadways, paved 440
robber barons 189, **363–364**
Robber Barons, The
   (Josephson) 291
Roberts, Cecil 452
Robinson, Henry L. 437
Robinson, Jackie 405
Robinson, Joseph T. 364

Robinson-Patman Act 24, 67, 102, **346**
Roche, James M. 293
Rockefeller, Andrews, and Flagler 163
Rockefeller, John D. **364–366**
  cartel formation 66
  Cyrus Eaton and 133
  Henry C. Frick and 173–174
  Henry M. Flagler and 163
  holding companies and 199
  Industrial Revolution and 211
  Ivy L. Lee and 244
  petroleum industry and 329–330
  Thomas A. Scott 376–377
Rockefeller, John D., Jr. 366
Rockefeller, Nelson A. 366
Rockefeller, William A. 365, 489
Rockefeller Bank 67
Rockefeller Foundation 366
Rockefeller Institute for Medical Research 366
Rockefeller University 366
Roebuck, Alvah 377
Rohatyn, Felix 244
Roosevelt, Franklin D.
  Louis D. Brandeis and 58
  consumer movement 102
  Export-Import Bank of the United States 141–142
  "Forgotten Man" radio speech **549–551**
  Hugh Samuel Johnson and 230–231
  John L. Lewis and 248
  Eugene Meyer and 272
  New Deal 205–206, 299–300
  NRA 298
  Public Utility Holding Company Act 342
  PWA 342–343
  radio industry 352
  regulation 360
  RFC and 358
  tariffs 422
  Volstead Act 459
  WPA 487
Roosevelt, Nicholas 412
Roosevelt, Theodore
  antitrust cases 24
  Edward H. Harriman and 196–197
  Panama Canal and 323

Pure Food and Drug Act 529
  John D. Rockefeller 365
  Jacob Schiff 375
  trust-busting campaigns 527
  UMWA 449
Roosevelt buzzard 298
Roots Glass Company 82
Rosenwald, Juilius 377
Rothschild, House of 47, 51–52, **366–367**
Rothschild, Nathan 367
Rowland Institute of Science 243
Royal African Company 395
Royal Dutch Petroleum 375
Royal House 470
Royal Navy 384
royalties, mining industry 273
rubber, synthetic 71, 121
rubber industry 188, **367–369**
Rubin, Robert 186
Rudolph the Red Nosed Reindeer 465
rugby football 405–406
Rule 415b 381–382
run-zone-clearance system 287
Rupert, Prince 495
Russell, William H. 419
Russo-Japanese War of 1904-05 375
R. W. Sears Watch Co. 377

S

Sachs, Sam 186
safety net 299
St. Louis Cardinals 172
St. Paul & Pacific Railroad 198
Salomon, Arthur 371
Salomon, Herbert 371
Salomon, Percy 371
Salomon Brothers **371–372**, 467
S&Ls. *See* savings and loans (S&Ls)
S. & M. Allen & Co. 80–81
San Francisco, regional stock exchange 358–359
Santa Fe Railroad 238
Saran Wrap production plant 72
Sarbanes, Paul 372
Sarbanes-Oxley Act 136, 372, **372**, 494
Sarnoff, David **372–373**
  Joseph P. Kennedy and 236
  radio industry 351, 353

RCA 346–347
  television industry 432
  Owen D. Young 490
Sarnoff, Robert 347
satellite communications 151, 354, **427**, **434–435**, 439, 471
savings and loans **373–374**
  crisis of 1988 494
  Depository Institutions Act 116
  Federal Home Loan Bank Board 152–153
  FIRREA 161–162
  government-sponsored enterprises 190
  junk bonds 231
  Resolution Trust Corporation (RTC) 361
Savings Association Insurance Fund 152, 161
savings banks 116, 374
saw blade technology 255–256
sawmills 472
SBA. *See* Small Business Administration (SBA)
scandals. *See also* corruption; fraud
  accounting and finance xi, 372
  Crédit Mobilier 354, 443
  "embalmed beef" 529
  mutual funds 292
  SBA 403
  trading 382
  Treasury bonds 239
  on Wall Street 414
scanning systems 431
Schecter Poultry Corporation v. United States 298
Schiff, Jacob 240, **374–375**
Scholes, Myron S. 55–56, 250
School of Public and International Affairs, Princeton 458
Schwab, Charles M. 64, **375–376**, 452
scientific advertising 4
scientific farming 249
Scioto land speculation 126
Scott, Thomas A. **376–377**
Scovill, Inc. 260
Scripps, Edward W. 304
Sears, Richard W. 377
Sears, Roebuck & Co. 240, **377–379**, 492
Sears Tower 377, 395
Sears Watch Co., R. W. 377
Seattle Computer Products 179
Seattle Pilots 172

SEC. *See* Securities and Exchange Commission (SEC)
secondary markets 92–93
secretaries 316–317
Securities Act (1933) **379–380**, 381, 493, 551–552
Securities Amendments Act 359
Securities and Exchange Commission (SEC) 551–552. *See also* Securities Act (1933); Securities Exchange Act (1934)
  Drexel Burnham bankruptcy 124
  Enron Corporation 136
  Financial Accounting Standards Board and 159–160
  and generally accepted accounting principles (GAAP) 181–182
  Joseph P. Kennedy and 236
  options markets and 319
  Sarbanes-Oxley Act 372
  Securities Exchange Act 381
  stock markets 415
  utility industry 342
Securities Exchange Act (1934) 379, **381–382**, 415–416, 493, **551–553**
Securities Investor Protection Corporation 416
securities underwriting and trading 123–124, 226–228, 379–380, 382
Sedition Act of 1798 301
Seitz, Peter 172
selective cutting 255
Selectric typewriter 441
self-censorship 301
self-directed retirement plans 292
self-regulation 360, 381
Seligman & Co., J. & W. **382–383**, 438
Semi-Automatic Ground Environment project 219
semiconductors 98
Seneca Oil Company 328
Separate Trading Receipts of Interest and Principal (STRIP) 438
September 11, 2001, terrorist attacks 12, 34, 494
serial photography 285
serums 336

Service Corps of Retired
    Executives (SCORE) 402
service industries, in
    antebellum South 400
set-aside contracts 402
set-aside land, farming 150
sewing machines 262, 291,
    393–394, 491
sexism 392
S. G. Warburg & Co. 119
sharecroppers 148
shared monopoly 65
shareholders 105
shark repellents 270
Shearson Hayden Stone 467
Shearson Lehman American
    Express 246
Shearson Loeb Rhoades 467
sheet glass 320
shelf registration rule 381
Shell Chemical 71
Shell Oil 330–332, 334
Shell Transport and Trading
    375
Sheraton group of hotels 180
Sherman, John 383, 527
Sherman Antitrust Act
    383–384, 527–528
    antitrust laws 23–24
    Clayton Antitrust Act and
        539–540
    passage of 492
    predatory pricing 341
    Standard Oil Company
        dissolution 534
    telecommunications
        industry 426
Sherman Silver Act 186
shipbuilding industry 207,
    235, 384–388, 390, 465
ship of inland commerce 100
shipping industry 323,
    388–392, 440, 478
Sholes, Christopher 440
Sholes and Glidden Typewriter
    440
shopping malls, suburban
    259–260
short-selling 415–416, 474
short-term debt 92–93
short-term financing 92–93
Shuttle. See Eastern Airlines
Siebert, Muriel 392–393
Siebert Financial Corporation
    393
Siebert Philanthropic
    Foundation 393
Siemens-Martin open hearth
    211
Silliman, Benjamin, Jr. 328
silver mining 276

Sinclair, Upton 291, 529
Singer, I. M. 262, 393–394
Singer Building 393–394
Singer Sewing Co. 291,
    393–394, 491
Single Market Program 140
sit-down strikes 368, 402, 445
skilled workers 444
Skilling, Jeffrey 136
skin color 399
skyscrapers 393, 394–395,
    409, 486
Slater, Samuel 208
slavery 107, 263, 302,
    395–401, 478
sleeping cars 343
Sloan, Alfred P. 31, 103, 183,
    401–402, 493
Small Business Administration
    (SBA) 402–403, 485
small businesses 260
Small Business Investment
    Companies 402
smelting 211
Smith, Adam 241
Smith, Al 394–395
Smith, John 273
Smith, Willoughby 430
Smith Barney & Co. 104, 372
Smith Corona 441
Smithsonian Agreement 169
Smoot, Reed 197
Snow White and the Seven
    Dwarfs (film) 120
soap 86–87
soccer 406–407
Social Democratic Party 114
socialism 16–17, 187
Socialist Party of America 114
social justice, income tax and
    205
social legislation 299–300. See
    also Great Society; New Deal
Social Security 299, 327–328
social theorists 457
Society of Motion Picture
    Engineers 431
software 97–98, 220–221,
    316, 430, 562–563
solid-state electronics 427
Solvay process 69
Soule, Samuel 440
Southern Pacific Railroad 196,
    375, 390, 443–444
Southern Power Company
    126
South Improvement Company
    65, 365
Southwestern Bell Corporation
    21
soy protein additives 128

Spalding, Albert 171
Spanish-American War
    303–304
Spartan Aircraft Company
    184
Spaulding, C. C. 297
speaking tours 479
specie payments 51
Specie Resumption Act. See
    gold standard
spectrum space allocation
    433
speculation
    Daniel Drew 122
    futures exchanges and
        74–75
    land 126, 341
    NYSE and 308
    reduction of 552
    stock markets 415
Sperry-Rand 97
Spitzer, Eliot 494
sports industry 171–173, 373,
    403–408, 434, 439
spot market 169
Spruce Goose 201
S. S. Kresge, Co. 239
stagecoach lines 469
stagflation 358
Staggers Rail Act 356, 409
Stamp Act 301
Standard & Poor's 112
standardization 261–262, 335,
    474
standard of living 400, 444
Standard Oil Company
    antitrust case against
        23–24, 81
    breakup 492
    cartel formation 66
    petroleum industry and
        329–330
    John D. Rockefeller 365
    Sherman Antitrust Act
        383
Standard Oil Company of New
    Jersey et al. v. United States
    534–539
Standard Oil of New Jersey
    365
Standard Oil Trust 163, 199,
    365
Standard Statistics Company
    112
Stanley, Harold 282
state-chartered banks 44
state-chartered savings and
    loans 374
state common law,
    federalization of 383
state insurance 213

state law enforcement 459
statements of financial
    accounting concepts
    (SFACs) 182
statements of financial
    accounting standards (SFAS)
    160, 182
state-sanctioned rate-setting
    215
states' rights 422
static electricity 430
steamboats 145, 174, 412, 491
Steamboat Willie (film) 120
steam power
    Industrial Revolution and
        208, 211
    locomotives 104, 412
    lumber industry 256
    railroads 354
    shipbuilding industry
        385, 387, 391, 456
    shipping industry 249,
        389
    steamboats 145, 174,
        412, 491
    United Fruit Company
        448
steel industry 409–411
    John Deere and 115
    Henry C. Frick and 173
    Industrial Revolution and
        211
    Henry J. Kaiser and 235
    Charles M. Schwab
        375–376
    shipbuilding industry
        385, 387
    shipping industry 389
    skyscrapers 394–395
    UMWA 451
Steel Workers Organizing
    Committee 410
Steinmetz, Charles 181, 349
Sterling, Ross 331
Stetson, John B. 411–412
Stetson University 411
Stevens, Edwin 412
Stevens, John 175, 412
Stevens, Robert 412
Stevens Institute of
    Technology 412, 423
Stewart, Martha 412–414
Stillman, James W. 79–80
stock brokers 413, 415
stock companies 106, 261
stock issues 42–43
stock markets 414–417. See
    also panics; specific exchanges
    analysis of 35–36
    George F. Baker 37

collapse after September
    11, 2001, terrorist
    attacks 494
collapse of 1987 176
crash of 1929 x, xi, 4, 38,
    45, 416, 493
crisis of 1893–94 279
declines 357
Daniel Drew and 122
William C. Durant 129
Cyrus Eaton and
    133–134
indexes 121–122
Samuel Insull and 213
manipulation of 457
mutual funds 292
NYSE and 308
options markets and
    319–320
reform of 436
regional exchanges
    358–359
regulation of 379–382
ticker tape 436
U.S. Steel Corp. 452
Western Union Telegraph
    Co. 470
Richard Whitney 474
stock options 55–56
stocks 99, 122, 319, 392
stock tickers. See ticker tape
stock valuations 415
stockyard districts 269
Stratojet, Boeing Co. 11
strikes
    anthracite 449
    in automotive industry
        361
    Pullman 114, 343
    in railroad industry 355
    in rubber industry 368
    Thomas A. Scott and 377
    sit-down 402, 445
    slavery and 398
    in sports industry
        172–173, 405–406
    in steel industry 173,
        375, 411, 492
    Taft-Hartley Act 421
    United Fruit Company
        448
    in wartime 248
    wildcat 421, 446, 451–452
Strong, Benjamin 37,
    417–418
Stuart, Harold 133–134
Student Loan Marketing
    Association (Sallie Mae)
    190
studio system, motion picture
    industry 287

styrene 121
submarines 174, 376
subsidiaries 107
subsidies. See government
    subsidies
suburban development
    and chain stores 66
    Interstate Highway Act
        226
    J. C. Penney & Co. and
        326
    Levittown and 246
    motion picture industry
        and 288–289
    purpose-built 246
Sudan tribes, and slavery 395
Sudduth, Horace 297
sugar trust 383
Sun 330–331
Sun Microsystems, Inc.
    562–563
Super Bowl 406
supercomputing 97
supermarkets 85, 191–192,
    268
supply-side economics 206
Supreme Court, U.S. 58,
    89–90, 492
Surface Transportation Board
    (STB) 225, 356, 409
Sustained-Yield Forest
    Management Act (1944)
    256
sustained-yield management
    252, 255
Sutter, August 418
Sutter, John A. 418–419
Sutter's Mill 418–419, 491
swap market 419–420
Swift, Gustavus 266
syndicates 380
synthetic chemicals 68–71,
    73–74
synthetic rubber 368

T

tabloids 305
Tabulating Machine Company
    95, 218–219, 492
Taft, Robert A. 421
Taft, William Howard 426
Taft-Hartley Act 248,
    296–297, 421, 493
Tainter, Charles Sumner 50
takeovers 64
talk shows 434, 476
tankers 385
Tappan, Lewis 110
Tarbell, Ida 290
Tariff Commission 198

tariffs 197–198, 205, 208,
    311, 422, 504
TAT-1 (transatlantic telephone
    cable) 427
Taurus automobile 168
taxes
    immunities between state
        and federal government
        263
    on income xii, 204–206,
        422–423, 493
    Ronald Reagan on 558
Tax Reform Act 206,
    422–423, 494
Taylor, Frederick Winslow
    423–424
Taylor, Moses 79
Teamsters Union 265
technological advances
    in advertising 7–8
    in coal mining industry
        451
    in motion picture industry
        285–286
    in moving goods and
        information 209
    in newspaper industry
        303
    NYSE and 308
    in shipbuilding industry
        384
    in telecommunications
        industry 427
    in television industry 434
    Sam Walton and 462
    Wells Fargo and 470
Ted Bates Agency 5
Telecommunications Act 353,
    428–429
telecommunications industry
    424–429
    Alexander Graham Bell
        21, 348
    convergence with
        computer industry 318
    deregulation of 118
    MCI WorldCom 488
    transatlantic cable 158
telegraphy 430. See also
    telecommunications
    industry
    Jay Cooke and 105
    credit-rating agencies and
        111
    Industrial Revolution and
        209–210, 212
    Samuel F. B. Morse and
        284, 491
    office machines 314
    radio industry 348
    ticker tape 436

Western Union Telegraph
    Co. 470
wireless 348
telephone ordering system 464
telephones. See also
    telecommunications
    industry
    FCC and 151
    first model 50
    Industrial Revolution and
        212
    National Do Not Call
        Registry 157
    networks 318
    office machines 314,
        316–317
    patented 492
    portable 318
    telephonic technology 50
    transcontinental 425
    Thomas A. Watson 465
    George Westinghouse Jr.
        472
television 430–435
    as advertising medium 5,
        233
    CBS 89
    Walt Disney and 120
    FCC and 151
    motion picture industry
        and 288–289
    RCA 346–347
    Charles Revson 362–363
    David Sarnoff 373
    Martha Stewart 413
    Ted Turner 438–439
Telex system 430, 471
"ten-gallon" hat 411
Tennessee Valley Authority
    (TVA) 310, 435, 453, 493
tennis 407–408
terrorist attacks 12, 34, 325,
    494
Texaco 331–333
Texas Air 132
Texas Company 330–331
Texas Railroad Commission
    330–331
textile industry 208–209
thalidomide 339
Thayer, John E. 238
theme parks 120
Theory of the Leisure Class, The
    (Veblen) 457
Thomas, Isaiah 301
Thomson, J. Edgar 376
3-D movie process 243
thrift institutions. See savings
    and loans
Thrift Supervision, Office of
    153, 161

Thunderbird automobile 167
ticker tape **436**
    consolidated 308
    Thomas A. Edison and
      135, 436
    introduction of 492
    NYSE and consolidated
      308
    stock markets 414
    Western Union Telegraph
      Co. 470
Tidewater Associated Oil
  Company 184
tie-in merchandise 285
timber. *See* lumber industry
timberland 472
Time (magazine) 437
Time on the Cross (Fogel and
  Engerman) 398
time standardization 470
Time Warner 413, **436–437**,
  439, 494
Tisch, Lawrence 89
Titanic disaster 349, 373
Title IX of the Higher
  Education Amendments
  408, 485
Title VII of the Civil Rights
  Act 485
Titon, William 259
TNT, Ted Turner and 439
tobacco 23, 211, 251, 397
Todd Shipyards 388
Toledo Glass Company 320
toll broadcasts 351
tombstone ads 380
tonnage 384, 386, 389–390
Toronto Maple Leafs 407
Tower Building 394
Townsend-Greenspan and
  Company 193
Toy Story (film) 229–230
tractors 148
trade agreements. *See* North
  American Free Trade
  Agreement (NAFTA)
trade "around the book" 359
Trade Expansion Act 422
trademarks **325–326**
trade policy, U.S. 141
trade unions. *See* labor
  organizations
T-rail 412
tramp vessels 389
tranquilizers 339
TransAmerica Corporation 37,
  42
transatlantic cable 157–158,
  424–425, 427, 470, 491
transcontinental railway. *See*
  railroads

transcontinental telegraph
  158
transistor technology 96
Transmission Control
  Protocol/Internet Protocol
  (TCP/IP) 223
Trans-Missouri Railroad case
  383
transport aircraft 12
Transportation Act (1940)
  225
traveler's cheques 15
Traveler's Group 371
Travelers Insurance Company
  467–468, 494
Travis, Bob 445
Treasury. *See* Department of
  the Treasury, U.S.
Treasury bills 437
Treasury bonds **437–438**
    Federal Reserve and 154
    5-20s 193
    investment banks and
      228
    scandal 239
    state tax exemption 263
    underwriting 81
Treasury Inflation Protected
  Securities (TIPS) 438
Treasury securities 371
Treatise on Money, A (Keynes)
  237
Tredegar Iron Works 398
Tri-Continental Corporation
  383
Trinity College 126
triple witching hour 176
Trippe, Juan 324–325
Tropical Radio and Telegraph
  Company 448
Troy Female Seminary 479
trucks 226, 256, 391, 409
Truman, Harry 272, 421
Trumka, Richard 452
trust busting era 24, 365
trust certificates 199
Trust Company of America
  245
trusts
    formation of 269
    holding companies 199
    investment 186
    money 37, 58, 91, 238,
      280
    regulation of 24, 365, 527
    sugar 383
truth in advertising movement
  53
Truth in Lending Act 157
Tunney, Gene 407

Turner, Donald F. 341, 384
Turner, Ted **438–439**
turnpikes **439–440**
Tuxedo Park 251
TWA (airline) 201, 494
TWX system 430
tying, prohibition of 82
typewriters 111, 135, 314,
  316, **440–441**, 492

U

UAW. *See* United Automobile
  Workers (UAW)
UHF (ultrahigh frequency)
  channels 433–434
UMWA. See United Mine
  Workers of America
  (UMWA)
UMWA Welfare and
  Retirement Fund 248
underground mining 278
Underwood, Frederick 138
Underwood-Simmons Tariff
  Act 205
Underwood typewriters 441
underwriters' syndicate 104
underwriting, new stock issues
  186
unemployment 154–155,
  339–340, 458
Union Carbide and Chemicals
  70
Union Carbide Corporation of
  New York City 121
Union Oil Company 377
Union Pacific Railroad
  443–444
    Edward H. Harriman 196
    Kuhn Loeb & Co. and
      restructuring of 240
    railroad industry and 354
    Jacob Schiff 375
    Thomas A. Scott 376
    Theodore N. Vail 455
unions. *See* labor organizations
Union Switch and Signal
  Company 471
United Airlines 493–494
United Association of
  Plumbers and Steam Fitters
  264
United Automobile Workers
  (UAW) **444–447**
    automotive industry 31,
      34
    International Harvester
      Company 222
    George Meany 265
    Walter P. Reuther 361
    Alfred Sloan 402
United Brands Company 449

United Corporation 281, 453
United Farm Workers of
  America 150
United Fruit Company 346,
  447–449, 490
United Independent
  Broadcasters, Inc. 352
United Light and Power 133
United Mine Workers of
  America (UMWA) 248,
  449–452
United Motors 401
United Press Association 304
United Press International
  (UPI) 304
United Rubber Workers 368
United States Football League
  (USFL) 406
United States Postal Service.
  See Post Office, U.S.
United States Rubber
  Company (Uniroyal) 367
United States v. E. C. Knight Co.
  90, 269–270
United States v. Henry S.
  Morgan et al. 283
United States v. Microsoft
  562–564
United States v. Northern
  Securities Company
  198–199
United States v. South-Eastern
  Underwriters Association
  215
unit trusts. *See* mutual funds
UNIVAC computer *95*, 96
universal charge card 15
universal service,
  telecommunications 428
University of Chicago 365,
  457
University of the City of New
  York 284
Unsafe at Any Speed (Nader)
  32, 103, 293
unskilled production workers
  444
urban flight 246
USA Today 307
U.S. Rubber Company 492
U.S. Shipping Board 386, 390
U.S. Steel Corp. 106,
  452–453, 492
    formation of 64
    Henry C. Frick and 173
    Elbert H. Gary and 178
    J. P. Morgan and 280
    J. P. Morgan Jr. and 281
    Charles M. Schwab 375
    steel industry 410

U.S. Vitamin and
  Pharmaceuticals Company
  363
U.S. v. Northern Securities 356
usury laws 91
US West 21
USX Corporation 452
Utah Copper Company 277
utilities industry **453–454**
  deregulation of 118
  Dow Jones averages 122
  Cyrus Eaton and 133
  J. P. Morgan Jr. and 281
  public utility commissions
    426
  regulation of 199, 213,
    342, 429, 493
  George Westinghouse Jr.
    471–472
  Owen D. Young 490

V
vacuum packing 84–85
Vail, Theodore N. 21–22,
  455–456
Vanderbilt, Cornelius
  456–457
  in cartoon 139
  Daniel Drew 122
  Erie War 138
  James Fisk Jr. and 163
  Robert Fulton and 174
  Jay Gould and 189
  and isthmus of Panama
    323
  robber barons 363
Vanderlip, Frank A. 79–80
Van Sweringen, M. J. and O. P.
  138
variety stores 239
Varitype 441
vaudeville 285
Veblen, Thorstein **457–458**
Velie, Stephen 115
Venator Group 486–487
venture capital 380, 402–403
Vermilye & Co. 119
Versailles, Treaty of 242
Versailles Peace Conference
  188
vertical integration 287
vertical mergers 270
veterans' mortgages 153
veterans' pension funds 327
VHF (very high frequency)
  channels 433–434
Viacom 413
Victor Talking Machine
  Company 352
Virginia Company 273
virtual trading markets 417

Visa card 42, 108, 493
Vitascope 285
Volcker, Paul 155, **458–459**
Volkswagen 33–34
Volstead, Andrew J. 459
Volstead Act (National
  Prohibition Act) **459–460**,
  493
Volta Laboratory 50
Voorhees, Daniel 419
vulcanization 367

W
*Wabash Railway Company v.
  Illinois* 89, 355
WABC television 434
wage and price controls
  461–462
Wagner, Franz X. 441
Wagner, Robert F. 297
Wagner Act 296–297, 421. *See
  also* National Labor
  Relations Act (NLRA)
Walker, James E. 297
Wallace, Henry 358
Wall Street. *See also* stock
  markets
    crises 416
    negotiable commission
      structure adopted 494
    NYSE and 308
    reform of 342
    Securities Act (1933) 380
    Securities Exchange Act
      (1934) 381
    Muriel Siebert 392
    tombstone ads 380
Wall Street Journal 48,
  121–122, 304–305, 307, 492
Wal-Mart 239–240, 462
Walt Disney Corporation 62
Walt Disney Productions
  229–230
Walton, Sam **462**, 493
Walton's Five & Dime 462,
  493
Wanamaker, John **463–464**
War Advertising Council 5
war bonds 103–104, 112, 382
Warburg Dillon Read 119
Ward, Aaron Montgomery
  464–465
war economy 446
War Industries Board (WIB)
  298
war loans 185, 240
Warner Bros. 287
War of 1812 44, 122, 437,
  456
War on Poverty 403
warplanes 13

Warren, Samuel 57
war reparations 490
warship construction 385
War Shipping Administration
  390
warships 384, 386
wartime construction program
  390
wartime production 446
Washington, Booker T.
  297–298
Washington Agreement 450
Washington Post 272
Wasserstein, Bruce 244
Waste Makers, The (Packard)
  103
Watergate 265
water power–driven mills 208
Watson, John B. 232
Watson, Thomas A. 50, 219,
  465
Watson, Thomas A., Jr. 219
Watson, Thomas J., Jr.
  466–467
Waxman-Hatch Act 338
W. Duke, Sons & Co. 23, 126,
  492
WEAF radio 351
"Wealth" ("Gospel of
  Wealth")(Carnegie) 63,
  520–527
wealth, pursuit of 184
Wealth and Commonwealth
  (Lloyd) 290
Webber College for Women
  36
Webster, Charles B. 259
Wedtech 403
Weeks Act (1911) 254
Weill, Alexandre 244
Weill, Sanford 371, **467–468**
Weimar Republic 124
Weinberg, Sidney 186
Welch, John F. 181, **468–469**
welfare managers 482
Wells, Henry 14, 469
Wells, Mary 7
Wells Fargo **469–470**, 491
Wells Fargo's Letter Express
  469
Wells Rich and Green 7
Western Electric Co. 22, 350,
  425, 455
Western Union Telegraph Co.
  424, 427, 455, **470–471**,
  491
Westervelt, George 56
Westinghouse, George, Jr.
  135, **471–472**
Westinghouse Air Brake
  Company 471

Westinghouse Electric Co.
  346, 425, 471, 490, 492
Weyerhaeuser, Frederick 253,
  255, **472**
Weyerhaeuser Company 255,
  492
Wharton, Joseph 473
Wharton School **473**, 492
Wheeler, Burton K. 529
Wheeler-Lea Act 529
Wheelwright, George 243
"when-arrived" trading
  175–176
Whiskey Rebellion 177
White, Edward D. 534–539
white pine, depletion of 254
Whitewater 403
Whitman, Meg 484
Whitney, Eli 107, 261,
  473–474
Whitney, Richard 452,
  474–475
Wholesome Meat Act (1967)
  293
Wiggin, Albert 67
wildcat strikes 421, 446,
  451–452
Wiley, Harvey W. 337
Willard, Emma 479
William Colgate & Company
  86
William D. Witter & Co. 124
Williams Act (1968) 270
Willis-Graham bill 151
Wilson, George 183
Wilson, Woodrow
  Roger W. Babson 35
  Bernard M. Baruch and
    49
  Louis D. Brandeis and 58
  Eugene V. Debs on 115
  FTC and 156
  Eugene Meyer and 272
  UMWA 450
  Owen D. Young 490
Wilson Dam, Muscle Shoals,
  Alabama 435
Wilson-Gorman Tariff Bill 205
windowpanes 320
Windows operating system
  179, 562
Winfrey, Oprah **475–476**
Wintel 98
wireless technology 346, 349,
  428–429
wire services 302, 304
WISH List 393
withholding system of taxation
  206
Without Consent or Contract
  (Fogel) 398

WJZ radio 351
Wolfson, James D. 459
Woman's Tea Company 480
women
    access to credit 482
    advertising industry 232
    in American business
        476–486
    business financing for
        483
    education 36
    entrepreneurship of 479
    Alexander Hamilton on
        employment of 505
    legal status of 482
    life insurance 217
    office machines and 316
    organizations for 393
    public service and 476
    as reformers 479
    as slaves 397
    in sports industry 408
    in UAW 446
    on Wall Street 413
    Wharton School and 473
    Oprah Winfrey and 475
women-owned businesses
    483–484
Women's Entrepreneurial
    Foundation 393
Women's National Basketball
    Association (WNBA) 408
Women's World Cup (soccer)
    408
wood. See lumber industry
Wood, Robert E. 377
wood consumption 252, 257
wooden sailing vessels 385,
    388–390

Woodruff, Robert 83
Woods, Tiger 408
Woolworth, Frank Winfield
    486–487. See also F. W.
    Woolworth Co.
Woolworth Building 394
word processors 316–317
worker benefits. See employee
    benefits
worker productivity 316–317,
    319, 423, 486
worker psychology 466
workers' rights 444–445, 462,
    486, 553
workforce 208, 266, 448
working capital 489
working-class citizens 299
working conditions 444
Works Progress
    Administration (WPA) 231,
    342–343, 487–488
World Bank 59, 272
WorldCom xi, 429, 488, 494
World Hockey Association
    407
World Series 404
World Trade Center 395
World Trade Organization
    (WTO) 422
World War I
    advertising 3
    airplane industry 12
    Boeing Co. during 56–57
    Colt Firearms and 88
    Henry Ford and 166
    Industrial Revolution and
        207
    J. P. Morgan & Co. and
        281

John M. Keynes and 237
pharmaceutical industry
    337
radio industry 349
railroads 356
rubber industry 368
Salomon Brothers 371
Charles M. Schwab 376
Benjamin Strong 417
telecommunications
    industry 426
Treasury bonds 438
UMWA 450
U.S. Steel Corp. 452
war bonds 112
World War II
    advertising 4–5
    airline industry and 10
    chemical industry 68–71,
        121
    General Motors Corp.
        183
    Howard Hughes and 201
    income tax and 206
    Henry J. Kaiser and 235
    Joseph P. Kennedy and
        236
    Kuhn Loeb & Co. 240
    labor federations 19, 446,
        451
    military-industrial
        complex 272
    motion picture industry
        288
    pharmaceutical industry
        337–338
    Polaroid Corporation 243
    radio industry 353
    RCA 347

rubber industry 368
shipbuilding industry
    386
shipping industry 390
steel industry 410
television industry 433
Treasury bonds 438
wage and price controls
    461
Thomas J. Watson
    466–467
World Wide Web (WWW; the
    Web) 99, 224, 428–429,
    494
Wozniak, Steve 229
WPA. See Works Progress
    Administration (WPA)
Wright brothers 492
Wriston, Walter B. 80
writers 487
WTBS (television station) 439

Y
Yablonski, Joseph A. (Jock)
    451
yankee peddlers 489–490
"yellow dog" contracts 553
yellow journalism 303
Yom Kippur War 333
Young, Owen D. 346, 490

Z
Zaharias, Babe Didrikson 408
Zenger, John P. 301
zero coupon bonds 438
zinc mining 273, 276
Zworykin, Vladimir K.
    431–432